THE STRATEGY OF THIS COMMENTARY

The primary goal of this structural commentary on the Gospel of Matthew is to show what *convictions* Matthew conveys to his readers. It is a commentary on Matthew's faith—on his system of convictions—that involves an unusual, but not technical, way of reading. The issues guiding our reading of each passage are briefly explained in this statement, which includes all the "technical" vocabulary used.

Since Matthew's convictions concern the ultimate meaning of individual and community life in relation to God and Jesus Christ, he cannot risk that they be misunderstood. Thus, when he directly states a conviction, he makes a *point* out of it. He tells both what he *means* to say and what he *does not mean* to say—so that his point, his conviction, might not be misinterpreted. Discovering Matthew's convictions is, therefore, a matter of *identifying in each passage the points Matthew makes by setting up explicit oppositions*—the narrative oppositions in his story.

In order to convey his convictions *to his readers,* Matthew also needs to express them in terms of his readers' presumed knowledge and belief. He does so in the parts of the text that do not include oppositions, by presenting his convictions in the form of *themes* that he develops for his readers. Since such themes express both the "old" (what the readers should already know) and the "new" (the convictions Matthew wants to convey), the themes involve *tensions.* These tensions signal where convictions are expressed in *thematic passages.*

A study of the oppositions and of the tensions allows us both to identify Matthew's basic convictions and to show how Matthew strives to convey his convictions to his readers. As a result, the meaning of each passage is clarified.

OTHER BOOKS BY DANIEL PATTE

Paul's Faith and the Power of the Gospel:
A Structural Introduction to the Pauline Letters

Preaching Paul

What Is Structural Exegesis?

A STRUCTURAL COMMENTARY ON MATTHEW'S FAITH

THE GOSPEL
ACCORDING TO MATTHEW

Daniel Patte

FORTRESS PRESS   PHILADELPHIA

Library of Congress Cataloging-in-Publication Data

Patte, Daniel.
  The Gospel according to Matthew.

  Bibliography: p.
  Includes index.
  1. Bible. N.T. Matthew—Commentaries. I. Title.
BS2575.3.P37 1986   226'.207   86–45218
ISBN 0–8006–1978–1

2554E86   Printed in the United States of America   1–1978

POUR ALINE

CONTENTS

PREFACE

Why did I decide to write a commentary on Matthew's faith after studying Paul's faith? Why not study Mark, Luke, or John? I could offer many reasons to explain my choice. Matthew is the Gospel of the Sermon on the Mount, a Gospel that through its magisterial discourses nourishes so richly the life of the church. It is also the Gospel that is spontaneously felt to be both deeply Jewish and painfully anti-Jewish, and thus a Gospel that is both attractive and repulsive. Similarly, it is the Gospel that seems the furthest removed from Paul. The teachings of Matthew and Paul seem so far apart that one might think that they represent two contradictory kinds of Christian faith—although their relationship is really much more complex than that.

I could add other reasons to explain my decision to study Matthew's faith. Yet all of them would explain why I am interested in Matthew, and not why I was driven to write this commentary. Indeed, my interest would not have become a fascination if it had not been nourished and fueled by the community of scholars to which I am privileged to belong at Vanderbilt University. To my colleagues, Professors Peter Haas, Fernando Segovia, and Mary Ann Tolbert, I owe the confidence to pursue such a project, a confidence that they give me by their generous appreciation of my work. Yet other partners in this scholarly community contributed even more directly to my study of Matthew. Fred W. Burnett, through his dissertation, "The Testament of Jesus-Sophia: A Redactional-Critical Study of the Eschatological Discourse in Matthew" (1979), kindled my interest for that Gospel by sharing with me his enthusiasm for his project. Gary Phillips's dissertation, "Enunciation of the Kingdom of Heaven: Text, Narrative, and Hermeneutic in the Parables of Matthew 13" (1982), transformed my interest into fascination by revealing to me the hermeneutical process at work in the Gospel of Matthew. In addition, through his theoretical and methodological work, Phillips prevented me from misconstruing Greimas's semiotic theory and structural exegesis; he forced me to recognize the fundamentally dynamic character of Greimas's model. Larry Vigen's dissertation, "To Think the Things of God: A Discursive Reading of Matthew 16:13—18:35" (1985), provided me with an important key for the interpretation of that central passage. Vigen's work taught me much through its original theoretical proposal concerning the "discursive structures," a part of semiotic theory that was much in need of development. His contribution on this theoretical issue is particularly significant for the study of the entire Gospel.

Similarly, the graduate students who participated in the several seminars devoted to the structural exegesis of the Gospel of Matthew over the last few years have contributed much more than they may think to the elaborations in this commentary. They quickly became partners in research, making many valuable suggestions concerning one passage or another, as I attempt to acknowledge in my notes. By their probing questions and their concern for rigor, they prevented me from forgetting that the semiotic theory we were using was a "theory" open to revision. Robin Mattison, by her insightful comments, forced us to look closely at the "Fatherhood" of God in Matthew. Judith Middleton repeatedly reminded us not to confuse the "ideal" disciples described in Jesus' teaching and the ever-struggling "actual" disciples; all the participants in the seminars kept me aware that as their teacher, I am nothing else than an "actual" teacher ever in need of being corrected by my students.

I am particularly indebted to two of my students. Jeff Tucker's excellent structural exegesis of Matt. 19:1—20:16 helped me refine a first draft of my own study of that important passage. He was also my teaching assistant. Because I could have total confidence in his pedagogical qualities when he was leading undergraduate students in their first steps in New Testament exegesis, and because he went much beyond the call of duty in helping me, he gave me both the time and the freedom of mind to complete this commentary despite a heavy teaching load.

Jonathan Kraus served as my research assistant. It is difficult to express in a few words the extent of his contribution to the preparation of this commentary. He spent two full summers preparing a semantic analysis (one of the stages of the formal structural analysis) of two-thirds of the Gospel, a semantic analysis that many times helped me correct oversights, imprecise statements, or outright errors in my own analysis. He also did a vast amount of bibliographical work and read critically a first draft of most of the commentary, challenging parts of my interpretation, suggesting better formulations, pointing out how the interpretation of a given passage needed to account for the proposal of one scholar or another. I owe him many notes and the reformulation of many passages of the commentary. Kraus was such an invaluable research assistant not merely because of his mastery of structural methods and of his command of the secondary literature, but also because of his remarkable knowledge of early Jewish literature, a knowledge particularly helpful in the semantic analysis of a text such as the Gospel of Matthew.

It was in struggling with the semantic system we were discovering in Matthew's Gospel that I found that the semiotic theory we were using needed to be refined. Fundamental theoretical research was necessary before a systematic structural analysis of Matthew could be performed. I was much helped in this theoretical research by conversations with Professor Jean Petitot (Ecole des Hautes Etudes, Paris), and by Professor Greimas's gracious encouragements. Without the confidence that my theoretical proposals made at least some sense—a confidence that Professor Greimas gave me— I would not have been able to focus all my attention on the interpretation of the Gospel itself.

The final form of this commentary owes much to the patient work of Pat Mundy. She typed a large section of the manuscript and proofread it. But her primary contribution was that of a careful editor who corrected my style and my English. David Landry prepared a bibliography out of the footnotes. Eli Fisher and Larry Jones read the proofs, and Eli Fisher prepared the index. John A. Hollar, of Fortress Press, helped me find the proper format for the commentary and greatly contributed to the further improvement of its style.

It is also with gratitude that I acknowledge the financial support of the University Research Council of Vanderbilt University, of Dean Russell Hamilton (Graduate School), and of Dean Jacque Voegeli (College of Arts and Science). Without their financial help the theoretical part of the research could not have been performed, and the manuscript would not have been completed by the deadline.

Finally, this work is dedicated to my wife, Aline. She knows why!

DANIEL PATTE
Vanderbilt University

ABBREVIATIONS AND SHORT TITLES

ANRW	*Aufstieg und Niedergang der Römischen Welt*
ATR	*Anglican Theological Review*
BAGD	Arndt, W. F., and Gingrich, F. W., *A Greek-English Lexicon of the New Testament and Other Early Christian Literature. A Translation and Adaptation of Walter Bauer*
BZ	*Biblische Zeitschrift*
CBQ	*Catholic Biblical Quarterly*
DSS	Dead Sea Scrolls
Evang. Theol.	*Evangelische Theologie*
EThR	*Etudes Théologiques et Religieuses*
HThR	*Harvard Theological Review*
IBA	Irish Biblical Association
ICC	International Critical Commentary
JBL	*Journal of Biblical Literature*
JSNT	*Journal for the Study of the New Testament*
NRTh	*Nouvelle Revue Théologique*
NovT	*Novum Testamentum*
NTS	*New Testament Studies*
NTSMS	*New Testament Studies Monograph Series*
RS/SI	*Recherches Sémiotiques/Semiotic Inquiry*
RSR	*Recherches de Sciences Religieuses*
RSV	Revised Standard Version
SBL	Society of Biblical Literature
Semeia	*Semeia: An Experimental Journal for Biblical Criticism*
TDNT	*Theological Dictionary of the New Testament*, ed. G. Kittel, G. Friedrich
TLZ	*Theologische Literaturzeitung*
ZNW	*Zeitschrift für die neutestamentliche Wissenschaft*
ALLEN	Allen, Willoughby C. *A Critical and Exegetical Commentary of the Gospel According to St. Matthew*
BEARE	Beare, Francis W. *The Gospel According to Matthew*
BERGER	Berger, Klaus. *Die Gesetzesauslegung Jesu. Ihr historische Hintergrund im Judentum und im Alten Testament*

BONNARD   Bonnard, Pierre. *L'évangile selon saint Matthieu. Com-
                   mentaire du Nouveau Testament* 1.
BROWN   Brown, Raymond E. *The Birth of the Messiah.*
GUNDRY   Gundry, Robert H. *Matthew: A Commentary on His Lit-
                   erary and Theological Art.*
KINGSBURY   Kingsbury, Jack D. *Matthew: Structure, Christology and
                   Kingdom.*
LAGRANGE   Lagrange, Marie-Joseph. *Evangile selon saint Matthieu.*
LOHMEYER   Lohmeyer, Ernst. *Das Evangelium des Matthäus.*
MEIER   Meier, John P. *Law and History in Matthew's Gospel.*
MINEAR   Minear, Paul S. *Matthew, The Teacher's Gospel.*
PRABHU   Prabhu, George M. Soares. *The Formula Quotations in
                   the Infancy Narrative of Matthew.*
SCHWEIZER   Schweizer, Eduard. *The Good News According to
                   Matthew.*
STENDAHL   Stendahl, Krister. *The School of Matthew and Its Use of
                   the Old Testament.*
STRECKER   Strecker, Georg. *Der Weg der Gerechtigheit.*
SUGGS   Suggs, M. Jack. *Wisdom, Christology and Law in Mat-
                   thew's Gospel.*
TRILLING   Trilling, Wolfgang. *Das wahre Israel: Studien zur Theo-
                   logie des Matthäus Evangeliums.*

A STRUCTURAL COMMENTARY ON MATTHEW'S FAITH

The subtitle *A Structural Commentary on Matthew's Faith* expresses both the specific character and the limitations of this work. As any *commentary*, it is intended to be consulted; special features are aimed at facilitating this use. It is nevertheless different from other commentaries because of its particular focus: *Matthew's faith.* A study of the Gospel According to Matthew with this focus demands a specific approach, namely, a *structural* reading which is presented here in a nontechnical way. Using a few structural principles enables us to identify in each passage the main points or convictions that Matthew makes in it for his readers. Then, when this passage is interpreted in terms of these points, important aspects of its meaning appear more clearly and the commentary gains a coherence that might warrant its reading from beginning to end.

A COMMENTARY ON THE GOSPEL
ACCORDING TO MATTHEW

As usual for a commentary, the comments on each passage have to be self-contained. In order to facilitate the use of this commentary, the subheadings reflect as much as possible the content of the pericopes, using traditional designations. To make it easier to locate the comments provided on given passages, the numbers of the chapter and verses discussed in the paragraphs have been noted in boldface. My comments on each section of the Gospel[1] are introduced by a presentation of *the main theme* of that section, which discusses, among other things, the context in which a given pericope needs to be understood in the Gospel.

Quotations are from the Revised Standard Version unless otherwise noted. I did not provide the complete text of the Gospel, assuming that the users of the commentary would have in front of them either a translation or the Greek text. More specifically, I assumed they would use an annotated version—such as the *Oxford Annotated Bible*—and therefore that I would not need to repeat the explanations found in notes of such versions.

Comments on a given section of the Gospel do not presuppose the reading of the comments on preceding sections. Yet they often refer to previous passages of the Gospel, because, in one way or another, these are related to the themes or points of the passage under study. In such cases the suggested references are not only to the passages of the Gospel but also to my comments on these texts. By the very fact that they are related to new passages, these earlier parts of the Gospel receive further interpretations. For instance, the passage regarding Jesus' baptism (3:16–17) appears in a new light when it is related, as it is in my comments, to Jesus' charge to the disciples: "Go therefore and make disciples of all nations, baptizing them" (28:19). For the convenience of the readers I provide a special kind of index, an index of biblical passages that are *mentioned outside the comments on the pericope to which they belong*.

The literary genre commentary demands that the comments on each passage designated by a subheading be mostly self-contained. I have striven to respect this constraint. Yet it prohibits any attempt to propose a systematic presentation of Matthew's teaching and, in our case, a systematic presentation of Matthew's faith. But, simultaneously, a commentary needs to be coherent. The discrete interpretations of various passages need to be consistent with one another, since we should assume that Matthew[2] himself was at least somewhat consistent in writing his Gospel.[3]

HOW THE COMMENTARY WAS WRITTEN

How does one proceed in writing a commentary? Because the literary genre commentary involves the twofold constraints of *self-contained comments* on each passage in a *consistent interpretation* of the Gospel, it may seem that the only reasonable procedure is to begin by elucidating what gives coherence to the Gospel. This is what the authors of most commentaries do by first publishing monographs or a series of articles. Such presentations are usually based on detailed exegeses of central passages or on certain distinctive features of the Gospel (e.g., its overall literary organization with a series of major discourses, or its use of Scripture),[4] passages and/or features perceived as providing a key for the understanding of the Gospel. Then, when the commentary is prepared, it is this overall interpretation of the Gospel that gives coherence to the commentary.

The procedure that I use in my study of Matthew's Gospel is exactly the opposite. This commentary was written *without* presupposing any overall understanding of the Gospel and its teaching. Yet I hope its readers will agree with me that it nevertheless presents a consistent interpretation of the Gospel.

My study of each passage aims at identifying the data that will need to be accounted for in a systematic presentation of Matthew's faith. So to speak, I identify the pieces of the puzzle which, later on, will need to be put together so that the complete picture might appear. This commentary does not include an overall presentation of Matthew's faith, not only because this literary genre does not allow it but primarily because it is only *after* completing the commentary that I will be able to envision it. It is therefore in a subsequent monograph that I plan to make a systematic presentation of "Matthew's faith" in which I will fully enter into dialogue and critically discuss other overall interpretations of the Gospel. Yet I believe this commentary presents a consistent interpretation of the Gospel. How can this be?

I stated that in writing this commentary I did not presuppose an overall understanding of Matthew's teaching; but I did not say that I wrote it without presuppositions. In fact, I presupposed all along that I knew what gives a basic coherence to the Gospel, namely, Matthew's faith, although I did not know at all what characterizes Matthew's faith. By focusing my comments exclusively on the way Matthew expresses his faith in each passage of his Gospel, I was confident that my interpretation would be coherent. Theoretically it should have the same coherence that the Gospel itself has.

Structural exegesis has a starting point that is quite different from traditional exegesis. Its starting point is a fundamental theoretical research regarding meaning or signification. This is the research field known as *semiotics*. This research is deliberately conducted as any fundamental theoretical research is in the physical sciences. It progresses by proposing a theory or model for a given phenomenon, which is tested in experiments or analyses and very often found wanting; then it is refined, further tested, further refined, and so forth. In this way, progressively, the theory takes shape, becomes more and more ascertained, and can find wider fields of application, although it always remains a theory open to further refinements. Through the research of A. J. Greimas and his collaborators, semiotic theory reached in 1978 a level of sophistication that made it possible to envision specific studies of religious texts.[5] In brief, it became possible to identify and describe six dimensions of the meaning of any discourse and to understand how they are interrelated. It then appeared that one of these dimensions involved nothing else than what is most characteristic of an "author's faith."[6] The implication of such a theoretical progress is that we know the formal features that express the author's faith in any discourse— with some variations related to genres. Just as it is possible to identify all the uses an author makes, for instance, of genitive absolutes when one knows the syntactical rules that define this Greek syntactical form, so it becomes possible to analyze any text so as to identify the characteristics of its author's faith when the semantic rules that govern the expression of an author's faith are known.

From this perspective, the preliminary research that I needed to do before writing this commentary was a formal analysis of the Gospel—rather than a study of the overall organization of the Gospel, or its Christology, or its ecclesiology, or any other feature perceived as giving coherence to the Gospel. Yet this formal analysis was not the mere application of a preexisting model. It also involved verifying the validity of this model and eventually refining it.

In my formal analysis of the Gospel, I first used the semantic rules that govern the expression of the author's faith as they were known in 1982 (and that I had used for the study of Paul's letters). In so doing, I was aware that I was using a "model" or "theory" which my analysis was further testing and verifying. As it turned out, I soon discovered that the existing theory could not account for certain features of the Gospel (both in the Sermon on the Mount and in narrative passages that I used as test cases). The semiotic theory needed to be refined. Consequently, I had to engage in semiotic theoretical research to find out how the theory needed to be modified so that it could account for these features while still being able to account for all the features of other texts (such as Paul's letters), as the previous formulation of the theory did. Thus one can readily understand that "complementing" the existing theory led to reconceiving the relationships between all the parts of the theory; from my point of view, it actually led to the clarification of several of these relationships. Professor Greimas kindly accepted the validity of these revisions of the theory, which actually did not contradict his theory but broadened it somewhat.[7] The first step of the research was therefore a theoretical quest aimed at confronting the existing model with Matthew's Gospel so as to verify the model and to refine it. The result was a new formulation of the theory regarding the generations of meaning in any discourse, including Matthew's Gospel. Then, by making use of this model, it became possible to make a complete formal analysis of the Gospel which would be the basis for the study of Matthew's faith as expressed in each passage.

A STUDY OF MATTHEW'S FAITH

The preceding remarks presuppose a specific definition of "faith." Here I need to explain what I mean by "faith." I have already attempted to do so in *Paul's Faith and the Power of the Gospel*.[8] Without repeating my case, I want to underscore that for me the most characteristic aspects of a "faith" is a "system of convictions." *Believing is holding to a system of convictions, or, better, it is being held by a system of convictions.* This can be readily understood when one remembers that the term "convictions," according to its etymology, designates what believers hold to be self-evident, that is, truths that do not depend upon a demonstration or an argument but rather impose themselves upon the believers. Consequently, convictions should not be confused with "ideas," including theological ideas that believers formulate through logical reasonings, deductions, and arguments. Rather, convictions have power over believers. They have the power to impose themselves upon believers and also the power to cause them to act in certain ways— at times in very eccentric ways. They motivate them, drive them, to follow certain patterns of behavior, because for the believers it is self-evident that this type of behavior is "good," that is, on shorter or longer terms it will bring satisfying, or euphoric, results, or at least will avoid bad, or dysphoric, results. Convictions have such a power over believers because, through their organization into a *system*, they establish for believers what they spontaneously perceive as their true identity as well as the true character of the world (the human community, the natural world, and their eventual relationship to a supernatural world) in which believers are to implement their identity. One can then understand why convictions have power over believers. Following one's convictions, being driven by them, is nothing else than "being oneself," implementing one's true identity. Conversely, when one's convictions are threatened in any way, one will do whatever is necessary to protect them. It is one's true identity, one's meaning in life, which is threatened.

These remarks are sufficient to explain how convictions are expressed in a text such as Matthew's Gospel. To begin with, since convictions have power over people, indeed the power to drive them to follow certain patterns of behavior in their daily life as well as in their speech-acts, it appears that an author's faith (system of convictions) is what gives a fundamental coherence to his or her discourse. This is why I could be confident that by systematically studying the convictions that Matthew expresses in each of the passages of his Gospel, my interpretation would be consistent. Since my study of the text is aimed at elucidating what gives coherence to the text—the author's faith—the results of my interpretation should reflect the very coherence of the Gospel itself.[9] But for this, the exegesis needs to be rigorous, that is, it needs to be exclusively concerned with the features of the text that express Matthew's faith. In sum, such an interpretation needs to follow certain rules that will help to identify Matthew's convictions; it needs to be a structural exegesis.

A STRUCTURAL COMMENTARY ON MATTHEW'S FAITH

My structural interpretation of the Gospel According to Matthew follows a few rules that are derived from Greimas's semiotic theory. In itself this theory is quite involved—as can be expected for a fundamental theory that describes the rules governing the generation of meaning in any discourse. Without this theory one could not have conceived the methodology I shall follow. But this methodology in itself can then be readily understood by reflecting quite concretely on the character of Matthew's Gospel.

First, there is the obvious—Matthew's Gospel is a religious text. One of the main functions of a religious text is to communicate a faith to the readers, either in order to strengthen the faith that the readers already hold or in order to transmit to them a new kind of faith. Furthermore, the faith that a text aims at conveying is the author's faith.[10] In other words, in the case of a religious text, the author's faith has a twofold role. On the one hand, it is what drives or motivates the author to write the text; as with any text, a religious text is "structured" by the author's faith in the sense that it reflects the fundamental patterns of the author's system of convictions. On the other hand, this faith is also what the author of a religious text intends to convey to the readers. Thus we can assert that, by writing his Gospel, Matthew intended to communicate the faith that he held and that held him and led him spontaneously to follow in his discourse the pattern of his system of convictions.

If a faith is what establishes someone's identity and the meaning and purpose of life for that person, then the significance of the preceding general observation is clear. The faith that Matthew aims at conveying to his readers is of the utmost importance for him. It is therefore something about which he wants to avoid any possible misunderstanding. While he might take the risk of being misunderstood on other matters, he cannot take the risk of being misunderstood on such matters around which revolve all the meaning and purpose of existence. But what do we do when we want to avoid being misunderstood? Quite commonly we do not only state what we want to communicate; we also stipulate *what we do not mean to say*, so as to remove any ambiguity. In other words, we more or less spontaneously set an opposition between what we actually want to say and what we do not want to say. So it is with the convictions that comprise the faith that the author of a religious text wants to convey. Oppositions set in the text are the primary mode of expression of such convictions, because the author cannot take the risk that they might be misunderstood. In the case of a religious text such as the Gospel, since these convictions are also what Matthew intends to convey, we can say that the main points that the text makes are conveyed by such oppositions. In sum, in order to identify the convictions or main points conveyed by the text, we need to find the oppositions that express them.

In any passage of a text, many kinds of oppositions can be perceived. Which among these express the author's convictions? First, we must distinguish between *implicit* oppositions and *explicit* oppositions. For instance, when the text refers to a "mountain" or to a "good deed," readers might perceive an implicit contrast with "plain" or the corresponding "bad deed." But note that in such cases readers are left free to set up the opposition themselves. Indeed, while "mountain" can be opposed to "plain," as I suggested, it can also be opposed to "city," to "sea," to "temple," or to any number of other things that are "not a mountain." It all depends upon which of the possible connotations of "mountain" is taken into consideration. Such implicit oppositions cannot be viewed as a direct expression of the author's faith, since the author allows the readers to select the opposition and the connotations through which that aspect of the text needs to be interpreted.

Alone, "explicit oppositions," that is, oppositions fully expressed in the text, *can be viewed as a direct expression of the author's convictions.*

Yet there are still several kinds of explicit oppositions in any given passage. We must distinguish between *semantic* and *narrative* oppositions so as to understand how they complement each other in order to express the author's faith. As we shall see, while semantic oppositions most directly express convictions, narrative oppositions signal what convictions fundamentally characterize the author's faith.

Convictions are expressed by *semantic oppositions*, that is, by oppositions that specify the connotations in terms of which a situation, a personage, a phrase, or a word needs to be understood. For instance, if in a passage "mountain" is explicitly opposed to "plain," "mountain" might need to be understood simply as a high geographical location—if other features of the text warrant this interpretation. But if in another passage "mountain" is explicitly opposed to "temple," "mountain" might need to be understood as another place where one can be in the presence of God. It is through such connotations (underscored by means of oppositions for situations, personages, phrases, or words) that specific views of the world, of human existence in relationship with the divine, of human community, of the purpose and meaning of life—in brief, specific systems of convictions—are expressed. In any given passage there are often many such semantic oppositions which express various convictions. But not all of these convictions are of equal importance for the author, who at any given moment might express views that he or she expects the intended readers to hold. Narrative oppositions signal which semantic oppositions express the convictions most characteristic of the author's faith.

Narrative oppositions, in contrast to semantic oppositions, are oppositions of actions. The role of narrative oppositions is quite different from that of semantic oppositions. In a story, narrative oppositions are what makes the story progress and what provides overall organization for the story—its narrative structure. For instance, without the misdeed of a villain, there would be no need for the counteraction of a hero who attempts to undo the villain's misdeed. Thus, without this opposition of actions there would be no story. When one notes that such conflicts can take the form of verbal clashes in polemical dialogue as well as the form of physical clashes, one can readily understand that such narrative oppositions provide the overall organization not merely of stories but also of more discursive texts, and even of pure discourses where the actions are often cognitive actions (e.g., knowing, teaching).[11] Since faith as a system of convictions imposes a specific pattern or overall organization on the believer's behavior, including his or her verbal and cognitive behavior (what he or she says or writes), and since narrative oppositions provide such a pattern or overall organization, it appears that *narrative oppositions directly reflect the author's faith.*

Narrative oppositions by themselves, however, do not express convictions that would provide a view of the world, of human existence in relation to the divine, of the human community, of the meaning and purpose of existence. By themselves they merely express convictions regarding the relative value of various kinds of actions. Yet they are almost always associated with semantic oppositions, concerning, for instance, what characterizes the respective agents of the actions (e.g., qualification, knowledge, helpers and allies, motivation, power and authority, title) as well as the respective locations and times of the actions. Then it can be understood that the basic convictions that characterize an author's faith are those expressed by the *narrative oppositions and the semantic oppositions attached to them.*[12]

PREPARATORY ANALYTICAL WORK

From the preceding remarks it is clear that a commentary aimed at elucidating the convictions that Matthew conveys in his Gospel needs to be prepared by an analysis of its narrative oppositions,[13] and first by their identification. To this end I have attempted to be as rigorous as possible by using the following criteria:

1. Both actions in each opposition must be explicitly expressed in the text. In other words, *two* verbs of action (which might be verbs expressing cognitive actions) are necessary. The only exceptions are cases where there is a clearly marked ellipsis (usually in order to avoid the repetition of the same verb).

2. The text must posit one of the actions as having a positive value and the other as having a negative value. This is not always easy to discern; in such cases we explain our reasoning. One common error is that of viewing as a narrative opposition the contrast between a blessing and a punishment (by God). Actually, in most cases, the punishment is posited as a just punishment; thus it has, according to the text, a positive value (even though it has, of course, a negative value for those who are punished). This is not therefore a narrative opposition.[14]

3. The two actions must be related; two totally unrelated actions cannot be opposed. In addition to the technical analysis,[15] I have asked myself: Would the reader spontaneously perceive this opposition? Practically, the two actions cannot be too far from each other in a passage, except in cases where it is strongly marked (i.e., by repetitions). One should not forget to take into account as narrative oppositions the polemical exchanges that are oppositions of verbal actions.

When such criteria are rigorously applied, it appears that there are in a given passage only a limited number of narrative oppositions, and at times very few. Since adding a nonexistent opposition is more misleading for the interpretation than omitting one, I have not taken into account oppositions about which I had doubts. Throughout the Gospel there are many narrative oppositions, as can be seen in the table of Narrative Oppositions (Appendix). This table uses the Greek verbs, since some narrative oppositions are not transparent in translation.

When the narrative oppositions have been identified, they need to be interpreted. By the identification of an opposition, the difference between the two actions expressed by the verbs has been identified. But the semantic component of the opposition still needs to be elucidated. Thus, regarding the subjects of the actions one must ask: In what ways are they opposed? At this stage of the analysis, one needs to take into account the entire description provided by the text of the subjects, their respective qualifications, knowledge (as expressed by their words), status (as expressed by titles, and by their relationships with other personages), as well as the description of the situations that are the immediate contexts for the opposed actions. At this stage of the interpretation, one needs to take note of all the *possible* connotations that each textual feature (such as a title) might have had in the cultural milieu of the text. Important results of historical research are thus taken into account here. Then, by studying the opposition as expressed by features of the text, one can recognize that the subjects (and the situations) are opposed through a number of connotations concerning one or several of the characteristics of the subjects and/or of the situations. One can then perceive how certain subjects and situations or, more specifically, how certain of their characteristics are perceived from the perspective of Matthew's faith. The opposition shows what are the particularly important connotations for Matthew that should be taken into account when interpreting these situations and the personages they involve. By means of each opposition Matthew underscores a specific point, a point concerning the system of convictions that he attempts to convey to his readers. By studying an opposition, we also identify one of the points made in a given passage.

One can also note that other characteristics of one or the other subject and situation are not relevant for the text in that they do not contribute to setting up the opposition—even though these characteristics might be most important according to our own preunderstandings. In this way the analysis allows us to suspend some of our preunderstandings.

The analysis of a single opposition most often produces few results. In the best of cases it involves a relatively abstract point on some discrete issue. We are left wondering: What is the significance of this point? In numerous cases the point itself is not clear, because there is a series of characteristics and connotations that can be viewed as participating in setting up the opposition. Then we are left with another question: Which, among this series of possible points, does Matthew want to underscore? Both these questions find answers when one remembers that Matthew's faith is a *system* of convictions expressed by a series of oppositions. These oppositions are correlated, that is, they complement and interpret each other in that they all follow a similar pattern. Actually, in a given passage a series of oppositions develops only one or two *main points*. Consequently, after the preliminary interpretation of each opposition by itself, we need to consider how these oppositions are interrelated—what do they have in common and what kind of progression is there from one to the next.[16]

In sum, I first attempted to identify all the narrative oppositions and to study them in a formal way. Then their correlations were noted and taken into account in a preliminary way. This yielded a vast and complex network of relationships among relatively abstract semantic features or connotations. This is the safety net that will allow us to control the next stages of interpretation, including the simplified structural reading which we present in the commentary.[17]

This study of the Gospel cannot be limited to the study of the narrative oppositions. As noted, there are relatively few such oppositions; in other words, many parts of the text are not involved in such oppositions. How should these parts be interpreted? One should remember that the oppositions allow us to identify the main points of a passage. This means that we can expect the rest of a passage to express these main points, but in another way.

Here we need to take into account that Matthew's Gospel as a religious text is an attempt to *communicate* these points or convictions to *readers*. As we know from experience, successfully communicating a message to a given audience demands that this message be expressed in a way appropriate for that audience. It needs to be presented in terms of what the audience knows (the readers' "old knowledge"), in a vocabulary, with images and symbols that make sense for the audience. In the case of Matthew's Gospel, the readers' old knowledge includes what they already believe and, as we progress in the text, the presumed knowledge that they have of what they have already read. One can then understand that while the narrative oppositions directly express what Matthew wants to convey to his readers, the rest of the text expresses the same points in terms of what he presupposes his readers know and/or believe.

This expression of the author's convictions in terms of the readers' old knowledge is what we shall call the *themes* of a passage.[18] Such themes, which often take a figurative form, are what readers perceive as the most striking message of the text. It is what makes sense for them, as, for instance, the figure of Jesus as a Moses-like teacher. But such themes should not be confused with the main points (or convictions). By presenting Jesus as a Moses-like teacher, Matthew aims at making a point about Jesus, and not merely saying that he was a Moses-like teacher, something that he presupposes his readers already know.

In terms of the readers' old knowledge, Matthew hopes to communicate to his readers something that he expects they do not know—something new. Otherwise, his discourse would be pointless. It is not the mere repetition of what the readers already know. Rather, the themes and the figures express something new in terms of the old knowledge of the readers. Consequently, the thematic parts of the text (parts not directly related to the narrative oppositions) necessarily include *tensions* between the "old" and the "new." These tensions take various forms, such as apparent contradictions, odd statements, or metaphors. Conversely, when we encounter such tensions, we can say that Matthew makes a point or conveys a conviction. When such a thematic expression of the point of a passage is considered by itself, it is often difficult to understand or to distinguish what is new (Matthew's own view) from what is old (the presumed view of the readers). But when one examines the oppositions, the main point of a given passage, what Matthew attempts to convey by the theme becomes clear. For instance, it becomes clear that through the figure of Jesus preaching the Sermon on the Mount, Matthew wants to affirm that in certain ways Jesus is Moses-like, as his readers believe. But he also wants to affirm that in certain ways he is not Moses-like, and that, for him, these are the more important characteristics of Jesus as teacher.

It follows, therefore, that our study of Matthew's Gospel needs to take seriously the readers' perspective. Practically, this means that we need to adopt the position of readers who begin their reading—without a prior knowledge of the content—at the beginning and progress from passage to passage until the end of the text; otherwise we will not be in a position to evaluate what Matthew presupposes they know. Such a reading will reveal the development of the themes of the Gospel.

Finally, it is important to identify the passages or sections that are discrete units in which Matthew makes certain points. From the perspective of the readers, these sections are unified by the development of a *main theme* (which expresses these points). In the most abstract passages, such a main theme is expressed in the form of a question, or of something that is puzzling for the readers, who are then led to raise the question: What does this mean? Obviously, the development of this theme is complete when this question is fully answered. In this way a section of the Gospel can be identified. Similarly, in more figurative passages, a theme might be posited by the proclamation of a promise or a command and fully developed when the promise is fulfilled or the command carried out. In narrative passages a section might be opened by a situation where there is a problem or a situation of lack; in such cases, the narrative section is fully developed and ends when this problem is corrected. Yet a narrative section can evolve, as is the case in tragedies, from a good situation to a bad one. In general, the opening part of a thematic section posits a certain kind of abstract or figurative situation and the concluding part of that section presents a *situation that is inverted*.

THE ORGANIZATION OF THIS COMMENTARY

In treating each major section of Matthew we will first present its "Main Theme." Since we follow the unfolding of the text of the Gospel, we will always know where the section begins. After a preliminary study of the opening part, we first seek to identify where in the subsequent text an inverted situation is to be found. Once we have identified this main theme, we describe how this theme is developed. In this way the relationship among the various subsections or pericopes and their subthemes is clarified.

Then we proceed to examine each pericope so as to show what is (are) the point(s) it makes. Here we examine "Matthew's Convictions" expressed in the section. First, we take note of the way in which each pericope expresses these convictions or points. If the pericope involves "narrative oppositions," our first task is to study these oppositions in order to identify the points Matthew makes, and then to try to understand how in the rest of the pericope—its figures, symbols, sayings—Matthew expresses these points in terms of his readers' old knowledge. Practically, this means that we show what Matthew attempts to convey by the teaching or the story presented in this pericope. In so doing, we always take into consideration how this pericope, its points, and its thematic features develop points and themes expressed in preceding pericopes and sections. If, by contrast, the pericope is *thematic*, that is, if it does not involve any narrative opposition, we have to look for "tensions" in the text that allow us to understand the points Matthew makes in terms of his readers' old knowledge. Such a pericope is also interpreted in terms of the points made in the preceding passages of the section. In a few cases, namely, when it is the opening passage of a section that is thematic, we must postpone the full interpretation of such a thematic passage, since it needs to be interpreted in terms of the points made in the section.

The preceding methodological remarks were necessary so as to explain the specific strategy that governs our comments. As the users of this commentary will soon discover, in practice the interpretation of the text can easily be followed. It is resolutely an interpretation of "Matthew in terms of Matthew," a strategy already used in certain redactional studies of the Gospel.[19]

Some may be surprised that I do not pay more attention to Matthew's sources and to the way in which he modifies them. I simply take seriously the fact that when an author duplicates a source and makes it part of his or her own discourse, he or she has appropriated that source. In other words, even when Matthew duplicates exactly what one of his sources says, this passage has to be viewed as expressing *Matthew's* convictions and views. Of course, modifications brought to a source signal more directly that Matthew is expressing his own point of view. But focusing too much on the differences distorts the overall perception that one has of Matthew's own point of view. The analysis we perform should spontaneously account for the characteristics of Matthew's Gospel. In practice, after completing a first draft of the interpretation, I made a synoptic comparison to verify whether or not I had accounted for all the differences between Matthew, Mark, and

Luke. In a number of instances, this verification allowed me to discover that my interpretation was not complete; in a note I then refer to the parallel text.

Similarly, some might be surprised that I have taken into account the historical context of the Gospel—for instance, early Judaism and the situation of the Matthean church—only in order to identify possible connotations of textual features. Actually, this is the issue of what Matthew expected his readers to know. But I primarily use *internal evidence* in order to determine what the readers know *according to Matthew*: Matthew is not writing to objective readers who could be identified out of what we know about this period (e.g., readers who would know the Dead Sea Scrolls and the deliberations at Jamnia). As any writer or speaker does, Matthew imagined an audience and made presuppositions concerning what it might or might not know. As we know from experience, this imagined audience is not necessarily the actual audience that we have in front of us. This means that we cannot assume that Matthew's Gospel directly reflects the *actual* situation of his church, and that the Gospel should be interpreted in terms of a reconstructed view of that church. This is why the historical context of the Gospel can only be used to identify the possible connotations that a term, a figure, a phrase, or a saying might have. But only those connotations used in Matthew to set up oppositions and thus to make one point or another, or to express this point thematically, are relevant and thus mentioned here. While I have consulted various historical studies of Matthew, I mention them only when they underscore connotations that the oppositions of the text showed to be relevant (at times, I also object to an interpretation).

The contribution of this commentary is limited to elucidating *the convictions that Matthew expresses in each passage and how they are expressed through the thematic features of that passage.* As one reads this Gospel, one progressively envisions the Christian faith in a very specific way; one discovers the richness of Matthew's faith in the goodness of the Lord. But this faith is not presented systematically, and many questions about it are not raised. They would have been distracting. In a subsequent monograph I will propose a systematic presentation of "Matthew's Faith." There I will address questions such as those concerning Matthew's theology, Christology, ecclesiology, eschatology, and ethics as well as raise questions concerning the relationship of Matthew's Gospel to the Judaism of his time and the kind of church that he presupposed.

NOTES ON INTRODUCTION

1. The term "Gospel" is used throughout as a shorthand designation for the "Gospel According to Matthew." The term "gospel" designates the teaching of Jesus—the gospel of the kingdom—and of the church.
2. The name "Matthew" is used throughout as a convenient designation for the

author or redactor of the Gospel without presupposing that he should be identified with the person mentioned in 9:9.

3. See Stanton, "Origin and Purpose," 1898. In a critical comment about the work of several scholars he notes: "Perhaps the evangelist was rather less consistent than some of his modern students." I do not deny that there are inconsistencies and other tensions in the Gospel. But I will argue that, for Matthew, they are part of the coherent and consistent expression of his faith. In other words, for Matthew, they are not actual inconsistencies. The challenge of any interpretation is to discover the perspective from which what could appear as inconsistencies contributes to the consistent and coherent presentation of what Matthew wants to convey. And this is not "explaining away these inconsistencies," as Stanton charges the redaction critics with doing.

4. See Stanton, "Origin and Purpose," for an excellent review of Matthean scholarship.

5. See Greimas and Courtés, *Sémiotique. Dictionnaire raisonné du langage*. Together with other collaborators of Greimas, I had access to the manuscript in 1978, and we began exploring its implications for our respective fields.

6. See D. and A. Patte, *Structural Exegesis*, 1–10; and Patte, "The Interface of Semiotics and Faith," *RS/SI* 2 (1982):105–29.

7. These theoretical proposals are published in the form of fourteen articles in Greimas and Courtés, *Sémiotique. Dictionnaire raisonné du langage*, vol. 2. In this work, see the article "Parcours génératif" by Patte, which refers to the dimensions of meaning that are the topics of the other thirteen articles. The basic issue concerns the relation between "veridictory" and "thymic" categories in "fundamental semantics." In Matthew's Gospel (and also, e.g., in certain Jewish texts and in Native American rituals and myths—i.e., in non-Western cultures), thymic categories (euphoric/dysphoric) have the primary role, while the current semiotic theory presupposed that "veridictory" categories (being/seeming, or real/illusory) always had the primary role, as is the case in most Western discourses. Allowing for this possibility demanded refining our understanding of the role of "modalities" in all the other dimensions of the "generative trajectory."

8. See Patte, *Paul's Faith*, 1–27.

9. I do not claim that Matthew's system of convictions exclusively provides the coherence of the Gospel. It is but one among several levels of coherence. Consequently, my comments do not necessarily exclude other interpretations that have found other principles of coherence. I will eventually enter into critical dialogue with other interpretations in a future monograph that will propose a systematic presentation of Matthew's faith.

10. I am assuming that Matthew's Gospel is not fraudulent or hypocritical. But even when this is the case, the text reflects its author's system of convictions, which drives the author to write such a hypocritical discourse. Features of the text—inconsistencies among different dimensions of meaning—reveal the hypocritical character of the text. I did not detect such inconsistencies in Matthew's Gospel.

11. In the case of pure discourses, such as a sermon, one could expect that the narrative oppositions would be primary verbal oppositions. Yet, as we shall see in studying the Sermon on the Mount, oppositions of physical actions found in exhortations often play a central role in the overall organization of the discourse; without such narrative oppositions the discourse would not progress.

12. Of course this statement has been demonstrated in a more technical way in theoretical arguments and verified by numerous analyses. See the fourteen articles mentioned in n. 7 for an updated theoretical argument.

13. For brevity's sake we shall use the phrase *narrative opposition*, or simply the word *opposition*, as an exclusive designation for the complex network of relationships formed by "a narrative opposition *and* the semantic opposition(s) associated with it." When at times we speak of other kinds of semantic oppositions, we use other designations for them (e.g., "contrast"). These conventions are necessary to avoid many repetitions, since narrative oppositions are, of course, the main focus of our study of Matthew's Gospel.

14. More technically, this is an *opposition* that would be written "A vs. B." There is a *difference*. But, on the *semiotic square*, the two terms would be in a relation of *implication*. See the entries concerning each of these technical terms in Greimas and Courtés, *Semiotics and Language*.

15. The actions are clearly related in three cases: when the performance of an action is opposed to the nonperformance of the same action (e.g., loving a person vs. not loving that person); when the same "object" is attributed to different "receivers" (e.g., loving friends and enemies vs. loving friends only); when different objects are attributed to the same receiver (loving enemies vs. hating enemies). See D. and A. Patte, *Structural Exegesis*, 26–27, 52–59. In these pages, other criteria used to test the validity of the identification of narrative oppositions are described: the two verbs must belong to the same narrative level; at least one of the two verbs must have a personal form (even in didactic discourses where, often, one of the verbs has an impersonal form—infinitive, or participle).

16. More technically, I also take into account the "levels" of the narrative or of the discourse (primary narrative level and interpretive level in stories, warranting and dialogic levels in discourses) to which the oppositions belong. The oppositions are correlated in one way with the oppositions belonging to the same level and in other ways with some of the oppositions belonging to the other level. It is when a passage involves two levels that one can say the passage makes two main points. Further verification of the analysis can be done by studying the semiotic squares formed by a series of oppositions. I have done such verifications only in places where the pattern did not appear clearly. For a complete presentation of this method as applied to narratives, see D. and A. Patte, *Structural Exegesis*, 11–93. For its application to discursive texts, see Patte, *Paul's Faith*, 1–29, 127–48.

17. For a presentation of this simplified method as applied to Paul's letters, see Patte, "Reading Paul so as to Hear the Gospel Anew," *Chicago Studies* 24 (1985):339–56.

18. This is what Greimas call the "discursive" dimension of the "generative trajectory," which includes the processes of "thematization" and "figurativization." See these entries in Greimas and Courtés, *Semiotics and Language*. The term "theme" is not used in the technical sense it has in Greimas's theory but rather with its common meaning—which encompasses Greimas's "theme" and "figure."

19. Cf. Stanton, "Origin and Purpose," 1895–1899.

THE ORIGIN OF JESUS, THE CHRIST, SON OF DAVID

THE MAIN THEME

At first it may seem that the opening chapter of the Gospel According to Matthew includes two distinct parts: the genealogy (1:1–17) and the story of the birth of Jesus (1:18–25). But it soon appears that these two parts are closely interrelated and that they need to be read as a unit. They develop the single theme of the origin of Jesus, as is suggested by the use of the same word, *genesis,* to designate both the genealogy (1:1–17) and the birth of Jesus (1:18–25).

This preliminary remark is confirmed by a first structural reading of the text which allows us to specify this theme. Such a reading is based on the simple observation that a text is written in such a way that after reading the first few lines, the readers will want to continue. The opening verses of a section create an expectation by positing a recognizable theme, the main theme that will be developed in the section. The section ends when this expectation is met; what was potential at the beginning is at last realized. Now, by juxtaposing the designation of Jesus as "Jesus Christ, the son of David, the son of Abraham" (1:1) with the words "Abraham begot Isaac" (1:2, au.), Matthew leads the readers to expect a development that will show not only how Jesus was "begotten" but also in which sense he can be designated as he is in 1:1. This theme will be fully developed only when this expectation of the readers will have been met, that is, when Jesus will have been born (a birth announced in 1:16 and 1:18, and realized in 1:25) in such circumstances that his name "Jesus Christ, the son of David, the son of Abraham" will have been justified at least in a preliminary way— since this designation could also be the theme of the entire Gospel. By the end of the chapter all these expectations are met; Jesus is born and receives the name "Jesus," and it has been shown that he is an extraordinary "son of David" (and thus "son of Abraham") for whom the title "Christ" is appropriate. We therefore conclude that 1:1–25 forms a first thematic section of the Gospel which can be studied in and of itself.

A first glance at the narrative oppositions suggests how they are related to the main theme of this section. There are only two fully manifested

narrative oppositions.[1] In 1:19–20a, the text opposes the intended action of
Joseph, that of divorcing Mary, which would have been a negative action,
to the positive action, that of taking Mary his wife (to his home). In 1:20b
(cf. 1:18) and 1:25, the text opposes two kinds of actions regarding the
conception of Jesus: the conception by the Holy Spirit, what took place,
and Joseph knowing his wife before she had borne a son, the action that
Joseph did not do. This shows that, for Matthew, there are two essential
events in this story: (a) *the adoption of Jesus by Joseph*, which meant that by
taking Mary as his wife he was giving his name to Jesus as well as taking
the responsibility of naming him (1:25); and (b) *the miraculous conception*, a
designation that is appropriate, since it is an extraordinary conception which
involves an intervention of the supernatural. While both of these events are
essential for Matthew, one is more fundamental than the other in the sense
that it is presupposed by the other. The issue of Joseph's relation with Mary
and its outcome, the adoption, presupposes the miraculous conception, already mentioned in 1:18. Thus the text itself shows that the most fundamental point (conviction) of the story is, for Matthew, and not merely
according to our preunderstanding, related to the miraculous conception,
even though the text does not describe how the intervention of the supernatural took place.[2]

A preliminary examination of the narrative oppositions, taking into consideration the consequences of the positive and the negative actions, begins
to show what is at stake in them. On the one hand, if Jesus had been
conceived by Joseph, he would be an ordinary human being; the text emphasizes that he is out of the ordinary, special, just as his conception was
extraordinary, since it involves a supernatural intervention which disrupts
the natural, human way of begetting children. On the other hand, if Joseph
had divorced Mary, Jesus could not be properly (i.e., legally) recognized
as "son of David," since he would not be adopted by Joseph, who is himself
called "son of David" by the angel (1:20). In sum, through the theme developed in 1:1–25 Matthew aims at presenting to his readers Jesus as an
extraordinary "son of David," as the Christ.

MATTHEW'S CONVICTIONS IN 1:1–25

Beyond the identification of the main theme of 1:1–25, our goal is to
discover what the convictions are that Matthew conveys to his readers by
developing this theme, or, in other words, what the points are that Matthew
makes in this text. These convictions are most directly expressed by the
semantic oppositions associated with narrative oppositions. We can anticipate that they concern, on the one hand, the character of the divine intervention by contrast with that of human procreation (1:20b, 25) and, on the
other hand, what allows Joseph to carry out the right action, taking Mary
his wife, by contrast with what would allow or motivate him to do the

opposite action, divorcing her (1:18–20a). Yet thematic passages—passages that do not involve any narrative opposition (the rest of the chapter)—also convey the author's convictions, although in a different way. In thematic passages the convictions are expressed in terms of the "readers' old knowledge," as envisioned by the author; the presence of the author's convictions, what is new for the readers, is signaled by the tensions they create by being introduced in the old knowledge of the readers.

1:1–17. The Genealogy of Jesus, the Christ, Son of David and of Abraham

There is no narrative opposition in 1:1–17. This means that Matthew expects his readers to be familiar with biblical genealogies and to find meaningful the association of Jesus with such a genealogy.[3] But right away Matthew's hand, recasting for his own purpose the readers' old knowledge, can be perceived.[4] He designates this genealogy according to its final entry—"The book of the genealogy of Jesus Christ,"1:1—rather than according to its first entry, as is the case in the Hebrew Bible (e.g., Gen. 5:1), where such a genealogy is called the genealogy of Abraham. This departure from biblical usage shows that Jesus is presented as the fulfillment of the sacred history of Israel and that Jesus as fulfillment is more important than those who precede him. By contrast the biblical genealogies give preeminence to the first progenitor. This first twist of the readers' expectation begins to specify in which sense Jesus is extraordinary; even though he can be called "the son of David, the son of Abraham"—a designation with which the readers were familiar, although not necessarily in this double form—he is greater than David and Abraham.

1:6, 17. Matthew's hand is also visible in the overall organization of the genealogy. David too is presented as greater than Abraham: he is the only one in the genealogy who is given a title, "David the king" (1:6); furthermore, the genealogy is divided into sets of fourteen generations (1:17), possibly according to the numerical value of the letters in the name "David."[5] Consequently, a first theme of this passage can be identified by the phrase "Jesus Christ, the son of David": Jesus, as fulfillment of the genealogy, is primarily "son of David the king"; he is the king of the "end" of the genealogy, the extraordinary "king of the end of time,"[6] the Christ (Messiah; 1:1).

1:16b. The hand of Matthew can again be seen in the last entry (1:16b), which disrupts the pattern set in the rest of the genealogy. In 1:2–16a, the active form of the verb "to beget" is used (literally, "Abraham begot Isaac . . . and Jacob begot Joseph," au.), while the passive form is used in 1:16b ("Joseph the husband of Mary, of whom Jesus was born, who is called Christ"). This last statement announces the story of Jesus' birth (1:18–25).

It leads the readers to contrast the ordinary conceptions of David and Joseph with the extraordinary conception of Jesus. They could now wonder whether the genealogy should be viewed as that of Joseph, who is called "son of David" by no less an authority than "an angel of the Lord" (1:20), rather than that of Jesus. In other words, the text creates a tension between the adoption and the miraculous conception. Is Jesus "son of David" merely because of his adoption by Joseph, who belongs to the biological lineage of David while Jesus does not? But Matthew clearly wants to say that Jesus is son of David both because of the adoption by Joseph *and* because of the miraculous conception, since he relates the miraculous conception to the genealogy (1:16). Even though Jesus' conception is extraordinary, it is not out of place in the genealogy.

1:3, 5–6. Other features of the genealogy that, because of their odd character, reveal once again Matthew's hand confirm the preceding observation and help us understand its implications. We refer to the strange notations regarding the mothers of four persons in an otherwise male genealogy: The mention of Tamar as the mother of Perez (Matt. 1:3) alludes to the tortuous way in which Judah begot Perez and Zerah (Gen. 38:6–30); Rahab, the mother of Boaz (Matt. 1:5), was the foreign prostitute who helped the Israelite spies at Jericho (see Joshua 2); Ruth, the mother of Obed (Matt. 1:5), was also a foreigner (see Ruth 4); the very designation of the mother of Solomon as "the wife of Uriah" (Matt. 1:6) reminds the readers of David's dubious behavior (see 2 Samuel 11). These four notations underscore that, far from being straightforward, the genealogy progresses in very unexpected ways and at times through strange roundabouts.[7] It is not a predetermined process by which the progenitors, because of their origin, would automatically and straightforwardly beget the next generation.

Reminded of these episodes, the readers can only marvel at the extraordinary ways in which the continuity of Abraham's line was maintained. They can only marvel at God's interventions which raised up children of Abraham with the help of these progenitors but also in spite of them.[8] It then appears why the miraculous conception of Jesus has its place in the genealogy. The generation of the other children of Abraham and of David is not merely the result of natural, human procreation but is also the result of supernatural interventions, as in the case of Jesus' birth. That the notations on the women refer to interventions of the divine is further confirmed when Matthew uses the same kind of phrase to speak of the "begetting" (or "conceiving," same verb in Greek: *gennaō*) "by" (or "of," same preposition in Greek: *ek*) Tamar (1:3), Rahab (1:5), Ruth (1:5), the wife of Uriah (1:6), *and the Holy Spirit* (1:20). Thus Jesus belongs to this genealogy, despite the miraculous conception and indeed because of it. He is "son of David," not merely because he has been adopted by Joseph (in which case one could say he is son of David thanks to Joseph and despite his conception by the Holy

Spirit) but because he fully belongs to this genealogy of people who are children of David and Abraham thanks to God's interventions.

Yet the contrast between the conception of Jesus and the rest of the genealogy remains; the conception of Jesus is even more extraordinary. What is new is that Jesus' birth manifests *without ambiguity* that it is *by the intervention of God* that he is son of David, son of Abraham, since there is no biological role of a human father. It demonstrates that one can be son of David (and of Abraham)—indeed, the true son of David, the Messiah—without being of the seed of David (and of Abraham). A son of David is not someone primarily characterized by a certain biological descendance but someone whose existence has been brought about by the intervention of God. A child of David and of Abraham is someone who owes his or her origin (*genesis*) to God. This is also expressed in 3:9, where John the Baptist warns the Pharisees and the Sadducees against presuming that they are children of Abraham because they are of his seed, and concludes: "For I tell you, God is able from these stones to raise up children to Abraham." Jesus is a child of Abraham (and of David) who has been brought to existence in this way. Thus it is because of his extraordinary birth that Jesus, the Christ, fully belongs to this genealogy.

In sum, despite appearances, the entire genealogy is fundamentally characterized by divine interventions. While the role of God might be overlooked in normal procreations, and even in the more exceptional cases marked by the role of the four women, it is now fully manifest thanks to the extraordinary birth of Jesus. But what is the nature and the purpose of these interventions of God? The following verses express it.

1:18–25. Jesus' Birth and His Adoption by Joseph

In this passage are found the most fundamental points. What is Matthew's understanding of Jesus according to this story? One could think that it amounts to saying that Jesus is the "Son of God."[9] But here Matthew does not use this title—it does not appear in the Gospel before 2:15 and 3:17. This makes us pause. Of course, it is not wrong to say that Jesus is the "Son of God," but, for Matthew, such a statement is quite ambiguous; acknowledging that Jesus is "Son of God" or that he is "Lord" may or may not be a valid confession of faith (see 7:21). This is why he chooses to tell a story through which he hopes to communicate convictions about Jesus to his readers so that they may confess their faith in a proper way. Thus we need to consider carefully the way he presents the story of the miraculous conception and adoption of Jesus in 1:18–25, that is, the way he relates his main points (expressed through the narrative oppositions, 1:19–20 and 1:25) to his readers' old knowledge (expressed in textual elements, 1:21 and 1:22–23, not directly related to the oppositions of actions). We shall first consider the verses that are not directly related to the oppositions, 1:21–23, before considering the most direct expression of Matthew's convictions in 1:18–20, 24–25.

1:21. Matthew explains to his readers the outcome of the miraculous conception and the reason for the adoption by appropriating a meaning of the name "Jesus" that, he presumes, they know: "she will bear a son, and you shall call his name Jesus, for he will save his people from their sins" (1:21). For Matthew, this is an unusual formulation of Jesus' role,[10] a fact which confirms that it is his readers' view that he recasts by setting it in this specific context. Yet note that Jesus is characterized, not in terms of his being or of his nature, but in terms of what he will do, his vocation: "he will save his people from their sins."

When considered in the context of the entire chapter, this presentation of the outcome of the miraculous conception as a person with a certain vocation is clearly in keeping with the logic of the rest of the text. By relating the miraculous conception to the genealogy, the text expresses that the children of David and of Abraham are not primarily characterized by a certain being, a certain nature, or a certain kind of descendance—since one can be son of David either through a biological descendance (as Joseph is, 1:20) or through a special intervention of God (as Jesus is). They are characterized as owing their origin to God. Similarly, Jesus, who is son of David, Messiah, because of his miraculous conception, is not himself characterized primarily by his nature but by the fact that he owes his origin to God. The explanation of the name "Jesus" shows that "owing one's origin to God" means "having received a specific vocation," the vocation to save his people from their sins. This is also what 3:7–9 expresses when the true children of Abraham are described as people doing certain things: they "bear fruit that befits repentance" (3:8), or, more generally, they bear good fruit (7:17). Whatever might be their mode of generation—whether they are natural children of Abraham or extraordinary children of Abraham—what characterizes them is a certain vocation. They are children of Abraham only insofar as they carry out this vocation. So it is with Jesus.

Jesus is Christ, Messiah, son of David, son of Abraham because he has a special vocation, that of "king of the end of time" who will save his people from their sins.

One might object: Why could we not also acknowledge that as a result of the miraculous conception Jesus has a divine nature and is a divine incarnation? Is this not implied as soon as one speaks of a conception by the Holy Spirit? For our Western minds, it is. But, as we begin to see, Matthew has a way of thinking, a system of convictions, which is quite foreign to us and is closely related to that of early Judaism. We have to accept the challenge of understanding the Gospel on its own terms, that is, of perceiving the Christian faith from the perspective of Matthew's system of convictions, even though it might be foreign to us. Not doing so would amount to betraying Matthew, and to distorting his message to the point that it would contradict his teaching. When a statement regarding Jesus' divine nature is read into 1:18–25, Matthew's view of the relationships of God to his creation and of human beings to God is misconstrued by the interpreters as much as it is by those who presume to say that they are children of Abraham because they are of his race (3:9).

These comments do not deny that Jesus is an extraordinary person as a result of his conception by the Holy Spirit. But in order to avoid imposing on the text our Western preunderstandings, we have to recognize that he is an extraordinary person, not because he has a special nature, but because he has special qualifications. By this distinction, we are saying that, for Matthew, Jesus is primarily characterized by his vocation. Whatever else characterizes Jesus belongs to the realm of qualifications, the qualifications necessary for carrying out this vocation. It is not because he is "Son of God" in the sense of having a divine nature that Jesus has, then, the vocation of savior, but it is because of his vocation that he needs to have, and also receive, extraordinary qualifications, indeed divine qualifications.

This distinction might seem exceedingly subtle, but without it one cannot understand central aspects of Matthew's faith and thus of his Gospel. In fact, when this distinction is not made, one is inexorably driven to make of Matthew's teaching a legalistic, fatalistic, or deterministic system— falsely so. Thus, if through his miraculous conception Jesus had first of all received a divine nature, then it would mean that he is fully determined by his nature which becomes his "fate." As divine, he could not but be the savior of his people; he would have to do what is predetermined by his nature. But it is clear this is not what Matthew means. Jesus is the "Son of God" in the sense that he is "called" by God (see 2:15), that he is "beloved" by God, and that he is the one with whom God is "well pleased" (3:17). He is not the puppet of a God who would have predetermined his existence; he is a person called by God for a specific and extraordinary vocation and given the means or qualifications to do it. He is a person free to respond to this call. Because he responds faithfully to this vocation (fulfilling "all righteousness," 3:15), he is "well pleasing" to God. As the "beloved Son" he is indeed in an intimate relationship with God.

Similarly, the mention of four women in the genealogy (1:3, 5–6) conveys that the unfolding of sacred history, even though it was the fulfillment of promises (in Abraham), was not predetermined and demanded new inter- ventions of God. We understand now that, for Matthew, these interventions involved the calls of certain persons, the women, to specific vocations. Thus, in brief, the pattern of promise-fulfillment, which plays a significant role in the Gospel, does not seem to involve, for Matthew, a deterministic view of sacred history, by contrast with what one finds in apocalyptic texts.[11]

1:22–23. The pattern of promise-fulfillment is also found in the last tex-

tual element not related to the narrative oppositions, 1:22–23, one of the
formula quotations we encounter throughout Matthew's Gospel.[12] These
verses express that the birth of Jesus (1:18–21) fulfills the prophecy of Isa.
7:14. Once again Matthew presupposes that his readers are familiar with
Scripture and view it as containing promises that are fulfilled in Jesus' time.
He appropriates and recasts his readers' presumed knowledge by introducing it at this point in the text, that is, *after* the story that the prophecy fulfills
has been told.[13] This is significant when one compares the formula quotations of Matthew with the *pesher Habakkuk*, one of the Dead Sea Scrolls
from Qumran. The similarities of interpretation between the two have long
been pointed out.[14] Both use not only the promise-fulfillment pattern but
also similar techniques of interpretation. Yet there is a difference: the *pesher*,
which originates in an apocalyptic community with a strongly deterministic
view of history,[15] almost always begins by quoting the biblical texts and
then describes the events in which they are fulfilled. Matthew describes the
fulfillment of the events and then points out the biblical prophecy that is
fulfilled. This order has the same effect as the reversal in emphasis that we
found in the genealogy, where the last entry, the fulfillment, is shown to
be greater than the first entry, the promise (see above, p. 18). In both cases
the order signifies not only that the fulfillment is greater than the promise
or prophecy but also, and conversely, that they do not predetermine the
fulfillment. (In *pesher* the prophecy is the blueprint that later history cannot
but follow.) Indeed, the events of Jesus' birth, results of divine interventions,
are aimed at fulfilling the prophecy according to God's purpose, as in 1:22:
"All this took place *in order that the word . . . be fulfilled*" (au.; note the
conjunction "in order that" and the passive form showing that the fulfillment is God's actions). Yet, for Matthew, the fulfillment of God's purpose
is not deterministic, although there is continuity between the prophecy (the
word of the Lord to the prophet) and the fulfillment (through God's interventions). But how can we make sense of this last statement, which seems
to involve an internal contradiction? It makes sense only in the case where
God and God's purpose are viewed in a very special way. Thus this theme
of the fulfillment of prophecies, or more generally of Scripture, which we
find directly expressed for the first time in these verses, serves notice that
we still need to understand Matthew's convictions about God and that we
might find them somewhat different from ours.

Much could be said about the relation of the formula quotation (1:22–
23) to the preceding verses.[16] But, for our investigation, it is most significant
to note that here Matthew expresses, in terms of his readers' old knowledge,
their knowledge of Scripture, the convictions conveyed by the opposition
in the stories of the miraculous conception and of the adoption. It is in this
light that the designation of Jesus as "Emmanuel," "God with us," needs
to be understood. Because of the parallelism with the explanation of the
name "Jesus," we must conclude that this new name refers to Jesus' vocation

rather than to his nature (see pp. 21–22). As the child Emmanuel of Isaiah's time was a "sign" of the active presence of God in the house of David (Isa. 7:13–17), so Jesus is the one through whom the presence of God is manifested among us. Jesus' vocation is both to save his people from their sins and to manifest God's presence.

Yet Matthew seems aware that it is somewhat awkward to call Jesus "Emmanuel." Properly speaking, it is not his name—a name never used elsewhere in the Gospel, nor in the New Testament for that matter. Thus he modifies the quotation in order to use an indefinite plural form ("they will call his name," au.), which amounts to saying something like, "One might want to call him Emmanuel." The fact that Matthew nevertheless chose this designation of Jesus and of his vocation is most important. This choice might indicate that, while satisfying his readers' expectations by mentioning the meaning of Jesus' commonly known name and by using the promise-fulfillment pattern with the prophecy of Isaiah,[17] Matthew deliberately chose to emphasize the name "Emmanuel" as a better expression of Jesus' vocation than "savior." "God with us" might be, for Matthew, a most significant designation of Jesus. It specifies the vocation of Jesus; while it can be said that it is a vocation to save his people from their sins, it might be more appropriate to say that it is a vocation to manifest God's presence among us.

The themes discussed above are the figurative, and thus indirect, expressions of Matthew's convictions. As such, they point toward these convictions and thus must be interpreted in terms of them. We have noted that these themes presuppose certain convictions about God, as could be expected, since such convictions are to be found in most kinds of faith. The question is thus: What is the specific view of God presupposed by Matthew's text? It is, of course, a central conviction of his faith, so central that we cannot hope to elucidate it on the basis of a single chapter of the Gospel. Yet the themes point toward other related convictions: Matthew's view of divine interventions, of divine presence, and of vocation. A study of 1:18–20, 24–25 should give us a glimpse of these convictions, since these verses express them more directly by associating them with narrative oppositions.

1:19–20a, 24. The narrative opposition between divorcing Mary (1:19) and taking Mary his wife (1:20a, 24) should help us better understand the theme of vocation. Since Joseph obeys a command from "an angel of the Lord," by studying this opposition of actions we can hope to understand what are, for Matthew, some of the conditions for the possibility of carrying out a vocation. What characterizes someone carrying out a vocation given by God? In order to address this question, leaving aside the narrative opposition per se, we need to examine the related semantic opposition that the text sets up between the description of Joseph as positive subject (taking Mary into his home) and the description of Joseph as negative subject (planning to divorce Mary). Note the way in which Joseph is characterized in each case:

Joseph, when taking Mary as his wife, is described as "son of David"; obeying (1:24), without fear (1:20), the command of the angel of the Lord who appeared to him in a dream; and being told by the angel that "that which is conceived in her is of the Holy Spirit."

Joseph, when wanting to divorce Mary, is described as "her husband"; "just," or righteous; "unwilling to put her to shame" (1:19).

A comparison of these two descriptions shows that the point about conditions for carrying out a vocation which Matthew makes by this opposition concerns three issues: (*a*) Joseph's status, either as son of David or as husband; (*b*) the reason for acting, either the command of the angel of the Lord or Joseph's righteousness; (*c*) a perception of the way in which the situation affects people, either as not to be feared or as potentially shameful.

We cannot say that this point concerns the kind of information that Joseph has, or does not have, about the situation; the text does not establish any opposition on this issue, since nothing is said regarding the kind of information Joseph has when he wants to divorce Mary. Of course, it is presupposed that Joseph knows something about the situation—he knows at least that she is pregnant—but Matthew does not specify what he knows. Did he know that Mary was pregnant as a result of the miraculous conception, since this is mentioned in 1:18, or did he think that she had committed adultery? The answer might seem obvious to us, even though the commentators are divided.[18] But since the text does not articulate an answer, we have to conclude that this is *our* question, prompted by our preunderstandings, and not that of Matthew. Similarly, we have the tendency to assume that by the phrase "that which is conceived in her is of the Holy Spirit" the angel explains to Joseph the circumstances of Jesus' conception. But, as most commentators note, this phrase does not describe how Jesus was conceived (*gennaō*) but rather the reason why Mary's pregnancy should not be perceived as shameful. "That which is conceived in her" is not shameful or impure but is "of the Holy Spirit," and thus holy (the Greek construction of this phrase underscores "holy"). For Matthew, information about what happened in a situation, a correct knowledge of the facts and the circumstances, is *not* one of the primary requirements for correctly fulfilling a vocation, that is, for doing the right thing. This knowledge might be helpful, but it remains secondary. It is another kind of knowledge or perception of the situation which is essential for Matthew.

The true conditions of possibility for carrying out a vocation are expressed by Matthew in the actual oppositions (i.e., the oppositions manifested on both the positive and the negative side by elements of the text). We have noted that the text opposes diverging evaluations of the same situation, Mary's pregnancy, either as something that is potentially shameful (a cause for disgrace and rejection by others if it is exposed, the literal meaning of the verb translated "to put to shame," 1:19) or as something that one should not fear. These evaluations express the ways in which the situation affects someone either positively or negatively.

At first, Joseph perceives the situation as shameful, that is, as having the potential of affecting negatively the people involved (Mary, and indirectly Joseph). But the angel of the Lord reveals to him that this is a wrong evaluation: the situation should not be feared; it should not be viewed as affecting negatively the people involved.

Thus, this opposition shows that, for Matthew, it is essential to discern the way in which a situation affects people, that is, whether a situation is euphoric (good in the sense of giving a feeling of well-being, here the feeling of absence of fear) or dysphoric (bad in the sense of giving a negative feeling, here the feeling of shame or disgrace). Of course, one needs to have at least some information about the situation in order to evaluate it; Joseph needs at least to be aware that Mary is pregnant in order to react negatively; similarly, the angel informs him that "that which is conceived in her is of the Holy Spirit" (1:20). Beyond this general awareness, knowing the precise facts involved in the situation is not necessary to carry out the correct vocation. Note that Matthew describes neither how the miraculous conception took place nor how Joseph imagined what happened. What is necessary is to have the correct evaluation of the situation, that is, the correct perception of the value that characterizes the situation—whether it is good or bad, holy or shameful. This is the basis for correct action.

Yet, how is it possible to have the correct evaluation of, or the correct feeling about, the situation? The other two oppositions express it. Joseph had a correct evaluation when "an angel of the Lord appeared to him in a dream, saying, 'Joseph, son of David, do not fear to take Mary your wife'" (1:20a). By contrast, he had an incorrect evaluation as long as he, the righteous Joseph, the husband of Mary (1:19), was on his own. In the latter case, Joseph's righteousness was of no help to him to gain the proper perspective of the situation. In fact, the opposition makes it clear that it is as "righteous" that Joseph makes an incorrect evaluation of the situation, and this even though his righteousness is the better righteousness (5:20) of a person who has mercy and compassion (5:38–48; 7:12) for someone else. This is indicated by his wanting to divorce Mary quietly so as not to expose her to shame (1:19). Yet such a righteousness is not enough. Something is missing or incorrect in it. Since this qualification of Joseph is opposed to a divine revelation, it appears that this righteousness is incorrect, because it is merely viewed in terms of human relationship. It is the righteousness of Joseph as *husband*, and thus quite possibly a righteousness viewed only in terms of contractual agreements—his contract with Mary—as obedience to the law.[19] Even this good righteousness can only lead to the wrong perception of situations. Conversely, it is only because of a special revelation from the divine, the revelation from "an angel of the Lord" and "in a dream,"[20] that Joseph can have the correct evaluation of the situation. More precisely, since

Joseph is called "son of David" (in contrast to "husband"), that is, since he is someone who owes his origin to interventions of God, we can say that the correct perception of the situation with the help of interventions of God is a part of what it means to be "son of David." In brief, a "son of David," a person in whose experience God intervenes (see pp. 19–20), has the qualification necessary for perceiving the true value of a situation, that is, whether it is truly good (euphoric) or truly bad (dysphoric).

In the case of Joseph, one can now understand what is, according to Matthew, the role of a divine intervention. As suggested earlier regarding Jesus, it is clear that the intervention of God has the purpose of establishing Joseph's vocation—of taking Mary as his wife and of adopting Jesus. One can also see that this is done, not by giving a new nature to Joseph nor by transforming the nature of a situation, but by providing Joseph with the proper qualification, namely, the correct evaluation of the situation. The perception of the euphoric character of the situation also involves perceiving what one should do about it, the vocation proper, which is thus simultaneously revealed.

Of course, we cannot generalize and say that, for Matthew, all the interventions of God are of this kind; we need to consider each case on its own terms. Yet the other intervention of God in this passage, the miraculous conception, establishes Jesus' vocation and also possibly provides him with some of the qualifications necessary for carrying out this vocation.

1:18, 20b, 25. The opposition between the conception by the Holy Spirit (1:20b) and Joseph knowing his wife, the action that Joseph did not do (1:25), does not help us specify what these qualifications are. The subjects of the two actions, the Holy Spirit and Joseph, are minimally described; there is no description of the Holy Spirit. Consequently, we only have a largely undefined opposition between the divine (the "Holy" Spirit as "God's" Spirit) and the human. Yet two observations are possible.

First, the divine is defined in terms of holiness, that is, in terms of a value (the ultimate euphoric value) rather than in terms of "being" (e.g., God's ultimate power in a miracle story). This allows us to understand a little better the phrase "God with us." The presence of God, whatever else it may be, is the presence of the Holy. This also means that it can be apprehended, as Joseph did, only through the evaluation of a situation with the help of a revelation. We can also understand the relation between the two names of Jesus. Jesus' coming among his people necessarily has the effect of transforming the characteristics of the human situation. Instead of being a situation characterized by the presence of sins, the unholy, it is now characterized by the presence of the Holy.

Second, even though the divine intervention is decisive, it is not complete in and of itself. The miraculous conception is complemented by the adoption of Jesus by Joseph. Even though the role of divine interventions in human affairs is now unambiguous in the miraculous conception, it does not abolish or bypass the role of human beings. The purpose of God's action—that Jesus be the son of David, the Christ, who will save his people and be the manifestation of the Holy among us—is realized only because Joseph received a vocation and accepted carrying it out. Note that it is Joseph who has the essential role of naming the child "Jesus" (1:21, 25). Does this observation mean that, for Matthew, this is a fundamental pattern according to which divine interventions are complete only when human beings accept the carrying out of the vocation to actualize them? In other words, does it mean that divine interventions are offered merely as potentials to be realized by human beings? Is this what is implied by the presentation of God's manifestation as a manifestation of the Holy to which human beings are called to respond rather than as the manifestation of an ultimate power that would impose itself upon human beings and transform them or their situations in a radical fashion? What is the view of God implied here?

Such are the questions that 1:1–25 raises, creating expectations that invite the readers to continue their reading with the hope that the rest of the Gospel will provide answers to these questions.

NOTES ON 1:1–25

1. We should not consider the incomplete or implied oppositions. Since the author takes the risk of letting the readers complete them, they do not express the author's fundamental convictions.

2. This is the case in Hellenistic stories about the extraordinary birth of heroes. See, e.g., BEARE, 70; BONNARD, 18–19; SCHWEIZER, 33. When we say that the miraculous conception is "more fundamental" than the adoption of Jesus by Joseph, we simply want to emphasize that the convictions involved in the former are more fundamental (and thus more abstract) than those expressed by the latter. Yet, as far as the theme of this passage (the expression of these convictions in terms of the readers' expectations) is concerned, it is clear that the adoption and the naming of Jesus play the major role in the passage.

3. Our investigation should not be confused with the form-critical and redaction-critical studies aimed at identifying the traditional material used in a text and how it is used in a text. Yet we take into account the results of such studies. For the present state of such studies, see PRABHU and BROWN.

4. The author's hand at work recasting, transforming, and twisting up the old knowledge of the readers can be perceived in the transformation of a common literary genre as well as in the places in the text where there are breaks in pattern or oddities.

5. In Hebrew, letters were also used as numbers. The three letters of David in Hebrew (daleth, waw, daleth = 4 + 6 + 4) have a total value of 14. This kind of interpretation found in the early Jewish literature is called gematria. See BEARE, 63; GUNDRY, 19; Johnson, The Purpose of Biblical Genealogies; Hood, "The Genealogies of Jesus," 1–15.

6. Concepts such as "end of time" and "Christ" or "Messiah" are largely undefined at this point of our study. As long as Matthew does not define such technical terms we need to consider them as unknown entities, which will be progressively defined by the text.

7. Yet this does not mean that Matthew considered these women as sinners. As Bloch shows in her study, Tamar was viewed in a very positive light: see Bloch,

"Juda engendra Phares et Zara de Thamar." From this, we can conclude with Beare and Brown that the other women were similarly lauded (note that Rahab is presented as an example of faith in Heb. 11:31 and as justified by her works in James 2:25): BEARE, 64; BROWN, 71–74.

8. BONNARD, 15.

9. See, e.g., KINGSBURY, 44; GUNDRY, 20; BROWN, 134. Note that my comments have nothing to do with modern or ancient objections to a *miraculous* conception, such as those discussed by BONNARD, 18–19. My only concern is to grasp the way in which Matthew understood this miracle and to avoid projecting upon the text the preunderstandings, whatever they might be, that we have about miracles in general and this miracle in particular.

10. While Jesus' vocation is somehow related to "sins," the function "saving from sins" is not emphasized in the Gospel of Matthew. See BEARE, 71.

11. See Patte, *Early Jewish Hermeneutic,* 159–67, and footnotes.

12. For a study of the formula quotations in Matthew, see STENDAHL, 97–127 and 183–206; Gundry, *Use of OT*; PRABHU.

13. This is true even though the formula quotation is situated before the end of the story is actually "performed." As Pesch has shown, Matthew follows a pattern (the "command-execution" pattern) that is also found with a formula quotation in 21:1–7: Pesch, "Eine alttestamentliche Ausführungsformel im Matthäus-Evangelium," *BZ* NF 11 (1967):79–95. For our purpose, it is enough to note that the angel's command already tells the end of the story. Thus this case (as well as 21:1–7, and also 2:15) can be assimilated to the case of other formula quotations where the quotation is found at the very end of the story.

14. STENDAHL, 183–202.

15. Patte, *Early Jewish Hermeneutic,* 159–67, 299–308.

16. Regarding the content of the prophecy, we note the close fit of its formulation (a somewhat modified version of Isa. 7:14 according to the LXX) with the description of the fulfillment in 1:18–21 (using phrases certainly borrowed from the quotation), a close fit that gives clues to the mode of redaction of the text. See STENDAHL, 97–99, 198–99; PRABHU, 229–53, and the bibliography in the footnotes.

17. The use of the promise-fulfillment pattern with a prophecy of Isaiah was quite common in early Christianity. Thus it is highly likely that Matthew presupposed that his readers were familiar with it. It is even possible that he presupposed that his readers were familiar with the application of Isa. 7:14 to Jesus, since Luke clearly also uses this text (see Luke 1:31) although without applying the name "Emmanuel" to Jesus.

18. Certain commentators defend the view, which has a long history, that Joseph was aware that Mary's pregnancy was the result of a miraculous conception; his hesitation was coming from his awe of the mystery: Pelletier, "L'annonce à Joseph," *RSR* 54 (1966):67–68; Léon-Dufour, *Etudes d'Evangile,* 67–81; GUNDRY, 21–22. The other view is more commonly supported; see, e.g., BROWN, 125–28; BEARE, 68.

19. There is considerable controversy regarding how *dikaios* should be interpreted in this passage. For a summary of the major scholarly opinions, see BROWN, 125–28, and his bibliography. It should be emphasized that, because of the unmistakable narrative opposition, "righteousness," as a qualification of Joseph, who wants to do the wrong action (divorce Mary), can only have a *negative* connotation in this passage. Several of the proposed interpretations are misleading because they are based upon the presupposition that this term has a positive connotation: see, e.g., Nolan, *Royal Son of God,* 123–30. Note also that the correlation of "righteous" and "husband" (parallel and opposed to the correlation of the "revelation in a dream" and "son of David"), which clearly appears in this twofold opposition, adds another argument to Brown's interpretation of this term as referring to someone obeying the law.

20. The opposition contrasts the human contractual relationship to the appearance of "an angel of the Lord . . . in a dream," underscoring in this way that it is a *supernatural* mode of revelation. For the frequent references to dreams as modes of revelation in the ancient world, see BEARE, 68–69.

FROM BETHLEHEM
TO NAZARETH

THE MAIN THEME

The second chapter of the Gospel constitutes a complete literary section. Even though one might be tempted to isolate the story of the Magi (2:1–12) from the story of Herod which follows, it soon appears that they are inextricably intertwined to form a story about Jesus, beginning with his birth "in Bethlehem of Judea in the days of Herod the king" (2:1) and ending with Jesus dwelling "in a city called Nazareth" in Galilee after the death of Herod (2:22–23). Thus, after the story in chapter 1 of the historical and divine origin of Jesus, chapter 2 presents a story that has as its main theme his geographical origin.[1]

Through this overall organization Matthew invites his readers to view Jesus' birth in Bethlehem of Judea (2:1) as raising expectations about Jesus which, surprisingly, will be met only in Nazareth of Galilee (2:22–23). Matthew may have been motivated by the need to explain why, at the beginning of his ministry (4:12–17), Jesus, the Messiah, son of David, came from such an unlikely place as Nazareth in Galilee rather than from a Davidic location, such as Bethlehem in Judea. But the effect for the readers is to underscore that what happened in Bethlehem, or more generally in Judea, is a promise, a potential that will be realized only in events taking place in Nazareth of Galilee or, more generally, beyond the boundaries of Judea. Jesus of Nazareth is the fulfillment of what is only potential in the son of David born in Bethlehem. It is therefore from this perspective that 2:23 and its obscure formula quotation, "That what was spoken by the prophets might be fulfilled, 'He shall be called *Nazōraios*,'" should be interpreted.

2:23. Numerous studies have been devoted to 2:23 in order to elucidate the meaning of *Nazōraios* (RSV: "Nazarene") in terms of traditions and biblical texts to which Matthew might have alluded (the quotation does not correspond to any known biblical text). The divergent proposals[2] do not necessarily exclude each other, since the very strangeness of the name is evocative rather than descriptive and therefore has several connotations.[3] Since *Nazōraios* conveys to the readers that Jesus' stay in Nazareth begins to actualize the promises contained in his birth in Bethlehem, two possible interpretations of *Nazōraios* appear to be appropriate. *Nazōraios* could be derived from *nazir*, "one consecrated to God by a vow" (see Num. 6:1–21),[4] in order to express that Nazareth is the place where it is made manifest that Jesus is a *nazir* like Samson, who was "made holy to God from [his] mother's womb" (see 1:18–25 and the LXX text of Judg. 16:17).[5] Yet *Nazōraios* could also be derived from *nezer*[6]—the "branch" as in Isa. 11:1: "There shall come forth a shoot from the stump of Jesse [David's father], and a branch shall grow out of his roots." It could signify that Nazareth is the place where it is made manifest that he is "son of David." In order to understand the main theme of this chapter, we need to find answers to the following questions: Are these interpretations valid? And if one or both are, in which sense does the move to Nazareth make manifest that Jesus is "holy" or "son of David"?

These questions cannot be addressed on the basis of 2:23 by itself. This verse and the questions it raises need to be understood in terms of the entire chapter, that is, in terms of the way in which Matthew develops the main theme, the theme "From Judea to Galilee," and in terms of the points Matthew makes by setting up a series of narrative oppositions.

Our study of these oppositions will show that the main points of this story concern Matthew's conviction about the true view of authority and the way it applies to Jesus the Christ, son of David, who, in 1:1–25, was presented as having a special vocation. It is now specified that one of the qualifications Jesus has in order to carry out this vocation is his authority. First, the text emphasizes that his authority must be acknowledged; it is *real authority which demands submission from people* (the Magi pay homage to him, 2:1–12). One must submit to his authority because it is a *supreme authority*, since it is associated (correlated) with the authority of the dream to which the Magi submitted (2:12): it is a supernatural authority, not a human authority. Furthermore, the text expresses one of the reasons why one can welcome Jesus' authority with joy and without fear, as the Magi did (2:10). True authority, divine authority, such as that which Jesus has, is not exerted through the use of (political) power or force as is Herod's authority, which through the use of power destroys and disrupts normal human life (see 2:13–16). Even though it is a real, indeed a supreme authority, God's authority respects the normal course of human affairs.

This brief summary of some of the conclusions we will reach and explain in our study of 2:1–23 suggests how the second chapter of the Gospel is related to the first and the significance of the movement from Judea to Galilee. The remarks regarding the characteristics of divine authority confirm our suggestion regarding 1:18–25; according to Matthew, divine interventions do not impose themselves upon human beings by disrupting the normal course of human affairs. Rather, they are calls, manifestations of vocations which human beings need to accept by submitting to them and carrying them out so as to complete God's interventions. On the other hand, we can anticipate that the movement from Judea to Galilee and the designation of Jesus as *Nazōraios* express the character of Jesus' authority. Jesus' authority is indeed that of the son of David born in Bethlehem, but the character of his authority is as unexpected as the fact that the son of David dwelt in Nazareth.

MATTHEW'S CONVICTIONS IN 2:1–23

This chapter of the Gospel divides itself into two parts: the Magi paying homage to Jesus (2:1–12); the exile to Egypt and the return from exile to Nazareth (2:13–23).

2:1–12. The Magi Pay Homage to Jesus

As we read these verses we notice several features of the story that Matthew expects his readers to find somewhat surprising, a signal that he expresses his convictions in terms of his readers' old knowledge. The exclamation "behold" shows that the readers might be surprised by the coming of the Magi (2:1) and the reappearance of the star that goes before them on their road to Bethlehem (2:9). Thus Matthew expects that the Magi, who have seen the newborn king's star and come to pay homage to him guided by that star, are enigmatic figures for his readers. We should not try to outwit the text by attempting to explain the precise identity of these personages and the nature of the phenomenon designated by the word "star."[7] The description that Matthew provides is enough for his purpose. It can be discerned by taking notice of the way in which he sets it in a context of elements with which he expects his readers to be familiar.

We note four features of the theme of the Magi. (1) The Magi are "from the East" (2:1), and thus non-Jews, Gentiles, since they are contrasted with "the chief priests and scribes of the people" (of Israel; 2:4). (2) They find meaning, indeed religious meaning (since it concerns the Christ), in the rising of a star (2:2)—a revelation discovered outside Scripture and contrasted with the religious meaning that the priests and the scribes find in Scripture (2:5). (3) From this observation of the star they learn that the "king of the Jews" is born, the approximate time of his birth (2:7), and its general location—the region of Judea, since the term translated "Jews" designates in Greek the inhabitants of "Judea" (2:2).[8] Yet they cannot find the Christ on the basis of this revelation alone. The revelation that they have needs to be complemented by the revelation in Scripture of the precise birthplace of the Christ (but not the time of the birth). Yet the validity of the revelation that the Magi received is shown by the fact that the star reappears (2:9) after they have been instructed according to what "is written by the prophet" and act accordingly (2:5–9). (4) Finally, on the basis of nonscriptural revelation, the Magi want to pay homage to the newborn king (2:2), while Herod "and all Jerusalem with him" (2:3) do not want to

pay homage to him, as is shown by their negative reaction to the news of
his birth (2:4).

2:3, 10. Matthew underscores this latter point by setting up a narrative
opposition that contrasts reactions to the news concerning the newborn
"king of the Jews." While Herod "was troubled, and all Jerusalem with
him" (2:3), the Magi "rejoiced exceedingly with great joy" (2:10), a joy in
response to the presence of the star which confirms the proximity of the
"king of the Jews." In a general sense the point made by this opposition
concerns opposite responses to Jesus' authority. The response of the Magi,
their great joy—comparable to Joseph's valid response, not fearing (1:20)—
involves the acknowledgment of Jesus' authority as king of the Jews (2:2),
an acknowledgment that leads them to pay homage to him with gifts (2:11).
The negative response of Herod and all of Jerusalem is one of fear; the
newborn king of the Jews is disturbing (2:3); his authority is perceived as
a threat that needs to be removed by his destruction (see 2:13, 16, 20).

Beyond this general observation, the text shows that the point Matthew
conveys to his readers concerns the conditions for acknowledging and accepting the authority of Jesus as "king of the Jews," Messiah, son of David.

Herod's negative reaction to the announcement of the birth of the Christ
is clarified by the contrast that the text sets up between the newborn king
(2:2), a phrase that means "one who is king by right of birth," and Herod,
who is "king" (2:1, 3) but not by right of birth. Matthew assumes, therefore,
that readers would identify Herod as the Idumaean usurper, indeed as a
conniving and ruthless tyrant (see 2:7–8, 16).[9] Thus one could expect that
Herod would be troubled by the news of the birth of the king of the Jews.
From his perspective, the Christ threatens his political authority. But why
should "all Jerusalem" be troubled with him (2:3)?[10] Since Jerusalem is
represented by its religious leaders in the second part of the same sentence
(2:4), and since the text contrasts two kinds of religious knowledge, we
have to conclude in this case that it is as religious authorities that they feel
threatened by the appearance of another religious authority—the Messiah,
the Christ. Thus Jesus' authority as Messiah is not accepted, and is even
rejected, by both the political and the religious authorities in Jerusalem. But
why?

It is striking that Herod and the Jewish authorities do not acknowledge
the authority of Jesus even though they seem to have almost all that is
necessary for doing so. From the Magi they know that he is born (2:2) and
the approximate time of his birth (2:7). They are able to recognize that the
"king of the Jews" mentioned by the Magi is the Messiah (2:4). They have
access to the revelation of Scripture which the Jewish religious authorities
know how to interpret correctly to determine where the Christ is to be
born.[11] We have to conclude that, despite their knowledge that he is the
Messiah, Herod and the Jewish authorities do not acknowledge Jesus as

their king, because, by contrast with the Magi, their will to do so has not
been established. This is not an attempt to psychologize the Jewish authorities but the recognition that one of the conditions for the possibility
of any action is that the subject's will to carry out this action be established.[12]
Then the question is: What establishes the will to pay homage to Jesus for
the Magi? Since they share their own information with Herod and the Jewish
leaders, who in turn share their own knowledge with the Magi, it appears
that the only difference between the two groups is that the Magi have seen
the star (2:3, 7, 9), while Herod and the Jewish leaders did not see it, although they heard about it. It is the seeing of the star that motivated the
Magi to journey to Jerusalem. In other words, it is a *revelation outside Scripture*, the star, that establishes their will to pay homage to Jesus, as is expressed in 2:2: "We have seen his rising star, and have come to worship
him" (au.).[13] The star is what motivates their action.

2:8, 12. Matthew underscores this point by opposing what the Magi did—
not returning to Herod after "being warned in a dream" (2:12)—to what
Herod wanted them to do—reporting to him where Jesus is (2:8). This
second point (conviction) of the story emphasizes that the will of the Magi
is established by a revelation in a dream—it is a submission to a supernatural
authority—and is not established by King Herod, a human authority.

From these observations we now draw several conclusions. First, for
Matthew, a revelation has, or should have, the effect of establishing the will
of people to act. As the revelation from the angel "in a dream" convinced
Joseph to act in a certain way (1:20–21, 24–25), so seeing the star (2:2) and
being warned in a dream (2:12) establish the will of the Magi. Similarly,
later in the text Joseph also acts according to what is revealed to him in
dreams (2:13–14; 2:19–21; and 2:22).[14] As we noted regarding 1:20–21, 24–
25, for Matthew a revelation is primarily the disclosure of the euphoric or
dysphoric character of a situation, a disclosure that leads the person to want
to act accordingly—since when one is truly convinced that something is
good one wants to appropriate it by acting accordingly, and since one wants
to avoid something perceived as bad. Consequently, one can say that such
a revelation is also a vocation, a call to do something.

Second, all the cases of revelations that properly establish the will of
people mentioned in chapters 1—2 are simultaneously *nonscriptural* (through
an angel, a star, a dream) and *confirmed by Scripture*. The relationship between
these revelations and the revelation in Scripture is clarified in 2:1–12. The
revelation in Scripture by itself does not establish the will, the true vocation
of a person (cf. the priests and the scribes); a revelation outside Scripture
alone can do it (cf. the Magi). Conversely, a revelation outside Scripture
does establish the will and vocation of a person, but the specific way to
carry out this vocation (where exactly the Magi need to go) or the specific

meaning (purpose) of this action (1:22–23; 1:15; 2:23) can be ascertained only with the help of Scripture.

More precisely, a revelation outside Scripture alone gives someone the possibility of truly recognizing Jesus' authority and therefore the will of submitting to it—paying homage to him, which is the same as worshiping him. Scripture cannot have this function, according to this passage. Yet without Scripture it would be impossible to find Jesus.

2:4–6. The ambivalent assessment of Scripture reflects a similar assessment of the Jewish leaders associated with Herod and of their religious authority. They are presented as having authority over the people by being described as "all the chief priests and scribes of the people" (2:4). They represent "Jerusalem" to which the Magi address their message (2:1–2) and which is troubled (2:3). In brief, the chief priests and the scribes are leaders of Jerusalem as a center of revelation, the place where people know the revelation of Scripture. But now, by being set in contrast with the star as a moving locus of revelation (both in the East and on the road to Bethlehem), Jerusalem appears as a static center of revelation, which according to Jewish expectations had "absorbing centrality . . . as the scene of revelation and redemption in eschatological speculation."[15] The text affirms Jerusalem as a center of revelation and thus the validity of the religious authority of the Jewish leaders who represent Jerusalem, but denies its "absorbing centrality."

The ambivalent assessment of the Jewish leaders' authority is further expressed by the words that Matthew puts into their mouths, that is, their answer to Herod (2:5–6, which includes the quotation). This answer involves a correct view, namely, that Jesus was born in Bethlehem, since he is the Messiah "son of David." But it also includes a view that is somehow incorrect, since it does not lead them to want to pay homage to the Christ. Matthew expresses the bias of the Jewish leaders by introducing three unexpected features in the quotation. The tension created by these features once again signals that Matthew expresses his convictions (what is new for the readers) in terms of his readers' presumed knowledge of Scripture.

First, contrary to what is announced by the opening formula, "for so it is written by the prophet" (2:5), the text quoted (2:6) is composite; it involves a citation from Micah 5:2 followed by a citation from 2 Sam. 5:2 (the last line of 2:6, "who will lead [as a shepherd] my people Israel," au.).[16] The use of 2 Sam. 5:2 has the effect of contrasting "the chief priests and scribes *of the people*" (2:4) with the Christ as leader of "[God's] people Israel." A second modification of the text of Micah is the phrase "by no means least," which emphasizes that Bethlehem should not be viewed as a place without status. The effect is that Bethlehem can be compared favorably with other religious centers and thus also with Jerusalem. Bethlehem and the leader coming from it are rivals of Jerusalem and its Jewish leaders.

Micah's text is also modified to read "Bethlehem, in the land of Judah" instead of "Bethlehem Ephrathah." This change brings about a repetition, in the quotation itself, of the name "Judah," which is also found in other forms in 2:1; 2:2; and 2:5. Why is Judea (or Judah) emphasized in this way? Note first that this repetition conveys that the "son of David" is a Judean king, and thus the "king of the Judeans [or Jews]" (2:2), a phrase that could be interpreted to mean that he is a king who would have authority only over the Jews. By presenting the Magi (non-Jews) as paying homage to Jesus, and thus manifesting that they submit to his authority, Matthew shows this interpretation to be wrong. Narrowly circumscribing Jesus' authority to Judea is wrong; even though he is the "son of David" from Bethlehem of Judea, his authority has a universal character. Yet, since all this emphasis on Judea is brought about in the words of the religious leaders, we can add that the text also conveys that Jesus' *religious* authority is not confined to the narrow scope of Judean/Jewish religious authority exclusively based upon the revelation in Scripture. Indeed, his authority is revealed in Scripture, but it is also revealed and manifested outside Scripture and outside its Judean context.

Finally, we note that for those who, like the Magi, properly recognize Jesus' authority as a divine authority it is a source of "great joy" (2:10). Why? In 2:1–12 this is not explained. The rest of the chapter expresses it while continuing to present how and where Jesus' authority can be recognized and acknowledged.

2:13–23. Exile to Egypt and Return from Exile to Nazareth

In the second part of the chapter, Matthew makes a new point by setting up a third narrative opposition. It is a little more difficult to identify than the two preceding ones because one of its subjects is undefined. Yet it is unmistakably underscored by a series of repetitions. The death of Herod (a passive action, but an action nevertheless) is emphasized by being mentioned three times (2:15, 19, 20) and is opposed by his killing of the children (2:16) in an attempt to put Jesus to death (2:13, 20). This is the classic opposition of the action of the villain (Herod) to the overcoming of the villain by the hero, who is here an undefined subject, whatever or whoever brings about Herod's death. For the readers of the Gospel, there is no doubt about who has the power of life and death over Herod: it is God. Therefore it appears that the third point made by this story concerns the *use of the power of life and death*. It contrasts the *passive* use of power by God which, so to speak, does not interfere with the natural course of events, or with normal human affairs, to the *active* use of power by Herod, which is destructive and disrupts normal human affairs (the life in Bethlehem and its region).

This opposition defines the character of divine authority by contrast with Herod's authority. The political and human authority of Herod is based on fear, indeed terror, that his use of the power of life and death inspires in people (see 2:16). Herod's authority is exerted through the use of disruptive and destructive power or force. By contrast, divine authority, which also includes the power of life and death over people, is exerted without making disruptive and destructive use of this power. It respects the normal course of human affairs. Consequently, divine authority need not be feared; it is not asserted by the use of power.

The opposition merely proposes a negative definition of divine authority; it is not like human authority which depends upon the use of power. Yet it challenges the readers' common view of authority. True authority, divine authority, is not based on the use (or the threat of use) of power.[17] Consequently, the recognition that Jesus has divine authority also demands abandoning one's commonly held views about authority: the views concerning political authority and also the views concerning religious authority. The readers have no difficulty rejecting Herod and his malicious and cruel use of authority. Yet they might reject the view of authority represented by Herod merely because it involves a misuse of power. Conceiving that authority might be manifested without power involves a complete reversal of the common view of authority.

Yet Matthew also invites his readers to reject the view of religious authority represented by the Jewish leaders, although they might not be inclined to reject these leaders despite the fact that they and their interpretation of Scripture are presented as accomplices of Herod (2:3–7). In brief, Matthew's point is that in order to be in a position of acknowledging Jesus' authority, a complete reversal of the common view of religious authority is necessary—including the authority of Scripture. Matthew conveys this point in terms of his readers' presumed knowledge, especially their knowledge of Scripture. He does so in the thematic parts of 2:13–23, the parts of the text not directly related to the oppositions, which in the present case include most of the passage. In the process he demands from his readers a reversal of their understanding of Scripture.

2:13–18. By mentioning Jesus' flight to "Egypt" under the guidance of "Joseph," Matthew summons his readers' knowledge of the biblical story of Joseph, who presided over Jacob/Israel's move to Egypt (see Gen. 46:2–4). Similarly, the reference to the return from Egypt associated with a king, Herod, seeking to kill the child (and who will kill children, 2:16), and to a hasteful departure "by night," evokes the exodus, out of Egypt, of God's people fleeing in a hasty departure by night (see Exodus 12) from a king, Pharaoh, who killed the male children of the Hebrews (see Exod. 1:15–22), a fate the child Moses escaped (see Exod. 2:1–10). The main purpose of this rich evocation of biblical themes is the typological identification of Jesus with Israel (Jesus as "new Israel"), who can then be presented as fulfilling the prophecy of Hos. 11:1, "Out of Egypt have I called my son."[18] In addition, the killing of the male children of Bethlehem and of "all that region" (2:16) is presented in 2:17–18 as the fulfillment of another tragedy of the history of Israel, the deportation into exile which is presented in Jer. 31:15 through the poetic evocation of Rachel at Ramah (in the region of Bethlehem), weeping over her exiled children who are "no more."[19]

Thus Matthew uses his readers' knowledge of Herod's ruthlessness and of biblical themes to develop the theme that expresses his convictions. We can recognize these convictions in the tensions provoked by the juxtaposition of all of these elements. The application of the biblical themes to the story of Jesus' escape from Herod's persecution has the effect of reversing the biblical themes. While Jesus is the fulfillment of Hos. 11:1 because he is called out of Egypt, it remains that the text describes an exodus out of Judea (a hasty departure at night) to Egypt as a land of refuge.[20] The killing of children by a tyrant takes place in Judea rather than in Egypt. The exiled Jesus is the one who escapes death, and those who remain in Judea are those who are "no more," while, according to Jer. 31:15, Rachel was weeping for her exiled children who were no more.

What is conveyed by these reversals can be understood when one keeps in mind the theme of the Magi (developed in 2:1–12 and evoked in 2:13 and 16). First, one can rightly perceive Jesus' true identity, and thus the true character of his authority, that of the "Son of God," only when one recognizes that he has been called out of Egypt. In other words, it is outside Judea that it is made manifest that he is the Son of God. Certainly, he is from Judea (2:1–12), and the fact that he is from Bethlehem does manifest his true identity and authority as the son of David, the Christ; but this Judean manifestation is not enough for people to acknowledge his true authority and to want to submit to it.

Jesus is the fulfillment of the history of Israel, but only when this history is interpreted correctly, that is, when one remembers that it is not limited to the history of the interventions and revelations of God in Judea. Israel is the special people of God, his son, because of God's interventions and revelations outside Judea during the exodus. The significance of Jesus as Son of God, son of David, Christ, Emmanuel, can be recognized and acknowledged only when one sees him as the fulfillment of that history, as a manifestation of God which transcends Judea and the revelations held by the Judean religious authorities.

Conversely, if he had remained in Judea, Jesus would be "no more" (2:18). He would simply be dead, killed by the ruthless king of Jerusalem who in this way would have removed the threat that this powerless "king of the Jews" was supposed to be for him. The massacre of the children evokes therefore the Passion story, where the political authority kills the "King of the Jews" (27:29, 37). This is not by chance. In the introduction and in the conclusion of his Gospel, Matthew expresses the same system of convictions with the help of similar themes.[21] Thus, if Jesus' identity—

that is also, his vocation as son of David and Emmanuel and thus Jesus as manifestation of God—were merely in Judea (his birth in Bethlehem, his ministry in Judea and Jerusalem), it could not have been acknowledged by people for what it really is, an authoritative manifestation of God to which one must pay homage and submit. He would be dead, a failure. But Matthew underscores that Jesus is the authoritative manifestation of God which can also be found beyond Judea, which transcends the boundaries of Judea and its religious system. It is *in Galilee*, and indeed in "all nations" (where he will be with his disciples), that the disciples can pay homage to him, that is, worship him by acknowledging his universal authority, the supreme authority in heaven and on earth (28:16–20). Similarly, it is only by recognizing that Jesus, born in Bethlehem of Judea, also belongs outside Judea that the true identity and authority of Jesus can be recognized according to chapter 2.

2:19–23. We have already commented on most of the features of this passage. It is enough, therefore, to note that Matthew continues to develop the themes we have discovered in 2:1–18. Jesus' true identity and authority need to be manifested outside Judea so as to be acknowledged for what they really are. This is what is achieved by Jesus' settlement in Nazareth, thanks to which he can be called *Nazōraios*.

We have seen that Jesus' identity involves having a real, indeed a supreme, authority not based upon power. It is not a political authority—involving the use of the power of life and death over people—comparable to the authority of Herod, or even to the authority of David the king. Indeed, he is the son of David, the Christ, but as long as this title is merely associated with Judea, it cannot be properly understood. Thus, beyond his designation as son of David by his birth in Bethlehem, he needs to be designated as "Son of God," but outside Judea so as to remove any hint that his authority might be based on power. His authority is derived from being *called* out of Egypt by the Lord and thus from his vocation: his authority is the special qualification he has in order to carry out a vocation. This qualification is also expressed by the title "Son of God." But how should it be interpreted? The designation *Nazōraios* gives us a first clue.

It should be clear by now that the term *Nazōraios* cannot be interpreted as simply meaning that Jesus' settlement in Nazareth demonstrates that he is the "son of David" (the "branch," *nezer*, out of Jesse's stump). At the very least, it shows what "son of David" truly means and thus explains who Jesus is beyond 2:1–12. Thus, without excluding the possibility that *Nazōraios* has connotations derived from *nezer*, this term needs to have other connotations, namely, those derived from *nazir*.

Jesus' settlement in Nazareth shows that he is one who was made holy to God from his mother's womb, as Samson was (Judg. 16:17). And thus, "Son of God" means that Jesus is *holy* as God is holy (the only designations of God in chapters 1 and 2 of the Gospel are "Lord," who has authority, 2:15, and "Holy," in the phrase "Holy Spirit" for "God's Spirit," 1:18, 20). Jesus' authority as Son of God to whom "all nations" (as represented by the Magi) need to pay allegiance is based upon his holiness, which is God's holiness. By carrying out his vocation of Emmanuel, that is, by being holy among us, Jesus brings about the presence of the Lord among us: he manifests the holiness of God among us.

We thus conclude that the move from Bethlehem of Judea to Nazareth of Galilee shows that Jesus' identity and authority may be understood as the presence of the Holy among us. Yet Jesus' authority can be properly recognized only when one acknowledges that the manifestation and revelation of God, which he is, fulfills Jewish expectations and, consequently, exceeds them. Born in Bethlehem of Judea, he is manifested as Son of God, as the holy one, outside Judea ("Out of Egypt have I called my son," 2:15) and in Nazareth of Galilee.[22] His authority as manifestation of the Holy is not exerted through the use of (political) power or force which disrupts normal human affairs and is destructive (as Herod's authority is). Jesus has this authority which demands allegiance even when he is powerless (a child threatened by political powers). But how should such an authority not based on power be conceived? We can begin to understand it by noting that Jesus, the holy son of God, is manifested both in Judea and outside Judea (Egypt and Galilee) as the revelation to the Magi is manifested both outside Judea (the star) and in Judea (the witness of Scripture). In other words, the revelation to the Magi is like the manifestation of Jesus' authority. The revelation to the Magi has the effect of establishing their will (what they want to do) by allowing them to perceive what is good (euphoric) and bad (dysphoric). Similarly, since Jesus is the manifestation of the Holy (the supreme good), when people are in the presence of Jesus, and acknowledge him for what he is, they are then in a position to perceive what is truly good and thus what they have to do. Thus, without the use of power Jesus has authority over these people. His very presence among them establishes what they can only want to do, their vocation. Yet, for this, they need to acknowledge that the holy one of God is manifested not only in Judea but also in Galilee. The revelation that Jesus represents cannot be limited to the realm of the old revelation to which the people have access. It is also manifested outside this realm, in unlikely places, such as Nazareth of Galilee.

NOTES ON 2:1–23

1. See Stendahl, *"Quis et Unde?"* Note also that the geographical movement from Bethlehem to Nazareth brackets the temporal movement (from the day of Herod to the time after his death), which explains the circumstances of the former.

2. These proposals are reviewed in BROWN, 209–13; and PRABHU, 193–216.

3. As Brown notes, we should not presuppose that *Nazōraios* had only one connotation; it could have involved a "wealth of possible allusions" (BROWN, 209).

4. Interestingly, it is only through the birth stories of Samson (Judg. 13:2–7) and of Samuel (1 Sam. 1:11) that we have concrete examples of the Nazirite practice. This is the interpretation proposed by exegetes such as Schweizer, "'Er wird Nazoräer heissen,'" 90–93. See also BONNARD, 30; Sanders, "*Nazoraios* in Matt. 2:23," *JBL* 84 (1965):169–72; PRABHU, 201–7.

5. Note also that Judg. 13:5 adds, regarding Samson, "He shall begin to save Israel from the Philistines" (lit. trans. of LXX), which is parallel to 1:21.

6. As proposed by STENDAHL, 198–99; and BROWN, 211–13.

7. These issues are extensively dealt with in many commentaries: e.g., LAGRANGE, 19–24; PRABHU, 261–93; BROWN, 188–96. In order to bring forth Matthew's system of convictions, we deliberately take into account such traditions only when the oppositions and contrasts in the text call attention to them.

8. This is further confirmed by the emphasis put on Judea in this passage. See Nolan, *Royal Son of God*, 107; and Lowe, "Who Were the IOYDAIOI?" *NovT* 18 (1976):101–30, esp. 118–19.

9. As noted by BEARE, 77. The text seems to presuppose a traditional knowledge that Herod the Great and his son, Archelaus (2:22), were ruthless tyrants.

10. This question should not be dismissed by calling upon traditions concerning Moses' infancy which describe the terror of both the Pharaoh and the Egyptians at the news that the birth of Moses would threaten the king's sovereignty. See BROWN, 174. The dissonance comes from the fact that Matthew calls upon his readers' traditional knowledge, which he twists in order to introduce his own perspective. The proposals by Bloch, Paul, Nellessen, and Brown, arguing for the use of Moses traditions, hold true as far as the origin of the *pre-Matthean* tradition is concerned. But as Prabhu and Nolan have convincingly demonstrated, in Matthew's text the Moses motif has been completely displaced in favor of other points (those concerning the issues of "authority"). Furthermore, Davies has demonstrated that Matthew is not concerned to establish a Jesus-Moses typology. See Bloch, "Quelques aspects de la figure de Moïse," *Cahiers Sioniens* 8 (1954):210–85; Paul, *L'Evangile de l'enfance selon S. Matthieu*, 153–61; Nellessen, *Das Kind und seine Mutter*, 64–65; BROWN, 114–16; PRABHU, 261–93; Nolan, *Royal Son of God*, 83–89; Davies, *Setting*, 5–93.

11. Even though the interpretation of Micah 5:2 as referring to the birthplace of the Messiah can be found in the Targum, it was not a common Jewish view (cf. John 7:27). See BEARE, 79.

12. Research in narrative semiotics has shown that, in order to act, a subject must have three modalities: "wanting," or "having to do" (what I call "will" without making this distinction); "being able to" (the helpers, the tools, the power, etc., needed to carry out the action); and "knowing" (various kinds of knowledge, including the know-how). See Greimas and Courtés, s.v. "Modalities," *Semiotics and Language*.

13. The different forms of the Greek phrases in 2:1 (*apo anatolōn*, a plural form) and in 2:2, 9 (*en tē anatolē*, a singular form) suggest that the latter should not be translated "in the East" (so RSV), but as referring to the "rising" of the star (the original meaning of the word also used to designate the East). See ALLEN, 12; BEARE, 77; cf. LAGRANGE, 23–24, who recognizes this possibility but dismisses the issue as unimportant. However, Matthew does not identify the star with "the East" (countries outside Palestine); it is also manifested in Judea. This is why I interpret the star as a revelation *outside Scripture* and not *outside* Judea.

14. The case described in 2:22 is slightly different, since Joseph is able to discern by himself the dysphoric character of the situation (Archelaus as king of Judea). So to speak, he has learned from the preceding revelations not only something about the situations under consideration but also *how to interpret correctly* on his own the character of a situation (the dream merely confirms his evaluation).

15. See Davies, *Gospel and Land*, 234. For a discussion of the early Jewish texts upon which this conclusion is based, see ibid., 223–34.

16. For a discussion of the relation of these texts to the Hebrew Bible and the LXX, see STENDAHL, 99–101; Gundry, *Use of OT*, 91–94; PRABHU, 261–67.

Note that the shepherd theme could have been found in Micah 5:4 but without direct link with "the people Israel."

17. These observations suggest that, for Matthew, someone's "authority" is *not* acknowledged because one recognizes that this person has "power." Once again, this conception goes against our preunderstandings. For instance, despite disagreements regarding the specific relation between power and authority, both Schutz and Holmberg follow the modern sociological view according to which power is the basis of authority; I acknowledge and submit to the authority of someone, because I recognize that this person has power, i.e., the ability to affect my situation by external constraint. This is precisely the view of authority that is rejected by our text. See Schutz, *Paul and the Anatomy of Apostolic Authority*, 21; and Holmberg, *Paul and Power*, 8, 134–35.

18. This has been variously noted by most commentaries: e.g., STENDAHL, 101; BROWN, 214–16; PRABHU, 216–28.

19. For a detailed discussion of the use of Jer. 31:15 in 2:16–18, see PRABHU, 253–61. See also BROWN, 214–23.

20. This is a perception of Egypt that itself is not foreign to the biblical tradition (1 Kings 11:40; Jer. 26:21), but the text clearly emphasizes the exodus theme by means of the quotation of Hos. 11:1. Cf. BROWN, 203.

21. Prabhu finds in chapters 1—2 and 27—28 the same pattern of five chiastically arranged scenes. See PRABHU, 173–76. But, as Nolan points out (*Royal Son of God*, 107–8), this literary pattern should not be interpreted to mean that chapters 27—28 is "a systematic re-reading or fresh application of the two initial chapters." More significant are the correspondences of themes as expressions of similar convictions.

22. Although Galilee and Nazareth are more than mere geographical notations, we have to agree with Strecker's negative conclusion that there is no way to defend that Galilee is, for Matthew, the symbolic land of revelation by contrast with Jerusalem and Judea, as Lohmeyer and Lightfoot have argued in different ways. Both Judea (and Jerusalem) and Galilee are lands of revelation and rejection, as Davies concludes from his well-balanced study. See STRECKER, 93–98; Lohmeyer, *Galiläa und Jerusalem*; Lightfoot, *Locality and Doctrine in the Gospels*; Stemberger, "Galilee—Land of Salvation?" (see his critical review of the proposals by Lohmeyer and Lightfoot); Davies, *Gospel and Land*, 221–43 (esp. 240–43).

FROM JOHN'S MINISTRY TO JESUS' MINISTRY

THE MAIN THEME

This new section, which begins with 3:1, unfolds until the end of the following chapter, 4:25, and thus includes the stories of John the Baptist, Jesus' baptism, his temptation, and the beginning of his ministry. The thematic unity can be seen when its beginning and its end are compared. Its introductory part, John's ministry (3:1–12), explicitly presented as announcing Jesus' coming (3:11–12), foreshadows Jesus' ministry in Galilee (4:12–25). Matthew makes it explicit by presenting Jesus as taking over John's proclamation: "Repent, for the kingdom of heaven is at hand" (3:2; 4:17). Furthermore, both John and Jesus fulfill "what was spoken by the prophet Isaiah" (3:3; 4:14–16), and both are associated with crowds of people from "Jerusalem" and "Judea" (3:5; 4:25; note also that "Jordan" is mentioned in both verses). Thus, John's ministry includes promises, potentialities that are fulfilled in Jesus' ministry, as is expressed by the differences between 3:1–12 and 4:12–25.

John is in Judea, Jesus in Galilee; we find again that the promises of Judea are fulfilled, or made manifest, in Galilee. John preaches in the wilderness (3:1); Jesus dwells in a town, Capernaum (4:13), and preaches in synagogues (4:23). John stays in one place, and people from Judea, and Judea alone, *come to him* (3:5); Jesus *goes to* various locations (from Nazareth to Capernaum, to the Sea of Galilee, 4:13, 18), indeed he is constantly on the move ("about all Galilee," 4:23) and is *followed* by people from Galilee and the Decapolis as well as from Jerusalem and Judea (4:25). Thus, as the static religious authority of Jerusalem was contrasted to the moving religious revelation represented by the star in 2:1–12, so here we find a static religious authority in Judea contrasted with a moving religious authority. John baptizes (3:6, 11); Jesus heals (4:23–24). John rebukes and rejects people (Pharisees and Sadducees, 3:7–10); Jesus calls people to follow him (disciples, 4:18–22).

The main theme of this passage can therefore be called "From John's Ministry to Jesus' Ministry." Yet what is the meaning of their differences? Is Jesus "mightier" than John (3:11)? If so, in which sense? And is it really a matter of might? Since John is rebuked by Jesus (3:14–15), can we trust his proclamation on this point? A quick glance at the differences between John's ministry and Jesus' ministry suggests that there is much more at stake than a question of might.

Our study of the relatively large number of narrative oppositions in 3:1—4:25 shows that Matthew makes all of them a series of points concerning the proper understanding of religious authority in the process of presenting his view of *the nature of Jesus' authority*. As we can expect from our reading of 2:1–23, his authority is precisely not to be understood in terms of might. We can summarize the conclusions of our study of the convictions expressed in 3:1—4:25 as follows.

1. Jesus' authority as "beloved Son" (of God) is publicly manifested when he "fulfil[s] all righteousness" (3:15). Fulfilling all righteousness is having a life that "befits" the present time, repentance, and God's word, because one's will is molded in the image of God's will, and this as a result of acknowledging and submitting to God, and God alone, as the supreme authority (4:10). Jesus' will is God's will in the strong sense that their wills are one, because Jesus exclusively submits himself to God as the supreme authority.

2. The authority of Jesus as Son of God is therefore primarily defined by his will. This is what the temptation story (4:1–11) expresses for Matthew. If the tempter could manipulate Jesus' will, Jesus would lose his authority because he would no longer fulfill all righteousness. By following the tempter's suggestion, and thus by acknowledging another supreme authority than God's, Jesus would have an authority, but it would be delegated by the devil, an inferior and deceitful authority (such as a political authority, 4:8–9, or the Pharisees' and Sadducees' religious authority, 3:7–10). But because his will (his vocation) remains fully identified with God's will through his unwavering submission to God's word and his full acknowledgment of the lordship of God, his authority is nothing else than God's authority. His authority is the superior authority which can even overcome the supernatural authority of the devil. And what other authority besides God's authority can overcome the devil's supernatural authority and reduce him to obedience (4:10–11)? Similarly, since the angels serve Jesus (4:11), they recognize in him an authority superior to theirs. Because his will is God's will, Jesus' authority is God's authority.

3. For Matthew, a person's will is always established by the person's submitting to the will of a supreme authority to whom the person pays allegiance—whatever or whoever might be this supreme authority, God, the devil, or eventually some other authority. A person's will is always established by the person's acceptance of a vocation from a supreme authority. Then the person shares the authority of the one whose will he or she has made his or her will. The difference in the authority that various persons have is, thus, nothing else than the difference that exists among the

supreme authorities they acknowledge. Thus, the Pharisees and the Sadducees have an authority that is of the same order as the deceitful supreme authority they acknowledge (3:7). By contrast, Jesus' authority is God's authority. The case of John points to a third possibility: someone who at times "fulfil[s] all righteousness" because his will is God's will, but at times does not do so, presumably because he or she acknowledges another supreme authority (see 3:14). Yet, with Jesus' help—by acknowledging Jesus' authority—John is brought back to the right path; his will is once again God's will; once again he shares in God's authority and is God's messenger. This also means that anyone who is called to submit to God's will—to make God's will his or her own—is by this very fact called to share in God's authority and thus to be a religious leader (as when John's admonitions are addressed to religious leaders, 3:7–10).

4. The will of those who make God's will their own is nevertheless not a will infused into them; it is not poured into passive recipients who would then be mere puppets of God. This will, which is manifested in the fulfillment of righteousness, must be established in each specific situation, and in terms of it, by Jesus, John, and good religious leaders. This is done by evaluating these situations in specific ways—as God would do it. It involves discovering what "befits" repentance (3:8), righteousness (3:15), and God's word (4:1–11, a point that will be developed in the Sermon on the Mount). It also involves evaluating a situation in temporal terms, that is, discovering what is fitting for the present (especially in contrast to the time of the eschatological judgment, 3:11–15). All this is done for the purpose of determining what is truly needed (3:14; 4:2–4; 3:7–8), that is, what is truly desirable (a good that one needs to have, something truly euphoric) and thus something that one will want to pursue (one's vocation). Yet such evaluation is done correctly only by those who submit to the authority of God's word delivered by someone (or something) who (which) shares in God's authority: for Jesus, God's word is Scripture (4:1–11); for John, it is Jesus' admonition (3:15); for religious leaders, it is John's admonition (3:8–10).

MATTHEW'S CONVICTIONS IN 3:1—4:25

As this summary of our conclusions shows, in this section (3:1—4:25) Matthew strives to convey to his readers an important set of convictions that we will better understand as we study each of its passages: the baptism of John (3:1–10), the coming of Jesus and his baptism (3:11–17), the temptation of Jesus (4:1–11), and the beginning of Jesus' ministry (4:12–25).

3:1–10. The Baptism of John

The description of John's ministry involves three narrative oppositions (found in 3:5, 7–9) through which Matthew underscores three convictions in a relatively short passage. We can expect that it is these same convictions that Matthew attempts to convey in the rest of the passage (3:1–4, 6, 10), that is, in the thematic parts of the text where Matthew expresses himself in terms of his readers' presumed knowledge. Since an understanding of the convictions underscored by this passage will help us in our interpretation of the thematic parts, we shall first consider the oppositions contained in 3:5, 7–9.

3:5, 7. The text first opposes "Jerusalem and all Judea and all the region about the Jordan" going to John (3:5) to the coming of "many of the Pharisees and Sadducees" (3:7).[1] In this way, the common people of Jerusalem and Judea are cast in a positive light; there is nothing wrong with Jerusalem and Judea in themselves, as chapter 2 already suggests. The problem is with the Jewish religious leaders, the Pharisees and the Sadducees, as had been mentioned but not specified in 2:1–12—the terms "scribes" and "priests" of 2:4 correspond to the party designations "Pharisees" and "Sadducees" of 3:7. Now Matthew clarifies what is wrong with them. It is not their Judaism, their Judean origin, which they share with the common people but the specific view of religious life that they have as religious leaders and that they manifest by their behavior.

3:7–8. The next narrative opposition underscores this point by contrasting what they do, "flee from the wrath to come" (3:7), with what they should do, "bear fruit that befits repentance" (3:8), that is, doing (good) actions that correspond to (or fit with) repentance. This opposition is somewhat puzzling. Why does John rebuke the Pharisees and the Sadducees for fleeing from the wrath to come? In itself, avoiding the eschatological punishment—the wrath to come, being cut down by the ax laid to the root of the tree (3:10)—is good. This is what John himself invites his hearers to do. What is wrong is that they have a purely negative, or defensive, attitude—they flee, strive to avoid—instead of doing something positive, or constructive—bearing good fruit. They believe that by fleeing they will avoid the dire consequences of the coming eschatological judgment. Paradoxically, warns John, by adopting such an attitude, they bring upon themselves the very judgment they want to escape (3:10). By contrast, they will be spared by having a life *suitable for (befitting) repentance*, that is, by bearing good fruit.

At this point, we cannot be more specific, since, in 3:7–10, "repentance" is an undefined term that, for the time being, we must consider as an unknown entity. Yet we can observe that the "baptism for repentance" (3:11) is refused to those who do not bear good fruit (3:7–8), and thus we conclude that it is reserved for those who "bear [good] fruit that befits repentance." Repentance is not the attitude of evil doers but of good doers.[2] This is why, for Matthew, there is nothing abnormal in the fact that Jesus was baptized.

His baptism does not indicate that Jesus was an evil doer but that he was bearing fruit that befits repentance.

The brief descriptions of evil doers and good doers proposed in 3:7–8 show what is, for Matthew, the basis for their respective attitudes. The evil doers are described as a "brood of vipers" (*gennēmata echidnōn*) to whom someone had suggested that they should flee the wrath to come. By contrast, the good doers would be following John's exhortation, the good exhortation of someone whose ministry fulfills the prophecy of Isaiah (Matt. 3:3; Isa. 40:3). There is no point in speculating about the identity of the "evil one" whom the Pharisees and the Sadducees follow. Once again we must respect the ambiguity of the text.[3] We can only note that by this opposition Matthew underscores that the origin of right and wrong actions is to be traced to whatever or whoever suggested these actions to people or, more precisely (according to the Greek verb *hypodeiknumi* in 3:7), to whatever or whoever *pointed* to them the orientation that their behavior should have.

For Matthew, what we do is the direct consequence of following the suggestion of a *supreme authority*,[4] that is, someone whose authority over us we acknowledge and whom we allow to define for us what are good actions which we should pursue. All actions, whether good or evil, are based upon our submission to one supreme authority or another. For Matthew, a person is fundamentally characterized by the kind of supreme authority that this person acknowledges. Thus, the Pharisees and the Sadducees are evil, because their behavior shows that they have submitted to an evil supreme authority. Furthermore, this evil supreme authority is deceptive, since it leads them to think that by acting as they do (fleeing), they will escape the wrath to come, while in fact this very action put them under that wrath.

3:9. What is wrong in the attitude of the Pharisees and the Sadducees is further expressed by the third narrative opposition, found in 3:9. "Do not presume to say to yourselves, 'We have Abraham as our father'; for I tell you, God is able from these stones to raise up children to Abraham," where "say[ing] to yourselves" is opposed to "I tell you." They wrongly believe that their ultimate worthiness on the basis of which they will be evaluated at the judgment is directly related to their nature (being) as biological descendants of Abraham (see 1:1–17). Indeed, those who will not be condemned at the judgment are children of Abraham. But biological descent in itself does not ensure that someone is a child of Abraham, as Pharisees and Sadducees were led to believe by the deceitful supreme authority to which they submitted. God can produce children of Abraham out of stones.

In sum, the main points in the story of John's ministry concern that upon which religious leaders[5] should base their behavior. Unlike the Pharisees and the Sadducees, who are misled by their allegiance to a deceitful supreme authority, those who listen to John, who is sent by God, since he fulfills the prophecy of Isaiah, that is, those who acknowledge God's authority, evaluate potential actions in terms of their suitability for repentance. Indeed, when one acknowledges God's authority, one does not evaluate the situation in which one is in terms of one's being (being a biological descendant of Abraham) but evaluates it in terms of a view of human experience that takes into account the role of God in it.

3:1–4, 6, 10. Since narrative oppositions can be found only in the confrontation with the Pharisees and the Sadducees, Matthew expects his readers to be familiar with most of the first part of the story concerning John's ministry. Specifically, Matthew expects them to be familiar with the following: John as the baptist carrying on his ministry in the wilderness (3:1); his call "Repent, for the kingdom of heaven is at hand" (3:2); the prophecy of Isa. 40:3, which it fulfills and which shows that John is the forerunner of the Lord Jesus (3:3); his garment (3:4) which recalls that of Elijah (see 2 Kings 1:8) and thus shows that he is the new Elijah who was to come before the Messiah (see 17:10–13); the fact that people "confessing their sins" were baptized by him in the Jordan River (3:6); and his eschatological message warning his hearers of the imminent coming of the judgment (3:10).

Matthew does not deny the validity of his readers' old knowledge. Indeed, he affirms it. Yet it must be properly understood. And thus, by recasting it in the light of his convictions (expressed by means of the narrative oppositions in 3:5, 7–9), Matthew transforms it, creating tensions within the text which demand that his readers reinterpret their old knowledge. Let us therefore consider the thematic verses both from the perspective of the readers and in terms of the convictions expressed in 3:5, 7–9.

3:1–2. A first tension is found in the introductory verses: it concerns time. The vague time reference, "in those days" (3:1), has little or no chronological significance. Its effect (as elsewhere in this Gospel) is to show that the theme of the new section (3:1–4:25) prolongs the theme of the preceding one (2:1–23). As we have noted, in both cases the main theme expresses that what is potential or promised in Judea is fulfilled in Galilee. But this vague time reference has also the effect of situating this episode in a past far removed from the readers. It is a special time when extraordinary events occurred, a sacred time comparable to that of the sacred history of Scripture.[6] Yet, is it not simultaneously the same time as the readers' time, since the coming of the kingdom is still expected in their present? Is it not still the time when "the kingdom of heaven is at hand" (3:2)? Thus, from the outset, a tension appears. John's time ("in those days") is a special time, but it is not the time of the ultimate eschatological fulfillment, the time of the kingdom understood as the time of the judgment, which is also "at hand" according to John's teaching: "Even now the axe is laid to the root of the trees" (3:10). This suggests that the time of Jesus' ministry should not be confused with the time of the eschatological judgment (a point that we will find again in 3:14–15). In other words, Matthew warns his readers that even though John's teaching about the kingdom is basically valid (since Jesus will repeat it, 4:17), it is misunderstood by John—and by the readers who would appropriate John's teaching without reinterpreting it—because the time of the kingdom is identified with the time of the judgment, when they must be distinguished. This also suggests that, whatever else the technical term "kingdom" means for Matthew, the coming of the kingdom should not be confused with the coming of the judgment. Furthermore, it would then follow that, during his ministry ("in those days"), Jesus is not the eschatological judge (see 3:14–15).

3:6, 8. A second tension concerns the nature of John's baptism as related to repentance. In 3:6, baptism is associated with confessing sins and possibly, therefore, with forgiveness of sins—yet Matthew does not use this phrase in this context[7]—while in 3:8 baptism is for the good doers bearing "fruit that befits repentance." Since the latter view is expressed by an opposition, and is thus a conviction of Matthew,[8] the former view is presupposed of his readers. The effect of this tension is that baptism is partly disassociated from confession of sins. Baptism is not to be understood primarily in relation to forgiveness of sins. How can this be? Is not baptism associated with repentance in John's preaching (see 3:1–2, 11)? Indeed, baptism must be understood in relation to *metanoia* (RSV: "repentance"). *Metanoia* means "changing one's mind." But in the light of our examination of the oppositions and of our observation concerning forgiveness we have to conclude that, for Matthew, this concept keeps the connotation of "turning" that it had in the prophetic texts. And it is not primarily a turning away (from sins) but rather a turning toward God, in obedience to God.[9]

The presentation of John's baptism expresses Matthew's conviction concerning the true believer's relationship to God; it is a relationship to the supreme authority whom they must acknowledge and to whom they must pay allegiance. Of course, when one turns toward God in submission, one turns away from one's sins and confesses them. But, for Matthew, such a confession of sins is pointless (it is "flee[ing] from the wrath to come"), if it is not part of the process of submitting one's entire life to God's authority.

3:3. In this context the quotation from Isa. 40:3 is to be read in a special way. It confirms that John is the forerunner of Jesus, the Lord.[10] But it simultaneously means that John's ministry prepares the way of the Lord God. Making ready and making straight the way of the Lord is bringing people to have lives that befit repentance (3:8), that is, ways or paths (of life) that fulfill all righteousness and that befit submission to the Lord God.

3:11–17. The Coming of Jesus and His Baptism

3:13–15. In the story of Jesus' baptism, we find a complex narrative opposition between Jesus, who comes to be baptized by John, and John, who at first does not want to baptize him but wants to be baptized by Jesus. John's first reaction when meeting Jesus involves the recognition that Jesus is superior to him, since he sees the need to be baptized by Jesus. Thus, for the readers who have just read 3:11–12, there is no doubt that John has identified Jesus as the one who is "mightier than I" (3:11); his request is an acknowledgment of Jesus' authority. But, simultaneously, there is something wrong in this identification of Jesus, since it leads John to propose a wrong action.

3:11–12. Jesus' gentle rebuke, a rebuke nevertheless, specifies what is wrong in John's understanding of his relationship with Jesus and thus in his understanding of who Jesus is: "Let it be so now; for thus it is fitting for us to fulfil all righteousness" (3:15). First of all, the timing is wrong in John's perception. John conceives Jesus as the mighty eschatological judge who "will baptize you with the Holy Spirit and with fire" (3:11), that is, who will destroy evil people in fire (3:12). The text does not deny this view of Jesus: he *will be* the eschatological judge. But it simultaneously underscores that, *"now,"* in the present (3:15), Jesus should not be perceived in this way. In the present, Jesus has authority over John, as is shown when John obeys him, yet it is not an authority based upon might or power that one exerts upon others; rather, it is the authority of someone who submits himself to his inferior. Furthermore, by submitting to John's baptism Jesus acknowledges its validity and the validity of John's vocation.

3:14–15. John's perception of the present situation is also wrong, because he does not have the proper view of what is "fitting" for it. By contrast, Jesus knows what is "fitting . . . to fulfil all righteousness" (3:15). John does not want to baptize Jesus; rather, he wants to be baptized by him because he evaluates the situation in terms of his need, "I need to be baptized by you" (3:14). By contrast, for Jesus, a right action is based upon an evaluation of the situation in terms of what is "fitting," or suitable, for the fulfillment of righteousness (another yet undefined term of Matthew). Despite the difference in terminology (in Greek), this is the same view as the one in 3:8 ("Bear fruit that befits repentance"). John falls into the trap against which he warned the Pharisees and the Sadducees. He fails to base his own proposed action upon an evaluation of what is *"fitting"* (for fulfilling righteousness, an attitude that is somehow related to repentance).

Fulfilling righteousness means to be doing something that has been established as a good behavior because of the evaluation of a situation in terms of time. What fits the fulfillment of righteousness at a given time might not be fitting at another time. Note that the text seems merely to make a distinction between the present and the eschatological future (the time of the judgment). Finally, observe that it is precisely when Jesus submits himself to a greater good that his authority is manifested; it is when it becomes clear that he wants to fulfill all righteousness that John obeys him.

3:16–17. These verses are not directly related to any opposition; they are thematic. Matthew calls upon his readers' knowledge. In other words, while he underscores by means of oppositions the significance of Jesus' baptism as befitting the present time and fulfilling all righteousness (3:14–15), he presupposes that his readers know that Jesus is God's beloved Son (3:17). He nevertheless signals that this public proclamation is extraordinary by twice using the exclamation "behold" (3:16–17). For Matthew's readers, the declaration by the voice from heaven that Jesus, upon whom the Spirit of God descends like a dove, is the beloved Son of God in whom God is well pleased, is certainly a rich revelation with many connotations. Matthew does not deny these other connotations, whatever they might be.[11] But for him, what is essential is to understand that the "beloved Son [of God]" is someone who fulfills all righteousness, someone who is totally submitted to God's authority and who himself has an authority comparable to that of God as is expressed in the temptation story. Note that, by wording the voice's saying in the third person, "This is my beloved Son," Matthew presents it as a *public* declaration, a form that is appropriate for the announcement of Jesus' authority.[12]

4:1–11. The Temptation of Jesus

4:1–2. The temptation episode is presented as a series of confrontations between the tempter and Jesus. The passage is almost entirely involved in narrative oppositions, each polemical exchange forming an opposition. The only significant thematic feature is that the temptation is cast in the context of a fast in "the wilderness" lasting "forty days and forty nights" (4:2). For the readers, this suggests that the temptation of Jesus is comparable to the temptation (testing) of Israel for forty years in the wilderness. Thus, as in 2:13–15, Jesus is presented as the new Israel, and here more specifically as the faithful Israel (in contrast to Israel itself which, in many ways, failed to remain faithful). But once again this identification of Jesus as Israel is not underscored by Matthew; this is not one of the points he strives to convey by means of oppositions; rather, he assumes that it is part of his readers' view of Jesus, and he affirms this view without specifying how he understands it.

4:1, 5, 8. The stage for the confrontations is set by a first narrative opposition that contrasts the Spirit's action—leading Jesus into the wilderness (4:1)—with the tempter's actions—taking Jesus to the pinnacle of the temple (4:5) and to a very high mountain (4:8). The Spirit of God and the devil are thus presented as manifestations of two supreme, supernatural authorities, which have some kind of power over Jesus[13] and are in contention for his allegiance just as John and the one who warned the Pharisees and Sadducees to flee are in contention for the latter's allegiance (3:7–8).

4:3. In the first temptation the devil is designated as "the tempter." This designation makes explicit his role and what is at stake in these confrontations.[14] First, a tempter attempts to convince someone to do something. Convincing someone to do something is not forcing the person to do something against his or her will (this would be coercion), but leading the person to *want to do something* (something not previously envisioned, or something else than what one is doing). Despite his physical power over Jesus, whom he can transport to various locations, the devil as tempter does not coerce Jesus; he confronts him with skillful words and discourses. Convincing does not deprive the person of his or her will but aims at transforming it; this is what the tempter attempts to do with Jesus. In addition, and in contrast to other kinds of persons who convince (e.g., preachers, teachers, leaders), a tempter has a negative connotation. A temptation is the attempt to change a person's will from good to bad, and thus it aims at causing the person to want to do something wrong. The designation of the devil as the tempter shows, therefore, that his confrontation with Jesus is a battle of wills, and since Jesus is victorious, the temptation shows what characterizes Jesus' will and upon what it is based.

4:3–4. In the first confrontation the tempter acknowledges that Jesus is "Son of God"[15] and interprets this title to mean that (*a*) Jesus has a supernatural power (to change stones into bread, as God can change stones into children of Abraham, 3:9) and (*b*) that he may want to use this power to satisfy his physical need (hunger). Doing so would demonstrate, from the devil's perspective, that he is indeed the Son of God. Jesus' response shows what is wrong with the tempter's suggestion, namely, a wrong interpretation of Jesus' situation of need. While the tempter had perceived his physical need, hunger, he had not recognized another kind of need; in order to live, human beings need "every word that proceeds from the mouth of God," as well as bread (4:4).[16] The tempter had perceived the hunger but not the cause of it, Jesus' fasting (4:2), which in this context appears to mean "nourishing oneself with God's word." Thus this opposition does not deny that, as Son of God, Jesus has a supernatural power at his disposal; nor does it deny that Jesus can use this power to satisfy his own need.[17] Rather, it opposes two evaluations of human needs, which are limited to physical needs for the devil and which include both physical and spiritual needs for

Jesus, with the understanding that the more important need is for God's word.

Why do human beings need God's word to live? What is its role? Jesus' response expresses it. To the tempter's attempt to define his will (what he should do), Jesus responds: "It is written." The first formula quotation (1:22) had made clear that, for Matthew, Scripture is "what the Lord had spoken," that is, God's word. Thus, because it invokes Scripture Jesus' response to the tempter amounts to saying: "I am not deciding what I should do on the basis of suggestions such as yours but on the basis of God's word." For Jesus, being Son of God is to acknowledge and submit to the supreme authority of God's word as expressed in Scripture. More generally, the evaluation of human needs, which is the basis upon which the will to act (one's vocation) is established, is properly done only when one acknowledges God's word as supreme authority and thus when one evaluates human situations in terms of God's word.

In this light we can now better understand the preceding points regarding the Pharisees and the Sadducees (3:7–8) and John (3:14–15). This first temptation confirms that what is wrong is not their attempt to have their needs met but the wrong perception of these needs. In order to "fulfil all righteousness" one must evaluate one's needs not only in terms of "the wrath to come" but also in terms of "repentance" and of God's word.

4:5–7. In the second confrontation the devil once again acknowledges that Jesus is the Son of God. But now he uses this title with the understanding that Jesus has of it according to his first response: the Son of God as someone who submits to the authority of Scripture. Thus, by quoting Scripture he justifies his suggestion that Jesus should jump from the top of the temple. Yet, for the second time, Jesus responds by quoting Scripture. This confrontation opposes two uses of Scripture and therefore two kinds of interpretations as well as two views of the authority of Scripture. In other words, this opposition specifies what is a proper view and use of Scripture in contrast to a wrong view of Scripture attributed to the devil. It is worth taking the time to understand in detail the point that Matthew expresses here; we can expect that it is related to the view of Scripture expressed in the Sermon on the Mount.

In 4:6 the devil quotes Ps. 91:11–12[18] as a promise of God's providential protection which would apply to the Son of God. Since he trusts Scripture and its promise, the Son of God should be confident that God would not allow him to suffer any harm. He could thus demonstrate his trust in Scripture by jumping from the top of the temple. Why not? Because, answers Jesus, "You shall not tempt the Lord your God" (4:7; Deut. 6:16).[19] In other words, you shall not do with God what the devil does with Jesus, namely, try to cause God to do something by manipulating his will. The strategy would indeed be the same. The devil attempts to cause Jesus to act according to his nature, that is, according to the way in which he conceives of himself. He is Son of God with supernatural power; therefore he should demonstrate it by using this power. He is the Son of God who acknowledges the authority of Scripture and consequently trusts its promises concerning God's protection; therefore he should take risks in order to demonstrate his trust in Scripture. The testing of God would follow the same pattern. God is a providential God, committed to protect those who abide "in the shadow of the Almighty" (Ps. 91:1). Therefore, by creating a situation in which he would need God's protection, Jesus would cause God to demonstrate his will and ability to protect him. This would be a manipulation of God's will.

Actually, the devil's use of Scripture involves a misunderstanding of the promises of Scripture. Rather than conceiving of Scripture as promise, the devil conceives of it as a means of testing faithfulness, a means of testing God's faithfulness but also a means of testing Jesus' (and by extension any believer's) faithfulness. Note that this opposition does not deny that one can trust the promises of Ps. 91:11–12 and of Scripture in general.[20] There is a significant difference between a promise and a means of testing. These two views involve quite different attitudes toward Scripture. As promise, it is a gracious gift of God. As a means of testing, it would be an instrument of judgment; it would be given so that people could test other people's faithfulness (as the devil does with Jesus). In view of 3:7—an appropriate correlation, since the devil attempts to establish Jesus' will, as the will of the Pharisees and the Sadducees was established by someone evil—we observe that people holding the view that Scripture is a means of judging others necessarily conceive of it as a means of avoiding condemnation for themselves; they use Scripture as a means "to flee from the wrath to come." In this perspective, Scripture could also be used as a means of protecting oneself. Thus it begins to appear that, for Matthew, it is wrong to conceive of using Scripture to protect oneself against harm.

In sum, the opposition of 4:5–7 denies neither the validity of the promises of Scripture and of Scripture as promise nor that it has authority over the true believers (Jesus) who need to submit to it, but it denies that Scripture is a means of testing. Furthermore, it denies that these promises need to be tested (as one tests an electric or electronic component to see whether it works). Trust in Scripture is based upon an acknowledgment of the lordship of God (see 4:7), that is, upon the acknowledgment that one needs to submit one's will to God's will as the supreme authority. Since this confrontation takes place in "the holy city" and on the pinnacle of the (holy) temple (4:5), God's authority is a holy authority which, as such, must be respected, not manipulated. Scripture is to be used to determine what one should do or not do in existing situations. But to conceive of one's action in terms of Scripture does not mean to set up situations demanding the fulfillment of the promises of Scripture. This is making a mockery of what is holy (as the devil does by using the holy city and the holy temple for his temptation). A valid interpretation of Scripture necessarily involves acknowledging the holiness of God as well as the goodness of God, who did not give Scripture in order to test believers.

4:8–10. The third temptation follows the same pattern, despite its differences from the two preceding ones. The devil does not refer to Jesus as Son of God, yet the temptation presupposes a view that Jesus should have of himself, namely, a view of himself as someone worthy of authority. (This view of Jesus was already expressed by John in 3:11–12 but was somewhat tempered by John's debate with Jesus, 3:13–15.) This third temptation involves two narrative oppositions (instead of one): on the one hand, the confrontation of Jesus and the devil; on the other hand, paying homage and thus allegiance to God or to the devil.

The confrontation opposes Jesus' authority to the devil's authority. Indeed, this time, in response to the devil's suggestion that he should recognize his authority, Jesus is not content to quote Scripture; he gives him a command, "Begone, Satan!" and the devil obeys (4:10–11). This first opposition signals that Jesus has an authority superior to that of the devil.

The second opposition expresses the nature of this authority. It is not the kind of authority the devil would give him, namely, a political authority over "all the kingdoms of the world" (4:8). It is, rather, the authority of someone who pays allegiance and homage, and indeed worships God, and God alone, as the supreme and holy authority, as Jesus expresses by quoting Deut. 6:13 (4:10).[21] In many ways this affirmation recapitulates the views expressed in the previous temptations: that Jesus' primary need is for God's word and that the lordship of God must be respected. Jesus' authority is thus delegated to him by the supreme authority, God, to whom he pays homage. He shares God's authority, since he can overcome the devil's supernatural authority and reduce him to obedience (4:10–11). He is served by angels (4:11), as God also is. Because his will is God's will, Jesus' authority is God's authority.

4:12–25. The Beginning of Jesus' Ministry

In this entire passage, there is not a single narrative opposition. It is, then, a thematic passage in which Matthew expresses his convictions in terms of his readers' presumed knowledge. This second part of the main theme of 3:1–4:25 presents Jesus' ministry as fulfilling the promises (or actualizing the potentialities) of John's ministry.

4:12–16. The relationship between John and Jesus is once again emphasized in 4:12; Jesus' ministry begins when John's ends tragically by his arrest.[22] But it is not merely the continuation of John's ministry. Jesus' ministry in Galilee fulfills a prophecy of Isaiah. This time it is Isa. 9:1–2 that is cited (Matt. 4:15–16) as an accomplished fact.[23] Jesus is the "great light," the Messiah, which "has dawned" on "the people who sat in darkness" and "in the region and shadow of death," and no longer the forerunner, the voice, described by Isa. 40:3. Furthermore, it is no longer a ministry limited to Judeans but a ministry to the Gentiles (cf. "Galilee of the Gentiles"). It is a ministry with universal dimensions, including both Jews and Gentiles (see 4:25).

But in which sense is Jesus "a great light"? This metaphor has to be interpreted in terms of the description of Jesus' activity in the following verses. In brief, he is "a great light" because he proclaims the good news of the kingdom (4:17, 23), calls disciples (4:18–22), heals the sick (4:23, 24), and teaches (4:23; 5:1—7:24). All these are positive activities, not negative ones such as the proclamation of the judgment by John.

4:17. Jesus' message is summarized in the very words attributed to John in 3:2: "Repent, for the kingdom of heaven is at hand" (4:17). But, for the readers, it is clear by now that this proclamation is not to be understood as John's words were; "repent" means turning toward God in obedience; and "the kingdom of heaven" should not be confused with the judgment. Jesus' proclamation of the kingdom is the proclamation of the good news ("gospel," 4:23). The kingdom is proclaimed as the coming of something good, which for the hearers is most desirable (not to be feared, not to be avoided). In fact, it is the ultimate blessing (5:3) which can be the goal of a person's life: that toward which one's entire life can be turned, the "great light" toward which those who sit "in darkness" (4:16) turn in hope. Then one can understand how receiving the good news of the kingdom and thus turning one's life toward the kingdom is related to repenting, since, for Matthew, repentance is turning toward God. Receiving the good news of the kingdom and repenting are actually the same thing. Thus it appears that "the kingdom of heaven" is simultaneously the ultimate blessing that one aspires to receive and the supreme authority to which one pays allegiance, namely, God's authority, the kingship or lordship of God. In sum, the proclamation that "the kingdom of heaven is at hand" is simultaneously a call to acknowledge the kingship of God, God's supreme authority, and an invitation to orient one's life toward what is good, the ultimate blessing which one wants to receive and which, consequently, establishes one's vocation—what one wants to do.

4:18–22. The calling of the first disciples takes on a special meaning in the context of 3:1—4:25. Instead of the rebukes that John issues to religious leaders who come to him (3:7–10), it is a positive injunction that Jesus addresses to lay people as they are at their workplace fishing and repairing nets; he goes to them and asks them to follow him in order to become religious leaders. Indeed, whatever else is meant by Jesus' saying, "I will make you fishers of men,"[24] it involves making true religious leaders out of Simon Peter and Andrew as well as of James and John. Thus, in contrast to John the Baptist, who appears as the forerunner of a judge, Jesus is presented as someone who addresses a call (a vocation). Furthermore, he does so with striking authority; he arrives, he speaks, they obey. One wonders about the disciples' motivations for obeying.[25] In the simple fact of Jesus' coming to them and calling them, Jesus' authority is manifested to them in such a way that they cannot but obey him. Jesus' presence and words are the presence of a supreme authority, of God's authority (see 4:11). Such is the authority of Jesus.

Through the juxtaposition of the call of the disciples with the proclamation of the kingdom (4:17), the command "Follow me" has special connotations. The proclamation of the kingdom, besides being a call to acknowledge God's kingship, also involves a reorientation of one's life toward the kingdom as the ultimate blessing. The command "Follow me" demands a similar reorientation: from a life oriented toward the demands of daily activities (fishing, mending nets with one's father) to a life oriented toward Jesus. Being a disciple is turning toward and following him who manifests the kingly authority of God.

What is suggested by this juxtaposition? That following Jesus means submitting to his authority and turning one's life toward the kingdom. In addition, this juxtaposition suggests that the proclamation of the kingdom is closely associated with a call to a specific vocation. As a call to reorient one's life toward the kingdom, this proclamation begins to establish the vocation of those to whom this proclamation is addressed. It calls them to direct their lives in a specific direction, the very direction in which Jesus' life is oriented; the proclamation of the kingdom is an implicit call to follow Jesus.

4:23–25. The concluding passage, a summary of Jesus' ministry in Galilee, shows once again how Jesus' ministry fulfills the potentialities of John's ministry. In the wilderness of Judea, John was preaching the imminent coming of the kingdom and its judgment; everywhere in Galilee, Jesus preaches "the gospel of the kingdom" (4:23) which is good news rather than the mere announcement of judgment. John baptizes; Jesus heals "every disease and every infirmity" (4:23–24); this is the manifestation of power that John expected from one mightier than he (3:11–12), yet it does not take the form of judgment and destruction but rather that of healing and restoration. In addition, Jesus performs a third action, "teaching" in their synagogues (4:23), that is, he takes over the task of the Jewish religious leaders who were denounced in 3:7 as unfit to do so.

Teaching, preaching the gospel of the kingdom, healing—these are the three tasks that Jesus carries out during his ministry. He does so as the one who comes to people and is followed by them; as the beloved Son of God who fulfills all righteousness; as the one whose authority is God's authority; as the one who makes present God's authority, lordship, and kingship; and thus as the one whose coming is the coming of the kingship of God among us, "God with us." By following him, people—disciples and crowds—orient their lives toward the only worthy goal, the ultimate blessing that the kingdom of heaven is. Indeed, "theirs is the kingdom of heaven" (5:3).

NOTES ON 3:1—4:25

1. In this section Matthew begins to use Mark and the source Q (texts also found in Luke and not in Mark). As was explained in the Introduction, we shall refrain from comparing the Gospels of Matthew, Mark, and Luke, since our goal is to identify Matthew's convictions. At this first stage of a long-term structural study of the Gospels, such a comparison is more distracting than helpful, since an author expresses convictions as much by choosing to make a literal use of a source as by modifying it. If the analysis is well performed, it should spontaneously account for the significant differences with the other Gospels and sources on the basis of the organization of the Matthean text in itself (and thus without being aware of these differences). In practice, after concluding the study of each section, I verified that these differences had indeed been accounted for. In a number of cases, such a verification led me to refine the analysis, and I made reference to the texts in Mark or Luke.

2. Incidentally, Josephus's presentation of John's view of his baptism is quite similar: "For John was a pious man, and he was bidding the Jews who practiced virtue and exercised righteousness toward each other and piety toward God, to come together for baptism. For thus, it seemed to him, would baptismal ablution be acceptable, if it were used not to beg off from sins committed, but for the purification of the body when the soul had previously been cleansed by righteous conduct" (Josephus *Antiquities* XVIII.5.2.116–19).

3. Because we cannot identify the "evil one" as a specific person does not mean that we should interpret the question of 3:7 as merely ironical. It is certainly ironical, mocking the Pharisees and the Sadducees. Yet the opposition (as well as other oppositions in chapters 3—4) makes it clear that one of the issues, for Matthew, concerns the kind of person or thing that influences one's choice of behavior. We have to disagree with the many commentators who treat the irony of the question as if no one could have suggested to the Pharisees and the Sadducees to flee the wrath to come. See, e.g., MEIER, 79; ALLEN, 24; LAGRANGE, 51; BONNARD, 35; note the guarded comment of BEARE, 93.

4. The phrase "supreme authority" is our effort to express a conviction of Matthew. By it we designate who or what suggests to people what are good actions which they should pursue and thus who or what establishes their will. We chose this phrase, on the one hand, because it is relatively vague and thus does not predetermine its meaning and, on the other hand, because it opens the possibility of conceiving of such an authority as part of a hierarchy—a supreme authority, a delegated authority given by the supreme authority to a person, who can further delegate it to other people.

5. In 3:7-9 common people are totally ignored. Pharisees and Sadducees (or scribes and priests) alone are addressed by John, who therefore describes the right attitude that religious leaders, and they alone, should have. It is the first instance of many in the Gospel of Matthew where the author seems exclusively concerned with defining good religious leaders. This means that all the intended readers of Matthew are in his view potential religious leaders. This is the first indication that Matthew aims at transforming his readers into disciples, or scribes of the kingdom (13:52) who will be religious leaders with a specific vocation (cf. 28:18–20).

6. See BONNARD, 31.

7. In contrast to Mark and Luke, who mention "forgiveness of sins"; cf. Mark 1:4 and Luke 3:3.

8. In this case it is quite certainly a conviction that was already expressed in the source Q (cf. Luke 3:7–8) appropriated by Matthew. But by choosing to keep the opposition present in the source, Matthew shows that he finds it an adequate expression of *his own* conviction.

9. See Dupont, "Repentir et conversion d'après les Actes des Apôtres," 422. The rest of this essay, a study of repentance according to Luke, provides a clear contrast with the view of repentance found in Matt. 3:1–10. Yet the idea of turning toward God is also present in Acts (ibid., 449–53) although it is related to other concepts.

10. As is indicated by the absence of "the paths of God" in the LXX quotation, so as to mention only "the Lord," who might be either God or Jesus.

11. On the biblical allusions involved in the declaration and the possible meanings of the description of its context (the voice from heaven, etc.), see BEARE, 99–104; BONNARD, 40.

12. Note the second person form in Mark 1:11 and Luke 3:22.

13. While it is clear that the tempter is in full control of Jesus' movements, and thus has a physical power upon Jesus, it is not clear what kind of power the Spirit exerts upon Jesus. *Anechthe* means "bringing up," but it could also mean "leading up." Several commentators, on the basis of synoptic comparisons, emphasize that Jesus is not manipulated by the Spirit: thus, BONNARD, 42–43; BEARE, 106–7; but see the cautious comment of LAGRANGE, 58.

14. In what follows, I am indebted to the semiotic analyses of this passage proposed by Calloud, *Structural Analysis of Narrative*; and Panier, *Récit et commentaires de la tentation de Jésus au désert*, esp. 19–110.

15. "If you are the Son of God" needs to be interpreted in the light of the next temptation as an acknowledgment, "Since you are the Son of God," rather than a mere expression of doubt (see 4:6 and my comments on this verse). Yet the temptation is challenging Jesus to demonstrate that he is Son of God; thus an element of doubt remains. See BONNARD, 44; GUNDRY, 55; BEARE, 109.

16. This is a quotation from Deut. 8:3 according to the LXX. With STENDAHL, 88; but against Gundry, *Use of OT*, 66–67. (I retain the long text despite the variant.)

17. With BEARE, 109–10; but against BONNARD, 44.

18. The quote is from the LXX. Cf. STENDAHL, 89; and Gundry, *Use of OT*, 67–68.

19. The quote is from the LXX. Cf. STENDAHL, 89; and Gundry, *Use of OT*, 68.

20. Consequently, the "again" in Jesus' response "Again it is written" should not be understood as expressing a rejection of the validity of one passage of Scripture on the basis of another.

21. A quotation that is neither in harmony with the Hebrew text nor with the LXX. See STENDAHL, 89; and Gundry, *Use of OT*, 68–69. The main change involves the introduction of the verb *proskuneō*, which is used not only in 4:9 (the devil's suggestion) but also in 2:2 and 2:11, recalling the Magi paying homage to Jesus.

22. This is also made clear by the way in which Matthew presents John's death in 14:3–12 as John's Passion. See Wink, *John the Baptist*, 28.

23. Matthew shows that the prophecy is accomplished by transforming all its future tenses into past tenses. See STENDAHL, 104–6; Gundry, *Use of OT*, 105–8; Wink, *John the Baptist*, 37–38.

24. See BONNARD, 50.

25. Luke, for instance, presents the call of the disciples after they have witnessed his preaching and a miracle (Luke 5:1–11). In such a case, one can understand why the disciples follow Jesus: they have witnessed Jesus' power. Yet, in Matthew, as well as in Mark 1:16–20, the very presence of Jesus and his command manifest his authority.

THE SERMON ON THE MOUNT

THE MAIN THEME

The Sermon on the Mount forms a complete thematic section, since it has an introduction (5:1–2) describing the situation in which Jesus' teaching is expected or needed and a conclusion (7:28–29) showing that the original expectation has been fulfilled. Before examining the Sermon itself, we need to consider the narrative framework in which Matthew expresses its overall purpose and meaning.

5:1–2 and 7:28–29. Narrative Framework of the Sermon

Matthew expresses the main theme of chapters 5—7 by describing the effect of the Sermon upon the hearers and thus the transformation of these hearers. The opening phrase, "seeing the crowds" (5:1), and the conclusion, according to which the "crowds" heard what "he taught them" (7:29), *suggest* that Jesus gives the Sermon for the crowds' sake. These crowds, "from Galilee and the Decapolis and Jerusalem and Judea and from beyond the Jordan" (4:25), "followed" Jesus because of his teaching, preaching, and especially his healings (4:23–24). In brief, the crowds recognize in Jesus someone with extraordinary power (as the devil did in 4:3) and follow him (as Simon Peter, Andrew, James, and John also do, 4:20, 22). But following Jesus because of his fame and his extraordinary healing power is not enough; they need to be taught by him and to receive his teaching. They need to recognize and acknowledge the true nature of Jesus' authority, first of all, as teacher; the proper recognition of his authority as healer will be the main theme of 8:1—9:34.

7:28–29. The point expressed by the only narrative opposition found in the framework of the Sermon concerns Jesus' authority. While Matthew expects his readers to know that one needs to acknowledge Jesus' authority— if for no other reason than that they have read the preceding chapters—he does not expect them to perceive this authority correctly. In his view, they still need to recognize the true character of Jesus' authority. Thus he opposes Jesus' teaching and the scribes' teaching (7:29); Jesus has an authority that the scribes do not have. In effect, Matthew develops the points he was making in chapters 1—4. Jesus has been presented as the Messiah, son of David, whose vocation is to manifest the presence of the Holy among us (chap. 1); as the "king of the Jews" to whom non-Jews pay allegiance and whose authority can be acknowledged only with the help of both biblical and nonbiblical revelations (chap. 2); as the beloved Son of God who fulfills all righteousness and shares in God's authority (chaps. 3—4). Thus he has the authority to teach, as well as to preach and to heal (4:23). Yet a teacher's authority is really established when, and only when, his or her teaching is received as authoritative by the audience. This is what 7:28–29 expresses. But by this opposition Matthew makes an additional point; Jesus' authority is such that the scribes can be characterized as lacking such an authority. His authority is different from that of the scribes.

Matthew further expresses this point (conviction) in terms of his readers' expectations, as is shown by a tension between 5:1–2 and 7:28–29 raised by the question: To whom is the Sermon addressed? To the crowds, as we noted above on the basis of 7:28–29 and of the phrase "seeing the crowds" in 5:1a? Or is it to the disciples alone, as is suggested by the statement: "When he sat down his disciples came to him. And he opened his mouth and taught them" (5:1b–2)? We examine two features of this passage.

5:1. First, by sitting down Jesus takes the customary position of a Jewish teacher, a scribe, or a rabbi.[1] In other words, in his teaching (by contrast with his preaching and healing), Jesus is presented as taking over the role of the scribes, as is also suggested by 4:23 as contrasted with 3:7–9. His teaching is an authoritative scribal teaching. But then a tension appears, since the opposition in 7:29 emphasizes that his authority is not like the authority of the scribes. Jesus is both scribe-like and not scribe-like. Does it mean that Jesus has an authority that the scribes should have, but that in fact they do not have because they submit to a deceitful supreme authority (see 3:7)?

Furthermore, by setting Jesus' teaching "on the mountain," Matthew suggests that Jesus is like Moses on Mt. Sinai, a view that he expresses in terms of his readers' expectations (since it is not involved in any opposition).[2] This typological identification of Jesus with Moses certainly had, for Matthew's readers, a rich meaning involving a specific understanding of Jesus' teaching. But by summoning this view of Jesus, Matthew only wants to make one point: he wants to specify that Jesus' authority is a Moses-like authority. Interestingly enough, in 23:2 Matthew describes "the scribes and the Pharisees" as sitting "on Moses' seat," that is, as having a Moses-like authority themselves. Consequently, by underscoring that Jesus' authority is different from that of the scribes in 7:29, Matthew might also convey that it is not a Moses-like authority. Thus Jesus would be both like Moses and not like Moses. Does this mean that, for Matthew, the teachings of Jesus and of the scribes have a similar, if not identical, function,[3] although

Jesus' teaching is far superior to that of the scribes? Our conclusion on the basis of 5:1–2 and 7:28–29 is that while Matthew does not want to reject completely the view that Jesus has a scribal Moses-like authority, a view that he assumes his readers hold, he does not want to affirm it without qualifications. We can expect that the Sermon itself will clarify this ambivalent point.

Second, we need to ponder what is conveyed by the tension between "disciples" and "crowds" as possible audiences of the Sermon. One of the terms reflects the old knowledge of the readers, while the other is introduced by Matthew. Since the term "crowds" is involved in the opposition of 7:29 and thus is part of a new point that Matthew strives to convey to his readers, we have to conclude that it is Matthew who introduced it. In other words, Matthew assumes that his readers thought that the Sermon was addressed to the narrow circle of disciples. This is the first time the term "disciples" is used in the Gospel. Matthew's readers would without doubt identify them as the four fishers who were called by Jesus to a vocation of religious leadership ("fishers of men") and "followed" him (see 4:18–22). As usual, Matthew does not deny his readers' view; as the content of the Sermon indicates, Matthew also thinks of it as addressed to disciples. But by describing the crowds' action in the same way as he describes the disciples (i.e., as following Jesus, 4:25), he presents the crowds as disciples,[4] or possibly as potential disciples. One does not need to be an ideal disciple to hear this Sermon. It is enough to be one who follows Jesus and thus recognizes in him some kind of authority.

Matthew then presents the Sermon on the Mount as demonstrating that Jesus' authority is both scribal and unlike that of the scribes, and both like and unlike that of Moses, and that this teaching is addressed to all his disciples, a group that includes international crowds (4:25), that is, a group not limited to the band of disciples that followed him during his ministry. These broadly defined crowds may include the readers, since Matthew expresses this view of Jesus' authority as a point that will be new for his readers. The Sermon is also addressed to the readers. Whoever the readers are, they are those who should acknowledge the authority of Jesus as teacher.

5:3—7:27. The Overall Organization of the Sermon

The narrative framework (5:1–2; 7:28–29) of the Sermon on the Mount demands that it be viewed as an authoritative teaching. Consequently, we need to ask: What makes it authoritative? How can Matthew write that "the crowds were astonished at his teaching" (7:28) and explain this astonishment by suggesting that they recognized that Jesus "taught them as one who had authority" (7:29)? Why does Matthew expect that readers will be ready to accept his new point that Jesus has a special authority as teacher?

One answer to these questions is that Matthew expects that crowds and readers will recognize that these words of Jesus have a special character, a special force, which demands a response from them. This is the very definition of a didactic discourse[5] which, when successful, causes hearers to accept its validity and to act accordingly because it is recognized as authoritative. This authority of the didactic discourse is conveyed by its special kind of argumentation. By redacting in the form of a sermon[6] sayings of Jesus gathered together from various contexts of his ministry (many of the sayings are found in different settings in the Gospel of Luke), Matthew presents this teaching as a didactic discourse which, it is hoped, will be viewed by readers as an authoritative teaching that they should accept.

Two characteristic features of didactic discourse are particularly important for our study of the Sermon on the Mount. First, in order to be convincing the discourse must establish a relationship between the "I" (the speaker) and the "you" (the addressees) so that the hearers will want to enter into this relationship. For this purpose, the "I" must be described and defined in such a way that the hearers might want to listen to, and obey, the speaker. The "I" must be perceived not merely as having authority but also as having a *good* authority, an authority to which hearers will want to submit. Similarly, the "you" must be described and defined in such a way that hearers will want to identify with the "you." In brief, the discourse must establish an "I-you" relationship so that hearers or readers will want to identify with the "you" of the discourse and accept as valid what the "I" says to the "you."

5:3–10; 7:21–27. A cursory reading of the Sermon reveals that the "I-you" relationship is indeed found in most of the Sermon in the form of direct addresses (e.g., "I tell you") and of exhortations (e.g., "Rejoice"). Yet two passages are in an impersonal style which does not express directly the "I-you" relationship: the introductory part (5:3–10, Beatitudes) and the concluding part (7:21–27). We suspect that these two passages play the special role of establishing the "I-you" relationship for the rest of the discourse. They are aimed at convincing hearers and readers to identify themselves with the "you," the disciples and the crowds (as potential disciples). They are spelling out reasons that should convince people to want to be disciples. (Consequently, we shall designate as disciples those who are addressed as "you" by the discourse; they are whoever will want to hear this teaching and do it.)

It is noteworthy that Matthew does not take for granted that by the end of the Sermon the hearers and readers will have been convinced that they should identify with the "you" since the concluding part (7:21–27) is also in an impersonal form. But this also shows that the discourse is organized in such a way as to come back to the original point, namely, convincing the hearers and readers to identify themselves with the "you." We recognize therefore a chiastic organization, A1–B–A2—where A1 is 5:3–10, B is the body of the Sermon, and A2 is 7:21–27. Furthermore, we have to expect that the body of the Sermon is also chiastically organized so as to bring the argument back to the same issues as those found in the introduction. This first observation provides an important clue for our understanding of the overall organization of the Sermon.

A second characteristic of didactic discourse is that it aims at causing the addressees to do something. This is clearly the case of the Sermon, as is emphasized in its conclusion (7:21–27). It is not enough to recognize the authority of Jesus (calling him "Lord, Lord") and to hear his teaching; one needs also to *do* what is commanded by this teaching.

5:20—6:21. What disciples should do is expressed in the central part of the Sermon (5:20—6:21). In brief, the disciples should have a righteousness more abundant than that of the scribes and the Pharisees (5:20), a behavior that is described in a series of exhortations and injunctions. This central part is clearly divided into two sections which are set in a framework. Whereas the first section (5:21–47) deals with the attitude that disciples need to have toward other people in order to have such a righteousness, the second section (6:2–18) focuses on the disciples' relationship with God. The framework in which these two series of exhortations are set presents the overall goal of this more abundant righteousness. The introductory statement (5:20) expresses in a negative form that, without such a righteousness, the disciples will not enter the kingdom of heaven. At the end of the first section (5:47–48) and at the beginning of the second section (6:1), the theme of the more abundant righteousness is again emphasized. The concluding statements (6:19–21) express in a positive form that the ultimate goal of such a righteousness is to have one's treasure in heaven and thus to enter the kingdom of heaven.

5:17–19; 6:22—7:12. These exhortations to a more abundant righteousness are preceded (5:17–19) and followed (6:22—7:12) by a teaching that expresses what conditions must be met in order to have a life characterized by such a righteousness. This well-balanced organization of the two parts that enclose the central teaching is signaled by the use of the rhetorical device of inclusion. The introductory verse, 5:17, expresses in a negative form the relationship of all this teaching with Scripture: "Think not that I have come to abolish the law and the prophets." With the view that Jesus abolishes Scripture, it is impossible to have a life characterized by true righteousness. The concluding verse, 7:12, expresses the same point in a positive form: "So whatever you wish that men would do to you, do so to them; for this is the law and the prophets." The condition of possibility for true righteousness can be summarized in this injunction which expresses the correct understanding of Scripture.

Still moving from the inside out, there are two additional steps in the chiastic organization of the Sermon.

5:11–16; 7:13–20. The vocation of the disciples is expressed in 5:11–16, where it is described as the vocation of people persecuted for Jesus' sake as the prophets were, of "salt of the earth" which should not lose its saltness, for then it is useless, and of "light of the world" which should not be kept in the narrow confines of a bushel. The vocation of the disciples is also expressed in 7:13–20. It involves finding "the narrow gate" and following the hard road "that leads to life" rather than taking the wide gate and the easy road, and bearing good fruit, as good trees do, by contrast with what the false prophets do.

Finally, as we noted both in the introduction (5:3–10) and in the conclusion (7:21–27), we find a description of who the true disciples are. Hearers and readers are not coerced into the role of addressees. They have to make the choice of identifying themselves as the "blessed" ones, that is, as disciples who shall not merely hear this Sermon but do what it teaches.

The Overall Organization of the Sermon on the Mount

A1—5:3–10. Beatitudes. Who the disciples are.
 B1—5:11–16. The disciples' vocation.
  C1—5:17–19. Conditions for implementing the vocation.
   D1—5:20. Introduction of antitheses (framing material).
    E1—5:21–47. Antitheses. The overabundant righteousness.
   D2—5:47–48. Conclusion of antitheses (framing material).
   D3—6:1. Introduction to next unit (framing material).
    E2—6:2–18. The overabundant righteousness.
   D4—6:19–21. Conclusion of preceding unit (framing material).
  C2—6:22—7:12. Conditions for implementing the vocation.
 B2—7:13–20. The disciples' vocation.
A2—7:21–27. Who the disciples are.

MATTHEW'S CONVICTIONS IN 5:3—7:27

5:3–10. The Beatitudes
Who the Disciples Are
(Part 1)

The first eight beatitudes (5:3–10), unlike the last one (5:11–12), do not include any opposition. They are expressions of Matthew's convictions in terms of his readers' old knowledge. Consequently, it is only at the end of the study of the Sermon (see p. 101) that we will be in a position to assess in which way the readers' old knowledge is both affirmed and transformed by Matthew. Yet several preliminary observations are in order.

Each beatitude involves two parts. The first part is the affirmation that certain people are blessed: "Blessed are the poor in spirit" (5:3). The second part, "for theirs is the kingdom of heaven" (5:3), explains why these people can be viewed as blessed and is thus a warrant for the preceding affirmation. This means that Matthew does not expect his readers to be convinced by the first part in itself; they would not readily recognize as blessed those who are "poor in spirit," "those who mourn," "the meek,"[7] "those who hunger and thirst for righteousness," "the merciful," "the pure in heart," "the peacemakers," and "those who are persecuted for righteousness' sake." Consequently, these affirmations are thematic expressions of convictions conveyed elsewhere in the Sermon through oppositions. We shall therefore interpret them later in terms of these convictions.

By contrast, the explanations (warrants) of the blessings are supposed to be convincing. Matthew expects his readers to acknowledge them as true blessings. The explanations of the first beatitude (5:3) and the last (5:10) beatitude are identical: "theirs is the kingdom of heaven." The use of the rhetorical device of inclusion shows that it is taken for granted that participation in the kingdom is the ultimate blessing. The other blessings (5:4–9) express specific instances of what it means to participate in the kingdom— namely, being comforted, inheriting the earth (i.e., having all one's needs met), having one's hunger for righteousness satisfied, receiving mercy from God, seeing God, being called "sons," or children, of God. Matthew assumes that the readers want to receive all these blessings. But these blessings remain quite ambiguous. They can be interpreted in many different ways, and there is no guarantee that the readers' understanding of these blessings coincides with that of Matthew. In fact, the opposite is certainly true, since there is a tension in the text; the first blessing and last blessing are in the *present* tense ("theirs *is* the kingdom"), while the others are in the *future* tense. Thus, either Matthew expects his readers to view the kingdom as belonging to the eschatological future, while he wants to affirm that it is *also* present, or vice versa. On the basis of these verses alone we cannot determine which is the case. Yet we have already found that the proper understanding of the relation between the present (now) and the (eschatological) future is crucial for Matthew. In 3:13–15, against John, Jesus denies that the present should be identified with the time of the eschatological judgment, a point that would seem to favor a view of the kingdom as future. Yet, simultaneously, Jesus takes over John's positive proclamation that "the kingdom of heaven is at hand" (3:2, 4:17). Matthew could therefore view participation in the kingdom as already possible in the present. Thus we cannot reach a definite conclusion about the view of his readers. But it is clear that Matthew can affirm that the kingdom is both future and present. From these verses, which do not include any opposition, the only thing we can say about Matthew's understanding of the kingdom is that it is presented as the ultimate blessing that the hearers and readers will want to receive.

Finally, the opening words of Jesus' teaching are presented in the literary form of a blessing. This is noteworthy, because blessings and curses (their negative counterpart) are words that have power; they have the power of positing a new reality.[8] Consequently, curses are feared by believers, while blessings are welcomed. This means that the speaker, Jesus, has a religious authority such that his words transform the situation of those to whom they are addressed; whatever was their situation, because of Jesus' words it is now posited as a euphoric situation. They are truly blessed; the kingdom is theirs. The beatitudes also convey that the purpose of Jesus' authoritative teaching as a whole is to bring about the new reality "blessedness" for all those who will set themselves in the position of receivers of this blessing. The beatitudes invite anyone in the crowds to join the ranks of those who are blessed by becoming "poor in spirit." In the process, they would join the ranks of those who acknowledge his authority—namely, disciples— and receive his teaching as authoritative. The beatitudes also signal that the rest of Jesus' teaching will help the readers to do so. In sum, the hearers and the readers are called by the beatitudes to become blessed ones, disciples.

5:11–16. The Disciples' Vocation (Part 1)

The beatitudes have shown who are the blessed ones, the true disciples. The very next verse (5:11), still in the form of a beatitude, takes the next step and assumes that "you," the hearers and thus also the readers, have identified themselves with the blessed ones and, more specifically, with those who are "persecuted for righteousness' sake" (5:10). As such they are now in a new relationship with Jesus; they are under his authority. He is in a position to exhort them, as the two imperatives "Rejoice and be glad" express here, and as he will do throughout the Sermon.

5:11–12. The fact that this last beatitude establishes the disciples and the readers as receivers of Jesus' exhortation(s) sheds new light on the rest of the beatitudes. The disciples' ultimate goal is to enter the kingdom, and for this purpose they must become poor in spirit. Yet, simultaneously, their actions or attitudes as disciples have another goal. They act "for right-eousness' sake" (5:10), or, better, "for Jesus' sake" (5:11), and ultimately for God's sake, since they act in this way so that people may "give glory to [their] Father who is in heaven" (5:16). In sum, the disciples' actions are simultaneously *for their own sake* (in order to be blessed, in order to enter the kingdom) and *for Jesus' sake and God's sake*. This means that the beatitudes and the Sermon as a whole do not merely spell out the conditions for en-trance into the kingdom, they also express how to serve Jesus and God.

We could say that being blessed, being disciples who (will) participate in the kingdom, is also being the *elected, chosen* people who have a specific vocation which involves doing something for Jesus' and God's sake. Could it be that the beatitudes (5:3–10) are an expression of the disciples' election, followed by an expression of their vocation (5:11–16) and of the "law" spelling out how to carry out this vocation (5:17—6:21)? The beatitude concerning Peter (16:17–19) suggests this, since it has the same organization: (a) Peter is declared "blessed" because something has been revealed to him by God, and thus because he has been chosen; (b) he receives a new name, "rock," which expresses his vocation (to be the one upon which the church will be built); (c) what he will do to carry out this vocation is then spelled out (16:19). This is not unlike the pattern we find in Exodus 19—20: (a) The way in which Israel was chosen by God's intervention is first expressed (Exod. 19:4–5); (b) Israel receives a new name designating its vocation, "a kingdom of priests and a holy nation" (Exod. 19:6); (c) and then the law is given (Exodus 20). From this perspective it would appear that 5:11–16 expresses the nature of the disciples' vocation by giving them more or less directly three names: prophets (like the prophets of old, 5:12), salt of the earth (5:13), and light of the world (5:14). Yet we need to note that these three names that designate their vocation are, interestingly enough, not directly involved in oppositions. And since the beatitudes themselves do not involve any opposition, it becomes clear that this entire pattern (election, vocation, law) reflects what Matthew presumes is his readers' view. It is in terms of his readers' old knowledge that Matthew presents the beatitudes as the affirmation of the disciples' election, then their vocation (and new names), followed by a law-like series of exhortations (5:17—7:12). It is for his readers' benefit that Matthew presents the Sermon on the Mount as the giving of a new covenant by a new Moses. This, however, is *not* Matthew's own view;[9] this is his readers' view that he can affirm to a certain extent but that he will also transform so as to convey his own convictions.

In order to elucidate Matthew's own view, and how he reinterprets his readers' old knowledge (their view of Jesus as giving a new covenant on a new Mt. Sinai), we need to examine the points he makes through the opposition of actions found in 5:11–12 and in 5:13–16.

5:11–12. The opposition of actions contrasts the response of the disciples with the action of their persecutors. They "rejoice" and are "glad" when people accuse them of being evil and, beyond this slander, persecute them. The opposition concerns, therefore, two evaluations of the disciples' situations. The disciples are those who act for Jesus' sake ("on my account," 5:11) and who can be recognized as associated with him. The situation of the disciples is perceived as good, or euphoric, by the disciples themselves, while other people (those not associated with Jesus) see it as evil, or dysphoric. Matthew's main point is that the disciples are those who are visibly associated with Jesus and who know how to evaluate their situation correctly, because they do so both in terms of "reward in heaven" (future reward, since it is "in heaven") and in terms of past sacred history ("the prophets who were before you"), that is also in terms of Scripture.

This opposition makes a twofold point. First, the evaluation of a *present* situation is correct only when it is done both in terms of the eschatological *future* (what will be in heaven, after the judgment) and in terms of *past* sacred history and Scripture. This point, made about Jesus in 3:13—4:11, is now made about the disciples. Second, the contrast between the disciples and those who persecute them underscores that the disciples are neither evil nor slanderous. Rather, they are like the prophets; they are prophets, as Matthew would expect his readers to say. Prophets are people who are persecuted for God's sake and who do not do evil things to others (and, presumably, do good things). This second point will be further underscored in 7:15–23, which emphasizes that the disciples as prophets are not those who merely proclaim the right things (and say "Lord, Lord") but those who also bear good fruits. Yet here it is primarily a negative definition; the disciples as prophets *are not* evildoers.

5:13–16. The metaphorical description of the vocation of the disciples as "salt of the earth" (5:13a) and "light of the world (5:14a), as well as the description of its goal that people "may see your good works and give glory to your Father who is in heaven" (5:16), is not directly involved in an opposition. Yet these verses involve two oppositions concerning the ways in which this vocation is implemented. As in the case of 5:11–12, these oppositions convey a point (conviction) that is in continuity with a point Matthew made in 3:11–15; it underscores that one needs to have a life that is suitable for or "fitting" one's vocation.

The first narrative opposition, "if salt has lost its taste, how shall its saltness be restored"? (5:13), is weakly marked and needs to be interpreted in terms of the second one, which is more clearly expressed: "Nor do [peo-ple] light a lamp and put it under a bushel, but on a stand" (5:15). This metaphor for the disciples' action contrasts those who act inappropriately by using something (a lighted lamp) in a way that *does not fit* its vocation (giving light) with those who act appropriately by using it in a way that *fits* its vocation. Thus we find once again Matthew's fundamental convic-tions regarding good attitudes, which are attitudes based upon the recog-nition of what is fitting or suitable in a specific situation. In chapters 3—4 we found that, for Matthew, a good attitude *fits* repentance (3:8), the present time (3:15), and God's word (4:4). Here a good action fits one's vocation. The disciples are those who know how to identify the action or attitude that fits their vocation—as salt, they should give salty taste to people; as light, they should be in a position to "shine" for those around them—and who act accordingly and thus fulfill their vocation.

These observations suggest that, for Matthew, attitudes that fit one's vocation are comparable to, if not identical with, attitudes that fit repent-

ance, the present time, and God's word, and consequently fulfill righteousness (3:15). It appears that turning toward God (repentance, see 3:8)
also means acknowledging one's true vocation; fulfilling all righteousness
also means fulfilling one's vocation; and nourishing oneself with God's word
(see 4:4) also means receiving and appropriating one's vocation.

From this perspective, we can now grasp how Matthew understood the
designations of the disciples' vocation. Instead of involving a negative attitude toward others (see 5:11–12), this vocation involves a positive action
for others, indeed all others ("the earth," "the world"). This vocation thus
has universal dimensions. It is so because this vocation is *for God's sake*; its
goal is to bring people, all people, to "give glory to [their] Father who is
in heaven" (5:16), a phrase that means basically the same thing as "sanc-
tifying God's name," a classical expression of the vocation of the chosen
people according to early Judaism[10] (see also 6:9). As the disciples can rejoice
(5:12), and thus give glory to God because they are "blessed," so people
can give glory to God when they see the "good works" of the disciples,
that is, when the disciples have a behavior that fits or is suitable for their
status as disciples. In such a case, according to the beatitudes, the disciples
are "blessed" (by God). This means that people can see not only "good
works" of good people but also of blessed people. Consequently, the designation of the disciples as "salt" and "light" expresses among other things
that *they are both blessed and a blessing for others.* And, indeed, "salt" has this
connotation in the Hebrew Scripture where it is associated with sacrifices
(see Exod. 30:35; Lev. 2:13); it is "pure and holy," and thus purifies and
sanctifies. Similarly, the metaphor "light" has, for Matthew, the connotation "blessing," since he used it in this way in 4:15–16 (Isa. 9:1–2) to
describe the coming of Jesus, the holy Son of God, in Capernaum.

In sum, by performing good works the disciples are blessed; they are
holy, manifestations of God's holiness, and thus a blessing for the world
(all the nations) which can then give glory to God. Such disciples are also
under Jesus' and thus God's authority, since they submit to Jesus' exhortations. If, for Matthew, the "kingdom" is not only what they are hoping
for (5:3–10) but is also the manifestation of the kingship of God (see 4:17),
then the disciples are already a manifestation of the kingdom insofar as they
submit to the kingship of God and perform good works thanks to which
people glorify God. "Theirs is the kingdom of heaven."

5:17–19. Conditions for Implementing
the Vocation

In this passage we find three oppositions that deal with Jesus' and the
disciples' vocations as related to Scripture. Because of the preceding oppositions we should expect that a correct view of one's relation with Scripture involves its evaluation in terms of time and in terms of what is suitable
for one's vocation. In fact, a first opposition (5:17–18) underscores that the

status of Scripture changes over time and thus that one's relation to Scripture is valid only insofar as one has a correct perception of the present time. The second and third oppositions (5:17 and 5:19) focus upon the view one should have of Jesus' and the disciples' vocations and how they are correctly or incorrectly understood according to the way the role of Scripture is conceived. Conversely, Scripture, which helps define the disciples' vocation, needs to be interpreted in terms of one's future place in the kingdom. In brief, 5:17-19 indicates that a condition of possibility for implementing one's vocation is a correct understanding of Scripture.

5:17-18. The authoritative teaching of Jesus ("Truly, I say to you," 5:18) is opposed to the way of thinking of false disciples ("Think not," 5:17). Note that it is not wrong to think that "the law and the prophets" (i.e., Scripture) will be abolished; Jesus himself says it (5:18). What is wrong is to think that the coming of Jesus signifies that they are already abolished, while Jesus affirms that this will be the case only when "heaven and earth pass away" and when "all is accomplished" (5:18).[11] As in 3:14-15, the incorrect view is based upon a wrong understanding of time. In the same way that the coming of Jesus is not to be confused with the time of the eschatological judgment (3:11-12), so it should not be confused with the time when the law and the prophets are abolished, that is, the end of the world. A correct view of the law and the prophets demands a proper time perspective, as is also the case when one wants to have a correct view of the situation of the disciples (5:11-12). The status of Scripture *in the present* can be correctly perceived only when it is evaluated in terms of the status of Scripture in *the eschatological future* and, as we can expect by analogy with 5:11-12, in terms of the status of Scripture in *the past* (see 5:21-48). In other words, the status of Scripture changes over time. In the past, it was given; in the present, it needs to be fulfilled; in the eschatological future, it will be abolished. Through the rest of the oppositions in this chapter (5:17-48), Matthew defines the status of Scripture in each of these periods by focusing upon Jesus' and the disciples' relation to it and, more specifically, upon the relation of Scripture to their vocation.

5:17. The second opposition contrasts two views of Jesus' vocation (what he has come for) as it relates to Scripture; Jesus has come to "fulfil" rather than to "abolish" the law and the prophets. What does this mean? The phrase "fulfilling the law and the prophets" can have many connotations and thus by itself is quite ambiguous, as shown by the many proposals concerning its possible meanings.[12] "Abolishing the law and the prophets" is no less ambiguous, despite that, in most instances, the meaning of this phrase is not perceived to be as difficult to assess. Yet Matthew narrows down the range of possible meanings of these phrases by defining them, to a certain extent, through the network of oppositions in which he sets them so as to integrate them into his system of convictions. We need to consider the opposition of 5:17 in itself but also in its relations to the oppositions of the preceding chapters; Matthew expects that his readers will remember the preceding points he has made.

When considered by itself, the opposition of 5:17 allows us to say that "to fulfil" is contrasted with "to abolish," that is, to dismantle, tear down, and thus make invalid, annul (according to the possible meanings of *kataluō*). Fulfilling means, therefore, having a constructive attitude toward Scripture and considering it important, and not null. Thus, this opposition contrasts not only two views of Jesus' vocation but also two views of Scripture. A wrong view of Scripture is associated with a wrong view of Jesus' vocation.

In the light of the oppositions of 4:1–11, which concern Jesus' attitude toward Scripture, we can say that fulfilling Scripture involves viewing it as authoritative, as God's word, and submitting to it by interpreting it correctly (contra the devil's use of Scripture). In this light, abolishing, tearing down Scripture, is related to viewing it as a means of testing God; as a means of testing or judging the faithfulness of other people (cf. the devil's view, 4:5–7); and as a means of fleeing the judgment (see my comments on 4:5–7 and its relationship to 3:7). Indeed, when one has this wrong view of Scripture, and wrongly understands Jesus' coming as the coming of the eschatological judgment (cf. 3:11–12), then one cannot but perceive the present time as a time when one does not any longer need to test God's promises (those found in the prophets, in particular), since they would be accomplished. In this perspective, Scripture would be useless; Jesus' coming would have made it purposeless. Similarly, when the law is wrongly conceived as a means of avoiding being condemned (fleeing from the wrath to come, 3:7), Scripture loses its purpose. It would be too late to try to use Scripture in order to avoid condemnation by carefully doing what the law demands, since the time of the judgment would have arrived. And, of course, Scripture as a means of judging (condemning) others would also be abolished, since the eschatological judge himself would be judging. The purpose of the law would have been dismissed by Jesus' coming. Thus the view that Jesus' coming would mean the abolition of the law and the prophets is based upon a wrong view of both the meaning of Jesus' coming and the role or function of Scripture.

Conversely, Jesus' fulfillment of Scripture is not such that it would make it useless. It involves a different view of Scripture. Jesus fulfills the law, but not because he wants to flee the judgment. His attitude is constructive, positive and not negative, because, for him, the law is not a means of judging other people. At the present time he is not coming as the eschatological judge. Rather, Scripture is "bread" (4:4), nourishment, that he and any human being need. *Fulfilling the law is allowing the law to mold one's will, to define one's vocation* (see 4:4), which determines the way one acts. Therefore, fulfilling the law is not merely doing what the law commands, obeying it;

this is the wrong view of fulfilling the law when one sees it as a means of avoiding condemnation at the judgment.[13] Similarly, Jesus fulfills Scripture as promise (the prophets). But these fulfillments are not a testing of God (cf. the devil's test of God, 4:5–7); human beings do not have control over this process of fulfillment. These are interventions of God taking place when and how God wants them to happen. Thus, fulfillments of the promises can be found only in someone who submits to God's will, that is, who fulfills the law in the sense of having a vocation defined and established in terms of the law. In brief, Jesus fulfills the prophets because of his vocation, because he is sent by God and has accepted this vocation by nourishing himself with the law.

Concerning the opposition between fulfilling and abolishing the law and the prophets, we conclude that fulfilling the law and the prophets *involves allowing Scripture to establish the vocation that one will carry out.* And since one lives in a specific time, the present, which should not be confused either with the eschatological future (as is expressed here) or with the past (as will be emphasized in 5:21–48), fulfilling Scripture necessarily involves interpreting the present in terms of Scripture as well as interpreting Scripture in terms of the present. A wrong view of Scripture can lead either to the view that Scripture is useless (abolished) in the present or to the view that fulfilling Scripture means simply obeying it (literally). Jesus' vocation (what he came for, 5:17a) is, on the one hand, established and defined with the help of Scripture (as a fulfillment of Scripture, 4:4) and, on the other hand, aimed at fulfilling Scripture, thus making it possible for others to allow Scripture to establish their vocation. Here we find the same pattern as in 5:3–16: as the disciples are *blessed* and have as a vocation to be a *blessing* for others, so in Jesus Scripture is *fulfilled* and his vocation aims at *fulfilling* Scripture.

5:19. The third opposition contrasts those who relax, or abolish, one of the least of the commandments and teach others to do so with those who do such a commandment and teach others to do so. This opposition is comparable to the preceding one, as is suggested by the Greek verb *luō* (RSV: "relax"; cf. *kataluō* in 5:17). Yet it shifts the attention from Jesus' vocation to the disciples' vocation, and from fulfilling or abolishing the whole of Scripture to doing or abolishing specific commandments, including the less important ones (i.e., the "iota" or "dot" of the law, 5:18, as metaphors for the least of the commandments).[14] In brief, the disciples' vocation involves doing specific commandments as Jesus fulfills Scripture. Doing the specific commandments is also doing Jesus' teaching about them and thus adopting Jesus' attitude toward Scripture.[15]

At first it may seem that doing a commandment and fulfilling Scripture are quite different. Yet despite the mention of performance in 5:19, both verses express the same basic point about the need to fulfill Scripture by interpreting it.[16] One can understand it when one notes that abolishing and doing a commandment do not stand by themselves; both are associated with "teaching others so." The correlation of abolishing and doing with teaching means that abolishing or doing a commandment is something that is teachable and taught, and thus something that needs to be argued or explained; in brief, it is the result of an interpretation. This is readily understood in the case of abolishing a commandment, translated relaxing it, a process that involves an interpretation. But this is also true in the case of doing a commandment, which should not be understood as performing a commandment literally (exactly as it is written and without interpretation)[17] but as performing a commandment according to its proper interpretation. Certainly, nothing, even the less weighty commandment, should be neglected in the law; all of Scripture remains authoritative. But fulfilling Scripture, or doing and teaching the commandments, involves a constructive attitude through which Scripture is applied to the present so as to establish the vocation that one will carry out. A proper acknowledgment of the authority of Scripture leads not merely to doing what is literally commanded by the law but to doing the vocation one receives by nourishing oneself with Scripture, a process that involves interpretation.

What is this proper interpretation of the law? Once again, it is somehow related to time. One needs to interpret the commandments in terms of the proper view of one's relationship to the future kingdom of heaven. Indeed, the text contrasts those who "shall be called great in the kingdom of heaven" and those who "shall be called least in the kingdom of heaven." Note that those who relax the commandments are not said to be cast out of the kingdom;[18] they will participate in it, although they will have a lower status. Whatever might have been the concrete situation Matthew had in mind,[19] this opposition means that attitude toward Scripture does not affect entrance into the kingdom but only one's place in it. Since being denied entrance into the kingdom (5:20) is what happens at the judgment, this means once again that, for Matthew, Scripture is not in itself a means of judgment.

In sum, the disciples' interpretation of Scripture, following Jesus' own interpretation, done in terms of the relation between their present and the future kingdom, defines and establishes their vocation. In order to perform this interpretation, they need a correct understanding of the status of Scripture in the present, as compared with its status in the eschatological future and in the past. They also need a correct understanding of their present, the time of Jesus, and thus of the meaning of Jesus' presence. In the present, Scripture is to be fulfilled, that is, used for establishing the vocation, and neither abolished nor merely interpreted literally—as one would do when one has a wrong understanding of Scripture as a means of judgment and as a means of testing God.

In 5:17–19, three conditions for implementing one's vocation are underscored. Only those who have the proper understanding of Jesus' coming (his vocation), of Scripture, and of the present time in relation to the eschatological future and Scripture (the past revelation) are in a position to fulfill their vocation.

5:20 and 5:47–48. Overabundant Righteousness as Condition for Entrance Into the Kingdom (Part 1)

The verses providing the frame in which the antitheses are set (5:20 and 5:47–48) involve an opposition that concerns opposite ways of fulfilling a vocation, that is, different kinds of righteousness.[20] This opposition moves beyond the preceding ones in that an overabundant righteousness is now the condition of entrance into the kingdom of heaven, and not merely what determines one's higher or lower status in the kingdom, as the attitude toward Scripture is. Our interpretation needs to account for this progression.

5:20, 47. The text opposes those who *do more than* the tax collectors and the Gentiles (loving both those who love them and their enemies) to those who *do not do more than* the tax collectors and the Gentiles (loving only those who love them, 5:47). This opposition echoes the warning in 5:20 which calls the disciples to a righteousness exceeding that of the scribes and the Pharisees, and thus contrasts the righteousness of ideal disciples with that of scribes and Pharisees.[21] Note that both parties have a righteousness. The difference is a matter of quantity; the disciples' righteousness is more abundant than that of the scribes and the Pharisees.[22]

This twofold opposition moves beyond the preceding one (5:19) in several ways. First, it is no longer a matter of attitude toward Scripture, but rather of righteousness. The text has moved from fulfilling Scripture to fulfilling righteousness (i.e., having an overabundant righteousness, such as loving one's enemies), and from relaxing the commandments to not fulfilling righteousness (i.e., having the incomplete righteousness of scribes and Pharisees as well as of tax collectors and Gentiles). Second, the consequences of these attitudes have changed. It is no longer simply a matter of the higher or lower rank one would have in the kingdom, but a matter of entrance into, or exclusion from, the kingdom. *An overabundant righteousness is the condition for entrance into the kingdom.* One's righteousness is what is decisive at the eschatological judgment. While Scripture and its fulfillment are not directly linked with the eschatological judgment, righteousness is.

The question then is: What is the difference between fulfilling Scripture (5:17), doing and teaching the commandments (5:19), and having a life characterized by an overabundant righteousness (5:20)? In order to address this question, we need to understand what is conveyed by the Greek verb *perisseuō* (RSV: "exceeds," 5:20) and by the corresponding adjective (*perissos*) in 5:47. As we suggested, it is a term referring to overabundance, to overflowing, to going beyond the normal boundaries; thus, it introduces here a metaphor, which needs to be understood in terms of the metaphors related to other oppositions.

Fulfilling Scripture and doing and teaching the commandments have as their primary purpose defining and establishing one's vocation. This is important, but it is not sufficient, as the metaphors of 5:13–16 express. One can have a lighted lamp, a vocation, and put it under a bushel, instead of putting it on a lampstand, where it can give "light to all in the house" (5:15). In terms of this metaphor, different uses of Scripture produce different lamps that are more or less efficient—more or less adequate definitions of the vocation. One should strive to have the better understanding of one's vocation, the understanding resulting from the proper use of Scripture; one's status in the kingdom depends on this. But whatever might be the specific understanding of one's vocation, it is essential to keep in mind that it is a lamp whose purpose is to give "light to all in the house" (5:15); it is "the light of the world" (5:14). Thus it needs to be put on a lampstand, so that this light can spread over "all in the house" or over "the world." In terms of the metaphor found in 5:20, one needs to let it overflow, go beyond narrow confines (the bushel of 5:15).

Consequently, we propose that *righteousness is the implementation of one's vocation, doing what fits one's vocation.* One can have a limited implementation of one's vocation, a narrow righteousness. Such is, according to Matthew, the case of scribes and Pharisees.[23] Such is also the case of tax collectors and Gentiles who correctly recognize that loving is part of what they should do (their vocation) but limit its implementation to loving those who love them. The overabundant righteousness is the implementation of this vocation by loving not only one's friends but also one's enemies (5:46–47). This righteousness overflows the narrow confines of the disciples' circle of friends and applies also to those outside this circle, their enemies. The disciples' proper implementation of their vocation is the fulfillment of "all righteousness," by doing all that fits their vocation (cf. 5:15), as Jesus did in 3:15.

5:48. Thus the disciples' overabundant righteousness is an implementation of their vocation to the broader possible dimension of the situation in which they find themselves. In so doing, disciples demonstrate that they are children of their Father who is in heaven who makes the sun rise and sends rain on the evil and the good (5:45), while, by having a narrower righteousness, other people demonstrate who they really are, that is, tax collectors and Gentiles, people who, for Matthew's audience, are not children of the Father. God's children are those who not only know and have appropriated God's will (even tax collectors and Gentiles have done so, since they love), but also strive to implement it completely by applying it to every aspect of their experience. Their righteousness is then complete, "perfect," as God's righteousness is. They are "perfect, as (their) heavenly Father is perfect" (5:48). Their righteousness, their way of implementing their own vocation is the same as God's way of implementing his own will. Thus, disciples with such an overabundant righteousness belong to the kingdom of heaven; they will enter into it. Note also that, for Matthew, God's righteousness is not to be thought of as a quality or as an aspect of God's nature, but as God's overabundant, perfect implementation of his will in his relation with the whole of humankind (the evil and the good, the just and the unjust, 5:45).

5:21-47. The Overabundant
Righteousness (Part 1). The Antitheses

This famous passage, known as the "antitheses," is the first part of the description of the overabundant righteousness that the disciples should have. From what precedes, we can anticipate that it describes what should be the disciples' *implementation of their vocation established with the help of Scripture*. Since one's vocation is nothing else than what one wants to do, one should not be surprised to find that the fulfillment of one's vocation involves its internalization. The disciples' vocation needs to become their will, their inner disposition. First, since their vocation is established with the help of Scripture, the internalization of their vocation includes the internalization of Scripture—a key point of this passage. On the basis of the correct understanding of Scripture and its role, one can then discover with the help of Scripture what one's vocation is and appropriate it so that it becomes what one wants to do. Second, this view of the role of Scripture as a means of establishing the disciples' vocation leads to a refusal to use God's word to judge or condemn others or, more generally, a refusal to use Scripture and God against others—another key point. Third, it follows that one of the characteristics of the disciples' vocation is the maintenance or (re)establishment of good relationships with others—the major point of the antitheses.

The six antitheses oppose "You have heard that it was said to [the people] of old" (5:21, 33, and in abbreviated form, 5:27, 31, 38, 43) to "but I say to you" (5:22, 28, 32, 34, 39, 44). This passage also includes five other oppositions (including that of 5:47; see above) related to the antitheses.

In the six antitheses the formal opposition concerns the transmission to "you" (would-be disciples) of two different messages about biblical commandments. But what are the specific points that Matthew makes by means of these oppositions? On the one hand, would-be disciples have received a knowledge of the commandments from hearing what has been said (by God, as the passive form indicates) *to the people of old*. In other words, their knowledge is secondhand, indirect knowledge; they appropriate what has been said to other people. On the other hand, Jesus expresses a knowledge that he has not received from anyone else. Thus the opposition might concern direct and indirect knowledge of the will of God. However, past authoritative teaching (by God to the people of old) is also opposed to present authoritative teaching (by Jesus).[24] Once again we find a temporal opposition, here between the present of Jesus' ministry and the past of the biblical revelation. The opposition might also be between a knowledge of the commandments as they are, a literal, narrow interpretation, and a knowledge of the commandments as radically and broadly interpreted.[25] Our examination of the antitheses will show how these possible points are conveyed by Matthew.

5:21–26. Here we find two oppositions: the first antithesis (5:21–22) and a secondary opposition in the material that illustrates the implications of the antithesis (5:22–26). The antithesis itself opposes hearing "You shall not kill; and whoever kills shall be liable to judgment" (see Exod. 20:13; Deut. 5:17; cf. Num. 35:12) to receiving Jesus' saying that "every one who is angry with his brother shall be liable to judgment." This is the opposition of two views of evil. Note that evil is defined in terms of judgment (condemnation). Evil is what makes one "liable to judgment," a phrase that is to be understood in the broadest sense to include both human condemnation (before the Sanhedrin, 5:22; before a judge who sends people to jail, 5:25) and eschatological condemnation (the Gehenna of fire, 5:22). Thus, evil is what has dysphoric, or bad, consequences for someone either now or in the future. Not implementing one's vocation as overabundant righteousness results in condemnation, while its implementation results in one's entrance into the kingdom (5:20).

In the former case ("You have heard"), evil is limited to an overt act (killing), while in the latter case ("I say to you"), evil includes both the overt act (Jesus does not deny that killing is evil) and an inner disposition (anger). In other words, overabundant righteousness is not limited to the realm of overt actions but also applies to the realm of feelings, inner dispositions, evil inclinations (evil *yetzer*). In the same way that Jesus has both a public and a private knowledge of the will of God—he knows what "you have heard" and has a personal knowledge of it—so the disciples should have a view of evil encompassing both public, overt evil (killing) and private, inner evil (anger).

Since killing and being angry are presented as having the same consequence, one needs to ask what view of evil allows Jesus to bring them together. It then appears that killing is the destruction of one's relationship with another person through physical annihilation of that person, while anger is a more subtle form of destruction of the same relationship. An evil inner disposition, anger against a person whom one should consider as a brother or a sister,[26] has the same effect as an overt evil act. Thus evil is the destruction of the bond that should unite two people.

This view of evil also means that when two people are estranged, one of them is to blame for this separation, since it is due to the evil inner disposition of one toward the other. But who should take the responsibility for it? The secondary opposition which contrasts those who insult others (5:22) and the disciple who should seek reconciliation (5:23–25) puts the burden squarely on the disciple's shoulders. The situation is quite ambiguous, as its description shows: "if you . . . remember that your brother has something against you" (5:23). In the light of what precedes, this means that your brother is alienated from you and is angry against you. But, in 5:24–26, it appears that a brother's anger should not be viewed as a reason to blame him for the estrangement; the disciple is somehow responsible for the estrangement, at least in the sense that he or she should be the one who strives to overcome it.

In sum, this opposition emphasizes that one should not conclude from the antithesis that when someone is angry with you, that person should be condemned—for having an attitude equivalent to killing. Even though the commandment and its broad interpretation express a condition of entrance into the kingdom, and are thus related to judgment, they should not be viewed as a means for condemning other people. The commandment and its interpretation apply only to "you" as disciples. They define the vocation you should carry out: you should not be angry against other people; you should reject all that alienates you from others. And when you are estranged from someone, your vocation is to strive to overcome this estrangement, to bring about a reconciliation. The negative expression of the vocation, not bringing about estrangement from other people, takes the positive form of reconciliation. Any rift between disciples and other people is the responsibility of the disciples. Reconciliation is their primary vocation, which takes precedence over everything else, including worship of God (offering a gift at the altar, 5:23). Not doing so is not having the overabundant righteousness and thus being excluded from the kingdom (and being condemned at the judgment, 5:26).

5:27–30. Here also we find two oppositions: the antithesis itself (5:27–28) and a secondary opposition (5:29–30). The second antithesis is quite similar to the first. Once again the view of evil is broadened in Jesus' saying. Adultery is not merely an overt, physical act but also a lustful inner disposition ("in [your] heart"). As previously, evil is defined as a wrong relationship between people, although it is now the wrong union of two people instead of the estrangement of two people.

The secondary opposition contrasts losing a limb (an eye, a hand), which is scandalous ("causes you to sin," 5:29–30), and losing one's whole body to Gehenna. The issue of judgment comes once again to the fore. In 5:21–26, it was underscored that the commandment and its interpretation should not be used to condemn others. Yet the commandment has a role regarding judgment. Fulfilling the law, in the sense of fulfilling righteousness (having overabundant righteousness), involves, for the disciples, applying the law to evaluate themselves but not in order to flee the judgment (3:7). Rather, it involves using the law to judge and condemn oneself, and carrying out this condemnation on oneself without waiting for the eschatological judgment.

5:31–32. The third antithesis continues the presentation of the view of evil which the disciples should have as they implement their vocation. After presenting a view of adultery focused on one's personal behavior, including one's inner lustful disposition and one's responsibility to judge oneself, the text considers the disciples' responsibility for other people's adultery. This is a shift comparable to the one found in 5:21–26, where the disciples have to assume the responsibility for any estrangement from others. Divorce is to be viewed as evil, insofar as it engenders a situation in which others will become adulterers. While divorce is permitted by Scripture (5:31; Deut. 24:1), disciples with overabundant righteousness need to take into account the effect of this action upon other people. Since "whoever marries a divorced woman commits adultery" (5:32), that is, is in a wrong union with the wife of someone else, a man divorcing his wife creates a situation in which she will be in danger of becoming an adulteress. Thus, disciples should not divorce. Yet if a situation of wrong union, whatever it might be,[27] already exists, then there is no objection to divorce; it would not create a situation that would cause others to engage in a wrong union, since this wrong union already exists. Beyond the rejection of wrong union (already found in the preceding antithesis), 5:31–32 also stresses that the disciples should preserve the good union that marriage is.

In the first three antitheses (5:21–32) overabundant righteousness aims at maintaining or (re)establishing good relationships with others with the recognition that inner dispositions are essential in these relationships and that disciples have to evaluate carefully their responsibility for these relationships so as to ensure that they are in no way the cause of evil relationships.

5:33–37. The fourth antithesis opposes "You shall not swear falsely, but shall perform to the Lord what you have sworn" (cf. use of Exod. 20:7; Lev. 19:12; Num. 30:3; Deut. 23:22) to Jesus' injunction "Do not swear at all." The term "swearing" covers the meaning of both "taking an oath" in order to confirm the truth of a statement and "taking a vow," that is, pledging that one will do something, solemnly declaring one's intention. The disciples should view any swearing as evil. Why? Because, as the rest of Jesus' saying (5:34–37) emphasizes, one always swears *by something or by someone other than oneself.* This is true even when you swear "by your head," because, in fact, you do not have control over what happens to you (5:36) and thus you actually swear by God. In this antithesis Matthew develops two of the points he made in the preceding verses.

First, there is the point regarding the disciples' relationships with other people. One of the reasons why swearing is evil is that it introduces someone or something in between them and those to whom they speak. It transforms a direct, open, frank relationship with others into an indirect one.

Second, people who swear attribute to someone other than themselves or to something the trustworthiness and validity of what they *say* and of what they *want to do*. This amounts to denying their own responsibility for their statements and intentions. Overabundant righteousness involves, for the disciples, taking full responsibility for what they say and for what they want to do. They cannot even hide behind God. Therefore, it appears that the disciples have to assume this responsibility because what they want to do is directly related to *their inner disposition*; it is, therefore, intimately linked with their own selves, not imposed upon them by someone or something else. It is fully theirs, and thus they must assume responsibility for it. Consequently, they should let their statements stand on their own, and "anything more than this comes from evil [or, the evil one]" (5:37). Anything more demonstrates that their will is not truly their own—their inner disposition. If their will is not this inner disposition which characterizes overabundant righteousness, it has an evil origin. The disciples' will—what they want to do, their vocation—might be offered or proposed by God (cf. the calls/commands to Joseph and the Magi in chapters 1—2), but it is not imposed by God. They have full responsibility for it.

5:38–42. The fifth antithesis opposes the *lex talionis*, "An eye for an eye and a tooth for a tooth" (cf. Exod. 21:24; Lev. 24:20; Deut. 19:21), to Jesus' injunction "Do not resist one who is evil." In the preceding antitheses the disciples' responsibility for maintaining and (re)establishing good relationships with others has been repeatedly emphasized, yet could be viewed as restricted to specific cases. In the fifth antithesis, instead of being verbal (as in 5:33–37), these relationships are concrete, and with people who mistreat the disciples—rather than with members of the community (as could be understood in 5:21–26).

Scripture could be viewed as providing the disciples with a ground to "stand against" (*antisthenai*; RSV: "resist") evil people. But this is not an appropriate use of Scripture for disciples with overabundant righteousness. Scripture has been used so far as a means for establishing their vocation and as a means for judging themselves (5:29–30). We noted earlier that, for Matthew, Scripture should not be viewed as a means of judging and condemning others. In the logic of these views, the fifth antithesis now affirms that disciples should not "stand against"—that is, should not seek revenge against—people who have done them wrong. Moreover, the disciples should not use Scripture against other people, even to protect themselves. Since the disciples' relationships with other people are an essential part of their vocation, they should maintain such relationships even when their terms are set by evil people who mistreat them.

Note that the four illustrations of the principle of nonresistance show that this is not a matter of passive submission to evil people. It is an active participation in the relationship as set by the evil people. Someone hits you, accept a second blow (5:39). Someone sues you for your shirt (*chitōn*, "undergarment"; RSV: "coat"), give also your "cloak" (5:40). You refuse to use Scripture against that person, and you give up the protection that it could have given you, since the biblical law (Deut. 24:10, 12–13; Exod. 22:25–26) prohibits taking away the cloak from a (poor) man. Someone compels you to do something (as the Roman soldiers often did; see 27:32), do more than what is asked of you. Someone asks you for money, give— whatever may be the situation. Such is the attitude of overabundant righteousness toward evil people.

5:43–48. The last antithesis carries these views of Scripture and of relationships with others to its logical conclusion. Even though Scripture would allow you to hate your enemies, "love your enemies and pray for those who persecute you." The active submission to evil people, the willful participation in a relationship with them even if it is detrimental to oneself, is truly overabundant righteousness when it also involves the proper inner attitude, love. In fact, the injunction "Love your enemies and pray" for them brings together the three points that Matthew emphasizes throughout the antitheses.

1. Love is an inner disposition.

2. It is an inner disposition toward others which underscores the fundamental value of the disciples' relationships to other people whoever they may be, including those who persecute them.

3. Praying for these persecutors introduces the relationship with God who gave Scripture, as is repeatedly expressed by the phrase "it was said" (the only portion of the introductory formula that is found in all the antitheses, cf. 5:31). Instead of seeking God's protection from their enemies, a protection that he could provide and that is offered in Scripture (see 4:6)— an attitude that would involve calling upon God and Scripture against their enemies—disciples pray for their enemies. They call upon God *in favor of their enemies.*

By loving their enemies and praying for them, as well as by letting their lives be governed by the inner disposition (the vocation) established with the help of Scripture which gives priority to their positive and active relationship with others, disciples have the overabundant righteousness, which makes them children of their Father in heaven (5:45). As such, they are perfect as their heavenly father is perfect (5:48) and belong to the kingdom of heaven (5:20).

At the conclusion of our study of the antitheses, the question remains:

How can anyone have a life characterized by such a righteousness? This question has often been raised and addressed from many perspectives.[28] According to our approach, we have to be content with what Matthew says on this issue, namely: (a) that a life characterized by overabundant right-eousness is the implementation of a vocation established with the help of Scripture; (b) that in order to be implemented, a vocation must necessarily be internalized—it needs to become the disciples' will, the inner disposition which governs their behavior.

Surprisingly, Matthew does not seem to envision that it might be difficult to follow this radical way of behavior. For him, as soon as people have truly appropriated the vocation they discover with the help of Scripture and have made it their own will, there is apparently no obstacle preventing its overabundant implementation (righteousness). Matthew does not seem to envision any obstacle to the implementation of such a vocation after it is appropriated. This is also true in the case of the confrontation between Jesus and the devil (4:1–11), where the issue of the power of the devil over Jesus is set aside as inconsequential as long as Jesus' will remains God's will. What would preclude someone from such radical behavior is whatever would prevent the appropriation and internalization of that vocation.

The question concerning the possibility of a life characterized by an over-abundant righteousness is nothing else than the question: How is this will established? How is the vocation defined and internalized? In 5:17–19, Mat-thew emphasizes the importance of the correct view of Scripture in this process. Furthermore, the antitheses underscore that Scripture should be viewed as a means of judging oneself (5:27–30) and that it should not be used against others, either for judging others or for protecting oneself against others (5:38–42). This is certainly one aspect of the sixfold oppo-sition between "You have heard that it was said to the [people] of old" and "But I say to you." Jesus' sayings contradict a literal use of the command-ments as a means of judging (condemning) others and as a means of pro-tecting oneself from evil people. But this opposition also underscores that the proper use and interpretation of Scripture is in terms of the distinction between past ("it *was said* to the [people] *of old*") and present ("But *I say* to you"). Somehow, in the present, there is something that is different as compared with the past and that sheds a different light on Scripture, thus leading to a different view of the vocation to which one is called by Scrip-ture. There is only one thing new in the present: the coming of Jesus (5:17) or, better, the presence of Jesus. Although it should not be confused with the presence of the eschatological judge (5:17–18; cf. 3:11–15), it is the authoritative presence of someone whose sayings are put on a par with God's words, of someone who can command the disciples (cf. the direct injunc-tions in 5:34, 39, 44). It is also the authoritative presence of someone who can say "Blessed are those . . ." and establish the reality "blessedness" for

the disciples, and of someone whose authority is recognized by the hearers
of the Sermon (7:29).

In brief, for Matthew, when one's vocation is established through an
interpretation of Scripture in terms of the presence of Jesus, and through
an interpretation of Scripture by the authoritative Jesus, then one has the
will (inner disposition) to have this radical behavior.

But why should the disciples ("you") accept this teaching of Jesus? Two
reasons (warrants) are given in this passage. In the first and second antitheses
(5:21–30), it is presupposed that the disciples will want to avoid the condemnation of the eschatological judgment, and in the last one (5:43–48) that
they will want to be children of their heavenly Father and thus enter the
kingdom (5:20). In other words, Matthew presupposes that would-be disciples (crowds and readers) have an eschatological conviction about the
judgment or, positively, the conviction that the ultimate good is participation in the eschatological kingdom. With such a conviction and the view
that the present is a special time (as compared with the past) because of
Jesus' authority, hearers should be convinced to receive Jesus' teaching, and
also to recognize it as authoritative, and to appropriate it. Then they should
be in a position to have overabundant righteousness. The only obstacle to
implementing the overabundant righteousness would then be whatever
would prevent someone from having such convictions (cf. 6:22—7:12).

6:1 and 6:19–21. Overabundant
Righteousness as Condition for Entrance
Into the Kingdom (Part 2)

The introductory (6:1) and concluding (6:19–21) statements which serve
as a frame for the second set of exhortations (6:2–18) express that this second
section continues the presentation of the overabundant righteousness that
the disciples should have and on the basis of which they will either receive
rewards in heaven or be condemned, if they do not have it.

In order to perceive that the introductory verse, 6:1, deals with righteousness, it must be translated literally:[29] "Beware of practicing your righteousness before human beings in order to be seen by them." As in the case
of 5:20 and 5:47–48, this introductory verse does not include any opposition.
But the closing statement, 6:19–21, opposes laying up treasures on earth,
where they will be worthless (destroyed by moth and rust, or stolen, 6:19),
to laying up treasures in heaven, where they will endure (6:20).

6:19–20. This metaphorical opposition needs to be understood in terms
of what precedes[30] and thus in terms of 6:1. In this context, laying up
treasures on earth means practicing one's righteousness before human
beings, that is, implementing one's vocation in such a way as to receive
praises from other people. This is receiving a reward (cf. 6:2, 5, 16), but
on earth rather than in heaven; this is gathering treasures on earth. But how

should we understand the term "reward" (*misthos*)? A reward is a recompense given to someone in return for an action. We need to make a distinction between (*a*) rewards such as salary or wages (the primary meaning of *misthos*), which is that for which one works and therefore what motivates the action; and (*b*) rewards such as unexpected gifts or recompense for an action that had another motivation. Both the metaphor of gathering together treasures on earth (6:19) and the comment that people practicing their righteousness before others (6:1) "have received their reward" (6:2, 5, 16) and will have no reward from God (6:1) show that "reward" is to be understood in this passage according to the meaning of wages. The hypocrites acted in order to receive praise from others, and they do receive it; they have their reward. The disciples will receive their reward (wages) from God. But why does Matthew emphasize rewards in the sense of wages in this passage (20:1–16 and 25:31–40 seem to indicate that the reward is unexpected)? This is not explained in 6:1–21; we will find the answer elsewhere (6:25–34).

6:21. Similarly, laying up treasure in heaven means practicing one's righteousness before God, who "will reward you" (see 6:4, 6, 18)—that is, in the light of 5:20, who will make you enter the kingdom of heaven. Thus, once again, overabundant righteousness is the basis upon which it will be decided whether or not someone will enter the kingdom. It then appears that 6:21, "For where your treasure is, there will your heart be also," was understood by Matthew as referring to future participation in, or exclusion from, the kingdom of heaven,[31] since "treasure" is, in this context, a metaphor for the reward (wages) one receives either from God or from other people. Consequently, the second part of 6:21, "there will your heart be also," means having one's inner being turned toward the kingdom of heaven and is more or less equivalent to "seek first his [your heavenly Father's] kingdom and his righteousness" (6:33), a theme developed in the following verses.

6:2–18. The Overabundant Righteousness (Part 2)

6:2–4. As 6:1 suggests, the disciples' relationship to God has now become the central point. This passage on almsgiving opposes the attitude of hypocrites, who want to be seen by people when they give alms so as to be praised by them, to the attitude of disciples, who should give in secret and they will be seen and rewarded by God. Through this multifold opposition, Matthew makes several points.

First, divine rewards are contrasted with human rewards—praises. This opposition, which is repeated in 6:5–6 and 6:16–18, expresses that divine rewards are more than praises; indeed, they are enduring treasures in heaven (see 6:19–21).

Second, God is described as seeing in secret by contrast with human beings, who can only see what is not secret. This opposition is also repeated in 6:5–6 and in 6:16–18, but with a notable addition, namely, that God "is in secret." Since the phrase "in secret" is contrasted with the hypocrites' intention to be seen by others, it should be taken as somehow referring to the disciples' intention, their inner disposition (cf. 5:21–48). Furthermore, since God "is in secret," this inner disposition is directed toward God. In brief, acts (almsgiving, prayer, fasting) done "in secret" are performed before God when one is turned toward God (cf. 3:8) rather than turned toward other people. Yet as the case of almsgiving shows—since it involves giving something to poor people—it is not a matter of having a purely spiritual attitude. It involves doing something concrete for other people (cf. 5:21–48), but not in order to receive something from others.

One can then understand how the text contrasts hypocrites and disciples. The Greek term for "hypocrites" (hypokritēs) is also used for "actors" in the theater; they are, therefore, people who act out a part but are not, in fact, the persons they pretend to be—they speak from behind a mask. They are people who do the right thing (almsgiving), yet without the proper inner disposition, which should be directed toward God. But their concrete behavior (sounding trumpet, etc.) shows what their actual inner disposition is. So it is also for disciples; by giving alms discreetly they show what their actual inner disposition is. When they give alms, they "do not let [their] left hand know what [their] right hand is doing" (6:3), a metaphorical expression of the unselfconscious character of the action. In other words, almsgiving is so much a part of the disciples' being, so much their inner disposition, that they do it with no ulterior motive.

6:5–6. These verses express the same points found in 6:2–4, but now about prayer, with the effect of focusing the attention on the disciples' relationship with God. Once again, what is wrong in the hypocrites' attitude is not the fact that they pray in public (see Jesus praying in the presence of his disciples and other people, 11:25–26; cf. also 18:19–20). What is wrong is their inner disposition; they "love" to pray in public (6:5). True prayer is characterized by an inner disposition expressed in a concrete attitude best illustrated by praying in one's room after having closed the door. Devotion, prayer, is being in direct relation with God. In the same way that relationships with other people need to be direct and without any intermediary, including God (5:33–37), so relationships with God need to be direct and without any intermediary.

Overabundant righteousness sets the disciples in *direct* relationships with *both* other people *and* God. The relationship with God cannot involve other people as intermediaries, as the relationship with others cannot involve God as intermediary. The relational network can best be represented as a triangular relationship.

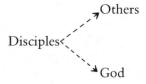

According to the antitheses (5:21–47), when one is put in relation with other people, for whatever reason, one needs to be totally devoted to establishing, maintaining, and protecting this relationship as an unmitigated relationship. Setting up an intermediary between oneself and others, even if this intermediary is God (cf. 5:33–37), is forfeiting true righteousness. This would amount to collapsing the triangular relationship into a linear one:

$$\text{Disciples} \rightarrow \text{God} \rightarrow \text{Others}$$

Similarly, one's relationship with God must be direct and cannot involve other people. It cannot take the following form:

$$\text{Disciples} \rightarrow \text{Others} \rightarrow \text{God}$$

In such a case, true relationship with God and true righteousness are denied. This is what is expressed in 6:2–6 and also in one of the meanings of the opposition of "You have heard that it was said to the [people] of old . . . but I say to you." A knowledge of God's will received through the intermediary of other people is not suitable for overabundant righteousness, but a knowledge received from God without intermediary is (as is the case of Jesus).

The following verses make two additional points about prayer (6:7–8, 13) and a point about forgiveness (6:14–15).

6:7–8. The Gentiles' (pagans') way of praying is opposed to that of the disciples. It is not necessary to "babble"[32] by using a multitude of words when praying. Such a practice shows what is wrong in their understanding of god (the false god[s] they worship). They believe they have to make god listen to them, to obey them (*eisakousthēsontai*; RSV: "be heard"). In other words, for them, at first god is not ready or willing to give them what they need; thus they must first convince him to be well disposed toward them. Note that this amounts to manipulating god's will (tempting god, cf. 4:7). Consequently, they need to multiply words; their prayer needs to be a long convincing discourse. By contrast, for disciples, God is a Father (the only designation of God in 6:1–21) who is described as knowing the needs of the disciples before they voice them. Since God is their Father, it is useless and superfluous to try to convince God to be willing to meet their needs. He knows them already, and as their Father, he already wants to meet them. He will not refuse good things (what they truly need) to his children when they ask for them (cf. 6:32; 7:7–11), and disciples have to express their needs to God. Indeed, if they are people who are truly in direct relationship with God as their Father in heaven, they should approach him with all their needs, with the confidence that, as their Father, he wants to provide them with what they need.

It then appears that, in 6:7–8, the direct relationship with God is further defined as the relationship of children with their caring Father and of the Father with his children. Note that God's fatherly relationship with human beings is not limited to disciples; "for he makes his sun rise on the evil and on the good, and sends rain on the just and on the unjust" (5:45). But, in the case of disciples, it is a two-way relationship; they relate to him as his children. They alone are truly his children. These verses also show that, unlike one's relationship with other people who might be unfriendly (cf. 5:38–44), one's relationship with God should never be viewed as antagonistic. Consequently, prayer is the acknowledgment that God is the Father. It should therefore begin with this acknowledgment: "Our Father who art in heaven" (6:9).

6:9–13. The Lord's prayer, despite its richness, includes only one opposition, in its last verse (6:13). The readers are thus expected to give their assent to this prayer or to know it. In order to elucidate how Matthew understands the Lord's prayer, we need to wait for a complete reading of the Sermon (see below, pp. 102–5). Yet, through his formulation of the last petition, Matthew makes a point for his readers. What God should do, deliver us from evil, is opposed to what God should not do, lead us into temptation (6:13).[33]

By this opposition, Matthew develops his preceding point. Since God is their Father in heaven, disciples can be confident that he will not only meet their needs but will also deliver them from evil. Thus, he is neither a god whom believers have to manipulate (tempt and test, see 4:7) so that he will want to be benevolent nor a god who manipulates the will of the believers by tempting them or causing them to be tempted, and/or put them to the test. Temptation does exist, and God might be the one who leads people into temptation, putting them to the test (cf. the ambiguous statement concerning Jesus' temptation, 4:1). Yet, for people in a children-Father relationship with God, for disciples who address this prayer to their Father, God is not a tempter, but, on the contrary, the one upon whom they can count to deliver them from the evil of temptation.

6:14-15. The parallelism of the disciples' relationship with God and with other people is the focus of attention in these verses. They should forgive those who have wronged them—an attitude directly related to not seeking revenge (5:38-42) and to loving one's enemies (5:43-47)—before asking for forgiveness from God with the expectation of receiving it (cf. 6:12). As in 5:43-48, the disciples' relationship with others (forgiving them) is directly linked with God's relationship with disciples (God forgiving them). In other words, while the disciples' relationships with other people and with God need to be carefully distinguished, so that both might be direct relationships, they are not unrelated. If disciples do not maintain and reestablish good relationships with others (whatever might be these people's attitude toward them), then they cannot be in a good relationship with God. While a good relationship with God (being blessed, being children of God, participating in the kingdom) is the ultimate goal that disciples seek, good relationships with others is the primary characteristic of overabundant righteousness. Without a proper relationship with others one cannot hope to be in a proper relationship with God. Thus, when one is in a situation where a choice needs to be made between worshiping God and seeking reconciliation with others, the latter must take precedence over the former (5:23-24).

Is this to say that forgiveness of others is a condition for receiving forgiveness from God? The text does not allow us to give any other answer than a positive one, even though many commentators hesitate, since such a view contradicts the distinctively Christian view according to which we forgive because God has first forgiven us.[34] Forgiveness of others as a condition for God's forgiveness is nothing else than a specific application of the general principle according to which overabundant righteousness is the condition for entrance into the kingdom (5:20). Certainly, it is wrong to view God as being antagonistic toward human beings (6:7-8), and thus disciples can count on their Father's forgiveness. But for this, they must be children of their Father in heaven; and they are his children only when they love, and thus forgive, their enemies (5:45). Clearly, this radical attitude of forgiveness is made possible by God's prior intervention, but, so far in the Gospel, this prior intervention has not been described as God's forgiveness. Rather, it is the presence of Jesus as the Holy among us (see 1:21-23 and 2:23) and as authoritative teacher (see 5:3-10, 21-48) that makes it possible.

6:16-18. The teaching on fasting reiterates the same points as those in 6:2-4 and 6:5-6. Note that these verses have the effect of underscoring the importance of the disciples' relationship with God, despite the fact that they must view their relationship with others as taking precedence over it. Purely religious acts (prayer, fasting) are necessarily parts of the disciples' overabundant righteousness.

Our study of 6:2-18 is not complete, since we had to postpone the interpretation of most of the Lord's prayer (see below, pp. 102-5). Yet we can take note of what makes this teaching convincing for disciples, crowds, and readers.

As in 5:21–47, Jesus' authority over "you" is strongly expressed by the series of injunctions in the imperative form (and equivalent forms). This is further reinforced by the use of the phrase "Truly, I say to you" (*amēn legō hymin*, 6:2, 5, 16). But what is new here, as compared with 5:21–47? In addition to calling upon convictions about the eschatological judgment and the kingdom as "reward," Matthew, in order to convince his readers, repeatedly calls upon convictions regarding God and his relationship to human beings. The organization of the argument is repetitious: The disciples should act in a certain way (the injunction). Why? Because God's way of acting is . . . (warrant). This pattern, which was found only twice in the preceding section (5:36, with an indirect reference to God, and 5:45), is found here with each injunction (6:1, 4, 6, 8, 14, 15, 18). It is not that Matthew expects his readers to have these convictions about God, since he conveys them to the readers by means of oppositions. But, for him, the exhortations to overabundant righteousness can be recognized as authoritative only when one has the proper view of God. More precisely, Jesus and his teaching will be acknowledged as authoritative only by those who have the proper convictions about the way God acts in the present (as the Father who is "in secret" as well as "in heaven") and in the eschatological future (giving eschatological reward). Thus, as in the case of 5:21–47, it appears that, for Matthew, all this teaching can be implemented by those who have the proper convictions—or inner disposition. We should not be surprised to find that the conditions of possibility of the overabundant righteousness concern the possibility for having such convictions.

6:22—7:12. Conditions for Implementing the Vocation

This part of the Sermon includes a series of sayings and teachings that, once again, certainly did not originally belong together. Whatever might have been their meaning in other contexts, these teachings take on a new meaning by the very fact of being strung together and of being set in the Sermon. As usual, it is this latter meaning which concerns us. For Matthew, they express a new series of conditions of possibility for implementing the vocation, that is, for having a life characterized by the overabundant righteousness described in 5:20—6:21.

In 5:17–19 it has been shown that such behavior is possible only for those whose vocation has been established on the basis of a proper understanding of Jesus' coming (vocation), of Scripture, and of the present time in relation to the eschatological future and Scripture (past revelation). In addition, 5:20—6:21 shows that this vocation must be internalized. Through a series of metaphorical statements, the following verses express other conditions for the implementation of one's vocation.

6:22–23. Since these two verses do not include any narrative opposition (there is no verb of action), they are thematic. Indeed, they are metaphoric and thus should be interpreted in terms of the readers' knowledge, including their knowledge of what precedes. Since these verses introduce a new part of the Sermon, they also need to be understood in terms of what follows.

Unlike 5:14–16 which includes both a twofold metaphorical statement and a clause (5:16b) explaining how the metaphor is to be interpreted—it refers to the disciples' good works—6:22–23 is totally figurative. Nothing in these verses expresses to what the metaphor refers—what is like a "sound" eye or a bad eye. Aspects of the metaphorical statement can be understood in terms of the preceding parts of the Sermon. Yet, it soon appears that central features of the metaphorical statement cannot be elucidated in this way. This metaphorical statement raises questions that lead the readers to look for answers in the following passages and thus determine the way in which 6:24—7:12 is to be read.

"The eye is the lamp of the body" (6:22a). Two features of this metaphor suggest how Matthew understands it. The "eye" is designated as a "lamp" that gives "light" (6:22b). In 5:14–16 the same images designate the disciples' vocation—"light of the world" and "lamp" to be put on a stand. Thus the metaphorical statement of 6:22–23 is somehow related to the disciples' vocation. Here, of course, what is discussed is the light or lamp of the body, not of the world. That the disciples' vocation needs to be internalized so as to be applied to one's entire experience (cf. 5:21—6:18) seems to be implied here in the statement that "your whole body will be full of light" (6:22b). Thus the metaphor of the eye as the lamp of the body expresses that the implementation of one's vocation (righteousness) is made possible by something—the eye—which affects the entire person's perspective (the light). Everybody has such an eye. But if your eye is bad, your entire body is darkness, and thus your vocation (giving light, 5:14–16) cannot be implemented. By contrast, if your eye is "sound," it can be implemented, for then your entire body is light. We can, therefore, conclude that the eye is a metaphor for that through which the vocation is internalized.

This provisional conclusion is far from being a complete interpretation of the metaphorical statement. It merely expresses what is the function of the eye, but does not explain what is the eye. The only thing we can say is that it certainly is an ability to perceive (to see) which can be either sound or bad. But we know neither what such an eye allows people to perceive nor what makes it sound or bad. Yet, the effect of this metaphorical statement is to focus our attention on all that the following passages have to say about "perception." *What* one perceives or does not perceive, and *how* one perceives it, determine whether or not one will be able to implement one's vocation. From this perspective it then appears that the following passages underscore the need to recognize what the Father is doing (6:25–34), to see what is evil or bad in ourselves (7:1–5), to distinguish what is holy from what is not holy (7:6), and what is good from what is bad for our children, ourselves, and others (7:7–12). As we shall see, such "perceptions" are necessary in order to implement one's vocation.

The metaphorical statement also focuses our attention on what would prevent people from having such a perception. This is expressed in 6:22–23 by the contrast between a "sound" eye and a bad eye. The only clue we have in these verses is the term *haplous*, which can mean "sound" but also "simple," "undivided," "sincere," "clear," and "generous."[35] All these connotations are possible since *haplous* is merely contrasted with the quite general term *ponēros* ("bad"). Nothing in 6:22–23 allows us to say which of these connotations is used by Matthew. But the following verse, 6:24, makes it clear that a sound eye is undivided (simple), an eye that does not give double vision (such as cross-eyed vision), as well as an eye that gives complete vision (a clear vision of one's entire experience).

6:24. This verse is also thematic and metaphorical. Despite obvious semantic oppositions, there is no narrative opposition (all the verbs concern wrong actions) which could clarify Matthew's point. This metaphorical verse plays therefore the same role as 6:22–23. It simply underscores that it is impossible to be a slave of two masters. Yet, since masters are people who dictate what slaves should do (their vocation), it is clear that this new metaphorical saying is directly related to the preceding one. In fact, it can be interpreted as explaining what it means to have a bad eye.

The situation described is that of a person with divided allegiance. When one's vocation is defined by two opposed masters (God versus mammon), one is bound to hate and despise one of the two masters and to love and be devoted to the other. One has then a twofold, divided vocation that one *cannot* implement because one cannot love and be devoted at once to these two contradictory masters. Because it is divided and contradictory, this vocation cannot be internalized and consequently cannot be carried out: "You cannot serve God and mammon."

It then appears that having a bad eye—which would prevent the implementation of one's vocation—is giving allegiance to two contradictory masters. It is perceiving in two masters, rather than in God alone, the authority to dictate one's vocation. It follows that a bad eye is a divided eye, a divided perception of who has the authority to establish one's vocation. Conversely, a sound eye is an undivided eye, the eye of someone who acknowledges only one master, God. Having a sound eye is perceiving God as the only one who should establish one's vocation.

This interpretation is confirmed by the contrast between God and property (one's possessions, i.e., mammon). It deals with that which dictates one's vocation, that is, what one wants to do or should do. Concern for one's possessions often dictates what one does! As long as this is the case, overabundant righteousness is impossible, since such a righteousness involves the readiness to give up at least a part of one's possessions (cf. 5:38–42; 6:2–4). God, and God alone, should be viewed as establishing one's vocation. The following verses explain why one can relax one's concern for possessions.

6:25–34. The first point (conviction) conveyed by this well-known passage is expressed by a narrative opposition: the exhortation "do not be anxious" (repeated three times, 6:25, 31, 34) *and* the descriptions of people who are anxious (an active verb in Greek, 6:27, 28). While concern for possessions seems to be a problem for rich people alone, by juxtaposing this teaching to the preceding verse Matthew shows that it is also a problem for poor people who are concerned about what they will eat, drink, and wear. This juxtaposition also has the effect of linking being anxious about one's life (*psychē*) with having a divided mind (two masters). In fact, *mē merimnate* ("do not be anxious") is related to a series of terms expressing division. Being anxious is having a divided mind.

The anxiety that must be overcome is not merely a worry about lacking food, drink, and clothing but ultimately a worry about one's life (6:25, 27) resulting from a wrong view of life. What is wrong is to think of life (*psychē*) and the body/person exclusively in terms of their physical reality, and thus in terms of physical needs. But life is more than food, and the body (the person) is more than clothing.[36] This is what was already affirmed in 4:4, "Man shall not live by bread alone, but by every word that proceeds from the mouth of God" (Deut. 8:3). As will be expressed in 6:33, true life is a life conceived in terms of God's kingdom and his righteousness. The argument underscores first, in 6:27, that anxiety does not help at all (either to prolong one's life or to add to one's stature). The main point is that the disciples should not worry, because they should trust in their heavenly Father who knows their needs (6:32; cf. 6:8). If God takes care of birds ("they neither sow nor reap nor gather into barns," 6:26) and of lilies of the field (6:28–30), how much more will he take care of you (6:26, 30).[37] This does not mean that the disciples should not work or that they should not have possessions.[38] This passage does not call the disciples to be like birds and lilies, but to *consider them* in order to understand that one does not need to worry. Human beings sow, reap, gather into barns (6:26), toil, and spin (6:29). But these activities can be performed either in anxiety and with "little faith" (6:30) or without anxiety and with faith in their Father.

6:32–33. This passage also expresses positively what the attitude of the disciples should be. They should seek their Father's kingdom and his righteousness (6:33); they should not seek food, drink, and clothing, as Gentiles do (6:32).[39] This opposition is particularly important because it specifies the disciples' relationship to God's kingdom and to God's righteousness. Because of anxiety for their own life—"little faith" (6:30b)—which finds

expression in concern for food, drink, and clothing, Gentiles make these
things the goals of their actions, their vocation. Conversely, because they
are not anxious about their life, because they have faith, disciples can allow
the kingdom and God's righteousness to become the primary goal of their
actions and thus to define their vocation. God's kingdom is not an unexpected gift, but the actual goal of the disciples' activities. It is the reward,
in the sense of wages, for which they work (cf. 6:4, 6, 18). It is the top of
the mountain that the climbers hope to reach and toward which each of
their steps is oriented. The kingdom is what is perceived by the disciples
as the ultimate good and thus what they want to obtain—the goal of all
their actions. Their vocation is seeking the kingdom in order to be blessed.
Seeking God's righteousness is another goal for the disciples' actions; this
phrase is another way of expressing their vocation. Their goal (vocation)
is having a life characterized by their Father's righteousness (overabundant
righteousness), that is, to be perfect as their Father is perfect (5:48); this is
the true understanding of life. As is expressed in 5:45 as well as here, God's
righteousness is manifested in his taking care of people as he also takes care
of birds and lilies. Seeking God's righteousness amounts, therefore, to seeking to have the overabundant righteousness characterized by active, positive
rapport with human beings, being a blessing for them. In this way, the
disciples will also be children of their heavenly Father (5:45), in a true Father-
children relationship with God, and thus inherit the kingdom. In sum, the
conjunction of the kingdom and of God's righteousness as goals of the
disciples' quest suggests (a) that being in the kingdom of heaven also involves being in a true Father-children relationship with God, and (b) that
the vocation of the disciples is twofold (cf. 5:11–16).

These observations help us better understand what Matthew means by
"kingdom" and how he can view it as both present ("at hand," 4:17) and
future. The kingdom of heaven is a place where people are in true Father-
children relationship with God: (a) because they are in God's presence, and
(b) because they acknowledge his authority and pay homage to him by
conforming their righteousness to his righteousness, implementing their
vocation as he implements his will. We can begin to perceive that, for
Matthew, the kingdom is not merely future (the eschatological kingdom)
but also present (cf. 4:17; 5:3, 10) insofar as God's kingship or lordship (his
fatherly authority and righteousness) is manifested in the present and acknowledged by people. Conversely, the disciples who make seeking the
kingdom and God's righteousness their vocation can be viewed as already
participating in the kingdom. They are indeed "blessed . . . , for theirs is
the kingdom of heaven" (5:3, 10).

Simultaneously, their vocation has another orientation established by
seeking God's righteousness. Indeed, they should seek the kingdom and
thus seek to be blessed. But this is the same thing as seeking God's righteousness and thus bringing blessings to other people. Being blessed is also

being a blessing (salt, light of the world, see 5:13–16), and thus pursuing one of these goals is also pursuing the other.

Coming back to 6:25–34, we conclude that this passage underscores that disciples can have a sound vocation which may be internalized so as to illuminate their entire experience, if, and only if, they are able to recognize the ultimate good they should seek first (6:33)—not food, drink, and clothing, but the kingdom and God's righteousness. These should be their primary goals, that which defines their vocation. The secondary goods—food, drink, and clothing— will be provided to them; their Father knows what they need. In order to recognize this twofold ultimate good (kingdom and righteousness), the disciples need what Matthew calls "faith," a positive attitude toward the situation in which they are. With such a faith they can *look at* (6:26; and learn the lesson from, "consider," 6:28) this situation with a "sound" (undivided) eye. By so doing, they can recognize signs of their Father's righteousness, in the way in which he takes care of the needs of the birds, of the lilies, and also in the way in which he makes his sun rise and sends rain (5:45). But this positive attitude, faith, does not deny the existence of problems, troubles, or evil (cf. 6:30). Indeed, there are troubles today (6:34), and one needs to deal with them. Yet one should deal with them from the positive perspective of faith rather than from the negative perspective of anxiety. The disciples' perspective on the future (tomorrow), and thus the orientation of their lives (their vocation), should be focused on the good things to come (the kingdom), not on the bad things to come.

7:1–5. Here there is an abrupt change in topic from the issue of the disciples' livelihood to that of their relationship with other people, but the point conveyed by the oppositions in 7:1–2 is directly related to the preceding points. In the same way that disciples should not have a negative attitude (anxiety) toward their own situation, so they should not have a negative attitude toward others. "Judge not, that you be not judged" (7:1), or better, "Do not condemn, that you be not condemned" at the eschatological judgment. This non-negative attitude toward others is part of seeking God's righteousness. Entrance into the kingdom, and thus overabundant righteousness, involves an attitude toward others that does not judge and condemn them (cf. 5:38–42). The injunction about not judging is justified by the observation (warrant) that "with the judgment you pronounce you will be judged, and the measure you give will be the measure you get" (7:2). Once again, the direct relation between what people do and their fate at the end of time is emphasized. Thus, 7:1–2 reiterates an aspect of the overabundant righteousness.

The following metaphorical statement, 7:3–5, seems to be in tension with what precedes. This is especially true of 7:5, since it seems to express that, after appropriate self-criticism, one may judge others.[40] But this verse does not use the verb "to judge." The tension exists only when we interpret taking the speck out of a brother's eye as presupposing a judgment. But this cannot be the case since, for Matthew, *judging means condemning*. What is described in 7:5 is not a condemnation. Disciples actually should not ignore the existence of evil (cf. 6:34). Indeed, they need to recognize it. But their attitude is to be positive rather than negative. In brief, condemning others (7:1–2) and helping others to take the speck or splinter out of their eyes (7:5) are not to be equated. This latter verse suggests for the first time (cf. possible allusions in 4:19 and 5:19) that helping brothers and sisters to have an overabundant righteousness is part of the disciples' vocation. Consequently, 7:5 means that in order to be in a position not to condemn others and yet to help others toward overabundant righteousness, one first needs to remove the log that is in one's own eye. Thinking that one can be truly righteous without first removing what prevents righteousness is being a hypocrite (7:5; cf. 6:2). Overabundant righteousness involves removing the log in one's own eye, that is also, cutting off and throwing away the limb that causes one to sin (cf. 5:29–30) without waiting for the judgment.

So far we have noted that 7:1–5 reiterates points concerning overabundant righteousness already found in 5:29–30 and 5:38–42: one should not judge others, and one should remove from oneself anything that causes sin. Yet the opposition between what hypocrites do (7:3–4) and what disciples should do (7:5) underscores the condition of possibility for the right attitude. The problem with hypocrites is that they do not remove the log in their own eye, *because they do not notice it*. We could wonder why Matthew makes it the main point of this passage by setting it up in this opposition, if we had not found him stressing similar points earlier (cf. 6:22–23) where the importance of a sound, undivided eye is underscored and where the importance of looking at and learning the lesson from a situation are stressed (cf. 6:25–34). For Matthew, *the fundamental precondition for overabundant righteousness* is taking notice, seeing what is wrong in oneself, or more generally, *perceiving correctly the distinction between what is good and evil, euphoric and dysphoric, holy and sinful* in the present situation (cf. 1:18–20; 2:1–12; 4:1–11), including in oneself (7:3–5).

7:6. The point just made is further expressed by 7:6. Since it does not include any opposition, it must be interpreted in terms of the preceding verses. Whatever might have been the meaning of this "strange" saying[41] in its original context, for Matthew it underscores that the disciples should recognize "holy" and precious things (pearls) for what they are and act accordingly, as they should recognize what is sinful or impure. The failure to do so leads to mixing holy things and impure things (dogs and swine), a confusion that can only have disastrous results.

What are these holy things (and pearls) and the impure things (dogs, swine, the log in one's own eye)? They are not defined in 7:1–6 but are hinted at in 6:25–34. These things that one should recognize (see) for what they are, as a precondition for overabundant righteousness, are, on the one hand, whatever is related to the kingdom and God's righteousness and, on the other hand, what is opposed to the kingdom and God's righteousness.

7:7–12. In this passage about prayer, a point is stressed by the opposition between people "who *know* how to give good gifts to [their] children" (7:11) *and* hypothetical, nonexistent, people who would *not know* how to do it and thus would give bad things ("stone," "serpent") to their children (7:9–10).

The effect of this opposition is to underscore that any human being, even an evil person (and anybody is evil as compared with God), has the ability to distinguish what is good and evil, euphoric and dysphoric, holy and impure, insofar as the person considers a situation from the perspective of parents envisioning the needs of their children, that is, could we say, from the perspective of the needs of their own flesh and blood. This last suggestion is prompted by the concluding saying which Matthew conceives as interpreting what precedes: "So whatever you wish that men would do to you, do so to them" (7:12). In other words, when you consider things from the perspective of what your children need and want, or from the perspective of what you wish for yourself, you know how to discern what is good from what is bad. This is the perspective, the "eye," the vision, which is the precondition for discovering what one should do (one's vocation), and thus for overabundant righteousness (carrying out one's vocation). This perspective, which allows one to perceive what is truly good and thus what one wants to do, has the same role as "the law and the prophets" have according to 5:17–19; both this perspective and Scripture are means of establishing the disciples' vocation.

The point that human beings, evil as they are, know how to give good things to their children is developed in the thematic part of this passage, the theme of prayer. If you know how to answer the request of your children, "how much more will your Father who is in heaven give good things to those who ask him!" (7:11), a statement that also expresses that you know what the good things are for which you need to ask. Since what is good is related to one's vocation and its fulfillment, and consequently to entrance into the kingdom, then the good things which will be given by God in answer to prayers are themselves certainly related to entrance into the kingdom. This is further suggested by the wording of 7:7: "Ask, and it will be given you; seek, and you will find; knock, and it will be opened." Knocking, as a metaphor for prayer, suggests asking to enter (into the kingdom). Seeking recalls seeking the kingdom and God's righteousness (6:33). In other words, this verse does not refer to prayer in general but to the specific petitions for the good things that one needs in order to fulfill one's vocation as well as in order to enter the kingdom itself. These are petitions for what one needs in order to have overabundant righteousness.

But what should the disciples ask for? Primarily, they should ask for a sound, undivided eye. They already know how to discern what is good and bad for their children and for themselves. The problem is that this vision is often impaired by concern for possessions and by anxiety for their livelihood. Consequently, they have a double vision; they confuse what is holy and impure and are led to perform nonsensical actions. But with a sound eye they would be able to distinguish what is holy and pure from what is impure and bad; they would be able to see God's righteousness manifested in their present and to recognize what is truly evil (including in themselves); then they could have the right vocation, seeking the kingdom and God's righteousness. In such a case, this vocation (vision of what they should do) would be established by a single master (since they would distinguish between a good master, God, and a false one, mammon), and thus they would be in a position to internalize it. Then they would have overabundant righteousness. Thus by the very fact of receiving a sound eye, they would be in a position to enter the kingdom and to be truly blessed, and simultaneously to be a blessing for other people.

But how does God respond to this prayer? How does God give a sound eye to the disciples? Clearly, Matthew wants to say that it is through Jesus and his teaching. In order to understand it, keep in mind the relation between 6:22—7:12 and 5:17–19, a relation strongly marked by the reference to "the law and the prophets" in both 5:17 and 7:12. A sound eye, the ability to perceive what is truly good (what you wish that people would do to you), is the law and the prophets (7:12). More precisely, it is the law and the prophets as properly conceived, that is, Scripture as *fulfilled* (5:17–19) in that it establishes the disciples' and Jesus' vocation. Since Jesus has come to fulfill Scripture (5:17), in his own teaching Scripture is fulfilled and establishes the disciples' vocation. His teaching is therefore the sound eye that the disciples need to receive. By appropriating Jesus' teaching, the disciples are in a position to distinguish between good and evil, holy and impure, in their present situation, and thus to discern and internalize their true vocation. Then, nothing prevents them from implementing this vocation in a life characterized by overabundant righteousness.

7:13–20. The Vocation of the Disciples (Part 2)

7:13–14. This new metaphorical passage opposes the few (disciples) who enter by the narrow gate and follow the hard or narrow road which leads to life (the kingdom) *and* the many people who enter by the wide gate and follow the easy or wide road which leads to destruction. What allows the disciples to enter the kingdom is the implementation of their vocation, described here as entering through a gate and following a road. Yet this narrative opposition does not concern either the implementation of the vo-

cation or the precondition for this implementation, but the broad characteristics of this vocation (gate, road).

The point of the opposition is that disciples are those who enter by a
narrow gate and follow a *narrow* road, a way involving many difficulties
and persecutions (RSV: "hard"; *thlibō*, from which we have the noun for
tribulation or persecution, *thlipsis*). The disciples' vocation involves persecutions, as was expressed in 5:11–12. These verses mix two metaphors
(gate and road) and thereby underscore that the disciples' vocation is not
limited to the entrance (into the kingdom, into a life of discipleship); it is
also an ongoing journey. As we noted about 5:11–16, the disciples' vocation
is not merely to be blessed (entrance into the kingdom, the gate) but also
to be a blessing for others (an ongoing process, the road). But in which
sense are the gate and the road "narrow" and "hard"? The opposition merely
emphasizes that the major problem is that the narrow gate is difficult to
find. Many do not find life because they do not find the narrow gate, and
consequently they enter by the wide gate and follow the spacious road. In
other words, the "many" do not recognize the narrow gate and the hard
road for what they truly are, the very issue underscored by the opposition
found in 5:11–12. They falsely perceive it as dysphoric instead of as
euphoric.

7:15–20. The passage about false prophets again mixes metaphors. These
people are described as being "in sheep's clothing but inwardly are ravenous
wolves" (7:15) and as bad trees bearing evil fruit (7:16–20). The opposition
of the trees bearing good fruit and those bearing evil fruit (7:17) underscores
that the fruit necessarily corresponds to the kind of tree that bears it. Thus,
thornbushes cannot produce grapes, thistles cannot produce figs, and bad
(rotten) trees cannot produce good fruit (7:16–18). This is also true of false
prophets; inwardly they are ravenous wolves, but even though they might
try to disguise themselves (in sheep's clothing), "you will know them by
their fruits" (7:16, 20). And since they do not bear good fruit, they will be
thrown into the fire (7:19, a repetition of John's warning to the Pharisees
and the Sadducees, 3:8). In other words, because they have a bad inner
disposition, because they have internalized a bad vocation (not that of a
prophet, cf. 5:12), these people can only be false prophets and do evil works.
By contrast, because they have internalized the right vocation, the disciples
are true prophets and do good works. The warning against false prophets
and the instruction about how to recognize them have the effect of defining
the disciples' vocation: they are called to be true prophets (cf. 5:12) doing
good works (cf. 5:16).

We might now begin to understand what is involved in doing good
works. At the beginning of the Sermon one might think that doing good
works involves a special effort on the part of the disciples (e.g., striving to
carry out commandments). But this is a misconception of what is involved,

and indeed a misconception of Jesus' teaching. Good works are good fruits which good trees spontaneously produce. Indeed, good works are the actions and attitudes described in 5:20—6:21 (a life of overabundant righteousness). But this central part of the Sermon should not be viewed as a law, that is, as the objective norms that one should carry out in order to escape the judgment and that one could use to condemn others. It is, rather, an illustration of the kinds of attitudes that people who have internalized their vocation, because they have a sound eye, spontaneously have. If they are good trees, that is, if they correctly perceive what is good and evil, holy and impure, and thus have found the narrow gate and the hard road, they will bear good fruits. Or, according to 5:13–16, if they are salt, they will transmit their saltness to the food in which they are put; if they are light, they will give light to all those around them; if they are blessed, holy, perfect as their Father is perfect, they will be a blessing for others. The only thing that would prevent the disciples from doing such good works would be: (a) not knowing how to discern what is suitable for their vocation; misunderstanding the meaning of Jesus' coming (5:17); and (b) not receiving from him the sound eye (his teaching).

7:21–27. Who the Disciples Are (Part 2)

Who then are the disciples? They are those who will not be rejected by the Lord Jesus at the judgment (7:23); they are not foolish people whose house, built on the sand, is destroyed in a great fall (7:26–27). Positively, they are wise people whose house, built on the rock, withstands floods and winds and does not fall (7:24–25); they are blessed and will enter the kingdom of heaven (7:21, cf. 5:3 and 10). Through the oppositions of this passage Matthew *contrasts* those who say "Lord, Lord" and do not do the will of Jesus' Father (7:21a) or who hear Jesus' words and do not do them (7:26) *with* those who say "Lord, Lord" and do the will of his Father (7:21b) or who hear his words and do them (7:24). Hearing Jesus' words, and even recognizing him as Lord, is not enough. Indeed, one can recognize Jesus' authority as the crowds did in Galilee. They had heard his teaching and his preaching and witnessed his healings (4:23). Because of his fame, they followed him (4:24–25). Thus they acknowledged his authority and viewed him as "Lord." They even prophesied and performed miracles in his name (7:22) and shared in this way in his authority. The point is: they have only acknowledged and shared in his authority as miracle worker; they have only acknowledged and shared in his power. As such, Jesus cannot acknowledge them ("I never knew you," 7:23), because, in fact, they do not truly know Jesus. They do not acknowledge his true authority, his authority as teacher. They hear his words, but do not do them! As is clear by now, if they do not do good works or do not bear good fruit, it is because they are false prophets, evildoers (7:22–23) who have not internalized his teaching. They are unable to do the will of God because they have failed to make it their own will. And they have failed to do so because they are unable to distinguish what is good (rock) from what is bad (sand). They do not know how to assess a present situation—the time of the building of the house—in terms of the future when floods and winds will come (cf. 5:17–18). In brief, they have heard Jesus' teaching but have failed to receive what it offers, a sound eye.

By contrast, the true disciples are blessed. They have received what Jesus' teaching offers: a sound eye; the ability to discern what is holy and good from what is impure and bad; the ability to internalize their vocation; God's will for them; and, therefore, entrance into the kingdom and blessedness.

CONCLUSIONS: THE BEATITUDES AND THE
LORD'S PRAYER

5:3–10. The Beatitudes

We now understand what it is to be "blessed." Those who are blessed are "poor in spirit" (5:3)—people who recognize that they are helpless without God's help. More precisely, they are people who do not assert their own will but are open to make God's will (7:21) their own will. Those who are blessed "mourn" (5:4)—people deprived of their loved ones who demanded allegiance, and thus people who are free to have only one master, God (6:24). Those who are blessed are the "meek" (5:5)—people who have no means to assert their rights against others and who can therefore accept that nothing, even Scripture, should be used against others (cf. 5:38–42). Those who "hunger and thirst for righteousness" (5:6) are the ones who eagerly look at everything around them for signs of God's righteousness and are thus ready to seek first God's righteousness (6:25–33). Those who are blessed are the "merciful" (5:7)—people who forgive others (6:14–15), love their enemies (5:44), and thus are children of their Father in heaven (5:45). Those who are blessed are "pure in heart" (5:8)—their heart is undivided, totally devoted to God and free from any other intention; they are totally turned toward God (cf. 3:8; 6:2–6). Those who are blessed are "peacemakers" (5:9)—people who seek reconciliation with others (5:23–26) and love their enemies (5:44). Those who are blessed are "persecuted for righteousness' sake" (5:10)—people whose overabundant righteousness can be recognized (5:20) and who follow the hard road (7:13–14). In brief, those who are blessed are the people who not only hear Jesus' words but also do them; who acknowledge his authority as teacher who gives them the ability to perceive what is good and bad, holy and impure, and thus to internalize the will of God. They are blessed because their attitude shows that their perception of what is good and evil (the "eye" that governs their lives) has not been revealed to them by "flesh and blood" but by the "Father who is in heaven" (see 16:17).

6:9–13. The Lord's Prayer

Some remarks regarding Matthew's understanding of the Lord's prayer are appropriate in concluding this study of the Sermon. It includes most of the themes through which Matthew expresses his main points in terms that his readers would readily accept, quite possibly because they already knew this prayer.

6:9a. The disciples should view God as "our Father who art in heaven" (6:9). In the context of the Sermon, this means that they should view God as the one who knows what they need before they ask it (6:8, 32) and who gives it to them (6:33; 7:11). God is also the one who gives sunshine and rain to the just and the unjust (5:45) and feeds the birds (6:26). In brief, God is their Father, the one who provides the disciples, as well as all the creation, with all the good things they need. God is also the one who will reward the disciples (6:4, 6, 18) and is present "in secret" with them. Thus, God is the provider of good things upon whom the disciples (children) can fully rely now as in the future. All the other possible connotations of God as Father (e.g., authority) are, at least in the Sermon, derived from this primary view of God as the provider of good things.

The first three petitions (6:9–10) ask God to bring about the ultimate outcome of the implementation of the disciples' vocation viewed from three different perspectives. When the disciples shall carry out their vocation, God's name shall be "hallowed," or sanctified; the kingdom shall have come not only for the disciples but for everyone; and God's will shall be done "on earth as it is in heaven," that is, his will shall be done by everyone on earth. The three last petitions (6:11–13) ask God to give to the disciples what they need to implement their vocation: daily bread, forgiveness, and freedom from temptation and evil. In brief, for Matthew, the Lord's prayer asks God to give to the disciples the good things they need in order to implement their vocation and to bring about the complete realization of the promised outcome of the implementation of their vocation. An examination of each petition in terms of the rest of the Sermon helps us understand it.

6:9b. "Hallowed be thy name," or "sanctified be thy name," is a petition about what should be, *for God*, the outcome of the disciples' implementation of their vocation (5:16). God's name is sanctified when people give glory to God. So, from the disciples' perspective, this petition means "Enable us to carry out our vocation so that people might glorify you and sanctify your name." Since the petition does not specify by whom God's name is to be hallowed or sanctified, it removes any limitation. God's name is to be sanctified not only by the disciples, not only by the limited number of people who "see your good works" (5:16), but by the "world" (5:14) or the "earth" (5:13), that is, by everyone.

6:10a. "Thy kingdom come" is a petition about what should be, *for the disciples,* the outcome of the implementation of their vocation. Disciples will enter the kingdom insofar as they have an overabundant righteousness (5:20); indeed, "theirs is the kingdom" (5:3, 10). The coming of the kingdom to the disciples is the blessing, the reward they (will) receive for implementing their vocation. The disciples are blessed, the kingdom is theirs. Yet, the absolute character of the petition means that the disciples ask that this blessing of the coming of the kingdom be for everyone, the world at large, and not merely for a small group of disciples. In the perspective of the Sermon it is clear that "kingdom" simply means the fullness of God's blessings as described in the beatitudes: being comforted (5:4); inheriting the earth (5:5; i.e., having all that one needs); having one's hunger and thirst for righteousness fully satisfied (5:6, because one is fully in the benefit of God's righteousness); having received mercy and forgiveness from God (5:7); seeing God (5:8), that is, being fully in the presence of God and enjoying full communion with God (something normally impossible for human beings; cf. Isa. 6:5); and being called children of God (5:9). This last blessing, being called children of God, suggests that the kingdom is also the manifestation of the kingship of God, his authority as king, since the children of God are those who submit to his will. But it is not to be conceived as some kind of objective authority—resulting from the power of the Father to impose his will upon his children by commanding them. The children of God are rather those who are *like their Father in heaven,* who share in God's perfection (5:48). The children of God do submit to God's authority, but it is because they are in communion with him, in his presence (since God is present with them "in secret," 6:4, 6, 18); they can "see God."

6:10b. "Thy will be done, on earth as it is in heaven." Disciples who carry out their vocation and implement Jesus' teaching do the will of God (7:21). For Matthew, this does not mean carrying out commandments viewed as external, objective norms for one's behavior. One does the will of God when God's will has become one's own will. But internalizing God's will involves appropriating God's view of what is holy, good, euphoric (what one wants to pursue) and of what is impure, evil, dysphoric (what one wants to avoid). Thus, by asking, "Thy will be done," the disciples ask that it be given to them to do God's will by appropriating it and internalizing it. And yet this petition has a universal scope. As "in heaven" everyone does the will of God, so it should be "on earth." This should be the outcome of the implementation of the disciples' vocation. They are to be "salt of the earth" and "light of the world" (5:13–16). As a result of carrying out their vocation, not only should God's name be universally sanctified and the kingdom be a universal blessing but also God's will should be universally done, since all would have made God's will their own.

In sum, in the first three petitions the disciples ask that God bring about the complete promised results of the fulfillment of their vocation. Then the second set of petitions ask God for what they need to carry out their vocation.

6:11. "Give us this day our daily bread" is somewhat difficult to understand because of the term "daily" (*epiousios*; used only in the Lord's Prayer). *Epiousios* could mean either "essential," thus "necessary" and "sufficient," or "for the morrow," thus "for the future" (including the eschatological future). While the eschatological meaning might have been original, in the context of the Sermon "essential" is to be preferred. This petition asks quite concretely for the bread necessary for one's subsistence. It asks God to give *today* what one needs. This petition is thus directly related to 6:25–34 (and 7:7–11). In 6:34 the disciples are exhorted not to be anxious about tomorrow, following the assurance that God will take care of their needs for food, drink, and clothing (6:31). In other words, this petition asks God to fulfill his promise to provide life-sustaining food. When God does this, day by day, it is all they need for carrying out their vocation, since they know they do not need to worry about the future. But if they lacked bread for their subsistence, they would be anxious and would not be free to seek the kingdom and God's righteousness. Unable to implement their vocation, they would have a divided allegiance to two masters. In brief, this petition asks quite directly that God as their Father provide disciples with what is necessary for their daily life. Then they will be free from anxiety and worry which would prevent the implementation of their vocation, and consequently the sanctification of God's name, the coming of the kingdom, and the doing of God's will.

6:12. "And forgive us our debts, as we also have forgiven our debtors." In view of the preceding and the following petitions, we can presume that this petition asks for something else necessary for the disciples so that they might carry out their vocation. God's forgiveness is not a precondition for doing good works such as forgiving others (cf. 6:14–15). All that is needed is a sound eye allowing discernment of what is truly good and evil. Thanks to this sound eye (what one has when one is free from anxiety, cf. 6:11), one can discover what one should do, including loving and thus forgiving one's enemies (5:44). And one is in a position to do these things. One also becomes aware of the evil that is in oneself (cf. 5:29–30; 7:3–5) and one is in a position to remove it. But even when one is doing these good things, one is still evil (see 7:11). One still needs God's forgiveness, so as to be "pure" and be in a position to "see God," since only those who are pure and holy can be in the presence of the Holy (the holy and the impure cannot be mixed, cf. 7:6). In other words, the disciples who have been enabled to carry out their vocation still need to be purified by God in order that the fulfillment of their vocation might have its ultimate result, the sanctification of God's name. When people see their "good works," they need to be able to recognize in them the presence of the Holy, the presence of God, so that they might *glorify God*. Thus it appears that forgiveness is viewed by Matthew as the purification of the disciples, what makes them a manifestation of the Holy for others (as Jesus is, 1:21–23).

6:13. "And lead us not into temptation, but deliver us from evil [or, from the evil one]" involves an opposition and makes a point concerning the way in which God relates to his children (see above, p. 88). In addition, this last petition asks, once again, for something the disciples need so that the implementation of their vocation might be complete and might bring about its ultimate desired results—the sanctification of God's name, the coming of the kingdom, the performance of God's will on earth as it is in heaven. This is a single petition asking for freedom from temptation and for freedom from the evil one as the tempter (cf. 4:1–11). Temptation by the evil one could prevent the disciples from continuing to carry their vocation to its end. Temptation as the attempt by the evil one to impose upon the disciples a new will (as was the case in Jesus' temptation) would undermine the disciples' implementation of their vocation at its most fundamental level. At the very least, it would mean that they would have two masters (6:24), two contradictory origins for their will, thus losing their sound eye and having a divided eye. It would become impossible for them to internalize God's will. They would be unable to bear good fruits and would become false prophets (7:15–20). They would be unable to do God's will, to receive the kingdom, and to sanctify God's name.

This last petition refers, therefore, to the very core of the Sermon, namely, that disciples are those who make out of God's will their own entire will. But they can do so only if God gives them the good things they need, namely, what it takes to have a sound eye and what it takes to preserve the soundness of their eye, that is, freedom from temptation.

NOTES ON 5:1—7:29

1. Davies, *Setting*, 423.
2. This observation is in agreement with Davies's conclusion that, even though Jesus is clearly presented as the "new Moses" in 5:1–2 and other parts of the Sermon, this is not Matthew's primary view of Jesus Christ. The discoursive organization of the text shows that this view of Jesus is one that Matthew expected his readers to have and that he modifies by setting it "into a deeper and higher context." Davies, *Setting*, 25–93.
3. Obviously, Jesus is more than a rabbi for Matthew. According to 4:23, there are two additional dimensions to Jesus' ministry: "preaching the Gospel of the kingdom" and "healing."
4. Cf. Edwards, "Uncertain Faith," 47–61.
5. Cf. Patte, "Method for a Structural Exegesis of Didactic Discourses," 85–97; idem, *Paul's Faith*, 127–28.
6. Even if Betz's proposal that the Sermon on the Mount was taken over from

a pre-Matthean source by the evangelist proved to be true, it would remain that Matthew appropriated, and thus *made his own*, the prior redaction of this document. Thus, our approach would be the same. Our concern is to understand the final redaction of the Gospel. But I have serious reservation regarding Betz's proposal. Many of the characteristics of the Sermon that Betz uses as evidence for his argument that the Sermon is pre-Matthean, I find later in the Gospel. See Betz, *Essays on the Sermon*.

7. The order of the second and third beatitudes is reversed in certain ancient manuscripts. This observation is significant for studies aimed at establishing the form of the beatitudes as received by Matthew and Luke. Thus Dupont (*Béatitudes* 1:251–57) concludes that it was composed by Matthew as an explanation of the first beatitude. But this order does not affect our interpretation aimed at elucidating Matthew's convictions.

8. Cf. Beardslee, *Literary Criticism,* 27ff. Since Jesus has been described as having religious authority, there is no doubt that the beatitudes need to be understood as authoritative religious pronouncements. Viewing them as merely congratulatory statements (as *"Heil!" "Wohl!"* or *"Félicitation!"*), as Strecker and Dupont do, is a trivialization of the beatitudes which leads to a misinterpretation of the entire Sermon. See Strecker, "Die Makarismen der Bergpredigt," *NTS* 17 (1970/71):255–75; Dupont, *Béatitudes* 3:672. Dupont is correct in stressing that the beatitudes are neither a promise nor a wish.

9. As Davies has shown, while the motifs "new exodus" and "new Moses" are present in the Sermon and its context, they are transcended by Matthew (*Setting*, 14–108). This demonstrates once again the complementarity of studies of the text in terms of its historical background and of its structural organization.

10. Patte, *Paul's Faith*, 100–104.

11. The phrase "till heaven and earth pass away" (5:18) must be interpreted temporally, as the RSV translation suggests, and as referring to the end of the world—rather than meaning "never," as similar phrases can be interpreted in Philo. The same is true of the second phrase "until all is accomplished." This interpretation is demanded because of the opposition as well as because of grammatical, philological, and other exegetical reasons. See Schweizer, "Noch einmal Mat 5, 17–20," 69–73 (an essay in which he revises his earlier interpretation, "Matth. 5, 17–20. Anmerkungen zum Gesetzesverständnis des Matthäus," *TLZ* 77 [1952]:479–84). His position (and that of his followers) has been convincingly refuted by Meier, a point of view that the structural analysis supports by showing the importance of the temporal perspective in chapter 5. See MEIER, 48–50. At this point in our reading, however, the analysis cannot support Davies's and Meier's main thesis (cf. Davies, "Matthew, 5,17–18," 428–56; MEIER, 57–65, 25–40), namely, that the future eschatological period mentioned in 5:18 should be identified with the period ushered in by the death and resurrection of Jesus. From the readers' perspective, in view of what precedes in the Gospel, the future period described in 5:18 can only be perceived as a period *beyond* history. The references in 5:3–12 to the eschatological future which concern the time *after* the judgment, the time of "reward in heaven" (cf. 5:12), necessarily lead the readers to perceive 5:18 in the same way. There is absolutely nothing in the text up to this point that would suggest an interpretation of this verse in terms of Jesus' death and resurrection. It is only through a retrospective reading of the Gospel from the perspective of the resurrection that the question involved in the thesis of Davies and Meier can be raised.

12. Cf. Barth, "Matthew's Understanding of the Law," 67–69.

13. Our analysis supports the conclusion of the commentators who note that, in 5:17, "fulfilling the law" does not mean primarily doing or obeying the law. Cf. MEIER, 73–81, and the bibliography in the notes. However, our analysis does not support the correlated conclusion that "fulfilling the law" should be understood exclusively as a "prophetic fulfillment," as Meier proposes. Rather, Matthew introduces a new perspective related to his view of vocation and what is suitable for it.

14. MEIER, 91–92. Beyond Meier's argument, this interpretation is further demanded by the study of the opposition of 5:19.

15. The "commandments" in 5:19 have been interpreted as referring either to the commandments of Scripture (in view of the correlation with 5:17–18) or to Jesus' commandments (the antitheses, 5:21–48, or all the teachings of the Sermon). The former view is that of a large number of commentators; the latter view is advocated by Betz (*Essays on the Sermon,* 48–49) following Grundmann (*Das Evangelium nach Matthäus*). The correlation between 5:17–18 and 5:19 and the shift from Jesus' vocation to the disciples' vocation show that this is not an either/or issue but rather a both/and issue. Furthermore, adopting Betz's view prevents any possibility of accounting for the relation between 5:19 and 5:20.

16. Against the view that these two terms are fundamentally different, because "fulfilling the law" would be said of Jesus in order to indicate his superiority over Scripture, while "doing the law" would be said of disciples to express their submission to it. Cf. LOHMEYER, 111–12; Betz, *Essays on the Sermon,* 48 n. 43. Establishing such a sharp contrast is impossible when taking into account the correlation of the two oppositions. Yet this does not mean that the two terms are identical. While the first expresses the "primary" interpretation (by Jesus), the second term expresses a "secondary" interpretation (by disciples following Jesus' teaching).

17. The view that Jesus demands a literal performance of the commandment, which is unfortunately found in many commentaries, is based upon an interpretation of 5:18 (and especially of the reference to the "iota" and the "dot" of the law) in isolation from its context. "Iota" and "dot" are interpreted literally (!) as referring to the smallest letters of the biblical text. But the mention of the smallest of the commandments in the next sentence shows that iota and dot refer metaphorically to the less important commandments. The misinterpretation of these terms generates unresolvable exegetical problems, namely, how to understand the contradiction between the teaching of Jesus demanding a literal fulfillment of the law and his own attitude throughout the Gospel, beginning in 5:21–48. See, e.g., BEARE, 138–42; and SCHWEIZER, 103–9.

18. As MEIER, 92–95, and Betz (*Essays on the Sermon,* 50–51) show, there is no way to interpret "least in the kingdom" as expressing exclusion from the kingdom, as proposed, e.g., by Schrenk, "Entolē," *TDNT* 2:548; by BONNARD, 62; by SCHWEIZER (p. 105) with hesitation.

19. An attack against Paul or against antinomian groups in the church is often inferred from 5:19 (e.g., Betz, *Essays on the Sermon,* 51). This could explain why Matthew does not want to condemn these people too harshly by excluding them from the kingdom. But such explanations are not sufficient in themselves; they do not explain how Matthew could envision the possibility of such a view of Scripture. Cf. MEIER, 95; and BEARE, 141.

20. As we have seen regarding 5:11–16 and its relation with 3:13–15, fulfilling righteousness and carrying out one's vocation can be identified with each other.

21. This second opposition is at once obvious and yet not fully expressed. Thus, we could not consider 5:20 as a direct expression of Matthew's convictions if it were not that the same opposition is fully expressed in 5:46–47.

22. *Perisseuō* (RSV: "exceeds") has a connotation of *quantity* rather than of quality. Cf. Dupont, *Béatitudes* 3:248–49. Thus the disciples' righteousness should be "more abundant," or be broader in scope than the scribes' and the Pharisees' righteousness, and not "better," or "higher," as Beare says (without really discussing his choice of terminology; e.g., BEARE, 142–45).

23. The phrase "scribes and Pharisees" should not be understood as an actual description of these Jewish leaders. This is a collective personage created by Matthew through which he refers not primarily to historical scribes and Pharisees but to all the "scribes and Pharisees" outside the church as well as inside the church whose attitude is, from Matthew's perspective, condemned by Jesus' teaching. Consequently, one should not attempt to interpret this and other verses in terms of what we know about historical scribes and Pharisees. In such a case, one is quite puzzled, since they were striving to implement their vocation in all the aspects of their lives (cf. Patte, *Paul's Faith,* 87–120). And thus commentators hesitate to interpret 5:20

to mean that an overabundant righteousness is the implementation of one's vocation in all aspects of one's life (by contrast with the Pharisees' narrow righteousness). Consequently, *against the text,* they interpret this verse as referring to a "higher righteousness," i.e., to a qualitatively better righteousness (by contrast with a *quantitatively* better one).

24. MEIER, 131–35.

25. Davies, *Setting,* 101–2, who follows Daube, *The New Testament and Rabbinic Judaism,* 55–62.

26. The text does not define at this point how "brother" (5:22, 23, 24) should be understood, since this term is not opposed here to any other term. Thus we have to respect the ambiguity of the passage and wait for texts that will define it.

27. The word *porneia* (RSV: "unchastity") is largely undefined in the text—it is not directly opposed to anything. Thus, as can be expected, it is interpreted in quite different ways (cf. MEIER, 140–50, and the bibliography in the notes). On the basis of the text, the only thing we can say is that it refers to some kind of wrong sexual relationship, but not exclusively to unchastity. It might also refer to incestuous unions such as those described in Lev. 18:6–18.

28. See, e.g., SCHWEIZER, 193–209, for a discussion of the various ways in which this question is raised and addressed.

29. The RSV text "Beware of practicing *your piety* before men" seems to be based on the textual variant that has *eleēmosynēn* (pious action, such as almsgiving, in which case 6:1 would only introduce 6:2–4) instead of *dikaiosynen.* With the great majority of scholars, I believe that, while one can explain the transformation of *dikaiosynē* into *eleēmosynē* (a term found three times in the verses that follow), the inverse transformation would be quite difficult to explain. Consequently, we consider *diakaiosynē* to be the original wording. For a discussion of this point, see Przybylski, *Righteousness in Matthew,* 78.

30. With BONNARD, 90. This metaphorical statement certainly might have a quite different meaning in other contexts. We of course are exclusively concerned with Matthew's understanding.

31. With SCHWEIZER, 162–63, who reaches this conclusion for different reasons.

32. According to Beare's excellent translation of 6:7: "Again, when you pray do not babble on like the Gentiles; they think that they will be heard for their many words" (BEARE, 167).

33. Note that this opposition is not found in Luke 11:4, since it does not involve the positive petition "but deliver us from evil."

34. See, e.g., BEARE, 177–78. The reference to the parable of the unforgiving servant (18:23–35) does not help, since ultimately the servant is not forgiven, because he has not forgiven.

35. According to *BAGD,* 85.

36. As Betz shows, there is a basic ambiguity in the use of the terms *psychē* and *sōma,* which he renders life/soul and body/person respectively (*Essays on the Sermon,* 104–7).

37. For a detailed explanation of the argument, see Betz, *Essays on the Sermon,* 107–14.

38. BONNARD, 93–94.

39. Cf. Betz, *Essays on the Sermon,* 114–15.

40. With this interpretation of taking the speck out of your brother's eye as equivalent to judging your brother, one is then led to conclude that either Matthew contradicts himself or that one should interpret 7:5 as an ironical statement which would mean that you may judge others only when you "first take the log out of your own eye," something that you cannot do. See BONNARD, 97. But this latter interpretation would contradict the rest of the Sermon which presupposes all along that the disciples are able to overcome whatever would prevent them from having a life characterized by overabundant righteousness.

41. It is a "strange" saying, especially when one fails to recognize the main point of the preceding verses and then cannot relate it to them. Cf. BEARE, 190–91; and BONNARD, 97–98.

JESUS AS MIRACLE WORKER

THE MAIN THEME

At first glance, it is difficult to perceive any unity in what appears to be a compilation of miracle stories and teachings in the form of dialogues. The unity is clearly not to be found in a narrative progression, in the sense that one event would need to take place before the next one can unfold. Consequently, if this passage is indeed an identifiable section of the Gospel, its unity is certainly provided, as in the Sermon, by a main theme that we should be able to recognize by comparing its beginning and its end.

An examination of 8:1–4 and 9:32–34 suggests that these passages are in fact the introduction and the conclusion of a thematic section, in the sense that the former describes a situation in which something is expected (and therefore not realized) and that the latter expresses the fulfillment of this expectation.

8:1–4. The healing of the leper (8:2–3) in the presence of the crowds (8:1) is concluded by the command of Jesus: "See that you say nothing to any one; but go, show yourself to the priest, and offer the gift that Moses commanded, *for a testimony to them*" (8:4, au.). This last phrase creates a tension in the text which signals the presence of a theme—the expression of Matthew's convictions in terms of his readers' presumed knowledge. Who are those designated by "them"? The readers would expect "them" to refer to the priests, but "priest" is in the singular and thus "them" refers to a collective anonymous subject which would include the crowds (8:1). But did not the crowds witness the cleansing? Then the exhortation to say nothing to anyone is surprising. Such a tension shows that Matthew develops a theme in order to express his main points (convictions) in terms of his readers' expectations.

What are the readers led to expect? When something is presented as "a testimony" (an evidence or, RSV: "a proof") for a group of people, the readers anticipate a response—either an acknowledgment or a rejection—by these people. More specifically, the readers are led to expect that people would acknowledge or reject the extraordinary character of Jesus' deed (cleansing the leper). This already suggests that the main theme of 8:1—9:34 concerns the *acknowledgment of the true character of Jesus' authority* as

109

manifested in miracles and other actions—rather than in his teaching as in the Sermon on the Mount (see 7:29).

9:32–34. This theme is apparent in 8:27;[1] 8:28—9:1;[2] 9:8;[3] 9:26;[4] and 9:31 (cf. 8:5–13), where we find various responses to Jesus' deeds. But none of these responses is presented as a definite assessment of the character of Jesus' authority. It is only in 9:33–34 that we find definite responses to Jesus' exorcism of the dumb demoniac. The crowds respond positively: they "marveled, saying, 'Never was anything like this seen in Israel'" (9:33). They acknowledge in a positive way the extraordinary character of Jesus' deed (and by implication, of all his preceding deeds) and thus his extraordinary authority. Similarly, the Pharisees acknowledge the extraordinary character of Jesus' deeds, although they have a negative evaluation of them: "He casts out demons by the prince of demons" (9:34). Indeed, Jesus has extraordinary power, but it is that of "the prince of demons."

From this rapid survey we conclude that the main theme of 8:1—9:34 concerns the acknowledgment of the extraordinary authority or power of Jesus as healer or performer of miracles, in the same way as the main theme of chapters 5—7 concerned the acknowledgment of the authority of Jesus as teacher.

Overall Organization

A first reading of 8:1—9:34 shows that this passage displays a well-balanced surface organization. It involves three groups of three miracle stories each (the third group could be viewed as having four miracle stories), the groups being separated by transition materials which serve either as conclusions or introductions to the three major units. Our analysis will show that this threefold surface organization reflects that, for Matthew, the proper acknowledgment of Jesus' authority involves three interrelated issues concerning three kinds of convictions. One of the main convictions expressed in the first unit (8:1–17) is that Jesus acts according to the faith of the supplicants, healing them with a word and from a distance if they have a great faith and healing by touching them in the case of a little faith. The second unit (8:18—9:13) underscores the divine power that Jesus exerts over natural forces (a storm) and over demons. In this way, Jesus' use of power among people, limited as it is by the faith of the supplicants, appears to be deliberate. Jesus is homeless and thus seemingly powerless because his acts are manifestations of God's mercy. By healing, calling sinners, and forgiving sins, Jesus performs acts of mercy which involve making himself vulnerable. In the third unit (9:14–34) the euphoric character and the newness of Jesus' ministry as a manifestation of divine mercy is further described and finally acknowledged.

1. *First Group of Miracle Stories.* 8:1–17
    1. The Healing of the Leper. 8:1–4

2. The Healing of the Centurion's Servant. 8:5–13
3. The Healing of Peter's Mother-in-Law. 8:14–15
Conclusion: Healings and Exorcisms as Fulfillment of Prophecy. 8:16–17

2. *Second Group of Miracle Stories.* 8:18—9:13
Introduction: Responses to Would-Be Disciples. 8:18–22
1. The Stilling of the Storm. 8:23–27
2. The Destruction of Demons in the Country of the Gadarenes. 8:28—9:1
3. The Healing/Forgiving of the Paralytic. 9:2–8
Conclusion: Call of Matthew and Controversy with the Pharisees. 9:9–13

3. *Third Group of Miracle Stories.* 9:14–34
Introduction: Controversy with John's Disciples. 9:14–17
1. The Raising of a Dead Girl and Healing of a Woman. 9:18–26
2. The Healing of the Two Blind Men. 9:27–31
3. The Healing of the Dumb Man. 9:32–34

MATTHEW'S CONVICTIONS IN THE FIRST GROUP OF MIRACLE STORIES. 8:1–17

Each of the three miracle stories in this first group is a healing, that is, a manifestation of Jesus' power in favor of human beings. Yet each of them has distinctive features directly related to the main points (convictions) Matthew wants to convey to his readers. The healing of both the leper and the centurion's servant emphasizes the faith of the supplicant, but in the latter case it is a greater faith and Jesus is not physically present near the sick servant, while in the former case Jesus touches the (unclean) leper. By contrast, the healing of Peter's mother-in-law does not involve any request (and thus not any mention of the faith of a supplicant), yet, as in the case of the leper, Jesus touches the woman; and as in the case of the centurion, there is a recognition of Jesus' authority, since after being healed Peter's mother-in-law serves him. As indicated in the conclusion (8:16–17), these three healings have been brought together by Matthew because he sees them as typical cases that exemplify certain aspects of the significance of Jesus' healings. More specifically, this first unit shows how Jesus' authority is defined by the way he interrelates with people in need of healings. He acts according to the faith of the supplicants. If the supplicants have great faith, a word is enough. But if the supplicants have little faith, he needs to touch them, and in the process take upon himself the uncleanness of the disease.

8:1–4. The Healing of the Leper

The point of this miracle story is expressed by the narrative opposition in 8:4. The cleansed leper should "go, show [himself] to the priest, and offer the gift that Moses commanded," instead of going to people and telling them what happened. This opposition expresses that Jesus' cleansing of the leper can be properly understood only when the ritual commanded by Moses is also fulfilled; the cleansing, together with the performance of the ritual (according to Lev. 14:1–32, it involves showing oneself to the priest, and bringing a gift), is a "testimony to them." By itself, the cleansing would not be a testimony about the true character of Jesus' deed. Why?

Since the priest's role will be to testify that the man is clean of leprosy (Lev. 14:7), one could understand that he will verify that the miracle did take place. But when one interprets 8:1–4 in terms of the context in which it is set by Matthew, and thus in terms of the following oppositions, it appears that this is not Matthew's point. Rather, the command to perform the ritual shows that, for Matthew, Jesus conceives his deeds in terms of the law, indeed as fulfilling the law rather than abolishing it (see 5:17). Yet this does not mean that Jesus follows the letter of the law when cleansing the leper; in fact, he touches the *unclean* leper and in so doing breaks the law (cf. Lev. 5:3). So then the point is that this deed which is beyond the boundaries of the law must be integrated into what is commanded by the law of Moses so as to be complete, and to be a testimony to the people. We have found this pattern elsewhere, especially in chapter 2, where what happened outside the realm of the authority of the law (the star in the East, Nazareth of Galilee) and what happened inside that realm (the revelation of Scripture in Jerusalem, Bethlehem of Judea) are shown to be necessarily complementary of each other. Here also, Jesus' healing involves an activity beyond the boundaries of the law; yet it should not be viewed as contradictory to the law but as a necessary complement of it.

Also note that by touching the leper, Jesus has, in a first way, overcome the separation of the leper from the rest of society (cf. Lev. 13:46). By stepping out of the boundaries of the law, Jesus has begun to achieve the goal of *the first part* of the ritual as described in Lev. 14:1–9, since by declaring a leper clean, the priest reintegrates the leper into society. It then appears in which sense Jesus' deed "befits" the law. The deed breaks the boundary between unclean people (lepers) and clean people (the rest of society), and in the process cleanses the unclean leper, as the first part of the ritual commanded by Moses does. But this deed of Jesus needs to be complemented by the ritual so that the reintegration of the leper into society might be complete. It is the leper as reintegrated into society by the ritual who is a testimony to the people of the true nature of Jesus' authority. A mere proclamation of the cleansing would merely lead people to acknowledge Jesus' extraordinary power, without providing any opportunity for understanding that its boundary-breaking character ultimately aims at the reintegration of people into society (the people of God).

The authority of Jesus is strongly expressed in the rest of the story (its thematic part). The leper coming to Jesus not only kneels before him but also calls him "Lord," which, in this context, is an acknowledgment of Jesus' authority. Yet, for the readers who have just been told that calling Jesus "Lord" is not sufficient (see 7:21–23), this acknowledgment of Jesus' authority is ambiguous. In fact, for the leper, Jesus' authority is nothing more than his power: "Lord, if you will, you can [you have the power to] make me clean" (8:2). Yet the authority displayed by Jesus is broader. It involves both the power to heal acknowledged by the leper ("I will; be clean," 8:3, where Jesus uses the leper's own words) and being in a position to command—expressed most forcefully by the direct discourse address, "See that you say nothing" (8:4).[5] In other words, a proper acknowledgment of Jesus' authority is more than an acknowledgment of his power.

8:5–13. The Healing of the Centurion's Servant

As in the preceding case, the main points (convictions) of this miracle story are not found in the healing itself but in the dialogue following the brief opening description (8:5) which involves two narrative oppositions. Through this passage Matthew makes two points that indicate that the transgression of the boundaries between clean and unclean set up by the law is not good in and of itself, but that it is *demanded by the kind of faith* the supplicants have.

8:7–10. The text first opposes what Jesus says he will do—go to the centurion's home and heal his servant (or child)[6]—to the centurion's reply that Jesus should not come to his home and that he need not do so for healing his servant (8:9–10). As compared with the point made by the preceding story, we find here what appears to be a curious inversion. In 8:3–4, the text views positively Jesus' transgression of the boundary separating unclean people from the rest of society by touching the leper. Similarly, Jesus' proposed action of going to the centurion's home would transgress the boundary between clean and unclean, since a Jew should remain separated from impure Gentiles such as the centurion. Yet this proposed action is now viewed negatively, since Jesus praises the centurion's counter-proposal.

We understand why this is the case when we keep in mind that what is marked positively in 8:3–4 is not Jesus' deed by itself (the touching and cleansing of the leper) but this action *as complemented* by the observance of what Moses commanded. In other words, transgression of the boundary between clean and unclean should not be viewed as good in and of itself; it is good only insofar as it leads to the reintegration of a person (the cleansed leper) in "clean" society. The opposition of 8:7–10 goes a step farther and underscores that, in fact, transgression of the boundary between clean (Jews) and unclean (Gentiles) is not even necessary. This is what is expressed by the detailed analogy that the centurion makes between his own authority and Jesus' authority (8:9). Jesus' physical presence with the sick servant is not necessary; his authority is such that a word from him is enough for performing the healing: "only say the word, and my servant will be healed" (8:8). Consequently, Jesus does not need to go to the house of the centurion, who is "not worthy to have [him] come under [his] roof" (8:8). Thus, from the centurion's perspective or "faith" (8:10), no transgression of the boundary between clean and unclean is needed. And indeed, by a word, Jesus heals the servant according to the centurion's faith: "be it done for you as you have believed" (8:13).

8:10–13. The second point that Matthew makes in this story concerns faith. As expressed in 8:2–4, the faith of the beneficiary of a healing by Jesus seems to play an important role for Matthew. As H. J. Held pointed out,[7] in all the healing stories (as distinguished from exorcism stories) found in the Gospel (with a single exception, 8:14–15), the initiative for a healing is taken by the beneficiaries, the sick person or friends, rather than by Jesus. Such requests for healing are not merely expressions of need. They also are expressions of faith (see 8:10, 13), and Jesus acts in a way that corresponds to the person's faith. Thus, here, Jesus says a word and the servant is healed "as you have believed" (8:13), that is, *according to the way* in which he believed. Yet we need to go beyond these observations which, as Held acknowledges, also apply to the healing stories in Mark and Luke. It is true that Matthew emphasizes the role of faith by his way of presenting the stories. But why?

In 8:10–13, Matthew defines for his readers the nature of faith by opposing the (great) faith of the centurion (8:13) to the lack of such a (great) faith in Israel (8:10).[8] It is not faith and an absence of faith that are opposed but two types of faith: the greater faith of the centurion and the lesser faith of Israel—which can be called "little faith" even though this designation will not be found before 8:26 (yet cf. 6:30). For Matthew, there are several degrees of faith. This opposition clarifies in a first way the difference between great faith and little faith. Great faith involves a trust in Jesus' authority such that one is confident that his power is effective against evil (illness in an unclean home) even when he is not physically present; it is the confidence that Jesus' word or command is efficient in itself. By contrast, the faith in Israel, little faith, involves a trust in Jesus' authority such that one is confident that his power is effective against evil only when he is physically present. Note, however, that Jesus' authority is still defined exclusively in terms of his (greater or lesser) power.

Since Jesus acts in a way that corresponds to the faith of the supplicant ("as you have believed"), a certain kind of faith requires from Jesus a certain mode of action. Thus the leper, a Jew, a member of the people of Israel, is a person with "little faith" (rather than great faith, as the centurion). Jesus, by using the very words of the request (8:2–3), acts according to the leper's faith. In other words, it is the leper's type of faith that demands that Jesus touch him and thus become associated with uncleanness. The transgression of the boundary between clean and unclean is demanded by the leper's type of faith, but it is not absolutely necessary, as the healing of the centurion's servant shows. When the supplicant has great faith, Jesus does not need to transgress this boundary and thus does not need to associate himself with uncleanness. Conversely, it becomes clear that it is because of the little faith of the supplicants (of Israel) that Jesus has to associate himself with uncleanness. According to this faith, Jesus can heal or cleanse only when he is in physical contact with the unclean person or the sick in an unclean home (here sickness and disease are directly associated with uncleanness). In the process of healing according to this faith, Jesus himself becomes unclean (see 8:17: "He took our infirmities and bore our diseases").

8:5, 11–12. These points (convictions) about Jesus' authority and its relation to the faith of the supplicants, which Matthew expects will be new for his readers, are expressed in terms of the readers' knowledge in the few elements of the text not directly related to the oppositions. That the scene takes place in Capernaum of Galilee (8:5) demands that the readers remember the points made by Matthew in chapters 2, 3, and 4 concerning Galilee. According to these chapters, it is in Galilee that the revelations received in Judea are completed. The saying in 8:11–12, concerning those who will come into the kingdom and those who will be excluded from it, does not include any opposition of actions[9] and thus is a statement that Matthew presumes his readers will readily accept. Matthew presupposes that his readers will identify themselves with the "many" who "will come from east and west and sit at table with Abraham, Isaac, and Jacob in the kingdom of heaven" (8:11).[10] This is the first suggestion that Matthew thinks of his readers as people who can identify themselves with Gentiles (people coming from east and west), either because they are from Gentile origin or because they have been excluded from the Jewish community (Israel). Matthew affirms this view of his readers but simultaneously conveys to them that they need to have the centurion's great faith rather than a little faith. In addition, it becomes clear that Jesus' ministry "in Israel" (among the Jews) will be fundamentally molded by the type of faith to be found there. Since he will only find "little faith" in Israel, in order to heal/cleanse and to carry out his vocation as "Emmanuel, God with us" (1:23), he will need to associate himself with uncleanness, indeed, to take upon himself Israel's (or more generally, cf. 8:17, "our") uncleanness.

8:14–15. The Healing of Peter's Mother-in-Law

In this brief miracle story an opposition is clearly expressed: Peter's mother-in-law was "lying sick" (8:14) *and* then "she rose" (8:15). For the first time, the text focuses on the healing itself rather than upon a dialogue about it. It opposes the situation of the patient before and after the healing. As a result, Jesus' role and power in the healing appears without ambiguity; the woman was sick, Jesus touches her hand, she is cured. Without Jesus she is sick; with Jesus she is well and serves him.

This is all we could say about the episode if it stood by itself. But for the readers these verses receive additional connotations from their relations to what precedes and follows. First, it appears that, despite the possibility of healing by a word or a command (8:13), Jesus continues to heal by physical contact, as he did in the case of the leper. Thus, one wonders whether touching the hand of the woman with fever has some of the connotations that touching the leper has. Could it be that, as in touching the leper he became unclean, so by touching the woman with fever he takes upon himself her fever? Then the readers would be led to understand in this perspective the following statement regarding the fulfillment of the prophecy of Isaiah (see 8:17). Similarly, the mention that the woman serves Jesus receives connotations from the preceding dialogue where the centurion described Jesus' authority by analogy to his own authority over his soldiers and his servants or slaves. For the readers, the fact that the woman serves Jesus appears as an acknowledgment of his authority (cf. the angels serving Jesus, 4:11). Furthermore, that she is presented as the mother-in-law of Peter, a disciple, suggests that by serving Jesus and acknowledging his authority over her she adopts the attitude of a disciple. This connotation is barely marked and should not be taken into consideration if Matthew did not introduce the theme of discipleship in the following verses (8:18–22). Then too one wonders whether this third type of healing initiated by Jesus— without request from anyone and thus without expression of a prior faith on the part of the patient—is not comparable to the calls to discipleship (cf. 4:18–22; 9:9); they too are fully initiated by Jesus. But would this mean that a call to discipleship is to be viewed as comparable to a healing? This suggestion, perhaps now far-fetched, is to be confirmed and specified in 9:9–13.

8:16–17. Healings and Exorcisms as Fulfillment of Prophecy

These verses, which do not involve any opposition, express the conclusion that the readers should be ready to draw from what precedes. The summary of Jesus' healing activity (either "with a word" or otherwise) on behalf of all kinds of sick people (8:16) underscores that the three preceding miracle stories (8:1–15) are typical and thus may be used to interpret all the other healing miracles of Jesus.

8:17. Consequently, the statement in 8:17 that by these healings Jesus fulfills the prophecy of Isa. 53:4 leads the readers to reinterpret not only 8:16 but indeed the three preceding miracle stories. Through his literal rendering of the Hebrew text,[11] Matthew gives to this isolated verse an ambiguous meaning which must be respected. On the one hand, "He took our infirmities and bore our diseases" may be read to mean that by his miracles Jesus *removed* the infirmities and diseases from the sick (without taking them upon himself).[12] This is indeed the case when the healings or exorcisms are performed "with a word" (cf. 8:5–13; 8:16). On the other hand, "He took our infirmities and bore our diseases" may also be understood to mean that Jesus took upon himself infirmities and diseases.[13] Obviously this does not mean that he took upon himself other people's illness— by touching the leper he did not contract leprosy. As the case of the leper shows, he shared with the leper what is, for Matthew, the fundamental characteristic of his disease, namely, uncleanness. We have difficulty understanding Matthew because of the distance that separates our modern way of thinking from his. For us, disease is primarily characterized by its fact and its nature (the infection by a virus, a bacterium, or another pathogen). For Matthew, it is a dysphoric state brought about by a dysphoric agent, such as uncleanness (a ritual or moral uncleanness) or a sinful condition (a condition of impurity; cf. 6:12; 6:14–15; 9:2–8). Thus, 8:17 also expresses that, in certain conditions—when Jesus heals not merely with a word but by touching the patient—Jesus takes upon himself what is the fundamental characteristic of our weaknesses and diseases, namely, their uncleanness; he becomes ritually unclean. Keep in mind that Jesus does so, not because he would not have the power to do otherwise, but because of the "little faith" of the supplicants.

In brief, when the supplicant's faith is great enough or when faith is not a factor (as in the case of exorcisms) Jesus simply removes the disease. In other cases, because the supplicant's faith is not great enough, he takes upon himself the uncleanness of the disease.

MATTHEW'S CONVICTIONS IN THE SECOND GROUP OF MIRACLE STORIES. 8:18—9:13

Jesus' authority has been perceived by the supplicants in 8:1–17 as a matter of (greater or lesser) power to heal. Yet the text also shows that Jesus' authority is not merely a matter of power but also a matter of *the way in which he uses this power*. He uses it according to the kind of faith supplicants have. As a consequence he transgresses or does not transgress the boundaries between clean and unclean as set by the law. As we will see, 8:18—9:13

carries this twofold theme a step farther. The range of Jesus' power is specified.

The miracle stories of the second group—the stilling of the storm (8:23–27), the miracle in the country of the Gadarenes (8:28–34), and the healing/forgiving of the paralytic (9:2–8)—describe quite different situations. The first one is a miracle over destructive forces of nature; the second one is a miracle over demons, that is, evil spiritual powers; and the third one is the healing of a human being. Thus 8:18—9:13 may be viewed as presenting the way in which the authority or power of the Son of man is exercised in three different realms: the realm of nature, the realm of evil spirits, and the human realm. The main points Matthew makes here are (a) that Jesus as the Son of man has absolute (divine) power over the forces of nature which threaten him and the disciples; (b) that the Son of man or Son of God has absolute (divine) power over the demons and that he has come to "torment" them; (c) in the case of human beings, he has the power to forgive and to heal in response to and according to their faith. His power over human beings is subordinated to the faith of the supplicants. In his relationship with human beings, Jesus, the Son of man, is presented as homeless and in an insecure position as if he were powerless (8:20). But since his miracles show that he has divine power, it is clear that Jesus' relative powerlessness in the human realm is deliberate. He chooses to use his divine power only in response to faith; such is his vocation. While he has come to torment and destroy demons (8:29), he has also come to call and heal sinners (9:12–13)—according to their faith. Since sinners only have a "little faith," this vocation demands that he take upon himself their infirmities and diseases and thus share the insecurity of their situation (8:20) outside the security of human institutions.

Discipleship involves following Jesus in the insecurity of his vocation (8:19–22) rather than in the security that his absolute power could provide. Note, however, that security and insecurity are defined in terms of the human realm and its interpretation of the law—a false perception of security and insecurity. In other words, discipleship involves more than a mere faith or confidence in Jesus' power—more than the greater faith exemplified by the centurion. Discipleship involves sharing the fate of the Son of man and his vocation. It involves acknowledging that his authority is primarily defined in terms of his vocation, and only secondarily by his power.

8:18–22. Responses to Would-Be Disciples

The second part of the transition material opens with a statement which includes Jesus' order "to go over to the other side" (8:18) that links 8:18–22 to the story of the stilling of the storm (8:23–27)—a description of what happens in the process of going to the other side—and to the story of the miracle in the country of the Gadarenes (8:28—9:1). Thus 8:18–22 is presented as the introduction to the second group of miracles.

Since Jesus' authority is comparable to (and greater than) that of the centurion who gives orders to his soldiers and slaves (8:9), the readers should not be surprised to find Jesus giving orders: he is entitled to do so! But there is something awkward in 8:18. First, to whom is the order addressed? This is not specified. Our knowledge of Mark 4:35 and Luke 8:22 leads us to presume that Jesus addresses the disciples, but this is not said here. Second, how is his seeing the crowds around him related to the order "to go over to the other side"? Our knowledge of passages such as Mark 3:9 leads us to presume that Jesus gave that order so as to escape the crowds,[14] but this is not said here. In fact, since the order is given to no one in particular, it is addressed to whoever in the crowds would want to receive it; it is an open invitation to *follow him* "to the other side."[15] Those who submit to this order and follow him will, in so doing, demonstrate that they are "disciples" (8:21)—people who follow Jesus after receiving an order to do so and who do what he teaches them. This is the only definition of discipleship found in the Gospel up to this point.

But what does following Jesus entail? This is specified by a series of oppositions in 8:19–27, first in 8:19–22 in which two would-be disciples are presented (two persons who want to follow Jesus but are corrected by him). In this way, Matthew sets up two oppositions through which he makes two points.

8:19–20. The opposition in these verses concerns the proper understanding of what is involved in following Jesus. Jesus' response emphasizes that following him means sharing his condition. Like him, the disciples—the ideal disciples[16] according to Jesus' teaching—will have "nowhere to lay [their] head[s]," that is, no home (hole, nest). They will be without the security provided by a home. What is wrong in the scribe's statement is that he conceives Jesus as a "teacher"—a view which could be that of the readers after reading the Sermon on the Mount—and that "wherever" Jesus is will be a secure place of teaching, a school, a hole, a nest. In other words, the scribe believes that he will find security in Jesus' teaching. But this is a wrong understanding of Jesus as teacher and of what is true security, and its true source. Jesus should be conceived as the "Son of man."

Here for the first time the title "Son of man" is used, and so we need to consider it as an unknown term. For the readers it might evoke many connotations (derived, e.g., from Dan. 7:13–14; 1 Enoch 37—71, or from uses of the phrase to designate a human being). Here "Son of man" is simply defined as "one who has nowhere to lay his head," in contrast to a "teacher."

8:21–22. A second person, described as "another of the disciples," addresses Jesus. In contrast to the ideal disciple described in Jesus' teaching, this actual disciple is cast in an ambiguous light. He acknowledges Jesus' authority—he calls him "Lord"—and asks his permission to do something. But he is mistaken in thinking that Jesus will give him permission to go and bury his father before obeying Jesus' order to go over to the other side. Because of the juxtaposition of these verses with the preceding ones, the disciple's request and Jesus' answer must be interpreted in reference to 8:19–20. Following Jesus, the Son of man, entails not only accepting being homeless as he is homeless but also giving up the security provided by "home" understood as the network of family relationships to which one belongs by fulfilling certain duties—including the most sacred duties, such as burying one's father. In the light of 7:8–11 (and 6:8, 25–32), where a "father" is described as being the provider of good things for his children, proper relationship to one's father is a guarantee of security. Thus, following Jesus, the Son of man, entails first of all—contrary to the disciple's expectation—giving up one's relationship to one's father, the provider of security.

When the relationship between 8:19–20 and 8:21–22 is recognized, it becomes possible to perceive how Matthew understands the response of Jesus, "leave the dead to bury their own dead" (8:22). First, observe that in the disciple's request it is not clear whether his father is already dead or simply sick (on his deathbed) or perhaps even simply old;[17] Jesus states that he is dead. The dead father can no longer provide security. Those who bury the dead ironically seek security where it is not, and thus are as good as dead themselves. Since the Jewish tradition preserved by the scribes makes burial of one's parent a sacred duty, the disciple who wants to bury his father is like the scribe who believes he will find security in Jesus' teaching. For Matthew, Jesus' response indicates that following Jesus, the Son of man, involves giving up the security of family relationship and duties, because it is false security.

Finally, note that the second person is described as "another of the disciples" (8:21). Since he was already a disciple (as the scribe of 8:19 was), it appears that, for Matthew, a first decision to follow Jesus is not enough. One needs constantly to become a disciple[18] by progressively discovering what is involved in following Jesus. Accepting the insecurity of a life with the Son of man by giving up false securities is only one step toward discipleship.

In view of the points made in 8:18–22, one can expect both a further description of what is entailed by discipleship—following the Son of man—and further characterization of the Son of man.

8:23–27. The Stilling of the Storm

The main theme of this miracle story is the stilling of the storm and thus Jesus' divine power over the forces of nature. Matthew assumes, in the light of the preceding miracles, that his readers will expect such a view of Jesus' power. For the new point (conviction) Matthew conveys to his readers by this episode, note the opposition: the disciples' call for help, "Save, Lord; we are perishing" (8:25) *and* Jesus' reproof, "Why are you afraid, O [people] of little faith?" (8:26). Matthew is primarily concerned with making a point about discipleship[19] or about what should have been the attitude and faith of the disciples in such a situation.

8:23–24. The first verse, which describes Jesus climbing into the boat and being *followed* by his disciples, suggests that this new point about discipleship is related to the points made in 8:18–22 where following Jesus has begun to be defined. In 8:20 and 8:22, the disciples were warned that following Jesus, the Son of man, involves sharing his fate and living in insecurity with him. Now the disciples in the boat with Jesus find themselves in a most insecure situation. "And behold, there arose a great storm on the sea, so that the boat was being swamped by the waves" (8:24).

8:25–26. The disciples' request seems quite appropriate. As the leper (8:2) and the centurion (8:5–6) did, they come to Jesus (8:25) and acknowledge his authority by calling him "Lord." They ask for his extraordinary help (a miracle) in a situation beyond their control. Jesus' response is therefore somewhat unexpected. First, he does not calm the sea right away;[20] rather, he begins by reproving the disciples. For him, calming the storm is not an urgent matter. Consequently, his saying appears to be the important thing. Second, on the basis of Jesus' reproof (8:26a), we might ask what attitude the disciples should have had. We have to conclude that they should not have awakened Jesus and they should not have been afraid of the storm, even though "the boat was being swamped by the waves" (8:24). Doing so is being a "coward" (*deilos*; RSV: "afraid") and having "little faith" (8:26; cf. 6:30). Positively, having faith would have meant they did not need to be anxious for their lives despite the threatening character of the situation, since they were with Jesus in the boat, even though he was asleep. In fact, as disciples following the Son of man who "has nowhere to lay his head" (8:20), they should have expected to be secure in apparently insecure situations. Thus, what is wrong with the disciples' attitude, their "little faith," is their failure to understand that they should expect to be in threatening situations and that they should not be anxious because Jesus has power even over the forces of nature. In the case of natural cataclysms, the situation of insecurity is only apparently threatening.

8:26b–27. We can now recognize the thematic features of 8:23–27. After reproving the disciples, Jesus performs the miracle they requested. As he previously did, with the leper and the centurion, he acts *according to the type of faith* of the supplicants. They have a "little faith," which involves trusting in Jesus only if he is visibly aware of the situation (awake) and does something about it, so Jesus gets up and calms the storm. He does so by rebuking "the winds and the sea" (8:26) and thus "with a word" (as in 8:13). For the readers (with their knowledge of Pss. 29:3–4; 65:7; 89:9; 93:4; 107:29;

124:1–5), this demonstrates that Jesus' power is divine power. As Yahweh has, so Jesus has power over natural elements such as the winds and the sea. Furthermore, Matthew concludes the story by noting that "men," not merely the disciples, "marveled, saying, 'What sort[21] of [person] is this, that even winds and sea obey him?'" (8:27). While the actual identity and authority of Jesus is not recognized, his divine power over the forces of nature is.

8:24. From the perspective of the readers, there is a small but significant tension in the text. Matthew refers to the "storm" as a *seismos*, which usually means "earthquake." The term evokes for the readers other texts and traditions with which they might have been familiar, as in texts describing cataclysms that will take place at the end of the world (see 24:7; 27:54; 28:2).[22] For Matthew, then, this story is typical not only of miracle stories but also of all the eschatological situations in which disciples (will) find themselves in grave dangers—an interpretation that would not be possible if the eschatological connotation was not found in other passages. Consequently, it appears that the insecure situations the disciples are invited to share with the Son of man by following him are eschatological situations. It follows that "Son of man" has an eschatological connotation. On the basis of this text, all we can say is that "the Son of man has nowhere to lay his head" (8:20) in that the eschatological cataclysms of natural elements are (already) unleashed against him, although they do not have power over him; rather, he has power over them. Those who follow him, the disciples as well as the readers (i.e., the church), share the Son of man's situation and thus should not be afraid. Even if they have only a "little faith," as the disciples had on the sea, in such situations they can count on the help of Jesus, the Son of man with divine power over natural cataclysms which are to be expected in the eschatological time, the time when the disciples follow the Son of man.

8:28—9:1. Destruction of Demons in the Country of the Gadarenes

This miracle story is not a healing story,[23] since the text does not mention what happened to the two demoniacs. Rather, its theme is the killing of the demons: "the whole herd rushed down the steep bank into the sea, and [they] perished in the waters" (8:32), a formulation suggesting it was the demons (plural subject of the preceding verb) that died as well as the herd.[24] We also need to note that the encompassing theme of this narrative is Jesus' arrival in the country of the Gadarenes (8:28) and his departure from it as a consequence of the negative reactions of these people to the miracle.

8:28–29. In this passage there is a single narrative opposition: the demoniacs were so fierce that "no one could pass that way" (8:28) *and* the demons acknowledged that Jesus has "come here" (8:29). The point (conviction) is that Jesus has the power or authority "to go" (*erchomai*) there, while the Gadarenes are unable "to go" on that road because the demons prevent them. The Gadarenes accommodate their lives to the fierce power of demons. There are areas of their country (of their lives?) over which they do not have control; their movements are limited by the power of the demons. By contrast, as the entire dialogue between Jesus and the demons underscores, Jesus has power and authority over the demons. Their first statement (8:29) is not primarily a formula of protection, an effort to use magic against Jesus,[25] but rather the recognition of Jesus' authority. Jesus is acknowledged as the "Son of God" and as the one who comes to "torment" the demons. This description of the purpose of Jesus' coming—his vocation—involves the use of a term (*basanizō* = "torment") that, once again (cf. 8:24), belongs to the vocabulary associated with the eschatological judgment.[26] The vocation of the Son of God is an eschatological vocation, that of tormenting and destroying demons, as is confirmed by the only defense used by the demons: "Have you come here to torment us before the time?" From the demons' point of view, Jesus should not torment them, because it is not yet the time of the judgment. But the demons are wrong. Now is the time when Jesus, as Son of God/Son of man, has the authority and the power to torment and destroy demons.

8:31–32. In their next statement (8:31), the demons are described as acknowledging that Jesus has such an authority, since they beg him to send them into the pigs (8:31). Finally, the way in which Jesus responds, by the command, "Go" (8:32), expresses once again his authority over them.

This is the third instance in which we find Jesus' vocation (the purpose of his "coming") specified in terms of time. In the first case (3:11–15) Matthew underscores that, for "now," Jesus is not coming in order to baptize people with fire; his present vocation is not that of the eschatological judge and tormentor, as far as human beings are concerned. In the second case (5:17–18) it is emphasized that he has not come to abolish the law and the prophets; his present vocation is not that of the eschatological prophet like Moses who will give a new law with the effect of abolishing the law and the prophets. After these two negative statements regarding Jesus' vocation as eschatological figure, we find in the third instance (8:29) a positive statement: he is the Son of God/Son of man whose vocation is to torment and destroy, but, for now, he exercises this role only vis-à-vis demons, not vis-à-vis human beings.

Similarly, this is the third passage in which Jesus is designated as "Son of God." In 2:15, this title appears in a context in which Jesus' authority is contrasted with Herod's political authority and thus is described negatively. Jesus' vocation as Son of God is not to disrupt the normal unfolding of human affairs by the use of destructive power as Herod does. The decla-

ration of the voice from heaven (3:17) is specified by the oppositions of the
temptation story (where the devil calls Jesus "Son of God," 4:3, 6); even
though the devil has the power to transport him to various places, one of
the points is that Jesus, as Son of God whose will is submitted to God's
will, resists the temptation; in so doing, he demonstrates that he is Son of
God and has authority over the devil (the devil obeys him, 4:10–11). Here
the demons acknowledge his authority as Son of God and his power over
them—the power of one whose vocation is to torment and destroy them.
Since in the preceding (8:23–27) and following (9:2–8) passages Jesus' power
is presented as divine, we conclude that the title "Son of God" is used here
to convey that Jesus has divine authority and power over demons.

   8:28–30. The rest of the story is Matthew's effort to convey these convictions to his readers in terms of their expectations. The theme of uncleanness (see 8:1–13) is found once again. Arriving in this country, Jesus
is met by unclean persons (two demoniacs coming out of tombs, 8:28);
there is a herd of unclean animals, pigs (8:30). This is a pagan country.

   8:34. The theme that provides the framework for the miracle story concerns Jesus' interaction with the Gadarenes and their negative reaction to
his destruction of the demons. The Gadarenes who beg Jesus to leave their
country (8:34) are the only ones described as being affected by the power
of the demons (8:28). What happened to the demoniacs as human beings is
not described. The Gadarenes recognize some kind of authority in Jesus—
all the people come out to meet Jesus (8:34) as they would do for a dignitary.
But they, the beneficiaries of the destruction of the demons, reject him.
Being a beneficiary of Jesus' power over demons (or over a storm, 8:23–
27) is not what brings people to acknowledge the true character of Jesus'
authority—they have little faith, and after the miracle they are simply puzzled (8:27).

   Finally, the concluding verse (9:1) shows Jesus, the Son of God/Son of
man with divine power over demons, submitting to the wish of the
Gadarenes.

9:2–8. The Healing/Forgiving
of the Paralytic

   The main theme of this story concerns forgiving sins, as indicated by the
crowds' reaction (9:8) and by the fact that forgiving is not directly involved
in a narrative opposition. By contrast, the healing itself is expressed in the
form of an opposition: 9:2 notes that the paralytic is "lying on his bed,"
while 9:7–8 shows him getting up, taking his bed, and going home. Furthermore, while the controversy that constitutes a second opposition (9:3–
6) focuses on Jesus' statement "your sins are forgiven," its primary point
concerns the respective attitudes of the scribes and of Jesus. The theme of

forgiveness of sins must therefore be interpreted in terms of the points made by these oppositions.

9:2, 6b–7. Since the first narrative opposition concerns the healing of the paralytic, it is clear that the point Matthew makes is about Jesus' power. Without Jesus the man is paralyzed; with Jesus and his power the man walks away. The beginning of the healing story follows the pattern found in the healings of the leper and of the centurion's servant and in the stilling of the storm. Jesus acts in response to, and according to, the faith of the suppliants (9:2). This faith is simply the confidence that Jesus has the power to heal.[27] The story underscores that the paralytic's original situation involves not only the inability to walk but also sinfulness, as well as lack of courage which indicates a deficient faith ("little faith"). First, the paralytic's deficiency in faith is both expressed and overcome by Jesus' exhortation: "Take courage, child" (9:2b, au.). However deficient the paralytic's faith might be, Jesus will act according to it. Then Jesus declares, "your sins are forgiven," not merely a statement describing an existing situation (such as, "your sins are forgiven by God, as the sins of everyone else are") but an *efficient word*, a word through which forgiveness of sins actually occurs at that moment. Jesus has the power to forgive sins (see 9:6). Since forgiveness of sins explains why the paralytic should take courage and trust that he will be healed, this declaration also indicates that *sins are part of his situation of infirmity*. A condition of sinfulness is directly related to a condition of paralysis. When sins are removed, one can be confident that paralysis will also be removed. Similarly, the question "For which is easier, to say, 'Your sins are forgiven,' or to say, 'Rise and walk'?" (9:5) indicates that the same kind of power is required for forgiving sins and for healing.

In view of earlier passages of the Gospel (6:12, where forgiveness of sins signifies purification, and 8:1–13, where healing is associated with cleansing and issues of ritual purity), and since Matthew closely associates forgiving sins and healing,[28] we conclude that here forgiving sins is also to be understood as a kind of purification rather than a cancellation of debts. It is the removal of an impurity, as healing is the removal of a disease; thus the same kind of power is needed to perform both acts. Jesus has the power—a divine power—both to forgive sins and to heal.

9:3–6. Matthew, however, makes an additional point. The opposition found in the controversy between Jesus and some of the scribes (9:3–6) concerns the character of Jesus' authority, not merely his power. It primarily concerns the attitude associated with the use of such power. Because 9:3 does not explain why Jesus' declaration is a blasphemy for the scribes[29] and because of the content of Jesus' response (9:4–6), the readers' attention is directed to something other than Jesus' power per se.

The scribes' reaction is based on a lack of true knowledge ("But that you may know . . . ," 9:6a), while Jesus has true knowledge ("knowing their thoughts," 9:4a). Jesus and the scribes are contrasted by the way in which they "know." The scribes know by "saying to themselves" (9:3); it is a self-centered knowledge. It is also a judgment (condemnation, cf. 7:1–5); it is thinking that someone else is evil—that Jesus is a blasphemer—because of an inner disposition that is itself evil ("thinking evil in your hearts," 9:4; cf. 5:28). They confuse good and evil (cf. 6:22—7:11), since they perceive Jesus as a blasphemer, while he is not. They perceive only evil in other people, and consequently they only have evil things in their hearts.

By contrast, Jesus has a different attitude. He perceives the evil in the scribes' hearts and the sins of the paralytic, but he also perceives the good that is in people—their faith ("when Jesus saw their faith," 9:2). Furthermore, he does not keep this knowledge for himself, as the scribes do, making their knowledge of evil a judgment/condemnation without the possibility of any appeal. He communicates this knowledge to the persons involved, and for their benefit. He perceives the (little) faith of the paralytic and of his friends and acts accordingly. He perceives the sins of the paralytic and in the very process of communicating this knowledge to him he removes this evil from him: "your sins are forgiven." Similarly, he perceives the scribes' evil thoughts, and communicates this knowledge to them together with what should remove this evil from their hearts: "'But that you may know that the Son of man has authority on earth to forgive sins'—he then said to the paralytic—'Rise . . .'" (9:6).

Jesus' authority to forgive sins, to remove evil, involves therefore (a) the ability to perceive correctly what is good and what is evil in others, (b) the will to share this knowledge with them and for their benefit, and (c) the power to remove the evil—the extraordinary, divine power to perform the forgiveness/purification of sins, the power to heal, which should also overcome the scribes' evil thoughts.

9:8. Most of the features of this passage are directly associated with the points (convictions) that Matthew conveys concerning the power and authority of Jesus, the Son of man, in human affairs ("on earth," 9:6). This is a God-given authority, as the crowds acknowledge (9:8). Yet the crowds' response creates a tension in the text which signals that Matthew calls upon his readers' expectations. The crowds praised God, "who had given such authority *to men*" (9:8, au. italics), while all the story led the readers to conclude that this authority had been given to Jesus, the Son of man. In fact, while the theme (the expression of convictions in terms of the readers' expectations) of 9:2–8 is that Jesus as the Son of man has such an authority, the points (convictions) that Matthew makes are primarily focused upon the specific character of this authority—what it accomplishes and how it accomplishes it—rather than upon who has it. Certainly, having this authority involves having a divine power. But it also involves an ability to perceive what is good and evil and a will to use this knowledge for the benefit of others, an attitude which, according to the Sermon on the Mount, disciples should also have. It thus appears that Matthew's conviction is that this authority is given by God not only to Jesus, the Son of man, but also to other people, such as disciples. This is what, according to Matthew, the crowds recognize and express.

Finally, as the emphasis on the crowds' response (afraid, glorifying God, 9:8) indicates, Jesus' declaration of forgiveness is presented as a stupendous or holy event. His declaration transgresses the boundaries of the scribes' understanding of Scripture as touching the leper did (8:1–4) and as going to the house of the centurion would have done (8:7–8). For the scribes, this is blasphemy. Jesus could have had the power to heal the paralytic without exposing himself to the attack of the scribes as he healed the *paralyzed* servant of the centurion (8:6). But by mentioning forgiveness of sins, he made himself vulnerable (cf. 8:20). His declaration of forgiveness, which is directly associated with the supplicant's faith, is comparable to touching the leper, a transgression of the law demanded by the supplicant's kind of faith. Thus, once again, in the human realm Jesus makes himself vulnerable by limiting the use of his power to what is appropriate for the situation, that is, by acting according to the ("little") faith of the people involved. This appears to be an essential characteristic of Jesus' authority.

9:9–13. Call of Matthew and Controversy with the Pharisees

9:9. The unit that began with 8:18–22 is concluded by 9:9–13; the latter passage deals with discipleship, as the introduction did. Furthermore, there is no doubt that, for the author of the Gospel, the call of Matthew (9:9) is directly linked with the controversy that follows, since it is echoed and explained by the last words of the controversy: "I came not to call the righteous, but sinners" (9:13). In brief, the call of Matthew, a man "sitting at the tax office" (9:9), is presented as the call of a sinner. Since tax collectors and sinners are closely associated with each other in 9:10, the phrase "tax collectors and sinners" could almost be read "tax collectors, that is, sinners."[30] When Jesus calls Matthew to discipleship he calls a sinner.

The juxtaposition of 9:9 and 9:10–13 creates a tension that reflects the tension expressed by the entire unit. The central part of 8:18—9:13 demonstrates that Jesus has divine power in all the realms of existence (the natural, the demonic, and the human realms); he has, with a word, the power to still the storm (8:23–27), to destroy demons (8:28–34), and to forgive sins and to heal (9:1–8). Thus the readers are not surprised by his power/authority over Matthew, the tax collector. A word, a command from Jesus, and Matthew follows him (9:9; as Peter, Andrew, James, and John did, 4:18–22). Such is the power/authority of Jesus. But then, how can it be said that "the Son of man has nowhere to lay his head" (8:20), and thus lives in insecurity? This tension is also found in 9:9–13. As Jesus has just demonstrated by calling Matthew, he has the power/authority to deal with such tax collectors and sinners from a distance—with a word. But in 9:10–13 he does not do so. So as to call sinners (9:13), he sits down at the table and eats with them, and in the process breaks the Pharisaic purity rules and becomes impure. Why? This is the question the text raises for the readers. It concerns once again the character of Jesus' authority over human beings, which must be understood in terms of his vocation (what he "came" for, 9:13). Thus we need to elucidate the points Matthew makes in these verses.

A first opposition is set up by the controversy between Jesus and the Pharisees (9:11–12). In addition, we find two closely related narrative oppositions in 9:13: calling righteous people *and* calling sinners; desiring mercy *and* desiring sacrifice (cf. Hos. 6:6).

9:13. Jesus' vocation is defined by his submission to God's will (cf. 4:1–11), since the reference to God's will, "I desire mercy, and not sacrifice" (see Hos. 6:6), is directly associated with Jesus' vocation. Consequently, the opposition found in this quotation and the opposition regarding Jesus' vocation are directly correlated. As God desires "mercy" rather than "sacrifice," so Jesus came to call the sinners rather than to call the righteous. It is from this perspective that we can grasp how Matthew understood both the quotation of Hos. 6:6 and Jesus' vocation.

Calling sinners is presented as a merciful act which is opposed to calling righteous people and offering sacrifices or partaking in sacrifices. This opposition expresses that calling sinners involves more than saying a word to them; it also involves being associated with sinners, indeed, eating with them, and consequently breaking the priestly laws of purity according to which any meal is like a sacrificial meal,[31] since sinners by definition do not follow these laws. As we have noted, becoming a disciple involves more than being willing to follow Jesus (8:19–22). Beyond the initial response to Jesus' command, one needs to be forgiven/purified from one's sins (cf. 6:12, 14–15). Consequently, Jesus' vocation vis-à-vis human beings, manifesting mercy to them, involves being associated with sinners (would-be disciples), and thus becoming impure (cf. also 8:1–17). This means becoming unfit to partake of a sacrifice—since, as is indirectly expressed in 8:4, one needs to be "clean" in order to "offer the gift that Moses commanded" (see Lev. 14:1–10). Thus, in order to be in a position to partake of sacrifices, one can be associated only with "righteous" (i.e., "clean") people. But wanting to remain pure so as to be in a position to partake of sacrifices and thus avoiding any association with sinners is not the will of God. For Jesus, this would be to betray his vocation. Mercy—calling sinners—demands from Jesus association with sinners, and thus sharing in their uncleanness. But why?

As the analogy of the physician (9:12) shows, this act of mercy is similar to healing and thus amounts to removing their sinfulness/uncleanness, that is, forgiving their sins. Yet the healing of the centurion's servant (8:5–13) demonstrates that Jesus has the divine power to perform this act with a word and thus without being directly associated with sinners and becoming impure. But the text underscores that removing sinfulness/uncleanness from a distance would not be an act of mercy; this is not what it means to be calling sinners. Calling sinners is an act of mercy only when Jesus forgoes the use of his divine power and associates himself with sinners.

9:10–12. The opposition between Jesus and the Pharisees clarifies this point. As in 9:1–8, it contrasts Jesus' attitude toward others with the Pharisees' attitude toward others. The Pharisees, by addressing *to the disciples* their criticism of Jesus' action (9:11) and thus not dealing directly with the person they perceive as evil, pose as judges who condemn *from a distance* (cf. 9:3). By contrast, Jesus directly addresses his opponents. His response both shows that their understanding is wrong (9:12) and provides the means to correct this misunderstanding (evil thoughts, 9:4): "Go and learn . . ." (9:13). Thus, once again, Jesus' response is not a condemnation. Jesus describes himself as a physician, a person who makes a distinction between healthy and sick people and who is needed by and acts for the benefit of the latter. Evil in people is not something to be condemned, but to be healed. He is not a judge (cf. 3:10–15) but a physician. For this purpose, Jesus cannot adopt the Pharisees' attitude; he cannot deal with the evil that he perceives (sin, uncleanness) from a distance. He has to allow sinners to come to him, and indeed to eat with him (9:10). Yes, he has the power to call sinners with a word, from a distance (8:5–13). But in order to fulfill his vocation as a manifestation of God's mercy, he needs to forgo the use of this power; he needs to be associated with sinners (9:10–13), to become unclean at their contact (8:3), and to take upon himself their diseases and infirmities (8:17). As such, he is the manifestation of God's mercy.

In sum, we can say that an acknowledgment of Jesus' power (the little faith of people in Israel, as well as the great faith of the centurion), while valid, is not in itself a complete acknowledgment of his authority. The true character of Jesus' authority can be recognized only when one understands his vocation. With the divine power that he has as Son of God/Son of man he could intervene abruptly and brutally in human affairs (as Herod did, 2:16–21) so as to remove all evil and impurity. But such an intervention would be condemnation and destruction (cf. 8:32), while his vocation is one of mercy according to God's will. This demands that he does what is appropriate for the present situation (3:15) and thus submits the use of his power to the people's little faith. As such, he is a manifestation of God's mercy; this is the fundamental characteristic of his authority. Paradoxically, this new manifestation of God transgresses the boundaries set by the law, between what is pure and impure. Jesus is the manifestation of God precisely when he becomes ritually impure according to the scribes' and Pharisees' understanding of the will of God. Thus, Jesus' true authority can be properly acknowledged only when one recognizes that his interaction with human beings is a new and merciful manifestation of God. The newness of his authority becomes the main point of the passages that follow.

MATTHEW'S CONVICTIONS IN THE THIRD GROUP OF MIRACLE STORIES. 9:14–34

9:14–17. Controversy with John's Disciples

The sudden appearance of John's disciples evokes for the readers the story of John and his ministry. In fact, the points (convictions) made in 9:14–17 are not unrelated to those Matthew made in 3:1–17. John's disciples associate themselves with the Pharisees. Even though they attack Jesus' disciples (9:14), their attitude is somewhat more positive vis-à-vis Jesus, since they address him directly.

Most of the features of 9:14–17 are related to three narrative oppositions and must be interpreted in terms of them. Jesus' disciples who are not fasting are opposed to John's disciples and the Pharisees who are fasting (9:14). This opposition is explained by three analogies: that of the wedding guests (9:15), of the unshrunk patch on the old garment (9:16), and of the wineskins (9:17). This latter analogy involves a twofold narrative opposition—putting new wine into old wineskins and both are lost, putting new wine into new wineskins and both are preserved. Another opposition is set up by the controversy between John's disciples and Jesus (9:14–15).

9:14–15. The opposition regarding fasting (9:14) as explained by the wedding guest analogy (9:15) underscores what is wrong in the attitude of John's disciples and the Pharisees: their *timing* and their perception of what is *fitting* for the present time (cf. 3:7–8 and 3:14–15). There is nothing wrong with fasting in and of itself (cf. 4:2; 6:16–18), and indeed "the days will come" when the disciples will fast. But when one is at the wedding feast with the bridegroom, it is not the appropriate time for mourning; fasting is thus identified with mourning. John's disciples and the Pharisees do not recognize that they are in the presence of the bridegroom and at the time of the wedding feast. They do not recognize the euphoric character of the present situation, and thus they mourn instead of rejoicing. But Jesus' disciples do, and thus they do not mourn. This point is directly related to those found in 8:17—9:13 and 3:14–15; in the present, Jesus should not be viewed as the eschatological judge bringing condemnation and torment, but rather as the bridegroom bringing "mercy" (9:13) and joy. The present of Jesus' ministry is a euphoric time contrasted with a future, dysphoric time when the bridegroom will be taken away—quite certainly a reference to the crucifixion (9:15).

9:16–17. The following analogies and the opposition of 9:17 develop the same point with a slightly different emphasis. Recognizing what is fitting for the present euphoric time also involves recognizing that the present includes something "new" by contrast with what is "old." The disciples are those who discern that Jesus' ministry and presence bring about something radically new, as compared with the old represented by both John's disciples and the Pharisees. What is "new"? In view of the preceding verses, it is Jesus' ministry as manifestation of God's *mercy* (cf. 9:13, a summary of all of Jesus' interrelations with sick and sinners). This radical newness does not fit with the old. Indeed, it has a power such that it tears apart or breaks the old. The unshrunk patch tears apart the old garment (9:16); the new wine causes the old wineskins to burst (9:17). The newness of the manifestation of God's mercy tears apart and breaks the old laws—that which "was said to the [people] of old" (see 5:21–47), or more specifically the ritual laws of purity as interpreted by the Pharisees which one follows in order to be fit to partake in sacrifices (9:13). "Mercy" demands from Jesus to be associated with sinners when calling them, to touch the leper and the sick when healing them, to blaspheme when forgiving their sins, indeed to take upon himself their diseases and their infirmities (8:17). This new manifestation of God's will breaks the old understanding of God's will. It is the manifestation of a power that has not only the positive effect of removing impurities (leprosy), diseases, and sins but also the destructive effect of tearing down the old, traditional views of what is truly euphoric, holy. What is truly the will of God, the will of the Holy One, is mercy. One can know what is appropriate, fitting to do, only when one recognizes that the euphoric manifestation of Jesus' power is also the new manifestation of the Holy. Truly acknowledging Jesus' authority involves not merely the recognition of his power but also that this power is a manifestation of divine mercy, a new manifestation of the Holy.

9:14–15. This point is further expressed by the third opposition, which is set up by the controversy itself (9:14–15). John's disciples, by the very fact that they address a question to Jesus, are characterized as not knowing what they should do or not do—as John was confused regarding whether he should baptize Jesus or be baptized by him (3:14–15). By contrast, as Jesus expresses in his response, his disciples have a clear perception of what they should do or not do; obviously, wedding guests *cannot* mourn (9:15). Because they acknowledge Jesus' authority, and thus because they acknowledge the new manifestation of the Holy in Jesus, (ideal) disciples know what they can do, their vocation. Once again, for Matthew, the recognition of what is truly good—here, Jesus as new manifestation of the Holy—establishes for people their will, what they want to do—their vocation.

9:18–26. Raising of a Dead Girl and Healing of a Woman

This twofold miracle story is closely tied to the preceding teaching by its opening phrase: "While he was thus speaking to them, behold, a ruler came . . ." (9:18). We can expect Matthew to develop the points presented in 9:14–17. We shall see that he does so by underscoring the power of Jesus and that it is inappropriate to mourn because of the newness Jesus brings.

For the readers, this story is similar to the healing of the centurion's servant (8:5–13). Someone with authority, "a ruler," comes to Jesus. Both by his attitude (kneeling) and by his words, he expresses his faith or confidence in Jesus' power (9:18), and Jesus *acts according to his faith*.[32] For the ruler, Jesus has the power to perform the miracle if he comes to his house and lays his hand on his daughter (9:18); so Jesus "followed" him to his house (9:19, 23) and "took her by the hand, and the girl arose" (9:25; cf. 8:15). Similarly, the woman with a hemorrhage has faith that Jesus' power is such that if she touches his garment, she will be "made well" (saved, 9:21). She touches his garment. Jesus acknowledges her faith—a deficient faith since Jesus' power is viewed merely as a quasi-magical power, and since he encourages her, "Take heart" (9:22, as in 9:2). Then he says, using the very word through which she expressed her faith, "your faith has made you well," and "instantly the woman was made well" (9:22). For the readers, the only thing new in this story, as compared with the preceding healings, is the magnitude of Jesus' power. The girl is dead—not merely sick— and he brings her back to life (9:18, 24–25). His power is even communicated by the fringe of his garment (9:20), although it is made efficient by Jesus' word—the woman is healed only after Jesus has addressed her (9:22).

9:18, 24. This point about Jesus' extraordinary power is expressed by the opposition found in the ruler's request—his daughter "has just died," but "she will live" (9:18)—and in Jesus' words, "the girl is not dead but sleeping" (9:24). Without Jesus, the girl dies and remains dead. With Jesus and his power, she is alive; death is transformed into sleep (a form of life).[33] Jesus has the power to bring dead people back to life, to transform death into life.

9:23–24. A second point is made through the opposition set up when Jesus confronts the people in the ruler's house (9:24). Jesus confronts them after *seeing* what they do (9:23), and thus after perceiving that what they do is inappropriate. The people mock him because they do not perceive that what they do (noisily mourning the dead girl) is not appropriate in the new situation created by the presence of Jesus with the girl. In the presence of Jesus (the bridegroom, cf. 9:15), one should not mourn, because one should perceive ("see"), as Jesus does, that the dysphoric situation (death) is subtly transformed into a non-dysphoric situation (sleep). In terms of

9:14–17, the mourners do not acknowledge that Jesus' authoritative presence brings something new into a situation and transforms it radically. Even after the miracle, although people recognize the power of Jesus, since "the report of this went through all that district" (9:26), there is no hint that they perceive the newness brought about by his presence.

9:27–31. The Healing of the Two Blind Men

9:29. For the readers, the story of the healing of the two blind men reiterates themes with which they are now familiar. Once again, it is emphasized that Jesus acts according to the faith of the supplicants: "According to your faith be it done to you" (9:29). This statement is similar to Jesus' concluding words to the centurion (8:13). Furthermore, the description of the two blind men and of the way they address Jesus—they follow him and cry, "Have mercy on us, Son of David" (9:27)—suggests to the readers that their faith might be a proper recognition of Jesus' authority. Are they not following him, as the disciples have been called to do (9:9)? Is not their cry a recognition that Jesus' healings are a manifestation of God's mercy (9:13)? Are they not acknowledging the newness of his ministry by greeting him as the "Son of David," that is, as Messiah? At last, it seems that these blind men's faith is the proper acknowledgment of Jesus' authority, a faith even more complete than that of the centurion, since they follow Jesus and acknowledge him as the merciful Son of David.

9:28. But Jesus' response shows that their faith is still exclusively a confidence in Jesus' *power* to heal them: "Do you believe that I am able to do this?" (9:28). And they affirm that it is indeed their faith: "Yes, Lord" (9:28b). Thus Jesus acts according to their "little faith"; he *touches* their eyes, as he touched the leper (8:3), a gesture necessary only when the supplicants' faith is not great enough.

9:30–31. As in the case of the leper to whom Jesus had said, "See that you say nothing to any one" (8:4), he commands the healed blind men: "See that no one knows it" (9:30). In 8:4 we noted that this command created a tension in the text. In 9:30 it is still puzzling for the readers. After a series of comparable miracle stories that do not involve any attempt by Jesus to prevent people from speaking about what happened, why should Jesus abruptly utter this command? Nothing in the story prepares the readers for it.

By describing the healed blind men as disobeying that order (9:31), Matthew sets up a narrative opposition, and thus makes a new point for his readers. In giving this order Jesus is shown to be an authoritative figure. He speaks to them "sternly" (*embrimaomai*, to be indignant), Matthew's way of saying that Jesus strongly emphasized the importance of his command. It expresses Jesus' authority, in contrast to the view of Jesus that the blind men have and that they spread—the view that Jesus has an extraordinary power, a misleading view of Jesus. Indeed, he has extraordinary power. But he also has an authority that these men do not acknowledge; they disobey him. Therefore their report about Jesus, positive as it is, fails to present him as he truly is. Despite their own words, they do not perceive that the fundamental characteristic of his authority is that he is the manifestation of God's mercy. They do not recognize the radical newness of God's manifestation in him.

9:32–34. The Healing of the Dumb Man

This last miracle story in this section of the Gospel is reduced to its bare minimum. "A dumb demoniac was brought to him. And when the demon had been cast out, the dumb man spoke" (9:32–33). Nothing is said about Jesus' interaction with the dumb man. Jesus' name is not even mentioned! Thus Matthew presents it as a typical miracle story which he asks his readers to imagine as being like the preceding ones. Consequently, the point that Matthew makes by setting an opposition between the crowds' and the Pharisees' response (9:33–34) concerns the evaluation not merely of this miracle but of all the preceding miracles.

9:34. The Pharisees' response shows a fundamental misunderstanding of Jesus and of his activity, as is clear from their words: "He casts out demons by the prince of demons" (9:34). This statement contradicts the view that Jesus' power is a divine power, a view that Matthew expects his readers to have in the light of 8:23—9:8. But, as our reading of 8:1—9:34 has progressively shown, the Pharisees misinterpret Jesus and his activity because they raise the wrong question. Actually, their statement shows that they primarily ask themselves a question concerning the nature and origin of Jesus' power. As long as one limits oneself to this kind of question, one cannot understand what is truly characteristic in Jesus and his activity, namely, what is his authority.

9:33. By contrast, the crowds acknowledge what is, for Matthew, the true characteristic of his authority: "Never was anything like this seen in Israel." In other words, Jesus and his activity are radically *new*. Furthermore, this manifestation is new "in Israel," new among God's people (2:6), the people to whom God manifested himself in the past, and to whom Jesus has come (2:20–21) despite their little faith (8:10). Thus, at last, the crowds acknowledge the true characteristic of Jesus' authority that Matthew progressively pointed out in 8:1—9:34. Jesus and his activity are a new manifestation of God in Israel, a manifestation of God and of his holiness in the form of *mercy* (9:13) rather than in the form of *judgment* and of commandments requiring ritual purity. As a manifestation of this new holiness—

mercy—Jesus breaks the old wineskins (9:17) represented by the old manifestations of holiness.

Because he is merciful, Jesus acts according to the little faith found in Israel: he touches the leper and the sick, he eats with tax collectors and sinners, he forgives sins. In so doing, he becomes impure, taking upon himself our infirmities and diseases (8:17) and becoming vulnerable to accusations of blasphemy (9:3). He is the Son of man who "has nowhere to lay his head" (8:20). He cannot but be viewed as unholy by those who adhere to the old manifestations of the Holy. And thus the Pharisees, who cannot but acknowledge his power, have to conclude that it has an unholy origin, namely, the prince of demons. Certainly, Jesus would have the power to come as a judge and to condemn and destroy the sinners that sick people and demoniacs are, as is demonstrated by his stilling of the storm and his destruction of demons. In so doing, he would remain ritually pure and fit to partake in sacrifices. Yet in such a case, he would not carry out God's will. By acting in a merciful way, he does. He makes God's will his own will, despite the cost and the temptation to do otherwise (4:1–11). But by the very fact that he makes God's will his own, he shares in God's authority (cf. 4:11). Acknowledging that he is a *new* manifestation of the Holy among us (cf. 1:23), a manifestation of God's mercy, is thus also acknowledging his authority, a divine authority.

NOTES ON 8:1—9:34

1. Here Matthew's text remains very close to Mark 4:41.

2. By contrast, in Mark 5:1–20 there is a long description of the response of people, including the healed demoniac, to Jesus' deed (Mark 5:14–20), concluded by the positive response of the people to whom the healed demoniac proclaimed what Jesus had done for him (Mark 5:20).

3. Cf. Mark 2:12, where people exclaim, "We never saw anything like this!" a statement not unlike the one in Matt. 9:33, which Matthew takes to be a positive acknowledgment of the extraordinary character of Jesus' deed.

4. Mark 5:42 (and Luke 8:56) reports the "amazement" of the parents.

5. The emphasis on the faith of the person to be healed, as well as the importance of direct dialogue in the miracle stories in Matthew, has been pointed out by Held's redaction-critical study (involving a close comparison of Matthew's text with his sources, Mark and Q). See Held, "Matthew as Interpreter." Beyond these observations, the structural approach allows us to ask what the points (convictions) are that are conveyed by these features.

6. This opposition remains even if Jesus' first statement, 8:7, is read as a question, as is sometimes proposed. In such a case we are dealing with a hypothetical action instead of a potential action. The difference in meaning is at the thematic level: it concerns Jesus' power or ability, a theme used by Matthew to make a point about his authority.

7. Held, "Matthew as Interpreter," 169, 239–41.

8. With the best manuscripts we read in 8:10 "with no one in Israel have I found such faith" rather than "not even in Israel have I found such faith." In addition, this first reading, which excludes more radically the possibility of such a faith in Israel, fits better the points (convictions) expressed in the rest of chapters 8—9.

9. The contrast between the fate of the Gentiles and of "the sons of the kingdom"

is between two *appropriate* retributions (and thus "good" retributions, from the perspective of the judge), even though the fate of the latter is dysphoric (being thrown into outer darkness, weeping, gnashing one's teeth). What would be opposed would be their respective actions, which are *not described* in 8:11–12.

10. With BONNARD, 116. This polemical statement against the Jews is thus the main theme of this passage (i.e., the aspect of the text that the readers will readily accept), yet it is not the main "point" (conviction) that Matthew wants to convey—a point that is new for his readers.

11. Here Matthew does not use the LXX translation which interprets this verse in terms of "sins." See STENDAHL, 106–7; Gundry, *Use of OT*, 109, 111.

12. Several commentators insist that this is the only meaning of this verse. Such is the case of BEARE, 211–12; GUNDRY, 149–50; SCHWEIZER, 217; Held, "Matthew as Interpreter," 259–61.

13. As other commentators interpret. See, e.g., LAGRANGE, 168–69; Dupont, *Béatitudes 3*: 518–19; STRECKER, 66–67.

14. To remove this ambiguity certain manuscripts (followed by RSV) add that these crowds were "great" (that is, numerous).

15. This is further shown by 8:23 in which obeying this order means that "his disciples followed him," as Held notes ("Matthew as Interpreter," 202). So also SCHWEIZER, 219, who asks: "Is this passage then meant to replace the omitted calling of the Twelve (Mark 3:17–19), and be a watershed separation between the ones who follow Jesus and those who do not?"

16. As Judith Middleton suggested to me, it is essential for the study of the Gospel According to Matthew to make a clear distinction between "ideal disciples"—those described in Jesus' teaching—and "actual disciples"—Peter, Andrew, James, and John.

17. BEARE, 214.

18. See Held, "Matthew as Interpreter," 203.

19. See Bornkamm, "Stilling of the Storm," 52–57; and Held, "Matthew as Interpreter," 203–4. Note that the miracle itself does not involve an opposition of actions (the great calm is not expressed by a verb of action).

20. By contrast with Mark 4:35–41 and Luke 8:22–25.

21. The Greek term *potapos* is difficult to render in English. It raises a question about the good or bad "quality" of something or someone, as the Latin *qualis* does. Here it raises a question concerning the euphoric quality of Jesus (as other terms do in 1:21–23).

22. As noted by Bornkamm, "Stilling of the Storm," 56.

23. By contrast with Mark 5:1–10 and Luke 8:26–39.

24. As noted by commentators: e.g., GUNDRY, 160; BONNARD, 122; Held, "Matthew as Interpreter," 174.

25. As is the case in Mark 5:7. See Held, "Matthew as Interpreter," 173–74.

26. BONNARD, 122, notes that it is used in Rev. 9:5; 11:10; 12:2; 14:10; 20:10.

27. By contrast with Mark 2:5 and Luke 5:20 where the faith or lack of faith of the paralytic is not mentioned.

28. As Held shows, this close association of forgiving and healing is brought about by Matthew's radical shortening of Mark 2:1–12 (where they are not as closely associated as in Matthew). Held, "Matthew as Interpreter," 175–78.

29. By contrast with Mark 2:7.

30. With BONNARD, 128.

31. According to rabbinic traditions, "if taxgatherers entered a house (all that is within it) becomes unclean," *Mishnah: Tohoroth* 7:6. As Jonathan Kraus pointed out to me, the Pharisaic rules that are broken are those for eating nonpriestly food in the state of priestly purity. In other words, for the Pharisees, table fellowship had a priestly connotation, a point particularly relevant here in view of 9:13. A sacrifice implied sharing a table with God. Any meal was then conceived of as participating in a sacrificial offering; thus the importance of the "blessings" related to meals (see *Mishnah: Berakoth*).

32. As usual for Matthew, Jesus acts according to the faith of the supplicant.

Matthew describes Jesus' acts or words in the very terms used by the supplicants. See Held, "Matthew as Interpreter," 163–299.

33. As the correlation between these two oppositions shows, it is not that death is nothing else than sleep but that death is transformed into sleep. The same conclusion is reached by BONNARD, 136.

REJECTION AS PART OF JESUS' AND THE DISCIPLES' MINISTRY

THE MAIN THEME

A new section of the Gospel begins with an almost verbatim repetition in 9:35 of the description of Jesus' overall ministry—teaching, preaching, and healing—found in 4:23. The verses that follow (9:36–38) describe Jesus' compassion for the crowds and indicate that other laborers are needed "into [the] harvest." Then Jesus sends the Twelve in mission (10:1–5a) and gives them instructions (10:5b–42). But where does this section end?

If this section was narrative in character—if it was organized according to the unfolding of a plot—it would be concluded by the description of the disciples carrying out their mission and coming back to Jesus with a report on the outcome of what they did. But nowhere in the Gospel do we find any mention that the disciples actually went on mission and came back to Jesus.[1] Thus, from the outset it appears that this section is *not* narrative in character. This should not surprise us. Even though it comprised stories, chapters 8—9 did not unfold according to a narrative plot; it was thematically organized. Similarly, the section beginning with 9:35 is thematically organized. In other words, this section has a pedagogical or didactic purpose. It certainly develops a theme—or cluster of themes—which, in the beginning of the section, is presented as difficult to understand. The end of the section will be found when this cluster of themes will have been fully explained and justified.

In view of 9:35—10:5, there is no doubt that the overall theme of this section is the instruction of the disciples so as to prepare them to carry out their mission. This is directly expressed in the discourse of 10:5b–42, aimed at instructing the disciples (11:1a). The discourse in 13:3–53 also clearly instructs the disciples; it trains them to be scribes for the kingdom of heaven (see 13:52). Perhaps then the section ends with the discourse of 13:1–53. We can also anticipate that the main themes of the section 9:35—13:53 concern characteristics of the disciples' ministry and its relationship to Jesus' ministry. A rapid overview of the entire section allows us to identify a series of units developing three main themes.

1. *The Sending of the Disciples to Crowds Who Are Like Sheep Without a*

Shepherd and Like a Harvest Without Laborers. 9:35—10:5a. This first unit
provides the context for the discourse that Jesus addresses to the disciples
whom he is sending in mission. Two features of this unit are noteworthy.
First, the role of the missionaries is described by two metaphors—shepherd
and harvester—which will prove to be designations respectively for a merciful and a judgmental aspect of their ministry. Second, Jesus gives to the
disciples the authority or power to perform miracles comparable to those
he performed according to chapters 8—9. The disciples' ministry will be
comparable to that of Jesus.

   2. *The Mission of the Disciples. 10:5b–42.* The discourse that begins in
10:5b is clearly delimited. It ends in 10:42, as is indicated in 11:1a: "And
when Jesus had finished instructing his twelve disciples." The first part of
the discourse (10:5b–15) describes the disciples' mission; it involves proclaiming the kingdom (10:7) and healing (10:8) as Jesus does. In other words,
through their mission the disciples should duplicate Jesus' ministry. Although the rest of the discourse (10:16–42) emphasizes that the disciples
should expect to be persecuted, a necessary part of their ministry, it continues to underscore the similarity of the disciples' ministry and that of Jesus
(cf. 10:24–25). In so doing, Matthew refers, for the first time in his Gospel,
to the Passion and the cross (cf. 10:38). So far there has been no mention
of any physical opposition to Jesus' ministry; there has been only one instance of verbal abuse (9:34), and a few doctrinal disputes (9:3, 11), in the
description of an overall successful ministry. Thus one wonders: Why are
the sending of the disciples and this discourse found at this location in the
Gospel?

   Since the chapters that follow describe a growing opposition to Jesus'
ministry, we are able to conclude that Matthew chose to describe opposition
to the disciples' mission before describing similar opposition to Jesus' ministry. We suspect that it is for a pedagogical reason, since Jesus' rejection
and his suffering on the cross are presented in 16:21–23 and elsewhere as
difficult for the disciples (and the readers) to understand. By first showing
that the persecution endured by the disciples (and the readers) has a purpose,
indeed, that it is a necessary part of their mission, Matthew hopes the meaning of the rejection and suffering of Jesus will be more easily understood.

   This suggestion begins to explain the link between the discourse of chapter 10 and the description of the growing opposition to Jesus in chapters
11—12. At this point, the Gospel is not organized narratively, that is, according to the unfolding of Jesus' story, but pedagogically.[2] First, in terms
of the experience that is closely related to his readers, Matthew expresses
what he sees as the main characteristics of the "Christian" ministry—the
ministry of both Christ and his followers. Then he develops these points
regarding Jesus' ministry.

   By contrast with what the readers might have expected after reading the
first nine chapters of the Gospel, such a ministry involves not only success

but also rejection. While it is bringing mercy to those who receive Jesus and his followers (see chaps. 8—9), it brings judgment to those who reject them. It is not merely a shepherd-like ministry (9:36) but also a harvester-like ministry (9:37–38), that is, a ministry that involves separating the "wheat" from the "weeds" (see 13:30, 41–43; cf. also 13:47–50).

On the basis of these preliminary observations on the introductory unit (9:35—10:5a) and the discourse (10:5b–42), we can identify the three themes that are developed in the entire section by way of questions:

1. Why does the ministry of the disciples and of Jesus involve such a judgmental component?

2. This leads to a second question. Why do certain people reject a ministry that involves the proclamation of the kingdom and healings (10:14–15)?

3. Finally, how is the disciples' ministry related to Jesus' ministry and to God's will? What is its goal? Why does it necessarily involve being re-jected and persecuted?

The last parts of the discourse address the questions of the third theme by emphasizing that rejection and persecution have the positive effect of broadening the disciples' mission so that it might reach the Gentiles (10:16–31). Rejection and persecution are thus an integral part of the "Christian" ministry because of the relationship between the disciples, Jesus, and the Father (10:32–42).

3. *Rejection of Jesus' Ministry. 11:1–30.* Chapter 11 further develops the three themes in terms of Jesus' ministry. It provides a first answer to the question: Why are certain people rejecting Jesus' ministry? In brief, they fail to interpret Jesus' deeds in terms of his teaching and preaching, as John (11:1–6) and the crowds do (11:7–19). When Jesus' ministry is rejected, a shepherd-like ministry which should bring about repentance, it becomes a judgment/condemnation for those (cities) who do not repent (11:20–24). The reason for the meekness of Jesus' ministry—it is an easy yoke—is then explained in terms of Jesus' relationship with his Father (11:25–30).

4. *Controversy Over Sabbath Observance. 12:1–21.* The controversies with the Pharisees over sabbath observance further develop the three themes. It is now emphasized that people reject Jesus' ministry because they have an incorrect understanding of God's will and of the way to fulfill it (12:1–8, 9–14). Negatively, this passage also underscores that, even though Jesus' ministry becomes a judgment when it is rejected, it is not a judgment/condemnation as the Pharisees' objections are (12:3, 10). Unfolding the concluding theme of 11:28–30, these controversies provide a concrete il-lustration of how the Pharisees make the day of rest a burden and of how Jesus makes the observance of the sabbath an easy yoke and a light burden. The formula quotation (12:15–21) makes clear that the three characteristics of Jesus' ministry—bringing judgment and justice, meekness and humili-ation because of rejections, and a special relationship with God—are ful-filling Scripture.

5. *Dispute Over the Nature of Jesus' Power and Authority. 12:22–50.* This passage further develops the three themes. A third explanation for the rejection of Jesus' ministry is provided (12:22–29). People reject Jesus because they misconstrue the origin of the power through which he performs his deeds. Ultimately, the reason for such a misunderstanding is a misconception of the relationship between power (deeds) and authority (including the authority of his words). The theme of Jesus' ministry bringing condemnation for those who reject it is further developed in 12:30–37. The meekness of Jesus' ministry—the "sign of the prophet Jonah" which calls people to repent (12:38–42)—is once again evoked. Yet in this passage the need for a voluntary response is emphasized through the example of the queen of the South (12:42), a description of what happens after an exorcism if it is not accompanied by a recognition of God's authority (12:43–45), and the mention that it is those who do the will of the Father who are Jesus' brother, sister, and mother (12:46–50).

6. *Teaching the Crowds in Parables. 13:1–53.* Jesus' discourse involves both a teaching to the crowds (13:3b–9, 24–35) and instructions for the disciples (13:10–23, 36–52). It emphasizes that the crowds cannot understand the mysteries of the kingdom (13:10–17) expressed in parables, as they do not understand Jesus' deeds and reject them. The crowds nevertheless should be taught in parables that reveal to them "what has been hidden since the foundation of the world" (13:35), a teaching they can receive—and that should not be confused with the mysteries of the kingdom. Why do people reject Jesus' and the disciples' ministry (their deeds and their teaching of the mysteries of the kingdom)? Because they have not truly received the basic teaching regarding things hidden from the foundation of the world. This is what the proclamation of the kingdom in parables addressed *to the crowds* aims at doing. The theme of the judgment/harvest is also developed (13:30, 39–43, 49–50), but it is now emphasized that disciples should not view their ministry as involving the condemnation of others. Their ministry involves a judgmental aspect (cf. 10:14–15), but it is a secondary effect of their positive, shepherd-like, ministry—when this ministry is rejected. Finally, the theme of the relationship between the disciples' ministry and Jesus' ministry is further specified. In fact, in his ministry and teaching Jesus is training the disciples to become scribes for the kingdom (13:52).

THE SENDING OF THE DISCIPLES
TO THE CROWDS:
MATTHEW'S CONVICTIONS IN 9:35—10:5a

The introductory unit does not include any narrative opposition. It is a thematic passage in which Matthew describes in terms of his readers' old knowledge the situation that led to the sending of the Twelve in mission. Nevertheless, such thematic passages express Matthew's convictions. These convictions are signaled by tensions in the text—what would be surprising for the readers. By identifying these tensions, we simultaneously identify the points (convictions) that Matthew expects his readers to find problematic because they are new for them.

The first verse, 9:35, is not a surprise for the readers, since it is the repetition of 4:23. Similarly, Matthew does not expect his readers to be surprised by 10:1, which states that Jesus gives to the disciples the power to cast out unclean spirits and to heal, and by 10:2–5a, which simply lists the names of the apostles sent in mission.

9:36–38. A first tension is created by the juxtaposition of the metaphor of the "harassed and helpless" crowds which are "like sheep without a shepherd" (cf. Num. 27:17 and 1 Kings 22:17) with the metaphor of the plentiful harvest with few laborers. According to the first metaphor, the crowds are described as lacking "a shepherd," that is, a single person who could be the leader of the people (like Joshua in Num. 27:17–18 or a king in 1 Kings 22:17); this leader would have the positive role of leading the people out of its desolate situation. The ministry or mission of the shepherd is one of "mercy," as is also expressed by the mention that Jesus "had compassion for" the crowds (9:36). By contrast, according to the second metaphor, several persons are needed, not just one person: "laborers," sent by the "Lord of the harvest." Furthermore, the laborers' role is ambiguous, rather than clearly positive, since the harvest is a traditional symbol for the eschatological judgment (cf. 13:24–30)[3] which involves condemnation and destruction for the "weeds" and blessing for the "wheat."

The juxtaposition of these two metaphorical statements prevents the readers from making a simple interpretation. The sheep and the harvest might indeed be the people of Israel, the Jewish crowds,[4] since Jesus' ministry takes place in their cities and villages where he preaches in *synagogues* (9:35). But what will be the predominant role? The positive role of a shepherd? Or the judgmental role of the harvesters? What will be the purpose of the disciples' mission? Will it be a shepherd-like mission, a positive mission? Or will it bring judgment and condemnation upon people?

10:1, 2–4. Only one thing is clear: the disciples' mission will be like that of Jesus. Jesus gives them power or authority "over unclean spirits, to cast them out, and to heal every disease and every infirmity" (10:1). In other words, their mission will be the same as Jesus' ministry described in chapters 8—9. This is further expressed in the charge found at the beginning of the discourse (10:7–8, a thematic passage), which specifies that they will also have to preach, "saying, 'The kingdom of heaven is at hand'" (10:7; cf. 3:2 and 4:17). The only part of Jesus' ministry that they are not yet (cf. 28:20) supposed to duplicate is his teaching.

In brief, the disciples' mission and Jesus' ministry are almost fully identified. Consequently, what was said about Jesus' ministry also applies to the disciples' ministry, and what will be said about the disciples' mission also applies to Jesus' ministry.[5] We conclude that even though it seems that 9:35—10:5a merely provides a context for the disciples' mission, it now appears to provide a context for Jesus' own ministry, as described in 11:1—13:53. Yet the question remains: Is this mission merely the positive mission of a shepherd, as Jesus' ministry was in chapters 8—9? Or does it also bring judgment and condemnation?

A second tension in the text is related to these issues: Why are the "disciples" (10:1) suddenly called "apostles" (10:2)? Could it be that these two designations are related to a twofold mission? But in which sense?[6] We can only conclude that this tension suggests that their mission is complex. Furthermore, part of the list of disciples/apostles (10:2–4) is new for the readers; only the names of Simon Peter, Andrew, James, John (see 4:18–22), and Matthew (9:9) had been previously mentioned. Moreover, the mention of "Judas Iscariot, who betrayed him," introduces a first direct allusion to the Passion.

These tensions and the questions they raise force the readers to recognize the ambivalence of the theme of this section: the character of Jesus' and the disciples' ministry. The purpose of this ministry is to meet the needs created by the present situation of "crowds." But the needs of the crowds are described in two apparently contradictory ways. The crowds are harassed and helpless, in need of a shepherd-like mission through which, it is hoped, they will receive both sustenance and guidance. The crowds are also a "harvest" in need of laborers who will separate the "wheat" from the "weeds," and thus in need of judgment. How can the disciples' ministry and Jesus' ministry have this twofold purpose and character and still be a coherent and meaningful ministry? And how is this twofold ministry related to the Passion? Such are the questions Matthew will progressively address in the following passages.

THE MISSION OF THE DISCIPLES:
MATTHEW'S CONVICTIONS IN 10:5b—42

When the beginning and the end of this second discourse are compared, its main theme, the mission of the disciples/apostles, appears in a somewhat surprising light for the readers. Both in 10:5b–13a and 10:40–42, we find a positive description of the mission and of the blessings that those who receive the disciples will have. But beginning with 10:13b until 10:39 the discourse focuses upon the rejection, indeed the persecution, of the disciples; their mission involves taking their cross (cf. 10:38). For the readers who have previously encountered a description of Jesus' ministry relatively free of confrontation, this is most surprising. After the questions raised by 9:35—10:5a, one suspects that there is a relation between the positive and negative attitudes toward the mission of the disciples (a mission that duplicates Jesus' ministry as described in the preceding chapters) and the "shepherd" and "judgment" roles that the disciples should have.

Even though this second discourse does not have the breadth of the Sermon on the Mount, it too is carefully organized by Matthew so as to express a series of new points (convictions).[7] It involves three main parts.

1. *10:5b–15. The Mission of the Twelve to "the Lost Sheep of the House of Israel."* The Twelve are charged to take the initiative *to go* to Israel. This mission has as its goal both the proclamation of the kingdom (in words) and the manifestation of the kingdom in concrete behavior (the way in which the Twelve carry out their mission). The hoped-for effect of this mission is that Israel will no longer be "harassed and helpless, like sheep without a shepherd." This shepherd-like mission is nevertheless a judgment or condemnation for those who are not "worthy," for those who reject the disciples and their mission.

2. *10:16–31. Persecution of the Disciples and Their "Mission" to the Gentiles.* The Jews, then the Gentiles, will persecute the disciples, who are "sheep in the midst of wolves." Yet it soon appears that being submitted to persecutions is not merely negative.[8] In fact, it is an integral part of the mission of the disciples; as a consequence of the persecutions by Jews, the disciples' mission is extended to reach Gentiles. But this mission to the Gentiles is not the simple repetition of the mission to the Jews with a new audience. To begin with, they do not take the initiative to go to the Gentiles; they are "dragged" before their authorities (10:18). As in the previous case, this mission is carried out both through a proclamation and through a concrete behavior. But rather than directly proclaiming the kingdom, the Twelve are called to witness (10:18–20). In other words, their mission has a different character.

3. *10:32–42. Relationship of the Disciples' Mission to Jesus' Mission.* This concluding part of the discourse, addressed to "every one," specifies the relationship between Jesus and the disciples. The disciples are those who "acknowledge" the authority of Jesus, the eschatological judge (10:32–33). The persecutions of the disciples (10:16–31) are shown to be a direct consequence of their association with Jesus' own mission (10:34–39). Then, in 10:40–42, the more positive aspect of the disciples' mission, bringing blessings for those who receive them (10:5b–15), is related to the blessings brought about by Jesus himself. In this way, the mission of the disciples is shown to be both similar and subordinated to that of Jesus.

Simultaneously, the theme of Jesus' suffering and death is implicitly introduced. The presentation of persecution as an integral part of the disciples' mission is also a first explanation of the rejection, suffering, and death of Jesus described in the chapters that follow. In addition to preaching the kingdom, teaching, and healing, Jesus' ministry involves suffering and being rejected. As the persecution of the disciples is a necessary part of their mission, so the rejection of Jesus, his suffering, and his death are a necessary part of what he came for (10:34). This discourse, as we will see, gives more than information about the nature of the disciples' mission; it also teaches us about Jesus' own vocation and the goal of his ministry.[9]

10:5b–15. The Mission to the Lost Sheep of Israel

10:5b–6. The opening statements of the discourse set up a narrative op-position; the disciples should go "to the lost sheep of the house of Israel," not to the Gentiles and the Samaritans. The Twelve's mission is to be ex-clusively directed to the house of Israel. But why?[10]

One could be tempted to say that the mission to Israel is appropriate ("fitting," 3:15) for the present time—the time of Jesus' ministry—while the mission to the Gentiles will be appropriate only after the resurrection (28:19). Yet these verses do not raise any issue concerning time, and when the text does so in 10:23 it will be in order to express that the mission to Israel will not be finished "before the Son of man comes."[11] Furthermore, as is expressed in 10:16–31, the mission to the Gentiles will take place almost simultaneously with the mission to Israel. Rather, the point that Matthew makes through this opposition concerns the Twelve's vocation as it relates to Israel, and their qualifications for carrying out this vocation. At first, what the Twelve have to offer in their mission is appropriate for "the lost sheep" of Israel but not appropriate for the Gentiles and the Samaritans— the mission to the Gentiles will require different qualifications that they do not yet have, namely, persecution. Thus the question becomes: According to the first part of the discourse, what do the Twelve have to offer that Israel does not have and needs?

We first notice that the Twelve are called "sheep" in 10:16. Thus they share something with the "lost sheep" of Israel. *They are sent to their own kind.* But they themselves are not "lost" sheep which are "harassed and helpless" and "without a shepherd" (9:36). On the contrary, they are "dis-ciples" to whom Jesus "gave" what they need for their mission, namely, the power to cast out demons and to heal (10:1). Consequently, being lost, harassed, helpless, and without a shepherd means in part being without someone who provides what one needs, that is, what one needs for carrying out one's vocation. Furthermore, the Twelve are "apostles" (10:2) sent forth by Jesus (10:5a), or laborers sent into ("cast out into") the harvest by the Lord of the harvest (9:38). The Twelve have a sense of direction, a goal, a specific vocation that they have received from Jesus or the Lord, while the sheep without a shepherd are without a leader (cf. Num. 27:17; 1 Kings 22:17) and thus are "lying down helpless" (*errimmenoi*, 9:36), without a sense of direction and thus without a proper vocation.

In this light, it appears that the Twelve are sent to Israel (and its twelve tribes?) because, by contrast with the Gentiles and the Samaritans, Israel is the chosen people, a people chosen for a special vocation.[12] But they are harassed, helpless, lost, because no one is there to guide them, to show them the way to go, to point them in the right direction. They have lost sight of the goal and purpose of their election; they do not know (any longer) their vocation. Simultaneously, they are deprived ("lost" and "harassed") because there is no one to give them what they need in order to carry out this vocation.

10:7–8. The Twelve's mission, which should meet the need of "the lost sheep of the house of Israel," involves two aspects. First, the Twelve are charged to proclaim to them, "The kingdom of heaven is at hand" (10:7). This proclamation has the effect of putting before "the lost sheep" what should be the ultimate goal of their lives, the ultimate blessing they should seek. "The kingdom of heaven" is indeed that toward which all the life of the chosen should be directed, as we have noted regarding Jesus' own proclamation of the kingdom (4:17), the beatitudes (5:1–10), and the exhortation to "seek first [the] kingdom" (6:33). The Jewish crowds, the sheep "lying down helpless" without a shepherd, are precisely people who do not seek the kingdom and therefore do not have a true sense of direction. The proclamation of the kingdom, it is hoped, will allow them to (re)discover what is the true ultimate goal of their lives, the kingdom. The lost sheep, who had been chosen for a special vocation, would then rediscover the goal of their vocation and would be called to carry it out. For Matthew, the proclamation of the kingdom is also a call to follow Jesus, a call to carry out a vocation of religious leadership (being "fishers of men"; see 4:17 in relation to 4:18–22). The proclamation of the kingdom should give to Israel the sense of direction it has lost, so that it might again carry its vocation for the benefit of the nations (Gentiles).

In addition, the Twelve are to "heal the sick, raise the dead, cleanse lepers, cast out demons" (10:8) as Jesus did according to chapters 8—9. In other words, they are to meet the needs of the "harassed" and "lost" (miserable, ruined, destroyed) sheep. As long as they are sick, lying dead, impure and thus outcast, or possessed by demons, they cannot carry out the vocation that the proclamation of the kingdom should have allowed them to (re)discover.

10:9–10. By means of a second narrative opposition, Matthew further underscores that the sheep *with* a shepherd—namely, the Twelve, and by implication the Jewish crowds after they have benefited from the mission of the Twelve—will receive all they need in order to carry out their vocation. The Twelve should not take anything (money, additional clothing) when going in mission, but trust that they will receive what they need for their sustenance (10:9–10). By taking what they need or by demanding rewards (wages) from those to whom they are sent (10:8b), they would show that they are "without a shepherd," without someone who provides for their needs.[13] They would be people anxious about their livelihood (food, drink, clothes, 6:25). Their life would be oriented by concern for sustenance instead of being oriented toward the kingdom. But as disciples sent by Jesus, they have a shepherd and thus should not be anxious (cf. also 10:19ff.). They have received freely (10:8b) all they need in order to carry out their vocation (10:1), and they can trust that they will continue to receive all they need. They are "worthy of [their] sustenance" (10:10b, au.) precisely because they have been sent by the Lord of the harvest. In fact, their being sent demonstrates that they themselves have received the message of the kingdom. Thus, this behavior is an integral part of their mission. It demonstrates and manifests the kingdom that they preach. It shows that their lives are totally oriented toward the kingdom as the ultimate blessing and that, as such, they are worthy of their sustenance. It shows that they have a shepherd, a Father, who provides what they need. In brief, their way of life demonstrates the trustworthiness of their proclamation of the kingdom.

10:11–14. Through a third narrative opposition Matthew specifies that the mission of the Twelve will have mixed results. Certain people or houses are "worthy" (10:11, 13) because they receive the Twelve and listen to their words (10:14); in such a case, the disciples should "let [their] peace come" upon these people and these houses. But when people are "not worthy," that is, do not receive the Twelve and do not listen to their message, they should "let [their] peace return to [them]" and "shake off the dust from [their] feet as [they] leave" (10:14), as a Jew does when leaving a pagan country and reentering the Holy Land.[14]

Through this complex opposition Matthew makes two interrelated points. First, he expresses that Israel will divide itself into two groups according to the response people give to the mission of the Twelve. Some will show themselves to be worthy because they receive the message of the kingdom—the only message the Twelve are charged to proclaim (10:7). They are people who redirect their life toward the only true goal, the kingdom. As such, they have a status similar to that of the Twelve; they are "worthy," as the Twelve are (10:10); they are no longer without a shepherd. The peace given to them by the Twelve remains with them; they are no longer harassed and lost sheep. But other people or houses of Israel show themselves to be "not worthy"; in fact, they show themselves to be like Gentiles: the Twelve shake off the dust from their feet when leaving them.

10:15. It then appears, and this is the second point, that the mission of the Twelve is simultaneously a shepherd-like mission—a positive mission, providing what the lost sheep need—and a judgmental mission—as laborers in the harvest (9:38). Indeed, they bring the good news of the kingdom. To the sheep that are lying down helpless without any true goal for their life, they show the ultimate blessing worth pursuing both by their behavior and by their words. This mission is in itself a true blessing; as a result of it, the lost sheep receive the peace they lack. But for those who do not receive the Twelve and their message, this mission becomes judgment. Those who are "not worthy" are separated from the "worthy." They condemn themselves, and indeed they will be treated more harshly "on the day of the judgment" than Sodom and Gomorrah (10:15). Clearly, the mission of mercy—the healings and exorcisms that the Twelve perform (10:8) as Jesus did (8:1—9:34) and the proclamation of the kingdom by the disciples (10:7) and Jesus (4:17, 23)—is not a mission proclaiming condemnation and bringing destruction, as the fire of the eschatological judgment will. But when people respond negatively to this merciful mission and its call to seek the kingdom, they condemn themselves.

10:16–31. Persecution of the Disciples and Their "Mission" to the Gentiles

At first, the sayings in this second part of the discourse seem loosely related to each other. The theme of 10:18–20 is clearly the persecution of the disciples by the Jews and the Gentile authorities. But why is it followed by a saying regarding hatred in the family (10:21), then by one regarding universal hatred (10:22), although the text returns in the following verses to the theme of persecution in the context of a mission to Israel (10:22b–23)? Similarly, the comparison of the fates of the disciples and of their master is somewhat surprising, since the master is not described as being under life-threatening persecution—he is merely called "Beelzebul" (10:24–25). And it is only after two sayings regarding what is hidden and will be revealed (10:26–27), which seem to be artificially tied to the main theme by the exhortation "Have no fear of them," that we find once again the theme of persecution in a court of (Gentile) authorities (10:28–33).

These tensions in the text make it clear that this passage does not merely aim at warning the disciples that persecutions can be expected (10:16–17, 23) and at exhorting them to endure until the end with the confidence to receive present (10:19) and future (10:22, 32) blessings and rewards. In fact, Matthew expects his readers to be aware that persecutions are part of the disciples' lot. Beyond this, by stringing together all these sayings, Matthew makes a series of points (convictions) regarding persecution. Being persecuted is, in fact, being in "mission," witnessing to the Gentiles and acknowledging Jesus before them, as is expressed at the beginning (10:18) and end (10:32) of this unit.[15] Consequently, as the oppositions show, the exhortations express how to behave so as to be saved (10:22) and be blessed (10:32) and also how to behave so as to "bear testimony" before the Gentiles (10:18) and thus how to be a blessing for the Gentiles.[16]

10:16–18. Here, without narrative opposition, Matthew describes the persecutions that the disciples will endure until the end (10:22)—in terms of his readers' expectations and of their knowledge of what they already read in the Gospel (esp. 7:15).[17] Matthew presupposes that his readers are aware that the lot of disciples, and of the church, involves persecutions (by the Jews).

When carrying out their mission, the disciples should expect to be persecuted, since they are sent "as sheep in the midst of wolves" (10:16). The Jews who are not worthy, which they show by not receiving the disciples and their words (10:14), are condemned by the disciples' mission, and, so to speak, lose their status as "sheep" and become "wolves."[18] Instead of joining the disciples in pursuing their true vocation as chosen people, and thus as "prophets" who will bring about the glorification of God (cf. 5:11–16), they are false prophets, wolves in sheep's clothing (7:15) that are dangerous to the true sheep. Thus the disciples ought to be alert and do everything they can to avoid falling prey to them. They should be "wise as serpents and innocent as doves" (10:16, where "innocent" means "pure," "unmixed" in a sense comparable to being "sound" in 6:22–23) and flee from one town to the next (10:23). Yet they will not be able to escape persecution; they will be delivered to the Sanhedrin and flogged in their synagogues (10:17).[19]

In the context of these persecutions by the Jews, the disciples "will be dragged before governors and kings for my sake, to bear testimony before them and the Gentiles" (10:18). In other words, there is a positive consequence to the rejection and persecution of the disciples by the Jews.[20] The mission of the disciples, limited to the "lost sheep of the house of Israel," is extended to the Gentiles as a result of the persecution by the Jews. Ironically and paradoxically the Jews as "wolves" contribute to the fulfillment of what should have been their true vocation (see 5:16)—they reject their vocation and persecute the disciples. When the disciples are dragged by the Jews before governors and kings, they are put in a position to witness to the Gentiles (10:18).

10:19–20. Witnessing to the Gentiles does not involve simply repeating the message about the kingdom they were charged to deliver to the Jews.[21] If this were the case, they would know what to say; but the text underscores that they do not know (10:19) and that the appropriate message will be given to them by the Spirit of their Father (10:20). The "mission" to the Gentiles is to be different from the mission to Israel,[22] because the Gentiles do not have the same needs as Israel. Far from being "harassed and helpless" and "without a shepherd," as the Israelite crowds are, the Gentiles are represented by their "governors" and "kings." Consequently, it appears that the major problem with the Gentiles is that they have a clearly defined purpose for their lives (since they have leaders), but a wrong one; that they have a sense of security provided by their institutions, but a wrong one;

that they acknowledge authorities, but wrong ones. Their needs are therefore different from the needs of the "lost sheep of the house of Israel." A proclamation of the kingdom to the Gentiles would miss the mark. Witnessing to the Gentiles needs to take place as a result of the persecution of the disciples, as Matthew expresses through a new series of narrative oppositions.

In 10:19–20 the text opposes the disciples as speaking while inspired by the Spirit and (false) disciples speaking on their own, that is, speaking their own words. In the same way that the disciples should not be anxious about physical sustenance (10:9–10; cf. 6:25–34), so they should not be anxious when speaking and witnessing before governors, kings, and Gentiles. Both the ability to speak and the content of their speech will be given to them by the Spirit of their Father. Being disciples involves knowing and trusting that *all* that they need will be provided for them. In this situation what they need is provided in the form of *the Spirit* of their Father. Here, for Matthew, the gift of the Spirit is the gift of the ability to speak with authority (the power to convince) and the gift of a message fitting the circumstances; it is the Spirit of their Father who will speak through them (10:20).

When they are dragged before the Gentile courts, the disciples should not be anxious about how they are to speak and what they are to say. The exhortation not to be anxious is not to be understood merely as soothing words for disciples afraid of persecution. It is also a charge to adopt a certain behavior which is an integral part of bearing testimony before the Gentiles, a behavior that demonstrates that they are children of their Father. Before governors and kings they bear witness to a higher authority; they bear witness to the kingship of their Father in heaven. By being anxious they would contradict their own verbal testimony.

In addition, by being anxious they would demonstrate that they are concerned about their own livelihood and that their words are efforts to avoid condemnation. They would show that it is for their own sake that they are before the Gentile authorities. By not being anxious about their own fate, they demonstrate that it is for Jesus' sake that they are before the Gentile authorities. This is already bearing testimony before the Gentiles. Furthermore, God, the disciples' Father, provides them with what they need, his Spirit (10:20). He takes care of them (see also 10:29–31); in brief, he is the true source of *security*. By being able to speak without fear, they manifest that their Father does indeed provide them with what they need "in that hour" (10:19).

10:21–23. These verses confirm the preceding observations. The opposition of being saved (by God, 10:22) and of perishing (at the hand of family members, 10:21) expresses a similar point in terms of family relationship. The disciples who will abide until the end—which is not far in the future, since it will happen before they complete their mission, 10:23—are those who put their trust in their Father instead of in family relationships. The family could be viewed as providing security (see 8:21–22), but for those who live for the sake of Jesus ("for my name's sake," 10:22), the family can no longer be viewed in this way. "Brother will deliver up brother to death, and the father his child . . . " (10:21). In other words, by being disciples, by living for the kingdom (cf. 10:7), people do gain the security provided by their Father in heaven and receive all they need; "theirs is the kingdom" (5:3, 10). But simultaneously, they lose all the security provided by human relationships—they are hated by those from whom they could have received security, namely, their family. Consequently, they can no longer live in the human realm characterized by its providers of security— here, the family, with a human father as its head, and, in 10:18–20, the governors and kings. They belong to, and live in, another realm charac- terized by another provider of security, namely, the Father in heaven; they live in the realm of the kingdom *of heaven* by contrast with the realm of human kingdoms, the human realm.

A last remark. The reference to the coming of the Son of man at the end of time in 10:23 is surprising for the readers. So far, they have encountered this title only in contexts associating it with Jesus' present ministry (8:20; 9:6). Consequently, this verse raises expectations regarding Jesus' escha- tological role, a theme to be developed in 10:32–33.

10:24–25. The preceding point—those who belong to the kingdom can expect hatred from all (10:22) and the loss of the security provided by human relationships—is now thematically expressed in terms of the readers' old knowledge. In the process a tension appears: the persecution of the disciples, including being physically dragged before Jewish and Gentile courts, is presented as comparable to verbal abuses of Jesus. So far in the Gospel the readers have encountered very little opposition to Jesus' ministry except for the comment of the Pharisees that "he casts out demons by the prince of demons" (9:34; cf. 12:24), which summarizes their negative evaluation of Jesus (9:3, 11). The comparison of Jesus' fate with the life-threatening per- secution suffered by the disciples alludes to the Passion and the cross (see also 10:4 and 10:38) and explains why the disciples can expect persecution. It also means that the points made regarding the disciples' persecution—it is a necessary part of their mission to the Gentiles—also applies to Jesus. The disciples duplicate Jesus' ministry not only through their preaching and healing (10:7–8) but also through the persecution to which they are sub- mitted. Consequently, the description of their rejection and persecution in this chapter is a first explanation of the reason and purpose of Jesus' own suffering.

Furthermore, disciple and teacher, servant and master (or Lord) belong together; they belong to the same realm, the realm of the kingdom, char- acterized by its specific sources of security and authority. Those who belong to the kingdom can expect hatred from "all" (10:22), as is already the case for the teacher and master/Lord (10:25) who called them to join him in his "household," in the realm of the kingdom. By being persecuted, they show themselves to be disciples of their teacher and Lord. This thematic restatement of the preceding point introduces another theme: the structure of authority and power. For disciples in the realm of the kingdom, their teacher or Lord is the true center of authority and power.

10:26–30. The preceding theme becomes the main point of these verses which oppose fear of those who persecute the disciples (10:26, 28a, 31) *and* fear of God (10:28b).

A first reason for not fearing persecutors is given in 10:26–27. These sayings about the hidden things that will be revealed[23] take a specific meaning from the fact that they are framed by exhortations not to fear persecutors (10:26a, 28). On the one hand, as 10:27 shows, they express what the disciples should not be afraid of doing: they should "utter in the light" and "proclaim upon the housetops" what Jesus told them "in the dark" or "whispered" to them. In brief, they should not be afraid of pursuing their mission,[24] which consists in proclaiming the kingdom (10:7) and witnessing, that is, showing that they act for Jesus' sake (10:18, 22), as will be underscored in 10:32–33. On the other hand, these sayings indicate that the persecutors do not know what the disciples have been told by Jesus (10:27). What is "covered" and "hidden" has not yet been revealed (10:26) to the persecutors: they do not yet know the message about the kingdom revealed by Jesus to the disciples. Thus they understand (misunderstand) everything in terms of the human realm instead of the realm of the kingdom. By fearing their persecutors, the disciples would show that they have the same misunderstanding as their persecutors. They would show that they do not believe that the vision of life revealed to their small group—a view of life in terms of the kingdom—will be shown to be the right one.

This is further expressed in 10:28–31, where it becomes clear that Matthew's main point concerns the realms over which two different authorities are exerted. Human authorities who persecute the disciples have only the power to kill the body (10:28a); the realm of human authorities is limited to the body. By contrast, God has the power to destroy both "body and soul" (10:28b). God's realm of authority, his "kingdom," includes therefore both body and soul.

But what do the terms "body" and "*psychē*" (RSV: "soul") mean? In 6:25 we noted that they are deliberately used in an ambiguous way to denote both an incorrect understanding of life and a true understanding of life. Here, we find the same kind of ambiguity reflecting the misunderstanding of life that the persecutors and those who fear them have because they do not view life in terms of the kingdom. Those who fear human authorities have an understanding of life limited to its physical dimension, the body.

By contrast, those who do not fear human authorities (and fear divine authority) have an understanding of life that includes both body and *psychē*. Disciples who have a life oriented toward the kingdom have this true understanding of life. Life encompasses both physical existence and participation in the kingdom, now and in the future.[25] It is "life as person" (*sōma*, "body," can also mean "person") perceived in terms of the ultimate blessing, the (future) kingdom toward which the disciples go. It is the "life as person in the kingdom" to which the disciples already belong. What they should fear is, therefore, the ultimate destruction of both body and *psychē*, the destruction in the Gehenna (10:28) of this "life as person in the kingdom."

Believing in the kingdom, trusting in the validity of what has been revealed to them by Jesus (10:26–27), means that the disciples should trust in the power of their Father (his kingship). Nothing that happens to the sparrows and to the hairs of their heads is beyond God's control (10:29–31). How much more so in the case of the disciples. The disciples, God's children, can therefore trust that nothing will happen to them that is not in accordance with the will of their Father. Thus, while persecutors are a real threat from whom they should seek to escape (10:16, 23), they can trust that their Father will take care of them (cf. 10:9–10).

Consequently, the disciples should not fear human authorities; rather, they should fear the One who has power over their "life as person in the kingdom" (body and *psychē*) and can exclude them from the ultimate blessing, the kingdom. Yet fearing God has also a positive connotation which remains here, even though it is not emphasized. The disciples should also fear God in the sense of submitting to his authority. While the realm of the kingdom involves a specific source of security, the Father as provider, it is also characterized by a specific center of authority to which they submit and which they "acknowledge" before other people by not fearing their persecutors.

In brief, by not being anxious about what they will say, and by not fearing those who kill the body but cannot kill the "soul," the disciples bear witness to several aspects of the realm of the kingdom to which they belong. They bear witness to their Father in heaven, who takes care of their needs; to his power and authority; to the fact that life in the realm of the kingdom is more than physical life since it extends to eternal blessings. In so doing, they challenge the Gentiles' view of life—understood exclusively in terms of the human realm. They make manifest before them what was hidden and whispered to them: the good news of the kingdom.

10:32–42. The Relationship Between Jesus' Mission and the Disciples' Mission

In 10:32 the style of the discourse changes. As was the case with the beginning and conclusion of the Sermon on the Mount (5:3–10; 7:21–27), the last section of this discourse is no longer addressed merely to "you," the Twelve disciples, but also to "every one who. . . ." This teaching is not merely for a few specially chosen disciples but for whoever (in the crowd, among the readers) will want to be a disciple. As this last section develops and reiterates points made earlier in the discourse, the relationship between Jesus and disciples and between their respective missions and vocations is specified.

10:32–33. The opposition concerning acknowledging or not acknowledging Jesus before human beings (i.e., before the court, 10:32–33) indicates that the disciples are those who not only submit to God's authority but also submit to Jesus' authority and "acknowledge" it before other people. This is what the disciples do when they demonstrate and express by their words that they carry out their mission for Jesus' sake (10:18) or in his name (cf. 10:22). They acknowledge before other people that they have been sent by Jesus (10:5) as well as by the Lord of the harvest (9:38).

In 10:32–33 this also means that Jesus is in a special position of authority in the realm of the kingdom. He is the one who will acknowledge the faithful disciples, and deny the unfaithful disciples, before the Father in heaven; he will decide their fate regarding their participation in the kingdom. He will be the eschatological judge. The structure of authority in the realm of the kingdom appears. Jesus, the eschatological judge, is subordinated to the Father (the Lord of the harvest, 9:38), and the disciples must acknowledge before human beings not only their Father in heaven (as they do by showing their trust in his power) but also Jesus, who gave them the power to heal and the message about the kingdom (10:1, 7) that he sent them to proclaim and manifest.

10:34–36. By contrast with chapters 3—9—in which Jesus was primarily portrayed as having the positive vocation of proclaiming the kingdom and of calling disciples, of healing the sick, and of teaching (9:35)—in 10:32–33 Jesus has been presented as the eschatological judge. Jesus has both a positive, merciful vocation and a judgmental vocation, as the disciples' mission is both positive and judgmental (10:5–15). This latter point is underscored in 10:34–36 by means of an opposition.

In 10:34, the text opposes Jesus who did not come to bring peace on earth but came to bring a sword. Jesus' vocation is to bring the good news of the kingdom and its blessing (9:35; cf. 4:23; 5:3–10). Yet this message is bringing not peace but dissension and, more specifically, dissension in the family (10:35–36). The text reads: "Do not think that I have come to bring peace *on earth*." In other words, this negative role of Jesus—bringing dissension, a sword—is qualified as pertaining to a specific realm, "earth," that is, to the human realm as contrasted with the realm of the kingdom. It is not excluded that Jesus brings peace in the realm of the kingdom, that is, to those who belong to this realm and are worthy of it. In fact, the parallelism between Jesus' mission and the disciples' mission (cf. 10:24–25) suggests it. In the same way that the disciples engender by their mission persecutions by the Jews and the Gentiles (10:16–20) and by their family members (10:21), so Jesus brings dissension "on earth," and especially in the family. Yet the disciples' mission involves bringing "peace" to those who are "worthy" (10:11–13), to those who receive them and their words and thus have accepted participation in the realm of the kingdom. But they do not bring peace ("let your peace return to you," 10:13) to those who do not receive them and their words and thus remain in the human realm ("on earth"). Similarly, for those who remain in the human realm, with its (wrong) view of the source of security and its center of power and authority, Jesus is a source of dissension, a sword.

10:37–39. The next two oppositions further underscore this point. In 10:37–38, the text opposes following Jesus to loving father, mother, son, or daughter more than Jesus. As is repeated three times, this is a matter of worthiness. Being worthy of Jesus is similar, if not identical, to being worthy in the context of the disciples' mission (10:11–13), that is, to being worthy of the kingdom. This means belonging to the realm of the kingdom. But now, when one loves a family member more than Jesus, one demonstrates that one lives according to the (wrong) system of values of the human realm; one still views the family as a source of security instead of placing one's trust in Jesus and in the Father in heaven. Such an attitude demonstrates that one does not belong to the realm of the kingdom, that one is not worthy of Jesus. By contrast, following Jesus involves taking one's cross (10:38)—that is, in terms of what precedes, accepting the carrying out of a mission (to the Jews) which is completed only when one is persecuted and when one witnesses (to the Gentiles) by showing that even in such situations one trusts in the Father in heaven. Following Jesus and carrying one's cross entail, therefore, participating in the realm of the kingdom with the proper view of who provides security. It also entails having the proper view of who has authority and power, namely, the Father in heaven and Jesus.

The complex opposition found in 10:39, about finding one's life (*psychē*) and losing it, underscores once again that Matthew's main point concerns the different perspectives that characterize the two realms to which one can belong. This is expressed by using the term *psychē* with an ambivalent meaning. In the phrase "he who finds his *psychē*" it is "life" as understood in the perspective of the human realm. But "it" in the phrase "will lose it" refers to "life" as understood from the perspective of the realm of the kingdom. The same comments apply to the second part of the verse.

This verse is not a strictly paradoxical statement; the two parts are not exactly parallel. Only when one loses one's life for Jesus' sake will one find it. In other words, "life" understood from the perspective of the realm of the kingdom is also necessarily a life for Jesus' sake. As the reader has seen (see 10:1, 5, 16, 18, 24–25, 26–27, 32–33, 37–38), the disciples participate in the realm of the kingdom only because they submit to the authority of Jesus, their teacher and Lord who sent them in mission, and when they acknowledge him before other people.

10:40–42. These concluding verses of the discourse do not include any opposition; they restate what the readers should have already concluded. First, since the disciples are sent by Jesus and act for his sake, those who receive them also receive Jesus (10:40a). It follows that by receiving Jesus they also receive the One who sent him, his Father (10:40b). Such is the case of the people who are "worthy" in that they receive the disciples and *listen to their words* (10:13–14), that is, acknowledge the authority of their proclamation of the kingdom. In other words, receiving the disciples, and thus Jesus and God, is acknowledging their authority, the structure of authority of the kingdom.

Second, receiving the disciples for what they are is also putting oneself to the benefit of the promises of the kingdom; it is participating in the realm of the kingdom where one can be confident of receiving from the Father the same reward as the disciples themselves, that is, the kingdom itself (5:3–10). And who are the disciples? They are prophets (10:41a), sheep among wolves (10:16; cf. 7:15), people persecuted for Jesus' sake (5:11–12). They are righteous (10:41b), indeed people with an overabundant righteousness (5:20ff.) who let their "light shine before men" (5:16), as is the case when they carry out their mission in the towns and villages of Israel (10:11–14). They are also "little ones." How should this term be understood? For this first occurrence, we note that these are disciples who have nothing and might even be in need of a cup of cold water (10:42). In view of the parallelism with the preceding designations (prophet and righteous person are related to the description of the disciples in 10:5–16), it is quite possible that the disciples are called "little ones" because they are deliberately without anything when they go in mission (10:10).[26]

If the "little ones" are disciples, it then may seem that 10:42 is addressed not to the disciples but to someone else (e.g., the crowd).[27] Yet this would be forgetting that we have found such a phenomenon in the entire concluding part of the discourse. Addressing the command to take care of the need of the little ones to "every one who . . ." (to whoever will want to be a disciple) implies that there are two kinds of disciples. On the one hand, there are the actual disciples, the Twelve with their less than perfect behavior—Judas Iscariot, who betrayed Jesus, is one of the disciples (10:4)! On the other hand, there are ideal disciples—the disciples as described in Jesus' teaching.[28] Then, it appears that the "little ones" are ideal disciples. The actual disciples are both those who should be received by others as they carry out their mission (see 10:14) and those who must receive the "little ones."

REJECTION OF JESUS' MINISTRY.
MATTHEW'S CONVICTIONS IN 11:1–30

The basic question raised in 9:35–38 was: How can Jesus' and the disciples' ministry be both like that of a shepherd and like a harvest? Both merciful and judgmental? The discourse in 10:5–42 indicated that this ministry becomes a judgment when their merciful proclamation and manifestation of the kingdom of heaven are rejected. Yet rejection and persecution are presented as an integral part of both the disciples' mission and Jesus' ministry. As a consequence of the persecution, they are brought to the Gentiles' rulers, a situation in which they should witness to Gentiles; the mission is extended to include Gentiles. But the fundamental question remains: Why are certain people rejecting the disciples and their mission? And, more important, why are they rejecting Jesus and his ministry? Partial answers to this question have been proposed in the discourse. Jesus' vocation was not to bring peace on earth, but a sword (10:34), because he proposes a view of life, and, more specifically, of security, which clashes with the human view of life. But this first answer is far from complete. Thus this theme is further developed in 11:1–30.

Despite narrative passages (such as 11:1–6, a short narrative unit), 11:1–30 is a didactic thematic unit. It takes the form of a discourse prompted by John's question—even though it is successively addressed to John's disciples (11:4), to the crowds (11:7), to cities that did not repent (11:20), and finally to the Father and to whoever wants to listen (11:15–30).[29] As in the case of the last part of each of the preceding discourses (7:21–27; 10:32–42), the last part of this discourse is addressed to an undetermined audience which includes the readers.

Matthew 11:1–6 raises a question: Why would people, including dedicated people such as John, doubt and be scandalized by Jesus? This section makes the point that it is because they consider Jesus' deeds *without taking into account his words*, his teaching and preaching. They take into account only one component of what constitutes the ministry of Jesus and of his disciples (10:7–14). The relation between 10:7–14 and 11:1–6 appears when we note that the rejection of the disciples is directly linked with the rejection of their *words*: "If any one will not receive you or listen to your words . . ." (10:14).

In 11:7–19 we find a similar issue, that of the rejection of John by the crowds, which is set on a par with the rejection of Jesus by the crowds. As is suggested by the reference to the "deeds" of Wisdom in 11:19—which echoes the reference to "the deeds of the Christ" in 11:2—the lack of recognition is once again explained in terms of the way in which "deeds" are interpreted by those who reject John and Jesus.

In 11:20–24 there is a condemnation to a fate worse than that of Sodom of the cities that did not repent and thus rejected Jesus and his message about the kingdom ("Repent, for the kingdom of heaven is at hand," 4:17), in spite of his miracles. What was expressed regarding the condemnation of those who reject the disciples and their message (10:14–15) is thereby amplified.

The concluding passage, 11:25–30, specifies the character of Jesus' ministry—an easy yoke and a light burden (11:30)—by emphasizing how it reflects the relationship of Jesus with his Father (11:25–27). The theme of this passage is not unlike that of 10:32–42, although the perspective is different.

11:1–6. John Questions Whether Jesus Is the Christ

These verses form a complete thematic narrative unit since they involve the transformation of an original situation, doubt, into a situation where this doubt is potentially removed. John, upon hearing from prison about the deeds of the Christ, sends his disciples with the question: "Are you he who is to come. . . ?" (11:3). This is an expression of doubt[30] that Jesus' answer should overcome, and thus John should no longer be scandalized by Jesus; he should be one of those who "takes no offense" at Jesus (11:6).

The transformation of doubt about Jesus into a situation in which doubt is potentially removed is the direct expression of the main point that Matthew wants to convey through this short passage. This point is expressed by an opposition between what John says (11:3) and what Jesus says (11:4). It concerns the reason for (or cause of) John's doubt and what is needed to overcome it.

John is in prison; he is persecuted, as the disciples and Jesus will be, according to 10:16–42. Thus he appears to be an ideal disciple of Jesus. Upon hearing "about the deeds of the Christ" (11:2), he doubts that Jesus is "he who is to come," the Christ. He is scandalized by Jesus; he takes offense at him (11:6). Why? The answer is to be found in the difference between the text's description of John and Jesus' response.

John has heard about Jesus' *deeds*, but this is not enough to convince him that Jesus fulfills the prophecies concerning the one who is to come (e.g., Isa. 59:20). According to Jesus' response, if John was to be told by his disciples what they "hear and see" (11:4), he would be convinced that Jesus fulfills the prophecies and is the Christ. What John's disciples "hear" is Jesus' teaching and preaching, and what they "see" are Jesus' deeds. The point that Matthew conveys in these verses is clear: John doubts and is scandalized—the first step toward rejection—because he takes into account only Jesus' deeds. As long as one has this attitude, one cannot properly understand these deeds. When, however, one takes into account both *Jesus'* *deeds*—his miracles, the healings of the blind, the lame, lepers, the deaf, and the raising of the dead (11:5a)—and *Jesus' words*—"the poor have good news preached to them" (11:5b)—then one is not scandalized by Jesus and does not reject him and his authority.[31]

In brief, one has doubts, is scandalized, and ultimately rejects Jesus and his ministry when one interprets Jesus' deeds in and of themselves rather than in terms of Jesus' preaching and teaching.

This conclusion regarding the point (conviction) conveyed by these verses is verified by the thematic portion of this passage (the part not directly related to the opposition). Once again we recognize how Matthew expresses his point in terms of his readers' old knowledge by taking note of the tensions in the text. For the readers, the description of Jesus' ministry in 11:1, strangely *limited to teaching and preaching*, is in tension with the verse that follows (11:2) which emphasizes that John heard . . . *about the deeds* of Jesus! Of course, the readers quickly adjust and refer to earlier chapters where deeds such as those mentioned in 11:5 are described. It means that Matthew presupposes that the readers would have the same attitude as John. Even when no deed is mentioned, they are primarily looking for deeds of Jesus. What John and the readers are looking for are "deeds of the Christ"— deeds that the Christ is supposed to perform according to their expecta- tions—as if the Christ could be identified merely by his deeds (as the people who are saying "Lord, Lord" do, 7:22). The text shows this attitude to be wrong, and the readers are reminded of the ambivalent character of John's attitude.

It is the third time that John is mentioned in the Gospel. In the first instance (3:1–15), although the validity of his ministry and of his proclamation of the kingdom was affirmed, he was presented as having a wrong under- standing of Jesus' vocation: he was expecting him to be here and now the vengeful eschatological judge. He failed to perceive Jesus' baptism as a proper action, because he did not recognize that it was an appropriate ful- fillment of Jesus' vocation or righteousness. In the second instance (9:14– 17) the disciples of John dispute the validity of a certain kind of behavior (not fasting) because they do not recognize the fundamental characteristics of Jesus' ministry, namely, its newness. In this third instance (11:1–6) John's failure is similar. He does not interpret Jesus' deeds correctly; he does not consider them in terms of his teaching and preaching. Consequently, he cannot recognize the true nature of Jesus' ministry; he cannot recognize Jesus as the Christ.

11:7–19. Relations Between John's and Jesus' Ministry

In this second passage, a discourse addressed to the crowds (11:7), there are only two narrative oppositions. Thus this relatively long passage makes only two points which are developed at length.

11:7–9a. The text makes a first point by opposing going into the wilderness in order to see a reed or an elegantly dressed courtier *and* going into the wilderness in order to see a prophet (11:7–9a). In brief, the crowds made the decision to go into the wilderness on the basis of a proper interpretation of the situation. They concluded that it was worthwhile to go there because they recognized that John was a prophet; it would not have been worthwhile going into the wilderness to see a reed shaken by the wind, and it would have been senseless to go there expecting to find a well-dressed courtier.

11:9b–19. Yet "this generation" (11:16, the crowds) rejects John by saying "he has a demon," because he is "neither eating nor drinking" (11:18), while Jesus emphatically acknowledges him as a prophet, indeed as more than a prophet (11:9–14).[32] This second opposition underscores that the crowds, despite their ability to make the decision to go and see the prophet John in the wilderness, refused to listen to him and rejected him. Why? At one level, the text clearly indicates that it is because they consider his actions and his ascetic behavior, "neither eating nor drinking," as contradictory to the behavior they expected from a prophet. Thus they reject him, saying, "He has a demon" (11:18). But this is not the true issue. It is not because they have a rigid understanding of the way in which a prophet should behave that they rejected John, since they also reject Jesus because of his behavior, and this even though he has exactly the opposite behavior (11:19). As in the case of the children of the parable (11:16–17), the issue is not that they do not want to play a given game or another but that they do not want to play at all.[33] In other words, it is not that they could not recognize a given behavior as appropriate for a prophet; rather, they simply did not want to recognize the kind of "prophets" that John and Jesus are. They are scandalized by, they take offense at, both John and Jesus.

Jesus' sayings about John (11:9–14), which are opposed to the crowds' sayings about John and Jesus (11:18–19), provide a more specific explanation for the rejection of John (and Jesus) by the crowds. The crowds *wanted to go* and see a prophet in the wilderness; this is why they went there! But what they found was a very special kind of prophet, indeed "more than a prophet" (11:9). In which sense? Keeping in mind that, for Matthew, this description of the rejection of John is also an explanation of the rejection of Jesus (see 11:19) and of the disciples (see 10:14), and furthermore that John proclaimed the message of the kingdom (3:2), we have to conclude that it is because he is associated with the coming of the kingdom that John is "more than a prophet." This is expressed in 11:10–15. As Jesus' coming—which brings the kingdom—is the fulfillment of prophecies (see 11:5 and the formula quotations throughout the Gospel), John's ministry is the fulfillment of the composite prophecy[34] of Mal. 3:1 and Exod. 23:20: "Behold, I send my messenger before thy face, who shall prepare thy way before thee" (Matt. 11:10). This means that he is the fulfillment of that other prophecy of Malachi which identifies this forerunner of the Messiah as Elijah: "Behold, I will send you Elijah the prophet before the great and terrible day of the Lord comes" (Mal. 4:5 [3:23 in the Hebrew]; cf. Matt. 11:14). Yet, as 11:10 expresses, John himself does not belong to the kingdom (11:11); he prepares the way for the One who will bring it. He does not belong to the realm of the kingdom (see the comments on 10:16–31), yet he is the greatest in the human realm ("among those born of women," 11:11). He is the climax of the period that preceded the coming of the kingdom: "For all the prophets and the law prophesied until John" (and including John, 11:13). He is "more than a prophet" because he is the one who prepares the coming of the kingdom as well as the coming of the Messiah. This is why he is rejected and persecuted (in prison, 11:2) together with those who belong to the kingdom (Jesus, and his disciples whoever they may be).

It is in this context that the saying "From the days of John the Baptist until now the kingdom of heaven has suffered violence, and [violent people plunder it]" (11:12) must be interpreted. Whatever might have been the original meaning of this saying,[35] Matthew's inclusion of it in a passage explaining the rejection and persecution of those who belong to the kingdom makes it clear that he understood it as describing hostility to the kingdom.[36] From the days of John, there are violence, rejection, and persecution against those who belong to the kingdom and thus against the kingdom itself.

In sum, the true cause of the rejection of John and of Jesus is neither a failure to recognize that they are "prophets" (people went out into the wilderness because they believed John was a prophet) nor objections to their respective behaviors or deeds, despite the claim of those who reject them. Rather, these people are scandalized by John and Jesus because of their association with the kingdom, or, more specifically, because of their proclamation of the kingdom—even though it is the proclamation of a "good news" (11:5).

11:7. These points are further expressed thematically for the readers in the parts of 11:7–19 not directly related to the oppositions and in the tensions displayed by the text. A first tension results from this discourse being addressed to "the crowds" (11:7). Up to this point in the Gospel the crowds were cast in a positive light, they followed Jesus (4:25), recognized his authority (7:28–29), and even acknowledged the newness of his ministry (9:33). Then unexpectedly they are identified as those who reject not only John (11:18) but also Jesus (11:19).[37] The readers are then led to reconsider the preceding chapters and to note that since 9:35 the crowds are cast in a less positive light. Jesus has compassion for the crowds which are harassed and helpless (9:36). Consequently, he sends his disciples to them in order that they might bring to them what they so desperately need: the message and the manifestation of the kingdom. But some in these helpless crowds reject the disciples and their message (10:14), as they reject John and Jesus (11:18–19). The crowds had recognized the authority of Jesus (see 9:33), as they had recognized that John was a prophet (11:9a); they followed Jesus (4:25), as they went out to the wilderness to see John (11:7–8). But they do not want to hear the message of the kingdom, and thus they reject Jesus as they rejected John.

11:15. This tension is maintained by a second thematic feature of this passage, the concluding remark of the first part: "He who has ears [to hear], let him hear" (11:15). Yes, it is possible that some in the crowds have ears that will allow them to understand and be willing to accept (11:14) that John is related to the coming of the kingdom, since he is Elijah. But most do not, and reject both John and Jesus under the pretense that their deeds are not fit for "prophets."

11:19. The concluding saying, "Yet wisdom is justified by her deeds" (11:19), can now be understood.[38] John's and Jesus' deeds are indeed manifesting "wisdom," the Wisdom of God, as the deeds of the disciples are the manifestation of the kingdom that they proclaim (cf. 10:7–10).[39] These deeds demonstrate the validity of the teaching; they are its concrete manifestation. Rejecting Jesus because of his deeds is rejecting the divine Wisdom of which they are the manifestation. This is failing to recognize the relationship between Jesus' deeds and his teaching, as John did (11:2–3). Then, it is impossible to recognize who Jesus really is, that is, the Christ (11:2), the Son of man (11:19), Wisdom (11:19).[40] In such a case one believes that one has to look for another (11:3), and one rejects the Son of man and Wisdom without being aware of the consequences.

11:20–24. Condemnation of Israelite Cities

Following the explanation of the actual reason for the rejection of John and of Jesus, the Son of man/Wisdom (11:7–19), the utterance of condemnation against the cities that did not repent amplifies the judgment expressed in 10:14b–15. Two oppositions clarify the reason for this condemnation.

11:21. Chorazin and Bethsaida, which have not repented despite the mighty works done in them, are opposed to Tyre and Sidon, which in the same circumstances would have repented (11:21). When one remembers that Jesus' and John's message about the kingdom is summarized in the exhortation "Repent, for the kingdom of heaven is at hand" (4:17; cf. 3:2), it is clear that the cities' failure to repent is the direct consequence of their failure to perceive the relationship between the Son of man/Wisdom's deeds *and his words*. But why do Chorazin and Bethsaida fail to do so? This is the question that the opposition addresses by contrasting them to Tyre and

Sidon. The only difference between the two groups of cities is that the first are Israelite cities and the latter are Gentile cities. The point that Matthew conveys by this opposition is that it is *because they are Israelite*⁴¹ that Chorazin and Bethsaida are unwilling (cf. 11:14) to relate Jesus' deeds and message and thus are unwilling to repent.

11:23. Why would Israelite people be unwilling to repent? This is the point made by the following opposition. It deals with the two possible fates of Capernaum: being exalted to heaven or being brought down to Hades (11:23). In itself, this verse indicates that the opposition concerns Capernaum's illusory expectation regarding what God will do by contrast with what he will actually do. Because of the relationship to the preceding opposition, these contrasting expectations are related to what establishes Capernaum's willingness or unwillingness (cf. 11:14, "if you are willing to accept it") to repent, that is, its perception of euphoric or dysphoric situations. Thus the point is that Capernaum is unwilling to repent, and thus rejects the Son of man/Wisdom, because it wrongly views its relationship with God as being euphoric. It perceives itself as having a privileged relationship with God which guarantees that it will receive eschatological blessings and will be exalted to heaven. It is this perception of one's relationship with God which leads to the rejection of Jesus and of the kingdom, and thus to condemnation. This interpretation is further confirmed by the fact that Matt. 11:23 alludes to Isa. 14:13–15, a reference the readers are certainly expected to recognize; this text unambiguously indicates that it is a matter of self-righteousness before the Lord: "You said in your heart, 'I will ascend to heaven. . . .' But you are brought down to Sheol."

The two points made by 11:20–24 are clear. Why are people rejecting Jesus, the Son of man, despite his miracles among them, and refusing to listen to his words and repent? Because they are Israelites and as such believe they are already in a privileged relationship with God which guarantees their exaltation to heaven. Far from perceiving themselves as "lost sheep of the house of Israel" (10:6) and "harassed and helpless" people (9:36) in need of the message of the kingdom and its manifestation (the deeds and miracles), and as being in need of repentance, that is, of turning toward the kingdom (cf. 3:7–8), they presume they are in a privileged relationship with God (cf. 3:9).

For the readers, and their knowledge of what precedes in the Gospel, this judgmental discourse recalls John's own invective against the Pharisees and the Sadducees (3:7–10). While, at first, Jesus' ministry appeared to be positive by contrast with the judgmental ministry of John (cf. 3:1—4:25), now Jesus' ministry is also judgmental. As John expected (3:11–12), Jesus is the eschatological judge, the Son of man: he proclaims condemnation. But he is (and will be) the eschatological judge when his positive, merciful ministry—both the proclamation of the kingdom and his merciful deeds—is rejected. It is as the humiliated and rejected Son of man (11:19) that he is the terrible eschatological judge who condemns the unrepentant to a fate worse than that of Sodom (11:24).

11:25–30. Jesus' Relationship with His Father, and the Character of His Ministry[42]

These verses are closely related to the rest of the discourse by the opening phrase "at that time" (11:25), a temporal notation that Matthew uses to signal the thematic unity of a pericope with another (as other temporal phrases did in 9:18 and 11:1) despite changes in style. Therefore this passage will need to be interpreted in terms of what precedes despite the fact that, instead of being addressed to crowds and cities, it is addressed first to God in a prayer of praise (11:25–26), then to undetermined addressees (11:27–30)—which is also the case for the concluding part of each of the preceding discourses (cf. 7:21–27 and 10:32–42).[43]

11:25–26. Jesus' prayer of praise to the Father expresses a relationship with God that is in sharp contrast with the Israelite cities' relationship with God (11:23). This relationship is no longer governed by a preoccupation with one's own exaltation and one's own eschatological fate (11:23) but is governed by what is well pleasing to God (11:26). Jesus' primary concern is to recognize and acknowledge how the almighty Father carries out his will, namely, by giving a privileged status—revealing certain "things"—to the "babes" rather than to the "wise and understanding."

11:27, 29. In the rest of the pericope Jesus presents himself not merely as Son of the Father (11:27) but also as one who assumes the position of a "babe," by being meek and "lowly in heart" (11:29). Jesus is therefore one of the "babes" to whom hidden things are revealed (11:27). Consequently, as "it was well-pleasing before" God (11:26, au.) that these things be revealed to babes, so Jesus is "well pleasing" to God precisely when he is meek and rejected.

In this light, the rejected Son of man described in 11:19 appears to be "well pleasing" to God; he fulfills the will of God. In other words, through its juxtaposition with the harsh condemnation of the Israelite cities that rejected the Son of man and his ministry (11:20–24), this passage (11:25–27) addresses the question: Why should the disciples' (10:6) and Jesus' ministry be exclusively directed to Israel, since it results in rejection? Chapter 10 had explained such a rejection in terms of its positive results: the disciples' mission is expanded to include the Gentiles (see 10:16–20). Here the answer to this question is simply: because such a ministry is well pleasing to God. It is according to God's will. Simultaneously, the themes of the relationship Father-Son-disciples (see 10:32–33) and of the revelation of hidden "things" (see 10:26–27) are fully developed.

The overall effect of 11:25–27 is that the rejection and humiliation of the Son of man by Israel is according to the will of the Father. Therefore it is not a failure! Thus, as he is rejected, Jesus can be thankful to the Father (11:25). As "Lord of heaven and earth," the Father would have the power to avoid such a rejection by imposing upon Israel the recognition of his Son. But it is his will that "these things" be hidden from the "wise and understanding," while they are revealed to the "babes." In view of the points made in 11:20–24, it is clear that it is the people of Israel (or more precisely, those in Israel who reject Jesus) who are ironically described as wise and intelligent; they are those who pretend to be in a privileged relationship with God (11:23) and thus who pretend to know the will of God; they *pretend* to be wise and intelligent. Since the "babes" to whom "these things" are revealed are contrasted with the wise and intelligent, they are simply defined by the text as the people who have no such pretension. They are "poor in spirit" (5:3), "lowly in heart" or humble (see 11:29), by contrast with the Israelite cities that presume to have a privileged relationship with God.

What are "those things" that are revealed to the "babes"?[44] From what precedes we conclude that they are the significance of Jesus' deeds. This revelation is the perception that Jesus' deeds, the deeds of the Son of man/ Wisdom, are manifestations of the kingdom proclaimed in Jesus' words. The juxtaposition of the sayings of 11:25 and 11:27 specifies that what is revealed to the "babes" is the Father: "No one knows the Father except the Son and any one to whom the Son chooses to reveal him" (11:27b). As has been repeatedly expressed in the Gospel, and more recently, as we noted in chapter 10, the kingdom and the Fatherhood of God are closely associated. Here they are identified. The manifestation and revelation of the kingdom are nothing else than the manifestation and the revelation of the Father.[45]

11:28. So far there has been no opposition in the passage.[46] But 11:28 opposes growing weary and being burdened to giving "rest." The point conveyed by this opposition concerns the qualification of Jesus as the one who gives rest as opposed to those (unspecified people) who burden others and cause them to grow weary.[47] Jesus is "gentle," or "meek" (cf. 5:5), and "lowly in heart" (11:29). Those who burden others are neither gentle nor humble in heart: they are haughty and full of pretension; they pretend to be wise and intelligent (11:25), like the Israelite cities condemned in 11:20–24. It then appears that the text alludes to Israel's leaders and the Pharisees who play a central role in the next chapter. Because they have such an attitude, they burden others with an excessive load, of the same character as their excessive view of themselves. By contrast, Jesus does not burden his followers with an excessive load, because he is like them; as they are "babes" without pretension, he is "meek" and "lowly in heart." Indeed, as they are weary, he is humiliated and rejected.

In view of the point made by this opposition, the theme of 11:25–30 is clarified. First, the "babes" who are chosen by the Son to receive the revelation of the kingdom and of the Father are those who are overburdened by the religious leaders of Israel. They are the people "harassed and helpless, like sheep without a shepherd" (9:36), or, more precisely, those who are "exploited and thrown down on the ground" (as the terms in 9:36 can be interpreted).[48] Thus it appears that the problem with the harassed crowds is not that they lack a shepherd but that they have bad shepherds, religious leaders who exploit them and make them collapse under an excessive burden because of their own pretentious view of themselves. It also appears that those who are "worthy" of the disciples (10:13), and are chosen by the Son (11:27), are those who, among the harassed and helpless crowds, perceive themselves as "babes." They are people who do not share the pretension of the religious leaders.

Jesus also gives them a burden. He puts upon them demands, a yoke—namely, that which is expressed in his teaching and ministry and which they are invited to learn (11:29a). For the readers, this teaching as a yoke that should replace the yoke imposed by the pretentious religious leaders recalls the Sermon on the Mount which demands from the disciples a righteousness that exceeds that of the scribes and the Pharisees (5:20). Yet Jesus' "yoke is easy" and his "burden is light" (11:30). Why? Similarly, how can it be said that by going to Jesus and taking his yoke upon oneself, one will find *rest* (11:28, 29)? The only explanation provided by the text is that it is because Jesus himself is "gentle and lowly in heart." For the readers this explanation does not resolve the questions; indeed, it underscores them. Obviously, this theme needs to be further developed, as it will be in the next chapter.[49]

CONTROVERSY OVER SABBATH OBSERVANCE: MATTHEW'S CONVICTIONS IN 12:1–21

A first explanation for the rejection of Jesus and of his ministry was provided in the discourse given in response to John's doubt (11:4–30). John, the crowds, and the Israelite cities failed to perceive the proper relationship between Jesus' deeds—miracles and attitudes that associate him with rejected sinners—and his message about the kingdom. A second explanation of the rejection is offered in 12:1–21. To the Pharisees, Jesus' deeds appear to contradict the will of God as they conceive it.[50] In other words, Jesus and his ministry are rejected because people have a wrong understanding of the will of God and of the way to fulfill it. These two explanations are related. In 12:1–21 Matthew continues to develop the themes of 11:25–30, although the new unit is more narrative in character—it involves a controversy about the action of the disciples (12:1–8), a miracle story and its consequences (12:9–14), and a formula quotation (12:15–21). This continuity is marked by the opening phrase, "at that time," which is used by Matthew along with other temporal notations to underscore that the following passage further develops the themes of the preceding pericope (cf. 9:18; 11:1, 25).

The thematic relation between 12:1–21 and 11:25–30 is multifold. The formula quotation (12:17–21) comes back to the themes of Jesus as "gentle" and "lowly in heart" (11:29) and as the one whose proclamation is hidden (11:25; 10:26–27).[51] Chapter 12:1–14 also prolongs the theme of 11:28–29. As we have noted, the readers are left puzzled by the repeated affirmation that by taking Jesus' yoke one finds *rest* (11:28–29). Now, in 12:1–16, the controversies concern the observance of the sabbath (the day of rest). In the perspective of 11:28–30, which opposed Jesus to those who overburden others with their teaching, these controversies provide a concrete illustration of the way in which the Pharisees make the day of rest a burden and of the way in which Jesus makes the observance of the sabbath an easy yoke and a light burden.[52]

12:1–8. The Dispute Over Plucking Grain on the Sabbath

Matthew's points (convictions) are expressed in this pericope by two narrative oppositions that concern the question: Why is it lawful according to Jesus, and unlawful according to the Pharisees, to pluck grain on the sabbath?[53] The first opposition contrasts the Pharisees' saying (12:2) with Jesus' response (12:3–8). The second opposition, embedded in the first, is found in the quotation of Hos. 6:6 in Matt. 12:7.

The first opposition concerns two issues, as Jesus' response makes clear. First, there is the issue of whether or not it is lawful to do what the disciples did on the sabbath (12:2, 3–5). Second, there is the issue of condemning other people: "You would not have condemned the guiltless" (12:7b), an issue also expressed in 12:2. As in 9:3 and 9:11, by addressing their criticism of certain people (disciples) *to someone else* (Jesus), rather than to the persons who are criticized, the Pharisees make their saying a condemnation or judgment without the possibility of any appeal, an attitude forbidden in the Sermon on the Mount (see 7:1).[54]

12:3, 5, 7. Why is it lawful according to Jesus to pluck heads of grain and eat them on the sabbath? According to Matthew, Jesus does not declare that the sabbath laws are abolished.[55] Jesus implicitly affirms the validity of these laws as scriptural laws *provided they are interpreted correctly*. The point made by the opposition concerns the interpretation of the law. As is shown by the repeated question "Have you not read. . . ?" (in Scripture or the law, 12:3, 5), a first problem with the Pharisees' interpretation is that they interpret the sabbath laws by the laws themselves rather than in terms of the rest of Scripture. Specific laws of Scripture must be interpreted in terms of God's will as expressed in Scripture as a whole. And once again (see 9:13), God's will is summarized by Hos. 6:6, "I desire mercy, and not sacrifice," a text the Pharisees fail to understand (12:7a).[56] Furthermore, for Jesus, the interpretation and observance of the law must take into account the concrete circumstances in which the people are, while, for the Pharisees, the law must be observed without regard for circumstances. They fail to take into account the hunger of the disciples (12:1) and thus their situation of need. This prevents them from perceiving that what David and his companions did when they were hungry—eating the bread of the Presence, which was not lawful to do (12:3–4; cf. 1 Sam. 21:1–6)—is a precedent that applies to the disciples.

Furthermore, in view of the opposition, Jesus' interpretation of the sabbath laws—or of any scriptural law, as in the case of David—is to be understood, not as setting limits to the application of the law, but as demonstrating its proper application. The Pharisees' interpretation of the law is wrong because they use it as a means of judging and condemning others (12:2 and 12:7b)[57]—a point that Matthew has already underscored in the temptation story (4:3–11) and the antitheses (5:21–46). This is why their teaching—including their teaching about the day of rest—is a heavy yoke and overburdening people (11:22). It puts a burden of guilt upon the guiltless (12:7b). By contrast, for Jesus, the law is to be used in order to establish one's vocation, to discover what one should do in specific circumstances so as to fulfill God's will, that is, "mercy" (12:7a). The disciples are hungry; thus God's will is that, even on the sabbath, the disciples' needs be met. At any rate, using the sabbath laws as a means of condemning others, especially the guiltless, would be contrary to the mercy which God desires.

12:5–6. For Matthew, there is more. The circumstances in which the disciples are is not merely a situation of need, their hunger. They are also with Jesus. Consequently, another scriptural precedent applies in their case, that of the priests who are breaking the sabbath laws (12:5) as they perform their service in the Temple, and yet are guiltless. The disciples are breaking the sabbath laws and are nevertheless guiltless because they are with Jesus, who is "something greater than the temple" (12:6). Thus the disciples' vocation, serving God with Jesus, is like the priests' vocation, serving God in the Temple. If the priests' performance of their vocation gives them the freedom to profane the sabbath, all the more so does the disciples' performance of their vocation, since Jesus is "greater than the temple."

12:7a. In which sense is Jesus greater than the Temple? This is expressed in 12:7a by the opposition found in the quotation of Hos. 6:6. Here we need to emphasize that Jesus is once again presented as the one who fulfills God's will (see comments on 9:13). By his ministry he manifests God's mercy. The Temple manifests God's presence—the bread eaten by David was a bread set forth before God (12:4), who is present in the Temple. In the Temple, God's presence is associated with sacrifices performed by the priests. Similarly, Jesus manifests God's presence—he is Emmanuel, the presence of the Holy among us (see 1:23). But in Jesus' case, God's presence is associated with mercy manifested by his ministry. Jesus, the Son of man—who eats with sinners (9:10–13; 11:19) and is rejected and humiliated (11:19)—is greater than the temple in that he manifests God's presence in a more appropriate way than the Temple, namely, as a merciful presence.

12:8. Consequently, "the Son of man is lord of the sabbath" (12:8). As the Temple and serving God in the Temple take precedence over the sabbath laws, so do the Son of man and serving God with the Son of man. Thus the hungry disciples who are with Jesus and are associated with his merciful ministry (see 10:1–8) need to apply the sabbath laws after interpreting them in terms of these circumstances. They can, and indeed must, break the sabbath laws, not only when they are in a situation of need, as David was, but also and primarily whenever it is demanded by the proper performance of their ministry, as the priests in the Temple do.[58] They even have a greater right to do so, since the one with whom they are associated is greater than the Temple. He is the Son of man, who, according to God's will, manifests the presence of God as mercy. But in which sense is such a Son of man "lord of the sabbath"? This pericope, 12:1–8, does not allow us to address the question.[59] But the following one, 12:9–16, does.

12:9–16. The Dispute Over Healing on the Sabbath

In this second pericope about the sabbath, two narrative oppositions express Matthew's points (convictions). The first opposition contrasts the Pharisees' saying (12:10) with Jesus' response (12:11–12). The second opposes Jesus' action, healing (doing good, 12:12–13) to the Pharisees' intended action, destroying Jesus (12:14). Most of the features of this pericope are directly related to the points made through the oppositions. Yet one feature is clearly thematic, betraying the tension between the readers' expectations and the new points that Matthew attempts to convey to them, namely, the strange statement found in 12:15: "And many followed him, and he healed them all." Are the readers to imagine that all the people in the crowds were sick? Or should they add "all who were sick"? We have to let the text puzzle us; the study of the points (convictions) conveyed by the oppositions should allow us to understand why this tension appears in the text.

12:10–11. As the formulation of the Pharisees' question (12:10) indicates, the "man with a withered hand" and his healing are used to make a more general point concerning healing on the sabbath—a point closely related to those of the preceding pericope (12:1–8). Once again, one of the issues concerns what is or is not lawful to do on the sabbath. According to Matthew, for the Pharisees it is not lawful to heal on the sabbath.[60] Yet they address their question with the expectation that Jesus will say it is lawful to heal during the sabbath, an answer that they plan to use in order to accuse him (12:10). In other words, their question makes use of their knowledge of Jesus' view to entrap him. In turn, Jesus makes use of his knowledge of what his opponents do or would do on the sabbath—"What man of you, if he has one sheep. . . ?" (12:11). In the case of an animal to which they attach great value—such as the one and only sheep someone owns—they do not hesitate to break the sabbath laws to rescue it (12:11).[61] They spontaneously know what is good to do (cf. 12:12b)—preserving what is valuable for them—even if it involves breaking the sabbath laws. In the context of their daily life, saving the valued sheep takes precedence over the sabbath. Why do they not recognize that healing a human being, who has a much greater value, also takes precedence over the sabbath?

The way in which the Pharisees are presented gives us a clue. Note that the name "Pharisees" is not used in 12:9–13. They are merely designated as the people to whom the synagogue belongs: "their synagogue" (12:9).[62] They are people who evaluate everything in terms of the synagogue as a place of religious gathering rather than in terms of the daily life and what they spontaneously do in it. As in 7:9–12, where it is emphasized that human beings know how to discern what is good for their children and that this perception is "the law and the prophets," so here the point is that in their daily life they know how to discern when it is appropriate to break the sabbath laws.[63] They know how to discern what has precedence over these laws and thus what is the very center of the law and the prophets: God's will, mercy. Yet they fail to do so. Why? The answer given in the Sermon on the Mount was: because their "eye is not sound" (6:23; cf. 6:22—7:12) and thus because of divided allegiance. Here, the fact that the Pharisees' question follows the mention of the Temple service (12:5) and the affirmation that God desires "mercy, and not sacrifice" (12:7) suggests that it is because they look at everything from a perspective that gives priority to sacrifice. As long as one seeks God's will through worship that is centered on sacrifice, as in the Temple, or on an observance of the law aimed at gaining God's favor so as to be exalted (as Capernaum did, 11:23), one cannot "do good." But one can "do good" if one seeks God's will, as one also does in the daily life—perceiving what is good for oneself (cf. 7:12 and 12:11).

Such an attitude does not exclude the possibility of worship but calls for a new center of worship, the merciful Son of man who is more than the Temple (12:6) and who, as such, is the lord of the sabbath. Yet the radical character of this pericope (12:9–16) and of the preceding one (12:1–8) should not be overlooked. They are a serious challenge to all religious institutions that give priority to the relation human-divine and consequently give a secondary status to the relation human-human—mercy. Since God, the Father revealed by the Son, is merciful, being children of the Father is being merciful, being for others, and true worship in the new temple should in no way interfere with the performance of good works (5:16; 7:17), activities that maintain or reestablish good relationships with others (cf. 5:23–24; 6:14–15) and especially mercy.

12:8. In this light, one can perceive how Matthew understands the saying that "the Son of man is lord of the sabbath" (12:8). It should not be interpreted in a negative sense, that is, in the sense that the Son of man has the authority to overrule or even abolish the sabbath. Rather, it must be interpreted positively: the Son of man has the authority (and power) to fulfill the sabbath (cf. 5:17). Indeed, the sabbath is the day par excellence on which God's will must be fulfilled. Thus the sabbath is the day on which one must show mercy without any restriction.

12:15. The Son of man, as lord of the sabbath, does this not only by healing—showing mercy to—the man with a withered hand but also by healing *all* those who follow him. In this light, the strange statement of 12:15 makes sense. Note that this verse has no temporal marker. Thus it is still on the sabbath, the day par excellence on which one needs to manifest mercy. And the Son of man does so in a magisterial way by healing *all of them* on that day.

12:11–14. A last point is conveyed by the second narrative opposition which contrasts the Pharisees' intended action, destroying Jesus (12:14), with the performance of an act of mercy, healing, doing good (12:12–13), and secondarily, with the act of the man rescuing his sheep (12:11). Through this opposition, Matthew makes a single but important additional point, which is underscored by the description of the Pharisees in 12:14: "The Pharisees went out and took counsel against him." The decision to destroy Jesus is not reached individually, by a single person, but by gathering together and taking counsel. By contrast, it is spontaneously—and thus without taking counsel—that the man makes the decision of rescuing his sheep on the sabbath (12:11). Similarly, Jesus simply knows what is good to do. In other words, if a decision needs to be the object of a deliberation among several people, it cannot be a good decision, a decision to do good and to show mercy. Indeed, one spontaneously knows—or feels—what is good to do when a merciful act is necessary and what that act should be. This is a point we found in the Sermon on the Mount (see 5:21–47). Either the will of God and the law and the prophets are internalized, become an integral part of the disciples' way of perceiving what is euphoric and dysphoric around them and in them, or they cannot be fulfilled.

In 12:9–14 this point is made in an exclusively negative way; the text merely describes the Pharisees' decision making (12:14). If one needs to take counsel for deciding to do something, the decision cannot be a good one. This does not mean that every spontaneous decision will be a decision to do good. In fact, the Pharisees' spontaneous decision to condemn the disciples (12:2) illustrates this last remark. Because the Pharisees perceive everything in terms of condemnation (cf. their use of Scripture, 12:2) and of "sacrifice" (12:7), their spontaneous reaction is to condemn others for the faults (trespasses) they perceive in them instead of wanting to show mercy to others so as to meet the needs they perceive in them. Thus a spontaneous perception and decision might be bad, against God's will. But in their daily life, that is, outside religious gatherings (the synagogue, 12:9, and their council, 12:14), even the Pharisees correctly perceive the needs around them and do good. In order to do good, one must therefore walk away from the synagogue and its gathering—as Jesus does (12:15)—and avoid gathering again to take counsel elsewhere (12:14).[64]

12:15–21. Jesus as Fulfillment of Prophecy About God's Beloved Servant

We have already begun discussing 12:15–16 which functions as the concluding part of the preceding pericope by developing the theme of the magisterial demonstration of mercy on the sabbath—since Jesus heals "them all" (12:15). Yet these verses also function as the introduction of the formula quotation. In the context of controversies with the Pharisees over the interpretation of Scripture, the first effect of this quotation is to confirm the validity of Jesus' view of Scripture.[65] It shows that his ministry is the fulfillment of God's will. As usual, Matthew quotes the prophecy after describing the events that fulfill it.[66] In this way the quotation functions as a thematic passage that reiterates certain points expressed earlier, underscoring them so as to lead the readers to expect that they will be further developed in the pericopes that follow.[67]

12:15–16. By withdrawing in the face of persecution (12:15), Jesus does what he commanded his disciples to do (10:23). The link between the mission of the disciples and Jesus' ministry is once again expressed. Yet, for the readers, the order "not to make him known" (12:16) is puzzling. Despite two similar orders (cf. 8:4 and 9:30), Jesus has been quite open about his ministry, and especially about the healing on the sabbath. But the formula that introduces the quotation makes it clear that, for Matthew, these verses from Isaiah are to be viewed as an explanation of Jesus' order. The Greek text reads: He "ordered them not to make him known *in order that* what was said by Isaiah be fulfilled" (12:16–17a).

Since the quotation of Isa. 42:1–4 does not follow any known Greek translation, it needs to be regarded as Matthew's own interpretation[68] formulated so as to clarify how the prophecy is fulfilled by Jesus' ministry. The central part of the quotation (Matt. 12:19) most directly explains Jesus' order "not to make him known," and his withdrawal: "He will not wrangle," he will avoid quarreling. One could simply understand that Jesus wants to avoid further controversies that a report about massive healings on the sabbath would have provoked. But the rest of this long quotation— the longest in the Gospel—shows that Jesus' order of silence touches on an essential characteristic of his entire ministry. Three main points about Jesus' ministry are emphasized.

1. The goal of the ministry of the Servant/Jesus is described as "proclaiming justice [or, judgment] to the Gentiles" (12:18b) and "bringing justice [or, judgment] to victory" (12:20b); consequently, "in his name will the Gentiles hope" (12:21). We are no longer surprised that the Gentiles are the ultimate beneficiaries of Jesus' ministry, since he is a great light for the Gentiles (4:15–16; Isa. 9:1–2); furthermore, the disciples' mission, which duplicates Jesus' ministry, has the Gentiles as its ultimate goal (10:16–18). And, is it not expressed in 11:21–22 that the Gentile cities, Tyre and Sidon, will receive justice from the Son of man "on the day of judgment"? Yet the context shows that this ministry, which has the Gentiles as its ultimate goal, is first carried out in Israel, and in humiliation.

2. Jesus carries out this vocation and fulfills the prophecy by *not doing* a number of things: "He will not wrangle or cry aloud, nor will any one hear his voice in the streets; he will not break a bruised reed or quench a smoldering wick" (12:19–20a). We recognize a point repeatedly made in different ways in the two preceding chapters. Beginning with the last phrases, it is clear that the Son who is "gentle and lowly in heart" and who gives rest to overburdened people (11:28–30) fulfills the prophecy about the Servant who does not break a bruised reed or quench a smoldering wick. Similarly, he does not attempt to impose himself and his ministry by force, by quarreling or shouting. He withdraws rather than confronting those who reject him (12:15–16), and asks his disciples to do the same not only in order to avoid persecution (10:23) but also as soon as people will not receive them or listen to their words (10:14). Indeed, he is rejected, humiliated, but he does not make a show of himself to avoid such a rejection; he does not proclaim his message in the streets, in public (12:19b). Rather, he quietly reveals it to those to whom he chooses to reveal it (11:27); to them, he tells his message in the dark, whispering (10:27).

Here a tension appears. Are not the disciples instructed to utter this message in the light and to proclaim it upon the housetops (10:27)? Is Jesus not expected to bring (forcefully) justice to victory (12:20b)? Yet, note that Jesus' forceful ministry is aimed at the Gentiles and that his instruction to the disciples (10:27) concerns their ministry among Gentiles—when they are dragged before governors and kings to bear testimonies before them and the Gentiles (10:18, 26–33). As in the case of the disciples' mission, we need to distinguish two phases in Jesus' ministry. The first phase is a ministry exclusively to Israel (see 10:5–6), a quiet, discreet ministry during which Jesus and his message are often rejected and during which, after making his case, he does not force the issue by wrangling or shouting but withdraws when confronted by rejection. He is the humiliated Son of man. By contrast, the second phase, which is still future, is a ministry to the Gentiles, a ministry when he brings judgment and justice to them. As a consequence of his rejection (see 11:20–24), as the Son of man, he is and will be the eschatological judge. Furthermore, this ministry to the Gentiles is and will be first carried out through the intermediary of the public and forceful witness of the disciples (10:16ff.).

3. Third, the Servant/Jesus has received all the necessary qualifications for carrying out this vocation.[69] He is in a special relationship with God and chosen by him (11:25–26 with 12:18a). In addition, the Spirit of God is upon him (see 3:16–17). The Spirit is thus presented as what gives to Jesus the ability (power and authority) to carry out his vocation—as it does for the disciples (see 10:20).

In sum, through this formula quotation Matthew emphasizes essential characteristics of Jesus' ministry as expressed in the first part of this section (9:36—12:16). Its overall effect for the readers is to confirm without ambiguity that Jesus' deeds—both his behavior and his miracles—fulfill the will of God, since they fulfill a prophecy. Jesus carries out in his ministry the vocation described in the prophecy, and the quotation confirms that God acknowledges him as his Servant in whom he is well pleased.

One can understand why Matthew found it necessary to underscore this point so emphatically. For his readers, the Pharisees' objections might appear to be weighty. Is it not right to criticize the breaking of the sabbath laws—the laws of Scripture—for so trivial a matter as plucking a few heads of grain and eating them and for a healing which could have waited without danger until the next day? By such a quotation, Matthew forces his readers to ponder the points he made and to discover that the clash between Jesus and the Pharisees has its origin in fundamentally divergent understandings of God's will. It is only with a proper understanding of God's will as mercy that one can recognize that Jesus is "greater than the temple" (12:6) and that "the Son of man is lord of the sabbath" (12:8).

DISPUTE OVER THE NATURE OF JESUS'
POWER AND AUTHORITY:
MATTHEW'S CONVICTIONS IN 12:22–50

A third explanation of the rejection of Jesus and his ministry is proposed in 12:22–50. As in 11:1–30 and 12:1–21, this explanation is related to the interpretation of Jesus' deeds, but here the recognition of the source of his power to perform miracles is at stake. People reject Jesus because they misconceive the origin of his power; they say it is Beelzebul rather than the Spirit. This unit explains the seriousness of this misconception which leads to blasphemy against the Spirit, the unforgivable sin. It also explains the cause of the misconception of the origin of Jesus' power—ultimately, a wrong view of power and authority—and how this misconception can be overcome.

This unit can be subdivided into four parts on the basis of the points that Matthew makes by setting up narrative oppositions. An introduction (12:22–24) presents the conflicting interpretations of a miracle by the crowds and the Pharisees. It is followed by a discourse (12:25–37) which can be subdivided into three parts. The discourse begins by showing why the Pharisees' interpretation is incorrect (12:25–29), goes on to show that their words are evil, indeed a blasphemy against the Holy Spirit, a blasphemy that will not be forgiven (12:30–32), and is concluded by warnings about the consequences of uttering such evil words (12:33–37). The third part (12:38–45) shows that in order to recognize the true nature and origin of the power at work in Jesus' ministry, one needs to recognize his authority even when he refuses to use his power. Furthermore, as the last part (12:46–50) shows, one needs to give up old conceptions of the household or kingdom of God and to acknowledge a new one.

12:22–24. Conflicting Interpretations of a Miracle

These verses oppose the crowd's question (12:23) to the Pharisees' saying (12:24), a question and a saying prompted by Jesus' healing of a blind and dumb demoniac. In order to understand the point conveyed by this opposition, note that the Pharisees' statement is addressed to the crowds. They are afraid of losing control over the crowds, who, because of the miracle, are "amazed," or, literally, "stand outside themselves" (12:23). The crowds are on the verge of abandoning their usual perspective, a perspective that leads them to acknowledge the authority of the Pharisees. In Jesus they begin to recognize another kind of authority: "Can this be the Son of David?" the Messiah (12:23).[70] It is therefore in order to preserve their own authority over the crowds that the Pharisees seek to discredit Jesus' authority by saying: "It is only by Beelzebul, the prince of demons, that this man casts out demons" (12:24). The point made by these verses is clear: Recognizing Jesus' authority requires one to abandon and reject other religious authorities, here the Pharisees' authority. This also implies that the group of people (kingdom, city, or household, see 12:25) over whom Jesus has authority is defined in a different way from the group of people (the Israelite crowds) over whom the Pharisees have authority, a point that will be underscored in the concluding part (12:46–50) of this unit.

12:25–37. True and False Views
of Authority: The Blasphemy
Against the Holy Spirit

12:25–29. The first part of this new discourse develops the preceding point by showing, through an opposition, what is the proper view of authority. The text opposes Jesus' utterance of two hypotheses: "if I cast out demons by Beelzebul" (12:27), the Pharisees' view, and "if it is by the Spirit of God that I cast out demons" (12:28), Jesus' view.[71] This opposition contrasts two views of the origin of the power used by Jesus: Beelzebul or the Spirit of God. Yet the point made by Matthew is broader, since it also concerns the power used in exorcisms by other persons than Jesus—such as the "sons" (followers) of the Pharisees (12:27). It then appears that ultimately the point made by this opposition addresses the question: Why do the Pharisees conclude that Jesus casts out demons by Beelzebul, the prince of demons?

For the Pharisees, the model for understanding authority and power is a prince who rules over his kingdom or city, or the head of a household who exerts authority and power over the household. According to this model, *one has power only over those who recognize one's authority*. One cannot expect to be obeyed by people who do not acknowledge one's authority! For the Pharisees, since the demons obey Jesus, it means that Jesus' authority is acknowledged by the demons and thus that he acts in the name of the prince of demons, Beelzebul (12:24, 27; cf. 9:34), or even that he is Beelzebul himself (10:25). We can even say that the Pharisees certainly view the relation of authority and power in the image of their own authority and power as religious leaders and as heads of households—as fathers.[72] They have power over the crowds only insofar as the crowds acknowledge their authority—thus their concern when the crowds begin to recognize Jesus' authority (12:24–25)! In this perspective, authority and power are one. The realm over which one has power is limited to the realm where one's authority is recognized and acknowledged. Conversely, recognizing the authority of someone is acknowledging that one is under the power of that person—a view that will be challenged in 12:38–45.

By contrast, for Jesus, the realm over which he has power is not limited to the realm where his authority is acknowledged. Here the model is that of God's power which is universal even though his authority is not universally acknowledged, as is expressed by the exceptional use of the phrase "kingdom of God" (12:28, rather than "kingdom of heaven"). It follows that the use of power changes character: it is primarily directed and exerted against alien powers—such as demonic powers—which threaten the realm where (God's and Jesus') authority is or should be acknowledged, and no longer exerted upon one's subordinates. It is an aggressive, expansionist use of power aimed at making the conquest of new territories for one's kingdom at the expense of alien powers—or at liberating these territories from the alien powers that subjugate them so that they might join one's kingdom. Thus it is a matter of plundering a strong man's—that is, Satan's—house (12:29), and, for this purpose, Satan's power needs to be neutralized or defeated. The strong man needs to be bound (12:29), the demons need to be cast out (12:28).[73]

Because of their view of power and authority, the Pharisees fail to perceive that the exorcisms and healings of Jesus—as well as those of the "sons" of the Pharisees and, by extension, of the disciples (cf. 10:1, 8)—are aggressive, destructive uses of power against evil powers. Then Jesus mocks their understanding of his exorcism and turns their argument against themselves ("[your sons] shall be your judges," 12:27b) by showing that from the Pharisees' perspective such a use of power would be as self-destructive as a civil war or as family strifes (12:25–26).

In view of these points (convictions) conveyed by the oppositions, we can understand the phrase "kingdom of God"; it is thematic, since it surprises Matthew's readers, who so far have encountered only the phrase "kingdom of heaven." The phrase "the kingdom of God has come upon you" (12:28b) is associated with the "Spirit of God" which, as we noted regarding 12:18, is closely linked with the power of God. From the preceding observations, it is clear that "kingdom of God" refers to an aggressive manifestation of the *power of God* which asserts itself against satanic and demonic powers. It is to be contrasted with the "kingdom of heaven" which, as we saw, refers to the *authority of God*—an authority which, at present, is not imposed upon people through the use of power but which people (should) recognize and acknowledge in the meekness and mercy of the Father and the Son.[74] Obviously, "kingdom of God" and "kingdom of heaven" are complementary. The liberation of human beings from demonic powers—the manifestation of the kingdom of God—is necessary in order to set up favorable conditions so that, without coercion, people might acknowledge the authority of the Father—the kingdom of heaven—manifested and revealed by the Son and later by the disciples. This is what is expressed by the parable of the strong man (Satan) whose house (people under Satan's power) is plundered after he is bound (12:29). Manifestations of divine power—the kingdom of God—and manifestations of meek authority—the kingdom of heaven—have the same ultimate goal, that of gathering together the kingdom, the people or household of God.

12:30–32. Now one can understand that, in its second part, the discourse opposes gathering with Jesus to scattering by being against him (12:30). Those who perceive that the use of power is directed against alien, satanic powers join Jesus in using power constructively, gathering a community, the people or kingdom of God. By contrast, those who conceive that power is also exerted upon one's own kingdom, city, or household—that is, those who conceive power as the expression of authority—divide, scatter the kingdom, the city, or the household. They work against the gathering of the kingdom, that is, against what Jesus' ministry is all about.

The negative formulation of 12:30—"He who is not with me is against me, and he who does not gather with me scatters"—shows that the point made by this opposition concerns primarily what it means to be irremediably against Jesus. Who are those who have reached the point of no return and can only be scattering? Who are those who have committed the sin or blasphemy that is not and will not be forgiven (12:31–32)? Since God desires mercy, as a rule "every sin and blasphemy will be forgiven" (12:31a). But there is one exception, the blasphemy against the Spirit (12:31b, 32b). A rejection of Jesus that denies that the power used in his miracles is the power of God, the Holy Spirit—and that blasphemously identifies this supernatural power with Beelzebul (or Satan)—will not be forgiven. This is the case of the Pharisees (12:24) and also of the Israelite cities that rejected Jesus despite his miracles (11:20–24). Already they are irremediably condemned because, by their blasphemy, they also deny the need for any intervention of God. As was the case with the Israelite cities (11:20–24), they are confident that they will be exalted, and thus do not believe they need to be freed from the power of the strong man, Satan (12:29).

Yet Matthew insists that the blasphemy against the Son of man will be forgiven (12:32a). Indeed, for Matthew, during his ministry Jesus is the Son of man as the one who manifests God's mercy by his meekness and humiliation and thus by his refusal to use power to impose himself (cf. 8:20; 9:6; 11:19; 12:8). Rejecting the Son of man does not necessarily involve denying the Spirit of God, God's power. Thus, in order to join Jesus in gathering the kingdom, one needs to acknowledge that gathering cannot take place as long as divine power, the Spirit, does not intervene and bind the strong man, Satan, and the demonic powers.

12:33–37. The two narrative oppositions of the concluding part of the discourse make two related points. The injunction "Either make the tree good . . . or make the tree bad" (12:33), the first opposition, underscores that people are responsible both for their good works—joining Jesus in gathering—and for their bad works—scattering and rejecting Jesus and the Spirit. In this new context, the saying (already found in 7:16–17) takes on an additional meaning; people are responsible for their view of the relationship between authority and power—what causes them to bear good fruit or bad fruit.[75] They can choose to reject the view of religious authority and power that the Pharisees have; then they will be a good tree and bear good fruit. A similar point is made through the opposition of "bringing forth good" and "bringing forth evil" out of one's treasure (12:35). One is responsible for what is in one's treasure. Yet, by contrast with the saying about laying up treasure in heaven (6:19–21), gathering such a good treasure is not practicing an overabundant righteousness but is its precondition, that is, making sure one has the proper view of God's authority and power. Then, out of the overabundance of one's heart, one speaks good things (see 12:34), and this is essential, since at the judgment people "will render account for every careless word they utter" (12:36), especially blaspheming against the Spirit. For this reason one must avoid adopting the attitude of the Pharisees—"brood of vipers" (12:34; cf. 3:7)—who appear to say good things while they are still evil, that is, while they still have the wrong view of religious authority, and thus deny both God's power and his authority as manifested in Jesus' ministry.

12:37. While 12:33–36 can be viewed as further expressing the main points of the preceding passage, this verse, "For by your words you will be justified, and by your words you will be condemned," is in tension with the readers' former knowledge. Indeed, in chapter 11 it was said that "wisdom is justified by her deeds" (11:19), not by her words. Similarly, in the Sermon on the Mount the verses following the saying about the good tree and its good fruit emphasize that one might be condemned even if one says the right words—"Lord, Lord," words that recognize the true power of Jesus—when one does not perform good works (7:21–23). In 11:19, 7:21–23, and other such passages, one is justified by one's deeds or works rather than by one's words, as in 12:37. Since by now the readers trust Matthew, who has demonstrated that he is reliable, they have to presuppose that these two types of statements in Jesus' mouth do not contradict each other. Thus they are led to interpret these sayings in terms of the points to which they are related. It then appears that 11:19 and 7:21–23 speak of Wisdom (Jesus) and of disciples as carrying out their vocation and being justified *when their works match their words*—the teaching of wisdom, the acknowledgment of Jesus as Lord. By contrast, 12:37 deals with the preconditions for doing good works, namely, acknowledging the power and authority of Jesus and of God and thus saying the right words about them. It is only if one can utter good words about Jesus' and God's power and authority that one can hope to be justified—by acting in accordance with these words. But if one speaks evil about Jesus' and God's power and authority, one is already condemned—the blasphemy against the Spirit—and one cannot do good works. Even though they are not sufficient—they need to be complemented by good works—*good words are necessary*.

12:38–45. The True Nature of Jesus' Authority. The Sign of Jonah

The opening sentence clearly connects with the preceding pericope:"Some of the scribes and Pharisees said to [Jesus], 'Teacher, we wish to see a sign from you'" (12:38). The Jewish leaders are presented as responding positively to Jesus' discourse and as taking seriously his warnings.

They want to be convinced that it is by the power or Spirit of God that he performs his miracles. Jesus' response (12:39ff.) shows that their question is fundamentally wrong, in spite of their good intentions. An opposition between the two sayings is thus established. The point made by this opposition addresses the question: How can one recognize that Jesus' power is God's power, the Spirit?

For the Pharisees the answer is: By seeing a "sign" from him, that is, by seeing an unmistakable demonstration of God's power. That "scribes" are involved and that they call Jesus "teacher" suggests that they expect this sign to establish the validity both of Jesus' power and of his authority as teacher. The Pharisees still identify authority and power (cf. 12:25–30), and for them one's authority as teacher is only at the measure of the power that one can use.

Jesus rejects this view and abruptly denies their request which is that of "an evil and adulterous generation" (12:39a). But simultaneously, Jesus points out what should demonstrate for them the divine origin of his authority and power: the "sign of the prophet Jonah" (12:39b–41) and his wisdom teaching (12:42); by contrast, the performance of signs (exorcisms) does not help; it renders matters worse for this evil generation (12:43–45).[76]

12:39b–41. Regarding the sign of Jonah the prophet, note that the text exclusively mentions staying "in the belly of the whale" or "in the heart of the earth" for "three days and three nights" (12:40; cf. Jonah 2:1). The emphasis is on the death, the powerlessness of Jesus, the "Son of man"— a title that consistently has this connotation (cf. 12:32). In spite of the number of days, which in other contexts is directly associated with the resurrection, in this passage the resurrection is not in itself part of the sign of Jonah as understood by Matthew.[77] The ultimate powerlessness of the Son of man, his death, is the ultimate sign of his divine authority. The sign of Jonah is also the proclamation of a message of repentance (12:41)—an integral part of the proclamation of the kingdom (cf. 4:17) by the humiliated Son of man. The people of Nineveh accepted such a message and repented; "this generation" should also be convinced by this message and thus repent. One can understand how these two aspects of the sign of Jonah are related when one recalls that, for Matthew, repenting is first of all turning toward God (cf. 3:8, 4:17), a *voluntary* submission to the authority of God (cf. 5:17–48)—since it involves making God's will one's own will. Preaching such a message of repentance can therefore be done only by someone who does not coerce people, by someone who is meek. Using power to bring people to submit voluntarily to the authority of God is a contradiction in terms. Similarly, the queen of the South comes to hear the wisdom of Solomon (12:42). She is not coerced to do so. She is a *queen*, a person who has power. She submits voluntarily to the wisdom teaching and thus to the authority of God.

12:41–42. In this context Jesus affirms that he is "greater than Jonah" (12:41), and "greater than Solomon" (12:42). Jesus' authority is comparable to and greater than that of the prophets—note that Jonah is called "the prophet" (12:39). It is also comparable to and greater than the authority of Solomon, the greatest teacher of wisdom in Scripture. Since the Pharisees recognize the authority of such prophets and teachers, Jesus' meekness, his preaching of repentance, and his teaching of wisdom (cf. 11:19) should demonstrate for them the divine source of his authority. Consequently, they should repent, turn toward God, and submit to God's authority as manifested in the ministry and teaching of the meek Son of man. But they do not, and thus will be condemned by the people of Nineveh (12:41) and the queen of the South (12:42).

12:43–45. An additional sign—another exorcism—would not help. In order to make this point, Jesus compares exorcism to the cleaning of a house—its effect is a house "swept, and put in order" (12:44b). This analogy is comparable to the presentation of exorcism as the liberation by the power of God of a territory for the kingdom and as the plundering of a strong man's house (12:24–30). But if, after the exorcism, the "house" is left empty (12:44), that is, if that person (or "this. . . generation," 12:45b) does not willingly submit to a new authority, the authority of God, if the house is not filled up by another authority, the unclean spirit comes back with other unclean spirits and the situation is worse than before (12:45). "So shall it be also with this evil generation" (12:45b). It is cleansed, liberated from demonic powers by Jesus' miracles. But because it does not seize this opportunity to turn toward God, the situation of this evil generation will become worse. It will be submitted to demonic powers even more than before.

In sum, liberation from demonic powers by interventions of divine power (the Holy Spirit) through Jesus' miracles is useless in and of itself, that is, as long as people who benefit from such a liberation do not respond by repenting, turning toward God, acknowledging and submitting to God's authority. Furthermore, it is not in the signs—miracles—in themselves that people can acknowledge the divine origin of Jesus' ministry but in his meekness as Son of man, in his preaching of repentance, and in his wisdom teaching. True religious authority is to be recognized in those who call to repentance—the voluntary turning toward God, the voluntary acknowledgment of God's authority—and thus who do not use power or coercion as they preach and/or teach people to repent. Otherwise their submission to God's authority would not be voluntary, it would not be repentance. But then, when one has acknowledged the divine authority of the meek Son of man's preaching and teaching, one can recognize that Jesus' mighty works are performed by the Spirit of God so as to bind the strong man,

Satan, who could otherwise have prevented the voluntary submission to the authority of God, repentance.

12:46–50. The Household of God

We have noted that the Pharisees rejected Jesus and his ministry because their incorrect view of authority and power was derived from other models of authority: a prince ruling over a kingdom or a city, or the head of a household (12:25). Acknowledging Jesus' authority and power demands a different and correct view of religious authority—a view based on a different model of authority, Jesus and his disciples as forming a new type of household (or family). In this context, the scene in which Jesus refuses to speak to his mother and brothers (12:46–50) receives a specific meaning. For Matthew, by his response (actually a non-response!) to the request of his mother and brothers, Jesus presents the household of God as a new model of authority.

Whether or not 12:47 is part of Matthew's text (12:47 is missing in important manuscripts), the text opposes designating Jesus' kinfolks as his mother and brothers (12:47 and 48a) and designating those who do the will of God as his mother, brothers, and sisters (12:49–50). The point is clear. One needs to give up the traditional view of the family and its structure of authority—Jesus does not accede to the request of his mother and brothers (12:46)—as was already expressed in 10:37. The new view of the family is one that involves conceiving of God as head of the family—as Father (12:50). The new family comprises those who submit to the authority of God and do his will, that is, make his will their will. This is not merely substituting God as head of the family in place of a human father (or a prince). Instead of being submitted to the authority of someone (father or prince) because that person has power upon them—in such a case authority is imposed upon people—the disciples willingly submit to the authority of Jesus and of his Father. In the case of a traditional family, one does not have any choice; one has to submit to the structure of authority of the family into which one is born. By contrast, belonging to the household of God is a matter of choice, of wanting to do God's will—something that one is not coerced to do. There are indeed manifestations of God's power, but they are such that they do not in and of themselves demand the allegiance of people to God's authority. True acknowledgment and submission to the authority of the Father in heaven necessarily involves a voluntary submission to his will, repentance (12:41).

In sum, the fundamental reason for the rejection of Jesus—and for calling him Beelzebul—is the failure of repenting, of turning toward God, and thus of acknowledging his authority and doing his will, because one holds to a wrong view of authority. According to this wrong view, one has no choice but to submit to the authority of someone either because one is coerced to do so (by a prince who uses power to this end) or because one is born into this structure of authority (natural family). Acknowledging Jesus' authority and God's authority demands a different view of authority, a view that recognizes that God does not impose the acknowledgment of his authority by people. It is only in this perspective that one can recognize the manifestations of God's power for what they truly are rather than viewing them as a means of convincing (signs, 12:38) or of coercing people to submit to God's and Jesus' authority.

TEACHING THE CROWDS IN PARABLES; MATTHEW'S CONVICTIONS IN 13:1–53

Chapter 13:1–53 begins with the words: "That same day Jesus went out of the house and sat beside the sea. And great crowds gathered about him . . . and he told them many things in parables" (13:1–3). The abrupt change of location—which is surprising, since the readers did not know that Jesus was in a house!—clearly marks the beginning of a new part of the section that began in 9:35. Once again we find a temporal phrase, "that same day," which signals that 13:1–53 belongs with the preceding unit (12:22–50). Furthermore, the formulation of the disciples' question in 13:10 indicates that the disciples seek to understand why Jesus speaks in parables to the crowds, because they see themselves as having to speak to the crowds as Jesus does. As our examination of 13:10 will show, Matthew clearly conveys that the passage beginning in 13:11 is an instruction given to the disciples to help them in their own ministry which involves speaking to the crowds as Jesus does (cf. 10:7). It is because they have been charged to go in mission to the lost sheep of Israel (10:6), the harassed and helpless crowds (9:36), that the disciples need to be trained as scribes for the kingdom of heaven (13:52). Thus the instruction of Jesus to his disciples in 13:1–53 is linked with those expressed in 10:5b–42. It follows that 13:1–53 must be interpreted in terms of its relations to 12:22–50—the preceding unit whose points it further develops—and in terms of 9:35—10:42, which introduces the section that 13:1–53 concludes.[78] As we shall see, Matthew presents 13:1–53 as an instruction by Jesus to the disciples about speaking to the crowds, as he did in 10:5b–42.[79]

In 10:1–42 Matthew deliberately presents the disciples' mission as duplicating Jesus' ministry. Their mission should involve the same kinds of deeds as Jesus' deeds: healings and exorcisms (10:1, 8), and behavior manifesting the kingdom—not taking anything with them (10:9) and having a specific attitude under persecution (10:16–42). It should also include the same proclamation as Jesus' proclamation: the disciples' "words" (10:14) about the kingdom (10:7). Such deeds and proclamation are closely related. This was one of the main points of 11:1—12:5 according to which Jesus and his ministry are rejected because people fail to understand his deeds in terms of his words, and especially in terms of his proclamation of the kingdom which is also a call to repentance. But, so far in the Gospel, there is no clear example of Jesus preaching the kingdom to the crowds. This preaching was merely presented in the summary formula: "Repent, for the kingdom of heaven is at hand" (4:17)—the Sermon on the Mount is an example of teaching (see 5:2; 7:29) as distinct from preaching (see 4:23; 9:35). Thus the disciples (and the readers as would-be disciples) have not yet been trained to preach. This is what the discourse of 13:1–53 does by providing examples of Jesus' preaching together with their explanation for the disciples.

When one reads this unit, keeping in mind its relations to what precedes it, one can understand why Matthew waited until now to present this instruction about preaching. As 10:5–15 already indicates, both deeds and preaching should manifest the kingdom of heaven. Thus, as the proclamation of the kingdom is the proclamation of the Fatherhood of God (God as trustworthy provider and as supreme authority), so the disciples' deeds—healings and not taking anything with them—need to manifest the Fatherhood of God. Conversely, the proclamation of the kingdom needs to be like the deeds. Thus before showing how one should preach the kingdom, Matthew took up the more concrete case of Jesus' deeds. He describes Jesus' deeds as ambiguous. To begin with, they include both mighty deeds (11:20)—manifesting God's power, the Spirit of God (12:18, 28)—and meek deeds—the behavior of the humiliated Son of man, the sign of Jonah (11:19, 29; 12:39–41). The mighty deeds by themselves do not bring about the acknowledgment of Jesus' authority. As long as people do not repent and do not acknowledge God's authority, the mighty works can only be misinterpreted, because the relation between power and authority is misconstrued (12:22–50). One first needs to acknowledge the authority of God as manifested in the meek deeds—the sign of Jonah; then, and only then, can one properly understand the role and purpose of God's Spirit in the mighty deeds. Thus, the mighty deeds need to be wrapped into, hidden by, hopelessly mixed up with, meek deeds—a source of puzzlement but also the only key for a proper understanding of the mighty deeds.

Similarly, as 13:1–53 will show, speaking about the kingdom of heaven and its coming necessarily involves speaking about manifestations of the power of God—mighty deeds, the mysteries of the kingdom. But as the mighty deeds are puzzling, so the mysteries of the kingdom need to be presented in a puzzling way; they need to be expressed in parables, since a knowledge of these mysteries cannot help acknowledge the authority of God. It is only when the authority of God will have been acknowledged that the mysteries of the kingdom will become understandable. These mysteries will only be understood by those who have already received another message about the kingdom, a message that will have allowed them to acknowledge the Fatherhood of God. This basic message about the kingdom is, for Matthew, also communicated by speaking in parables. While the crowds cannot understand the mysteries of the kingdom expressed by the parables, they can understand the other part of the message conveyed by the parables, namely, "what has been hidden since the foundation of the world" (13:35).

This is what 13:1–53 will show. For our purposes, it is essential to recognize the overall organization of 13:1–53. Changes of addressees divide it into four parts:

Introduction. 13:1–3a.

1. Parable of the sower (*to the crowds*). 13:3b–9.
2. Teaching about speaking in parables and explanation of the parable of the sower (*to the disciples*). 13:10–23.
3. Parables of the weeds, of the mustard seed, and of the leaven (*both to the crowds and to the disciples*). 13:24–35.
4. Explanation of the parable of the weeds, parables of the treasure, the pearl, the net, and the householder (*to the disciples*). 13:36–52.

Conclusion. 13:53.

13:3b–9. The Parable of the Sower

Matthew 13:3b–9 has to be considered as a complete discourse unit addressed to the crowds since Jesus speaks to his disciples after these verses. In view of the following discussion about what the crowds can or cannot understand, one needs to consider how these verses can be interpreted apart from the following explanations. In so doing, we put ourselves in the position of the crowds who, according to 12:46, have heard the preceding dispute with the Pharisees.

These verses, when read by themselves, are puzzling. Yet the story of the parable makes sense. Despite repeated failures due to hostile elements—birds (13:4), sun (13:6), thorns (13:7)—the sower is more (a hundredfold) or less (sixtyfold or thirtyfold) successful in his enterprise (13:8). For the readers and their knowledge of the risks that farmers have to expect in their work, this story in itself is not surprising, except for the yields; a hundredfold, sixtyfold, and thirtyfold are extraordinary yields. Then when reading 13:9, "He who has ears, let him hear," the readers have to stop. Did they hear? What does Jesus want to teach by such a parable? Why did he tell such a story?

The readers are consequently led to interpret the parable in terms of the preceding chapters. The repeated failures of the sower are easily linked by the Pharisees with the rejections of Jesus and of his message. Is this a parable told so as to promise the ultimate success of Jesus and of his ministry? Yet the presentation of the yields in decreasing order, from a hundredfold to thirtyfold (13:8b), does not appear to be an appropriate figure for unmitigated success.

This incertitude in the interpretation of the parable is not removed, as is usually the case in other passages, by the discovery of points underscored in the text by narrative oppositions. Indeed, in Matthew's presentation of the parable of the sower there is a single multifold narrative opposition. The seeds falling on good soil (13:8) are opposed to the seeds falling along the path (13:4), on rocky ground (13:5), and upon thorns (13:7).[80] But the point made by this opposition can only be expressed in the form of a question: Why are certain seeds falling on good soil and others on bad soil? Actually, there is no clear answer. Is it because the sower is sometimes a good sower and at other times a bad sower who does not know how to discern bad soil from good soil? But nothing in the text suggests any criticism of the sower's action which is described as a single action (13:3–4). Then, are there other factors? If there are, why are they not mentioned? Is this a pointless story? The concluding verse, 13:9, clearly indicates that this is not the case.

13:10–23. Expressing the Mysteries of the Kingdom in Parables. Explanation of the Parable of the Sower

13:10. "Why do you speak to them in parables?" This question has a twofold effect. First, by formulating it, the disciples set themselves on Jesus' side over against the crowds, "them"; the contrast of disciples and crowds, one of the main points of 13:1–53, is thus posited.[81] Second, the question shows that the disciples' concern is with the way of speaking, speaking in parables, rather than with the meaning of a specific parable.[82] In sum, the disciples are presented as being concerned by pedagogical issues. They want to understand why and how Jesus speaks to the crowds, because they see themselves as being in the same relationship with the crowds as Jesus is. They themselves have been charged by Jesus to speak to the crowds (10:7). The very formulation of 13:10 links the following discourse with the charge to the disciples to go in mission to the lost sheep of Israel (10:6), the harassed and helpless crowds (9:36).

The question of 13:10 also suggests that the disciples are puzzled because Jesus speaks in parables, a puzzlement which already presupposes that the crowds—together with the readers—do not understand this kind of speech. This issue is the topic of the points made in the first part of Jesus' answer.

Two sets of narrative oppositions are found in 13:10–17. The first opposes the crowds who "do not see" and "do not hear," even though, in another sense, they see and hear (13:13, 14–15) *and* the disciples who see and hear (13:16).[83] The second opposes the prophets and the righteous people who do not see and hear specific things (13:17) *and* the disciples who see and hear these things (13:17).

13:13–16. In order to understand the point of the first opposition (13:13, 14–15 vs. 13:16) we need to consider how the text distinguishes the disciples from the crowds. To begin with, what the disciples see, hear, and know, and what the crowds do not see, do not hear, and do not know, is what is expressed by the parables, namely, the mysteries of the kingdom of heaven (13:11).[84] In view of the verbs used, these mysteries are manifested both in deeds, which can be seen, and in speech, which can be heard. But, for Matthew, mysteries of the kingdom are not all that can be seen and heard about the kingdom. It is emphasized in 13:12 that the knowledge of these mysteries is given to the disciples because ("for") they already have a certain knowledge about the kingdom.[85] The knowledge of the mysteries is a *surplus of knowledge about the kingdom*: "For to him who has will more be given, and he will have abundance" (13:12a). Here Matthew makes a distinction between two levels of knowledge about the kingdom: a primary or basic knowledge about the kingdom, and a surplus knowledge which is available only to those who have the basic knowledge. Since the crowds do not have this basic knowledge about the kingdom, they will not receive the surplus knowledge, the mysteries. What they have will be taken away from them (13:12b). But what does this mean?

The thematic presentation of this first point in terms of the readers' old knowledge creates several tensions. What can be taken away from those who have nothing? How is the quotation of Isa. 6:9–10 in Matt. 13:14–15 related to the preceding verses?[86] What is conveyed by the designation of the disciples as "blessed"? In order to be in a position to address these questions, we need to consider the related point expressed by the opposition of the disciples to the many prophets and the righteous (13:17).

13:17. This second opposition expresses another condition for receiving the knowledge of the mysteries of the kingdom. Note that according to the text, the only difference between the disciples and the prophets and righteous is *the time* in which they live: prophets and righteous belong to the past, the time of the Hebrew Scripture; the disciples belong to the present, the time of Jesus. In order to see and hear the mysteries of the kingdom, one needs to be in the present time, the time of Jesus, the time when the kingdom is manifested. Since they do not belong to this time, prophets and righteous cannot see and hear the mysteries, even though they "longed to see . . . and to hear" them (13:17). Except for this question of time, prophets and righteous had what is needed to know the mysteries. And what did they have? Like the prophet Jonah (12:41), they had the message that allows people to repent, to turn toward God acknowledging his authority without coercion. Like Solomon (12:42), the wise and righteous par excellence, they had wisdom, a knowledge of God's will which allows people to be righteous.[87] It is this twofold knowledge that made them long to see and hear the mysteries of the kingdom, a longing that is not satisfied merely because they belong to the wrong time in history.

13:12b. We can now better understand what Matthew says about the crowds. They belong to the right time, the present of Jesus. But they are prevented from seeing and hearing because they lack this longing for the mysteries of the kingdom. Furthermore, they do not long for the mysteries of the kingdom, because they do not have the twofold knowledge (the prophetic knowledge about repentance and wisdom) that the prophets and righteous had, a twofold knowledge which is nothing other than what we called the basic knowledge of the kingdom. The crowds have failed to appropriate the basic teaching of Scripture (in the Prophets and the wisdom books), that is, what was given to them in the past, including their election and vocation as the chosen people. Consequently they are without direction, without true longing—they are not oriented toward the kingdom. They are "harassed and helpless, like sheep without a shepherd" (9:36)! And so they are not qualified to be given the mysteries of the kingdom. Ultimately, what they have—Scripture and their election—will be taken away from them in an indeterminate future (13:12).

But 9:36—10:15 hints that condemnation of the crowds is not immediate. For Matthew, 13:10–17 does not express a final condemnation and rejection of the crowds.[88] Otherwise, there would be no reason to go and preach the kingdom to them as Jesus charges his disciples to do (10:7) and as he does himself (e.g., 4:17; 11:1). But this preaching of the basic message of the kingdom should not be confused with the telling of the mysteries of the kingdom. The crowds are not yet ready for it. Thus the second part of the proclamation of the kingdom, the proclamation of the mysteries, must be both made available to them for the time when they will be ready—when they will be disciples—and yet made unavailable. It needs to be expressed in parables so that hearing, they might not hear, in the same way that they see and do not see these mysteries of the kingdom in Jesus' deeds that they are unable to understand because of the parable-like ambiguity of these deeds (cf. 11:1—12:50).

13:14–15. In this perspective, the quotation from Isa. 6:9–10—it reexpresses a point in terms of the readers' knowledge of Scripture—is both quite appropriate and creates a possible tension. In the LXX translation selected here by Matthew,[89] this prophecy is appropriate in the sense that it reexpresses the situation of the crowds described in the preceding verses— hearing but not understanding, and so forth. Yet the LXX translation keeps the responsibility for this situation on the crowds (e.g., "their eyes they have closed") rather than reading it as a condemnation, as is the case in the Hebrew text where God commands the prophet to "make the heart of this people fat" and to "shut their eyes" so as to make sure they will not repent and be healed. Consequently, the concluding part of the prophecy, "lest they should perceive . . . and turn for me to heal them," is no longer a condemnation but is the deliberate choice of the crowds who refuse to repent—as Matthew repeatedly expressed (cf. 11:20–24; 12:41).

Thus, for Matthew, speaking in parables is not condemning the crowds not to hear. According to 13:13, it is *because* the crowds do not see, do not hear, and do not understand that Jesus speaks to them in parables.[90] They have put themselves in a position where they are not yet ready to hear the mysteries of the kingdom. And this will remain so as long as they do not become disciples by receiving and appropriating the basic message about the kingdom. If they would appropriate this message which is already found in Scripture, if they would accept repenting, then they would long for the kingdom and its mysteries and would understand the parables.

13:18–23. The explanation of the parable of the sower is addressed to the disciples. This obvious fact is significant in itself. Matthew has emphasized that the disciples are not like the crowds. In terms of 13:10–17, they have the basic knowledge of the kingdom; they have repented. Yet they need explanations in order to hear the parable of the sower (13:18). This means that hearing (and seeing) is not spontaneous or automatic as soon as one has appropriated the basic knowledge of the kingdom and has repented. One still needs to be taught and learn how to interpret the parables[91]— and how to interpret Jesus' deeds which are parable-like. One needs to be trained as a scribe for the kingdom of heaven; one needs to be made a disciple (cf. 13:52). The explanation of the parable of the sower, indeed the entire discourse of Jesus to the disciples, is training them to be scribes for the kingdom.

The single opposition of the parable (13:3–7), the seeds falling on different kinds of soil, has been replaced in the interpretation by two interrelated narrative oppositions. On the one hand, not understanding the word (13:19)—and immediately receiving the word with joy (13:20) which is presented as similar to not understanding it—is opposed to understanding the word (13:23). On the other hand, being unfruitful (not bearing fruit, 13:22) is opposed to bearing fruit (13:23). What happens is therefore clear. The point of the parable—which remained undefined in 13:3–7—is now made explicit. What is this point? Both the person who understands and the person who does not understand (or falls away, or is unfruitful) "hear the word of the kingdom" (13:19, 20, 22, and 23). The difference between the two groups concerns what they do with the word, and consequently their inability or ability to make it bear fruit.

13:19. In the case of the seeds sown along the path, the focus is on the receiver of the seed—the soil, the hearer of the word. While that person is deprived of the word by "the evil one," who comes and snatches it away, the receiver of the word remains responsible. It is because that person "does not understand it" that the evil one comes, not vice versa.[92] The failure to understand the word cannot be blamed on the evil one, who ends up controlling the life of such people—and on any other outsider, for that matter.

The person who hears the word is fully responsible for understanding or not understanding the word. But what does this involve? Note that the word is "sown in [the] heart," that is, in the place where someone's will is established. Consequently, understanding the word means appropriating it, internalizing it into one's heart (cf. 5:21–44). It means allowing the word to establish one's will, one's vocation, what one wants to do. This first case does not explain what prevents a person from understanding the word. But the following cases can do it, now that it has been stated that the person who receives the word is responsible for appropriating the word.

13:20–21. In the case of the seeds sown on rocky ground, the text becomes more specific. The person receives the word *with joy* (13:20), a joy contrasted with the "tribulation or persecution . . . on account of the word" (13:21). This is to say that the word of the kingdom is wrongly perceived by this person as good news which should only bring blessings and good things to those who receive it. In such a case, of course, one can immediately receive it (13:20); one readily accepts it, since one thinks that its blessings are obtained without cost. But when one is confronted with what the word entails, as immediately as one received it one "falls away" (13:21). Even though the word of the kingdom is good news, gospel (cf. 4:23; 11:5), its true understanding involves the recognition that commitment to the word brings about tribulation and persecution, as 10:14–33 indicates concerning the disciples' mission.

13:22. Since the case of the seeds sown among thorns is involved in a different opposition (about not bearing fruit and bearing fruit), it makes a point that moves beyond the preceding one.[93] Even though one might have received the word and be committed to it despite the tribulation and persecution it brings about, one remains fruitless if one's life is simultaneously characterized by "cares of the world" and "delight in riches." In effect, in such a case one attempts to serve two masters, an impossibility (see 6:24–32). In order to bear fruit, one should not have cares of the world and delight in riches. Or, to put it positively, one needs to have the attitude presupposed by the command given to the disciples as they go in mission: "Take no gold, nor silver, . . . no bag for your journey" (10:9–10).

13:23. The relations between chapters 10 and 13 suggest that, for Matthew, bearing fruit is having a successful mission which is possible if, and if only, the disciples recognize that preaching the word of the kingdom (cf. 10:7, 14) entails rejection and persecution, and giving up cares of the world and delight in riches (cf. 10:9–10).

Now one can begin to understand what the phrase "word of the kingdom" (13:19) designates, namely, the basic message about the kingdom which the disciples should proclaim to the crowds (10:7). Matthew further suggests it by the contrasting juxtaposition of Jesus' exhortation *to the disciples*, "Hear then the parable" (13:18),[94] with the description "when any one hears the word of the kingdom" (13:19), which refers to a hearing by an indefinite person, someone in a crowd.

Because of Jesus' explanation, the disciples can hear and understand the parable, the mysteries of the kingdom—not to be confused with the basic knowledge of the kingdom. What are these mysteries? A knowledge about why certain people receive the basic message of the kingdom and become fruit-bearing disciples, and mainly why other people do not do so? No, it is not because "the evil one" is overpowering and "snatches away" the word, making it impossible for this people to repent. Rather, it is because they do not want to repent (cf. 13:14–15, 19), or because they misconceive the good news of the kingdom as promising a life without tribulation and persecution (13:20–21), or again because they let the cares of the world and the delight in riches be a primary concern in their lives (13:22). Such is a first mystery of the kingdom, mystery that the crowds who have not yet repented do not need to hear but that the disciples (including those from the crowds who repent) need to know as they carry out their mission. Indeed, they need to be aware of what causes the rejection of their message so as to be able to design a mission that will appropriately confront the situation. In their preaching of the kingdom, the disciples need to *convince*— they need to change the will of those who, so far, did not want to repent. They also need to make sure that it is clear that the proclamation of the kingdom does not promise a life free of suffering—as they do by witnessing that it is for Jesus' (and the kingdom's) sake that they are persecuted (10:18–20). They also need to warn people that receiving the gospel necessarily involves giving up cares for the world and one's riches—as they demonstrate by not taking anything with them when going in mission (10:9–10).

By comparing the explanation of the parable of the sower (13:18–23) with the parable itself (13:3–7), one may begin to grasp what is meant by "hearing and understanding" the parables—the proper interpretation that the disciples should make. What happened in the passage from the parable to its interpretation? First, it is striking that the multifold opposition of actions of the parable—about seeds falling on different soils—formally disappears; falling is no longer found in the explanation. Yet the seeds and the soils become even more important; indeed, the whole point of the explanation concerns those who hear the word. A displacement of the center of meaning takes place. For the readers—and the crowds—the actions of falling on different soils were perceived as signals that the main point concerned the agent of the action, the one responsible for making the seeds fall on different soils, the sower. Then the parable was impossible to understand. The crowds did not realize that with strange stories such as the parables— and unusual deeds such as those of Jesus—the way of perceiving (hearing and seeing) needs to be out of the ordinary. Confronted by the actions of these stories and deeds, one should not begin by asking: What are the qual-ifications of the one who acts? Who is he? What is the origin of his power? These were the very questions raised by John in 11:3 and by the crowds and the Pharisees in 12:23–24! By beginning with these kinds of questions one reaches meaningless conclusions! As the explanation shows, the point, the mysteries of the kingdom, is not to be found in what brings about the actions and deeds—the agents, the origins of the actions—but rather in their results, their effects, that is *seeds on a path, on rocky ground, among thorns, on good soil.* This is exactly what Jesus does in his answer to the Pharisees in 12:25–29, which amounts to saying: First, consider the result of the actions, namely, the destruction of the kingdom of Satan, and then you will be able to speak about the origin of my power! It is only after focusing one's at-tention upon the results of the actions—seeds on different soils—that one can understand the meaning of the parable. Thus the explanation under-scores by its oppositions what the soils do with the seeds or word (13:19–20) or what the seeds do with the soils (13:22–23), and in the process it becomes clear that the mysteries of the kingdom concern what people do with the word of the kingdom which they hear.[95]

13:24–35. Uttering Things Hidden
Since the Foundation of the World
in the Parables of the Weeds,
the Mustard Seed, and the Leaven

The third part of the discourse,[96] which presents three additional parables, is apparently addressed to the disciples, since, following a speech explicitly addressed to them, it is introduced by the words, "Another parable he put before *them*" (13:24). Yet these parables are also addressed to the crowds, as is specified in 13:34–35, that is, after the parables.

For the readers, this unfolding of the text functions as a trap. In the preceding verses they identified themselves with the disciples who hear and understand the parable of the sower as they listen to or read its explanation by Jesus.[97] Now, because of the ambiguity of 13:24, the readers are led to believe that these new parables are addressed to the disciples and therefore that they, the readers, are in a position of fully hearing and understanding them. By allowing the text to guide them, as they did in 13:18–23, they will be able to understand the mysteries of the kingdom that these parables convey, will they not? But 13:34–35 reveals that these parables were ad-dressed to the crowds and that the readers have been surreptitiously led to read these parables as the crowds hear them. Yet they have understood them, have they not? This means, then, that the crowds themselves receive a teaching from hearing the parables. Of course, this teaching is not a knowl-edge of the mysteries of the kingdom—which is reserved for disciples, and will be given in the explanation of the parable of the weeds (13:36–43). As

13:34–35 specifies, what the crowds (and the readers) can directly understand are things "hidden since the foundation of the world."

This game which Matthew plays at the expense of the readers is not frivolous. It shows why Jesus speaks in parables to the crowd. As 13:3–17 indicated, the crowds are unable to understand the main point of the parables, namely, the mysteries of the kingdom that they reveal. But one should not conclude from this that the parables are totally meaningless for the crowds, as seemed to be the case with the parable of the sower. Besides the mysteries of the kingdom that the parables convey *to the disciples,* there is in the parables a teaching *for the crowds.* On the basis of our discussion of 13:10–17, we can anticipate that the parables convey to the crowds the basic knowledge of the kingdom ("the word of the kingdom") that they need to appropriate in order to become disciples.

13:24–30. *The parable of the weeds* is actually presented by Matthew in a way that is meaningful for the readers/crowds. In it Matthew sets no fewer than four narrative oppositions so that there will be no way for the readers/crowds to miss its multifold point. This parable makes for them a point about the kingdom (13:24), even though they will not understand the mysteries of the kingdom that this same parable conveys to the disciples (cf. 13:36–43).

13:24–28a. The text first opposes the action of the man who sowed good seed (13:24, 27b) to that of his enemy who sowed weeds (13:25, 28a). This opposition concerns the fact that besides the good owner of the field, there is an enemy who craftily sows weeds among the wheat, the good seeds sown by the owner. The point expressed by the description of the enemy as contrasted with the owner is that this enemy and his work are *hidden.* He acts while people are "sleeping," and, his work done, he goes away (13:25); he is not seen by anyone. Furthermore, at first and for a long time, no one takes notice of the weeds; it is only much later, "when the plants came up and bore grain," that "the weeds appeared" and thus became visible (13:26).

The conflicting interpretations of the situation by the servants (13:27a) and by the householder (13:28a)—a second opposition—make the point that, contrary to the householder, the servants were not aware of the enemy's role. They wrongly thought that everything in the field was the result of the activity of the owner—whom they call "Lord" (au.), possibly expressing that he has full authority not only upon them but also upon the field and what happens in it. The servants' questions express their surprise, indeed their confusion, when they discover weeds, evil, in the field of the owner. They do not understand the origin of evil; for them, evil should not exist. But the householder reveals to them that an enemy is the cause of evil.

13:28b–30. Two additional points are made in the second exchange in which the servants propose to go and gather the weeds and the householder forbids them to do so. A first opposition concerns the servants, who believe they know what the householder wants ("Then do you want us . . . ?" 13:28), while the householder shows them that they do not know what he wants ("No," 13:29). For the servants, as soon as one discovers a manifestation of evil, it is self-evident that it should be removed; one's will, one's vocation, is to react against what is evil so as to condemn it and destroy it. The presence of evil demands *active judgmental interventions* against it. But the householder's response shows that this view is totally wrong: one's will or vocation should be established in terms of the manifestation of good, that is, in terms of what it is good to do vis-à-vis the wheat. Far from being a reaction against evil, one's vocation should manifest one's concern for the good; one first needs to consider what will be the consequence of one's action for the wheat. The disciples' vocation is to be established in terms of the kingdom, as the ultimate good—by repenting, by turning oneself toward the kingdom. In other words, one cannot become a disciple—and have the proper vocation—as long as one thinks that one's vocation should be primarily negative, judgmental, a vocation to fight evil. (Note that the disciples' vocation as manifested in their mission described in 10:5b–15 is first of all positive; it becomes judgmental when it is rejected, and not because it aims at judging and condemning.)

The fourth opposition involves the proposed action of the servants— gathering the weeds (13:29)—and the householder's command: "Let both grow together until the harvest" (13:30). The action proposed by the servants is not wrong in itself; the weeds must be gathered and burned (see 13:30). What is wrong is the timing. Now is not the time to do so; it will be done at the time of the harvest. This point has been repeatedly made, first in 3:14–15: one's vocation is to do what is fitting for the present time, and now is not the time of the (active) judgment. Now is the time of mercy (9:13; 12:7), the time to let both grow together, the time when "your Father . . . sends rain on the just and on the unjust"(5:45).

Thus for the readers/crowds the parable of the weeds reveals that from the beginning, from the time of the sowing, evil existed even though it was hidden and appeared only at a later time; that its origin is an enemy of the householder; that one's vocation is not to be a reaction against the presence of evil, a punitive vocation; and that one's vocation and actions must be fitting for the present time, and established in terms of what is good. As is clear, this is the basic message about the kingdom, "the word of the kingdom," addressed to the crowds by Jesus in his preaching and teaching which are a call to repent and to turn toward the kingdom. But it includes a new element: the revelation—the uncovering of something hidden—that an enemy is at the origin of evil.

Both the parable of the mustard seed (13:31–32) and that of the leaven

(13:33) do not include any opposition. They do not make any new point. Rather, for Matthew, they are the thematic development of the preceding points; the readers should interpret them in terms of what they already know, and most directly in terms of the parable of the weeds.

13:31–32 The sowing of *the mustard seed* (13:31) is thus associated with the sowing of the good seed in the preceding parable. But the juxtaposition of the two parables brings about tensions that signal the points Matthew emphasizes for his readers by twisting their expectations. While the parable of the weeds underscored that the existence of the weeds and their origin were hidden by contrast with the wheat of which the servants were aware, now the good seed is itself described as "the smallest of all seeds" (13:32), and thus as hardly visible. Furthermore, the preceding parable had emphasized the simultaneous, and thus apparently equal, growth of weeds and wheat (13:30). Now the mustard seed, the good seed, is presented as growing into the greatest of the plants—into a shrub or tree with branches big enough for birds to make nests in them (13:32). Thus this word about the kingdom is the revelation that the manifestation of the kingdom is originally very small and hardly visible, and yet its growth will far surpass the growth of evil.[98]

13:33. Similarly, the *parable of the leaven* (13:33) assimilates the good, the kingdom, to something originally hidden—the leaven hidden by a woman in a great amount of flour (the three "measures" mentioned might amount to forty pounds of flour). One could think that the leaven would be lost in all this flour and overwhelmed by it, as the thorns choked the good seed (13:7, 22). But it is the hidden and miniscule leaven that makes the whole of the flour rise. Despite its small, hidden beginning, the kingdom will succeed in affecting and transforming all that seemed to threaten it.

13:34–35. Matthew comments on this discourse of Jesus to the crowds in a concluding statement about speaking in parables which one is tempted to interpret in terms of 13:10–17. But the point expressed by the opposition of 13:34 (speaking in parables and speaking without parables) is quite different.[99] The opening phrase "all this" refers to what was expressed in the three preceding parables, as is specified by the quotation of Ps. 78:2.[100] By means of the parables, Jesus utters "what has been hidden since the foundation of the world" (13:35), that is, the hidden existence and origin of evil since the beginning, the hidden character of the kingdom which, in the beginning, is like the smallest of the seeds or like a small lump of leaven hidden in a great amount of flour but which will surely triumph—becoming the largest plant and making the whole dough rise. "All this" is said, communicated by Jesus, *to the crowds*. These are not mysteries of the kingdom that the crowd could not understand. Rather, these are parts of the basic message about the kingdom to which the crowds have access and which will be taken away from them if they do not repent (13:12). Other parts of this basic message about the kingdom can be expressed without parables (e.g., the Sermon on the Mount), but the things hidden since the foundation of the world must be communicated to the crowds in parables. In such a case, even for the crowds, the parables do not conceal; rather, they reveal. Far from being kept from the crowds, these hidden things should be proclaimed "in the light" and "upon the housetops" by the disciples (10:26–27), even though these hidden things (including the revelation of the Father) will be received only by the "babes," by those who have been chosen by the Son (11:25–27), that is, by those who will become disciples. But these hidden things are not the whole message of these parables. The same parables also reveal for the disciples mysteries of the kingdom, as is explained in the following verses.

13:36–53. Explanation of the Parable of the Weeds. Parables of the Treasure, the Pearl, the Net, and the Householder

The mention that Jesus "left the crowds and went into the house" with his disciples (13:36) clearly separates this part of the discourse from the rest. Without any ambiguity, it is exclusively addressed to the disciples. Thus the readers anticipate that they will at last find in these verses a new dimension of Jesus' teaching, his revelation of the mysteries of the kingdom to the disciples beyond what was expressed in 13:18–23. But the formal characteristics of 13:36–53 show that these expectations are somewhat misguided. Indeed, there is only one opposition of actions here! Matthew underscores a single point. Most of this passage is thematic. Matthew presupposes that his readers understand most of this teaching on their own, in terms of what they already know—the mysteries of the kingdom should not be new for the readers. If they remember what has been previously expressed in the Gospel, the readers should readily understand all that is expressed in 13:36–53. To the question "Have you understood all this?" they should be able to answer together with the disciples: "Yes" (13:51). This means that Matthew invites us to interpret 13:36–53 in terms of what precedes in the Gospel—the first part of chapter 13, but also the entire section, which began in 9:35.

13:37–43. In the *explanation of the parable of the weeds*, Matthew sets the pattern that needs to be followed for reading the concluding part of the discourse. He does so by preserving in the explanation a single opposition out of the four oppositions of the parable: "He who sows the good seed" (13:37) is opposed to "the enemy who sowed [the weeds]" (13:39). But the point is quite different. The sower of the good seed must be identified with "the Son of man" (13:37) and the enemy with "the devil" (13:39). While the identification of the enemy as the devil, the evil one (13:38), was expected, it is surprising that the Son of man be identified as the owner of the field, the householder who sows the good seed at the time of the creation (since it is something hidden "since the foundation of the world," 13:35). There is a temporal displacement from the parable to its explanation.[101] The mysteries of the kingdom do not concern what was "hidden since the foundation of the world"—they are not revelations about "what is old" (see 13:52), what prophets and righteous of the Old Testament already knew (see 13:17). Rather, the mysteries of the kingdom concern the Son of man, and what happens and will happen in his ministry and until the end of the world—they are revelations about "what is [and will be] new" (13:52; cf. 9:14–34).

There is no difficulty in recognizing that this observation also applies, in retrospect, to 13:18–23. Although it was not the point that was emphasized, the identification of the seed as "the word of the kingdom"—what Jesus (and the disciples) preaches—relates the explanation of the parable of the sower to the ministry of the Son of man (and of the disciples). Thus 13:36–53 is the conclusion of the discourse in parables (13:1–53). Furthermore, the emphasis on the newness of the ministry of the Son of man also links 13:36–53 with 9:33 which, as we noted, made a point of the newness of Jesus' ministry, which the Pharisees rejected (9:34). It then appears that 13:36–53 is also the thematic conclusion of the entire section 9:35—13:53 which develops both the negative theme of rejection and the positive theme of the newness of the Son of man's ministry and what it entails. This is confirmed by the fact that, as we shall see, both the theme of the judgment (the harvest, 9:37) and that of the positive ministry of Jesus and of the disciples (a shepherd-like ministry, 9:36) are also emphasized in 13:36–53.

13:40–41. The rest of the explanation of the parable of the weeds in 13:37–43 involves two features that are surprising for the readers. First, so far in the Gospel, the title "Son of man" was used to describe Jesus during his ministry as lowly, humiliated, and merciful (see 8:20; 9:6; 11:19; 12:8; 12:32), except in 10:23 which suggested without elaboration that the Son of man will have an eschatological role and thus raised for the readers a question without providing any clear answer for it.[102] Now, 13:40–41 explicitly states that the Son of man will have a role "at the close of the age." "The Son of man will send his angels," and they will carry out the destruction of the evildoers. Thus, the Son of man has great power and authority; at the end of time, far from being the meek and merciful personage he is during his ministry, he will use this power and authority in a terrible judgment. Furthermore, he is described as having a "kingdom" (13:41b) which is nothing else than "the world" (13:38a).[103] By contrast with the "kingdom of [the] Father," which is exclusively comprised of righteous people (13:43), the kingdom of the Son of man includes both righteous and evildoers—since the evildoers will be gathered by the angels "out of his kingdom" (13:41). Thus in the present (before the end of time) he is the lowly and merciful Son of man who tolerates evildoers.

13:41–43. A second feature that is surprising for the readers is the identification of the good seed and of the weeds. In the parable itself, the readers are led to associate themselves with the servants and their questions.[104] In the explanation, the servants disappear—only the reapers, identified as "angels," remain (13:39, 41)—and the good seeds are identified as "the sons of the kingdom" (13:38) with whom the readers now associate themselves. The effect of this additional displacement is comparable to what happened in the case of the explanation of the parable of the sower. Once again, as the contrast between "sons of the kingdom" and "sons of the evil one" (or "of evil," 13:38) suggests, and as is emphasized in the descriptions of their judgment in 13:41–43, the focus is upon what people do. The basis for the judgment is not their origin, whether they have been sown by the Son of man or by the devil, but their righteousness (13:43) or the fact that they are "causes of sin" (scandalous) and perform evil actions (13:41).[105]

In sum, the mysteries of the kingdom as expressed in 13:36–43 are primarily revelations that Jesus is not merely the meek and merciful Son of man during his ministry but also the eschatological Son of man, the wrathful judge at the end of time (cf. 10:32–33; 11:20–24), and that this judgment will be based upon what people do. Jesus is indeed the Lord of the harvest (9:37), and what people do during and in response to his present ministry (and that of his disciples) predetermines what will happen when he will come as the eschatological judge (cf. 10:13b–15). The following parables will underscore other mysteries of the kingdom, namely, those which concern how people should respond to the present ministry of the Son of man.

13:44–45. In the context of this discourse to the disciples, *the parable of the treasure and the parable of the pearl* must be interpreted as revealing mysteries of the kingdom, that is, as concerning the present of Jesus' ministry and, more specifically, the positive aspect of his ministry—the shepherd-like ministry of Jesus (and his disciples, cf. 9:36; 10:5–13a). It involves showing people *how to discover* what is hidden (13:44; since the foundation of the world, 13:35), such as a treasure (13:44) or a pearl of great value (13:45). The point of these parables is to show how people should fully devote themselves to the appropriation of this ultimate good. Once again the emphasis is put on what these people do: selling everything—giving up any other concerns (cf. 10:9–10; 13:22)—to devote themselves fully to the pursuit of this ultimate good.

13:47–50. *The parable of the net* brings together several of the preceding themes. The casting of the net and the gathering of "fish of every kind"

(13:47) correspond to Jesus' ministry and the kingdom of the Son of man which include righteous and evildoers. Then, as is specified in 13:49–50, the sorting of the good and bad fish—when the net is full and has been drawn ashore, that is, at the completion of time—is the eschatological judgment, when the evil ones will be thrown into the fires (13:50).

13:51. "Have you understood all this?" They said to him, "Yes." By now the disciples (and the readers) know why Jesus speaks in parables to the crowds; it is in order to reveal to them what was hidden from the foundation of the world. They also know how to interpret the parables so as to receive the message they contain for them as disciples—the mysteries of the kingdom concerning what is new in Jesus' ministry, how people respond to it, and how it is related to the eschatological judgment. Consequently, they also know how to interpret Jesus' deeds—by contrast with John, the crowds, and the Pharisees, who do not know how to do it (11:1—12:50). Actually, they should recognize that, by analogy with the parables, these deeds have a twofold purpose. Like the parables, these deeds aim at revealing to the crowds what was hidden from the foundation of the world, what the prophets and righteous of the Hebrew Bible knew—the Fatherhood of God, the kingdom of the Father as ultimate good, as treasure, as the exceptional pearl, as well as the existence of evil and its origin in the evil one (distinct from God). The disciples also understand that, like the parables, Jesus' deeds and his entire ministry through its meek and merciful character reveal who is blessed and who is condemned, and thus what will happen at the eschatological judgment. Those who radically reject Jesus' ministry are irremediably condemned (11:20–24; 12:31–32). For others, those who are simply puzzled by Jesus' deeds—John, the crowds—there is only one way of avoiding this fate: considering Jesus' deeds in terms of his preaching and teaching (11:1–19). If they appropriate his "word of the kingdom," this word of old, this call to repent, to turn toward God and his kingdom (12:38–42), and thus if they repent, they will understand these deeds. They will understand that they are the deeds of the Son of man who will also be the eschatological judge.

13:52. Understanding all of this, the disciples are like scribes[106] "trained" (made into disciples) for the kingdom of heaven (13:52). They have now a treasure of understanding which includes both "old" things—what was hidden since the foundation of the world, what needs to be preached and taught to the crowds—and "new" things, the mysteries of the kingdom about Jesus' ministry and its relationship to the judgment, which is to be revealed only to disciples. Thus, according to the circumstances—according to whom they speak—the scribe "trained for the kingdom . . . brings out of his treasure what is new and what is old" (13:52).

NOTES ON 9:35—13:53

1. By contrast with Mark and Luke; cf. Mark 6:12–13, 30 and Luke 9:6, 10; 10:17. See Beare, "Mission of the Disciples and Mission Charge," *JBL* 89 (1970):3.

2. So far we found only two sections that are narratively organized: chapters 2 and 3—4. On this issue, see BONNARD, 7–8; and GUNDRY, 10.

3. See also Matt. 3:12; Joel 3:1–13; Isa. 27:12–13.

4. Against GUNDRY, 180, who says they symbolize all the nations (i.e., Gentile nations).

5. See S. Brown, "Mission," *ZNW* 69 (1978):78–79. Brown provides a chart of verbal correlations between the functions and experiences attributed to the disciples in the discourse of chapter 10 and to Jesus throughout the Gospel.

6. S. Brown ("Mission," 76) following Schweizer (*Matthäus und seine Gemeinde*, 154) interprets the choice of the word "disciples" for the apostles in this section as a deliberate identification of the apostles of the past and the members of Matthew's present community.

7. See Gaechter, *Die literarische Kunst im Matthäus-Evangelium*, 40–43. He sees a chiasm in the structure of 10:5b–42.

8. See S. Brown, "Mission," 88.

9. In other words, Christology and ecclesiology are closely interrelated in this unit. This observation is against the common tendency of scholarship to separate them. See Kingsbury, "Form and Message of Matthew," 67–68, 71, for this dichotomization. Christology is the determinative factor for Kingsbury. S. Brown ("Mission") stresses ecclesiology in his assumption of the transparency of the disciples for Matthew's community. Neither pays enough attention to how the two are integrated. Our structural exegesis confirms Stanton's view of chapter 10 as a prime example of how "Matthew's ecclesiology is grounded in his christology." See Stanton, "Origin and Purpose."

10. For a critical discussion of the alleged contradictions between "Judaistic and universalistic tendencies" in Matthew's Gospel, see Tagawa, "People and Community in Matthew," *NTS* 16 (1969–70):154–55.

11. See S. Brown, "Mission," 79. See also Dupont, "Vous n'aurez pas achevé les villes d'Israël," *NOVT* 2 (1958):228–44, for a discussion of what this logion meant in the tradition and in the Gospel.

12. This interpretation diverges from those interpretations which are based on the presupposition that Matthew's references to "the disciples" or "the Twelve" are transparent allusions to Matthew's own community. See Luz, "The Disciples in the Gospel According to Matthew," 98–128. S. Brown ("Mission," 90) views "Israel" as Matthew's own Jewish-Christian community, and sees in 10:18 and 10:23 references to two *contemporary* missionary groups (one to "Israel," and one to the Gentiles) separated in space. STRECKER, 196, and TRILLING, 99–103, see in 10:5–6 a reference to one of two different missionary groups *separated in time*. This particularistic mission to Israel reflects an earlier stage of development of the Matthean community. For all these scholars, the disciples of Jesus are an allegory for the Matthean community. See also Stanton, "Origin and Purpose," 1928. From a structural perspective, one cannot move directly to a *Sitz im Leben* from allegedly "transparent" characters taken out of their complex narrative context.

13. Against S. Brown ("Mission," 86–87), who views the "restless movement" and lightly loaded traveling primarily as a sign of eschatological urgency.

14. See Meier, *Matthew*, 211, and footnote.

15. S. Brown ("Mission," 88) acknowledges that the disciples witness "through their suffering" but does not consider this witnessing as a part of their mission. He claims that it is not clear whether the phrase "bear testimony" before the Gentiles has a positive or negative connotation. But since this suffering is comparable to the cross (10:38), it amounts to saying that the cross does not have a positive connotation.

16. This is a fundamental characteristic of Matthew's system of convictions expressed in 5:11–16. Seeking to be blessed, or discovering that one is blessed in the

present, is simultaneously being a blessing for others as well as serving God and Jesus. Seeking the kingdom and seeking righteousness (serving others and God) are one and the same thing (6:33). Here, in a situation of persecution, when they adopt a certain behavior in order to be saved and blessed and when they receive blessings from the Father (10:20), the disciples also "bear testimony" before the Gentiles. They are manifesting the kingdom before them; they are in "mission" to the Gentiles.

17. Against STRECKER, 41, who sees at 10:17 a shift in these from the past historical sending out of Jesus' disciples to the suffering Matthean community (perhaps at an earlier Palestinian stage of development).

18. With S. Brown, "Mission," 87, n. 53.

19. STRECKER, 30, and many others after him make much of the pronominal adjective "their" as a linguistic means of excluding the Jews from the boundaries of the Matthean community. Cf. S. Brown, "Mission," 87, n. 53; SCHWEIZER, 243.

20. Cf. S. Brown, "Mission," 85.

21. With S. Brown, "Mission," 88.

22. Various solutions have been proposed for this distinction between Jewish and Gentile missions. Some, following Strecker and Trilling, understand Matthew to have separated them according to a salvation historical scheme: first to the Jews, then to the Gentiles, after the Jewish rejection of Jesus. Cf. SCHWEIZER, 235. S. Brown ("Matthean Community," *NovT* 22 [1980]:218) views "the twofold representation of the mission in Matthew's gospel" as an "irenic approach" toward bringing together the sides opposed within the Matthean community over the controversial issue of the Gentile mission.

23. They are similarly associated with sayings about persecutions in Luke 12:2–9, while in Mark 4:22 a similar saying is set in a quite different context (teaching in parables). As usual, our aim is to show how Matthew understood these sayings, by taking note of the way in which he set them in the entire discourse, 10:5–42.

24. BONNARD, 151–52.

25. With KINGSBURY, 159. Quoting Edwards (*Sign of Jonah*, 49–51), Kingsbury calls this the "eschatological correlative" of present ethic. Cf. also Keck, "Ethics in the Gospel of Matthew," *Iliff Review* 40 (Winter, 1984):54–55.

26. With Schweizer, "Matthew's Church," 138.

27. As proposed by Edwards, *Matthew's Story*, 36.

28. As suggested to me by Judith Middleton.

29. Green, "The Structure of St. Matthew's Gospel," *Studia Evangelica* 4 (1968):48. He views this chapter as a discourse in order to challenge Bacon's fivefold discourse scheme.

30. Cf. Dupont, "L'ambassade de Jean Baptiste," *NRTh* 83 (1961):805–21, 943–59. He recognizes that Jesus accuses John of being scandalized. Yet Dupont proposes a different explanation for this doubt by interpreting it in terms of John's possible expectations according to a historical reconstruction.

31. These deeds and this preaching are described in 11:5 in a way that makes clear that they fulfill prophecies such as those found in Isa. 35:5–6; 29:18; and 61:1. But, for Matthew, the point of this saying is not that John has failed to interpret Jesus' activity in terms of Scripture but rather that he has failed to consider Jesus' deeds in the light of his teaching and preaching.

32. On this passage, see Edwards, "Matthew's Use of Q in Chapter 11," 257–75, and SUGGS, 31–61.

33. With Bonnard, 164, and other commentators, I interpret the parable so that "this generation" is identified with the children who do not want to play. This interpretation is demanded by the relations among the parable and the following verses. The invitation to dance corresponds to Jesus' festive ministry ("eating and drinking"). The invitation to mourn corresponds to John's ascetic ministry ("not eating and not drinking"; note the association of fasting and mourning in 9:14–15). As with the parables of the kingdom, the introductory formula—here, "To what shall I compare this generation?" 11:16—should not be understood as suggesting

that the correspondence is with the first personage mentioned in the parable. The comparison is rather between the situation of this generation and the overall situation presented in the parable. See also Jeremias, *Parables*, 160–65; Perrin, *Rediscovering*, 86, 119–21; Linton, "The Parables of the Children's Game," *NTS* 22 (1976):159–79.

34. STENDAHL, 49–53.

35. See Perrin, *Rediscovering*, 74–77.

36. Thiering emphasizes that this attack against the kingdom originates in the context of "doctrinal disputation." See Thiering, "Are the 'Violent Men' False Teachers?" *NovT* 21 (1979):297.

37. In order to avoid this problem, Luke makes sure "this generation" is identified as the Pharisees and the lawyers (cf. Luke 7:29–30). But in Matt. 11:16 this phrase can only designate the crowds.

38. We take this sentence to be Jesus' concluding comment regarding the whole first part of the discourse because "her deeds" echoes the mention of "deeds of the Christ" in 11:2. Yet it could also be understood as the conclusion of the statement by those who reject Jesus. In such a case, it needs to be read ironically: We know that Wisdom is justified by her deeds, but obviously being a glutton, a drunkard, and a friend of tax collectors and sinners are not deeds worthy of Wisdom! According to this interpretation, Jesus would still be identified with Wisdom, but less emphatically, since it would be said by those who reject him.

39. With Johnson, "Reflections on a Wisdom Approach," *CBQ* 36 (1974):58. Johnson's comment is part of an argument criticizing Suggs's suggestion that Matthew *identifies* Jesus with Wisdom. Cf. SUGGS, 129–30.

40. Cf. Burnett, *Testament of Jesus-Sophia*, 84–92. Burnett shows in greater detail why, in Matthew, Jesus is identified with Wisdom, although he was not identified with Wisdom in Q. See also his bibliography in notes. For objections to this view, see Johnson, "Reflections on a Wisdom Approach." See Meier, *Wisdom*, 76–78, who underscores the relation between "Son of man" and "Wisdom." As he notes, it is somewhat surprising that the title "Son of man" be associated with humiliation and rejection (yet cf. 8:20), since he was conceived as the "glorious eschatological champion or judge," a view that is still recognizable in 9:6 (the Son of man has authority to forgive, as a judge would), and in 10:23 (which refers to the coming of the Son of man at the end of time). By contrast, Wisdom was conceived as rejected and humiliated. Note that the following passage describes Jesus as passing judgment over cities, and thus assuming the function of Son of man as judge. From our perspective, we have to note that this passage uses in a balanced way three titles for Jesus: Christ, Son of man, and Wisdom.

41. Since all the cities (or villages) mentioned are in Galilee, one could think that the opposition contrasts Galilean and Gentile. In the present context of a discourse amplifying 10:5b–15 where Israel is opposed to the Gentiles (and Samaritans, cf. 10:5b–6), we have to conclude that the opposition contrasts Israel (Judea and Galilee) with the Gentile world.

42. See SUGGS, 77–97. See also Davies's comparison of this passage to the Dead Sea Scrolls, in "Knowledge," in *HThR* 46 (1953):113–39.

43. SUGGS, 77–83, reviews the arguments for treating 11:25–30 as coming from a liturgical *Sitz im Leben* and concludes that 11:25–27 may be liturgical in its pre-Matthean Q origins but that 11:28–30 is definitely a Matthean interpolation.

44. Davies ("Knowledge," 137–38) says that "these things" refer to "eschatological secrets." Cf. also SUGGS, 88–89.

45. This verse also expresses the special relationship of Jesus with God. He is the Son of God, as is emphasized by KINGSBURY, 63–65.

46. Hiding and revealing in 11:25 and the similar contrast in 11:27 are not oppositions of actions, because both actions in each pair are positive; they are either God's action or according to God's will (although some have negative consequences for the receivers).

47. See Betz, "The Logion of the Easy Yoke and of Rest," *JBL* 86 (1967):10–24.

48. Cf. E. Schüssler Fiorenza, *In Memory of Her*, 134–41. She identifies the "heavy laden" as the socially "outcast" and "marginal people." The Jesus movement's "sophiology" marks a theological "alternative ethos" in direct opposition to the "dominant religious ethos." Schüssler Fiorenza, however, sees this as a pre-Matthean phenomenon, since in her historical model the earliest egalitarian Jesus movement eventually degenerates into a patriarchal betrayal of its origins.

49. Schüssler Fiorenza (*In Memory of Her*, 142) views the "yoke" of Jesus as a "symbol of discipleship" to "Sophia-Jesus." Cf. also SUGGS, 96. But such an explanation does not clarify why and in which sense this yoke is *easy*.

50. See MINEAR, 177.

51. Against STRECKER, 85, who believes that the formula quotations are "pedantic additions" superficially connected by later non-Matthean hands to the narrative context.

52. See MINEAR, 178.

53. See Levine, "The Sabbath Controversy," *NTS* 22 (1975–76):480–83.

54. Note that, as in 9:1–8, Jesus' response is not a judgment/condemnation. While he does reprove the Pharisees, he gives them the possibility of changing attitude by offering them a teaching about Scripture and its interpretation.

55. With Barth, "Matthew's Understanding of the Law," 104. In Mark 2:23–28, the same controversy seems to imply that the sabbath laws are abolished by Jesus. Cf. Goulder, *Midrash and Lection*, 17–18, 328.

56. See Meier, *Vision*, 84.

57. Ibid.

58. See Davies, *Setting*, 456–57.

59. Against KINGSBURY, 106.

60. The Pharisees' question is phrased in general terms, that is, as if healing on the sabbath were forbidden whatever might be the circumstances, and without reference to the man with the withered hand, as several commentators note when comparing Matt. 12:10 with Mark 3:2. For the relation of Matthew's presentation of the Pharisees' question with Rabbinic teaching, see Levine, "The Sabbath Controversy," 480–83.

61. MINEAR, 180, suggests that this example might be a thematic recollection of Israel's own situation as lost sheep (10:6).

62. See S. Brown, "Matthean Community," *NovT* 22 (1980):193–221. He questions the interpretation that this expression means that Matthew and his community are no longer in actual dialogue with Jews.

63. A similar point (conviction) is made in both 7:9–12 and 12:11–12 despite the differing Greek vocabulary.

64. See MINEAR, 179–80, for a similar interpretation of the significance of Jesus' "exits" (in a discussion of Jesus' exit from the Temple in 24:1a).

65. With BONNARD, 177.

66. See my comments on the first formula quotation in 1:23.

67. On the relation of this formula quotation to its context, see Rothfuchs, *Erfüllungszitate*, 72–77; and Cope, *Matthew, A Scribe Trained for the Kingdom of Heaven*.

68. For the relation of Matthew's text with the Hebrew, the LXX, the Targum, and other translations, see STENDAHL, 107–15, and GUNDRY, 229-30.

69. Cf. Hill, "Son and Servant," *JSNT* 6 (1980):2–16.

70. On Matthew's special association of the title "Son of David" with Jesus' healing and exorcising ministry, see Duling, "The Therapeutic Son of David," *NTS* 24 (1978):392–409.

71. Formally the narrative opposition is between two verbal actions, "Jesus *said* to them . . . if I cast out demons by Beelzebul" (12:25, 27), a restatement of the Pharisees' saying (12:24), and "Jesus *said* to them . . . if it is by the Spirit of God . . ." (12:25, 28).

72. According to this view, power and authority are so closely associated that they can be identified with each other, a view that Matthew repeatedly has rejected since the beginning of the Gospel (see chapters 2; 8; and 9).

73. Thus the parable of 12:29 can refer either to Jesus' assault on the demonic

realm or to the Jewish leaders' assault on Jesus and the kingdom (cf. 12:30). Cf. KINGSBURY, 150.

74. As was expressed in chapter 2, in the Sermon on the Mount, and in many other passages. We have noted about 8:23—9:8 that Jesus uses divine *power* in order to dominate and defeat cosmological and demonic powers but *not* in order to coerce human beings to recognize his authority.

75. Cf. Gerhardsson, "'An ihren Fruchten sollt ihr sie erkennen,'" *EvT* 42 (1982):113.

76. See Edwards, *Sign of Jonah,* 95–105.

77. Against Justin's interpretation (*Dialogue* 107.1) and the many commentators who followed him, among whom are Edwards (*Sign of Jonah,* 99–100), GUNDRY, 243–45. With BONNARD, 184. Interpreting the sign of Jonah as referring to the resurrection contradicts the very points that Matthew makes in all of this section, 12:21–50, and in many other passages. It would presuppose that the recognition of the authority of God results from a mighty deed of God which convinces and coerces people to believe—the view that Matthew has struggled to reject since the beginning of the Gospel.

78. By contrast with Kingsbury (*Parables,* 16), who with most commentators regards Matthew 11—12 as the immediate context of Matthew 13.

79. Against Kingsbury (*Parables,* 13–31), who interprets it as an "apology" of Jesus addressed primarily to the Jews. See also Minear, "The Disciples and the Crowds," *ATR* Supp. Ser. 3 (1974):28–44. Although our respective interpretations of chapter 13 are significantly different, my interpretation owes much to the work of Gary A. Phillips, "Enunciation of the Kingdom of Heaven;" idem, "History and Text," *Semeia* 31 (1985):111–38. The differences are due to Phillips' exclusive use of discursive structures.

80. The apparently slight redactional changes in the text of the parables (especially in Matt. 13:8) as compared with Mark 4:3–9 have the significant effect of removing several oppositions and ultimately of changing the point made by the parable. In Mark the oppositions concern growing and not growing, yielding and not yielding, points that one could have expected Matthew to emphasize. Since these oppositions are no longer found in Matthew, the opposition concerning the seeds falling on different soils appears. I am indebted to David Landry's excellent insights.

81. So Kingsbury, *Parables,* 39. But he fails to see the significance of the fact that it is the disciples who attribute to the crowds the differentiating epithet "them."

82. As is emphasized by BONNARD, 193; and Dupont, "Le point de vue," 233–34.

83. Dupont ("Le point de vue," 236–37) has well identified this opposition. Consequently, he shows that 13:16 needs to be interpreted together with 13:10–15 rather than together with 13:17. Because he does not discuss the relations between 13:10–16 and 13:17, however, his conclusions remain incomplete. Similarly, Kingsbury (*Parables,* 38) recognizes the opposition. But he interprets it as an opposition between the Jews and the disciples.

84. Kingsbury, *Parables,* 42. He recognizes that the disciples have a special knowledge here, but on the basis of a synoptic comparison with Mark.

85. Against BONNARD, 194, who assumes that what the disciples already have is a knowledge of the mysteries of the kingdom rather than another kind of knowledge about the kingdom. Then the second part of 13:12 has to be interpreted as a paradoxical (or nonsensical!) statement; for Bonnard, what is taken away from the crowds is their "emptiness"!

86. Kingsbury, *Parables,* 38–39. He argues that this formula quotation is a later non-Matthean interpolation.

87. The pair prophet/righteous of 13:17 is parallel to and recalls the pair prophet/wisdom of 12:41–42. For Matthew, Solomon is before all a teacher of wisdom, and thus a righteous person, rather than a king. Thus the pair prophet/righteous is more appropriate than prophet/king found in Luke 10:24. Cf. Cothenet, "Les prophètes chrétiens."

88. STRECKER, 106, by interpreting 13:12 in terms of 25:29 and its context,

concludes that 13:12 expresses a judgment that is the anticipation of the eschatological judgment. I agree that the same logion is found in both passages. But they receive quite different meanings from their respective contexts. My only point is that the judgment expressed in 13:12 does not need to be viewed as a final condemnation—in agreement with Dupont, "Le point de vue," 235.

89. On the peculiar character of this formula quotation, see STENDAHL, 129–32; Gundry, *Use of OT*, 116–18; Dupont, "Le point de vue," 236, n. 35; Van Segbroeck, "Les citations d'accomplissement dans l'Evangile selon Matthieu."

90. By contrast with Mark 4:12, which reads "*so that [in order that]* they may indeed see but not perceive."

91. Against Kingsbury, *Parables*, 49–50, it appears that Matthew is presenting a "theory of parabolic speech."

92. With GUNDRY, 259; against BONNARD, 197. Bonnard reads 13:19 (and 13:4) in terms of the parable as found in Mark 4:3–8 and of Mark 4:15!

93. This is further expressed by the emphasis put on bearing fruit in 13:23, "This is he who hears the word and understands it; he indeed bears fruit."

94. The Greek text underscores that this exhortation is specifically addressed to the disciples: "You, therefore, hear . . ." Although Dupont ("Le point de vue," 238) identifies the "word of the kingdom" with the "mysteries of the kingdom"— as most commentators do (cf. BONNARD, 197) because of their incomplete interpretation of 13:10–17—Dupont notes the tentativeness of this identification, implicitly acknowledging the contrast involved in this juxtaposition.

95. For other interpretations of this passage, see Marin, "Essai d'analyse structurale d'un récit-parabole," *EThR* 46 (1971):35–74; Via, "Matthew on the Understanding of the Parables," *JBL* 84 (1965):430–32; and Gnilka, "Das Verstockungsproblem nach Matthäus 13:13–15," 119–128.

96. On this passage, see Smith, "The Mixed State of the Church in Matthew's Gospel," *JBL* 82 (1963):149–53.

97. See Edwards, *Matthew's Story,* 48

98. See Dahl, "Parables of Growth," 164–65.

99. With BONNARD, 203; but against GUNDRY, 269.

100. On this quotation from the LXX, see STENDAHL, 116–18; and GUNDRY, 270–71.

101. As there is in the parable itself the image of growth. See Dahl, "Parables of Growth," 164–65 and notes.

102. The description of the condemnation of the cities (11:20–24) associates Jesus, who is previously designated both as Son of man and as Wisdom (11:19), with the eschatological judgment. Yet these verses do not give any specific role to the Son of man at the eschatological judgment.

103. There is much discussion among the commentators to know whether the kingdom of the Son of man is the church or the world. For a discussion of this issue, see Dupont, "Le point de vue," 224–29 (and his detailed bibliography in the notes). As Dupont concludes, when one takes into account the details of the descriptions provided by the text (without importing foreign elements into it), this kingdom can only be "the world."

104. This is in part the effect of the direct discourse in 13:27–30.

105. Of course those who are from bad origins do bad works. But those who are from good origins (such as the good seeds, the word, in 13:18ff.) might still do bad works.

106. The verse from which Cope borrowed the title of his book (*Matthew, A Scribe Trained for the Kingdom of Heaven*). I agree with Cope on the importance of this concept for Matthew. Matthew's entire Gospel is aimed at training scribes "for the kingdom."

FAITH, LITTLE FAITH, AND UNBELIEF

THE MAIN THEME

A new section begins in 13:54. Its opening pericope (13:54–58) tells the story of Jesus in his own country, followed by the story of John's death (14:1–12), the feeding of the five thousand (14:13–21), and then the crossing of the lake of Gennesaret (14:22–23). But where does the section end? In order to discover the end we need to examine the opening pericope (13:54–58). It then appears that the theme of the story of Jesus in his own country is expressed by its conclusion: Jesus performs few ("not many") miracles in Nazareth "because of their unbelief" (13:58). The conclusion of this section should therefore express that Jesus performs many miracles somewhere else. This is what we find in 14:34–36, a pericope which presents many miracles taking place in Gennesaret following a pericope regarding "belief" (14:31–33). We therefore conclude that 13:54—14:36 forms a complete section.[1]

The introductory (13:54–58) and concluding (14:34–36) units of this section stand out from the central unit (14:1–33) because all the pericopes of 14:1–33 are closely tied together to form a narrative development—the introductory and concluding units could stand by themselves. Actually, it seems that a quite different story begins with the introduction of Herod in 14:1. Yet Matthew marks the thematic link of this story with the preceding pericope by his habitual use of the temporal phrase "at that time." Similarly, at first it seems that there is very little connection between the crossing of the Lake of Gennesaret (14:22–23) and the scene in Gennesaret (14:34–36). Yet, once again, a temporal phrase, "when they had crossed over" (14:34), links them. Thus, for Matthew, the central unit (14:1–33) somehow explains why there are few miracles in Nazareth and many in Gennesaret. More specifically, it should explain how the original situation characterized by unbelief and few miracles is transformed into a situation where there is faith and many miracles (14:34–36).

MATTHEW'S CONVICTIONS IN 13:54—14:36

13:54–58. Jesus in His Hometown

Here Matthew opposes Jesus to the people of "his own country"[2] (i.e., his hometown) through their polemical statements (13:54, 57). This opposition indicates why people reject Jesus' authority and his teaching; it specifies the reason for "their unbelief" (13:58).

Jesus "taught them in their synagogue" (13:54a). In view of the preceding discourse (13:1–53), this phrase takes on a particular meaning. Jesus teaches them a synagogal message (one to which they already have access, see 13:12), "what is old" (13:52), the basic "word of the kingdom" (13:19) which is appropriate for the crowds. Furthermore, Jesus views this message as a prophetic teaching; he speaks of himself as a prophet (13:57). It is therefore a call to repent (cf. 12:41), a call to turn toward God and the kingdom. By contrast, the people—the "crowds" of Jesus' hometown—want to know the mysteries of the kingdom. They want to know the origin of Jesus' authority as teacher (the origin of his wisdom teaching) and the origin of his power as manifested in his miracles (13:54b). As we know from 13:36–52, the answer to their question would be that Jesus is the Son of man whose authority and power need to be understood in terms of his role as the eschatological judge; the issue of his authority and power is not so much a matter of origin as of eschatological role. Since they are people of Jesus' hometown, however, they know his family origin; he is the son of the carpenter, and his mother and his brothers and sisters are among them. (13:55–56). This knowledge leads them to raise questions regarding the origin of Jesus' authority and power and to refuse to acknowledge his authority and power. They are scandalized in him and by him (13:57a). For them, then, the prophet is "without honor"; consequently, they do not listen to his message. The very formulation of 13:57 with its double negation has the effect of underscoring that this is the case only "in his hometown [au.] *and* in his own house"—a phrase ambiguous enough to include not only Nazareth but also anyone who considers Jesus in terms of family relationships (see 12:46–50). As long as one considers Jesus in terms of family relationships, one cannot but be scandalized by Jesus. The only possibility is "unbelief" (13:58), that is, here, not honoring a prophet. It follows that belief involves giving honor to the prophet, listening to his message and repenting (see 12:41).

Matthew concludes the pericope by noting that Jesus "did not do many mighty works there, because of their unbelief" (13:58). Note that Matthew does not say that Jesus did not perform any miracles, but that the number of his miracles was limited. We can understand this concluding thematic statement[3] in terms of what Matthew pointed out earlier regarding miracles (which the readers know). Jesus' deeds (miracles) are meaningful if, and only if, they are interpreted in terms of his teaching (11:1–19). It follows that, when this teaching is not received and there is unbelief, such deeds would be pointless.

14:1–12. Herod Puts John the Baptist to Death

Three themes found in 13:54–58 are developed here: Herod seeks an explanation for Jesus' deeds; he does not listen to a prophetic teaching; and he overemphasizes family relationships. In other words, Matthew further expresses the preceding points rather than making new ones in this thematic passage.

14:1–2. As the people of Jesus' hometown did, Herod the tetrarch[4] seeks an explanation for Jesus' miracles: "why these powers are at work in him" (14:2). But, by contrast with these people, who were simply puzzled and scandalized (13:54, 57a), Herod comes up with an explanation by identifying Jesus with John the Baptist raised from the dead (14:2). This is a more positive explanation than that of the people of Jesus' hometown; it recognizes that Jesus' power has a supernatural character.

14:3–11. But, as these verses show, Herod's statement is in no way an acknowledgment of Jesus' authority. The identification of Jesus with John the Baptist indicates that Herod would treat Jesus as he treated John. It is not impossible that Matthew would expect his readers to see in the story of John's death a prefiguration of Jesus' death, since he assumes that his readers know about the Passion (cf. 10:38).[5] But the main theme is that Herod would have the same attitude toward Jesus and his teaching as he had toward John and his teaching. Herod put John in prison (14:3) and "wanted to put him to death" (14:5a) because, unlike the crowd, he did not consider him a prophet (14:5b)[6]—he did not acknowledge the authority of his prophetic teaching. As we have suggested regarding 13:57, such a teaching is a call to repentance, a call to change the orientation of one's life, as is clearly indicated by the summary of John's teaching to Herod: "It is not lawful for you to have her [your brother's wife]" (14:4).

Finally, as 14:4 and 14:6–9 show, the rejection of the prophetic teaching and the killing of John are directly caused by an undue emphasis on family relationships which then become incestuous (14:4) and monstrous. In order to make this case, one only needs to list the references to family relationships in 14:6–9: "Herod's birthday" (a celebration of one's family origin); "the daughter of Herodias" (his brother's wife, now his wife); this daughter "pleased Herod" (an overvaluation of the relation with her which leads to the oath, 14:7); the girl is "prompted by her mother" (14:8) and brought John's head to her mother (14:11). In the process other social relationships are distorted. The fear of the crowd which Herod had and which prevented him from putting John to death is dismissed (14:9); consequently, the role of the crowd in preventing evil (14:5) is set aside.[7] By contrast, the social relationship of Herod with his guests when he does not want to retract his oath in front of them is valued more than John's life and more than his relationship with the people he governs.

In sum, the story of Herod and of the death of John (14:1–12) has the effect of reinforcing and generalizing the point made by 13:54–58. One is inevitably bound to reject Jesus and his prophetic teaching, not only when one considers Jesus in terms of normal family relationships (13:54–58) but also when one attributes too much value to one's family relationships and to social relationships in general. Matthew has already expressed a similar point in 8:21–22 and 10:21, 34–39 by underscoring that when one gives precedence to family relationships over one's relationship with Jesus it is impossible to be a disciple. In 13:54—14:12 it becomes clear why this is the case. It is impossible to believe as long as one views family and social relationships as the basis and the norm for one's life. Family and social relationships should not be the basis upon which one discerns the value of a teaching nor the basis upon which one decides what is good or evil. When one's vocation, one's way of life, is based upon family and social relationships, one cannot but have evil behavior, indeed monstrous behavior.[8] In such a case, family and social relationships occupy the place and play the role that one's relationship with the Father in heaven or the kingdom should occupy and play. It is thus impossible to listen to the prophetic call to repent and to orient one's life toward God and the kingdom. This is unbelief. And thus one can only be scandalized (13:57) by Jesus (or John) and by his deeds.

14:12–21. The Feeding of the Five Thousand

14:12–14. After the story of the death of John at the hand of Herod, the story of Jesus' response to the news of John's death (14:12–13) takes on new meaning. Withdrawing "from there" (14:13)—the place where Jesus would be in danger of being persecuted by Herod—is to flee persecution (cf. 10:14, 23)! But, withdrawing "to a lonely place apart" (14:13) where Jesus is joined by crowds coming "from the towns" (14:13) is also to *withdraw from society*.[9] It is to go to a place where one is free from social relationships; a place where social relationships do not and cannot play the central role they play in society; a place where it is possible to turn toward the Father and to believe. Actually, the fact that the crowds "followed him . . . from the towns" (14:13) shows that they believe, or at least are ready to believe. The phrase "[Jesus] saw a great [crowd]; and he had compassion on them" (14:14a) recalls 9:36. It is a crowd in need of his ministry and worthy of it—they came out of their towns to follow him. They have at least a little faith, and thus he heals their sick (14:14b)—an act of mercy which demands some faith from the beneficiaries (see 8:1—9:34).[10]

In the story of the feeding of the five thousand, there are two narrative oppositions through which Matthew makes new points. These points underscore and specify the theme expressed in 14:12–14 (and 14:1–11).

14:15–16. The point made by the first opposition—the disciples suggesting that Jesus dismiss the crowds (14:15) and Jesus' refusal to do so (14:16)—concerns the evaluation of the situation of the crowds by the disciples and Jesus. The disciples and Jesus agree that the crowds need food at that time of the day, the evening. The question is: How can this basic need be met? For the disciples, the crowds' present location, with Jesus in "a lonely place," is inappropriate. In order to meet this basic need, they need to be in society—in "villages"—and there to follow the rules for life in society—buying food for themselves (14:15). Jesus' answer contradicts this view: "They need not go away; you give them something to eat" (14:16). Thus, contrary to what the disciples think, the crowds' basic need for food can be met here in this lonely place, outside society. Despite the point of 13:54–58, that one should not evaluate Jesus' ministry in terms of usual social and family relationships, and despite the theme of 14:1–11 according to which the respect of social conventions leads to monstrous behavior, one could still think that society and its way of life are necessary in order to have one's basic needs met. But Jesus' answer is unambiguous. One does not need society even for that purpose. The disciples can and should take the place of society and play its basic role, as they take the place of the family (12:46–50) insofar as they are true disciples doing the will of the Father in heaven (12:50), or, and this amounts to the same thing, insofar as they submit to Jesus' authority (doing what Jesus orders them to do, 14:16).

14:17–18. The second opposition—the disciples' objection (14:17) and Jesus' response (14:18)—and the rest of this feeding story clarify this point. For this purpose Matthew plays with the word "here" (14:17 and 18). For the disciples, what Jesus asks them to do is impossible, because "here," in this lonely place, they have very limited resources: five loaves and two fish (14:17). But Jesus answers: "Bring them here to me" (14:18). "Here" is now the place where Jesus is. It is because they are with Jesus that the disciples are truly disciples and can play the role one might think society alone is able to play.

14:19–21. When they perceive that they are not merely in a lonely place but also with Jesus, the disciples can then bring their limited resources to Jesus, who "looking up to heaven gave thanks" (14:19, au.) and gave the loaves back to the disciples. There was enough, indeed more than enough (14:20), for the disciples to feed a huge crowd (14:21).[11] In brief, the disciples can play the basic role of society, providing food, because through Jesus' intervention (thanksgiving) their meager resources are multiplied by heaven—the "heavenly Father" who knows that people need food (6:32) and will give good things "to those who ask him" (7:11).

The point that Matthew develops in the first part of this section (13:54—14:21) now appears. To receive the basic message about the kingdom and thus turn toward God and orient one's life toward the kingdom, one must not consider Jesus and his teaching as one considers someone in society—in terms of family relationships for instance. One should be ready to abandon such a societal/familial perspective, not only because of its monstrous excesses (as in the story of Herod) but also and primarily because one does not necessarily need family and society. From a human perspective, it seems that one cannot survive outside society, which alone can provide for one's basic needs—food (and security; cf. 8:18–22)—and thus without respecting the norms and way of life of that society. But from the perspective of the kingdom, the Father in heaven is the one who truly provides for one's basic needs (see 6:25–34; 10:9–10; 10:19–20), and he does so through the disciples, those who are with Jesus and who do the will of Jesus and his Father.

The disciples, as a group of people under the authority of Jesus and of the Father, take the place and basic role of society. Through them the Father provides for the basic needs of the crowds. Jesus has an intermediary role, as in 10:32–33 and 11:27. On the one hand, he is the one who gathers the crowds (they followed him and he healed their sick, 14:13–14), makes the crowds sit (14:19), and dismisses them (14:22–23); he gathers the crowds in a lonely place, creating a situation that demands that the disciples play the role of society. On the other hand, he is the one to whom the disciples bring their resources so that he might present these resources to heaven, and thus it is through him and because of his presence that (the Father in) heaven provides the disciples with what the crowds need. In sum, the point of this episode is that the disciples can play the basic role of society when they acknowledge that the situation in which they are with the crowds is fundamentally characterized by Jesus' presence ("here to me," 14:18). As long as they do not do so, they can only put their trust in society and in its ability to provide what is needed in a situation, rather than acknowledging that heaven can provide it and rather than becoming those through whom divine providence is manifested. With such a point of view, the disciples cannot have "faith"[12] as the next pericope expresses.

14:22–33. Jesus and Peter Walk on the Lake of Gennesaret

In this episode, Matthew makes two points that generalize those expressed in the previous one. In 14:22–23 Matthew further expresses the relationship of Jesus with the crowds (it is twice stated that he is the one who dismisses them) and with his Father in heaven (he prays by himself).

14:24–27. A first opposition is created by the exchange between the disciples, who "were terrified, saying, 'It is a ghost'!" (14:26) and Jesus, who "spoke to them, saying, 'Take heart, it is I; have no fear'" (14:27). As in the preceding cases (see 14:15–18), this opposition concerns the interpretation of a situation brought about by Jesus, who ordered the disciples to go ahead by boat (14:22) and then "came to them, walking on the sea" (14:25). The point is clear. As long as the disciples do not recognize Jesus, they are absolutely terrified. But the opposition also shows what allows the disciples to recognize the presence of Jesus "here." Seeing Jesus is not sufficient; by itself this sight terrifies them. They also need to hear his words, "it is I" (*egō eimi*, 14:27). They need to hear his words as addressed to them: the words of Jesus as "I" addressing the disciples as "you," the authoritative words of someone who exhorts and commands them, "Take heart; . . . have no fear" (14:27).

14:28–30. A second opposition between Peter walking on the water (14:29) and Peter beginning to sink (14:30) makes a complementary point. Once again the situation is brought about by Jesus—here by Jesus' command to Peter (14:29a; note that Peter does not want to do anything without Jesus' command, 14:28). The point concerns "faith" and "little faith," that is, faith with doubt (14:31). Faith acknowledges the presence of Jesus as the one who commands the disciples to do what appears to be impossible and obeys his command. It is only if Jesus gives such an order to him that Peter will acknowledge the presence of Jesus: "Lord, if it is you, order me to come to you on the water" (14:28, au.). This is a faith that involves trusting in the presence of Jesus as Lord, as the one who has both the authority to command and the power to give the disciples the ability to do what is commanded. And Peter walks on water (14:29). But, for this, the disciple also needs to abandon the usual, human way of looking at such a situation. Simultaneously acknowledging another power (the wind, 14:30) amounts to losing the ability to do what is commanded by Jesus. This is "little faith," a faith with doubt, a faith with a divided mind (14:31). Such a little faith prevents one from carrying out one's vocation—what was commanded by Jesus. But a little faith is enough to call upon Jesus, the Lord, for help (14:30).[13] Jesus responds by reaching out his hand (14:31), as he responded to the cry for help of people with little faith (see 8:1—9:34).

14:31b. Yet Peter is rebuked by Jesus for his "little faith." As a disciple, especially as the one who represents the disciples, he needs to have more than a little faith. He needs to have full faith in order to carry out Jesus' order, to do as Jesus did—walk on the water (14:26, 29) or meet the needs of the crowds. In retrospect it appears that when the disciples were ordered to feed the crowds (14:16) they were ordered to do as Jesus did. As Jesus had compassion on the crowds so the disciples have compassion on the crowds which they indicate by their suggestion to Jesus (14:15). As Jesus met the needs that he perceived at that time by healing the sick (14:14), so the disciples should meet the crowds' needs (14:16). But for this they need to have full faith and totally abandon the human view that society alone can provide for the basic needs of such a great crowd since their own resources are too limited, and that natural elements overpower human beings (14:30). Being a disciple with such a full faith involves acknowledging that Jesus has the divine power to save, heal, and feed the crowds—and thus that he is Lord. It also involves acknowledging that Jesus has authority to command, and trusting that he gives the disciples the power to do what he commands—by sharing his power with his disciples.

Matthew concludes the pericope by mentioning thematically (without making a point by means of an opposition) that "those in the boat worshiped him, saying, 'Truly you are the Son of God'" (14:33). The readers are left on their own to interpret this statement which remains ambiguous. Is this an expression of full faith or of little faith? Other people, people with little faith, knelt before Jesus (e.g., 8:2; 9:18)! Demons acknowledged that Jesus is Son of God (8:29)! Yet the "truly" suggests that this is the expression of a greater faith than the faith of those in the boat when Jesus calmed the sea for the first time; in that case, they simply "marveled, saying, 'What sort of man is this . . .'" (8:27).[14]

14:34–36. Jesus Performs Many Miracles at Gennesaret

In the perspective of what precedes, the theme of the concluding verses of the section 13:54—14:36 can easily be understood. First, people of the region of Gennesaret bring to Jesus "all that were sick" (14:35). Jesus does not go to their villages, in their society; they come to him. Second, these people have faith that Jesus has power to heal their sick. This is a faith comparable to the faith that the disciples should have. They believe that it is enough to touch the fringe of his garment (14:36), as the woman with a hemorrhage did (9:20–22). Their faith is quite comparable to Peter's faith when he walked on the water (before beginning to sink). As Peter asks Jesus to order him to go to him on the water (14:28), so they beseech Jesus to allow them to touch the fringe of his garment (14:36a). As Peter walked on the water (14:29), so all those who acted accordingly "were made well" (14:36b). It is a faith that does not demand any direct intervention of Jesus besides his permission.

These people from the region of Gennesaret are far from the "unbelief" of the people of Jesus' hometown. They have faith, and many healings occur when they are in the presence of Jesus—"here" with Jesus—touching the fringe of his garment. By contrast, in Nazareth among people who were unbelievers, not only was it Jesus who needed to perform miracles but he performed only a few (13:58). Thus, for the readers, it is clear that the people of the region of Gennesaret do not consider Jesus from a human perspective, that is, in terms of family and social relationships.[15]

NOTES ON 13:54—14:36

1. Gaechter (*Die literarische Kunst im Matthäus-Evangelium*, 29–30) treats 14:1—16:20 as a complete unit on the grounds of its "symmetric" and "chiastic" structure. A structural approach aimed at identifying the pattern "inverted/posited contents" finds two sections, 13:54—14:36 and 15:1—16:12, which are then shown to com-

plement and balance each other. Many features of Gaechter's "symmetry" and "chiasm" are thereby taken into account.

2. Matthew avoids designating Jesus' own country as Nazareth, possibly because of the positive light in which he has cast "Nazareth" in chapter 2.

3. The statement of 13:58 is not directly related to the opposition of 13:54, 57; it expresses in terms of the readers' old knowledge—including what they have read in the preceding chapters—the point/conviction expressed by the opposition.

4. Herod "the governor of one-fourth of the territory" (the meaning of "tetrarch") is Herod Antipas the governor of Galilee and Berea.

5. See Meier, "John the Baptist," *JBL* 99 (1980):400; and Trilling, "Die Taufertradition bei Matthäus," *BZ* 3 (1959):271–89. See also Wink, *John the Baptist*.

6. While there is no formal opposition of actions in 14:5—wanting to kill and fearing the crowd are not formally opposed—the readers are led to perceive one by supplying "he did not kill him" (something that Matthew does not want to say!). Thus, although Matthew *does not* make a point in this verse, the theme of Herod's radically negative attitude against John is underscored (by contrast with Herod's ambivalent attitude in Mark 6:14–29).

7. For Matthew, the mention that Herod "was sorry" (14:9) can only mean that he was sorry about what such an act would mean for his relationship with the crowd.

8. This does not mean that God's commandment regarding honoring one's father and mother should not be observed (cf. 15:4). In the next section a more positive view of family relationships will be expressed so as to prevent the readers from understanding 13:54—14:36 as a total rejection of family and social relationships. The point: they should not take the place of one's relationships to God, Jesus, and other disciples.

9. With Meier, "John the Baptist," 400.

10. With Held, "Matthew as Interpreter," 285.

11. Note the role of the disciples as described in 14:19. Jesus "gave the loaves to the disciples, and the disciples gave them to the crowds." See Held, "Matthew as Interpreter," 182.

12. With Held, "Matthew as Interpreter," 183. However, Held's conception of faith is less concrete and more dogmatic: "The notion of faith in the synoptic miracle stories is understood as a rule as 'trust in the miraculous powers of Jesus'" (p. 279).

13. With Held, "Matthew as Interpreter," 295.

14. See KINGSBURY, 66–67. By presupposing the conventional interpretation of the boat of the disciples as an allegory of Matthew's church, Kingsbury infers from 14:33 that "Son of God" is the definitive confession of Matthew's church.

15. Cf. Held, "Matthew as Interpreter," 296. Our interpretation agrees with Held's, with two fundamental exceptions. First, Held does not interpret deficient faith as resulting from the overevaluation of family and social relations. Second, Matthew's reference to "little faith" or faith in the face of "impressions deriving from experience which contradicts what faith desires from God" is not to be explained exclusively by the identification by the post-Easter church of its own experiences with those of the disciples before Easter.

JESUS AND THE TEACHING
OF THE PHARISEES

THE MAIN THEME

A controversy between Jesus and the Pharisees and scribes "from Jerusalem" (15:1–9) opens a new section. The Jewish authorities condemn[1] the disciples for not washing their hands before eating (15:2). Jesus counterattacks by calling them "hypocrites" (15:7)[2] because they "transgress the commandment of God for the sake of (their) tradition" (15:3). Yet this answer does not address directly the issue raised by the Pharisees and scribes. What should be the disciples' attitude toward the teaching of the Pharisees and the scribes? Is "the tradition of the elders" (15:2) to be totally rejected? Or only their hypocrisy? Furthermore, for the readers, Jesus' argument that God's commandment about honoring father and mother must be obeyed is in tension with the points of the preceding section (13:54—14:36) which underscored that family and social relationships should be set aside to make room for "faith."

The following pericope (15:10–20) explains the initial dispute, first to the crowds, then to the disciples and Peter. In the process the attack against the Pharisees is clarified and the significance of the dispute is generalized. The text emphasizes that the disciples are "still without understanding" (15:16), and there is no indication that, after Jesus' explanation (15:17–20), the disciples understand what he said about the teaching of the Pharisees. It is only in 16:12 that it is stated that "they understood," at the end of a passage (16:1–12) in which the Pharisees, now associated with the Sadducees, reappear as central characters. At first, the two intervening pericopes— the Canaanite woman (15:21–28) and the feeding of the four thousand (15:29–39)—seem totally unrelated to this dispute. Yet, as is clearly indicated in 16:7–10 which refers to the feeding story, these pericopes address the questions raised by the introductory pericope (15:1–9) so as to lead to the disciples' correct understanding of what should be their attitude toward the Pharisees and their teaching.

These observations suggest that the section that begins in 15:1 ends in 16:12; its theme deals with Jesus' and the disciples' relationship with the Pharisees and their teaching. Yet this section is also closely related to 13:54—

215

14:36. Several of the points made in the preceding section are further developed in 15:1—16:12.

The preceding section began by mentioning that Jesus "taught in their synagogue" (the synagogue of the people of his hometown, 13:54). This phrase meant that Jesus' teaching was a prophetic teaching that the people should have heard at the synagogue. It also had the effect of separating Jesus from the synagogue ("their" synagogue)—a theme which had been repeatedly mentioned (4:23; 9:35; 10:17; 12:9) but without becoming a central issue.[3] Now it becomes one of the main themes of the new section which in 15:1-20 and 16:1-12 sharply opposes Jesus' teaching to the teaching of the Pharisees, scribes, and Sadducees—the Jewish authorities in charge of the synagogue and the Temple. In 13:54-58 Matthew emphasized the *continuity* between Jesus' teaching and the teaching available through the prophets to the Jewish people. Now he underscores the radical *contrast* between Jesus' teaching and actual Jewish teaching—"the teaching of the Pharisees and Sadducees" (16:12). Yes, there is continuity, but there is also contrast. Conversely, the sharp contrast between faith and family/society presented in 13:54—14:36 gives way in 15:1—16:12 to a positive relationship (continuity) between faith and family/society. While faith requires one to abandon a certain view of familial and social relationships, it does not deny the importance of these relationships.

MATTHEW'S CONVICTIONS IN 15:1—16:12

15:1-9. Jesus and the Tradition of the Elders

This episode includes no fewer than four closely interrelated narrative oppositions, a signal that something important is at stake for Matthew.

15:2-3. The polemical dialogue (15:2a and 15:3a) opposes the Pharisees and scribes "from Jerusalem" and Jesus. In both cases, the first parts of the sayings are interpretations of situations described in their second parts: the disciples' action, not washing their hands when eating (15:2b); and the Pharisees' and scribes' teaching regarding what is dedicated to God as not available for one's parents (15:5). Since other features of these sayings are underscored by the other oppositions, the point made by this opposition simply concerns the basis upon which one establishes that an action is a transgression.[4] For the Pharisees and the scribes it is on the basis of "the tradition of the elders" (15:2), while for Jesus it is on the basis of the law and the prophets; he quotes one of the Ten Commandments (Exod. 20:12; 21:17) and Isa. 29:13 in Matt. 15:4, 8-9.[5] This opposition does not necessarily involve a complete rejection of "the tradition of the elders."[6] It simply says that it is not the proper basis for evaluating someone's behavior; Scripture, God's word (15:6) is.[7] The problem with the Pharisees and the scribes—religious authorities "from Jerusalem"—is that they attribute to the tradition of the elders the status and role that Scripture alone should have.

Another opposition contrasts the disciples transgressing the tradition (15:2b) and the Pharisees transgressing God's commandment "for the sake of your tradition" (15:3b)—a phrase repeated in 15:6 regarding the Pharisees making void God's word. Thus the tradition is now directly opposed to God's commandment.[8] Yet the main point expressed is that the tradition is no longer called "the tradition of the elders" but "your tradition." While the Pharisees claim that it is the tradition of the elders, it is now presented as their own teaching. Consequently, Jesus' saying is not necessarily a direct attack against the tradition of the elders itself. The point made by the opposition concerns *the origin of what one uses as authority*. The disciples (15:2) are under Jesus' authority, the authority of someone else. By contrast, the Pharisees are under the authority of a tradition of which they are themselves the author; so to speak, they are under their own authority.

15:4–5. As the opposition between "God said" (15:4, au.) and "you say" (15:5a) further indicates, the tradition that the Pharisees use instead of Scripture when evaluating other people's behavior is not merely nonscriptural; it is against Scripture, against God's word because it is their own teaching, a human teaching.[9] As the last phrase of the quotation from Isa. 29:13 further underscores, they "teach as doctrines human precepts" (15:9, au.).[10]

15:4–9. The last opposition underscores what is contradictory in these two teachings. God's word requires one to honor one's father (15:4), while the Pharisees teach that one does not need to honor one's father[11] if one declares that something is dedicated to God (15:5b–6a). This opposition needs to be interpreted in terms of the quotation of Isa. 29:13 which is tied to this opposition by the verb "to honor" (15:8).[12] When one submits to God's command (15:4), one honors one's father, and simultaneously one honors God (cf. 15:8a), the Father in heaven; thus one's heart is close to God (cf. 15:8b) and one can truly worship God (cf. 15:9a). By contrast, when one declares that something is dedicated to God, one honors God with one's lips (15:8), that is, through one's declaration. Yet this is not truly honoring God, because one does not submit to God's command but rather to a human teaching. When one does not honor one's father, one cannot truly honor God, and this shows that one's heart is far from God (15:8b).[13] When one declares that something is dedicated to God, one is also worshiping; but since it involves making void God's word, such worship is in vain (15:9a).

In sum, the Pharisees and scribes are "hypocrites" because they confuse their own teaching, their own will (established in their "heart," cf. 15:8b), with God's commandment and his will.[14] And thus when they want to honor and worship God, they do so in vain.

15:10–20. What Comes out of the Mouth Defiles

At first it seems that the explanation of Jesus' response to the Pharisees is to be subdivided into an explanation to the crowds (15:10–11) and one to the disciples (15:12–20). But a closer look shows that it should be subdivided into (1) an explanation to the crowds and the disciples (15:10–14), and (2) an explanation to Peter (15:15–20). Even though Peter represents the disciples, his question changes the issue. This is confirmed by the narrative oppositions which show that the second part of the pericope begins in 15:15. There are four oppositions. In 15:11 and 15:18–20 we find two parallel but distinct oppositions between not defiling *and* defiling a person. There is also an opposition between the crowd which is exhorted to "hear and *understand*" (15:10) *and* the Pharisees who hear the word and are *offended* (or *scandalized*, 15:12). A study of this latter opposition—and of the related opposition between the disciples' saying (15:12) and Jesus' response (15:13)—will show that 15:10–14 needs to be treated as a first subunit.

15:10–14. In 15:10 the crowd is presented as potentially able to understand Jesus' saying (15:11). By contrast, the disciples report to Jesus that the Pharisees are "offended" (scandalized) by this saying (literally, "by hearing the word," 15:12). This opposition is comparable to the one in the explanation of the parable of the sower, where the same Greek vocabulary expresses that the seed sown on rocky ground "hears the word" and is scandalized and that the seed on good soil "hears the word and understands" (see 13:20–21, 23). In 15:10–11, as in 13:20–21, 23, Jesus' response explains why people are not able to understand (cf. 15:13–14). But this explanation is somewhat different. Those who do not understand, the Pharisees, are a "plant which my heavenly Father has not planted" and which "will be rooted up" (15:13), a description that reminds the readers of the parable of the weeds (13:24–30). The Pharisees are irremediably bad plants; they are "blind guides" who can only fall with those whom they guide (15:14b). There is no hope that the Pharisees will understand "the word"; they are fundamentally evil.[15] By contrast, instead of being let alone (15:14a), the crowd is "called" by Jesus to him. They are not bad plants; they are not fundamentally evil. One can hope that the crowd will hear and understand the word—the explanation given by Jesus.

The related point made by the opposition between the disciples' saying (15:12) and Jesus' response (15:13) begins to cast the disciples in a negative light. Since it follows Jesus' word to the crowd, the disciples' statement is presented as a warning that such a teaching to the crowd irritates the Pharisees. For the disciples, in his ministry which is also their ministry, Jesus should be cautious and take into account the Pharisees' reaction; he should not antagonize them.[16] This implies that he should not speak to the crowd as he does (15:10–11). Jesus' response is similar to the response of the master to his servants in the parable of the weeds. As the master ordered his servants to let the weeds grow (13:29–30), Jesus orders his disciples to let the Pharisees alone (15:14a). In this case the point is that Jesus and his disciples should carry out their ministry without taking into account the Pharisees and their reactions. Respecting the Pharisees' feelings would be to avoid challenging their ministry to the crowd. But they are "blind guides," and thus they mislead the crowd. Jesus who, by his teaching to the crowd, offends the Pharisees, is thus presented as a sure guide for the crowd.

What should the crowd (and the readers) understand from Jesus' teaching (15:10–11)? The opposition between not defiling and defiling in 15:11 ("what goes into the mouth" does not defile; "what comes out of the mouth" defiles) needs to be interpreted in terms of 15:1–9. It is clear that "what goes into the mouth" is food, what one is eating (cf. 15:2). But what comes out of the mouth and defiles? In terms of what precedes, it has to be a teaching—a human teaching (15:9b) or honoring God with one's lips (15:8a), declaring that something is dedicated to God even though it makes void God's word (15:5–6). Thus what defiles is what comes out of the mouth of those who do not submit to God's command and transgress it (15:3)—bad plants, weeds, the Pharisees and the scribes.

In view of 13:24–35 we see why the saying of 15:11 is presented as understandable by the crowd. It expresses "things hidden since the foundation of the world" which the crowd can learn from the parables, namely, the origin of defilement. This defilement is the teaching of those who do not submit to God's command. Matthew 15:11 is also an implicit call to reject such a teaching and thus to submit to God's command.

15:15–16. For Matthew, however, there is more in a parable than its lesson for the crowd about the origin of evil. It also reveals to the disciples the mysteries of the kingdom (13:11), a lesson concerning the present and future implications of the presence of evil (and of the kingdom). This is what Peter and the disciples do not understand—although they should have understood it (15:15–16)—and what Jesus explains to them.

15:17–20. The explanation of 15:11 in 15:17–20 turns on the parts of the body and their respective functions. The effect is that the point made by the opposition emphasizes that the origin of "what comes out of the mouth," the origin of evil, is *the heart* (15:18–19). In this way, the only feature of Isa. 29:13 that had not yet been fully accounted for—"their heart is far from me" (Matt. 15:8b)—is used for interpreting the polemical dialogue between the Pharisees and Jesus. As a consequence, what defiles is shown to be much more than declaring something dedicated to God against

God's command, but indeed anything that comes out of a heart far from God (cf. 15:8b): "evil thoughts, murder, adultery, fornication, theft, false witness, slander" (15:19). The heart is where one's will is established. Thus if the heart is evil, far from God, instead of internalizing God's command (see 5:21–47), it produces "evil thoughts," evil intentions (such as looking at a woman lustfully, see 5:28), an evil will which can only engender evil actions and thus is as evil as the actions.

In this list, all the evil actions concern relationships with other people— as was the case in the antitheses (5:21–47).[17] As declaring something dedicated to God amounted to breaking the good relationship with one's parents commanded by God, so "murder, adultery, fornication, theft, false witness, slander" (15:19) destroy various kinds of good relationships among people in a society.[18] Such actions make a society an evil society—"an evil and adulterous generation" (12:39; 16:4). These actions amount to making "void the word of God" (15:6) instead of fulfilling it (cf. 5:17).

By contrast, "to eat with unwashed hands" (15:20), as well as eating food that is said by the law to be impure (15:17), does not defile. Thus, as in 9:10–13 and 12:1–8, ritual laws of Scripture are set aside. But unlike these other texts which express that Jesus does so because God desires "mercy, and not sacrifice" (9:13; 12:7), here the point is primarily negative.[19] Any behavior that destroys good human relationship in society is against the will of God; it demonstrates that these people's heart is far from God, and thus what comes out of their heart defiles them by the very fact that it denies them any possibility of being in good relationship with others—the over-abundant righteous described in 5:20–48.[20]

15:21–28. Jesus and the Canaanite Woman.

In this episode we are in a new location, the region of Tyre and Sidon (15:21)—outside Israel, whose center is Jerusalem (cf. 15:1). There is a new interlocutor, a Canaanite woman (15:22), who sharply contrasts with the Pharisees and the scribes as Jewish religious authorities (15:2).[21] The shift in situation is so abrupt that the narrative continuity is barely maintained; the presence of Jesus and of his disciples provides it. But the juxtaposition of the dialogue between Jesus and the Canaanite woman with the dialogue between Jesus and the Pharisees and its explanation suggests a thematic continuity, an *antithetical* continuity.[22] This is further suggested by the theme of "bread" and "eating" (cf. 15:1–20)[23] which plays a central role in the concluding and decisive exchange[24] between Jesus and the Canaanite woman (15:26–27). Finally, Jesus concludes by declaring that the Canaanite woman, a pagan, has "great" faith (15:28), while he had declared that the Pharisees, the Jewish religious authorities, make void the word of God and are hypocrites (15:6–7). The Pharisees are presented as an example of "unbelief" (see 13:58), and the Canaanite woman as an example of great faith.

Consequently, the points Matthew makes in 15:21–28 are related to the points made in 15:1–20.

15:22–24. For the readers, this story is perplexing. The woman's call for mercy, addressing Jesus as "Lord, Son of David" (15:22), seems most appropriate. But why does Jesus refuse to respond (15:23a)? Is this non-response of Jesus a rejection of the woman's request, which then would be wrong? Would a first opposition be set between her saying and Jesus' refusal to answer? The rest of the story shows that this is not the case, since finally Jesus grants the woman's request (15:28). There is in fact no opposition between 15:22 and 15:23a. By contrast, the exchange between the disciples and Jesus (15:23–24) involves an opposition. The disciples were wrong in suggesting that Jesus send the woman away (15:23b), as the polemical character of Jesus' answer shows: "I was *not* sent except to the lost sheep of the house of Israel" (15:24, au.). But this answer demands that the readers reinterpret the disciples' petition. Obviously, Jesus does not understand them to say that he should merely dismiss the woman without granting her what she wants; otherwise his response would be meaningless. Rather, the disciples' words need to be understood as a request that Jesus dismiss the woman by granting her what she wants.[25]

As in the previous episode (15:12–17), the disciples are cast in a negative light. The issue is the same. For them, it would have been prudent not to teach the crowd in a way that offends the Pharisees (see 15:10–12). Now it would be expedient to grant this woman's request so as not to be importuned by her. For the disciples, one should conduct one's ministry by acting in a way that would avoid anything that could displease people; one should avoid disquieting confrontations. But, for Jesus, this is precisely not the way of conducting one's ministry. He does not act in response to people's reactions or wishes but acts according to *what he was sent for* (15:24a), according to his God-given vocation. He is totally devoted to his vocation, whatever might be the reaction of the Pharisees (15:12). Since he was sent "to the lost sheep of the house of Israel"—which are lost because they are led by "blind guides" (15:14)—he teaches the Jewish crowd (15:10–11). Similarly, since he "was sent only to the lost sheep of the house of Israel," he has nothing to say to this pagan woman (15:23a), even though she acknowledges that he is the "Lord, Son of David," the Jewish Messiah, and even though she might be bothersome by her cries (15:22, 23b).[26]

15:25–28. A second opposition appears in the following exchange between the woman and Jesus. To her renewed request (15:25), Jesus' response is a refusal to do what she asks (15:26). But the woman's following response (15:27) leads him to change his mind and to grant her request (15:28). Thus Jesus' original response to the woman (15:26) is opposed to her own statement (15:25, 27), as is shown by Jesus' concluding saying (15:28). His first

statement to the woman expresses by means of a metaphor that granting
the request of this pagan woman would be wrong if it would result in a
limitation of Jesus' ministry to Israel (15:26). Positively it also expresses
that Israel has a privileged status; even though the Jews are "lost sheep,"
they are "children" of God, while the pagans are "dogs." Jesus' ministry—
especially his healings—is "bread," blessing, for Israel, which should not
be diverted to the pagans.[27] One might wonder why this is the case. According to 9:35—10:20 the proclamation of the kingdom and the healings
that manifest it as mercy are exclusively directed to the lost sheep of Israel
because of their special needs resulting from their special status and vocation. Israel has a role in the mission to the Gentiles, even if it is the
paradoxical role of rejecting and persecuting the disciples who then are in
a position to witness to Gentiles (10:16–20).[28] The point is simply that
healing Gentiles would divert Jesus from his vocation toward Israel, a privileged people, and this would be wrong.

In her response (15:27), the woman does not deny—indeed, she affirms—
that taking away what is for Israel would be wrong.[29] She acknowledges
the special status of Israel as the masters of the dogs and her own status as
among the dogs. A remarkable humility. But she is not ready to give up.
As Jesus is like a father giving bread to his children—a father who knows
how to give the good things his children need (see 7:11)—so she is a mother
who has resolved to obtain what her daughter needs—bread/healing. Evil
(pagan) as she is, she knows what is good for her child (see 7:11). Taking
care of one's children is "the law and the prophets" (7:12), as much as
honoring one's parents is (see 15:4). Such a human, secular wisdom is not
opposed to the will of God, and thus not to Jesus' vocation. The validity
of this secular wisdom is further demonstrated by the woman's prolongation
of Jesus' metaphor. She points out that the dogs also eat bread in the form
of crumbs falling from their masters' table; in this way the dogs' needs are
met without depriving the children.

It is in the light of these points that Jesus' concluding statement, "O
woman, great is your faith," and the healing of the woman's daughter
(15:28)—a thematic verse—need to be understood. What is having a "great
faith"?[30] It involves acknowledging that Jesus is "Lord" (15:22, 25), that
he has the divine power to help those in need. It involves acknowledging
and understanding the specificity of Jesus' vocation—a Jewish vocation as
Son of David, sent to the lost sheep of Israel (15:22, 27). But "great faith"
also involves understanding, with the help of one's (non-Jewish) secular
wisdom, how Jesus' vocation can be appropriately carried out in a specific
situation. Thus it involves understanding how Jesus' vocation "fits" a specific situation, by contrast with John who had not understood it (cf. 3:13–
15).[31]

The healing of the woman's daughter by a word—as in the case of the
centurion's servant (8:13)—also demonstrates *how Jesus carries out his voca-*

tion. Clearly he does not let the situation dictate what he should do or not do for the sake of avoiding confrontations (15:12–14, 22–24). Yet he takes into account the situation. For Jesus, carrying out his vocation does not mean following to the letter a certain formulation of this vocation—as if in total abstraction from the existing situation. His vocation is carried out in different ways in different situations: here, he heals the daughter of the Canaanite woman (15:28) when it becomes clear that it is "fitting" his vocation "to the lost sheep of the house of Israel" (15:24). Jesus' objection to his disciples does not mean that his vocation should be implemented without taking into account the situation. What is at stake is how one should take into account that situation so as to decide how this vocation should be implemented. For the disciples, one should take into account the "negative" features of the situation: the negative reaction of the Pharisees (15:12); the fact that the woman's cries are bothersome (15:23). For Jesus, one decides how to implement one's vocation, not on the basis of such negative features, but on the basis of the "positive" features of that situation—here the woman's "great faith." By her behavior and her words, the Canaanite woman manifests a human, secular wisdom which Jesus identifies as "fitting" his vocation, and thus as a manifestation of God's will ("great faith") as his vocation is.[32] It is on this basis that he decides to act, to implement his vocation. Thus, a proper implementation of one's vocation involves discovering what, in a given situation, fits one's vocation—positive aspects of this situation, secular manifestations of God's will.

15:29–39. The Feeding of the Four Thousand

Matthew 15:29–39 and 14:13–21 both include a scene of healing in the wilderness (14:13–14; 15:29–31) followed by the feeding of crowds (14:15–21; 15:32–39). But significant differences show that 15:29–39 develops the themes and points of 15:1–28. The points made in 14:13–21 by two oppositions disappear. In 15:29–39 a single opposition remains, but the point it underscores is quite different; it develops the points made in 15:1–28 and prepares for those of 16:1–12. In sum, 15:29–39 should be primarily interpreted in terms of its immediate context rather than by comparison with 14:13–21. Each of the two feeding stories contributes to the development of specific points and themes of the section of the Gospel to which they respectively belong.

15:32–34. Even though 15:29–39 is primarily thematic, it includes one opposition: the disciples' objection (15:33) is opposed to Jesus' statements (15:32, 34). By contrast with the similar opposition in 14:13–21 which dealt with the disciples' relations to society, here the mention of society (villages, buying) is absent. The opposition underscores that Jesus has the power to accomplish his will. Jesus is unwilling to send the crowds away hungry because of his compassion for them (15:32). Thus Jesus' will, his vocation, is one of mercy and compassion for the crowds, "the lost sheep of the house of Israel" (cf. 9:36; 15:24). The disciples do not question the validity of what Jesus wants to do—it is a proper implementation of his vocation based upon an evaluation of the situation. A perception of the crowds' needs shows that, here, compassion involves feeding the hungry crowds. But the disciples doubt that Jesus has the ability to carry out this vocation. By this opposition, Matthew underscores the additional and complementary point that Jesus has the means to accomplish his will—not sending the crowds away hungry, and thus feeding the crowds in the wilderness. By contrast, the disciples think that it is impossible to do so in the wilderness because there is not enough bread; for them, Jesus does not have the means to feed the crowds.

This point is not new in the sense that Jesus' power has been repeatedly underscored in preceding chapters. Yet its repetition in 15:32–34 complements certain of the points[33] expressed in 15:10–28. In 15:12–14 Matthew has underscored that Jesus and the disciples were not to allow the Pharisees' reaction to limit their ministry; they were to carry out their vocation in spite of the Pharisees' objections. The following points, in 15:23–24 and 15:26–28, underscored Jesus' total devotion to his vocation which he carries out in terms of what is "fitting" in each situation, but without concern for the eventual negative effects for himself and the disciples. In view of Jesus' determination to carry out his vocation, only one thing could prevent him from so doing, namely, not having the means or power to carry out his vocation. Jesus' words and the feeding of the crowds (15:32–39) demonstrate to his disciples (and to the readers) that Jesus does have the power to implement his vocation as demanded by any given situation. He has, in the wilderness, the power to feed large crowds with seven loaves of bread and a few small fish.

15:29–32. In reference to the preceding pericopes, one is not surprised that the themes through which this point is expressed also develop the themes of 15:1–28. The description of Jesus' return to Galilee (15:29) identifies the crowds as Jewish crowds,[34] that is, as "the lost sheep of the house of Israel" (15:24) toward whom Jesus' ministry is directed. The description of Jesus as sitting on the mountain (15:29) reminds the readers of the opening verses of the Sermon on the Mount (5:1) and thus suggests that he not only healed all their sick from all kinds of diseases (15:30) but also taught the crowds (see 15:10).[35] This is further suggested by the mention that the crowds remained with him for three days (15:32). In brief, Jesus' ministry, which includes both teaching and healings, is directed to "the lost sheep of the house of Israel." Since the people of Israel already know the God of Israel, it can then acknowledge that these healings are gifts from God: "they glorified the God of Israel" (15:31). Pagans, such as the Canaanite woman, are not able to do so as long as they do not know the God of Israel—a knowledge they can only gain through a mission that originates in Israel (chap. 10). This explains once again why Jesus' ministry—his proclamation of the kingdom both in words and in deeds—is exclusively directed toward Israel (cf. 15:24 and 10:5–6).

As for the rest of the story, note that Jesus has a much more central role in it as compared with his role in 14:15–21. In 15:32, it is Jesus (rather than the disciples) who takes the initiative and points out the need of the crowd. Yet once again Jesus associates the disciples to his ministry. While the crowds come to Jesus (15:30) and sit down at his command (15:35), after he gives thanks Jesus gives the bread and the fish to his disciples, who in turn give them to the crowd (15:36)—a point underscored in 14:16–19. Consequently, what is conveyed in 15:29–39 concerning Jesus' ministry also applies to the disciples' ministry even though the text is almost exclusively focused upon Jesus' ministry—how he implements his vocation (compassion) for the lost sheep of the house of Israel and his power to carry it out.

16:1–12. The Disciples Understand
What Jesus Told Them About the Teaching
of the Pharisees

16:1–4. The first part of this pericope did not originally include 16:2b–3 (it is not found in important manuscripts).[36] It opposes "the Pharisees and Sadducees," who are asking for a sign from heaven (16:1), to Jesus, who refuses to give them a sign "except the sign of Jonah" (16:2a, 4). Matthew's point made by this opposition develops the preceding point (15:32–34). The disciples had doubts concerning Jesus' power to carry out his vocation, without denying the validity of this vocation, that is, what he was sent for by God or by heaven. Now the Pharisees and the Sadducees are described as tempters (16:1, as the devil is in 4:3).[37] As religious Jewish authorities, who hold their authority and vocation as leaders of Israel to be God-given ("from heaven"), they contest not only Jesus' power—his power to perform signs—but also and primarily his religious authority. They deny that his authority and vocation are "from heaven" and thus that he can perform "a sign from heaven."

Of course this means that the Pharisees and the Sadducees have failed to recognize the healings (15:30–31) and the feeding of the crowds (15:32–39) as signs from heaven. This is the point that is underscored in the added material (16:2b–3), which is summarized by 16:3b: "You know how to interpret the appearance of the sky, but you cannot interpret the signs of the times."[38] The main point is that the Pharisees and the Sadducees, far from being legitimate religious authorities, are "an evil and adulterous generation" (16:4a), that is, "plant[s] which [the] heavenly Father has not planted" (15:13). Their authority is not "from heaven." Consequently, they are unable to recognize Jesus' deeds as signs of heaven and to glorify "the

God of Israel," as the crowds did (15:31). And thus "no sign shall be given to [them] except the sign of Jonah" (16:4). A demonstration of Jesus' power would be of no avail—they would not recognize it as "from heaven." Unlike the disciples, they do not recognize that he is sent "from heaven," by the God of Israel. Yet "the sign of Jonah" will be given to them. As in 12:39–41, the sign of Jonah is the death of Jesus (not his resurrection), who, like Jonah, proclaims a message of repentance. Rather than being a manifestation of power, the sign of Jonah as a true "sign from heaven" is a manifestation of powerlessness.[39] As in preceding chapters, the true authority of Jesus is not to be confused with his power. It needs to be acknowledged first of all in his powerlessness, as the sign of Jonah. In 12:39–41, Matthew emphasized that acknowledging Jesus as the sign of Jonah is repenting, submitting to Jesus' authoritative proclamation and teaching. This latter point is not expressed in 16:1–4; it is an aspect of the point made in 16:5–12.

16:5–12. In the concluding verses of this section (15:1—16:12), Matthew strongly makes a single point by an opposition that is expressed no fewer than three times: first in the opposition of two sayings—Jesus' saying (16:6, 8) *and* the disciples' saying (16:7); then in the same form in 16:12b; and in the opposition of not understanding (16:9, 11) *and* understanding (16:12a).

Jesus warns his disciples against "the leaven of the Pharisees and Sadducees" (16:6)—against their teaching (16:12). Since they are fundamentally evil, "an evil and adulterous generation," their teaching is evil, "leaven" as symbol of *impurity*.[40] Their teaching is thus contrasted with the sign of Jonah: the call to repentance of the one who is greater than Jonah (12:41), the call to *purify* oneself and to turn toward God. But the disciples misunderstand this warning. They display the same concern as in 15:33, a concern for the means—bread—to satisfy their needs. They feel guilty for not having taken bread with them—any means of subsistence. This is having "little faith," that is, not having the kind of faith they should have as disciples trusting that "the laborer deserves his food" (10:9–10), the faith that God will take care of their needs, as he did in the feeding of the five thousand and of the four thousand (16:8–10). Because they are concerned with food, because they are "anxious about [their] life, what [they] shall eat" (6:25), and thus do not trust in the power from heaven and in their heavenly Father, they fail to understand Jesus' teaching. They fail to understand that Jesus speaks about what is truly important: teaching, religious teaching. It is because of a "teaching" that one either has access to the kingdom and its blessings (see 5:1—7:29) or is led to perdition, falling into a pit (15:14).

In sum, the point of this threefold opposition of 16:5–12 is that as long as one is anxious about bread and life, one cannot understand Jesus' warning about the bad teaching of the Jewish authorities. The feedings of the crowds should be, for the disciples, a sign from heaven, a manifestation that one does not need to be anxious because "your heavenly Father knows that you need" food and other things (6:32). And thus after witnessing the feedings of the crowds, the disciples should be ready to understand what Jesus told them about the teaching of the Jewish authorities (see 15:1–9). They should not be anxious because the Pharisees are offended by Jesus' teaching (15:12) and because they represent a threat for Jesus and for them. If they had this faith, rather than a "little faith" (16:8), they could understand that the entire teaching of the Pharisees and of any Jewish religious authority, including that of the Sadducees, is fundamentally evil. Instead of leading people to repentance (as the sign of Jonah does), and thus instead of leading them truly to honor God and to worship God, such a teaching leads their hearts away from God and thus leads people to honor God with their lips and to worship in vain (cf. 15:8–9).

NOTES ON 15:1—16:12

1. As we noted regarding 9:3 and 9:11, for Matthew the fact that negative comments about someone's behavior are addressed to someone else makes these words a condemnation without appeal, the kind of judgment that is against God's will (cf. 7:1). By contrast, when such negative comments are directly addressed to the people concerned (cf. Jesus' words in 15:3–9), they are not a judgment/condemnation but a call to repent.

2. It is the first time the term "hypocrite" is used to designate the Jewish authorities (in 6:2, 5, 16 the term is used in a more general way). See BERGER, 500–502, for a discussion of Matthew's special usage of the term "hypocrite," esp. in the context of 15:1–20.

3. See KINGSBURY, 66, 153. He claims that this theme has already been fully developed in chapters 11—13.

4. With BERGER, 500.

5. According to the LXX; see STENDAHL, 54–58.

6. Against BERGER, 505.

7. A narrative opposition makes a point that shows what is *contradictory* (and not *contrary*) to something. This is affirming that "the tradition of the elders" is not Scripture, and thus that it should not be construed as having the same authority as Scripture. But this is not to say that "the tradition of the elders" is necessarily antithetical to Scripture and without value. BONNARD, 227, correctly makes this point on historical grounds but without establishing it in terms of the text—a remark that suggests, once again, both the difference and the complementarity of structural and historical exegetical approaches. Despite his opposite conclusion, K. Berger points out that there is a double opposition: an opposition between "command of God" and "command of men" (15:4, 5), and between the transgressed tradition and the transgressed commandment (15:2a, 3b). See BERGER, 499–500.

8. More technically "tradition" and "God's commandment" are in a contrary relationship on the square formed by several narrative oppositions. With GUN-DRY, 303, who reaches this conclusion on the basis of comparison with Mark 7:6a, 8–9; and with BERGER, 499, who notes that the opposition is a Matthean re-working of Mark's version.

9. Against Meier, *Vision*, 102, who claims that Jesus revokes a law of Scripture "without any argumentation" on the basis of his own transcendent authority.

10. With BERGER, 502, who says that Matthew's redaction of the whole tradition makes the Isaiah quotation fit more closely to the entire pericope than Mark's.

11. The best manuscripts do not include "or his mother" in 15:6a (RSV:15:5b).

12. See BERGER, 499, who notes that Matthew's scriptural argument is an attempt to ground scriptural interpretation upon the rules of the Ten Commandments, in this case, the Fourth Commandment.

13. If BERGER, 499, is right, even the phrasing of the human tradition in the form of Septugintal "sentences of law" marks Matthew's emphatic condemnation of the Pharisaic teachers' human presumption.

14. These comments, therefore, go beyond Berger's interpretation of hypocrisy which focuses on the disparity between apparent, outward public religiosity and actual inward unrighteousness. See BERGER, 500–502.

15. With BERGER, 504, who notes that the Pharisaic opponents are unteachable.

16. Against Meier, *Vision*, 103, who claims that the disciples' question about food uncleanness was prompted by their "obtuseness."

17. It might not be by accident that the order of the evil actions approximately follows the order of those discussed in 5:21–37 (with the addition of "theft"). Note that the list of evil actions in 15:19 is somewhat different from the one in Mark 7:21–22. As Jonathan Kraus pointed out to me, Matthew's redaction of Mark's vice list focuses on "sins of the mouth," that is, "wicked plots," "false witnesses," "slanders." In agreement with BERGER, 503.

18. The last term in this list could be translated "blasphemy" instead of "slander" (RSV). But this latter translation is demanded by the rest of the list and the plural form of all these terms in the Greek text.

19. With BERGER, 505, who refutes the proposals of Hummel (*Auseinandersetzung*, 46) that Jesus makes only a special halakhah about handwashing; and Barth ("Matthew's Understanding of the Law," 88) that Matthew opposes handwashing "not because of a rejection of the tradition altogether, but on the basis of the law." As Berger correctly notes, neither Hummel nor Barth perceives the specific focus of the polemic against Pharisaic teaching *as such*, because of their presuppositions about Matthew originating from a Jewish-Christian community. See also STRECKER, 30.

20. Thus, against Meier, *Vision*, 103, for Matthew, Jesus' abrogation of the food laws is warranted by Jesus' correct interpretation and argumentation, not by his transcendent authority to revoke the laws.

21. TRILLING, 104, sees the contrast between the believing pagan woman and "unbelieving Israel" in general by interpreting this passage in terms of the centurion pericope (8:10–13).

22. With Anderson, "Matthew: Gender and Reading," *Semeia* 28 (1983): 11.

23. Note that the Greek text of 15:2 mentions that the disciples were not washing their hands "when they *eat bread*" (au.) and that 15:20 refers back to the accusation of the Pharisees.

24. Another theme of the preceding pericope, "talking," "what goes out of the mouth." As Barth points out, "the form of the narrative makes it clear that it is not the miracle as such that was important but the *conversation which* the healing brought forth" ("Matthew's Understanding of the Law," 199). Barth also sees a thematic connection between the previous pericope about what is clean and unclean, though he exclusively attributes that connection to the pre-Markan synoptic tradition.

25. As the translation of the *Jerusalem Bible* suggests.

26. With Kingsbury, "'Son of David.'" *JBL* 95 (1976): 601. For him the title "son of David" characterizes Jesus primarily in his function as Messiah sent specifically to Israel and as miraculous healer, especially of "no-accounts" in Israel. However, because Kingsbury stresses Matthew's "apologetic" use of the title, and because of his general view that Israel is a lost cause, he does not adequately account for Matthew's insistence on the preserving of the strict lines between Jew and Gentile as manifested in the discussion of Jesus and the Canaanite woman.

27. Against Kingsbury ("'Son of David,'" 601), who can see nothing positive on the Jewish side of Matthew's contrast between Jew and Gentile in the story of the healing of the Canaanite woman's daughter. For Kingsbury (*Parables*, 31), beginning in chapter 13, the Jews have lost their privileged status "for having spurned their Messiah."

28. With TRILLING, 105, who says further that this is not to be attributed to a "Jewish-Christian tendency" on the part of Matthew but to a "theological necessity."

29. With TRILLING, 104, who points out that, in Matthew's redaction, 15:27 is not, strictly speaking, a request, nor a contradiction of Jesus, but rather an expansion of his words, in which, however, the woman shifts the focus from "dog" behavior to "master" behavior.

30. Cf. Held, "Matthew as Interpreter," 279.

31. Note that all of these features of a "great faith" are already present—although in a more implicit way—in the case of the centurion in 8:5–13. TRILLING, 104, proposes an interpretation of "faith" in 15:21–28 and 8:13 as being that characteristic in Gentiles which renders the otherwise exclusive mission of Jesus to Israel accessible to Gentiles. He does not, however, fill out the content of this faith in the same manner.

32. Anderson ("Matthew: Gender and Reading," 10–11) stresses that the supplicant as a *woman* and as a *Gentile* signifies the "marginality" of the source of such a faith and initiative. This is to say, in our own terms, that according to the readers' old knowledge, the woman's gender and non-Jewishness qualified her secular knowledge as marginal, as apparently insignificant. But this secular, marginal knowledge is shown to be significant—through the tension created by a text which describes this Canaanite woman as changing Jesus' mind.

33. The new point in 15:32–34 belongs to the interpretive level. Consequently, it complements the points of 15:10–28 which are on the interpretive level, and not those which are on the primary narrative level.

34. Since Galilee is the only location mentioned, by contrast with the text of Mark 7:31 which locates Jesus in Decapolis, on the other side of the Sea of Galilee.

35. See KINGSBURY, 56–57.

36. Especially Sinaiticus and Vaticanus. With many commentators, we consider that 16:2b–3 has been added by a scribe on the basis of Luke 12:54–56, in agreement with BONNARD, 237, but against GUNDRY, 323.

37. The parallelism between the designation as tempters of the Pharisees and Sadducees in 16:1 and of the devil in 4:3 is even more striking when one notes that the first temptation (4:3) concerns feeding with bread—transforming stones into loaves of bread—while 16:1 follows the feeding of the four thousand with seven loaves of bread.

38. With Edwards, *Sign of Jonah*, 105.

39. Against Edwards (*Sign of Jonah*, 105), who interprets it as referring to Jesus' Passion *and* resurrection, though with an emphasis on the aspect of suffering.

40. See Windisch, "*Zymē, zymō, azymos*," *TDNT* 2:902–906.

JESUS BEGINS TO SHOW THAT HE MUST GO TO JERUSALEM

THE MAIN THEME

This new section[1] begins with the well-known episode of Peter's confession at Caesarea Philippi (16:13–20) followed by the first announcement of the Passion, to which Peter violently objects (16:21–23). The latter verses constitute an important turning point in the Gospel in that the disciples (and the readers) are confronted with a new perspective. So far in the Gospel, and this is still the case in 16:13–20, the disciples and the readers were asked to understand who Jesus is and how they should relate to him in terms of his teaching, preaching, and healings, and of his role as eschatological judge. But now in 16:21–23, for the first time, it is in terms of Jesus' death and resurrection that they are asked to understand who Jesus is and how to relate to him.[2]

The initial reaction of the disciples is expressed by Peter's total rejection of the *possibility* of the Passion: "God forbid, Lord! This shall never happen to you" (16:22). Thus the theme of these introductory passages is the refusal to envision the possibility that Jesus, "the Christ, the Son of the living God" (16:16), must "suffer many things from the elders and chief priests and scribes, and be killed" (16:21). Consequently, this section will be concluded when the disciples will accept the possibility of Jesus' Passion, an acceptance that will complete the theme posited in 16:13–23. This conclusion is found in the second announcement of the Passion. That Jesus will "be delivered into the hands of men, and they will kill him, and he will be raised on the third day" (17:22–23a) is a reality they can no longer escape. This is expressed by their attitude: "They were greatly distressed" (17:23b). Certainly, the disciples still have a negative evaluation of forthcoming events. But they are now convinced that Jesus' fate necessarily includes his Passion.

If we have correctly identified the main theme of this section, a theme posited in 16:13–23 as a lack which is overcome in 17:2–23, it follows that, for Matthew, the intervening material (16:24—17:21) somehow explains what makes it possible for disciples (and readers) to accept the necessity of Jesus' Passion.

MATTHEW'S CONVICTIONS IN 16:13—17:23

16:13–20. Peter Replied, "You Are the Christ, the Son of the Living God"

Matthew here[3] makes two interrelated points, first by opposing what people (16:13–14) and the disciples (16:15–16) say about Jesus, then by opposing "flesh and blood," which did not reveal to Peter his answer and the Father who did (16:17).

16:13–16. In the first opposition, two groups of people and their respective views of Jesus are contrasted. The first group, designated by the general term "human beings" (RSV: "men"), is described as being in a relatively distant relationship with Jesus: "Who do men say that the Son of man is?" (16:13). By contrast, the disciples are presented as being in an intimate "I-you" relationship with Jesus: "Who do *you* say that I am?" (16:15). The people who remain at a distance from Jesus, as observers, identify him as John the Baptist, Elijah, Jeremiah, or other prophets (16:14). They recognize in him a man sent by God, whose teaching and deeds are from God. But they fail to recognize him as "the Christ, the Son of the living God" (16:16); they fail to recognize his intimate relationship with God. By contrast, through their spokesman Peter, the disciples who are themselves in an intimate relationship with Jesus acknowledge Jesus' intimate relationship with his Father. Matthew's point is clear. People who observe Jesus and his ministry *from a distance* can recognize him as a man sent by God, but they can only conceive his relationship with God as a somewhat *distant* relationship. By contrast, disciples who are in an *intimate relationship with Jesus* by sharing his ministry can recognize his *intimate relationship with God,* as expressed by the phrase "Son of the living God" (cf. 11:27).[4] It is also this relationship that the title "Christ" primarily designates in the present context.

16:17. In Jesus' response to Peter's confession, the opposition underscores that such a confession is possible only it if is revealed by "my Father who is in heaven." "Flesh and blood" do not reveal it. Those who are in an intimate relationship with Jesus and confess his intimate relationship with the Father have also received (and receive) revelations from the Father. Conversely, people who remain distant observers of Jesus do not receive such revelations from the Father; they are limited to the knowledge provided by "flesh and blood." They are limited to their own knowledge, which is incomplete and ultimately false, since it does not involve the recognition of the intimate relationship of Jesus with the Father. Yet, while being in an intimate relationship with Jesus appears to be a necessary condition for receiving revelations from the Father, it is not a guarantee of it; Peter alone confesses that Jesus is the Christ, the Son of the living God, and he alone is declared "blessed" for having received this revelation from the Father. In order to confess Jesus' sonship, one needs to be a disciple. But being a disciple is not sufficient; one still needs to receive a revelation from the Father.

16:18–19. The rest of Jesus' saying regarding Peter does not include any other opposition. Although these statements seem important, they do not involve points that Matthew views as significant enough to be specified by means of an opposition. Consequently, these verses are tantalizingly ambiguous and are open to a variety of interpretations—attempts at reconstructing the meaning that these statements might have had before being used by Matthew. Indeed, these verses are a thematic expression of Matthew's preceding points in terms of the readers' old knowledge ("church" refers to a reality that belongs to the readers' experience). We want to try to understand how these verses further develop the preceding points.

First, observe that the overall form of the address to Peter follows a covenantal pattern which Matthew assumes to be reflecting his readers' point of view (see 5:3–19). The beatitude about Simon Bar-Jona is the affirmation that he is chosen (elected) for a specific vocation expressed by a new name, "Peter" the rock upon which Jesus will build his church (16:18), involving certain duties spelled out in a law, binding and loosing on earth (16:19). In terms of 16:13–17, this thematic presentation of the role of Peter as the foundation upon which the church will be built further expresses his relationship with both Jesus and "heaven." Peter, who together with the other disciples is in intimate relationship with Jesus and has been charged to prolong Jesus' ministry in a mission (10:1–8) is now presented as participating in Jesus' continuing ministry in the period of the church. Yet even in this period beyond Jesus' ministry, his own activity will remain primary. Peter will not build his own church; rather, Jesus himself will build that church with the help of Peter, and it is Jesus' church. Thus Peter will continue in the relation of a disciple to the Christ (16:13–16). Similarly, Peter is in a special relationship with the "Father who is in heaven" from whom he received a revelation. Consequently, he also is the one whose actions "on earth" will have effects "in heaven" and he will receive "the keys of the kingdom of heaven" (16:19). Thus Peter, the rock upon which the church will be built, will remain in the privileged relationship with heaven manifested by his confession.

From this perspective, we can suggest how Matthew understood the metaphorical statements found in 16:18–19, which might originally have had different meanings for his readers. Considering the phrase "the gates of Hades shall not prevail against it" (16:18b, au.), we first note that Hades is the opposite of heaven. Since through Peter the church is related to heaven, it will triumph over Hades—the church will conquer the realm of Hades or the church will resist the attack from the realm of Hades.[5] The former option seems preferable both because of the metaphor—the *gates* of Hades are defensive (not offensive) features—and because of the relation between the church and Jesus' ministry. As Jesus' exorcisms are attacks against the demoniac powers associated with the realm of death (cf. 8:28–34) and are the conquest of the satanic kingdom (cf. 12:25–29), so the church will not be prevented by the gates of Hades from conquering the realm of Hades (perhaps in the sense of freeing the dead from it).

Similarly, "the keys of the kingdom of heaven," the authority of binding and loosing on earth and in heaven,[6] needs to be interpreted in terms of the relation between the church and Jesus' ministry. It is by his preaching and especially by his teaching (see the Sermon on the Mount) that Jesus either offers the possibility of entering the kingdom or excludes people from it (see 5:20). Consequently, as Jesus has the authority to teach what is binding and not binding in the law (see 5:21–48, and the preceding section, 15:1—16:12) and thus what the conditions are for entrance into the kingdom, so will Peter. "The keys of the kingdom" are the authority to teach as Jesus does. "Binding and loosing on earth as in heaven" means interpreting former expressions of God's will (in the law, and possibly in Jesus' teaching) so as to show "what is fitting for now" in a specific situation of the church's experience. Of course, since such a teaching will apply both on earth and in heaven, the teacher (here Peter, but all the disciples in 18:18) needs to be in a special relationship with heaven.[7]

16:20. This verse with the interdiction given to the disciples to tell anyone that Jesus is the Christ is somewhat puzzling for the readers. Why is this interdiction given? For the readers, the effect is that they are stopped in their reading. Something is amiss. In this way they are prepared to recognize that, for some reason, the disciples are not ready to proclaim that Jesus is the Christ, the Son of the living God.[8] The following verses suggest that although the disciples can *say* (cf. 16:15!) together with Peter that Jesus is the Christ, nevertheless they do not yet fully understand what this means.

16:21–23. Jesus Announces His Passion and Resurrection. Peter's Reaction

Here one is first struck by the highly emotional character of Peter's reaction (16:22) to Jesus' announcement of the Passion (16:21)—a first opposition—and by the harshness of Jesus' response—which contains an opposition between thinking human things *and* thinking the things of God (i.e., "having human intentions" *and* "having the intentions of God," 16:23, au.). In addition, in the announcement itself, making Jesus suffer and killing him are opposed to raising him (16:21). The fact that three points are made in three verses shows the importance of this passage for Matthew.

16:21–22. Through the first opposition Matthew underscores the significance of Jesus' statement that "he must go to Jerusalem and suffer many things . . . and be killed" by opposing it to Peter's elliptical exclamation, *hileōs soi* (RSV: "God forbid") which could be rendered "God be merciful to you" (16:22). Such a translation makes clear that Peter's response is comparable to the second temptation (4:5–6), where the devil suggests that God will not want his Son to suffer any harm. For Peter, God is merciful; consequently, going to Jerusalem to suffer and die cannot be his will for the Christ, his Son. Jesus' response, "Get behind me, Satan!" (16:23a; cf. 4:10), confirms that Peter's suggestion is indeed to be understood as a temptation, as an invitation to forgo doing what is truly the will of God. In short, the opposition underscores that Jesus' statement according to which "he *must* go to Jerusalem and suffer . . . and be killed" expresses not only that this is God's will (God's plan for Jesus) but also that he is determined to carry out God's will. It is not a fate that Jesus, willing or not, would have to follow, but rather something that Jesus accepts to do. He has made God's will his own will. This means that he perceives that going to Jerusalem, suffering, and dying is indeed good to do, ultimately euphoric (the Passion is followed by the resurrection), and thus worth pursuing (see 4:1–11). This point is further expressed by the opening words of the pericope: "From that time Jesus began to show his disciples that he must go . . ." (16:21a). The need to go to Jerusalem is something that must be understood even though it is hard to understand. And thus Jesus explains it, shows it, and demonstrates it to his disciples. For Matthew, this is not a teaching for everyone (the crowds)[9] but an explanation reserved for the disciples. It is one of the mysteries of the kingdom that the disciples alone can understand (here, as in 13:1–52, Matthew avoids the verb "to teach").[10] Thus Jesus' statement aims at helping the disciples to perceive that going to Jerusalem, suffering, and dying is euphoric, despite the appearances, and thus something they will want to pursue together with Jesus, joining him in the path to the cross (see 16:24–26). But this particular mystery of the kingdom is hard to understand and will demand more than a single explanation; here Jesus merely "began to show" it to his disciples.

16:23. This first explanation of what is God's will for Jesus is clearly not sufficient for Peter. He opposes it, and in so doing plays the role of Satan. He is a tempter and thus a scandal (RSV: "hindrance") for Jesus. This latter concept, found in 5:29–30 and 13:21, 41, 57 (see also 11:6; 15:12), is thereby clarified. A scandal is something or someone that has the potential of causing someone to turn away from fulfilling God's will.[11] Peter is a scandal for Jesus because his intentions—his will, his thoughts—are not those of God but of human beings (16:23). Actually, by refusing to accept that the suffering of Jesus is part of fulfilling God's will, Peter puts himself on the side of the "elders and chief priests and scribes" whose actions (making Jesus suffer many things, killing him) are directly opposed to God's action (raising Jesus, 16:21). Even though they are religious leaders in the holy city of Jerusalem and call upon God's authority, as Peter does ("God be merciful to you," 16:22, au.), their actions and intentions are not inspired by God; they are purely human in origin and thus against God.

In order to have the intentions of God, to have as one's will God's will, one needs to perceive that going to Jerusalem, suffering, and dying is God's will, and that it ultimately is a good that one may want to pursue. Yet this first demonstration by Jesus is not sufficient either for the disciples or for Matthew's readers. The following pericopes will continue this demonstration—to be completed only at the end of the Gospel.

16:24–28. Taking up One's Cross and Following Jesus

By presenting Peter's objection as a temptation, Matthew has underscored that the necessity of going to Jerusalem, suffering, and dying is a matter of perceiving what is ultimately good and thus worth pursuing. It is a matter concerning the proper establishment of Jesus' will as fulfillment of God's will. Matthew 16:24–28 specifies that it is also a matter concerning the proper establishment of the *disciples' will*: "If any one wants to come after me . . ." (16:24a, au.); "For whoever wants to save one's life . . ." (16:25a, au.).

16:25–26. This point is underscored by a twofold opposition between saving one's life and losing it. Wanting to save one's life (16:25)—not accepting suffering and dying as Jesus will do, not being willing to deny oneself and take up one's cross (16:24)—amounts to a wrong understanding of "life." It is having an understanding of life limited to the human realm (see my comments on 10:39 and 6:25). In such a case, one does not perceive that saving one's life, or trying to protect it at all cost by accumulating goods for the sustenance of one's life—gaining the whole world (16:26)—is not a good worth pursuing. Indeed, ultimately one will lose one's life—the life limited to the human realm, the only life in which one participates, according to this point of view. This is establishing one's will on the basis of a human point of view on life; this is having human intentions, as Peter did (16:23b).

16:25b, 27–28. By contrast, those who lose their life *for Jesus' sake* "will find it" (16:25b). Their will has been established in relation to Jesus; they want to follow Jesus and thus want to act for his sake. These ideal disciples (by contrast with the actual disciples such as Peter) perceive the ultimately euphoric character of the way to the cross, and thus its necessity—they accept to follow Jesus by denying themselves and taking up their cross.[12] They also have a proper understanding of life as not merely limited to the human realm. Thus when considering what is euphoric and dysphoric regarding one's life, what one would want to pursue or to avoid, they also take into account the part of life that is beyond the human realm.

Peter objected to the way to the cross without taking into account that this series of events does not end with Jesus' death but with his resurrection (16:21b). People want to save their life because life is limited to the human realm. By contrast, ideal disciples should decide what they will do by taking into account the dimension of life that is beyond the human realm. As they should take into account the resurrection in order to evaluate the way to the cross, so they should take into account the eschatological judgment when evaluating what they should do with regard to their own life (16:27). In fact, the two are closely linked, since it is the resurrected Christ, "the Son of man . . . in the glory of his Father," who will be the eschatological judge. Thus, when deciding what to do, the ideal disciples have to take into account that the Son of man "will repay every man for what he has done" (16:27b). They should not hesitate to do so, since Jesus strongly affirms ("Truly, I say to you") that "the Son of man [is] coming in his kingdom" in the near future, namely, before some of those standing here die (16:28).

In sum, understanding that the Christ, the Son of the living God, must suffer and die is the same as understanding that one's life is not limited to the human realm but includes life after death. It is precisely because he is the Son of the living God, in intimate relationship with the Father, that the Christ can accept without anxiety the way to the cross; he fully trusts in his Father, who will resurrect him and whose glory he will share as the eschatological judge (cf. 16:27). Similarly, for the disciples, having a view of life that is not limited to the human realm simultaneously involves (1) not being anxious about life because of their trust in the Father (the condition for overabundant righteousness and thus for entering the kingdom of heaven; see my comments on 6:25–34), and (2) truly following Jesus by denying themselves and taking up their own cross. Confessing that Jesus is the Christ the Son of the living God is not therefore simply being able to say it (cf. 16:15–16)—simply knowing who Jesus is—but having a perception of Jesus and of one's life in terms of their relationship with the Father and the kingdom. From this perspective, one perceives what is truly euphoric and dysphoric, and thus one can have "intentions," a will, which are God's intentions (cf. 16:23b), God's will. By acting accordingly, even though one might lose one's life, one finds it.

17:1–8. The Transfiguration

In the story of the transfiguration,[13] Matthew develops the preceding points by opposing (1) Peter's saying (17:4) *and* the saying of the voice from heaven (17:5), and (2) the disciples falling on their faces and being afraid (17:6) *and* the disciples rising and having no fear according to Jesus' injunction (17:7–8).

17:2–5. Once again Peter is given a privileged status. As he had been singled out to receive from the Father in heaven the revelation that Jesus is the Christ, the Son of the living God (16:17), Peter is one of the three disciples who have been specially chosen to witness Jesus' transfiguration— an epiphany, a manifestation of the divine in Jesus whose "face shone like the sun, and his garments became white as light" (17:2). But once again Peter exhibits a deep lack of understanding of this new revelation by adopting a human point of view (cf. 16:23). He does acknowledge Jesus' authority, addressing him as "Lord" and speaking to him with deference, "If you wish . . ." (17:4a). But, as people were associating Jesus with John the Baptist, Elijah, Jeremiah, or another prophet (16:14), so Peter associates Jesus with other prophets when he proposes to "make three booths here, one for you and one for Moses and one for Elijah" (17:4). As these people did, so Peter considers Jesus as having a status similar to that of the great prophets of the past; they are servants of God who remain human and are in need of human dwellings.[14] Indeed, Jesus speaks with Moses and Elijah. Peter fails to recognize that his transfiguration manifests that Jesus is in a unique and intimate relationship with the Father in heaven—as the voice proclaims (17:5) by repeating its public proclamation at Jesus' baptism (3:17). Note that, here, rather than being described as a "voice from heaven" (3:17), the voice is described as coming from "a bright cloud" (17:5a), bright, luminous as Jesus' garment and as his face (17:2).[15] Thus the brightness of the transfigured Jesus might be a figurative representation of his intimate relationship with the Father—the saying shows that it is the voice of the Father. The saying (see my comments on 3:17) emphasizes the intimate relationship already suggested in 16:16. Jesus is not only the Son but the "beloved Son, with whom I am well pleased" (17:5b).[16] This phrase conveys the two-way intimate relationship—the Father loves him, and what he does pleases the Father—which 11:27 expressed in another form. The voice further emphasizes Jesus' authority by adding "listen to him" (17:5b). In this way it is specified that it is not enough to acknowledge Jesus' authority as that of great prophets like Moses the lawgiver and Elijah—as Peter does (17:4a). His authority is properly acknowledged when it is recognized as the authority of the Son in intimate relationship with the Father.

17:6–9. The second opposition underscores the role of Jesus as mediator between heaven and the disciples—as long as the disciples have the human perspective displayed by Peter in 17:4. The disciples cannot stand hearing the voice from heaven. This direct revelation from heaven is too much for them and results in a great "fear," a panic. Instead of being put in relationship with heaven by this direct revelation from heaven, they fall on their faces (17:6); they turn away from heaven. But by listening to Jesus' command (see 17:5b) and by being touched by Jesus (as the people who have little faith and are healed by Jesus are, see chaps. 8—9), the disciples can overcome that fear, rise, and lift up their eyes (17:7–8).[17] Note that in 17:9 the disciples see Jesus *alone*. It is Jesus in his human form, no longer Jesus transfigured in the company of Moses and Elijah,[18] who can alone be seen without fear by the disciples. As long as the disciples have a human perspective (17:4),[19] they can receive the revelation from the Father (as Peter did, 16:17)[20] only because they are in intimate, physical relationship with Jesus (the touch, the "I-you" direct relationship expressed by his words, see also 16:15).

In sum, the story of the transfiguration shows that because of their human perspective, the disciples are unable to recognize the significance of the transfiguration as a manifestation of Jesus in the glory of his Father. They also are unable to relate directly with heaven and to receive a revelation from it. The pericopes that follow (17:9–13 and 17:14–20) will show that these deficiencies of the disciples are major obstacles for accepting the necessity of Jesus' Passion and will aim at overcoming these deficiencies.

17:9–13. "Tell No One the Vision, Until the Son of Man Is Raised"

The dialogue between Jesus and the disciples "as they were coming down the mountain" (17:9) involves two points that show why, for Matthew, the disciples failed to recognize the significance of the transfiguration, a failure directly related to their lack of understanding of the necessity of Jesus' suffering, death, and resurrection (16:21).

17:9–10. The first exchange involves an opposition, since the disciples object ("Then why. . . ?" 17:10a) to Jesus' command not to tell anyone "the vision, until the Son of man is raised from the dead" (17:9b). By this command, Jesus links transfiguration and resurrection. This confirms the observation[21] that what the disciples have seen is something like the Son of man "in the glory of his Father" (16:27), that is, like the Son of man after the resurrection.[22] Consequently, it is not yet time to say that Jesus was manifested in this way on the mountain. This also shows that, for Matthew, one of the major obstacles to be overcome so as to be in a position of understanding the necessity of Jesus' suffering and death is a lack of belief in the resurrection. It is on this point that the disciples object.[23] When they ask, "Then why do the scribes say that first Elijah must come?" their objection can only be related to the resurrection. By his command, Jesus presupposes that the resurrection of the Son of man will take place in the relatively near future (also conveyed by the phrase "on the third day," 16:21), since after this event they will be allowed to speak of the transfiguration. Taking once again the side of the scribes (see 16:22), the disciples object that one cannot expect the resurrection of the Son of man in the near future because "first Elijah must come."

17:11–12. Matthew underscores the fact that the scribes "did not know" Elijah (17:12) by opposing it to the disciples who understand that Elijah already came in the person of John the Baptist (17:13). According to Jesus' statement (17:11), what prevents an understanding of the possibility of the resurrection of the Son of man in the near future is not a wrong knowledge of Scripture but rather an inability to apply it to the present. They are correct in saying that Elijah must come first: "Elijah does come, and he is to restore all things" (17:11). But the scribes misunderstand the time.[24] Consequently, they fail to recognize that Elijah has already come, and fail to recognize him. Since the disciples' saying and Jesus' response allude to Mal. 3:23 (Matt. 4:5), the scribes are presented as knowing Scripture but not as knowing how it applies to the present. By contrast, the disciples, with the help of Jesus' teaching—something the scribes miss—can understand the time and thus how Scripture applies to the present. They recognize that Elijah has already come in the person of John the Baptist (17:13).

This recognition is essential for understanding the necessity of Jesus' suffering, death, and resurrection for two reasons. First, as the preceding opposition emphasizes, if Elijah has indeed already come, then one can conceive of the resurrection of the Son of man in the near future. Then one can envision that the sequence of events that begins by going to Jerusalem does not end with Jesus' death but with his resurrection, a perspective that allows one to accept the necessity of the Passion. Second, as 17:11b indicates, if John was Elijah, then he can be viewed as a precursor of Jesus (see 3:11). Then John's suffering and death can be viewed as a prefiguration of Jesus' own suffering at the hand of the scribes, which demonstrates in another way that the Passion is according to God's will. But, for Matthew, the primary point is the first one. When the possibility of the resurrection can be envisioned—since Elijah has already come—then the Passion can be accepted. Jesus does not need to try to save his life; by losing it, he will find it (16:25)!

17:14–20. "Why Could We Not Cast Out the Demon?"

For Matthew, there is another major obstacle that would prevent the disciples from accepting the necessity of Jesus' death: Jesus would no longer be with his disciples. Through Jesus and their intimate relationship with him in his physical presence with them, they can receive revelation from the Father (16:17) without fear/panic (17:7–8). Actually, they can be in a relation with the Father that is not unlike Jesus' relation with the Father ("Our Father who art in heaven," 6:9) and carry out a ministry similar to that of Jesus, including performing the same type of miracles (10:1–8). But what will happen if Jesus departs? Will they not be unable to do all this? Will they not lose their ability to look toward heaven, as was the case on the mountain as long as Jesus did not touch them and speak to them (17:6)?

This seems to be the case, as is shown by what happened to the disciples in Jesus' absence (17:14–20). But then Jesus' departure, his Passion, cannot be good, cannot be God's will even if it leads to his resurrection!

In 17:14–20 Matthew makes two points that underscore that in Jesus' absence the disciples should not find themselves unable to carry out their ministry. This should not and need not be so. Even in Jesus' absence, the disciples should be able to heal and perform exorcisms. Their powerlessness was due not to Jesus' absence but to their lack of faith.

17:14–18. The story of Jesus' healing of the epileptic boy is a typical healing story,[25] except that the boy's father reports that the disciples were unable to heal his son (17:16). In the process an opposition is set between healing (17:18) *and* not healing (17:16), an opposition that is repeated in another form when not being able to cast out the demon (17:19) is opposed to "nothing will be impossible to you" (17:20). The first opposition contrasts Jesus' ability to perform the exorcism with the disciples' inability. But Jesus' words in 17:17 specify that the disciples' inability is not due to his absence, as is shown by the exclamations "How long am I to be with you? How long am I to bear with you?" Even in the absence of Jesus, the disciples should have been able to perform this exorcism. The true reason for their inability is that the disciples are part of (associate themselves with) this "faithless and perverse generation"—as they associated themselves with the people who have a wrong understanding of who Jesus is (16:14; 17:4) and with the scribes (17:10). What characterizes human beings is, for Matthew, both their faithlessness—not believing in God's power—and their perversity (17:17a). For Matthew, not acknowledging the power of God means that one cannot perceive what is truly good (what God does). Consequently one cannot but fail to pursue good things. One has human intentions and ends up with a perverse, misled behavior.

17:19–20. The second opposition makes the positive point. If the disciples are truly disciples—if they have faith, if they trust in the power of their Father (cf. 6:25–34)—there will be no limit to their ability to carry out their ministry: "if you have faith as a grain of mustard seed . . ." (17:20). The problem is that the disciples have only a "little faith"; they acknowledge Jesus as Lord but do not believe in Jesus' power when he is not physically present (by contrast with the centurion, cf. 8:5–13).[26] Ideal disciples should have true faith, not the little faith.

17:22–23. The Second Announcement of the Passion and the Disciples' Distress

Following the demonstration that the resurrection is a possibility and that the disciples will not be helpless when Jesus departs, the second announcement simply presents the Passion as a series of events which will take place:

"The Son of man is to be delivered into the hands of men . . ." (17:22). The disciples now accept the Passion as something that will happen, even though they cannot yet perceive it in a positive light, as something good: "And they were greatly distressed" (17:23).

As a consequence, the announcement of the Passion takes a different form. The opposition between killing and raising Jesus now opposes God to human beings in general who have just been described as this "faithless and perverse generation" (17:17). It is no longer specified that it is "from the elders and chief priests and scribes" (16:21) that Jesus will suffer many things; he "is to be delivered into the hands of men" (17:22). Jesus' opponents lose definite identity. Similarly, and more important, Jesus loses his role as a person. Instead of being presented as a person making the decision to go to Jerusalem, and thus deliberately choosing to do what is according to God's will ("he must go to Jerusalem," 16:21), here the Son of man is totally passive. He does not initiate anything; things happen to him. Of course, the two announcements do not contradict each other. By choosing to go to Jerusalem he chooses to submit himself to whatever people will do to him. But in 17:22–23 Matthew emphasizes the passive submission of Jesus to what is to be and thus to both (perverse) human beings and God. This theme will be carried forward in the next section.

NOTES ON 16:13—17:23

1. In my comments on 16:13—17:23 I am indebted to the work of Larry Vigen, "To Think the Things of God." Our respective interpretations are different. He studied exclusively the discoursive dimension of the text. I study Matthew's system of convictions. Yet many of my insights are derived from his work.

2. In the preceding chapters, Jesus' cross and death are explicitly mentioned only in 10:38, as part of an explanation of the disciples' persecution, and in 12:40, about the sign of Jonah which, for Matthew, is primarily the preaching of repentance. In both cases, these are passing remarks and do not demand from the readers an overall interpretation of Jesus and of one's relationship to him in terms of his death. KINGS-BURY (21–36) interprets 16:21 as the turning point which introduces the third part ("the reason and finality of Jesus' suffering, death and resurrection") of his tripartite structuring of Matthew's Gospel.

3. See Kingsbury, "The Figure of Peter," JBL 98 (1979): 67–83. See also Brown, Donfried, and Reumann, eds., Peter in the New Testament, 75–107; Kunzel, Gemeindeverständnis, 180–93, 196ff; Burnett, "Characterization in Matthew."

4. Cf. KINGSBURY, 122.

5. Commentators argue in favor of one or the other of these interpretations. For instance, the former is advocated by BONNARD, 245, while SCHWEIZER, 341–43, advocates the latter.

6. On the possible original meaning of this tradition, see the thesis of Hiers, "'Binding' and 'Loosing,'" JBL 104 (1985): 233–50. His suggestions (246–48) regarding Matthew's understanding of these verses are not incompatible with our interpretation.

7. With STRECKER, 206; and Schweizer, "Matthew's Church," 129–55. See also Kingsbury, "The Figure of Peter," 67–83.

8. The interdiction prepares the readers for what will appear as the "disconcerting inconsistency" between 16:17–18 and 16:23 regarding the portrayal of Peter. Cf. Stanton, "Origin and Purpose," 1929.

9. As is the case in Mark 8:31, where it is presented as a public *teaching*.

10. With SCHWEIZER, 345.

11. This definition holds true even in the cases of 11:6 and 15:12, where Jesus is perceived as a scandal by people such as the Pharisees. Jesus is thus perceived as causing people to turn away from fulfilling "God's will," but of course in this latter case it is "God's will" as wrongly understood by the Pharisees. See Zumstein, *La condition du croyant*, 175–78.

12. In the phrase "Let him deny himself and take up his cross and follow me" (16:24) the two "ands" have to be understood as explicative and could be rendered in English by "that is," and not as the expression of a logical sequence. With BONNARD, 249–50.

13. See Feuillet, "Perspectives," *Biblica* 39 (1958):281–309; and Pederson, "Proklamation," *NovT* 17 (1975):241–64.

14. Peter's proposal to build "booths" might be a thematic allusion to the Feast of Booths (cf. Lev. 23:42) to which the temporal notation "after six days" of 17:1 might also refer since the Feast of Booths is six days after Yom Kippur. So BONNARD, 254–55. Feuillet relates the imagery to the Shekhinah, the divine Presence as manifested in the traveling Tabernacle (an interpretation also suggested by Jonathan Kraus). See Feuillet, "Perspectives," 294–96. But with Pederson ("Proklamation," 260), we have to say that these are no longer the points Matthew wants to emphasize for his readers.

15. Feuillet ("Perspectives," 295) views the image of the "bright cloud" as an Old Testament allusion both to the divine voice coming from the midst of a cloud at Sinai (Exod. 24:16–17 and Deut. 5:19) and to "wisdom" (Ecclus. 24:4, 8), who is located on a column of cloud and pitched her tent among human beings.

16. With Feuillet, "Perspectives," 297.

17. With KINGSBURY, 68. However, he sees the pattern of the disciples' fear and Jesus' comforting as merely the typical marks of a "christophany" (cf. 14:22–33).

18. We could say that the transfigured Jesus is like "the Son of man [who] is to come with his angels in the glory of his Father" (16:27), as pointed out by Larry Vigen.

19. It is important not to generalize this point—as if the physical relationship with Jesus in human form was necessary for receiving revelation from God and being in relationship with heaven. In fact, Matthew wants to emphasize that such a relationship with heaven is possible for the disciples after Jesus' departure (his death and resurrection) as is already expressed in 16:19 and will be underscored in 17:14–20.

20. Pederson ("Proklamation," 261) also recognizes an allusion in the transfiguration scene to the opposition found in 16:13–16.

21. See n. 18, above.

22. My point has nothing to do with the suggestion made by scholars who argue that the transfiguration story is a misplaced resurrection tradition. See Carlston, "Transfiguration and Resurrection," *JBL* 80 (1961):233. My point is simply that Matthew in his own text relates transfiguration and resurrection.

23. With Fitzmyer, "More About Elijah Coming First," *JBL* 104 (1985):295–96. He makes such an observation in the context of an argument in support of Faierstein ("Why Do the Scribes Say That Elijah Must Come First?" *JBL* 100 [1981]:75–86), and against the view that the statement regarding Elijah should be read as primarily expressing that he is the forerunner of the Messiah, a view based on the unfounded presupposition that this was a common expectation in Judaism. This latter view has been most recently defended by Allison ("Elijah Must Come First," *JBL* 103 [1984]:256–58). Yet note that while the disciples' objection (17:10) bears upon the coming of Elijah as preceding the resurrection, and not upon Elijah as forerunner of the Messiah, for Matthew, John/Elijah is nevertheless the forerunner of Jesus (cf. 17:12).

24. Ironically, John the Baptist also failed to understand the present time. Cf. 3:13–15.

25. By contrast with the text in Mark 9:14–29 which presents such an exorcism as extraordinarily difficult to perform.

26. This point is clearly shown in Larry Vigen's analysis of the discursive structures of this passage. See Vigen, *To Think the Things of God.*

RECEIVING LITTLE ONES AND FORGIVING AS BLESSINGS

THE MAIN THEME

"And they [the disciples] were greatly distressed" (17:23). "They [the servants] were greatly distressed" (18:31). These statements echo each other; they mark the beginning and the end of a new section, as is indicated by the great difference in the situations that distress respectively the disciples and the servants. In order to identify the theme of this section—which begins with the Temple tax episode (17:24–27), includes the discourse on church life (18:1–35), and concludes with the parable of the unforgiving servant (18:23–35)—we need to consider why the disciples were distressed.

In the preceding section (16:12—17:23), the disciples (and the readers) have learned to recognize that the Passion is a necessity. One perceives that the Passion is God's will, and thus necessary, when one views it in terms of the proper understanding of "life" (cf. 16:24–28); of the possibility of the resurrection (17:1–13); and of the possibility for the disciples of carrying out their ministry in the absence of Jesus (17:14–20), if they have faith. But the disciples still do not perceive the Passion in a positive light. They still do not understand that it is something good about which one does not need to be distressed.

How are the disciples (and the readers) to perceive that being "delivered into the hands of men" and being killed is something intrinsically good, about which they should not be distressed? This demands a fundamental change of "heart" (cf. 18:35), a total reversal of their perception of what is good and bad, of what is euphoric and dysphoric. The preceding part of the Gospel (1:1—16:12), through its presentation of Jesus' ministry and of his teaching and proclamation of the kingdom, provides the perspective that should allow the disciples to perceive the Passion in a positive light. But their reaction shows that they have not yet appropriated this teaching about the kingdom. They do not yet know how they as disciples should relate to the presence of evil (cf. 13:1–53). It is this fundamental change of perspective that Matthew hopes to achieve by means of the last part of his Gospel.[1]

Changing the disciples' and the readers' fundamental convictions about what is good and bad cannot be done by a single statement about the Passion.

244

In fact, it is only when the disciples and the readers perceive all the areas of their life in terms of this new view of what is good and bad that they will be able to perceive the Passion in a positive light. Thus we should not be surprised to find that the basic points that express this new view are developed in terms of quite different situations, issues, and topics.

This is what Matthew begins to do in 17:24—18:35.[2] Note that the disciples' distress is in response to an announcement of the Passion which describes Jesus' passive submission and self-denial. This theme is carried forward in 17:24–25a, where Jesus submits himself to the half-shekel (or double drachma) tax. This submission to the Temple tax is not unrelated to Jesus' submission to human beings (17:22), among whom are the chief priests (16:21). In his comments on this issue (17:25b–27), Jesus emphasizes the deliberate character of his submission to the Temple tax since he and his disciples are not obligated to pay it but are "free" (17:26a).[3] He further explains why it is good to submit to such a tax; the purpose of this submission is to avoid scandalizing (17:27a) others.

The significance of this statement for a correct understanding of the Passion will appear only when it is taken to apply not merely to the specific case of the Temple tax but to a series of cases presented in 18:1–35—including the disciples' life since their ministry and attitude should duplicate that of Jesus (as repeatedly expressed: e.g., 10:1–8 and 16:24). The theme expressed in 17:24–27 is developed in 18:1–35, the discourse on church life, to the point that its application is generalized and that the statement about Jesus' self-denial can be understood to mean: "It is good to deny oneself (16:24) by submitting to others in order to avoid scandalizing them." If one could fully understand this, then one would perceive that it is good that Jesus denies himself and submits to the people who will make him suffer and will kill him. One would no longer be "greatly distressed" by the announcement of the Passion (17:23). Indeed one would be greatly distressed, as the good servants of the king are in 18:31, when someone, for the sake of self-preservation, does not submit to someone else's request. Furthermore, one would understand that the disciples' own self-denial is not merely something necessary so that they might be blessed at the eschatological judgment (16:24–27) but also something fundamentally good and thus something they will joyfully want to do.

One should not be surprised to find that Matthew uses his habitual pedagogical approach; he seeks to demonstrate this point about the Passion by first taking the case of the disciples (see my comments regarding the relation of chapter 10 to chapters 11—12). Thus Matthew first develops the case of the relationships of the disciples with their brothers and sisters. When it will be understood that self-denial and submission to brothers and sisters are good, then a great step will have been taken toward understanding Jesus' self-denial.

From this perspective, one recognizes that the theme of self-denial for the sake of others is developed in various ways in 18:1–35. Humbling oneself like a child and not despising one of these little ones (18:1–14) are forms of self-denial for the sake of others. Similarly, forgiving others (18:15–35) especially when it is unlimited (18:21–22) is a form of self-denial and of submission to others—being in a good relationship with others despite their sins against us, and thus suffering what they do to us. Even when limits are finally put on forgiveness (18:17; 18:23–35), the value of self-denial is affirmed. It is because the good servants of the king, with whom disciples and readers can identify, are "greatly distressed" by the lack of self-denying compassion displayed by the unmerciful servant, that the latter is not forgiven. Self-denial and submission to others is now perceived as good, while efforts at self-preservation at the expense of others are perceived as bad and distressing.

MATTHEW'S CONVICTIONS IN 17:24—18:35

17:24–27. Jesus and the Temple Tax

17:24–25a. The story of the payment of the Temple tax is thematic because it does not contain any opposition.[4] For the readers, whose expectations are repeatedly betrayed, this story is unsettling. The question of the collectors of the Temple tax (17:24) is clearly polemical, as one could expect from Jewish officials after reading the controversies of preceding chapters (e.g., 15:1—16:12). They anticipate a negative answer, and so do the readers. But there is no controversy! Peter affirms that Jesus pays the Temple tax (17:25a).

17:25b–27a. Jesus' opening question to Peter, "What do you think, Simon?" (17:25b), again misleads the readers. For them, this question following Peter's quick answer to the Jewish tax collectors seems to indicate that his answer was wrong—as one could expect from Peter, who is less than trustworthy (cf. 16:22–23; 17:4). This evaluation seems to be confirmed when Jesus specifies: "From whom do kings of the earth take toll or tribute? From their sons or from others?" (17:25b). Obviously, as Peter expresses, the answer to this question is "From others" (17:26a). And Jesus confirms it by noting "Then the sons are free" (17:26b). Does this not indicate that Peter's response to the tax collectors was wrong? The implication that the readers are called to draw is that Jesus and his disciples, as sons of the king of heaven, are not obligated to pay the Temple tax, since this would be paying tax to their Father.[5] Thus one might conclude that Peter was wrong in affirming that Jesus pays the Temple tax. But the next verse shows that he was right: Jesus does pay the tax (17:27).

The effect of all these tensions is to underscore the reason for paying this tax. Jesus does not pay it because he is obligated to do so. He is free from this obligation.[6] Rather, he submits himself to the Temple tax and thus to the demands of the Jewish authorities "in order not to scandalize them" (17:27a, au.).

Once again this explanation is in tension with the readers' expectations. Earlier when the disciples had reported to him that the Pharisees were scandalized by his teaching, Jesus had responded by an additional attack against them (15:12–14). He was not concerned by the fact that he scandalized them by his teaching. Then why does he now want to avoid scandalizing these Jewish tax collectors?

We should not try to supply an answer to this question on the basis of this pericope by itself. The readers should be puzzled. The phrase "in order not to scandalize them," which expresses the reason for submitting oneself to the Temple tax, begs for an explanation. It posits the theme of the section (17:24—18:35). When it will have been shown why not scandalizing others is so important that one should not hesitate to deny oneself and submit to others *and* what are the eventual limits of such an attitude, the presentation of the theme will be complete.

17:27b. Finally, the way in which Jesus pays the Temple tax is full of irony.[7] As the miracle of the fish with a shekel (or stater) in its mouth shows, in the case of the children of heaven the money necessary for paying the tax is provided by the king of heaven himself! This is another reason for Jesus and his disciple not to scandalize the tax collectors. The cost of their submission to the tax is covered by God! Thus, ultimately, submitting to the tax—which usually involves denying oneself the use of a sum of money—is no denial at all.[8]

18:1–14. Becoming Like a Child and Not Despising the Little Ones

The discourse on church life (18:1–35)[9] is closely linked with 17:24–27 by a temporal phrase, "at that time" (18:1). Matthew frequently uses such a device (see 9:18; 11:1; 12:1; 13:1; 14:1; 16:21) to signal that what follows develops the theme of the preceding pericope.[10] This is the case once again as the first part of the discourse indicates through its emphasis on not "scandalizing one of these little ones" (18:6, au.) and through its subsequent discussion about scandals (18:7–9). By juxtaposing sayings and teachings that originally belonged to diverse contexts,[11] Matthew shows that for him these sayings and teachings need to be interpreted together and in terms of each other. Once again, he has carefully edited this discourse so as to make certain points—the very points that will develop the theme formulated in 17:24–27.[12]

In 18:1–14, after a discussion regarding who is the greatest in the kingdom, namely, "whoever humbles himself like this child" (18:1–4), we read a saying regarding receiving a child and not scandalizing the little ones (18:5–6), an apparent shift of topic. The verses that follow (18:7–9) are linked

with 18:6 through the theme of scandals; but while 18:7 speaks of scandalizing others, 18:8–9 shifts focus and speaks of being scandalized. Then,
18:10–14 further develops the theme of the little ones first in a saying (18:10),
then through the parable of the lost sheep (18:12–13), which is concluded
by a saying (18:14) that, as we shall see, once again involves a shift of
perspective. Yet all these sayings and teachings together contribute to explaining why the disciples must strive toward self-denial and submission
to others.

18:1–4. Jesus' discourse is prompted by the disciples' question, "Who is
the greatest in the kingdom of heaven?" (18:1). In Matthew's presentation,[13]
Jesus does not object to this question, since he answers it after placing a
child in their midst (18:2). Although Jesus' answer might have been quite
unexpected for the disciples, Matthew does not set up an opposition that
would contrast Jesus with the disciples. Rather, he contrasts those who will
not enter the kingdom (18:3) with those who will be the greatest in the
kingdom (18:4) by opposing "unless you turn and become like children"
(18:3) *and* "whoever humbles himself like this child" (18:4). The point is
that being like a child is a prerequisite for greatness in the kingdom (18:4b),
indeed for entering it (18:3b). Yet, and this is the essential, people—that
is, would-be disciples—are not spontaneously like children. They must
become like children by turning away from what they are, by humbling
themselves.[14] Self-denial, giving up what one is, is a prerequisite for participating and being great in the kingdom.

18:5–6. The opposition of "whoever receives one such child" (18:5) and
"whoever scandalizes one of these little ones who believe in me" (18:6, au.)
specifies in several ways the point made by the opposition of 18:3–4. First,
this new opposition describes children as in need of being received by others
(18:5). Thus, for Matthew, children are before all "dependents"; they depend upon others for support and are also at the mercy of others. Consequently, becoming like a child is to recognize oneself as not being self-
sufficient. One acknowledges that one needs the support of one's Father in
heaven, as children count on the support of their human father for their
sustenance and security. Turning and becoming like a child is, therefore,
turning toward the heavenly Father and trusting that he knows what one
needs (6:8, 32). But it is also putting oneself at the mercy of other people
who may or may not receive you (18:5), and indeed who may scandalize
you (18:6). This is what was already expressed in 10:9–14. By not taking
gold and other means of self-support (10:9–10), the disciples demonstrate
their trust in their heavenly Father. Simultaneously, they put themselves at
the mercy of others who may or may not receive them (10:14) and may
even persecute them (10:16 ff.). Becoming like children means giving up

any pretense at self-sufficiency and giving up whatever ways and attitudes one could use to be self-sufficient.

The opposition in 18:5–6 also indicates that when Matthew speaks about children he has in mind not merely actual children (such as the child whom Jesus puts in the midst of the disciples) but also those who are like children even though they are adults—"these little ones who believe in me" (Jesus, 18:6). At first, one could be tempted to identify these little ones as disciples since they believe in Jesus.[15] Yet this would be forgetting that those who believe in Jesus and his power are not merely the (ideal) disciples (cf. 17:20) but also the people in need of his help—the sick, the relatives or friends of sick people (cf. chaps. 8—9). For Matthew, believing in Jesus and his power, and thus saying "Lord, Lord" (see 7:21–23), is a necessary part of discipleship; but it is not sufficient. Consequently, for Matthew, the "little ones who believe" in Jesus form a relatively large group which includes both disciples and others who view themselves as needing help from Jesus (and God) and trust in his power.[16] It is precisely those who are like children and see themselves as being in need of support and help who believe in Jesus. It appears that becoming like children is a condition for believing in Jesus—a necessary step toward discipleship.

Finally, through the opposition in 18:5–6, Matthew contrasts those who receive one such child (18:5) with those who scandalize the little ones (18:6). Those who receive a child do so in the name of Jesus. They are therefore (ideal) disciples who do what Jesus taught them and will be received by him, that is, who will enter the kingdom. Consequently, it is only when people have become like children—and thus when they view themselves as dependents in need of support (from the Father) and thereby put themselves at the mercy of others—that they can receive a child or a little one. Such people will be the greatest in the kingdom (18:4). Conversely, as long as one does not turn and become like a child, one cannot but scandalize the little ones and the children, that is, cause them to turn away from God (18:6a). In such a case, it would be better for these people to drown themselves (18:6b, see below).

18:7–9. After emphasizing that scandals will come (18:7a), the following sayings (18:7b–9, already found in 5:29–30) identify the people through whom "scandal comes" (18:7b, au.), the people who scandalize the little ones. They are people who are themselves scandalized by something—a hand, a foot, an eye (18:8–9). In the same way that people who have become like children can receive children and little ones, so people who are scandalized can do nothing but scandalize the little ones.

But who is being scandalized? On the basis of 18:8–9 we can say that the people who are scandalized are those who have not (yet) given up a hand, a foot, or an eye. They are people who do not miss an important organ, something that gives them a feeling of wholeness, of self-sufficiency. Conversely, those who turn, becoming like children by humbling themselves (18:3–4), are those who give up an important part of themselves, a hand, a foot, or an eye (18:8–9).

18:6–7, 8, 9. Why would people want to humble themselves, becoming like children by mutilating themselves, giving up important parts of their life or of their being? As is expressed through an opposition repeated three times in different forms (18:6–7; 18:8; and 18:9), it is because "it is better" to be received by Jesus and to enter life than to be thrown into the eternal fire of Gehenna. Death by drowning in the sea (18:6b) is even better than this eschatological punishment, being consumed in eternal fire instead of entering life.[17] In brief, people should want to become like children in order to be blessed rather than cursed at the eschatological judgment.

Yet, for Matthew, there is another reason for becoming like children; it is more important than one's eschatological fate. By becoming like children, one becomes able to receive children and little ones in Jesus' name (18:5–6). Indeed one should not merely act in order "to flee from the wrath to come"—the negative attitude which characterizes the Pharisees' and Sadducees' behavior (3:7). One should also have a positive constructive reason for acting. Here it is for the sake of receiving children that one should humble oneself, because as long as one does not become like children one cannot receive children; one will only scandalize them.

It follows that in order to *want* to become like children, one needs not merely to be convinced that it is better regarding one's eschatological fate but also to be convinced that receiving children is something ultimately good in and of itself, something worth pursuing whatever might be the cost. This point was already expressed in 18:5–6. Now, in 18:10–14, Matthew further develops it by introducing sayings that explain what receiving children in Jesus' name means and why it is an ultimate good worth pursuing.

18:10. A first saying expresses that despising the little ones, and consequently not receiving them, is actually missing a blessing, because the little ones are blessed (cf. 5:3–6). They are in a special and intimate relationship with the Father, a relationship that is described by the phrase "in heaven their angels always behold the face of my Father who is in heaven" (18:10b). By receiving the little ones who are in a special relationship with the Father, one shares in their blessedness.

18:12–13. It remains that these little ones are like children; they are in need of support from others. According to the parable, they are "lost sheep" (cf. 9:36; 10:6; 15:24) who need the help of the shepherd/owner. The contrast between the "lost" and the ninety-nine that are not lost emphasizes that the only good situation for a sheep is to be with the flock—a thematic point which will be developed in 15:14. The narrative thrust of the parable (taken by itself, 18:12–13) does not concern the transformation of the situation of the lost sheep, but that of the owner, who, having one hundred sheep, is deprived of one that is lost (18:12) and then finds it (18:13).

For the disciples (and the readers), there is nothing surprising or new in this parable.[18] Through their basic human knowledge of how people behave they should be able to anticipate the unfolding of the story, as is indicated by its interrogative and hypothetical formulation and the introductory phrase, "What do you think?" (18:12a). Obviously, in order to find the lost sheep, the owner abandons the rest of the flock (18:12). And obviously, if he finds it, "he rejoices over it more than over the ninety-nine" (18:13). The story further expresses the preceding points. Taking care of the lost sheep (the little ones) demands abandoning the rest of the flock (what one has). This is what is involved in turning, becoming like children, and humbling oneself like a child.

What is underscored by the parable taken by itself is the greater joy felt in finding the lost sheep. In other words, abandoning the flock—self-denial—is something one should want to do because of its eventual joyful outcome. The owner of the sheep does not hesitate to abandon the flock because of his anticipation of the great joy at finding the lost sheep. Similarly, disciples should not hesitate to humble themselves in order to receive the little ones, because they should anticipate the great joy involved in receiving them. Receiving the little ones is for them something good (euphoric) and thus something they should want to pursue. Furthermore, ultimately it does not cost anything, since, after all, one is not deprived from the ninety-nine that never went astray—as it did not cost anything for Jesus and Peter to pay the Temple tax (17:27b)! In other words, one has everything to gain (a greater joy) by receiving the little ones.[19]

18:14. The following saying both prolongs and creates a tension with what precedes, as can be expected in a thematic passage—a passage (18:10–14) in which Matthew does not make new points by means of oppositions but rather expresses preceding points in terms of what he assumes his readers know. In 18:14 the perspective changes. Instead of focusing upon what is good for the disciples (the owner of the flock), this new saying focuses upon the need of the little ones: "So it is not the will of my Father who is in heaven that one of these little ones should perish" (18:14).

The effect of this tension is to underscore that wanting to pursue what is truly good for oneself is the same thing as wanting to carry out God's will and thus wanting to provide the little ones with what they need, namely, escape from destruction.[20] In terms of what precedes, what brings great joy to the owner is also what provides the lost sheep with what it needs—being found and being received by others. As was expressed in the Sermon on the Mount, God's will is nothing else than what is truly good for people, and thus what people will want to do for their own sake—doing God's will is being blessed now and in the future. But, simultaneously, God's will is that people do what is good for others: "So whatever you wish that men would do to you, do so to them" (7:12). God's will is that none of these little ones should perish. As the owner of the flock in the parable does, so God wants to find the lost sheep and will greatly rejoice when finding it. Disciples should do the same thing both because it is God's will that they should be a blessing for those in need (the little ones) and because they can anticipate that such self-denying action will bring to them, here and now, great joy (18:13) since they will share in the little ones' blessedness (18:10) and, in the eschatological future, blessings of the kingdom rather than the punishment of being "thrown into the eternal fire" (18:8–9).

18:15–35. The Benefits of Forgiving Others

In the second part of the discourse, Matthew gathers together a series of teachings and a parable that concern interrelationships among members of the community, interrelationships among brothers and sisters (18:15–22), or, in the parable of the unforgiving servant, among fellow servants (18:23–35). This second part of the discourse further develops the points of the first part.

18:15–17. At first, one wonders how the instructions concerning what to do when a "brother sins against you" (18:15) are related to the preceding teaching. Their abrupt introduction in the discourse creates another tension. This signals that Matthew calls upon his readers' old knowledge—presenting something that he expects them to know and to accept, but doing so in such a way that their old knowledge is marshaled as additional evidence for the points he is making through the discourse. This observation is confirmed by the anachronistic use of "church" which shows that Matthew refers to a rule of church discipline that he certainly expected his readers to know.[21]

In its original form (the tradition to which Matthew alludes) this rule specified the steps to be taken to reprove a sinner in the community: first a one-to-one reproof; then, according to Deut. 19:15 (quoted in Matt. 18:16), a reproof with two or three witnesses; and finally a reproof before the entire community, which, if it was not heeded, led to exclusion from the community. The goal of such a reproof of sinners was not primarily to exclude sinners from the community but to bring them to acknowledge their sins and to repent (as Luke 17:3–4 emphasizes). Understood in this way, the rule is far from advocating the self-denial for the sake of those who have gone astray, which is emphasized in 18:1–14. It involves demanding that others—the sinners—humble themselves rather than that one humble oneself.[22]

Without denying the overall validity of this rule of church discipline, Matthew uses it to underscore a point that demands an understanding of this rule from a new perspective. He does so by setting up an opposition between the sinner who "listens" (18:15b) and the sinner who "does not listen" (18:16a, 17a, 17b). Through this opposition Matthew underscores that the motivation for going and showing one's sins to a brother or a sister is not primarily to cause one, the sinner, to humble oneself and to repent. Although the phrase "if he listens to you" certainly implies that the sinner will also repent, it is significant that Matthew does not use this verb here. Indeed, for him, the primary motivation for going and showing one's sins to a brother or a sister is to gain a brother or a sister (18:15b). In the process, what is emphasized is not the sinner's need—the need to repent and to be part of the community—but the disciple's need. The disciple is in need of brothers and sisters. If one of them sins against the disciple, the problem is not so much the harm done to the disciple but the fact that the disciple is in risk of losing a brother or a sister, as is the case when a sinner becomes for the disciple as a Gentile (a foreigner) and as a tax collector (someone who exploits and abuses you). Thus the elaborate process for reproving a sinner should not be viewed as being carried out primarily for the sinner's benefit—even though it also has this role—but primarily for the benefit of the disciple who should perceive that having sisters and brothers is the ultimate good that one should pursue.

This effort to gain a brother or a sister is not necessarily successful. The sinner might not listen. Matthew does not deny the necessity of the rule for church discipline. There is a specific condition that must be met to be worthy of the status of brother or sister; it is expressed by the verb "to listen." One needs to be willing to listen to one "brother," to two or three of them, or to the whole church. One needs to be willing to remain in the network of relationship that links brothers and sisters of the community; one needs to show that one values this relationship by listening to other members of the community.

18:18–19. In this context, the statements regarding the authority of the disciples (as church members) to "bind" and to "loose" (18:18) and regarding prayer (18:19) take a special meaning. First, note that these two sayings are closely linked by the repetition of the phrases "on earth" and "in heaven." As the disciples' binding and loosing are effective both on earth and in heaven (18:18), so it is only if two disciples agree "on earth" to ask something, that the Father "in heaven" will do it (18:19).[23] Matthew wants his readers to read these verses together.

Consequently, binding and loosing should not be conceived as something that the disciples could do by themselves. Ultimately, it is Jesus' Father who does it, as it is Jesus who builds the church even though Peter has an authoritative role in this process (16:18–19). The disciples bind and loose by asking the heavenly Father to do so. Nevertheless, according to Jesus' solemn promise ("Truly, I say to you," 18:18a, 19a), their prayer and pronouncement regarding binding and loosing is in itself authoritative because it is what the disciples ask which will be done by the Father.

One should also note that the authority of binding and loosing is attributed to the disciples in general, no longer to Peter alone, as in 16:19. More significantly, this authority is attributed to *several* disciples who need to exercise this authority in agreement with each other (18:19), so that their binding and loosing might have an effect not only on earth but also in heaven. The condition is that "two of you agree" (18:19). It is only if one has a brother or a sister—the only kind of person with whom one can truly agree on religious matters—that one has the authority to bind and to loose!

In this perspective it begins to appear why gaining a brother or a sister is so important for a disciple and thus why it is something that the disciple wants to strive for. Gaining a brother or a sister is also gaining the authority to bind and to loose, and thus it is receiving the very authority that Jesus has now during his ministry (see my comments on 16:18–19). Simultaneously, because of the conjunction of 18:15–17 with 18:18–19, this authority to bind and to loose is the authority to exclude people from the community (by declaring as binding a certain commandment) or to readmit people in the community (by loosing a commandment, by declaring that a sin is forgiven). The very authority that one receives by virtue of being in agreement with a brother or a sister is the authority that one should use in order to do everything possible to gain a brother or a sister (18:15–17), an eventual gain that would further ensure that one will continue having such an authority. Thus the juxtaposition of 18:18–19 to 18:15–17 begins to clarify why it is of ultimate importance for the disciples to gain brothers and sisters. Without them, they would not have the authority necessary for carrying out their ministry.

18:20. But there is more. Having brothers and sisters with whom one can agree about asking something of Jesus' Father also means having brothers and sisters with whom one can gather together in Jesus' name. Then, according to Jesus' promise (18:20), by having such brothers and sisters one gains something else, indeed the ultimate blessing for disciples of Jesus: the presence of Jesus in their midst.[24]

For the readers, who, according to Matthew's presuppositions, are quite familiar with Jewish teaching, the promise of 18:20 certainly evoked many connotations. If they were aware of the rabbinic teaching, according to which "If two sit together and words of the Law [are spoken] between them, the Divine Presence rests between them,"[25] then they could understand that gathering in the name of Jesus takes the place of gathering to study Torah. Such a point would be in agreement with Matthew's earlier points according to which Jesus and his teaching take the place of Scripture

("It was said to the [people] of old. . . . But I say to you," 5:21–48; cf. also 12:41–42). Furthermore, the presence of Jesus in the midst of his disciples would be comparable to the divine Presence. This would be in agreement with Matthew's affirmation of the intimate relationship of Jesus with his Father and that he is "God with us" (1:23).[26] Yet these are views of Jesus that Matthew presupposed that *his readers* had—he presupposed that they viewed Jesus as a new Moses teaching a new Torah (cf. above, pp. 60–65). Without denying the validity of these views, Matthew primarily aims at making other points that are somewhat in tension with these views. His concern is not to make a point about the nature and role of Jesus but rather to show that having, and thus gaining, brothers and sisters is something truly good that the disciples should want to pursue.

18:21–22. It is this very point that Matthew underscores once again in the polemical exchange between Peter and Jesus (an opposition). By asking how many times he should forgive a brother who sins against him (18:21), Peter demonstrates that he did not understand Jesus' preceding teaching. For him, forgiving is costly. First, you get hurt by someone; then, by forgiving you give up the right to ask for reparation, even if the reparation is merely revenge, such as depriving the sinner of your friendship. Forgiving is being magnanimous. Is not Peter very generous when he offers to forgive the same brother for sinning against him seven times? Yes, Peter agrees to adopt a self-denying attitude, to suffer quite a lot from someone else. But there are limits, aren't there?

Jesus' answer (18:22) amounts to saying that there are no limits to forgiving.[27] Why should there be? By forgiving, one does not lose anything. On the contrary, one gains something, and indeed something very good; one gains a brother and therefore the possibility of enjoying the presence of Jesus in their midst. Actually, if a brother or a sister sinned against you, you incurred a loss. But the true loss is not what has been stolen from you (if the sin was a theft) or what you have been deprived of by the action of the sinner. The main loss, the only true loss, is the loss of a brother or a sister. And thus it is what you should strive to regain, and the way to do so is by forgiving. Then why should one want to limit the number of times one forgives? Why should one deprive oneself of something good? Such is the way of perceiving what one should do, what is truly good, what one wants to do, when one considers everything in the perspective of the kingdom of heaven (18:23b).

As the rule of church discipline (18:15–17) expresses, however, wanting to go to someone who has sinned against you and being ready to forgive that person (18:22) does not mean that one will automatically gain a brother or a sister. The offender needs to respond to your offer to reestablish a good relationship. Otherwise, despite your efforts the person will "be to you as a Gentile and a tax collector" (18:17). Being brothers and sisters is a two-way relationship. But the (ideal) disciples (by contrast with Peter) are those who will make the first step toward reestablishing this relationship, a self-denying step prompted by the will to forgive, even though the outcome might be rejection by the sinner.

18:23–35. By introducing here the *parable of the unforgiving servant,* Matthew further underscores these points. The parable opposes the attitude and actions of the king who shows mercy by releasing his servant and forgiving his debt (18:26–27, 33b) *and* those of the unmerciful servant who does not want to show mercy and puts his fellow servant in prison (18:30, 33a).

This multifold opposition would simply repeat the preceding points if it were only expressed in 18:26–27 and 18:30, that is, if the parable ended in 18:30. By his attitude and actions as described in 18:23–27, the king shows that he attaches greater value to the ongoing relationship with his servant—a relationship that would have been lost if the servant had been sold (18:25)—than to the satisfaction of seeing his servant being punished and making reparation for his deed against him. Note that the description of the king wishing to settle accounts with his servants and confronting one of them with the seriousness of his debt by ordering his punishment (18:23–25) corresponds in many ways to the disciple going and reproving the brother who has sinned against him. Actually 18:15–17 presupposes that the disciple expresses in the original confrontation the consequences of the sin: that the sinner will be like a Gentile and a tax collector to the disciple, a situation comparable to the servant losing his status as servant by being sold. By contrast, through his attitude toward his fellow servant as described in 18:28–30, the unmerciful servant shows that he holds the opposite view, a wrong view.

But the repetition of this opposition in 18:33, "Should not you have had mercy on your fellow servant, as I had mercy on you?" adds a new dimension. By contrast with 18:22, which underscored that one should be ready to forgive brothers and sisters an unlimited number of times, it is now expressed that there are limits to forgiveness. The servant by his unmerciful and unforgiving attitude toward his fellow servant demonstrates that he is not worthy of receiving forgiveness.[28]

This servant is wicked and thus not worthy of forgiveness, because, even though he had been forgiven, he did not forgive. But how should such a statement be understood? Does it mean that people, and the disciples in particular, are under obligation to forgive because they have first been forgiven by God or by Christ, as this parable is at times interpreted?[29] Such an interpretation which transforms forgiving into an obligation, a law that stands above and beyond the disciples, would contradict all that Matthew said concerning the internalization of God's will (cf. 5:21–48; see also 18:10–14) which 18:35 again expresses by speaking of forgiving "from your heart."

Furthermore, it would contradict 6:14–15, which underscores that one will be forgiven by the Father if, and only if, one forgives others.

Matthew's point is discerned by a closer look at the opposition. Why according to the text did the king forgive the servant and the servant did not forgive his fellow servant? The text makes it clear that the king is not swayed by the servant's promise to repay his debt (18:26). This debt is so huge (ten thousand talents, the equivalent of millions of dollars) that there is no way he could conceivably repay it; and the king cancels the debt (18:27). Rather, the king acts "out of pity"; he has compassion; he is moved by the plight of his servant. This is empathy, the identification with someone else's feeling, making one's own the pain of the other. Such a compassion presupposes an intimate relationship with the other and thus that this relationship is valued more than a huge amount of money that one has lost because of the other. Forgiveness preserves this relationship or reestablishes it. In 18:27 we have, therefore, the image of a king in close relationship with his servants and thus the image of a tightly bound community composed of king and servants. We find this same image in the description of the servants who report to the king the unmerciful servant's behavior (18:31). That they are "greatly distressed" shows their compassion for the second servant and their deep disappointment at the lack of compassion of the unmerciful servant; by reporting their distress to the king, they show their close relationship with him.

By contrast, the servant does not show any compassion for his fellow servant who implores him (18:29–30). He is brutal, "seizing him by the throat" (18:28), and insensitive. The minuscule debt (one hundred denarii, the equivalent of a few ten dollar bills) makes it clear that his attitude is not even caused by a significant loss. His attitude toward his fellow servant demonstrates that he is not really part of this tightly bound community. The bond that unites the servants among themselves and with the king is broken by the unmerciful servant.

Thus the unmerciful servant is not worthy of forgiveness simply because he does not see any value in participating in the closely bound community. He does not value his relationship with his fellow servants, and therefore does not value his relationship with the king. He does not want to participate in the relationship that exists among the servants (who are therefore called "fellow servants") and the king, a relationship that forgiveness aims at reestablishing. Forgiving him is thus pointless.

In sum, one should want to forgive one's fellow servants, one's brothers and sisters (18:35), because it is a gain or a blessing. It is participating in the intimate community composed not merely of fellow servants but also of the king. When servants are in this relationship, when they "are gathered in [Jesus'] name," he is part of their community, he is in their midst (18:20). All of these are positive reasons for forgiving—they should cause the disciples to want to forgive *from their heart*, that is, because they really and deeply want to do it, since it will give them great joy (18:13). This is not a law that stands above the disciples and that they simply must obey. It is perceiving things from the perspective of the kingdom and, as a consequence, having internalized God's will.

Negatively, God's will remains God's will, and thus not doing it is to expose oneself to the wrath of God. The unmerciful servant is punished (18:34), and his punishment without end (when will he have repaid, from his prison, all of his huge debt?) evokes the eschatological judgment to which will be submitted those who scandalize the little ones (18:7–9). But fear of the judgment (wanting to flee it, 3:7) cannot be the motivation to forgive. As expressed in 18:34, it is only if one forgives *from one's heart* that one will escape the fate of the unmerciful servant. One will escape eschatological punishment only if one truly wants to forgive because one perceives that it is a gain—of brothers and sisters, and of the presence of Jesus—and thus because one perceives in one's heart that forgiving is a good thing to do.[30]

NOTES ON 17:24—18:35

1. My characterization of the last part of the Gospel (16:21—28:20) is similar to Kingsbury's "Suffering, Death, and Resurrection of Jesus Messiah." He does not, however, recognize its rhetorical purpose, namely, to change the disciples' and the readers' fundamental convictions about what is good and bad (euphoric and dysphoric). See KINGSBURY, 161.

2. In my comments on 17:24—18:35, I am once again indebted to the work of Larry Vigen, "To Think the Things of God."

3. Thompson (*Matthew's Advice*, 62) believes that Matthew stresses Jesus' and Peter's *freedom* from the Temple tax. Thompson views the wish not to offend "the Jews" as a kind of afterthought, which he later uses to establish the historical setting in the Matthean community vis-à-vis the council of Jamnia (68, 246). He does not see the importance for Matthew of Jesus' submission in spite of his freedom.

4. The only possible narrative opposition would be between the true kings of the earth who take taxes from others and hypothetical kings who would take taxes from their sons (17:25). But it is weakly marked and does not appear to make any significant point. Thus it can be discounted, especially in a passage that plays with the readers' expectations, misleading them into thinking that there are oppositions only to show them that these are not actual oppositions.

5. With Thompson, *Matthew's Advice*, 59.

6. There is no need to extrapolate from this passage a view of the Temple, as Thompson does when he affirms "that the Temple is no longer the center of community and that its sacrifices are no longer necessary to reconcile man with God" (Thompson, *Matthew's Advice*, 59). Such comments, which are not necessarily wrong, have the effect of focusing our attention away from the text and away from the points (convictions) Matthew wants to convey.

7. Thompson (*Matthew's Advice*, 50) downplays the importance of the miracle and thus misses the irony.

8. However strange it may seem, this thematic point will become one of the main points of the section (cf. 18:15–21).

9. Thompson (*Matthew's Advice*, 258) gives a good summary of the various positions. Scholars usually view this passage as a "community rule," emphasizing one or another connotation of such a concept and therefore using different phrases to designate it. See TRILLING, 122–23, and Bonnard, "Composition et signification," 139. Thompson's own position is that "these instructions are better classified as

wisdom sayings or advice rather than as regulations or prescriptions for a 'community-order' (*Gemeindeordernung*)" (266). We also conclude that these are not regulations and prescriptions. See also W. Pesch, "Die Sogennannte Gemeindeordnung Mt. 18," *BZ* 7 (1963): 235.

10. With Thompson, *Matthew's Advice*, 83–84, 99.

11. See BEARE, 373.

12. This is the thesis of Thompson's book. He assumes, however, that Matthew constantly reasons from general principles to specific applications. Such an approach leads him not to take into account the unfolding of the "discourse." See Thompson, *Matthew's Advice*, 254. By contrast, Bonnard is particularly sensitive to how Matthew's "discourse" works according to its own rules. See Bonnard, "Composition et signification," 112; and BONNARD, 267–79.

13. For a comparative study of 18:1–6 with the other Gospel texts about becoming like a child, see Patte, ed., *Kingdom and Children* (*Semeia* 29, 1983). My structural analysis of these texts may be compared with the studies of the same texts by Robbins and Crossan which, despite their innovative character, remain historical in orientation.

14. That is, it involves an *active will*. Paradoxically, self-denial is the act of will to be passive, to restrain oneself. With TRILLING, 108.

15. Note that 18:6 is the only place in the Synoptic Gospels where the phrase "who believe in me," i.e., "*in Jesus*," is to be found. Yet we have observed in chapters 8—9 that "faith" is clearly understood by Matthew as trust in Jesus' power.

16. With Thompson, *Matthew's Advice*, 119.

17. Note that 18:6 does not describe a punishment. Drowning in the sea with a great millstone around one's neck "would be better" than incurring the punishment in Gehenna. As Jonathan Kraus suggested to me, for Matthew death as the *absence of life* in this world is a way of escaping the eschatological punishment, the *deprivation of life* in the insatiable life-consuming fire of Gehenna. This seems to be a peculiarly Jewish mythic conception of the power of fire to feed on living things. "No wonder," he added, "the ovens at Auschwitz horrified the imagination of Jews even more than the gas chambers."

18. There is no opposition in this story and thus no new point for the readers. The only possible opposition would be that of "went astray" (18:12) and "never went astray" (18:13). However, despite the RSV translation, in Greek these are expressed by the same verb in a passive form (passives of *planaō*) which, therefore, describe situations (or states) rather than actions.

19. Against TRILLING, 112–13, we need to recognize that the parable taken by itself emphasizes the owner's joy, rather than interpreting it right away in terms of 18:14. In so doing, one removes the tension, and then one cannot perceive Matthew's point.

20. With TRILLING, 113, who asserts that the concern for the "little ones" is a concern for people who are actually needy (and not "poor in spirit").

21. As TRILLING, 113, points out in a comparison of these rules with 1QS, the *correctio fraterna* is already known to the Matthean community as a dominical saying (18:15), even as it is known to the Qumran community from Lev. 19:17. Trilling also uses the expression "Let that one be to you as a Gentile and a tax collector" (18:17) to show that the form comes neither from Jesus nor from Matthew himself, but from a Jewish-Christian stage of the tradition of Matthew's church. The passages 2 Cor. 13:1–2 and 1 Tim. 5:19–20 seem to refer to a similar rule, a fact which suggests that such a rule was known in the early church.

22. Through their efforts to find the original meaning of the sayings, commentators have the tendency to present this understanding of the rule as if it were Matthew's. Cf. BONNARD, 273–75; SCHWEIZER, 370–74; BEARE, 379–80; GUNDRY, 367–68; TRILLING, 120.

23. As TRILLING, 121, summarizes, the image of the church, which stands behind these words, has a threefold structure: the Father in heaven, who grants a request; Christ in the middle; and the fellowship of his believers, the community united by its confession of him.

24. With TRILLING, 120, who sees the sequence of 18:18–20 as the expression of an emergent church consciousness.

25. *Mishnah: Aboth* 3:2 (Danby's trans., 450). It is a saying attributed to "R. Hanina the Prefect of the Priests," a first-century rabbi, but of course recorded in the *Mishnah* much later than the writing of the Gospel According to Matthew.

26. See Thompson, *Matthew's Advice*, 198.

27. It is possible that Matthew expected his readers to see in the number "seventy times seven" (or "seventy times") a paradoxical allusion to the limitless desire for revenge mentioned in Gen. 4:23–24 about Lamech.

28. Saying, as the king does, that the servant is "wicked" (18:32) amounts to saying that he is not worthy of forgiveness, as 18:34 shows. The concept of worthiness, found in 3:8 and 10:10–13, 37–38, is related in these passages to repentance, receiving peace, and being with Jesus.

29. Compare, e.g., BONNARD, 277; and MEIER, 134.

30. Bonnard views this parable as a warrant or a threat of what will happen to one who does not follow the instructions regarding forgiveness. See Bonnard, "Composition et signification," 119.

HARDNESS OF HEART, BAD EYE, AND GOD'S GOODNESS

THE MAIN THEME[1]

19:1–2. "Now when Jesus had finished these sayings, he went away from Galilee and entered the region of Judea." These words of transition and verse 2, which describes great crowds following Jesus and being healed by him, are significant. Even though they do not express the main theme of this new section, these verses are thematic since they do not include any opposition. Here Matthew calls upon his readers' knowledge, particularly what they have read earlier in the Gospel, in order to draw their attention to the new points he will make in the passages that follow.

The mention that Jesus leaves Galilee and enters Judea suggests to the readers that he is *on his way* to Jerusalem and that he begins to do what he must do according to 16:21: "He must go to Jerusalem and suffer many things." The itinerary might surprise the readers; he goes from Galilee to "the region of Judea beyond the Jordan" (19:1). Could it be that Matthew expects his readers to understand that in so doing Jesus avoids going into Samaria, as he had commanded his disciples to avoid the towns of Samaria (10:5)? This would suggest that even though he is on his way to Jerusalem, Jesus pursues his usual ministry—a ministry that the disciples are supposed to share and that is directed to "the lost sheep of the house of Israel" (10:6; 15:24). This suggestion is supported in 19:2 when Jesus is described as being followed by the crowds and performing healings, a description similar to those found in 4:23; 9:35; 14:13–14; and 15:30 regarding Jesus' ministry in Galilee. Furthermore, the readers' attention is drawn to the concluding phrase, "he healed them there," because it literally says that Jesus healed all the crowds and not merely their sick. One should not of course understand this statement literally. Yet the readers have been stopped and should take note what Matthew stipulates: it is "there" that he healed them. For some reason it is important to recognize that on his way to Jerusalem (and already in Judea) Jesus continues his usual ministry. For Matthew, the Galilean ministry and the Judean ministry—including the Passion—are a single ministry: what will happen in Judea should be interpreted as a continuation of the Galilean ministry. Is Matthew signaling in 19:1–2 that what will happen in Judea needs to be interpreted in terms of the Galilean ministry so as to be properly understood? We suspect that this is the case: Matthew has underscored this point in chapter 2, and again in chapters 3 and 4. What takes place in Judea can make sense only in the light of what happens in Galilee.[2]

19:3—20:16. A first overview of the pericopes that follow suggests this continuity; there is nothing here that could not have taken place in Galilee. As they did in 16:1, Pharisees come to Jesus in order to test him (19:3). As they have begun doing in Galilee by showing their little faith (8:26; 14:15; 14:31; 15:33; 16:8) and increasingly so since the first announcement of the Passion (16:22), the disciples question the validity of Jesus' teaching (19:10; 19:25). Or they do things that interfere with Jesus' ministry although they should have known better (19:13). Furthermore, Jesus' teaching deals with themes we have already encountered in his Galilean teaching.

Most significantly, one notes several parallels with the Sermon on the Mount. Jesus' response to the Pharisees' question about divorce (19:4–9) is comparable to 5:31–32. In Jesus' final words to the rich young man, the phrase "if you would be perfect" (19:21a) reminds the readers of 5:48: "You, therefore must be perfect, as your heavenly Father is perfect." Furthermore, in 19:21b a reference to having "treasure in heaven" is a parallel of 6:20 (closely linked with 5:48 in the organization of the Sermon). The whole discussion regarding wealth (19:21–24) reminds the readers of the saying about mammon (6:24), and the image of a camel going "through the eye of a needle" (19:24) is similar to that of a narrow gate that few will find (7:13–14). Finally, one should note that following the sayings about treasures in heaven (6:19–21) and preceding the saying about mammon (6:24), Matthew introduced sayings about the sound eye (6:22) and the bad eye introduced by the phrase "If your eye is bad" (6:23, au.). The metaphor of the bad eye, which played an important role in the Sermon and referred to the impossibility of discerning what is truly good, is found in the concluding verse of the parable of the workers in the vineyard, where we read: "Or is your eye bad because I am good?" (20:15b, literal rendering; RSV: "Or do you begrudge my generosity?").

Matthew is not simply repeating here what he has previously expressed. By stringing together a series of pericopes—probably not together originally in the same context[3]—Matthew pursues a pedagogical goal. He develops a theme that is certainly related to the themes and points of the preceding section (17:24—18:35). The relation of the first pericope (19:3–9) to the preceding discourse can readily be perceived in 18:35: if the disciples do not forgive brothers and sisters "from [the] heart," they will be punished, as the unmerciful servant has been. Now, in 19:8, it is because of their "hardness of heart" that the Pharisees were given by Moses the commandment regarding divorce (19:7). It is because of their "hardness of heart" that they cannot follow God's will which they know or should know and which Jesus repeats for them (19:4–6).

It soon appears that the issue of "hardness of heart"—the character and nature of this predicament—is the main theme of 19:1—20:16. Thus, by their question (19:9) the disciples demonstrate that they have hard hearts, as they further show by rebuking the people who bring children to Jesus (19:13). In this light, it becomes clear that the dialogue with the young rich man (19:16–22) and the following discussion with the disciples (19:23–30) address the issue of the nature of hardness of heart. It is not primarily a lack of knowledge of God's will. It is a much more fundamental problem. Hardness of heart is what prevents people from doing God's will, and it affects not only the Pharisees but also potentially everyone, including the disciples. This interpretation is confirmed when Matthew proposes the parable of the workers in the vineyard (20:1–16) as a key for understanding 19:1–29—he frames it by repeating (with a significant change) the saying of 19:30 in 20:16. Now we see that one of the main points of the parable concerns what causes people to have a bad eye: "Or, is your eye bad because I am good?" (20:15, au.). Since bad eye and hard heart are equivalent metaphors for what prevents people from doing God's will, it becomes clear that it is the problem of evil in human beings which is raised; this is the theme of this section.

As we noted regarding 18:35, for Matthew, doing God's will "from your heart" means doing it as a result of having internalized God's will by recognizing that something (e.g., forgiving) is truly good and thus worth pursuing. Consequently, having a hard heart or a bad eye is being unable to perceive what is truly good according to God's revelation and thus being unable to make God's will one's own will. The source of such a hardness of heart (or bad eye) is ultimately the inability to accept or envision the goodness of God—God who "from the beginning" gives good gifts to human beings (19:3–9); God about whom Jesus says, "One there is who is good" (19:17); God who, like the householder, rhetorically asks angry servants, "Is your eye bad because I am good?" (20:15, au.).

As we proceed to read this section, it is important to keep in mind that Matthew asks his readers to reinterpret 19:1–30 in the light of the parable of the workers in the vineyard (20:1–16), the proposed key to understanding the preceding chapter. This means that important aspects of the meaning of 19:1–30 will be discussed in the context of the interpretation of the parable.

MATTHEW'S CONVICTIONS IN 19:3—20:16

19:3–9. Marriage and Divorce: A Debate with the Pharisees

The polemical dialogue between Jesus and the Pharisees about divorce involves a teaching similar to the one in 5:31–32—in both cases divorce is associated with adultery (19:9). Here Matthew makes yet different points by setting up a series of oppositions.

19:3–5. The point made by the first polemical exchange is seen in a comparison of the two statements. The Pharisees ask whether it is "lawful to divorce one's wife for any cause" (19:3b).[4] Jesus answers by pointing out that because of what is written in Scripture the Pharisees should not have to ask this question (19:4–5). Actually, the Pharisees are not seeking to be taught by Jesus. They are testing him (19:3a). They know what the proper answer to their question is! Jesus' response indicates that he knows that the Pharisees are testing him. Their question also reveals an inappropriate attitude. They are so exclusively concerned by what is lawful, by what one has to do or not do, that they do not pay attention to other aspects of Scripture. They do not take into account what Scripture says about what God has done "from the beginning." For them, one's behavior should be based upon considerations concerning a law that one should obey. For Jesus, one should perceive what is good to do or what should be avoided by considering what the Creator has done "from the beginning."

One may be puzzled by this latter phrase which is repeated in 19:8; one would have expected *"in* the beginning." The readers are stopped long enough to be reminded of the comparable phrase in 13:35, "since the foundation of the world." The crowds as would-be disciples can learn from the parables what took place "since the foundation of the world," and thus can learn to distinguish the good things done by the Creator (the sower, 13:24) from the bad things done by the enemy (13:25). This is what the prophets and the righteous people of Scripture already knew (13:17) and therefore what the Pharisees also should have learned from reading Scripture. It then appears that the Pharisees' preoccupation with "what is lawful" prevents them from reading Scripture in such a way as to recognize the things "hidden since the foundation of the world" (13:35). They do not recognize what are the good things God has done "from the beginning" (19:4), the basis for establishing what one should or should not do.

By presenting the words of God in Gen. 2:24 regarding marriage as a direct consequence ("for this reason") of the way God created human beings according to Gen. 1:27, Jesus' answer (Matt. 19:4–5) shows that God's will for human beings should be deduced from what God has done for them.[5] Now, by definition, what God did at the creation is good ("it was very good," Gen. 1:31). Thus marriage—leaving father and mother, being joined to his wife, and the two becoming one flesh—is itself a good gift of God; it is a direct consequence of the way the two were created. Matthew's point about marriage and divorce is therefore similar to the one he made about forgiveness of others in 18:15–22. That point could be summarized by the question: Why would one want to deprive oneself of something good (brothers and sisters) by limiting the number of times one should forgive?

Similarly here, if one takes the creation of human beings as "male and female" to be good, then its consequence—marriage—is also to be viewed as a good gift from God. Why then would one want to ask whether it is permitted to divorce? Why would one want to deprive oneself of a good gift from God? Why would one want to deprive oneself of a part of oneself— of one's "flesh" (19:5b)? The only reason for this attitude is that one does not perceive of marriage as a good gift from God and that consequently one views as good the possibility of separating oneself from one's wife (divorce from a patriarchal perspective). This ignores what is written in Scripture about the creation.

19:6. The last part of Jesus' response further opposes the action of God joining man and woman to the action of those who would put them asunder either by divorcing their spouses or by advocating divorce. The point is simple, but most powerful. For Matthew, such people are directly opposed to God. They would undo what God has done.

19:7–9. The second polemical exchange between the Pharisees and Jesus sharpens the preceding points. According to the Pharisees, Jesus contradicts Moses' *commandment* regarding divorce (Deut. 24:1; Matt. 19:7). But Matthew says more. By presenting the Pharisees' new question just after the saying "What therefore God has joined together, let [no one] put asunder" (19:6b), Matthew conveys that the Pharisees not only object to Jesus' saying but also deliberately challenge the authority of the Scripture quoted by Jesus; they challenge what God said and did "from the beginning" (19:4).[6]

At first it seems that Jesus' response confirms that there is a conflict between the two scriptural teachings: "Moses allowed you to divorce your wives, but from the beginning it was not so" (19:8b). Contrary to the Pharisees, however, Jesus does not refer to Moses' teaching as a commandment but as a *permission* or a *concession* because of their "hardness of heart" (19:8a). Moses' teaching and what was "from the beginning" cannot be opposed because they do not have the same status. This specific teaching of Moses is not a commandment but a concession.[7] Furthermore, Jesus does not fault Moses for having made this concession; it was demanded by the situation, that is, by the hardness of heart of the people.

Since the Pharisees are personally designated as those who have hard hearts, all their sayings and attitudes (in this passage) are to be viewed as examples of what people with hard hearts think and do. Hardness of heart confuses a concession with a commandment and as a consequence challenges the words of the creator God in the name of Moses' teaching; it rejects God's will (19:7); it undoes what God has done (19:6); and it is unable to perceive that marriage is a good gift from the Creator (19:3–5). Hardness of heart makes one unable to recognize what is truly good and thus unable to make any valid distinction between good and bad (euphoric and dysphoric).

19:9. Jesus' concluding statement is thematic (it does not include any opposition) and thus expresses the preceding points in terms of the knowledge of readers who should recall the saying in 5:32. But the saying is adapted to its new context so as to express the new point that Matthew made in 19:7–8. That the divorced woman will become an adulteress is left out; here Jesus admonishes men who would divorce their wives. If they did not have a hard heart and thus did not confuse concessions and commandments, then they would understand that the commandment against adultery applies to a man who, after divorcing his wife, marries another. For Matthew, however, there is an exception: "except for unchastity" or except for the case of some other kind of wrong union.[8] Since this phrase is not involved in any opposition, it remains largely undefined. In its present context, it refers to some kind of bad situation.[9] Someone who does not have a hard heart—people able to discern good and bad—should be able to recognize that certain situations are so bad that such a marriage can no longer be viewed as a blessing, a good gift from God. In such cases, when people have already put asunder what God has joined, but only in such cases, divorce is allowed.

19:10–12. The Disciples' Response: Then It Is Better Not to Marry

19:10. The disciples' reaction confirms that, for Matthew, the exception formulated in 19:9 does not weaken in any way the rigor of Jesus' teaching about marriage and divorce.[10] Once again we find an opposition between the disciples' saying and Jesus' response.[11] The disciples do not reject Jesus' teaching, but they draw the wrong implication from it (as Peter did in 18:21–22). They think that Jesus has conclusively demonstrated that divorce is against God's will, and they do not want to transgress God's will. But by concluding that it is better not to marry, they show that they cannot conceive of marriage without the possibility of divorce. In effect, they associate themselves with the Pharisees; they show their hardness of heart. They do not perceive the union of man and woman as a good gift from God, a blessing that one should want to preserve. Rather, for them, what is good is what benefits the man by himself. Because of their hardness of heart, what is ultimately good or bad is (wrongly) associated with man conceived as *independent* from woman.

19:10–11. The opposition between the disciples' statement and Jesus' response broadens the issue. The disciples reason as follows. Something is good or bad according to the way it affects an *individual person*. Relations with other persons are conceived in a negative light because they have the potential of affecting an individual person negatively. Then, since it is next to impossible to free oneself from such relations (e.g., to free oneself from the bonds of marriage), it is better not to enter into such relations. By contrast, if they would not have a hard heart and would consider marriage from the perspective of what God did from the beginning, then the disciples would perceive that what is ultimately good, God's gift, is the state of being in relation with others—including marriage.

19:11–12. The twofold point of Jesus' response is then understandable. First, the ability to receive and accept "this saying" (i.e., Jesus' preceding saying about marriage and divorce) is itself a gift from God. In order to accept marriage as being a good gift from God, one needs to have received another gift from God—a sound heart. Since not everyone will be given the latter gift, not everyone will be able to accept Jesus' saying about marriage and divorce.

Just as the disciples did not deny the validity of Jesus' teaching while rejecting its underlying assumption regarding what is good and bad, so Jesus does not deny the validity of the disciples' proposal while rejecting its underlying assumption. Jesus acknowledges that abstaining from marriage and thus from sexual union can also be perceived as good, if it is properly conceived. This is suggested by the latter part of Jesus' response (19:12) in the opposition between being made eunuch from birth or by other people and making oneself a eunuch for the sake of the kingdom of heaven—a point closely related to the preceding one due to the concluding phrase, "He who is able to receive this, let him receive it" (19:12b). Being made a eunuch by a birth defect or by other people is the worst thing that may happen to a man; it is the loss of one's manhood. It is being deprived of sexual relationship—a good gift from God. This deprivation cannot be viewed as good! It is a loss. Similarly, not marrying because one values one's independence more than marriage, as the disciples suggest (19:10), is dismissing and losing the good gift offered in the sexual union of marriage.

Yet Jesus affirms that giving up sexual relationship—celibacy—for the sake of the kingdom is good. Why? First, celibacy is not adopted on the basis of a self-centered view of what is good or bad. It is not adopted because it would be more beneficial to an individual who conceives what is good or bad for the self in isolation and independence from others. Celibacy is adopted in terms of the kingdom of heaven.[12] Far from denying the value of relationships with others, acting for the sake of the kingdom involves acknowledging that a good relationship with others is the ultimate good that one needs and wants to seek. This was expressed in 5:21–48 (a passage that includes the teaching about divorce which has been repeated in 19:9) and in 18:15–35. In such a case, therefore, even though one is deprived of the goodness of sexual union and marriage, celibacy is good: far from denying the goodness of relationship with others, it is adopted for the sake of one's relationship with others in the realm of the kingdom.

"Let the one who is able to receive this receive it" (19:12b, au.). Here, what is to be received is the saying concerning celibacy for the sake of the kingdom. Not everyone can receive it. Only the (ideal) disciples—those who have received the teaching about what took place "from the beginning" (what was "hidden since the foundation of the world," 13:35) and about the mysteries of the kingdom (13:11)—are able to receive it. In order to receive this teaching about celibacy for the sake of the kingdom, one needs to recognize that the goodness of the kingdom (the blessing of relations with others) is similar to, and thus can be substituted for, the goodness of marriage and sexual relationship. To be aware of this similarity one needs to have received a full understanding of the kingdom; one needs to have understood the mysteries of the kingdom!

19:13–15. Jesus Blesses the Children

This brief pericope opposes rebuking those who bring children to Jesus and not preventing the children from coming to him. Thus, once again, Matthew opposes the disciples to Jesus. The new point is clearly related to the preceding points. Despite Jesus' earlier teaching about children (18:2–6), the disciples fail to perceive that "to such belongs the kingdom of heaven" (19:14b). The disciples show their hardness of heart; they are unable to perceive what is good to do or not do. For them, as it is better not to be involved in a marriage relationship (19:10), so also it is better for Jesus not to be involved in a relationship with children (19:13b). They do not act for the sake of the kingdom in that they fail to acknowledge that relationship with others is the supreme good that should be sought. For them and their hardness of heart, independence, freedom from relationship with others, is the ultimate good to be preserved.

For Jesus, involvement with others, and indeed dependence upon others—a situation in which one values one's relationship with others—is what characterizes participation in the kingdom. Consequently, children, who totally depend upon others for their livelihood, are the very model of people who belong to the kingdom. This is especially true in the case of these children who are brought to him "that he might lay his hands on them and pray" (19:13); they need a blessing from God through Jesus. These children are presented as dependent not merely upon human beings but also upon God. They belong to the kingdom. They receive from Jesus, who himself belongs to the kingdom, the blessing they need (19:15).

19:16–30. The Rich Young Man.
Conditions for Inheriting Eternal Life

The pericope beginning with 19:16 does not end before 19:30.[13] The story of Jesus' encounter with the young rich man (19:16–22), which is concluded by the departure of the young man, is the direct occasion for Jesus' teaching to his disciples about rich people (19:23–24). In turn, this teaching prompts a polemical dialogue between the disciples and Jesus (19:25–26); it leads Peter to raise a question regarding the eschatological rewards of the disciples to which Jesus gives an answer (19:27–30). In this long and important pericope Matthew sets up only three narrative oppositions: the polemical dialogue between the man and Jesus (19:16–17); Jesus' order to the young man to follow him as opposed to the young man's departure (19:22–23) which is also contrasted with the disciples who followed Jesus (19:27); and finally a polemical dialogue between the disciples and Jesus (19:25–26). These oppositions establish Matthew's points, and the rest of the pericope needs to be understood in the light of them.

19:16–17. The first opposition is set by the surprisingly polemical response of Jesus to someone who approaches him and asks, "Teacher, what good . . . must I do, to have eternal life?" (19:16)—apparently a legitimate question. This unidentified man expresses by his question that he does not know "what is good" to do. He is very much like the disciples, who did not know that it was good to let the children come to Jesus (19:13) and like the Pharisees, who did not know that marriage is a good gift of God and thus that divorce is not good (19:3–9). But because of their hardness of heart, Pharisees and disciples are unaware that they do not know what is good, and are in fact sure they know what is good to do—this is true even in the case of the Pharisees, since their question aims at testing Jesus rather than learning something from him (19:3). By contrast, this man is aware that he does not know what is good to do and that such a knowledge is essential for receiving eternal life. He appears to the readers in a much more positive light than the Pharisees and the disciples. Actually, he raises the very question that the readers might want to raise after reading the preceding pericopes. Since hardness of heart (19:8) is not knowing what is good to do, and since even the disciples seem to be in this predicament, his question means that he wants not to have a hard heart. What can be better than this? And what can be better than to ask Jesus to teach him what is good to do?

Jesus' polemical answer comes, therefore, as a surprise: "Why do you ask me about what is good? One there is who is good" (19:17). The only issue about which the readers could expect an objection from Jesus is the man's use of the phrase "eternal life" instead of "kingdom of heaven." But Jesus does not object to the man's view, according to which in order to receive eternal life one needs to do what is good, since he adds: "If you want to enter life, observe the commandments" (19:17b, au.). What, then, is wrong in the man's request?

Before this question is addressed, a few remarks about the entire dialogue between the young man and Jesus are necessary. It is often said that Jesus' initial exclamation expresses his humble submission to God and that his teaching is merely the interpretation of God's will as expressed in Scripture.[14] Such comments are not incorrect, but they fail to account for the opposition and thus miss the point Matthew makes by it. They presuppose that Jesus provides the man with what he needs and requests, namely, the *knowledge* of what is good to do.[15] But, and this is the point made by the opposition in 19:16–17, what the man needs is something other than the knowledge of what is good. It is true that by his teaching Jesus can provide the man with the knowledge of what is good to do. But this knowledge will not help him to do what is good and to receive eternal life; despite Jesus' teaching (19:18–19, 21), by the end of the story the young man has not gained what he really needs. As Jesus indicates ("If you want to enter life," 19:17b, au.), what the young man really needs is the *will* to enter life.

What is wrong with the man's question is not merely that he addresses it to the wrong person—to Jesus instead of to God[16]—but primarily that he asks the question at all. If one has to ask the question about what is good to do, one shows that one cannot do it. If the man truly knew and acknowledged the goodness of God, he would know what good deed he must do to have eternal life and therefore would not need to ask the question! The second part of Jesus' answer (19:17b) shows that the man might lack one of two things: either he might not know that he should "keep the commandments" of God or he might not truly want to enter life ("If you want to enter life," au.). In either case, acknowledging the goodness of God would have met the need expressed by his question. Either it would have led him to perceive that God's commandments teach what is good to do[17] or it would have caused him to want to have eternal life with such a good God.

19:18–20. By his second question ("Which?"), the man appears to believe that what he lacks is a sufficient knowledge of the commandments. This implies that he truly wants to enter eternal life.

Jesus does not criticize the man either for this or the following question. To the man's query regarding which commandments he should observe, Jesus answers (19:18–19) by giving a list of selected commandments, including several of the Ten Commandments and the commandment to love one's neighbor as oneself (Lev. 19:18). All of these commandments concern relationships with other people rather than the relationship with God as in the first part of the Decalogue. Similarly, Jesus does not express any surprise when the man confidently says that he has observed all these commandments and asks what he is still missing (19:20).

These three verses (19:18–20) do not include any opposition; they are thematic. Matthew assumes that his readers can understand them on the basis of their old knowledge. Yet a few oddities or tensions signal that Matthew introduces aspects of his convictions (points) in this otherwise readily understandable material. All the commandments quoted are from the Decalogue except one ("Love your neighbor"). This will be directly related to the next point. A second surprise comes when the unidentified man is suddenly identified in 19:22 as a "young man," and this at the time when he said: "All these I have observed; what do I still lack." After the pericope about the children (19:13–15) and its point concerning the dependence of children, for the readers this "young man" appears somewhat like a child. As children who belong to the kingdom do, so he acknowledges that he lacks something. Yet his statement also suggests that he is not a child; he has a past, a time during which he has observed the commandments. Thus this "young man" appears as an ambivalent figure. In certain ways he is still a child, but in other ways he is no longer a child. So does the kingdom belong to him?

19:21–22. A second opposition appears when Jesus challenges him to be perfect by selling what he possesses, by giving it to the poor, and by following him; but "he went away sorrowful."

After hearing Jesus' response to his questions, the young man knows what is good to do. As the readers also know after reading the Sermon on the Mount (and especially 5:20–48 and 6:19–21), so he knows that truly fulfilling the commandments—having the overabundant righteousness which is the condition for entrance into the kingdom—involves giving up everything for the sake of one's relationship with others. Actually it involves giving everything one has to the poor (19:21). Loving one's neighbor as oneself (see 19:19b) is the "perfect" fulfillment of the commandments. But the problem is that he cannot do it or that he does not want to do it, as his *sorrow* shows. In a sense he wants to enter life, but he perceives that he will not obtain it because he does not want to do what is necessary for that purpose; "for he had great possessions" (19:22b). Yes, he perceives eternal life, a treasure in heaven, as a good worth pursuing. But he also views his great possessions as something that he wants to keep—a good without which he cannot envision his life.

Thus the young man's effort to overcome hardness of heart fails. He mistakenly thought that hardness of heart (what he still lacks, 19:20) was just a matter of *not knowing* what is good to do. But Matthew's point is that this is not the problem. Even though one may know what is good to do, nevertheless one may still have a hard heart. Hardness of heart is a problem of will, of wanting. Not having a hard heart is perceiving what is truly good "from [the] heart" (cf. 18:35), so much so that it is what one wants to pursue at all cost; it is the ultimate good beside which everything else is valueless. Not having a hard heart is being totally committed to this ultimate good. But being a "young man" both childlike and adultlike, both wanting the kingdom and wanting one's possessions, is having a hard heart. In spite of his own statement (19:16), he does not really have the will to enter life. He is not "perfect," his will is not totally identified with God's will—as it would be if he were convinced of the ultimate goodness of God and thus of the goodness of eternal life with God.[18] The young man's will (or heart) is divided between God and mammon (see 6:24; as a bad eye also is, see 6:22–23).

19:23–26. From Jesus' remark that it will be difficult for rich people to enter the kingdom (19:23), more difficult than for a camel to go through the eye of a needle (19:24), the disciples conclude that if it is so, then no one can be saved (19:25). As the opposition created by Jesus' response (19:26) shows, the disciples are not incorrect in generalizing Jesus' comments by applying them to everyone, and not merely to "rich" people; it is not to this aspect of their exclamation that Jesus objects. Everyone is in the same predicament. From the disciples' perspective (from a human perspective), if what Jesus said to the young man and about rich people is right, then it is impossible for human beings to enter the kingdom just as it is impossible for a camel to go through the eye of a needle.

In effect the disciples recognize that the tragic situation described by Jesus is that of those who fail to give up everything for the sake of the kingdom because they do not perceive it as the ultimate good. This is the problem of the hardness of heart (19:8), and the disciples acknowledge it in all seriousness. As Matthew pointed out through the story of the young man (19:16–22), hardness of heart is not simply a matter of lack of knowledge which could be overcome by the mere appropriation of a teaching about what is good. Such knowledge does not help, as the case of the young man demonstrates. But "who then can be saved"?

Jesus' answer is clear. As long as one thinks only in terms of human abilities, as the disciples do, it is impossible to overcome the predicament of a hard heart, and thus it is impossible to be saved, to enter the kingdom. "But with God all things are possible" (19:26b). In other words, it is only through an intervention of God that people can perceive what is truly good and may want to pursue it from their heart (18:35), and thus be saved.[19]

19:27–30. Peter's question and Jesus' response, a thematic passage, need to be interpreted in terms of what precedes, since this pericope does not add any new point; it simply confirms and further explains what preceded. First, Peter's statement that the disciples have, contrary to the young man, left everything and followed Jesus confirms that people can indeed do what Jesus asked the young man to do. They can do so, even though they are far from knowing in every situation what is good to do (cf. 19:10; 19:13) and far from understanding all of Jesus' teaching (cf. 19:25). They are the demonstration that God does intervene to make it possible for people such as the disciples to leave everything and follow Jesus. As explained in 19:29, leaving everything and following Jesus does not mean simply giving up one's possessions, but also giving up one's family for Jesus' sake.

There is, however, a subtle tension that recalls one of Matthew's earlier points. In the list of family members that the disciples have abandoned for Jesus' sake—brothers, sisters, father, mother, children—one person is absent—the wife. As noted in my treatment of 19:10–12, Matthew is ambivalent on this issue. Giving up marriage, and thus a wife, for Jesus' sake is not necessarily required from everyone who follows Jesus.

A question remains: "What then shall we have?" (19:27b), that is, what will be the eschatological rewards of the disciples? In answer Jesus describes the disciples as sharing the glory of the Son of man, sitting on thrones as he will, and participating in the eschatological judgment by judging the twelve tribes of Israel (19:28). This also means that it *will* become manifest that the disciples who have left everything—they are poor and lowly—are in a leadership position over Israel.

But a new tension appears. The next saying no longer speaks of the disciples alone but of "every one who has left" everything for Jesus' sake. Such people will be richly blessed, receiving a "hundredfold" (of what they have left) and eternal life. Why is there a sudden shift from the disciples to "every one" who follows Jesus? Presumably this means that the promises of eschatological blessings are for a much broader group than the disciples.[20] When one reads the next verse, one wonders if there is not more.

For the readers, 19:30 is puzzling: "But many that are first will be last, and the last first." Only one thing is clear. This saying concerns the eschatological judgment ("will be"). Certain people who are here and now "first" will be "last" as a consequence of the judgment, and vice versa. Furthermore, the form of the saying is that of a warning, since this eschatological reversal is not systematic—it will affect "many" people but not everyone. It is also primarily addressed to the "first," people in some kind of privileged situation who risk to lose it by becoming "last." But who are those who are presently "first" and "last"? First and last in terms of what? Are the "first" those who have first left everything for Jesus' sake, that is, the first who were given by God to do so (19:26), the disciples? In this case, the "last" would be all the others ("every one," 19:29) who also left everything for Jesus' sake. Or are the "first" those who are now in a position of power and superiority (the twelve tribes of Israel? 19:28) and the "last" lowly people (the disciples and other followers of Jesus)?

As readers we are puzzled and cannot resolve the ambiguity of this verse. But the verse plays an important role in the understanding of this section. It forces the readers to stop and to wonder whether or not they have missed something. Furthermore, since it is repeated, although in an inverted form, in the conclusion of the parable of the workers in the vineyard (20:16),[21] this puzzling saying in 19:30 draws the readers' attention to the parable. Indeed, it tells the readers to view the parable as providing the key for understanding a major point they may have missed, even though it is expressed in Jesus' teaching to the young man and the disciples (19:16–30) and possibly in the entire chapter (19:1–30).[22]

20:1–16. The Parable of the Workers in the Vineyard[23]

Since the preceding verse suggests that the parable presents a major aspect of the meaning of 19:16–30 (and possibly of 19:1–30), we need to pay attention to the points Matthew makes in it by means of narrative oppositions, and then consider how these points explain 19:1–30.

There are four such oppositions in the parable. First, the householder's action of hiring workers (20:1) is opposed to the fact, according to the last workers' statement, that no one hired them (20:7). Second, receiving one denarius (20:9, 10b) is opposed to receiving more, as the first workers expected (20:10a). This second opposition is closely related to, but should not be confused with, the third one; it opposes "agreeing" (for a denarius a day) (20:14; cf. also 20:2) and "thinking" (that they will receive more) (20:10a). Finally, a fourth opposition is set up by the polemical dialogue between the first workers (20:12) and the householder (20:13–15).

20:1–7. At the beginning of the parable, note the somewhat unrealistic character of the situation that is described. Throughout the day, the householder goes out to hire workers for his vineyard (20:1–5). This is surprising, yet it can eventually be understood by imagining a time (such as harvesttime) when the owner of a vineyard has an urgent need for workers. But the exchange with the eleventh hour workers (20:6–7) is even less realistic. They contend that no one hired them (20:7). How could the householder have failed to see them and to hire them in his previous trips to the marketplace? And how did he know they have been standing idle all day long at that place (20:6)? Yet he does not challenge the validity of their explanation and sends them to his vineyard (20:7b). Nothing in the text suggests that they were lazy and avoided being hired, as the readers might imagine in order to explain the odd situation.[24] Does it mean that the householder's query (20:6b) and his order sending them into the vineyard are expressions of his compassion for the plight of these unemployed people?

These tensions lead the readers to pay close attention to this first part of the parable. It then appears that the exchange between the householder and the eleventh hour workers in 20:5–7 is designed to underscore what is involved in not being hired (20:7) by contrast with being hired (20:1)—the first narrative opposition. Not being hired is being "idle," a situation that is presented as highly undesirable, since these people have waited all day long at that place, eagerly hoping they would be hired by someone. This undesirable situation, idleness, can be overcome only if someone else intervenes. Someone needs to hire them.

The first point made by this parable can then be understood. The hiring process, including the hiring of the first workers, is cast in a peculiar light. Of course, hiring workers involves making a contractual agreement with them; they will work in the vineyard, and for their services the householder will pay them "a denarius a day" (20:2). From the perspective of this contractual agreement, the householder has a need and the workers provide what he needs; the wages are the acknowledgment that they render such a service to the householder. As the case of the eleventh hour workers reveals, the hiring process also meets the needs of would-be workers. By hiring them, the householder offers them, indeed gives them, something they very badly need; being hired by the householder is a most desirable situation. In brief, the householder needs workers in his vineyard; the workers meet his need. People who are idle need work; the householder meets their need. The hiring process is beneficial to both the householder and the workers in the same way that seeking the kingdom is both being a blessing for others and for God and being blessed (see my comments on 5:3–16).

When this first point is understood, the unfolding of the story makes sense. That the householder goes out even at the eleventh hour to hire people demonstrates that what he was doing in the morning, and also at the third, sixth, and ninth hour—that is, what he was doing "from the beginning" (cf. 19:4, 8)—was giving these people something they needed; he also obtained what he needed by making a contractual agreement with people who will work in his vineyard.

The first part of the parable is therefore not without relation to the first part of the section (19:3–9) which emphasized that what God did from the beginning, creating "them male and female," is a good gift from God. The effect of the parable is to generalize what was said about marriage in 19:3–9; now it applies to whatever God did and does "from the beginning." It is simultaneously related to 19:17b–21, where Jesus emphasizes that the young man must keep the commandments, which can be viewed as corresponding to the contractual agreement.

20:8–10. At the beginning of the second scene (the workers receiving their wages), according to the command of the householder the "last" (the workers last hired) are paid their wages before the "first" (20:8). This reversal of order reminds the readers of the saying in 19:30. Thus the "first" who will be "last" are the workers hired in the morning. Simultaneously Matthew reinforces the previous point through the opposition of "receiving one denarius" as the eleventh hour workers do (20:9) with "receiving more than one denarius" as the first workers expect to receive (20:10). It is now absolutely clear that the householder did not hire people only because he needed their work. He also hired them because they needed to have work and wages. The householder is generous. Being hired is not merely entering a contractual agreement. It is also receiving a gift from the householder, the twofold gift of work in the vineyard and of wages. By contrast, if the first workers would receive more than a denarius, if the wages were proportional to the amount of work, then the workers and their service would merely be viewed as being needed by the householder, who would pay them according to the amount of service rendered. But this is the wrong perspective. While workers are givers of services for which they are compensated, they are simultaneously receivers of a gift, work and wages.

Once again, this point parallels those made by 19:3–9, where Jesus emphasized that people should view themselves as receivers of the good gift of marriage. Yet this parallelism casts the Pharisees in a new light. Their eagerness to know what is "lawful" (19:3) which leads them to see commandments even where there is no commandment (they confuse a permission with a commandment, 19:7–8) shows that they conceive of themselves exclusively as workers in a contractual agreement with God, or better, as servants of God in the sense of people who provide a service needed by God. Then one has to wonder whether the young man's initial question, "What good deed must I do, to have eternal life?" (19:16), should not be read in a similar way. Even though it is not the point made in 19:16–17, is not eternal life viewed by the young man as wages for services rendered to God? Is this not implied by his use of the phrase "eternal life" instead of "kingdom of heaven" and by his question, "All these I have observed; what do I still lack?" (19:20)?[25]

20:10, 13b. The third opposition between what the first workers think or suppose (20:10) and what they agreed upon with the householder (20:13b) makes a quite different point. By asking the first workers, "Did you not agree with me for a denarius?" (20:13b), the householder shows that their expectation of receiving more than a denarius is incorrect even from their own perspective.[26] Precisely because they view work in the vineyard exclusively as a service for the benefit of the householder, they should view their being hired as a contract for services and appropriate wages. Consequently, from their perspective, they should expect to receive what was agreed upon in the contract.

20:10–15. This point is carried farther by the complex opposition created by the polemical exchange between the first workers (20:10–11) and the householder (20:12–15). After receiving a denarius, the first workers grumble against the householder and accuse him of injustice since he has made the last workers equal to them who have given much of themselves by bearing "the burden of the day and the scorching heat" (20:12). One of the points made by the householder's response is that, even if one conceives of their being hired as a contract for a service, one cannot accuse him of injustice. He abided by the terms of the contract; he gave them what was agreed upon. Even from their own narrow perspective, they should be able to perceive that he is not unjust. By considering his action exclusively from this contractual perspective, they should also see that he gave to the eleventh hour workers more than was required. They should recognize and understand that he was generous and that what he gave to the last workers was a gracious gift (cf. 20:15). Even if they do not understand that their own hiring was a gift from the householder as well as a contract, then they should at least understand that the hiring of the eleventh hour workers was a gift.

The first workers have false expectations; they are angry against the householder and accuse him of injustice. Why? As we saw, it is not because of their incorrect understanding of their own hiring (see 20:13). They should understand that the householder was generous and that he has the right to do with his belongings whatever he chooses, as the rhetorical questions of 20:14b–15a indicate. They *should* understand all this, *but they do not!* In other words, and this is the point made by this concluding opposition, there is another reason for their anger, which is expressed by the last rhetorical question: "Or is your eye bad because I am good?" (20:15b, au.).[27] In brief, *they cannot accept that the householder be good.* And because of this they have a bad eye (cf. 6:23); they are totally unable to make a correct distinction between what is good and bad (see my comments on 6:22—7:12).[28] This is why they are unable to conceive that the householder's action vis-à-vis the last workers was a gift, an act of generosity, and why they construe it as an injustice. They are unable to understand that the householder considered them as his "friends," or "companions" (20:13b), those with whom he wants to be in a personal relationship, an "I-you" relation (note the relation between the "I" and the "you" in the singular in 20:13–15).[29] Therefore, they are unable even to imagine that the contract for their services in the vineyard was also a gift from the householder.

It is clear that a bad eye and hardness of heart (19:8) are the same thing, since the consequence of these predicaments is in both cases the inability to recognize good gifts for what they are. Because of their hardness of heart the Pharisees conceive of their relationship with God exclusively in contract terms—in terms of what is lawful to do and of commandments (19:3, 7)—as the first workers considered their relationship with the householder.

We can then understand why Jesus speaks to the Pharisees and the young man in terms of the law. As the first workers should have been able to perceive the true character of the householder's action despite their incorrect view of their relationship with him, so also the Pharisees should be able to perceive that marriage is a good gift from God despite their exclusive concern for the law.[30] So it is in terms of the law that Jesus shows them that divorce is against God's will since it leads to adultery (19:9). Should not this show them that from God's perspective marriage is good? Similarly, Jesus refers the young man back to the commandments that he already knows and observes (19:17b–20). But the source of the inability to understand and do what is good is not merely a lack of knowledge. The Pharisees, the young man, and the disciples (19:10, 13) could overcome such a lack of knowledge with the help of the scriptural law that they strive to fulfill. The source of their inability to recognize good gifts, the source of their hardness of heart, of their bad eye, is that they neither accept nor envision that God be good. And yet, "One there is who is good" (19:17). As long as one does not have a change of "heart" (or of "eye") through the recognition and acceptance of God's fundamental goodness, there is no hope for salvation (19:25).

But how can one truly acknowledge and accept God's goodness and be saved? "With human beings this is impossible" (19:26a, au.). Being one of the first workers, people who work hard in the service of God, does not help. And how could it help? As long as one does not acknowledge God's goodness, one is bound to misconstrue this work as a mere service to God, and to exclude that it is also a gift from God? As long as one strives to serve God without recognizing that being in his service is a gift from him one can only be angry with God and be alienated from God.[31]

20:16. How can anyone be saved? Indeed, with human beings it is impossible. The first workers striving to serve God cannot be saved. These are the first who will be last (19:30; 20:16). And who are they? The Pharisees who strive to serve God without acknowledging the goodness of his gifts (19:3–9). The young man who can say, "All these I have observed" (19:20). And also possibly the disciples as described in 19:10 and 19:13. The first who will be last are all those who do not acknowledge and accept God's goodness, and therefore have a hard heart and a bad eye, which in turn prevent them from perceiving the goodness of God.[32] This is a "Catch 22" situation, a diabolic circle from which one cannot escape and which necessarily leads to alienation from God.

So how can anyone be saved? How can one truly acknowledge and accept God's goodness? The formulation of the concluding verse (20:16) is no longer judgmental by contrast with its earlier formulation in 19:30. It begins, "The last will be first" (instead of "The first will be last"). There is hope even for the "last." "With God all things are possible" (19:26b). People hired at the eleventh hour are the last who will be first. Because of their dire situation they have to recognize their being hired for what it is: a manifestation of the goodness of the householder. Who will be saved? Who are the last who will be first? The children and those who are like them (19:13–15). Indeed, since they are totally dependent on others, they have to count on the goodness of others and of God—otherwise everything is impossible. Those who are like children have left everything for Jesus' sake (19:29). Without home and family, without possessions, they must count on the goodness of God. Such people can recognize God's gifts for what they are. Consequently they are not alienated from God. Those who are like children, without anything for Jesus' sake, are the last who will be first.[33]

NOTES ON 19:1—20:16

1. My interpretation of 19:1—20:16 owes many insights to the unpublished paper of Jeffrey T. Tucker ("On Following Jesus, Hardness of Heart, and the Goodness of God"). I revised an earlier draft of this part of the commentary in view of this paper and helpful critical comments by Jonathan Kraus.

2. This observation will be confirmed in the chapters that follow, in which Matthew's description of Jesus' ministry in Judea involves the same features—proclamation of the kingdom, teaching, and healings—as his ministry in Galilee.

3. A rapid glance at a Gospel Parallels shows that two passages, 19:10–12 and 20:1–16, have no parallel in Mark, without speaking of numerous other differences between Matt. 19:1–30 and Mark 10:1–31.

4. The phrase "for any cause" can be understood to mean either "for any reason a man wishes" or "for any reason whatsoever." With SCHWEIZER, 381, and BONNARD, 281, I think that the former option is preferable, since in this case the question presupposes that divorce is allowed and that the only problem to be resolved concerns the reasons that may be invoked to divorce one's wife—the view implied by the Pharisees' second statement (19:7). But even if one chose the latter option, one would have to understand that by this question—which then would be about whether or not it is permitted to divorce—the Pharisees were testing Jesus while believing that divorce is permitted.

5. With BERGER, 570–71.

6. If the order of Jesus' sayings was reversed, as they are in Mark 10:1–12, then the text would not convey that the Pharisees deliberately challenge the validity of God's words.

7. With BERGER, 571.

8. See a discussion of this phrase in my comments on 5:32.

9. Against Barth ("Matthew's Understanding of the Law," 94–95), one cannot infer from this verse that the Old Testament law held complete validity in the community of Matthew. The issue is rather that of a fundamental conflict in interpretation. Here the interpretation of the law should be based upon a perception of the goodness of God's work and will, a point that Barth misses. Our comments are relatively close to those of BERGER, 572, who is critical of Barth's view.

10. With BONNARD, 284; but against STRECKER, 132.

11. While Berger sees that the eunuch sayings and the marriage sayings are connected by the theme of marriage, he misses the continuation (refigurativization) of the theme "hardness of heart" because he does not account for the opposition between the disciples' sayings and Jesus' sayings. See BERGER, 573.

12. BERGER, 573–74, suggests that this view is partly shaped by early Jewish concepts of ritual purity (cf. Wisd. of Sol. 3:13–14) and by the practice of celibacy in early Christian prophetic groups.

13. The question about having "eternal life" (19:16) is not answered until 19:29, where a similar phrase is used, as pointed out by Jonathan Kraus.

14. So, e.g., BONNARD, 287; and Edwards, *Matthew's Story*, 70.

15. See Frankemölle, *Jahwebund*, 293. He recognizes an opposition, yet he interprets it as an opposition between Old Testament righteousness according to the law and Matthean "perfection," a right relationship between the disciples and God. We shall see that this cannot be the case.

16. Confusing Jesus with God, by calling Jesus "good," is the point of the opposition in Mark 10:17–18. Note the different text of Mark.

17. This perception would also reveal to him what is good in what God has done "from the beginning" (cf. 19:4–6). Frankemölle (*Jahwebund*, 293) sees the issue primarily as one of right relationship with God.

18. The meaning of "being perfect" in this pericope is much debated. See, e.g., BERGER, 446–53; TRILLING, 194–96; Frankemölle, *Jahwebund*, 292; Kunzel, *Gemeindeverständnis*, 247–48. These scholars strive to interpret this phrase in terms of Old Testament, Jewish, or Hellenistic traditions which, for us, simply suggest *possible* connotations. As usual, we give priority to the relations in the text. Our con-

clusions are closer to the positions of Berger and Trilling, and especially the latter, who notes that "perfect" has the connotations of the Hebrew expression "perfect heart."

19. With Kunzel (*Gemeindeverständnis*, 247). He calls this sort of intervention of God an "experience of God as Father" which works as the summons to be perfect.

20. With BERGER, 439, 459.

21. Thus scholars who want to study the parable *of Jesus* exclude 20:16 along with 19:30 as Matthean. See Jeremias, *Parables*, 36–37; Dodd, *Parables*, 92; Crossan, *In Parables*, 112. Crossan also says that 20:14–15 is also a Matthean addition. This claim is supported by our analysis: these verses are indeed the key for the understanding of 19:1—20:16.

22. Against Tolbert (*Perspectives*, 60), who claims that the parable does not fit its context in Matthew's Gospel. This comment would be valid when the parable is limited to 20:1–13 (as it is for Crossan). But for her the parable is 20:1–15.

23. My interpretation of the parable owes much to Jonathan Kraus's observation that "the point of the parable is in part to resolve a perceived opposition between 'service to God' and 'gift of God.'"

24. This is the interpretation of Jeremias (*Parables*, 37, 136–37).

25. See BERGER, 458–59, who interprets the basic tension in the synoptic tradition of the rich young man as that between apocalyptic theories of reward and the ethics of the Old Testament love commandment and of the Decalogue.

26. With Crossan, *In Parables*, 114.

27. This literal translation is essential so as to perceive the relation of this verse with 6:23, where the phrase "your bad eye" (au.) is also found, and with 19:17. The RSV rendering, "Or do you begrudge my generosity?" makes it impossible to perceive these relations and consequently to understand how this parable is related to 19:1–30.

28. The interpretation of 20:15b in terms of the Sermon on the Mount is demanded not only by the use of the phrase "your bad eye" (6:23) but also by all the references to the Sermon on the Mount in this section. See our introductory remarks on the main theme of this section. Even though he is primarily concerned with the study of the parable "of Jesus," Crossan perceptively makes similar points to ours about the way in which Matthew integrates the parable into its context. See Crossan, *In Parables*, 112–13.

29. Of course the term "friend" is also reproachful, as Jeremias notes (*Parables*, 139).

30. Via (*Parables*, 154) terms the workers' attitude a "legalistic understanding of existence."

31. In my opinion the parable does not set up a contrast between the merit system of the law and the graceful goodness of the Gospel, as argued by Jeremias (*Parables*, 139) and Via (*Parables*, 154–55). Rather, for Matthew, the contrast is between a view that the law and its merit system are to be interpreted in terms of the goodness of God and the view of the law and its merit system by themselves.

32. This set of correlations *within the text* is to be contrasted with the correlations made in traditio-historical studies. Cf. Jeremias, *Parables*, 38.

33. It is not excluded that those who have been presently rejected (20:14a), they who were first and have become last, might in turn become first.

GOING UP TO JERUSALEM
AND THE TEMPLE

THE MAIN THEME

"As Jesus was going up to Jerusalem"[1] he said to the Twelve: "Behold, we are going up to Jerusalem" (20:17–18). The repetition of this phrase, often used with the connotation "going to worship at the Temple,"[2] signals that the section beginning with these verses ends with the scene describing Jesus in the Temple, the "house of prayer" (21:13), where he is acclaimed by children (21:15–16).

By retelling Jesus' journey to Jerusalem, Matthew continues to unfold the points and themes of the preceding section. In 20:17–19 and 20:20–28, the issue is in part what being "first" means for Jesus as well as for the disciples. In this context the limit of Jesus' authority is underscored, while the extent of his vocation, giving his life "as a ransom for many" (20:28), is specified. The scene that follows, the healing of two blind persons who are first rebuked by the crowds (20:29–34), reminds the readers of the scene when the disciples rebuked people for bringing children to Jesus (19:13–15). The crowds failed to recognize that Jesus' vocation is to manifest the goodness (or mercy) of God. As a consequence, in the following scene (21:1–11), the crowds' acclamation, "Hosanna to the Son of David!" cannot be trusted by the readers. Actually the entire scene of Jesus' entrance into Jerusalem is most ambiguous. The proper understanding of this acclamation will appear only when children will repeat it. The Temple scene (21:12–16) makes clear that Jesus is Son of David in that he manifests God's mercy and goodness. As a consequence he can be acknowledged only by those who do not have a hard heart, namely, children.

MATTHEW'S CONVICTIONS IN 20:17—21:17

20:17–19. The Third Passion Prediction

As compared with the preceding predictions (16:21; 17:22–23), the third one is more detailed; the respective roles of the chief priests and scribes and of the Gentiles are specified. But the main difference is the omitted emphasis that Jesus "must go" or "is to be delivered." This announcement no longer

281

seeks to convince the disciples of the necessity of the Passion. It presents the disciples as joining Jesus on his way to Jerusalem.[3]

20:18. Since this verse opposes God's action, raising Jesus, *and* the actions of priests, scribes, *and Gentiles*, it contrasts God and human beings in general. Coming after passages that contrasted the goodness of God and the hardness of heart or bad eye of (certain) human beings (20:1–16), this opposition carries forward these points. By their actions the chief priests, the scribes, and the Gentiles display their hardness of heart. Unable to recognize the goodness of God and of his gifts, they condemn to death someone they take to be bad while he is good; they mock someone they take to be "last" (and thus ridicule) while he will be "first" (cf. 19:28—20:16). Because of his goodness, however, God will raise him. He who is last—condemned, delivered to the people without control over his own destiny, scourged, and crucified—will be first. Consequently, the chief priests, the scribes, and the Gentiles are the "first" who will be last. But what about the twelve disciples? By joining Jesus *on the way to Jerusalem*, are they among the last who will be first? Do they acknowledge the goodness of God, and thus are they free from hardness of heart and able to leave everything (cf. 19:21–22, 29)?

20:20–28. The Ambition of the Sons of Zebedee and of Their Mother

The request of the mother of the sons of Zebedee—also the request of her sons (Jesus responds to them in 20:22–23)—shows that the answer to the preceding question is not as obvious as it might have seemed.

20:21–23. While the ten other disciples are "indignant at the two brothers" (20:24), Jesus' response to the request is more nuanced. First, he encourages the mother to formulate her request (20:21a). In the polemical dialogue[4] that follows (20:21b–23), Jesus does not directly object to the desire expressed by the request to be seated on his right and left hand in his kingdom (20:21b)—the desire to share his authority and glory, to be "first" in the future. Actually, Jesus has promised his disciples that when he "shall sit on his glorious throne" they "will also sit on twelve thrones, judging the twelve tribes of Israel" (19:28). What the disciples are indignant about (20:24) is that the sons of Zebedee want to be "first" among the "first," among the Twelve, that is. But this is not Jesus' (and Matthew's) concern. For him the issue is that they do not know what they are asking (20:22a).

What they do not know is specified in Jesus' question: "Are you able to drink the cup I am to drink?" (20:22b). Although the metaphor of the cup that Jesus is about to drink appears here for the first time in the Gospel, the readers should interpret it as referring to the Passion. This is shown by the question itself which indicates that the disciples have to do the same thing that Jesus is about to do—go to Jerusalem and ultimately be crucified (20:18–19). What they do not know is that by asking to share his glory and authority in his kingdom, they also ask to share his Passion, to be persecuted as he will be. But are they *able* to do so? The affirmative answer of the sons of Zebedee (20:22b) is not contradicted by Jesus; indeed, they will drink his cup (20:23a).[5] After all, they are already *going up to Jerusalem* with him (20:18a) without objecting as Peter did (16:22) and without being distressed as the disciples were (17:23).

There is something else awry in the request of the sons of Zebedee and their mother. They incorrectly believe that Jesus has the authority to grant their request (20:23b). Matthew's second point concerns a misconception about Jesus' authority. By speaking of his kingdom the mother has presupposed that Jesus will have full authority over what will take place in it. Since her request follows directly the announcement that he is going up to Jerusalem (20:18a), and ignores that he will suffer there (see 20:22), it seems that the mother and her sons expect him to take power at Jerusalem as the Messiah. He will be the king to rule over his people with absolute authority. Without denying that he will have a kingdom, Jesus' answer underscores that the supreme authority remains his Father's; his authority remains subordinated to and limited by the authority of his Father. It is the Father alone who prepares and assigns places in the kingdom; God alone makes it possible for people to be saved (19:26), not Jesus. The authority of Jesus should not be confused or identified with that of the Father. Jesus does not take the place of the Father!

20:25–28. These verses are presented as a general lesson for all of the disciples, a lesson which Jesus draws from the preceding dialogue. Despite the ten disciples' indignation (20:24), once again Jesus does not object to the desire of being "great" among the disciples. This is a good goal which he implicitly encourages them to pursue.

For Matthew, the point of these sayings is expressed by the opposition between the rulers of the Gentiles who "lord" over others and exercise power over them (20:25; cf. 20:28a) *and* the disciples and Jesus who are great when they serve others (20:28b; cf. 20:26b–27). Greatness, being first, is to be viewed in the community of the disciples exactly in the opposite way as it is understood among the Gentiles. Being great or first is being servant or slave of others. Furthermore, being servant of others also means giving one's life for others—"as a ransom for many" (20:28b)—giving one's life for the sake of others. But the main point of this opposition is that the disciples should have such a view of greatness and serve others because they imitate Jesus ("even as the Son of man came not to be served," 20:28a), by contrast with the Gentile rulers who do not have Jesus as a model.[6]

In sum, as in 20:22, the issue is whether or not the disciples are ready to drink Jesus' cup, to share in his Passion. Are they? Do they know what true greatness entails? Or do they share the Gentiles' view of greatness, which, according to Jesus, they know (Jesus says to them: "*You know* that the rulers of the Gentiles . . . ," 20:25a)? After all, what does it mean to share in Jesus' Passion?

Finally, these sayings underscore that the Passion is the culmination of Jesus' vocation (what he came for)—a vocation to serve others. It is for the sake of others that Jesus, the Son of man, will suffer and give his life "as a ransom for many" (20:28b). The preceding chapter has emphasized that the disciples should give up everything (19:29) so as to be saved (19:25), that is, so as to receive blessings for themselves. Consequently, one could forget that giving up one's life—as in Jesus' Passion—is also and primarily for the sake of others. Jesus' (and the disciples') entire ministry is first of all an act of mercy, an act aimed at meeting the needs of others. It is "to give his life as a ransom for many." Furthermore, this phrase suggests to the readers that, in so doing, Jesus fulfills the prophecy of Isaiah concerning the Suffering Servant (Isa. 53:11–12), as he also did in his healing ministry in Galilee (see Matt. 8:17, which quotes Isa. 53:4).

20:29–34. Healing of Two Blind Persons near Jericho

This healing story reminds the readers of the similar story in 9:27–31. In both cases, two blind persons "cried out" using the same phrase, "Have mercy on us, Son of David!" (9:27; 20:30, 31), and Jesus heals them by touching them (9:29; 20:34). These repetitions literarily link this episode of Jesus' Judean ministry with the healings in Galilee described in 8:1—9:34. As we have noted, because of the people's limited faith, Jesus had to *touch* them when healing them. In the process he fulfilled the prophecy of Isaiah: "He took our infirmities and bore our diseases" (Isa. 53:4; Matt. 8:17). As 20:28 already suggested, through these thematic features Matthew conveys that Jesus' Passion is the culmination of his ministry of mercy, a ministry that involves healings as one manifestation of compassion toward people in need.

Yet the present story includes new features through which Matthew makes two points by introducing two narrative oppositions. The blind persons who cry out (20:30, 31b) are opposed to what the crowd would like them to do, stay silent (20:31a), while the crowd who rebukes them (20:31) is contrasted to Jesus who calls them (20:32).

20:30–31. The cry of the blind persons, "Have mercy on us, Son of David!" (20:30b), is both an expression of their faith that Jesus, as Son of David, the Messiah, has the power to heal them[7] and a request that he be merciful toward them. According to the crowd, they should remain quietly seated by the roadside while Jesus is passing by (see 20:30a). For the crowd, their cry is inappropriate. But why? Is it because they should not expect compassion from the Son of David? Or is it because they should not have faith that Jesus, the Son of David, has the power to heal them? Since the crowd "followed him" (20:29), we can infer that it has faith in Jesus and his power as Son of David, as the proclamation in 21:9 confirms. For the crowd, however, it is inappropriate for the Son of David to be stopped *on his way to Jerusalem* to take care of handicapped people. This might be an indication that the crowd has a view of Jesus' power and authority similar to that of the sons of Zebedee and their mother—the powerful Messiah who goes to Jerusalem to establish his kingdom (cf. 20:21) according to the model of the kingdoms of "the rulers of the Gentiles" (cf. 20:25). In this way the crowd is presented as having the same kind of misconceptions about Jesus' authority and power as the disciples had—misconceptions that Jesus attempted to correct in the preceding dialogue with his disciples (20:20–28).

20:31–32. The second opposition, between the crowd who rebukes the blind persons and Jesus who calls them, underscores Jesus' compassion (20:34a) by contrast with the crowd's lack of compassion. The similarity between the crowd's and the disciples' attitudes is further emphasized. As in the case of the disciples who rebuked the children (see 19:13–15), the crowd that follows Jesus (20:29) excludes from its privileged ranks people viewed as unworthy of following Jesus. Even though the group of Jesus' followers is large and is now "a great crowd" (20:29), it views itself as an exclusive group of privileged people. But this view involves lack of compassion for people who would slow down the progress of the march toward Jerusalem following Jesus.

By contrast, Jesus, the Son of David, is first of all someone who has compassion, over against the crowd's expectation about the Son of David. Compassion demands that Jesus stop (20:32a), take the time to ascertain their needs (20:32b–33), and meet the needs of the handicapped people by healing them (20:34a). As a consequence, they are now included in the group of Jesus' followers: and they "followed him" (20:34b). Jesus' act of mercy toward them is therefore twofold: he removes their infirmity and, in so doing, gives them the possibility of being included in the group of his followers.

21:1–11. The Entry Into Jerusalem

In this passage there is not a single narrative opposition. It is therefore a thematic passage in which, rather than conveying new points, Matthew expresses previous points in terms of his readers' presumed knowledge of this story, ones that can be recognized in the tensions displayed by the text.

21:1–7. The first part involves a well-known tension expressed by its concluding phrase which most unrealistically describes Jesus as riding on *both* the ass *and* the colt.[8] The effect of this unrealistic description is to call the readers' attention to the quotation of the prophecy (21:4–5) that it fulfills. Matthew restates a point he had already made in terms of his readers' knowledge of Scripture and a tradition involving the mention of two asses.[9] The story of Jesus' entrance into Jerusalem on an ass that has a colt can be understood in many different ways (e.g., as a triumphal entry demonstrating the kingship of Jesus). But by pointing out that Jesus' entrance into Jerusalem fulfills the prophecy of Zech. 9:9, Matthew underscores the meekness of Jesus.[10] He does so by providing his own rendering of the prophecy in a wooden literal translation of the Hebrew text which omits parts of the text.[11] No, it is not the triumphant entrance into Jerusalem of a powerful and victorious king—as the omitted words would have expressed, and quite possibly as his readers might have understood it. Rather, it is the entrance of someone who is meek and lowly. In brief, Matthew restates the point he made in 20:25–28. Unlike the rulers of the Gentiles who "lord over" people, he came not to be served but to serve; he is "meek," as riding on an ass and on a colt demonstrates.

21:8–11. Since the first part (21:1–7) emphasizes Jesus' meekness, for the readers, the second part of the story appears to be in tension with the first. Now the crowd seems to understand this entrance as a royal procession. People spread their garments and branches on the road (21:8) and acclaim Jesus: "Hosanna to the Son of David! Blessed is he who comes in the name of the Lord! Hosanna in the highest!" (21:9).

Once again Matthew assumes that this acclamation is well known to his readers.[12] It is an expression of praise which designates Jesus as the Messiah, Son of David. Matthew does not deny this view of Jesus. By creating this tension, however, he warns his readers that this acclamation needs to be correctly interpreted; the context in which this acclamation is set—a triumphal royal procession—might be misleading.

Furthermore, in this second part of the story (21:8–11), Matthew gives the main role to the crowds: they spread garments and branches on the road (21:8), precede him and follow him (21:9a), acclaim him (21:9b), then answer the question of the people of Jerusalem (21:11). This last verse suggests that the crowds are not from Jerusalem. They have come with Jesus from Jericho. For the readers, such crowds are not trustworthy, since against Jesus' wish they rebuked the two blind persons even though they called Jesus "Son of David" (20:31) as the crowds do.[13] The crowds are further discredited by the answer they give to the people of Jerusalem who inquired "Who is this?" (21:10): "This is the prophet Jesus from Nazareth of Galilee" (21:11). Is this all that they can say after acclaiming him as the Son of David? For them, is Jesus only a prophet (cf. 16:14)? Or do they mean the eschatological prophet (whose name happens to be "Jesus from Nazareth in Galilee")? This latter alternative is not impossible, since the crowds respond to people ("all the city") who are agitated (21:10), as if they expected a momentous, eschatological event. But how is this response related to the crowds' acclamation of Jesus as the Son of David (21:9)? It is clear: Matthew wants to affirm that Jesus is the Son of David. But simultaneously he warns the readers against the understanding of this title and of Jesus' entrance into Jerusalem that is implied by the crowds' actions and words. Such an understanding might not be totally false, but at best it is full of ambiguity.

21:12–17. Jesus in the Temple

Just after the ambiguous story of Jesus' entrance into Jerusalem,[14] Matthew presents Jesus in the Temple: there, he drives out the merchants and the money-changers (21:12–13), heals the blind and the lame (21:14), and is acclaimed by children as the Son of David (21:15–16). In this way Matthew shows that, for him, this scene is the perspective from which the entrance into Jerusalem should be properly understood.[15] This is further shown by Matthew's two points that remove any possible ambiguity.

21:12–13. A first point is made by means of the opposition found in the words that Jesus addresses to those he is driving out of the Temple: "It is written, 'My house shall be called a house of prayer'; but you make it a den of robbers" (21:13). This combined quotation of Isa. 56:7 and Jer. 7:11[16] opposes those (especially Jesus) who call the Temple a house of prayer *and* the merchants who make it a den of robbers. The point is clear: It is in the name of Scripture and a correct view of the function of the Temple that Jesus drives out those who make possible the cult as it is practiced. In the process, Jesus rejects the cult as it is practiced, with its emphasis on paying the Temple tax with the proper money, and on sacrifice (e.g., of the doves). Such a cult is contrary to the will of God as expressed in Scripture, and implicitly denies that the Temple is God's house. As he shows by driving out the merchants, Jesus has the authority to reestablish the proper kind of cult in the Temple.[17]

21:14. What is the proper cult? What are the proper activities in the Temple? According to the quotation, praying should be the main activity. But Matthew does not describe Jesus as praying. Rather, Jesus heals the blind and the lame who have come to him "in the temple" (21:14). Healings in the Temple instead of the traditional cult! After reading the story of the healing of the two blind persons (20:29–34), repeatedly called an act of "mercy," the reader should recall that Jesus twice quoted Hos. 6:6 (see Matt. 9:13; 12:7): "I desire mercy, and not sacrifice." In order to fully appreciate this comment, it is important to note what constitutes such acts of mercy. Regarding the healings near Jericho, we observed that the act of mercy was actually twofold. Jesus opened the eyes of the blind persons; he removed their infirmity. But he also included in his group of followers these two persons who were excluded and could only sit on the roadside.[18] Similarly here, by emphasizing that it is "in the temple" that the blind and the lame follow Jesus and are healed, Matthew indicates that by this act of mercy they are included among those who can now participate in Temple cultic activities.[19] If the readers know—Matthew expects them to know—that according to 2 Sam. 5:8 "the blind and the lame shall not come into the house," a text that was interpreted in early Judaism as excluding them from the Temple,[20] then they can fully appreciate the significance of Jesus' act of mercy. By healing them, Jesus not only removes the infirmity of the blind and the lame but also (re)introduces into the worshiping community those who were excluded from it.

Consequently, Jesus' action in the Temple is twofold. He drives out of the Temple and thus excludes from it those who are presently inside, those through whose trade worship as sacrifice was made possible. Once again (see 20:20–28), the "first" are the "last" (and thus excluded, 19:30—20:16). But he also opens the possibility for the excluded, the blind and the lame, to come into the Temple and makes them fit for worshiping in the Temple. Thus the "last" (the excluded) are "first."

21:15–16. The second opposition is set up by the polemical dialogue between the chief priests and scribes and Jesus. The chief priests and the scribes do not object either to Jesus driving the merchants from the Temple or to his miracles (RSV: "wonderful things") that they witnessed (21:15a). Their only objection is to "the children crying out in the temple, 'Hosanna to the Son of David!'" (21:15b–16a). For them it is inappropriate that Jesus be praised as Son of David. On the basis of what they have seen, Jesus' activity in the Temple and especially his healing of the blind and the lame, they cannot conclude that such praises are appropriate and thus that Jesus is the Son of David, the Messiah.[21]

Jesus' reply points out that their inability to recognize the validity of the children's praise is due to their ignorance or lack of understanding of Scripture: "Have you never read . . . ?" (21:16b). This is the same reproach that Jesus took to the Pharisees in 19:4 and to the young man in 19:7, and that the householder took to the first workers in 20:13. In other words, as we noted about 20:17–19, the chief priests and the scribes are afflicted with hardness of heart; they do not acknowledge God's goodness. Consequently, they cannot recognize someone performing acts of mercy as God's Messiah, the Son of David who manifests God's goodness. Because they do not acknowledge God's goodness and mercy, and therefore have another view of God, they are unable to recognize a manifestation of God, even though it is found in the place where God is supposed to act—the Temple. Matthew contrasts the chief priests and the scribes with children, and this confirms that, for Matthew, the Jewish leaders have a hard heart. Children who typify those to whom the kingdom belongs (cf. 19:13–15), and thus those who do not have a hard heart and acknowledge the goodness and mercy of God, are those who can utter proper praise. They utter their praise according to God's will, the praise that God prepared for himself, as is expressed by Ps. 8:3 which Jesus quotes:[22] "Out of the mouth of babes and sucklings, you prepared for yourself a praise" (Matt. 21:16b, au.).

Jesus is the Son of David, the Messiah, because he manifests the mercy of God. His entrance into Jerusalem is that of a meek, or "humble," personage (21:5). And so he is to be praised by shouts of "Hosanna to the Son of David!" as the crowds correctly did (21:9), although, like the mother of the sons of Zebedee (see 20:21–22), they did not know what they were saying.

NOTES ON 20:17—21:17

1. Or, according to other manuscripts, "As Jesus was about to go up to Jerusalem."

2. See BONNARD, 294.

3. This is also expressed by the shift from the third person discourse in 16:21 and 17:22–23 to the plural first person ("we") in 20:18 which associates the disciples with Jesus' Passion.

4. There are two interrelated oppositions in these verses: the polemical dialogue (what the mother and Jesus say, 20:21b, 22a) and what the mother expects Jesus to do, commanding that her sons sit at his right and left hand in his kingdom (20:21b) as contrasted with Jesus' statement that he cannot do it, that it is not his to grant (20:23b). For the sake of brevity we discuss them together.

5. In spite of this pericope's tendency to assimilate the fate of Jesus to that of the disciples, Trilling is right in seeing that Matthew also stresses something about the peculiarity or uniqueness of Jesus' Passion, but not in 20:23. See TRILLING, 34.

6. Neither Strecker nor Trilling, who believe that Matthew's Gospel may be directed to Gentiles, has anything to say about this opposition which involves a negative assessment of Gentiles.

7. Compare my interpretation of the title "Son of David" throughout this section with Duling, "The Therapeutic Son of David," NTS 24 (1978): 392–409; and Chilton, "Jesus ben David," JSNT 6 (1980): 101.

8. The original reading of 21:7b is "he sat on them." In various ways the manuscripts attempt to make this phrase more realistic by writing, e.g., "he sat on it." Similarly, RSV translates "and he sat thereon," dismissing in this way the unrealistic feature of the text.

9. With STENDAHL, 118–20, 200.

10. With Rothfuchs, Erfüllungszitate, 82–83.

11. See STENDAHL, 118–20. Matthew's translation allows him to describe Jesus as riding both on the ass and on the colt. Omitted from Zech. 9:9 is the additional description of the personage as "triumphant and victorious" (according to the Hebrew, as translated here by RSV), or "just and savior" (according to the LXX). Note also that the introduction "Tell the daughter of Zion" is borrowed from Isa. 62:11.

12. As STENDAHL, 64–66, suggests, it might have been the rendering of a liturgical hymn in use in early churches.

13. Chilton ("Jesus ben David," 105) stresses that "Son of David" is the messianic title given to Jesus by those who express the prevailing "Jerusalem theology of his day." But the children also use this title.

14. Mark and Luke do not juxtapose the stories of Jesus in the Temple and his entrance into Jerusalem.

15. With Hummel, *Auseinandersetzung,* 97.

16. See STENDAHL, 66–67.

17. Matthew is not saying that the Temple cannot be a locus of divine activity. With Hummel, *Auseinandersetzung,* 82, 96–97.

18. With Lohmeyer as cited by Hummel, *Auseinandersetzung,* 96.

19. Against Hummel, *Auseinandersetzung,* 96–97; but with Lohmeyer, whom he cites.

20. This exclusion of the blind and the lame from the worshiping community (cf. also Lev. 21:18–19) is mentioned in the Dead Sea Scrolls (1QSa 2:19–25; 1QM 7:4–5; Damascus Document 15:15–17) as well as in the *Mishnah* (*Hagigah* 1:1). See SCHWEIZER, 408; GUNDRY, 413. While the structural exegesis supports their interpretation according to which the text alludes to 2 Sam. 5:8 and to the exclusion of the blind and the lame from worship at the Temple (because of the relation between the opposition found in 21:12–14 and the preceding opposition in the text which happens to be in 20:31–34), it does not provide any ground to assume that the words of 2 Sam. 5:8 are from David. In other words, while this interpretation is quite suggestive, and might have occurred to the original readers of the Gospel, here Matthew does not make a point of contrasting David and the son of David.

21. The readers can easily envision that the chief priests and the scribes are also indignant because the proclamation of Jesus as "Son of David" is a challenge to their own authority in the Temple. But the opposition merely emphasizes the validity—"perfect praise"—of the children's words, a validity that the chief priests reject.

22. The quotation of Ps. 8:3 in Matt. 21:16 follows exactly the LXX, an exceptional case in Matthew, who is not hesitant to modify the biblical texts. Therefore I propose to translate the verse literally, despite its awkwardness. See Rothfuchs (*Erfüllungszitate,* 25), who explains this phenomenon as coming from Matthew's tradition rather than from his redactional work.

BY WHAT AUTHORITY ARE YOU DOING THESE THINGS?

THE MAIN THEME

In the concluding part of the preceding section, the Temple scene (21:12–17), the chief priests and the scribes failed to recognize Jesus as the Son of David. This point is developed in this new section which begins in 21:18, but from a different perspective. In 21:12–17, the lack of recognition of Jesus as the Son of David was viewed from Jesus' perspective. For him, it is a problem directly related to failing to know and understand Scripture and failing to acknowledge goodness and mercy as fundamental characteristics of God. By contrast, from the perspective of other people, it is an issue of authority and power. For them, the Messiah, Son of David, should have special power and authority.

In 21:20 the disciples raise a question concerning Jesus' power in the context of a pericope—the cursing of the fig tree (21:18–22)—which, by its odd character, also raises questions regarding the purpose of Jesus' use of power. Then in 21:23 the chief priests and the elders raise the question of the origin of Jesus' authority. This question prompts a substantial response, involving the discussion of John the Baptist's ministry (21:25–27; 21:32) and three parables: the two sons (21:28–31), the wicked tenants (21:33–41), and the wedding feast (22:1–14). In this context, Jesus' own perspective is reintroduced. It soon appears that the questions that had been raised regarding the origin of his power and authority display a wrong understanding of "authority." But the main theme of this section is clear: in the same way that only one is good (19:17), so only one has power and authority—namely, God. Everyone else, including Jesus, the Son of David and the Son of God, does not have authority. They can do authoritative actions only when such actions manifest their acknowledgment of God's authority. Any other view of authority leads to the rejection of God's servants and even of his Son (21:33–46), and to a denial of God's authority (22:1–14).

This theme is posited by the puzzling, and apparently arbitrary, use of power made by Jesus when he curses the fig tree (21:18–19). It is concluded by a similarly puzzling, and apparently arbitrary, use of power by the king when he condemns a person who has no wedding garment (22:11–14). And yet, with the proper understanding of power and of authority conveyed by the entire section, the readers are able to make sense of these two puzzling incidents.

MATTHEW'S CONVICTIONS IN 21:18—22:14

21:18–22. The Cursing of the Fig Tree

21:18–19. This brief description of Jesus' action as he was returning from Bethany to Jerusalem—a thematic passage—is puzzling for the readers. The disciples ask a question: "How did the fig tree wither at once?" (21:20). But the question for the readers is: *Why* did Jesus do it? Making the tree wither (destroying it) because he did not find fruit on it when he was hungry appears to be an angry, arbitrary, and excessive use of power. One could understand the violence involved in driving merchants out of the Temple, overturning their tables and furniture (21:12). Such an action had a clear reason and purpose. The Temple needed to be restored to its proper function and Jesus needed to make room for people—the blind and the lame—who had been excluded from it. But such a violent use of power against a fig tree seems out of character for Jesus. It appears to be vengeful and self-serving, since the only offense of the tree was that it did not provide what Jesus needed for himself. Is not Jesus supposed to use his supernatural power to meet the needs of others through merciful acts, such as the healing of the blind and the lame? Furthermore, that he was "hungry" (21:18) reminds the readers of the other time when Jesus was hungry and yet refused to use his power to satisfy his hunger, as the tempter suggested to him (4:2–4).[1] Why then this destructive use of power against a tree that did not provide fruit which would have satisfied his hunger?

The readers are puzzled. A new theme is posited. The cursing of the fig tree will only make sense in retrospect after one reads the concluding verses of the section (22:11–14), which describe yet another destructive and apparently arbitrary use of power. As we shall see, the time of the coming of the Son (and of the "servants")—"now"—is the time when fruits are to be produced (21:34–40); it is also the time of the wedding of the Son, a time when people need to wear wedding garments (22:2, 11). Not doing so is to bring destruction upon oneself, to expose oneself to the same fate as the fig tree. The cursing of the fig tree appears then as a parabolic act which prefigures what will be expressed in parables.

21:20–22. For the readers, the disciples' question about the fig tree misses the main issue. The only thing that impresses them is that the fig tree "withered at once" (21:19b, 20b)! This tension shows that in 21:20–22 Matthew makes a new point and that the dialogue between the disciples and Jesus should be viewed as polemical, as setting up an opposition that expresses this point. In effect, Jesus rebukes the disciples for not knowing how he performed this miracle. His answer (21:22) suggests that the disciples raised their question because they "doubt" and do not have the appropriate kind of faith, and consequently because they consider that Jesus' deed is extraordinary (cf. their amazement, 21:20a).

Matthew's point is that such a deed should not be viewed as something that Jesus alone can accomplish because he would have some kind of extraordinary power—a power that would be an intrinsic part of being the Son of David (or the Son of God). Implicitly Jesus denies that he has special powers (by contrast with what the readers might have assumed). All that he has is faith, a faith that the disciples could and should also have. Thus the disciples should be able to duplicate what Jesus did to the fig tree, and do things that are even more extraordinary—such as casting a mountain into the sea. For doing thusly they must have faith without doubt (21:21); they need to trust in God's power when asking something from God in prayer (21:22). And since it is "in prayer" that one asks for such things, it now appears that Jesus himself has performed the miracle by asking it in prayer. In sum, it is not Jesus' power that made the tree wither at once, but God's power. What characterizes Jesus as the Son of David is not some kind of extraordinary intrinsic power but a faith without doubt which disciples could also have.

21:23–32. By What Authority Are You Doing These Things?

Here Jesus is teaching in the Temple (21:23). Since he also healed there (21:14), we notice how Matthew presents Jesus' ministry in the Temple as a continuation of the Galilean ministry. Yet Matthew makes several new points by setting up oppositions in the polemical dialogue and discourse that follow.

21:23–25a. Through the first polemical exchange Matthew opposes the chief priests now associated with "the elders of the people" to Jesus. The question of the chief priests and the elders, which concerns the origin of Jesus' authority, seems quite appropriate. It presupposes that such an authority is not an intrinsic quality of Jesus but was *given to him* (21:23b)—one of the points Matthew underscored in 21:20–22 about his power. The answer to their question can only be that Jesus' authority is either "from heaven or from human beings" (21:25, au.), as Jesus suggests in his counterquestion. Consequently, for the readers, there is no doubt that it is God who gave Jesus his authority and power.

But what is the point made by this opposition? In order to understand it we need to compare the words of the chief priests and the elders (21:23b) with those of Jesus (21:24–25a). A first difference is that the chief priests and the elders single out Jesus' authority, which for them is a special case.

By contrast, Jesus associates his authority with that of John, since he will not say who gave him authority as long as they do not answer the same question about John and his baptism. Thus, in the same way that the power which Jesus uses is also available to the disciples (21:20–22), so receiving authority from God is not a privilege exclusively reserved for Jesus. Jesus implies that John the Baptist has received authority from God. And, in the light of 21:20–22, one should not view John as another exceptional case because of his unique place in sacred history.[2] Rather, he is one example among many possible examples of people receiving authority from God (such as the disciples, cf. 10:1, 5–15).

There is another important difference between the two statements. Even though the chief priests and the elders correctly view authority as something given to someone and not as an intrinsic part of someone's being, for them once it has been received this authority characterizes that person. For them, Jesus *has* an authority, and with it he does certain things. By contrast, Jesus does not speak of *John's* authority but rather of the *authority of his baptism*: "The baptism of John, whence was it"? (21:25a). In other words, authority, for Jesus, is attached to an act, to what a person does, rather than to the person. The person does not have authority; what a person does, such as the baptism performed by John, is authoritative.

21:25b–27. This subtle but important point is clarified by the two oppositions that are set up by the deliberation of the chief priests and the elders (saying "from heaven" and saying "from human beings," 21:25b–26, au.) and by their second polemical exchange with Jesus (21:27). Because these oppositions are so closely related they need to be treated together.

In order to understand Matthew's point, notice that he describes Jesus' opponents as people who have authority. They are "*chief* priests" and "elders *of the people*," people who have authority over people. In this light it appears that, in their deliberations (21:25b–26), they are exclusively concerned with the effect their answer (and Jesus' anticipated response) will have on the audience, the people over whom they have authority. They are not seeking the truth but a face-saving argument. In brief, they are seeking to preserve their authority as chief priests and elders of the people.[3] For them, authority is something that one has, a possession that needs to be preserved, a status that distinguishes a person from "the people" or from "the crowd," that is, from persons without authority. But preserving one's authority is something quite delicate to do. Thus "they debated among themselves" (21:25b, au.), exchanging words so as to find what they should say so that their words either would show their authority—by winning the argument—or at least would not impair their authority. For them, the right answer is simply the answer that chief priests and elders of the people should give in order to maintain their authority over the people. Other issues, such as the truth of the matter, are totally irrelevant. "So they answered Jesus,

'We do not know'" (21:27a). This is the right answer: words that do not commit them to anything, words that are face-saving ("authority"-saving!).

By contrast, words, for Jesus, do not need to be debated. He has said that he would answer their question only if they answered his own (21:24). They did not do it. Therefore he does not tell them by what authority he acts (21:27b). Similarly, as his opponents anticipated, if they had answered that John's baptism was from heaven, he would have challenged them by pointing out that, since they did not believe John, their attitude is contradictory to their words (21:25b).[4]

In sum, Matthew's point is that as long as one considers one's words, what one says, as that through which one saves or loses face (or "authority" viewed as a possession, the person's status), such words cannot be truthful. In such a case, one's authority is from human beings, since it depends upon the way in which the people will perceive one's words. Consequently, one's words need to be carefully deliberated (plotted!), since they are the very expression of one's authority, one's worthiness. By contrast, it is only if they are directly linked with what one does that words can (eventually) be truthful. Words cannot be truthful if they are neither a commitment to do something nor a reflection of what one does or has done. From such a perspective, words are secondary as compared with one's actions, since they should reflect what one does, will do, or has done. One's actions are what actually manifest one's authority, and thus one's relative worthiness as a person. Consequently, the validity of words, their truthfulness, depends upon the quality of the action that they should reflect and the degree to which they are consistent with past, present, or future actions.

21:28–31a. It is then clear that, with the *parable of the two sons*, Matthew further develops the preceding points. The opposition between the two sons is clearly marked.[5] The first son[6] goes to the vineyard to work (21:29), whereas the second does not (21:30). The point is clear. Doing the will of the father (21:31), and not one's words, is the criterion by which one is judged to be worthy.[7] What one says, even if it is the right thing—presenting oneself as a good and obedient son (21:30)—does not guarantee or establish one's worthiness. If one's good and valid words are not followed by actions consistent with these words, one is not worthy.[8] But if one has uttered the wrong words—presenting oneself as a bad and disobedient son (21:29)—and then repents and does what one was asked to do, one is worthy despite one's original words.

The chief priests and the elders, who are asked to interpret the parable ("What do you think?" 21:28a), condemn themselves and their view that it is through one's words that one's authority or relative worthiness is established and sustained. By their answer (21:31a), they concede that one's authority and worthiness are manifested by one's actions. It is also possible that the readers would take the mention of the first son's change of mind or repentance as an allusion to the teaching of John the Baptist (see 3:1–12).[9] Ironically, by their response the chief priests and the elders would implicitly affirm that the worthy person is the one who repented, as John urged people to do. In brief, they would affirm the validity of John's teaching.

21:31b–32. These verses are clearly presented by Matthew as an application of the parable to the case of the chief priests and the elders. It includes an opposition between Jesus' opponents who "did not believe" in John and the tax collectors and the prostitutes who "believed" in John (21:32). There is also another opposition that interweaves the parable and its explanation (21:29, 32b). Before studying the points made by these two oppositions, we need to understand what Matthew means by "believing" and, more specifically, by "believing John," a phrase repeated three times in 21:32. Because of its particular character, the second opposition will help us understand it.

The opposition that interweaves the parable and its explanation opposes the first son, who changed his mind and went (21:29), to the chief priests and the elders, who did not change their mind and thus "did not believe" (see 21:32b). The opposed actions are twofold. Changing one's mind is opposed to not changing one's mind; and going and doing (what the father asked) is opposed to not believing. This means that, for Matthew, believing is equivalent to going and doing (what the father asked). As we have observed about 21:25b, believing belongs to the category of actions, because, for Matthew, it is accepting a vocation. In this light, we can understand what the phrase "believing John" (21:32) means. Note that here John is not described as preaching—giving a command to which one could say yes or no. He is not identified with the father of the parable—actually, the "father" is God. Rather, the text says: "John came to you in the way of righteousness" (21:32a).[10] In other words, it is the worthiness of John's actions, his righteous behavior, which is emphasized; he is presented as a model of worthy behavior.[11] We therefore conclude that "believing John" means recognizing that his behavior is a model of righteousness, and accepting walking in the way of righteousness by patterning one's behavior according to his behavior which is authoritative. "Believing John" is to recognize what one's behavior should be—as the first son did when he changed his mind (21:29).[12]

When this is recognized we can understand how the explanation (21:31b–32) is related to the parable (21:28–31a). The opposition in 21:32a between those who "believed" and those who "did not believe" concerns people who either acted properly or did not—and not people who said either yes or no. In other words, the chief priests and the elders in 21:32a are like the second son, who said yes and did not go and work. As their very position as religious leaders shows, at first they said yes to God's command to go and work for him in his vineyard, Israel. But this work involved "believing John," accepting walking in the way of righteousness according to the model that John's behavior is. But they did not do so; they failed to do what they had promised to do. By contrast, the tax collectors and the prostitutes are like the first son. At first, they said no to God, refusing to work for him; they are tax collectors and prostitutes (evil people). But then they "believed John"; they recognized John as a model of righteousness and agreed to follow the way of righteousness: they not only repented (as John urged them to do, see 3:2) but also bore "fruit that befits repentance" (see 3:8), a condition that John required for baptizing people. Thus, doing what the Father asks involves recognizing in the behavior of other people (such as John) authoritative models of righteousness.[13]

But the explanation goes a step farther: "and even when you saw it [that tax collectors and prostitutes believed], you did not afterward repent and believe [John]" (21:32b). The chief priests and the elders are now contrasted with the first son, who repented (21:29). After their failure to do what God expected from them—a failure comparable to that of the second son—they had a second chance. This first failure is treated as if it were that of the first son—saying "no" to God. They still had the opportunity to repent. That tax collectors and prostitutes believed was another call to "believe John" and thus to change their mind. They should have perceived it and thus should have believed in John as the first son repented; but they did not. The point Matthew makes by opposing the first son (21:29) to the chief priests and the elders (21:32b) is that the latter did not even realize they had said no to God. They did not recognize that when the tax collectors and the prostitutes believed it was a call to repentance which God addressed to them and to which they refused to listen. This is why the tax collectors and the prostitutes who believed John will go into the kingdom before the chief priests and the elders.

The action (believing) of the tax collectors and the prostitutes is authoritative, as John's action—his baptism and walking in the way of righteousness—also is. Their "believing John" is an authoritative call to repentance that the chief priests and the elders should have heeded. Authority—from heaven—is so much linked with the actions of people (rather than with the persons) that even the actions of people as worthless as tax collectors and prostitutes can manifest such an authority and thus be authoritative. Consequently, authority from heaven is manifested not merely in Jesus' actions but also in the actions of John and of the tax collectors and prostitutes.

21:33–46. The Parable of the Wicked Tenants

We need to read the parable of the wicked tenants and its explanation in the light of the preceding points so as to elucidate how Matthew understood this passage[14] and what convictions he expresses through it. With the introductory "Hear another parable" (21:33a), Matthew presents it as a prolongation of the polemical dialogue between Jesus and the Jewish leaders who, as in 21:31, are invited to draw the conclusion of the parable (cf. 21:41) and thus to condemn themselves. Furthermore, the concluding verses of the pericope (21:45–46) state that the parable is about the "chief priests and the Pharisees."[15]

The theme of the parable is that a householder plants a vineyard and lets it out to a first group of tenants (21:33) and finally lets it out to other tenants (21:41b). Matthew expresses the theme in terms of his readers' presumed knowledge.[16] As is clear from the description of the planting of the vineyard in 21:33, which is a quasi-quotation of Isa. 5:2, Matthew expects his readers to know this prophetic text and to interpret the vineyard as a reference to Israel which has been planted with much caring love by God.[17] In this perspective, the parable is read as an allegory of the history of the relationship of God with his rebellious people and their leaders (the wicked tenants). This relationship becomes progressively worse as the servants (the prophets) repeatedly sent by God (21:35–36) are *beaten*, *killed*, and *stoned* (21:35). These three verbs express by their succession the aggravation of the situation; death by stoning is the worst. In this same perspective, the son who is finally sent, rejected, and killed (21:37–39) is Jesus, the Son of God. And the other tenants to whom the vineyard is let out (21:41) could be the Gentiles and thus the church[18]—*if the vineyard is then interpreted to be the kingdom* (cf. 21:43).

Notice, however, the tension created by this last verse. It can be interpreted in the way we just suggested only if one abandons the identification of the vineyard with Israel, which was the starting point and the basis for the above interpretation of the parable![19] This tension shows that the preceding interpretation is only one of several meanings of the parable. Matthew does expect his readers to understand the parable in the perspective of their old knowledge. But he also introduces in it his own perspective, his own convictions; these are the points which, for him, the parable makes in the context in which he chose to set it. Although he keeps exactly the same set of narrative oppositions that are in Mark 12:1–12, through them he makes different points, if for no other reason than to prolong the points made in Matt. 21:28–32.

21:34–35, 41, 43. The text first opposes what should have happened, the servants receiving the fruit (given to them by the tenants, 21:34), to what actually happened, the tenants beating, killing, and stoning the servants (21:35). This opposition is related to 21:41 (other tenants giving the owner the fruits in their season) and to 21:43 (the kingdom will be given to "a nation producing the fruits of it"). The point of this opposition is expressed by the contrast that it sets between the wicked tenants and the ideal tenants (as envisioned by the owner, and later described as "other tenants" and "a nation"). This point is related to the points found in 21:28–32. The servants are sent by the owner; consequently, by going to the tenants they do the will of the owner, God. This amounts to saying that the servants go to the tenants "in the way of righteousness" (21:32), as John did. The wicked tenants recognize that the servants are sent by the owner—since the text notes that they take "*his* servants" (21:35). Consequently, the tenants recognize that the servants come and act in the name and with the authority of the owner. But they nevertheless beat them and kill them. The tenants rebel against the owner, denying him any authority over them. But why? A first reason is clearly that they do not want to give fruits to the owner. They reject the owner's authority and suppress those who represent his authority, because they work for themselves. In the process, they deny that the possibility of working and having fruit has been given to them by the owner who has carefully planted the vineyard—the means through which fruit can be produced.

By contrast, ideal tenants would acknowledge the authority of the owner and thus of his servants. At "the season [time] of fruit" (see 21:34a), they produce fruits for the owner—both in the sense of exhibiting and giving the fruit to the owner (21:41) and in the sense of bearing fruit (21:43). This play on the English word "producing" (not present in the Greek) attempts to render what is expressed both by 21:41 and by 21:43, as well as to account for the ambiguity of the phrase "when the season [time] of fruit drew near" (21:34a). In Matthew's formulation, the servants are sent while it is not quite "the time of fruit." By this somewhat unrealistic feature of the story— the servants should have been sent "at the time of the fruit," harvesttime, not before—Matthew subtly leads the readers to take notice of the point he sees in this parable and further expresses in 21:43. The ideal tenants are supposed to produce fruit of the kingdom, bear fruit for the owner, *when the servants' coming* has shown them that it is "the time of fruit."[20] It then appears that Matthew understands the parable as unfolding the points made in 21:28–32. Note that in the parable of the two sons, the father says, "Son, go and work in the vineyard *today*" (21:28b). Similarly, the Jewish leaders were supposed to do the right thing (believing) *when* John came to them (21:32a) and *when* they saw that tax collectors and prostitutes believed (21:32b). In effect, the coming of someone walking "in the way of righteousness" (John, tax collectors and prostitutes, the servants) is to be perceived as an authoritative mandate to bear fruits of the kingdom (21:43).[21] It means that now is the time to bear fruit for the owner (or the kingdom).[22] This is what the wicked tenants—and the chief priests and the Pharisees— do not want to do. They refuse to acknowledge and submit to the authority of the owner because *now* they do not want to produce fruit for the owner/ God, that is, fruit of the kingdom.

21:37–38. The next opposition between what the owner says when sending his son (21:37) and what the tenants say about it (21:38) develops the preceding point further. It adds two new features. First, the rejection and killing of the son removes any possible ambiguity: the tenants do reject the owner's authority since they do not even respect his son. Second, it becomes clear that they do so because they want to appropriate the heritage for themselves. This also means that they do not want to work for the owner; they want to work *for themselves*.

21:35, 39, 41. Finally the parable opposes the tenants who killed the servants (21:35) and the son (21:39) to the owner who will kill the wicked tenants (21:41). The point of this opposition is that the wicked tenants have completely misjudged the situation and what would be good for them. Their project is totally futile and vain. Common sense should make them realize that their dream of keeping the fruit for themselves by killing the servants and of taking the heritage by killing the son can only result in their own destruction. Despite all their own wickedness, the chief priests and the Pharisees themselves can draw this conclusion of the parable!

21:42. In the quotation of Ps. 118:22–23, which follows as a first explanation of the parable, we find an opposition between the builders who rejected the stone and the Lord who made it become the cornerstone. The verb translated "rejected" means "rejected after evaluation" (*apodokimazō*), as a coin is rejected as valueless when it is recognized to be counterfeit. This means that the point made by this opposition concerns the ability to perceive the value of something or someone. The builders—and thus the wicked tenants as well as the chief priests and the Pharisees—are unable to recognize the value of the stone and reject it as valueless. By contrast, for the Lord and also for those who praise him in this psalm, the stone is of great value and can be used as the keystone of the building—"and it is marvelous in our eyes" (21:42b).

This point made by the text of Psalm 118 fits well with the rest of Matthew's points.[23] The problem with the wicked tenants, and with the chief priests and the Pharisees, is that they are unable to perceive what is simultaneously truly good for them (a useful stone) and worthy of honor—as the keystone is. Actually, they can recognize that the son, Jesus, is indeed the son of the owner, the Son of God, who therefore manifests the authority of God even more directly than the servants. Similarly, they can recognize that the servants, John, the tax collectors and prostitutes who repented, are walking "in the way of righteousness" and that they manifest the authority of God. But these manifestations of the authority of God do not have, for them, any value whatsoever and are therefore not worthy of honor. Ultimately, they fail to acknowledge God's authority. This is the same point that was made by the parable of the workers in the vineyard (see 20:15), but this time it concerns the issue of the acceptance or rejection of God's authority rather than God's goodness. Although they can draw the conclusion that the tenants' project was futile because they acknowledge the destructive power of God which will be manifested at the judgment (21:41), the chief priests and the Pharisees do not acknowledge and accept God's goodness and authority as manifested in his Son, because they do not know and understand Scripture (21:42a).

21:45–46. It is against their own best judgment therefore that they reject the Son, Jesus, whom they perceive as a threat to them and who speaks against them (21:45). They want to arrest him (21:46). They, who have just condemned the wicked tenants, want to do what the wicked tenants did. But for the time being they are prevented from doing so by the crowds who, despite their limitation, perceive in Jesus someone sent by God, a prophet (21:46b). When we read that the chief priests and the Pharisees "feared the multitudes," we need to recall 21:26 where the same phrase is used. Once again, it is because they are afraid of losing their own authority over the people that they act as they do—although, in the present case, the result is positive; they do not arrest Jesus.[24]

22:1–14. The Parable of the Marriage Feast

Jesus' discourse to the chief priests and the Pharisees continues with the telling of a third parable, the first part (22:1–10) of which is similar to the preceding one.[25] As in the parable of the wicked tenants (21:33–41), the first called (the first tenants, the invited guests) end up being last, excluded (cf. 20:13–16).[26] In both cases, the privileged people, tenants and invited guests, do not want to do something that is requested by a person in authority (owner or king) through his servants who are then mistreated and killed; these privileged people are excluded (from the vineyard in which they were or from the wedding feast they never entered), and their place is taken by other people (other tenants, new guests). But then, the parable of the wedding feast adds a new and surprising dimension: one of the new guests is also excluded (22:11–14).

This break in the pattern runs so much against the readers' expectations and seems so out of place—how can a person brought into the wedding hall from the street be expected to have a wedding garment?—that one might be tempted to discount these last verses. Yet, as we have repeatedly noted, such tensions signal that at such places in the text Matthew conveys major points (convictions) that are surprising for the readers because they involve a view unknown to them—a view that Matthew strives to convey to them. In brief, the concluding verses, 22:11–14, should be considered an integral part of Matthew's parable; they express its main point.[27]

22:2–3. The points expressed by the first series of oppositions can be readily understood since they develop those presented in 21:33–46. The text first opposes, on the one hand, the servants calling the invited guests who are asked to go "to the marriage feast" (22:3a)—ideal invited guests should go—and, on the other hand, the fact that they do not go (22:3b). The contrast is between the ideal and the actual invited guests. As the text underscores, the latter *do not want* to go. While it is not explained here why they do not want to go, the text suggests why they should. First, they are called by servants who do so in the name and with the authority of the king. Yet they are not ordered to go. What they should do is not imposed upon them, as would be the case if they were commanded to do it. They are left free to make up their own minds. But it is fully expected that they would go because of the character of the invitation. They are invited by a king to the "marriage feast of his son" (22:2). They are honored by the king who chose to ask them to come and share in his joy; they are the privileged group of "those who were invited" (22:3a). Thus they should *want* to go. Conversely, responding to such an invitation is what they should do in order to honor the father of the bridegroom and because they respect him. They should voluntarily pay homage to the king and acknowledge the honor and privilege he bestowed upon them by inviting them. By not wanting to go, the invited guests show that they do not view such an invitation as an honor or privilege. They deny the superior status of the one who invited them, and thus his authority as king.[28]

As we have repeatedly noted in the Gospel (see chap. 2), the proper kind of authority—such as Jesus' and God's authority—is not manifested by a demonstration of power. The king does not give a command. True authority is, rather, manifested in the form of an invitation to a marriage feast, in the form of a privilege, an honor, bestowed upon people who are then expected to accept it and to respond to it. And if they recognize this invitation for what it truly is, they should want to respond positively to it. Why would they refuse to be honored? The invited guests cannot recognize that such an invitation is an honor bestowed upon them.

22:4–5. The second opposition is again between the ideal invited guests, who should "come to the marriage feast" (22:4b) according to the second invitation by the servants, but who instead "went off" to their farm or business (22:5). The point appears when one takes note of what the servants are asked to say to the invited guests: "Behold, I have made ready my dinner, my oxen and my fat calves are killed, and everything is ready" (22:4). Although they have not recognized that the invitation was an honor bestowed upon them, surely they will want to come if it is pointed out that good food has been prepared. It is a great feast, and they will enjoy it! But the invited guests are totally indifferent (RSV: "they made light of it," 22:5a). They have better things to do. Taking care of their own farm or business is more important for them.[29] The invited guests fail to recognize at its just value the goodness of the feast prepared for them by the king.

The good that they prepare for themselves through their own work in their farm or business is incomparably better than any good the king might have to offer them, so much so that the feast appears to them as totally valueless.

The point that Matthew makes here is particularly important. For Matthew, the basic cause of "hardness of heart" and "bad eye"—what prevents one from accepting the kingdom and entering it—is the lack of recognition (and thus of acceptance) of the goodness of God (see my comments on 20:15). Now, the indifference toward God's goodness is shown to be the result of the false conviction and illusion that what one can obtain for oneself by one's own work is the greatest good one can expect. While this point has been implied in previous passages, here for the first time it is stated clearly.

22:6–7. These verses oppose the invited guests who kill the servants (22:6) to the king's troops who kill those murderers (22:7). Those who do not recognize the goodness of the feast offered by the king are people who, when they are not engaged in their own business, engage in senseless, unjustified violence. They seize, mistreat, and kill the servants who, in the name of the king, were not doing them any harm but were actually graciously offering them something good. This violence can only mean that the servants and the goodness of the feast that they offer are perceived by the invited guests not only as valueless but also as a threat, as something that might destroy them and what has ultimate value for them (the good that they pursue for themselves by their work). By construing the goodness of the king as a threat and by becoming "murderers," they bring upon themselves the destructive anger of the king. And this anger cannot be escaped since the king has "troops" and the destruction will engulf their city (in fire). Their senseless violence shows them to be totally unable to distinguish between real and imaginary threats of destruction.

22:8. The comment that the invited guests were "not worthy" is to be taken as a summary of all that precedes. People are "not worthy" when they recognize neither the honor the king bestows upon them nor the goodness of what he offers them; they deny both the authority and goodness of the king.

22:9–13. But the marriage feast and all its good food (oxen, fat calves) remain ready (22:8a); they are available for other guests. The conclusion, 22:9–14, describes what happens when the wedding hall is filled with people who were not originally invited. The point of these verses is expressed through the opposition of the king who addresses a question to a guest without a wedding garment (22:12a) and the guest who remains speechless (22:12b). For Matthew, the king's question and his subsequent action are justified. For some reason (here, the lack of a wedding garment) this new guest is "not worthy," as the invited guests were; he is condemned (22:13) as they were. This suggests that what is wrong with the new guest and with the invited guests is similar. But the text allows us to be more specific.

As the first guests were, so the new guests are people whom the king's servants "call [to come] to the marriage feast" (22:9, au.), even though they are not "invited" guests but rather whomever the servants can find in "the thoroughfares" (22:9a). They are not select people, but people of all kinds, "bad and good" (22:10). According to the king's order to call to the marriage feast "as many as you find" (22:9), the servants "gathered all whom they found" (22:10). Yet the servants do not simply round up people and bring them to the wedding hall whether they want to come or not. The text makes clear that the servants follow the king's order. Therefore the people they gather are those who respond positively to their call to come to the marriage feast. "Many are called" (see 22:14a), and many respond positively. But why are they responding and going to the wedding hall?

According to the first part of the parable, there are two reasons for accepting the invitation to come to the marriage feast (see 22:2–3; 22:4–5). One might want to accept the invitation either because one is honored by it and wants to honor the king (see 22:2–3), or because one wants to partake in the good food of the feast offered by the generous and good host (see 22:4–5). When this is kept in mind, it appears that to wear a "wedding garment" is to honor the king in response to the honor of being invited. In other words, a guest without a wedding garment is a person who accepted the invitation to come to the marriage feast because it is the occasion to enjoy a good, indeed a great, meal. Those who go to the marriage feast for this reason recognize and acknowledge that there will be good food and that the king gives good things and is generous. In brief, they acknowledge the goodness of the king, an acknowledgment that finds expression in an action (going to the marriage feast).

Such an acknowledgment of the goodness of God is a *necessary* condition for overcoming "hardness of heart" and "bad eye," which prevent participation in the kingdom (see the comments on 19:1—20:16). But the point of the parable and of 21:18—22:14 is that acknowledging the goodness of God is *not sufficient*. One also needs to acknowledge the *authority* of God, an acknowledgment that finds expression in an attitude (wearing a wedding garment) that is different from the attitude of simply acknowledging his goodness. Without such an acknowledgment of God's authority and the will to honor him as motivation for one's actions, no participation in the kingdom (now and in the future) is possible. One is cast "into the outer darkness" where people "will weep and gnash their teeth" (22:13).

22:14. "For many are called, but few are chosen." This conclusion broadens the scope of the parable. The guest without a garment is not an exception, as the parable might lead one to think. The king's coming into the wedding hall "to look at the guests" (22:11) is not so much aimed at excluding unworthy people but at choosing those who are worthy to remain. This election is actually the second step of a two-step process. First, servants are calling people to the marriage feast, inviting them to come as an acknowledgment of both the authority and goodness of the king. People ignore and reject this call, especially those who are part of the select group who were first invited. Others readily accept it, especially the common people, those who are in particular need of God's goodness (e.g., children; cf. 19:13–15). Then the king himself comes and chooses among those who have accepted the call of the servants. Those who are ultimately chosen and not excluded are those who acknowledge the king's authority as well as his goodness and demonstrate it by their behavior.

Acknowledging God's authority is the necessary condition for ultimate participation in the kingdom and thus for benefiting from his goodness. For this, however, one needs to recognize, as Matthew pointed out in 21:18–46, that God is the only one who has authority. All others, including the Son, are authoritative only insofar as their actions are authoritative—that is, if these actions are performed in the name of God.

NOTES ON 21:18—22:14

1. The temptation story (4:1–11) raises the question of the proper use of power by Jesus as Son of God, just as 21:18–19 raises the question of the proper use of power by Jesus, who has just been designated as Son of David.

2. Against BONNARD, 311.

3. With Edwards, *Matthew's Story*, 74.

4. Note that we are led by the text to view "believing in John" as an attitude, to be classified with actions. This is what people do, by contrast with what they say. It is so because, for Matthew, believing is accepting a vocation, that is, accepting doing something. This observation will be confirmed by the use of "believing John" in 21:32 as a parallel to "doing" in the parable of the two sons (21:28–31a).

5. With Tolbert (*Perspectives*, 77), who sees the opposition as a fundamental component of the parable's formal plot structure.

6. I follow here, for the readers' convenience, the RSV which, with most recent translations, is based on the text found in certain good manuscripts. But other manuscripts, equally good, have a text in which the order of the sons is reversed: the first son says he will go and does not, while the second says he will not go but does. I would argue that this second form of the text is the original text of Matthew because of its consistence with the semantic and discursive organization of the context. Yet I would agree with Tolbert that the original form of the parable (i.e., the parable apart from the context of Matthew's Gospel) is the form used in the translations, as Tolbert demonstrates convincingly by considering it in terms of "parallel plot type." See Tolbert, *Perspectives*, 130.

7. With TRILLING, 189–90.

8. One should also note that the second son addresses his father as "lord," a designation that at once expresses the recognition of his authority but also a certain lack of personal involvement: he simply acknowledges that he will go because his father as authority figure, "lord," ordered him to do so. By contrast, the first son, despite his refusal, acknowledges that his father's request demands a personal involvement, making his father's desire his own will. Thus, the second son reminds us of the teaching found in the Sermon on the Mount: "Not every one who says

to me, 'Lord, Lord,' shall enter the kingdom of heaven, but he who does the will of my Father who is in heaven" (7:21).

9. Even though the verb translated "he repented" is *metamelomai* in 21:28 rather than *metanoeō* as in 3:2, an additional reference to John the Baptist in 21:32 makes it probable that Matthew expected his readers to identify "changing one's mind" and "repenting."

10. See STRECKER, 187, who draws the title of his book from this passage.

11. With STRECKER, 187.

12. We could also say, with BONNARD, 313, that here, "believing John" and "repenting" are almost synonymous.

13. See TRILLING, 188, who notes that the "will of God" implies the strongly theocentric direction of all human activity. The basic direction of ethics goes toward God, the Father.

14. As usual, our only concern is to show how Matthew understood the parable rather than to attempt to elucidate its original meaning.

15. In spite of the change of name, this is the same group as precedently: for Matthew, "the Pharisees" are "the elders of the people." We noted that this latter designation was used in 21:23 in order to indicate that they were religious authorities.

16. In this part of the text, despite the appearances, there is no (formal) narrative opposition. Indeed, letting out the vineyard to the first tenants(21:33) cannot be viewed as negative or wrong—it is the subsequent behavior of the tenants which is negative!—and, consequently, it cannot be opposed to letting out the vineyard to other tenants (21:41).

17. SCHWEIZER, 413–14, notes that, as compared with the version of the parable in Mark 12:1–12, Matthew has emphasized the features that suggest such a reading of the parable.

18. So SCHWEIZER, 414, and GUNDRY, 429.

19. The great diversity of interpretations of 21:41 by commentators who have more or less followed the suggested line of interpretation for the rest of the parable demonstrates the difficulties the readers have with this verse. See BONNARD, 316–17.

20. Dillon believes that "the pairing of the *statement* of the present reality of sacred history with an *exhortation* to bear its fruits is indication of a fundamental tension in Christian consciousness, viz. between the realities of *calling* and of *task*, between the *indicative* and the *imperative* of divine election." See Dillon, "Tradition History," *Biblica* 47 (1966): 34.

21. As the people during John's ministry had to "bear fruit that befits repentance" (3:8).

22. The "time of fruit" should not therefore be identified with the time of the eschatological judgment, as Bonnard suggests by interpreting this phrase in terms of 13:30. See BONNARD, 315.

23. There are here images from a "royal theology." But this is not the main point for Matthew. Against Nolan, "The Heir Unapparent," *Proceedings of the IBA* 4 (1980): 84–95.

24. While noting its audience (i.e., the chief priests and the Pharisees) in the text, Matthean scholars tend to be preoccupied with how this parable defines the "new Israel" over against the "old Israel." For instance, see TRILLING, 55–65, and Frankemölle, *Jahwebund*, 247–56. They propose insightful analyses of the way in which this parable socializes its Matthean communal audience to the continuities and discontinuities of its identity as the new people of God, and the ethical obligation to bear fruit. While all this is true, these analyses do not show how Matthew mediates this socialization of the new people through the function of the parable in the polemic between Jesus and the Jewish leaders.

25. See Dillon, "Tradition History," 5.

26. This observation about the first and the last also applies to the parable of the two sons if its original Matthean form is that of the manuscripts in which the first son is the one who says yes and does not go. This is one of the reasons that makes me believe that this version is the original one (see above, n. 6).

27. Against Via (*Parables*, 129) and most other commentators, who see these verses as a separate parable inappropriately joined to the wedding banquet parable, and thus an indication of pre-Matthean traditions. Via seems to dismiss the tradition-critical evidences for the Matthean language and provenance of 22:11–13, adduced by Barth, "Matthew's Understanding of the Law," 59–60, n. 9.

28. Via emphasizes the general issue of the guests' misinterpretation of the contextual situation. But he does not locate it specifically in the misinterpretation of the goodness of the king's authoritative status, as we do by examining the oppositions closely. See Via, *Parables*, 131.

29. In the Greek text this point is clearer than in the RSV translation. The phrase translated "[they] went off, one to his farm" (22:5) can be more literally rendered "[they] went off, one to his *own* farm."

WHOSE SON IS THE CHRIST?

THE MAIN THEME

In the preceding section (21:18—22:14), Matthew has underscored that God alone has true power and authority and thus that the Son of David should not be viewed as having power and authority in and of himself. It is God's power that the Son of David uses and God's authority that he manifests. In this new section (22:15–46), Matthew clarifies this view of the Messiah and his authority by presenting a series of scenes in which Jesus demonstrates the authority of his teaching by silencing all his Jewish opponents—Herodians, Sadducees, and Pharisees.

The theme of this relatively brief section is posited by the statements of the disciples of the Pharisees: "Teacher, we know that you are true, and teach the way of God truthfully" (22:16). This section concerns the authority of Jesus' teaching. Yet Matthew warns the readers that the Pharisees' statement, despite its positive character, is not trustworthy. He first mentions that their goal is to trap ("entangle") Jesus (22:15) and then notes that Jesus is "aware of their malice" and that they are "hypocrites" (22:18). Consequently, the readers are led to ask the question: What is the proper understanding of Jesus as a teacher, he who has been designated by the trustworthy children as the Son of David (21:15)? The answer is provided in 22:41–45: the Son of David is also the "Lord" of David.

This answer makes sense only when one notices that Matthew develops this theme through a succession of four confrontations with the Jews. In the first three, the Jews seek to trap or test Jesus by asking him to address controversial issues: that of the Roman tax (22:15–22), of the resurrection (22:23–32), and of the "great commandment," the one that expresses the essence of the law (22:33–40). In the fourth, it is Jesus who asks the no less controversial question regarding the Messiah: "Whose son is he?" (22:41–46). At first these four confrontations appear to be simply juxtaposed with each other, a collection of teachings about controversial issues. But since Matthew presents them together,[1] we can be sure he sees a relation among them. For him, all of them develop the same point, namely, that the role of God's authority and power in human affairs must be accounted for if one wants to reach a proper understanding of the issues raised about Roman tax, the resurrection, Scripture and the "great commandment," and the Messiah, Son of David.

MATTHEW'S CONVICTIONS IN 22:15–46

22:15–22. Render to Caesar What Is Caesar's and to God What Is God's

The interpretation of this pericope depends on the way it is read. Should the statements of the disciples of the Pharisees (22:16–17) and of Jesus (in 22:21) be understood at face value or as ironical? By considering the perspective that the text asks the readers to adopt, we conclude that these statements are ironical.

22:16–17. The opening words of the disciples of the Pharisees, "Teacher, we know that you are true . . ." are clearly flattering. They acknowledge that Jesus' teaching is truthful because it is characterized by the integrity that comes from teaching "the way of God truthfully" without allowing anyone to influence one's teaching (22:16). For disciples of the Pharisees, this is the highest compliment one can pay a teacher. Yet these words are uttered by people who intend to trap Jesus. Furthermore, for the readers, the beginning of their question—"Tell us, then, what you think" (22:17a)— is full of irony. They use the very phrase that Jesus used to entrap the Jews in 21:28 (cf. 21:31, 40)! How could they imagine they would be successful in turning the very stratagem against Jesus that he used to make them condemn themselves! Then it appears that their flattering description of Jesus as truthful teacher should be taken with a grain of salt. First, they do not really believe that Jesus is such an excellent teacher. Furthermore, such a description of Jesus' teaching is based upon *their own view* of an excellent teacher, a dubious viewpoint. Thus these words about Jesus as teacher are certainly both true and false; they certainly involve a misrepresentation of Jesus' actual teaching.

22:21. Similarly, Jesus' teaching about the Roman tax is to be read as an ironical statement. This is shown by the fact that Matthew presents it just after the parable of the wedding feast. According to this parable, this acknowledgment of God's authority involves leaving aside one's own possessions and one's means of gaining them (farm and business, see 22:5).[2] Such an acknowledgment is a prerequisite for participating in the kingdom. In this light, for the readers, Jesus' statement "Render therefore to Caesar the things that are Caesar's, and to God the things that are God's" (22:21) can only be understood as an ironical response to an ironical question (22:17). Giving "to God the things that are God's" (22:21b) is nothing else than to acknowledge God's authority and honor him by one's life. In such a case, one renounces other allegiances, including one's allegiance to one's possessions. In paying taxes to the Romans one acknowledges that Caesar has authority, but limits Caesar's authority to the things upon which his image and his inscription are stamped: Roman coins such as a denarius, things that by comparison with the kingdom (the feast) are valueless. And thus, why not give "to Caesar the things that are Caesar's"!³

22:16–19. The point Matthew makes by this pericope is understood when one notes that the irony of Jesus' response is not directed against Caesar but against the disciples of the Pharisees and the Herodians (22:16), two groups in favor of paying taxes to the Romans. In short, the point of this pericope is expressed by the polemical dialogue (22:16, 18) which contrasts Jesus and his opponents. The latter are presented as "disciples" of the Pharisees who call Jesus "teacher," who affirm that they know that Jesus teaches truthfully the way of God because he teaches without allowing people to influence him, and who question him about what is lawful (22:16–17a). It is thus clear that Matthew is concerned with the kind of knowledge Jesus' opponents claim to have ("we know") and not to have (their question). By contrast, Jesus is "aware of their malice" (22:18). For him, the response to their question is not to be found by calling upon a previously received knowledge but by examining what is used to pay the tax (22:19).⁴ In brief, a valid knowledge of what is good or bad is based upon an evaluation of the interrelationship among people. Thus Jesus knows that his interlocutors are "bad." Valid knowledge also concerns whether or not an action denies God's authority and is based upon what is involved in the action.

22:16–17. The Pharisees have an incorrect view of Jesus as teacher because they believe he bases his teaching on "the way of God" viewed as an abstraction. For them such a teaching is "true," valid, when it is kept separate from one's relationship with people—caring for no one and not regarding the position of people (22:16). But this is a complete misunderstanding of Jesus' teaching. By his response⁵ he demonstrates that his teaching does take into consideration to whom he speaks—whether they are good or bad people. Similarly, rather than asserting what is right or wrong in the form of an ever valid truth (what is "lawful," 22:17), he asks people to discern whether or not an action is valid by examining what is concretely involved in that action, so as to understand whether or not it would prevent one from honoring God. Jesus' teaching—a "situation teaching"—is so different from the view that the disciples of the Pharisees had of it that, "when they heard it, they marveled" (22:22).

Why is it not appropriate to teach "the way of God" in abstraction from concrete situations? On the basis of 22:15–22 we can already answer that it is so because in such a case one ignores the place of God's authority in the present situation. The next pericope (22:23–32) suggests that such an attitude also involves denying the role of God's power in the present situation.

22:23–32. God Is Not God of the Dead
But of the Living[6]

In the debate between Jesus and the Sadducees about the resurrection from the dead, Matthew makes a complex point. While the oppositions are the same as those in Mark 12:18–27, in this context they express a specifically Matthean point.[7]

There are two interwoven oppositions. The polemical dialogue opposes the Sadducees' saying (22:24–28) *and* Jesus' saying (22:29–32). In addition, the Sadducees "who say that there is no resurrection" (22:23) are opposed to "what was said to you by God" (22:31b), namely, "I am the God of Abraham, and the God of Isaac, and the God of Jacob" (22:32, a quotation from Exod. 3:6),[8] a statement which the text claims to be a reference to the resurrection.

22:24, 29. Jesus' first response expresses what is at stake in this passage: "You are wrong, because you know neither the scriptures nor the power of God" (22:29). In what sense do the Sadducees misunderstand Scripture? How is this related to the Pharisees' misunderstanding of Jesus' teaching (22:15–22)? In what sense do they misunderstand the power of God? And how are these two misunderstandings related?

Jesus' opponents again do not understand Scripture (see most recently 21:16, 42). But what is incorrect in their understanding of Scripture? It is only after a careful reading of the pericope that we will be able to find the answer to this question. In 22:29 the text simply indicates that it is incorrect to interpret what Moses said about levirate marriage (or brother-in-law's marriage) as a proof that there is no resurrection. Furthermore, the words in Matt. 22:24 are hardly a quotation of either Gen. 38:8 or Deut. 25:5.[9] This law is rather a free formulation of what is expressed in the scriptural texts. By phrasing the Sadducees' words in this way, Matthew begins to express the point that is more directly expressed in other verses.[10]

22:23, 31–32. There is something else the Sadducees do not know: the power of God. They do not believe in the resurrection (22:23), against what God says in Scripture (22:31–32). This is clearly one of the main points. What is "the power of God" that they are ignoring, and how is it manifested for Matthew?

Matthew's point about the power of God is expressed through the opposition between the Sadducees' statement and Jesus' response. The opposition becomes clear when we identify the issues about which there is disagreement. Beside the issue of the resurrection itself, there is a disagreement about what will be the relationship between women and men "in the resurrection." The Sadducees presuppose that it will be the same as it is now, and thus that marriage will still govern the relationship of women and men. But in their example the woman would be simultaneously married with each of the seven brothers (22:28)—a situation that is impossible according to the law of Moses and proves for them that there is no resurrection. For Jesus, the Sadducees misconstrue the relationship of women and men in the resurrection; then they will be "like angels in heaven" and will not marry (22:30). This means that the Sadducees have ignored that God has the power of transforming the relationship between women and men by making them like angels. The main effect of God's power is that it makes it unnecessary to marry: "For in the resurrection they neither marry nor are given in marriage" (22:30a).

22:24–28. The abolition of the need for marriage is thus a major manifestation of the power of God. But how is it related to the resurrection? The answer lies in 22:24–28. For the Sadducees, marriage is exclusively described as the means of having children. This is the goal of the levirate marriage law which aims at ensuring that a man who dies without children will nevertheless have descendants. By marrying the widow, the brother will "raise up children for his brother" (22:24b). In this view, a man (either the first husband or one of his brothers) and his power to procreate are necessary in order to have descendants. For them, it is exclusively through human power (to procreate) that one can hope to have descendants. The abolition of the need for marriage would be for the Sadducees the abolition of the very means to have descendants—for them this is unthinkable. Thus they cannot believe in the resurrection because levirate marriage, and marriage in general, would not have any place in it.

For Matthew, such a view ignores the power of God, a point he makes by playing on words. According to Matthew's formulation, the brother must marry the widow in order to "raise up children for his [dead] brother" (22:24b). In so doing, Matthew uses the verb "to raise up" (*anistēmi*), which refers to "resurrection" (*anastasis*).[11] In other words, the raising of the dead (cf. 22:31a) performed by God is taking the place of the raising up of children for a dead man performed by a man. We could say that the power of God as manifested in the resurrection will ensure somebody's survival, the very thing that levirate marriage aimed at ensuring through the human power to procreate.

22:31–32. The rest of Jesus' answer means that, because of the way in which the text of Exod. 3:6 is formulated, one should conclude that Abraham, Isaac, and Jacob are "living" and not dead (22:32b). But Jesus' words also mean that in the patriarchs the "raising" power of God is (and was) manifested.[12] The mention of Abraham and of *his descendants*, Isaac and Jacob, is not without relation to the effort to ensure descendants for a dead brother (22:24). Furthermore, the reader is reminded of the genealogy which opened the Gospel (1:2–16). The genealogy made the point that it was not only through human procreation that Abraham's descendants were ensured.

The power of God was also at work so as to ensure the succession of generations.

In sum, Matthew's first point is that the power of God, which the Sadducees ignore, is both the power to raise the dead, which will be manifested at the resurrection, and the power to raise children for people. This power was operative in the past and is operative in the present, either in conjunction with human power to procreate (1:2–16a) or independent from it (1:16b, 18–25).[13] The Sadducees deny the power of God. For them, only human beings have the power to ensure the continuance of their "seeds" (RSV: "children" for *sperma* in 22:24b and 25).

The point about Scripture can now be understood. The Sadducees misinterpret Scripture because they fail to hear what it says about the power of God. They fail to understand that God was at work in the history of the descendants of Abraham that Scripture tells. Since they do not recognize the role of God's power in human affairs, they view the law as the only important medium of God's activity in Scripture. For them, the commandments are God's will for people which express what they, and they alone, *can do* for themselves. Although they acknowledge the limitations of human power and ability—six brothers fail to raise up children for their dead brother—nevertheless they do not envision that God might intervene directly.[14]

22:33–40. The Great Commandment

The exchange between the lawyer and Jesus regarding the "great commandment" could easily be construed as amicable.[15] Jesus does not appear to challenge the validity of the lawyer's question. But Matthew clearly signals that this is a polemical dialogue since he notes that the lawyer was testing Jesus (22:35).[16] Thus there is an opposition between a lawyer (a Pharisee) and what he says (22:34–36) *and* Jesus and his response (22:37–40). In the lawyer's question, "Teacher, which is the great commandment in the law?" (22:36), something is wrong. But what? The point Matthew makes by this opposition will appear when the lawyer's question is understood in terms of the context in which it is set.

22:33–34. Since the question is intended to "test," or tempt, Jesus, the description of the Pharisees in 22:34 suggests hostility to Jesus. That they "came together" (*synagō*, 22:34b) suggests that they are plotting against Jesus as in 22:15. Furthermore, their reaction to the news that Jesus has silenced the Sadducees (22:34a) can only appear to be negative by contrast with the positive response of the crowds (22:33). Against the traditional view of the Pharisees as being in discord with the Sadducees, a view that Matthew's readers might have had, Matthew describes the two groups as united against Jesus.[17] In the present context, this means that the Pharisees reject Jesus' preceding teaching and take sides with the Sadducees. In order to understand what is wrong in the lawyer's question, we therefore need to clarify how the two preceding pericopes are related to the polemical dialogue about the great commandment.

In the discussion about the Roman tax (22:15–22), the Pharisees have been presented as not knowing how to distinguish what is good from what is bad, what would honor God from what would deny his authority. This is so because they viewed "the way of God" as an abstraction totally removed from human affairs. It then appears that the Pharisees' view is closely related to the Sadducees' view of life which denies the role of God's power in human affairs (22:23–28). This is why Matthew describes the two groups as united. The Sadducees also fail to recognize the role of God's power in Scripture and in the history of the descendants of Abraham. For them, the law is the central part of Scripture; it expresses "the way of God." For them, the law expresses not merely what people should do, but also what people are alone able to do for themselves. In holding such a view they implicitly deny the role of God's power. In brief, according to these two pericopes, both the Pharisees and the Sadducees acknowledge the authority of the law over human affairs; it is "the way of God," the way to have a good life by doing for oneself and others what is good. But, for them, the authority of the law is so great that any interpretation of it influenced by consideration for people and concrete situations is a denial of its divine authority. God's way must be carried out in human affairs, but human affairs must not affect God's way which remains immutable. God's way and human ways have to remain distinct, separated. For the Pharisees, and the Sadducees, the law delimits a human realm where the way of God needs to be implemented by people who are then fully in charge of their destiny. For them, the human realm is separated from God's realm; it is a realm in which people have to rely on their own power (as the Sadducees do).

22:36–40. Is this such a wrong view of the law which is implied by the lawyer who tests Jesus by asking: "Teacher, which is the great commandment in the law?" (22:36)? An examination of Jesus' response shows that it is. First, note that Matthew emphasizes the close relationship of the commandment to love the Lord God (quoted from Deut. 6:5)[18] and the commandment to love one's neighbor (Lev. 19:18).[19] Actually, they are on equal footing; the second is "like" the first one (Matt. 22:39a), that is, both similar to it and equal in importance with it. They are not separable. Together, they are the "great commandment":[20] "On these two commandments depend all the law and the prophets" (22:40). Yet these two commandments remain distinct. They should not be identified with each other. Loving God should not be reduced to loving one's neighbor! Loving God is an act of love distinct from loving one's neighbor, and vice versa.

The correlation of these two commandments expresses that one's relationship with God and with one's neighbor are similar. As one should love

God with one's whole being—"with all your heart, and with all your soul, and with all your mind" (22:37)—so one should love one's neighbor as oneself (22:39). By emphasizing the relation between the two commandments, Matthew indicates that, for Jesus, people can be in relationship with God as they are in relationship with their neighbors. In other words, God should not be viewed as distant, separated from human beings as the Pharisees and the Sadducees assumed according to 22:15–33. On the contrary, even though he is "the Lord," he is as close as one's neighbor (Greek: *plēsion* means "close by"). God is involved in the human realm as a neighbor is. Thus one can be in the same relationship—love—with God as with one's neighbor.

What is Matthew's point? The Pharisees (and the Sadducees) totally misconstrue the relationship between God and human beings. For them there are two separate realms and thus one's relationship with God cannot be compared with one's relationship with one's neighbor.[21] By contrast, for Jesus these two relationships are alike, and thus God is present ("close by") with human beings as the neighbor who shares someone's daily life. In the same way that the life of their neighbor is necessarily interwoven with their life and necessarily affects it, so it is with God's involvement in their life. The twofold commandment demands that they acknowledge the participation of God and of their neighbor in their life and that they participate in this relationship with their whole being by loving both God and their neighbor.

Finally, note that this twofold commandment is not merely "the great commandment in the law" about which the lawyer inquired (22:36): "On these two commandments depend [or hang] all the law and the prophets" (22:40).[22] This statement underscores that the law should not be isolated from the rest of Scripture, as the lawyer as well as the Pharisees and the Sadducees did.[23] Separating the law from the prophets amounts to separating God from human beings, and thus denying his involvement in human affairs.

22:41–46. Whose Son Is the Christ?

22:46. Matthew's concluding points in the section that began in 22:15 are to be understood in terms of the preceding comments on 22:15–40. Note that while the Pharisees unsuccessfully tried to trap Jesus by asking him "What do you think?" (cf. 22:17), it is now Jesus who addresses this question to the Pharisees (22:42). In so doing, he silences them once and for all: they were unable to answer his second question, and from that day no one dared "to ask him any more questions" (22:46).

The question concerns the Christ: "Whose son is he?" (22:42a). In the exchange that follows between the Pharisees and Jesus, Matthew sets up two oppositions. First, what the Pharisees say about the Christ, he is "the son of David" (22:42b), is opposed to what David says about him, he "calls him Lord" (22:43, 45). The point is clear. The Pharisees' understanding of the Christ as son of David is somehow incorrect because, contrary to David, they are not "inspired by the Spirit" (22:43). The Pharisees have an exclusively human knowledge, one that people have when they are "gathered together" (22:41) and thus that they receive from each other. Consequently, as the Sadducees did in 22:23–28, they think of descendance (the Christ) strictly in terms of human procreation and lineage; consequently, the Christ is "the son of David." By contrast, David is inspired by the Spirit. In such a case, one takes into account the involvement of the divine in human affairs. From this perspective, the Christ is no longer exclusively perceived in terms of human lineage. One also recognizes the authority of the Christ—the authority as Lord that he receives from God.[24] As the quotation from Ps. 110:1[25] in Matt. 22:44 shows, it is the Lord (God) who bestows the authority of Lord to the Christ ("my Lord") by making him sit at his right hand.

The second opposition, between what Jesus says to the Pharisees in 22:43–45 and the Pharisees who are unable to answer him (22:46), clarifies this point. Jesus does not deny that the Christ is son of David. This is not the issue. His questions are: "How is it then" that he is the Lord of David? (22:43); and "how is he his son?" (22:45). The question concerns *what makes it possible* for the Christ to be both Lord of David and son of David. The Pharisees do not know the answer to this twofold question because they do not take into account the "prophets." This is shown by the description of Ps. 110:1 as a saying of "David, inspired by the Spirit," that is, as a scriptural text that is to be understood as a *prophecy*. And it is this prophecy which reveals the role of the divine in human affairs. It is because God intervenes and bestows authority to the Christ that he is simultaneously Lord of David and son of David. As expressed in 22:15–40, the Pharisees, however, ignore the role of God in human affairs. For them, God's relationship with human beings is limited to the giving of the law. They ignore the prophets and thus do not recognize that the "law and the prophets" are summarized in the twofold commandment which shows that God is as close to people as their neighbors are (22:40). And thus they are unable to answer Jesus' question.

The Jewish leaders are silenced by Jesus (22:46). They do not dare to ask him any more questions. From their perspective, each of their preceding questions was a trap because it was dilemma without a clear-cut answer. They expected, therefore, that Jesus would entangle himself by answering their questions—alienating each time a part of his audience. But Jesus showed them that each dilemma can easily be resolved when one takes into account the role of God in human affairs. And since any objection to such affirmations would be a denial of God and of his power, they are silenced.

NOTES ON 22:15–46

1. Throughout this section Matthew closely follows Mark 12:13–37. Yet he did not hesitate to transform the text he found in Mark so as to make his own points.

He chose to keep these pericopes together because they express his own convictions which he makes sure to convey by modifying Mark's text in key passages.

2. Because one needs to acknowledge simultaneously the goodness of God.

3. One should not seek in this pericope a complete doctrine of the relationship between church and state. The ironical character of the Matthean form of this saying prevents such an interpretation, whatever might have been its original point (possibly a statement against the Zealots who refused to pay taxes, and thus a rejection of their totally negative view of the state; cf. Bornkamm, *Jesus*, 120–24). See BONNARD, 322–23.

4. In Jesus' order "Show me the money," the verb (*epideiknumi*) suggests that the coin should be shown for the purpose of being examined with the expectation that it would provide the evidence (as in a court proceeding).

5. As we noted in the comments on 21:18—22:14, Jesus' authority is shown in his actions, and here in the manner of his response to his opponents. In this sense, we agree with Beilner that Jesus does not speak about his authority. See Beilner, *Christus und die Pharisäer*, 131.

6. For the interpretation of this pericope, I am indebted to Jonathan Kraus's analysis.

7. While the commentators recognize that Matthew aims at discrediting the authority of both the Pharisees and the Sadducees, they do not pursue the question to know why they are bad authorities according to Matthew. See, e.g., Hummel, *Auseinandersetzung*, 20; BONNARD, 323–36; BEARE, 440–41.

8. In a form close to the text of the LXX. See STENDAHL, 71–72.

9. See STENDAHL, 69–71.

10. Matthew's formulation of the law is somewhat different from its formulation in Mark 12:19.

11. See Cohn-Sherbok, "Jesus' Defense," *JSNT* 11 (1981): 64. Cohn-Sherbok suggests that Jesus does not use "rabbinic" methods of argumentation. While it is true that Jesus' argument (according to Matthew) does not follow any of the seven *middot* of Hillel, the use of word play to make a point is also typical of Jewish exegesis (although other groups also use word play).

12. Commentators usually emphasize only the first point that Abraham, Isaac, and Jacob are living. See, e.g., Doeve, *Jewish Hermeneutics*, 106.

13. Cohn-Sherbok ("Jesus' Defense," 66) recognizes that it is possible to interpret Jesus' argument in this way. Yet he dismisses it.

14. The points in this passage set up the plausibility and right interpretation of Jesus' resurrection. "Resurrection" is to be understood as the manifestation of "the power of God," a power misunderstood by those who "know neither the scriptures nor the power of God" (22:29).

15. Such is the case in Mark 12:28–34.

16. Against Hummel (*Auseinandersetzung*, 52), who claims that because this is a stereotyped opposition it does not present a clash of substantive ideological differences.

17. We end up with an interpretation similar to that of Hummel (*Auseinandersetzung*, 20). For him, however, the two groups are united because in the time of Matthew the distinction between Pharisees and Sadducees was irrelevant.

18. This is a part of the Shema quoted without its introductory phrase and with variation from the LXX. See STENDAHL, 72–76.

19. Quoted exactly from the LXX. See STENDAHL, 76–77.

20. With SCHWEIZER, 425–26; and BONNARD, 329.

21. Note that these opinions are those of the Pharisees and the Sadducees as constructed by Matthew's text, that is, as Matthew believed them to be. We are not making any claim regarding the "rabbinic" position about these topics. For such discussions, see Barth, "Matthew's Understanding of the Law," 77; and TRILLING, 207.

22. See BERGER, 229–30. On the basis of Hellenistic Greek parallels and the context of the Matthean passage, Berger interprets this verse to mean that "all the law and the prophets can be (logically) deduced from these two commandments."

23. As Berger argues, the expression "the law and the prophets" (22:40) is not a technical designation for the written content of the Jewish scriptural canon. Rather,

this expression is used in some Hellenistic Jewish texts to refer to the "totality of the prescriptive will of God." See BERGER, 202–32, and esp. 224.

24. With Frankemölle, *Jahwebund*, 170. He correlates the concept of sonship presupposed in such christological titles as "Son of David" or "Son of God" with the proper structures of human relationships in Matthew's ecclesiology. In brief, he finds a thematic link between sonship in terms such as "Son of David" and "sonship" as an aspect of discipleship—a point that our structural exegesis confirms. By contrast, most other commentators interpret this pericope with regard to the sociological relationship that is said to exist between the Jewish groups mentioned in the passage and Matthew's community. For instance, see STRECKER, 120; Hummel, *Auseinandersetzung*, 121; BONNARD, 330.

25. From the LXX with a small variant. See STENDAHL, 77–79.

CONDEMNATION OF FALSE RELIGIOUS AUTHORITY

THE MAIN THEME

Beginning with 23:1 Matthew presents a discourse by Jesus "to the crowds and to his disciples" *about* the "scribes and the Pharisees." Whether or not the Pharisees are still present—22:45–46 does not say they have departed—23:1–2 does not leave any doubt. This discourse cannot of course be addressed to the Pharisees, since it teaches the crowds and the disciples that "the scribes and the Pharisees sit on Moses' seat" (23:2). We might be tempted to overlook this opening statement since a large part of the discourse seems to be directly addressed to the scribes and the Pharisees; 23:13–36 contains invectives introduced by "Woe to you, scribes and Pharisees, hypocrites!" (23:13, 15, 16, 23, 25, 27, 29). Because they are included in the discourse, the "woes" are to be viewed as a rhetorical device used to convey a point to the actual addressees, the crowds and the disciples.[1]

The conjunction of crowds and disciples as addressees of Jesus' discourse surprised the readers at the beginning of the story of Jesus' ministry (see 5:1). By now it should be expected. Although the disciples have a distinct vocation (see Matthew 10) and are in a closer relationship to Jesus, they are as much in need of Jesus' teaching as the crowds are. We have noted that Matthew depicts the crowds in a way similar to the disciples. Both groups are followers of Jesus who often display an inaccurate, if not totally wrong, understanding of Jesus' mission and authority. For instance, as the disciples rebuke the children (19:13–15), so the crowds rebuke the two blind persons (20:29–34); as the disciples cannot be trusted to have a correct understanding of Jesus' journey to Jerusalem (16:2–23; 17:23; 20:20–22), so the crowds, despite their enthusiastic proclamation of Jesus as the son of David "who comes in the name of the Lord" (21:9), cannot be trusted to understand the meaning of Jesus' entry into Jerusalem (21:8–11). In Matthew's presentation, Jesus shows by his discourse (23:2–39) that he does not trust the crowds and the disciples to have understood what was at stake in his ongoing disputes with Jewish leaders since his entrance into Jerusalem (21:14—22:46). Thus he speaks to them about the scribes and the Pharisees, explaining why these religious leaders should not be followed (23:2–12) and why they

319

should be rejected as cursed (cf. "woe to you," 23:13–36), until the time when they will join the crowds (and the disciples) in saying "Blessed is he who comes in the name of the Lord" (23:37–39; cf. 21:9).

The development of this section's theme is essentially negative. It is a presentation of what constitutes false religious authority as exemplified by the scribes and the Pharisees. The "woes" to the Pharisees, however, should be taken by the actual audience—crowds and disciples, and readers—as solemn warnings regarding false religious authorities, whoever they might be, lest they be tempted to follow them. Simultaneously, it is a warning to those among the disciples, crowds, and readers who might be tempted to adopt such attitudes and behavior so as to accede themselves to positions of authority and of leadership (cf. 23:8). Is this not the kind of religious authority the sons of Zebedee wanted to have (cf. 21:20–28)? Nonetheless the main goal of the discourse is to cause crowds, disciples, and readers to reject the authority of people who practice such behavior as those listed in the "woes," for instance.

There is nevertheless a positive dimension to the development of this theme. This rejection of false religious authorities aims at affirming a true kind of religious authority. The entire discourse begins with a positive statement regarding the authority of the scribes and the Pharisees. They "sit on Moses' seat" and one should practice and observe what they teach (23:2–3). The true authority of Christ and of those who follow him is underscored in 23:10–11. Furthermore, in the concluding parts of the discourse (23:32–36, 37–39) Jesus' authority, even over those who reject him, is emphasized and becomes the main theme. And in the concluding verses (23:37–39) of this terrible chapter, there is a ray of hope. The rejection of such false authorities and of those who follow them is not irremediable. A day will come when Jerusalem will again have the opportunity to welcome the one "who comes in the name of the Lord" (23:39b).

Since the scribes and the Pharisees are presented as typical examples of such false authorities, one cannot avoid the conclusion that this discourse is an attack against the Jewish leaders, even though it is simultaneously an attack against similar kinds of religious authorities in the Christian community. For Matthew, affirming Christ's authority and acknowledging true religious authorities in the Christian community involve rejecting the kind of authority typified by the Jewish authorities. But the use of this chapter as the basis for an anti-Semitic attitude, which involves a rejection of Judaism as a whole, runs contrary to the convictions Matthew attempts to convey to his readers. Matthew also wants to affirm the validity of Jewish authorities (23:2–3). Furthermore, those who are "killing the prophets and stoning those who are sent to [them]" (23:37) will one day say "Blessed is he who comes in the name of the Lord" (23:39). It now appears that the chapter can be divided into four parts: 23:1–12 (practice what they tell you, but not what they do); 23:13–31 (the "woes"); 23:32–36 (Jesus affirms his authority over the Pharisees); 23:37–39 (condemnation of Jerusalem and a promise of restoration).

MATTHEW'S CONVICTIONS IN 23:1–39

23:2–12. Practice What They Tell You, But Not What They Do

23:2–3. For the readers, there is a tension in these verses which signals that Matthew both expresses himself in terms of his readers' old knowledge and makes a new point which challenges their expectations. Jesus' exhortation to "practice and observe all that [the scribes and the Pharisees] tell you" (23:3a, au.) seems to be contradicted by the very next verse which says that "they bind heavy burdens, hard to bear, and lay them on men's shoulders" (23:4). For the readers, this latter verse suggests that the Pharisees' teaching is a wrong teaching that people should not have to bear. Actually, it reminds them that Jesus said his own teaching was a light burden (11:28–30), and that he warned against the "leaven," the teaching, of the Pharisees (16:11–12). Consequently, the readers are left puzzled. What does 23:3 mean? As confirmed by the following negative statements about the Pharisees' teaching, Jesus' exhortation cannot mean that one should literally do "all" that the Pharisees teach. Only one thing is clear: Matthew wants to convey a point by this verse.[2]

23:3. Now it should not be surprising to find Matthew making a point in 23:3 by opposing doing what the Pharisees "tell you" to doing what "they do" (this is what the hearers should not do). The crowds and the disciples should acknowledge the authority of the scribes and the Pharisees insofar as they speak as people who "sit on Moses' seat" (23:2). As such they teach the law of Moses, and thus what they say is authoritative and should be observed by Jesus' followers.[3] This is a necessary point after the preceding disputes between Jesus and the Pharisees; they might be taken to mean that Jesus rejected the law of Moses together with his opponents who invoked the law in defense of their position. Neither the law nor the authority of those who teach it should be rejected! All the law that scribes and Pharisees are charged to teach should be practiced and observed.[4]

23:3b–6. But what the Pharisees do should not be viewed as authoritative; it should be rejected. Why? Because "they say and do not do" (23:3b, au.). In the light of 23:2, this means that they themselves do not observe the law of Moses, and this in two ways, as the following verses show. First, they are not doing what they tell other people to do (23:4). But then their interpretations of the law become very demanding, "heavy burdens." Since the Pharisees "do not want to move [these burdens] with their finger" (23:4, au.), let alone carry them, they do not even notice that they are imposing too many demands upon others. In so doing, and this is the main point, they misuse their authority as people sitting "on Moses' seat." As Matthew has repeatedly emphasized since 4:1–11 and 5:17–48, the law is properly used when it helps to establish one's own will (one's vocation, and thus one's authority). But they use it to impose heavy burdens upon others, to dominate them.[5]

Second, as 23:5–6 indicates, the Pharisees' manner of practicing the law is not appropriate; "they do all their deeds to be seen by men" (23:5) and love to be honored by other people (23:6; cf. 6:1–6). The objection is that "*all*" their deeds are done for the sake of appearance. It is to be expected that, because they are religious authorities sitting on Moses' seat, *some* of their deeds will express their authority (e.g., in teaching they have to display their superior knowledge of the law). But when "all" their deeds—prayer with phylacteries and fringes (see Exod. 13:9 and Deut. 6:8) and sitting at a table or in the synagogue—are aimed at displaying or affirming their authority so that other people will recognize it, once again the Pharisees misuse their authority. Their deeds and attitudes show that they have a false view of authority; they believe that authority is something that belongs to them and that they must strive to preserve by making sure other people acknowledge it (see the point of 21:23–27).

In sum, the scribes and the Pharisees as teachers of the law have authority, because what they teach, the law, is authoritative. But they do not have a true authority when, by their deeds, they usurp the authority of the law so as to have authority over other people. Having a true authority as teachers of the law would be fulfilling the law (5:17), allowing the law to establish one's will, what one should do, and doing it.

23:7–8. Matthew develops this point by opposing the Pharisees who love "being called rabbi" (23:7) to Jesus' followers who "are not to be called rabbi" (23:8a).[6] Jesus' followers should not allow themselves to be called "rabbi" because "you have one teacher, and you are all brethren" (23:8b). This latter clause shows that Matthew understands the term "rabbi" as an honorific title which could be rendered by the phrase "my great teacher." By loving to be called by this title, the scribes and the Pharisees show that they have a false view of authority. Instead of acknowledging the authority of the one who gave the law by using the title "rabbi" for him, they usurp this title for themselves. Furthermore, the Pharisees "love" (23:6a) to be called rabbi, which shows that this desire for recognition is the motivation for "all" that they do (23:5a). By contrast, Jesus' followers should acknowledge that there is only one great "teacher" worthy of the title "rabbi," namely, God.[7] Consequently, they should view each other as brothers and sisters, people with equal status under the authority of a father.

23:9–11. This point is developed thematically in terms of the readers' knowledge and also in terms of their situation. One of the effects of the direct address to the audience (crowds, disciples, and readers) is to reinforce the point that this discourse is not only a denunciation of the Pharisees but also a warning to the Christian community, particularly its leaders.[8] Thus 23:9 not only indicates that alone the Father in heaven is worthy of being called "father" but also generalizes the preceding point. The beginning of this verse, "do not call each other father" (23:9a, au.), shows that calling other people by the title reserved for God is as wrong as seeking to have oneself called by such a title.[9] In other words, the fundamental problem is not that people want to have their authority recognized but that the authority of God is not recognized and acknowledged (see the points of 21:18—22:14).[10] Similarly, 23:10 does not just repeat the preceding point about the title "master" (or "leader"). It also expresses that someone else besides God is worthy of an honorific title, namely, the Christ. He is the "leader" (or "master") of his followers, and thus he has authority over them. But it is a special kind of authority, as Matthew expresses by juxtaposing this verse about the Christ to the teaching (which the readers already know, see 20:26) regarding "the greatest among you" who is "your servant" (23:11). The authority of Christ is not like the false authority of the Pharisees. Unlike the Pharisees who impose their authority over their followers by dominating them (putting upon them heavy burdens, 23:4), the Christ makes himself a servant of his followers (and thus his burden is light, 11:28–30).[11]

23:12. Thus Matthew is able to conclude with the general saying "whoever exalts himself will be humbled, and whoever humbles himself will be exalted" (23:12). The point made by the opposition between "exalts" and "humbles" suggests that a false view of authority due to no acknowledgment of God's authority leads one to attribute authority to oneself (self-exaltation). True authority can be received only from God, the one who will humble and exalt. In other words, authority can be *received* only by one who fully acknowledges God's authority, and consequently *sees oneself as not having authority*. Such is the person who humbles oneself. The problem with the Pharisees is that they exalt themselves; they attribute to themselves authority instead of humbly acknowledging that their teaching has authority only because of the authoritative law of Moses which it transmits. Consequently, they are humbled, cursed, as the "woes" express.[12]

23:13–31. Woe to You, Scribes and Pharisees

In the main theme of 23:1–39 the series of seven "woes" serves a rhetorical function—to warn Jesus' followers against adopting the Pharisees' view of authority and against allowing themselves to be guided by bad authority.[13] The opening thematic phrase "Woe to you, scribes and Pharisees, hypocrites!" should therefore be understood in terms of what the readers already know, namely, the preceding verses. Consequently, the Pharisees are "hypocrites" because, while they teach the law of Moses and affirm its authority, by their deeds aimed at asserting their own authority they deny its authority.[14] They only pretend to acknowledge the authority of the law, God's authority. Each of the "woes" develops the preceding points in its own way.

23:13. The opposition between shutting the kingdom and allowing people to enter it underscores that the Pharisees' false view of authority causes their vocation and ministry to become an anti-vocation and an anti-ministry. Their vocation should have been to allow people to enter the kingdom (23:13b), the same vocation as that of the disciples who received "the keys of the kingdom" both to shut it *and to open it* (binding and loosing, see 16:18–19; 18:18) for those who are worthy to enter it ("those who would enter," 23:13b). By their ministry, however, the Pharisees exclude not only themselves but also everyone else from the kingdom. This restates the seriousness of the failure to acknowledge the authority of God (cf. 22:1–14). Not only does one condemn oneself but also one prevents others from entering the kingdom. And how could it be otherwise, since entering the kingdom is to acknowledge the kingship of God, his authority, as Matthew has repeatedly told us in preceding chapters?

23:15. In the light of the first "woe," the second one is seen to involve an opposition. The Pharisees are carrying out their vocation when they strive to make proselytes—they "traverse sea and land to make a single proselyte" (23:15a); making a proselyte is bringing people to recognize the authority of the law, and thus of God. But, then, they make this proselyte "twice as much a child of hell" (Gehenna, 23:15b) as themselves. In brief, they lead this proselyte to deny the authority of God.

23:16–22. Consequently, the third "woe" designates the scribes and the Pharisees as "blind guides" (23:16a) and contrasts them with the Christ, who alone is a trustworthy leader (23:10). The point here is expressed through a twofold opposition. Swearing "by the gold of the temple" (23:16b) and "by the gift that is on the altar" (23:18b), the only oaths that are binding for the Pharisees, are opposed to swearing "by the altar" (23:20a) and "by the temple" (23:21a), oaths that, for Jesus, are binding.[15] For the readers who remember that Jesus taught the disciples not to swear at all (5:33–37), the concluding verses of this pericope (23:20–22), which describe the proper way to make an oath, seem to contradict the earlier teaching. Such tension further underscores Matthew's new point which the opposition already signals.

The point is clear. Once again the Pharisees fail to acknowledge the authority of God. Now the opposition underscores a basic characteristic of God's authority, namely, "holiness." The Pharisees fail to recognize what

"made the gold [gift] sacred [holy, 23:17, 19]." The foolishness and blindness (23:17a, 19a) of the Pharisees are caused by their inability to distinguish
among degrees of holiness, and thus of authority, because they fail to raise
the question of the origin of holiness. The gold in the Temple is holy. But
that which makes it holy, the Temple, is more holy than the gold. And if
they had recognized this, then they would also recognize that God, who
makes the Temple holy, is ultimate holiness, the source of all holiness (cf.
23:21–22). The same point is made about the altar and the gift on it (23:18–
19).[16]

The concluding verses (23:20–22) underscore an additional point. According to these verses, the Pharisees are in fact partially right! An oath is
binding not because it is made "by the temple" or "by the altar," but because
it is made by what is "*in* the temple" and "*on* [or above] the altar." In other
words, they are on the right track—they guide other people in the right
direction. But they are blind, and thus cannot see that "on" or "above"
(same word in Greek, *epanō*) the altar there is *more than* the gift. "He who
swears by the altar, swears by it and by all the things which are above it"
(23:20, au.). These "things" include the gift which is on the top of it, but
also "heaven" which is above it (the throne of God), and ultimately God
who sits "on" it (23:22). Similarly, "he who swears by the temple, swears
by it and by him who dwells in it" (23:21). Swearing by the Temple is
swearing by what is "in the temple," but they fail to see that what is in the
Temple is not merely the gold but primarily God; it is his house. Thus the
Pharisees are hypocrites who fail to acknowledge the authority of God; they
fail to recognize the Temple and the altar as manifestations of the holiness
of God. They fail to recognize that things in the human realm (temple, altar,
gold, gift) are in relationship to heaven. Such is, for Matthew, the Pharisee's
hypocrisy.[17]

23:23–24. The fourth "woe" opposes neglecting "the weightier matters
of the law, justice and mercy and faith" (23:23a) and doing them "without
neglecting the others" (23:23b). The point is similar to the preceding one.
As they fail to recognize the relative degree of holiness of temple, altar,
gold, and gift, the Pharisees fail to recognize what are the most important
matters in the law. Among these we find "mercy," singled out as the most
basic characteristic of God's will through the quotation of Hos. 6:6 in Matt.
9:13 and 12:7. The preceding term, "justice," certainly needs to be interpreted in this light, not as condemnation (as in 5:21; 10:15; and 23:33), but
as the justice or right that wronged people should receive, a justice that is
an act of mercy. Similarly, "faith" should be understood as "faithfulness
to the will of God" and not as faith in Jesus.[18] Because they do not recognize
justice, mercy, and faithfulness to be the weightier matters of the law, the
Pharisees devote much effort to fulfilling minor points of the law—tithing
even the most insignificant things, such as herbs (mint, dill, cummin)—

and do not fulfill the most important matters. Note, however, that the text does not say that the minor matters (tithing) should not be done. "You ought to have done" justice, mercy, and faithfulness "without neglecting the others" (23:23b). Avoiding swallowing a camel does not mean one should swallow a gnat (cf. 23:24)!

23:25–26. The fifth "woe" develops the negative counterpart to the preceding point by opposing cleansing "the outside of the cup and of the plate" (23:25) to cleansing "the inside" (23:26). By cleansing exclusively the outside, the Pharisees show that they are not able to recognize the most important impurities. As they are unable to recognize what are the weightier matters of the law, so they are unable to distinguish among various degrees of uncleanliness. Several points are underscored. First, impurity is not merely "outside" (the Pharisees' view) but also and primarily "inside." The mention of "cup" and "plate" suggests that the Pharisees have a view of impurity limited to ritual impurity and cleansing (dietary laws). Second, the most important impurity—the Pharisees do not recognize it—is precisely the opposite of "justice, mercy, and faith" (23:23): extortion and robbery, injustices committed against other people; and lack of self-control or self-indulgence (rather than "rapacity," RSV), that is, lack of faithfulness to the will of God.

In sum, the failure to recognize the most important matters of the law also involves the failure to recognize the most important uncleanness, and consequently where this uncleanness is to be found. In the process, the cup and the plate become a metaphor of the entire person.[19] The most important impurities are located "inside" the person (not "outside") since they are attitudes, unjust and self-indulgent behavior, which manifest the will or inner inclination of that person.[20] It does not mean that outside impurities should not be cleansed. But when inside impurities are cleansed, then outside impurities will also be cleansed (23:26b).[21]

23:27–28. The sixth "woe," which does not involve a new opposition, thematically restates the preceding point with a new metaphor: "whitewashed tombs." The Pharisees, by doing the less important matters of the law, might appear to be clean and righteous. But like tombs full of human bones and uncleanness, they are fundamentally unclean. In this context, the inner uncleanness is further explained. Ultimately, it is "inner *anomia*." It is not merely "iniquity" (so the RSV), but the absence of the law inside the person. "Hypocrisy" therefore is an inner condition; it is not having internalized the law, not having made the law one's will or inner inclination. As long as this is the case, any effort to carry the law can only result in *apparent* righteousness, not in actual righteousness.

23:29–31. The last "woe" includes an opposition between the Pharisees who say that they would not have associated themselves with the murderers of the prophets (23:30) *and* the Pharisees witnessing against themselves that they are the children of these murderers (23:31). In light of the preceding "woes,"[22] for Matthew, the Pharisees deceive themselves and believe that their actions demonstrate them to be on the side of the prophets rather than on the side of their murderers. In 23:23 they were presented as believing that their actions, such as their fulfillment of the commandment regarding tithing, demonstrate that they are on the side of the law. Now, in 23:29, by building tombs and adorning monuments they believe that they honor the prophets and the righteous and that they acknowledge their authority. Once again, however, these are gestures that are only concerned with the "outside" (23:25), appearances (23:27), what other people can see (23:5). Therefore such gestures demonstrate that they do not truly acknowledge the authority of the prophets and the righteous. A true acknowledgment of their authority would involve appropriating their teaching! By their actions they demonstrate that they would have been on the side of the murderers rather than on the side of the prophets (23:31). The point is that the Pharisees as "hypocrites" are not conscious that they are rejecting the authority of the prophets (and the law).[23] On the contrary, they believe that through their actions they acknowledge the authority of the prophets, even though these very actions demonstrate the contrary.

23:32–36. Fill Up the Measure of Your Ancestors

The concluding part of the discourse surprises the readers with a sudden change of style. Jesus now speaks in the first person, "I." This tension is a thematic expression of an important point that Matthew makes in 23:32–36 in terms of the readers' knowledge. They have just read the preceding part of the discourse, the "woes" (23:13–31), in which the Pharisees, their actions, and their teaching were described and evaluated. It was a second and third person discourse. The speaker remained outside the discourse. As a consequence, even though the woes were direct invectives involving and manifesting the speaker, they were presented, it seems, as statements with a kind of objective and absolute validity; they are justified by objective descriptions and evaluations of the Pharisees. The "woes" appeared as curses decreed by an authority that transcends the speaker, Jesus, and thus as divine decrees. But now in the last part of the discourse (23:32–39), the speaker enters the discourse and plays a direct role by using "I." For the readers, the effect is an astonishing quasi identification of Jesus ("I") with God.[24] This effect is further reinforced by the last "woe" (23:29–31). It repeatedly mentioned "the prophets" and "the righteous" of the past who were *sent by God*. Now in his opening statement in the first person, Jesus says: "I send you prophets and wise men" (23:34). Jesus plays the same role as God. So Jesus suddenly appears not only as the one who has the authority to proclaim God's curse upon the Pharisees but also as the one who himself has the authority to curse them and bring about the realization of this curse.

As Jesus displayed his authority over the crowds and the disciples by exhorting them to "practice and observe whatever [the Pharisees] tell you, but not what they do" (23:3) and to avoid being called rabbi as the Pharisees do (23:8–10), so too he affirms his authority over the Pharisees by exhorting them to fill up the measure of their ancestors (23:32). Of course, this exhortation is ironical. The Pharisees, by contrast with the crowds and the disciples, are not inclined to obey Jesus. They do not acknowledge his authority, as they did not acknowledge John's authority—a comparison suggested to the readers by 23:33 where the Pharisees are described in terms reminiscent of 3:7: "You serpents, you brood of vipers, how are you to escape being sentenced to hell?" (23:33). Even though they do not want to acknowledge it, Jesus' authority over the Pharisees is nevertheless quite real. According to Matthew, Jesus will make them do what he asks, even if they do not want to do it! By sending to them prophets, sages, and scribes, whom they will reject, Jesus will make them "fill up the measure" of their ancestors. These prophets, sages, and scribes are the disciples who have been called prophets and righteous (a term equivalent to sages) in 10:40–42 and scribes of the kingdom in 13:52.

23:33–35. When this thematic expression of Matthew's point is understood, the opposition that further conveys it can readily be understood. The text opposes Jesus, who sends to the Pharisees prophets, sages, and scribes (23:34a), and the Pharisees, who "drive them away from town to town" (23:34b, au.).[25] The point is clear: Jesus who sends the prophets does so as one who has the authority and the power to make the Pharisees demonstrate their fundamental wickedness and thus to make them condemn themselves to Gehenna. By contrast, the Pharisees (falsely) believe they have the power to escape Gehenna (23:33). Ironically, the only use they make of this power is to kill, crucify, scourge, and drive away prophets, sages, and scribes sent by the one who has divine authority and power—namely, Jesus. In this way the Pharisees associate themselves with their ancestors who murdered the prophets and the righteous; "all the righteous blood shed on earth" (23:35) will come upon them (23:35). They are sentencing themselves to hell (23:33).

The Pharisees' predicament which finds expression in the hypocritical behavior described throughout the discourse is rooted in their failure to acknowledge God's authority. They are unable to make the proper distinction among various degrees of righteousness and of uncleanliness. They also fail to acknowledge Jesus' authority. The latter is worse than the former. By refusing to acknowledge Jesus' authority they fill up the measure of their ancestors (23:32) and irremediably condemn themselves. But this situation is not without hope, as the last pericope (23:37–39) suggests.

23:37–39. Until You Say "Blessed Is He Who Comes in the Name of the Lord"

Readers are once again surprised by this concluding pericope. The discourse is no longer addressed either to the crowds and disciples or to the scribes and Pharisees, but to Jerusalem. Since Jerusalem kills the prophets, the readers are to associate Jerusalem with the Pharisees; both have that attribute. This association broadens Jesus' opponents. But in what way?

Another tension suggests it. Jesus ("I") presents himself as playing the same role as God, not only in the present (as in 23:32–36) but also in the past—the time when prophets were sent to and killed by Jerusalem (23:37).[26] Thus Jesus exercised his divine authority and power throughout the history of Jerusalem—also in a time before the scribes and the Pharisees. For the readers, this description of Jesus' activity in 23:37, together with the earlier mention that he sends sages, or "wise men" (23:34), may suggest that Jesus is to be identified with God's Wisdom who was with God since the beginning of the world.[27]

In this pericope, Matthew makes two points: First, he opposes Jesus wanting to gather Jerusalem's children (23:37a) *and* Jerusalem's children not wanting to be gathered (23:37b).[28] He also opposes Jerusalem killing and stoning the prophets (sent to them by the Lord, 23:37a) *and* Jerusalem welcoming the one who is coming in the name of the Lord in the future (23:39).

23:37–38. The point of the first opposition is that Jesus often wished to gather Jerusalem under his wings (23:37). From Jesus' perspective, Jerusalem needs protection and security—as a brood needs the protection offered by a hen's wings. Without him and the protection he can provide for Jerusalem's children, their "house is forsaken [and desolate]" (23:38).[29] Yet Jerusalem's children reject this offer despite its goodness; from their perspective, they are not in danger. They do not envision that without Jesus' protection they will be forsaken and desolate, and consequently they do not see the need for protection.

23:37–39. Because of her blindness to her precarious situation, Jerusalem both refused the help offered by Jesus (Wisdom) and rejected the prophets sent by the Lord.[30] But, and this is the positive side of the point made by Matthew in 23:37 and 39, there is a ray of hope. Jerusalem is forsaken, abandoned (23:38). The departure of Jesus (23:39a) means also the departure of Wisdom, of God's presence announced by the prophets that Jerusalem rejected (cf. Jer. 12:7, a text that Matthew might have expected his readers to remember). But a day will come when Jerusalem will again have the opportunity to welcome the one "who comes in the name of the Lord" (23:39b; cf. 21:9 and Ps. 118:26). By recognizing the authority of Jesus as he returns and by acknowledging the authority of the one in whose name he comes, Jerusalem as well as the scribes and the Pharisees will escape their hypocrisy and blindness which lead them to the utter destruction of Gehenna.[31]

In sum, the only hope for the scribes and the Pharisees, as well as for the crowds and the disciples to whom the discourse is addressed, is to acknowledge the authority and the goodness of the one "who comes in the name of the Lord," Jesus. When one does so, one is then enabled truly to acknowledge God's authority, as well as to distinguish what is truly important in the law—justice, mercy, faithfulness—and what is truly unclean—injustice and unfaithfulness. Then one can no longer be a hypocritical Pharisee. One's acts are done for the sake of God, not for being seen by other people.

NOTES ON 23:1–39

1. With Garland, *Intention of Matthew 23*, 37; and Edwards, *Matthew's Story*, 80.

2. As usual, our concern is to show what meaning effect the text, as it stands, has for the readers. Since 23:3 seems to contradict what they have read earlier, which is now part of the readers' knowledge, this verse should be seen as expressing a new point that Matthew wants to convey. By contrast, commentators who interpret the text in a historical perspective view 23:2–3 as a tradition that "date[s] from a period when the Christian community was still trying to live strictly according to the Jewish Law" (SCHWEIZER, 430). See also STRECKER, 138; Van Tilborg, *The Jewish Leaders in Matthew*, 136; Kunzel, *Gemeindeverständnis*, 164. They all set up an opposition or tension between the point of a pre-Matthean tradition and Matthew's redaction. I do not object to this assessment. But when Schweizer concludes from it that these verses do not express Matthew's point of view, I object. Why did Matthew keep these verses in his text? Why did he introduce them into his text, since they are not found in either Mark or Luke? We have seen time after time the freedom with which Matthew uses his sources, including the biblical texts. If Matthew chose to use this tradition in this formulation, it is precisely because it is important for him—as Frankemölle (*Jahwebund*, 295) notes.

3. The term "scribes" also expresses this point; these are people whose vocation is to teach the law. Furthermore, as Frankemölle (*Jahwebund*, 100) notes, Moses may have here the connotation "teacher" rather than "originator" of the law. This is why Matthew associates the scribes with the Pharisees. For the sake of brevity, we shall use the single designation "Pharisees."

4. With BONNARD, 334; and Garland, *Intention of Matthew 23*, 55.

5. With Bornkamm, "End Expectation and Church in Matthew," 61; and BONNARD, 335. Once again we find here Matthew's conviction regarding the necessary unity of words and deeds. See Lategan, "Structure and Reference in Mt 23," *Neotestamentica* 16 (1982): 81.

6. As is also noted by Frankemölle (*Jahwebund*, 99–101). Most other commentators, by focusing on the origin of the different traditions juxtaposed by Matthew in these verses, do not account for the way in which Matthew links them. See, e.g., BONNARD, 336–37.

7. The opposition demands that the "one teacher" be identified as God (or eventually as Moses) rather than as Jesus. Note also that in the preceding chapter it is by the Pharisees that Jesus is designated as "teacher," a sign that this designation is not necessarily appropriate. Against Frankemölle, *Jahwebund*, 101, and TRILLING, 36.

8. With Garland, *Intention of Matthew 23*, 63.

9. See Schüssler Fiorenza (*In Memory of Her*, 149–51) for an interpretation of 23:8–11 as a rejection of patriarchal structures in the community in a pre-Matthean

tradition. But, as Robin Mattision pointed out, this is based on a questionable reconstruction of the tradition. As far as we are concerned, this rejection of patriarchal structures is still Matthew's point.

10. See above, pp. 292–305.

11. With Frankemölle, *Jahwebund*, 100.

12. Against Garland (*Intention of Matthew 23*, 89), who calls the woes a "proleptic final judgment" and rejection of the "false leaders as a recalcitrant Israel."

13. See Garland (*Intention of Matthew 23*, 65–67) for a discussion of the range of meanings scholars have attributed to the "woes."

14. Many scholars find the switch from "hypocrites" in six of the "woes" to "blind guides" in 23:16 problematic. It has been explained as reflecting a difference of traditions. See, e.g., TRILLING, 200–202. Thus scholars do not see these two epithets as relating the Pharisees' hypocrisy to their authority as such (as 23:2–3).

15. The opposition can also be understood as being between what the Pharisees "say" (23:16a) and what Jesus says (the questions in 23:17 and 19 imply a direct address by Jesus to them).

16. With Hummel, *Auseinandersetzung*, 79.

17. With Hummel, *Auseinandersetzung*, 79. Yet we cannot follow Hummel in his argument opposing Matthew's views to that of historical rabbis on the basis of questionable evidence. Again, we should keep in mind that Matthew's text is not concerned to paint a historical picture of Pharisees and scribes, but to attack bad types of religious authorities typified by Pharisees and other people as well.

18. For a similar interpretation of "justice, mercy, and faithfulness," see BONNARD, 340.

19. With TRILLING, 200–201, this "woe" combines both literal and metaphorical elements of inner and outer cleanness to make thematically a point about hypocrisy.

20. By implication, justice, mercy, and faithfulness are "done" (23:23), when they are themselves internalized, becoming the will of the person, as was expressed in 5:21–48.

21. Against BONNARD, 341; but with GUNDRY, 465–66. The last clause of 23:26 is introduced by *hina*, which has to be understood in its final sense, "in order that," "so that" (other senses of *hina* demand other types of constructions).

22. BONNARD, 341–42, proposes to interpret 23:31 in terms of what follows (23:32). This case proves that the Pharisees would have been on the side of the murderers of the prophets because they themselves will murder the Christ. But the interpretation of 23:31 in terms of the preceding "woes"—which Bonnard mentions as a less likely possibility—better accounts for the construction of the text. The difficulty in perceiving the relationship between 23:30 and 31 might be caused by an Aramaic or Hebrew origin of this saying which could have been based on puns on Hebrew words, as suggested by SCHWEIZER, 443.

23. With TRILLING, 202–3.

24. With Frankemölle, *Jahwebund*, 101–02.

25. The RSV translation, "persecute from town to town" (23:34b), without being incorrect hides the opposition between sending and driving away.

26. With TRILLING, 86.

27. This identification of Jesus with Wisdom has been emphasized and discussed at length by Burnett (*Testament of Jesus-Sophia*, 49–80, 169–182). See also his bibliography, and Frankemölle, *Jahwebund*, 254–55.

28. This opposition is clearer in the Greek where the verbs "I wanted" and "you did not want" are emphasized.

29. The words between brackets are missing in important manuscripts.

30. With Frankemölle (*Jahwebund*, 357), who suggests that the times distinguished by the phrase "you will not see me again, until you say" (23:39) are distinguished not merely temporally but also qualitatively. Thus when he contrasts Matthew's sacred history perspective to a "linear temporal" one, he is making a point similar to ours. Matthew contrasts situations, not points in time.

31. Against STRECKER, 114, and, following him, TRILLING, 87, and KINGS-

BURY, 86 and 156. To most commentators, 23:39 with 21:43 mark the unmitigated
rejection of the old Israel and its replacement by a new Israel, the church. Few seem
to take seriously the specific form of this attack against Jewish *authorities*, rather
than on Judaism or Israel (see again 23:2–3). The lament over Jerusalem is a lament
over people who follow bad authorities and are forsaken until they finally acknowledge the proper kind of authority. The problem with these interpretations is that
they too quickly seek a historical context for the text. As Lategan has pointed out
regarding this chapter, it is essential to avoid falling into the trap of the "referential
fallacy." This chapter involves a redescription of reality, and therefore about what
is described we have to say, "It was and it was not." In sum, I fully agree with
Lategan's objection to the many redaction-critical studies. "The relationship between text and reality cannot be clarified by a direct mapping of textual contents
on to reconstructed situations of origin'" (76). See Lategan, "Structure and Reference
in Mt 23."

WATCH, FOR YOU KNOW NEITHER
THE DAY NOR THE HOUR

THE MAIN THEME

This last major discourse of the Gospel is clearly set apart from the pre-ceding one by a change of location and of audience: "Jesus left the temple and was going away" (24:1); "the disciples came to him privately" (24:3). In contrast with the discourse about the Pharisees and the nature and cause of their hypocrisy (23:1–39), addressed to both the crowds and the disciples, the discourse concerning the end of time (24:1—25:46) is addressed only to the disciples.[1] We recognize the pattern that we have found in 13:1–53. The matters concerning the past and the origin of evil, "What has been hidden since the foundation of the world" (13:35) and therefore what occurred throughout sacred history—such as the rejection of the prophets by Jeru-salem and the Pharisees—is revealed to the crowds as well as to the disciples. By contrast, the mysteries of the kingdom (13:10–17), including what will happen at the end of time (13:36–52), are revealed only to the disciples.

For the readers, the significance of this shift in audience is clear. It is not because they are better or more trustworthy than the crowds that the disciples alone receive this teaching about the mysteries of the kingdom. As we have noted (see The Main Theme of Matthew 23), Matthew pur-posefully underscores that crowds and disciples are very much in the same position; both groups are followers of Jesus who frequently misunderstand his ministry and teaching. What distinguishes the disciples from the crowds is that the former have a special vocation—a mission to Israel and to the Gentiles (cf. 9:36—10:42). Consequently the readers are led to expect that this teaching about the mysteries of the kingdom is something the disciples need to receive in order to carry out this specific mission.

These preliminary observations help us perceive how Matthew expected his readers to understand 24:1–4a. These verses not only provide a narrative setting for the discourse but also express its theme.

24:1–4a. In 24:1–2 an opposition is set up between the disciples, who "point out to [Jesus] the buildings of the temple" (24:1), *and* Jesus, whose response is clearly polemical ("But he answered them . . .", 24:2). It is a puzzling opposition because Matthew[2] does not describe why the disciples pointed out the Temple to Jesus or what was their view of the temple. Consequently, the point of the opposition is somewhat vague. For Matthew, however, it is an effective way of reminding the readers that the disciples are not trustworthy. But since Jesus emphasizes that the temple will be utterly destroyed we surmise that the disciples implied by their gesture that the temple would endure. Jesus rebukes them for pointing out the buildings of the Temple to him, without seeing (or understanding) "all these" things. They did not perceive the actual reality of the Temple which already includes its forthcoming destruction.

The significance of 24:1–2 appears as soon as we read the question addressed to Jesus by the disciples in 24:3: "Tell us, when will this be, and what will be the sign of your coming [parousia] and of the close of the age?" This question concerned with the time of the end; the knowledge of the "sign" of Jesus' coming and of the end is what would allow one to recognize *when* the end is arriving. Note that the disciples associate three events: the destruction of the Temple (when the "house" of God in Jerusalem "is forsaken and desolate," 23:38); Jesus' parousia (i.e., his glorious return when Jerusalem will say "Blessed is he who comes in the name of the Lord," 23:39); and the end of time. For the readers, the relation of this question to the lament over Jerusalem (23:37–39) is thus clear.

But how should the readers understand the question of 24:3? They might be positively impressed. For the first time, the disciples acknowledge that the return of Jesus is directly related to the end of time.[3] But the preceding verses (24:1–2) warn the reader—the disciples are still not trustworthy. Furthermore, the suggestion that the time of the destruction of the Temple is also the end of history when Jesus will come back seems to contradict the description of these two events in 23:37–39. There the destruction of Jerusalem and of the Temple appears to be separated by an undetermined amount of time from Jesus' glorious return. Consequently readers are led to expect that other features of the disciples' question are incorrect. In brief, readers should be ready to view Jesus' response—the entire discourse—as a polemical statement rejecting the disciples' question and its implications. This is precisely what happens. Consequently the opposition between what the disciples say (24:3) and what Jesus says (24:4—25:46) underscores the theme of the entire discourse. A survey of this theme's development shows that once again Matthew has carefully organized the discourse.

A warning about being led astray by false christological claims (24:4–5) opens the discourse. This already suggests that the disciples' view expressed in their question could lead them into error.

To the suggestion that the time of the destruction of the Temple is the end of time, Jesus responds negatively: wars and other destructions (24:6–8), including the destruction of the Temple, will occur, "but the end is not yet" (24:6b), "this is but the beginning of the sufferings" (24:8b, au.). The proper identification of the time when "the end will come" (24:14) is given in the conclusion of a pericope describing persecutions of the disciples, wickedness within their community, and what will happen if they endure (24:9–14). Furthermore, since wickedness and false prophets are to be found within the community of disciples, the issue of the trustworthiness of the disciples is again raised. How can one distinguish faithful disciples from wicked and false disciples? This latter theme will be one of those developed in 24:45—25:30.

The time of profanation of "the holy place" (24:15) appears to be identified with "the beginning of the sufferings" (24:8b, au.), the time of the destruction of the Temple and of wickedness within the community. The profanation of "the holy place" has nevertheless a special significance, especially for the elect who should "flee" and "not turn back" (24:15–22). It is a time when the elect are scattered. This subsection of the discourse describes the unfolding of time until the end when the elect will once again be gathered (24:31). In the process, the discourse gives a negative answer to the question regarding the "sign of your coming" (24:3), a question that implied that the disciples should look for this sign. Jesus' answer underscores that *one does not need to look for it*. The sign of the Son of man and his coming will be readily recognizable by everyone and is not, therefore, to be looked for in one place or another (24:23–27). Consequently the elect should not think they have to take the initiative to gather together at one place (around the presumed location of the Christ, 24:28). They will be gathered together from the four corners of the world—where they should be!—by the angels of the Son of man (24:31).

The parable of the fig tree (24:32–36) emphasizes that on the basis of the preceding teaching one should be able to recognize in a general way that the end of time is approaching. But 24:36 underscores that no one, not even the Son, knows the "day and hour," the actual time of the end and of the coming of the Son of man. The Father alone knows. Any answer that one could have for the disciples' question about the time of the coming of the Son of man and of the end can only be false and misleading. The disciples' question betrays an attitude that excludes the only valid attitude (watchfulness, making sure that one is ready) as first expressed by the comparison with the days of Noah (24:36–44).

This point is developed by three parables. The parable of the servant entrusted with supervision (24:45–51) expresses that not knowing the day and hour does not mean that one should act as if the master will never come back. The parable of the ten maidens (25:1–13) underscores that being ready involves taking into account that the waiting for the coming of the bridegroom might be longer than expected. The parable of the talents (25:14–30) shows that watchfulness and readiness are active (and not passive) attitudes. Finally, this general point is specified in the description of the judgment by the Son of man (25:31–46).

This concluding pericope fully overturns the original question of the disciples. The discourse has shown that their preoccupation for the time of the end and of the coming of the Son of man can only be misleading. One does need to be concerned about the end and the coming of the Son of man. But the essential is not "when" it will occur—no one except the Father knows when it will be—but rather "what" it will entail (the separation of the sheep from the goats, 25:32) and "how" this judgment will be conducted (25:34–46). This is what one needs to know in order to be ready for that time, whenever it might be. Furthermore, the identification of the time of the parousia with the end of the world is shown to be narrow-minded, and thus wrong. Of course, it is at the end of time that the Son of man will come in his glory—one meaning of the term "parousia." But the term "parousia" also designates the presence of the Son of man. This is a presence which is not necessarily recognizable, and therefore it is useless to look for its signs.

MATTHEW'S CONVICTIONS IN 24:4—25:26

24:4b–5. Take Heed That No One Lead You Astray by Using My Name

The introductory verses of the discourse set up an opposition between the disciples who should avoid being led astray (24:4b) and the many who will be led astray (24:5). The point made by these verses[4] is significant. In contrast with the disciples who will not be led astray if they heed Jesus' teaching and warnings, many will be led astray by false christs *who will be using Jesus' name*. This means that this discourse is not a warning against Jewish apocalyptic movements—people who would claim to be the Christ without acknowledging Jesus. Rather, it warns against apocalyptic movement among the followers of Jesus—against people in the community who would claim to be the Christ-Jesus.[5] For Matthew, the actual danger of apocalyptic speculation is *within* the church and results from a misunderstanding of Jesus as the Christ. Thus the points Matthew wants to make in this "apocalyptic" discourse will be primarily about Christ and the way in which disciples need to relate to him (already suggested by the disciples' question concerning "the sign of your coming," 24:3).

24:6–14. The Gospel Will Be Preached and Then the End Will Come

First the text specifies that certain events—wars, famines, earthquakes, tribulation—should not be construed as signs that the end of time has arrived (24:6b–8). It then describes the event—the proclamation of the gospel throughout the whole world—which will take place before the end comes (24:14).

24:6–8. Since they do not include any opposition, the first verses of the pericope are thematic and need to be interpreted in terms of what the readers know, in terms of the preceding verses. The disciples are exhorted not to be alarmed by rumors of war, because "this must take place" (it is according to God's will), and because "the end is not yet" (24:6). This already suggests that these words are related to Jesus' solemn ("Truly, I say to you") prophecy about the destruction of the Temple (24:2), prophecy that the disciples wrongly associated with the end (24:3). The striking parallelism of the expressions "stone upon stone" (24:2, au.), and "nation upon nation" and "kingdom upon kingdom" (24:7, au.), leads the readers to relate the destruction of the Temple to the wars respectively described by these expressions. But now the destruction of the Temple is set in the broader context of wars and other calamities—natural or cosmic calamities, earthquakes and famines—which will take place not merely in Jerusalem but "in various places" (24:7b). Yet "all this is but the beginning of the sufferings" (24:8, au.).[6]

24:9–14. More significant for Matthew is the tribulation that will directly affect the disciples (24:9–14). This is underscored by the opposition between the many who will fall away (be scandalized, 24:10) and "he who endures to the end" (24:13). The first point made is that all disciples will be persecuted and hated "for my name's sake" by "all nations" (24:9). Yet it is not only these persecutions which the faithful disciples need to endure and which scandalize many of them; "wickedness is multiplied" (24:12a); the first who fell away bring about the fall of others. As a consequence of the persecutions which bring about the falling away of disciples, "wickedness" enters the community of Jesus' followers.[7] This wickedness includes betrayal and hatred within the community (24:10b), false prophets (inside the community, 24:11), and the disappearance of love (including the love that should characterize the community of disciples, 24:12). All this wickedness inside the community is also a cause of scandal which will lead many to fall away. Those who endure until the end and will be saved, relatively few (so the singular in 24:13) as compared with the many who will fall away, are those who will somehow be able to remain unshaken by this wickedness both from outside and from inside the community. But the text does not express why they will be able to endure. Rather, it emphasizes what they will be doing. In the midst of all this wickedness, they will continue preaching the gospel of the kingdom, until the time it "will be preached throughout the whole world, as a testimony to all nations" (24:14). This preaching of the gospel of the kingdom is the opposite of all the wickedness described in 24:9–12. It is offered as a witness to the nations, as a response to the persecutions and hatred of the nations. This implies that the preaching of the gospel of the kingdom is also a positive response to the betrayal, hatred, and lack of love in the community (24:10, 12), as is clear from all that Matthew has underscored in previous passages regarding the kingdom and love. It is also the opposite of what the false prophets proclaim (24:11); it is a preaching which does not lead astray.

The coming of the end (24:14b) is related to this proclamation of the gospel. The coming of the end is not merely something that "must" and will happen because of God's sovereign actions; it also depends on the disciples' faithful fulfillment of their mission. And the context in which this mission needs to be fulfilled is that of a time of wickedness and persecutions. As 10:16ff. expresses, such persecutions are necessary so that the mission might be extended to "all nations" (24:14).[8]

24:15–31. The Scattering of the Elect and Their Gathering from the Four Corners of the World

It is necessary to recognize that 24:15–31 forms a complete subsection in order to understand the points Matthew makes. The passage begins with the scattering of the elect (24:16–20) and concludes with their gathering from the four corners of the world (24:31).

24:15. Matthew opens this subsection with a cryptic statement—as the phrase "let the reader understand" (24:15b) expresses—: "So when you see the desolating sacrilege spoken of by the prophet Daniel, standing in the holy place" (24:15a). Note that this statement (which refers to Dan. 9:27; 11:31; 12:11) is linked with what precedes: "So [or, consequently] when you see . . ." (24:15a). In other words, the time in question is the one that was earlier designated as "the beginning of the sufferings" (24:8b, au.), the time of the wars, of the persecutions by all nations, as well as the time of wickedness in the community. Consequently, this statement refers either to the profanation of the Temple (the literal meaning of "holy place") or to the profanation of the community of the disciples (the new "holy place"), or more likely to *both*; both belong to this time when sufferings have begun and when it is not yet the end.[9]

24:16–18. Matthew makes a first point, which further clarifies the cryptic statement of 24:15. He opposes fleeing to the mountains (24:16) *and* going down to (and into) the house (24:17) and turning back (24:18). Immediate and hurried flight away from the "desolating sacrilege," that is also, from tribulation and persecution (cf. 24:21), is the only hope the disciples have for survival. The opposition suggests that one needs to abandon everything, all one's possessions which are in the house (24:17), even one's coat (24:18). Thus the disciples run away without anything as they are to be without anything when they go in mission (see 10:9–10). Fleeing from Judea also involves running away from and abandoning "the holy place" (the Temple), the place that one treasured because there one was in the presence of God, the Holy. Now that this holy place—be it the Temple or the community of disciples—has been profaned, one should flee from it and not turn back. The disciples need to be ready to abandon everything, including what they held to be the most sacred.

24:19–21. Three thematic verses (24:19–21) develop the preceding point in terms of the readers' old knowledge. Matthew 24:21, which underscores the intensity of the tribulation, is a quasi quotation from Dan. 12:1, a text Matthew's readers should recognize. Furthermore, we read that the disciples should pray so their flight may not be "on a sabbath" (24:20). Matthew here presupposes that his readers observe the sabbath in a strict way (according to many Jewish teachings, the sabbath could be broken in life-threatening situations such as persecutions), and this despite 12:1–8 (where the Son of man is lord of the sabbath).[10] At the same time, 24:19–21 reinforces the preceding points. The disciples should be so totally ready to abandon everything that only circumstances beyond their control—being pregnant, breast-feeding, bad weather, and the sabbath—should prevent them from fleeing. Thus the disciples should "pray that [their] flight may not be in winter or on a sabbath" (24:20).

24:22. The opposition—between "those days will be shortened" and the hypothetical case according to which they are not shortened—underscores two points. First, it becomes clear that the time when the disciples must flee is actually an extended period. This time is not limited to one specific day (e.g., when the Temple is profaned), and thus it is certainly related to a succession of profaning events such as those described in 24:6–12. Second, this opposition means that in this time of tribulation the disciples ("the elect") are not abandoned by God. God shortens these days "for the sake of the elect." In other words, God has control over what happens and, even though he allows this great tribulation to occur, God makes sure that the elect will be spared. This also means that the flight and scattering of the elect happens according to God's plan.

24:23–28. In the following pericope the text opposes what people wrongly say (24:23a, 26a) to Jesus' warning (24:25). The point is clear. The false disciples believe that one is to expect the Christ to come in one or another location—"here" or "there" (24:23), "in the wilderness" or "in the inner rooms" (24:26), outdoors or in a house in a city. They believe that persons who perform great miracles in these locations are christs or prophets. But these are false christs and false prophets who attempt to lead the elect astray (24:24). The true disciples, the elect who have the proper understanding of the Christ, believe that he is the Son of man whose coming will be visible everywhere at once, as lightning is (24:27). In terms of the preceding points, even though they are scattered, the elect will not miss the coming of the Son of man. Fleeing from "the holy place," whatever and whenever it might be, cannot be construed as going away from where the Son of man will come. He is not coming to a specific "holy place"!

24:29–31. The following pericope is closely linked with the preceding one (24:23–28) in that their respective last verses are opposed. In 24:28 eagles gather together around a corpse. In 24:31 the elect are gathered by the angels of the Son of man. Matthew's point is thematically expressed in traditional apocalyptic imageries (cf. 24:29–31) with which he expects his readers to be familiar. The false disciples (the "eagles") gather together in specific places around false christs (a corpse). By contrast, the elect believe that the coming of the Son of man will be visible from everywhere (24:27)—that his "sign" will be spontaneously recognizable by "all the tribes of the earth" (24:30a)—and that all will see "the Son of man coming on the clouds of heaven with power and great glory" (24:30b). Consequently, rather than gathering themselves in one place, the elect are scattered to the four corners of the earth. But when the time comes, they will be gathered by the angels of the Son of man (24:31).

The points of this subsection (24:15–31) need to be related to those of the preceding subsection (24:6–14). As we noted, in 24:6–14 Matthew underscored that the coming of the end, and thus of the Son of man, depended on the disciples' fulfillment of their mission to preach the gospel of the kingdom "throughout the whole world" (24:14). Now the conclusion of the following subsection underscores that the disciples will be scattered to the four corners of the world from which the angels will gather them (24:31) at the coming of the Son of man. Then the overall point Matthew makes becomes clear. The scattering and flight of the disciples because of the great tribulation will result in the proclamation of the gospel of the kingdom to the whole world! The profanation of the "holy place" and persecutions have the effect of sending the disciples in mission farther and farther away from Judea. But the great persecutions will contribute to the propagation of the Gospel only if two conditions are met: the disciples need to be faithful by accepting to leave behind all their possessions and thus to go without anything (24:16–18; cf. 10:9–10); and they need to avoid being misled into "turning back" and gathering at specific privileged places because of false beliefs about the Christ and his coming (24:23–28).

24:32–36. The Parable of the Fig Tree

24:32–33. This short thematic pericope may be viewed as a summary of the preceding points for the readers' sake, and in terms of their old knowledge. First, the "beginning of the sufferings" (au.) (see 24:6–12 and 15–28) is comparable to the time when the branch of the fig tree "becomes tender and puts forth its leaves" (24:32). "All these things" (24:33) announce the coming of the end (the coming of summer in the parable) in a relatively near future. This point is reexpressed in 24:34: "Truly, I say to you, this generation will not pass away till all these things take place."

24:34, 36. At first the readers might understand the statement of 24:34 as a prophecy according to which *all* the events described by Jesus in 24:6–31—including the coming of the Son of man—will take place before the generation of Jesus' time will pass away.[11] However, as soon as 24:36 is read, a tension appears. The prophecy seems to be contradicted since Jesus now affirms that no one, not even he, knows when "these days" (the end) will occur. Again Matthew juxtaposes what the readers know with another view on the same topic. The readers have then to stop so as to resolve the tension. Rereading the parable of the fig tree and the prophecy, they discover that they have failed to interpret the prophecy in the light of the parable, as Matthew invites them to do by using the phrase "all these things" in both 24:33 and 24:34. In the parable "all these things" clearly refers to events that announce the coming of the end and thus take place *before the end* and before the coming of the Son of man. Thus one is led to conclude that "all these things" that will take place in the time of the first generation are "the beginning of the sufferings" (24:8, au.; note that the phrase "all these things" introduces this verse), that is, the events described in 24:6–26. In sum, "this generation will not pass away" until the beginning of the sufferings takes place, while the events of the end and the coming of the Son of man (24:29–31) will take place later on.[12] But the tension is not fully resolved; despite 24:36, Jesus is still suggesting an approximate date for the end, which will occur soon after "the beginning of the sufferings."

24:35. The saying "Heaven and earth will pass away, but my words will not pass away" (24:35) reminds the readers of the important place in all these eschatological events of the preaching of the gospel of the kingdom, Jesus' words (cf. 24:14). In spite of all these apocalyptic events the gospel will endure.

24:37–44. Watch, for You Do Not Know the Day

The comparison of the coming of the Son of man with the coming of the flood in the days of Noah (24:37–41) and with the coming of a thief (24:42–44) does not include any clear opposition. This pericope continues, therefore, to unfold the theme of 24:36 (no one knows that day) in terms of the readers' old knowledge, and prepares for the next point that Matthew wants to convey in 24:45–51.

24:37–41. It had already been emphasized that the disciples should not look for specific signs of the coming of the Son of man (24:27) which will be unexpected, causing people to mourn (24:30). The comparison with the days of Noah (24:37–41) goes a step farther by stressing that the people in those days were pursuing an undisturbed life, "eating and drinking, marrying and giving in marriage" (24:38), as people will be doing (24:40–41) when the Son of man comes. In other words, the coming of the Son of man is totally separated from the wars and other such tribulations with which the disciples associated the coming of the Son of man (24:3). These might be signs that the end will occur in a relatively near future (cf. 24:32–33), but the actual time of the end might occur without wars and tribulations.

This first comparison also introduces a new theme, the coming of the Son of man in judgment. For the readers, the mere mention of the flood already evokes the judgment and condemnation of wicked people in the time of Noah. But in the description of these people's life, nothing is said either about their wickedness or about Noah's righteousness. No such opposition is set. Similarly, it is not explained why one man is taken and the other left in the field (24:40) and why a woman is taken and the other is left at the mill (24:41). In this way, the coming of the Son of man in judgment is strongly emphasized. The grounds on which one is to be judged ("taken" or "left" out) remain totally undefined.

24:42–44. The comparison of the coming of the Son of man with the coming of a thief thereby stresses the necessity of watching (24:42) and of always being ready (24:44). Since the coming of the Son of man involves a judgment, something to be feared if one is not ready for it, one needs to "watch," to adopt the attitude that someone has when the time at which a thief will come is known. But since the arrival time of the eschatological judgment is not known, one needs to have this attitude all the time.

24:45–51. The Parable of the Servant Entrusted with Supervision

Matthew makes a first point concerning what is involved in being watchful by opposing the wise servant who gives food to his master's household (24:45–46) to the wicked servant who beats his fellow servants and eats and drinks with the drunken (24:49).[13] Matthew's main concern here is to make a point regarding the delay of the parousia. That the Son of man is not coming soon for Matthew's readers (the church of his time) should not be taken to mean that he is not coming. By contrast, the wicked servant acts as if his master will never come back; he does not carry out his master's orders because he "says to himself, 'My master is delayed'" (24:48). He acts as if his master will never ask him to account for his behavior. For Matthew, despite the delay of the parousia, one should be fully aware that the Son of man and the judgment will come, and this at a time that no one expects. One should be watchful and ready at all times.

A second point made by the same opposition is that being watchful and ready is an *active* attitude, one of carrying out the mission received from one's Master. In the parable this involves feeding the household of the master at the proper time (24:45), the designated times before his coming. As for the disciples (servants), being watchful might mean bringing to other people the gospel of the kingdom both in preaching (24:14) and in actions (cf. 10:5–13). Not doing so is to lose one's status as "servant" (or disciple); one will be punished just like the "hypocrites" (those who refused to be disciples, cf. 23:13–30; 24:51). Being a disciple, one who will be blessed (not condemned) at the coming of the Son of man, means being "faithful" and "wise" in carrying out the mission that one has received from him (24:45).

The question of 24:45, "Who then is the faithful and wise servant?" conveys that it is not clear who can be counted among the "faithful and wise" disciples. In this way Matthew develops the theme of 24:4–12, which implied a mixed community of disciples. In such a community it is difficult, although essential, to distinguish between faithful disciples and wicked disciples (false prophets). The parable provides a first criterion. Only those who are carrying out their mission—feeding people "at the proper time"—and are found doing so at the unexpected coming of the Son of man are truly disciples, people worthy of being blessed (24:46).

25:1–13. The Parable of the Ten Maidens

This parable[14] makes a series of new points that develop the point made in the parable of the servant entrusted with supervision (24:45–51). It therefore needs to be interpreted in terms of the immediately foregoing and the first part of the discourse (24:3–44). The opening phrase (25:1) indicates that this is a parable of the kingdom of heaven (cf. Matthew 13), but it refers to the kingdom at the end of time ("then") rather than in the present.

25:3–4. The opposition of the five foolish maidens who "took no oil with them" (25:3) and the five wise maidens who "took flasks of oil with their lamps" (25:4) expresses the first point. Both groups take lamps, what maidens who will meet the bridegroom need to have to be part of the wedding party. So all of them appear to be part of the wedding party, just as people might appear to be servants or disciples according to 24:45–51. Yet the question of 24:45 (cf. 24:4–12) is again pertinent: "Who then is the faithful and wise servant" or maiden? The opposition makes clear that she is the maiden who takes into account that there might be a delay and so takes additional fuel for her lamp, a flask of oil. To be watchful then means to anticipate a delay of the parousia; one is to be ready for a future.

25:5–6, 10. The text now opposes the wise maidens responding to the call to go and meet the bridegroom (25:6) and entering the marriage feast with him (25:10b) *and* the foolish maidens who proceed to buy oil from dealers (25:10a). Here the timing of one's action becomes the central issue.

Note that both the wise and the foolish maidens dozed off and slept because the bridegroom was delayed (25:5); they are not rebuked for doing so. Being inactive and even sleeping is not necessarily not being watchful.[15] The maidens are not expected to be on the alert for signs of the coming bridegroom; "a cry" will alert them (25:6a). As such the maidens are like ideal disciples who should not look for signs of the Christ (24:23–26) because his coming will be universally recognizable (24:27). This is not what it means to be watchful, in contrast with what the actual disciples thought (24:3). To be watchful means to be "ready" by having done, "at the proper time," what is necessary (taking oil for one's lamps), just as the wise servant fed his fellow servants "at the proper time" (24:45). To prepare at the time of the bridegroom's coming is too late because one thereby moves away from the bridegroom instead of toward him.

Matthew still does not specify what it is the disciples (servants, maidens) are supposed to do "at the proper time." The metaphors of feeding one's fellow servants and taking a flask of oil for one's lamp still need to be elucidated (we suspect it has something to do with their mission of proclaiming the kingdom; cf. 24:14).[16]

25:8–9. A third opposition is now set by the polemical dialogue between the foolish (25:8) and the wise maidens (25:9). The refusal of the wise maidens to help the foolish ones strikes us as rude and insensitive, especially since it is not even certain that it is not enough oil for all of them: "Perhaps there will not be enough" (25:9).[17] But the point is clear. At the time of the bridegroom's coming it is too late, not only to try to do what one should have done but also to receive help from others.

25:11–12. The wise maidens' attitude is vindicated by the bridegroom's own response to the foolish maidens in the concluding polemical exchange (25:11–12). They call him "Lord, lord" (25:11; cf. 7:21–22). But he responds "I do not know you" (25:12; cf. 7:23).[18] As the wicked servant is identified with the hypocrites—he is like those who refused to be disciples (24:51)—so the foolish maidens are not recognized by the bridegroom as belonging to the wedding party.

To be watchful (25:13) is not a matter of staying awake and being constantly on the alert for signs of the coming Son of man so as to do the right thing at the last minute. Rather, it is to do right now what is required by one's status as a member of the wedding party—as disciple.

25:14–30. The Parable of the Talents[19]

The third parable in this series further develops the points of the two preceding parables (24:45–51; 25:1–13). It too does not specify the nature of the disciples' mission; the text provides few clues about how to interpret the "talents" that a man going on a journey gave to his servants (25:14–

15). The mission represented by the activity of the good servants remains largely undefined.[20] The talent was of course a huge sum of money (ten thousand denarii, i.e., ten thousand daily wages, cf. 20:2); by entrusting these talents to his servants, the man "entrusted to them his property" (25:14), just as the master entrusted his servant with his household (24:45). But the point of the parable does not concern the amount of money involved—each servant receives "according to his ability" (25:15b). Rather the parable underscores that the talents entrusted to the servants are valuable for the man and what the servants do with it.

25:16–18. A first opposition contrasts what the five talent servant and the two talent servant do, making more talents (25:16–17) *and* what the one talent servant does, hiding his master's silver in the ground (25:18). On the basis of these verses alone, what distinguishes the good servants from the wicked one? In contrast to the parable of the ten maidens, it is neither when they act—all of them act "at the proper time" (i.e., "immediately")[21]— nor that the good servants acted whereas the wicked servant did not act. The point instead concerns whether their action with the talents is appropriate or not.

The good servants "traded" with their talents, a sum of money and thus something to be used to trade and do business. In sum, the good servants' action fits the nature of what they have received. This is an *appropriate* use of talents which results in the increase of the original sum. By contrast, the wicked servant "dug a hole in the ground and hid his master's silver" (25:18, au.).[22] In this case, the designation of the "talent" as "silver" is significant. In a way, the third servant's action is once again appropriate; silver metal or silver ore belongs to the ground! Thus, it is fitting to dig a hole in the ground and put it there. This action is wrong, however, because it is not silver that the master gave the servant, but a talent, a sum of money. In other words, the wicked servant totally misconceived the nature and use of what he received. As a consequence, although the silver is preserved, the talent does not increase.

25:19–25. Next, the text opposes what the good servants say (25:20, 22) and what the wicked servant says (25:24–25) to their master when he returned "after a long time" (25:19). The point concerns the respective attitudes of the servants toward their master. The good and faithful servants acknowledge what the master had done for them: he "entrusted" (same verb as in 25:14) talents to them. In other words, they show that they have a correct perception of what their master had done and of the trust in them that such an act involved—he "entrusted to them his property" (25:14). By contrast, the wicked and "hesitating"[23] servant does not acknowledge what his master had done and also shows that he has a different perception of the master. He is "afraid" (25:25a). He does not perceive his relationship with the master as euphoric—a relationship that brings "joy" (see 25:21, 23), a trusting relationship initiated by the trust that the master has in his servants and that culminates in the master sharing his joy with his servants (25:21, 23). Rather, the wicked servant perceives it as a dysphoric relationship, something to be feared. Instead of perceiving his master as "gentle and lowly in heart" (cf. 11:29), a fitting description for one who entrusts his property to others, he perceives him as harsh or severe (25:24). And thus the only thing the wicked servant sees is that his master will benefit from the work of his servants without having done anything himself: "reaping where you did not sow, and gathering where you did not winnow" (25:24b). The master does not deny this latter point! He does benefit from the work of his servants; he does reap where he has not sowed and does gather where he has not winnowed (25:26). In other words, this aspect of the wicked servant's perception of his master is correct. It is the misconception of his master as harsh rather than as "gentle and lowly in heart" that makes the third servant wicked.

In sum, the wicked servant is one who misconceives the true nature and usefulness of what he has received—he treats a talent as if it were silver ore. He also fails to perceive the true character of his master, his goodness. By contrast, good and faithful servants correctly perceive the nature of what they have received and use it accordingly, and acknowledge the true character of a master who entrusted his property to them.

25:25–27. A last opposition contrasts what the wicked servant has done, hidden the talent in the ground (25:25), and what he should have done according to his master, thrown his silver to the bankers (25:27).[24] The point is that the wicked servant acted out of fear (25:25a) rather than on the basis of what he knew about his master (25:26b). Clearly he did not fully understand his master's intention: he did not expect the master to share his joy and authority with his faithful servants (25:21, 23); he did not recognize his goodness (cf. 20:1–16). On the basis of his partial knowledge that the master has *authority* over his servants and expected them to make a profit for him in his absence, the wicked servant should nevertheless have deduced what he needed to do. In brief, failing to recognize his master's goodness should not have prevented the servant from acknowledging his master's authority and understanding what he should have done. Not recognizing the master's goodness—his good intentions—is not, therefore, in itself condemning the servant to fail. The wicked servant has therefore no excuse for not discerning what he should have done. It is because he imputed to the master bad intentions—perceiving him to be a harsh man and fearing him—that he failed. And he has no excuse for viewing his master in this way.

25:28–30. The thematic description of the punishment of the wicked servant (25:28, 30) and the saying "For to every one who has will more be given, and he will have abundance, but from him who has not, even what he has will be taken away" (25:29) draw the conclusion of the parable for the readers. By now they would expect such a punishment (cf. 24:51), and the substance of the saying of 25:29 is already expressed in 13:12. Readers are thus invited to associate what Jesus said about his teaching in parables to the crowds (the context of 13:12) with the parable of the talents. The crowds are very much like the wicked servant. They do not understand the mysteries of the kingdom—the ultimate goal of what God does and will do[25]—just as the wicked servant did not fully understand his master's intention. But it remains that, like the wicked servant, the crowds have a partial knowledge—they are in a position to know what was hidden from the foundation of the world (cf. 13:34–35). Like the wicked servant, the crowds have no excuse for not discerning what they should do. And if they adopt the same attitude toward God as the wicked servant adopted toward his master, and end up not doing what they should do because they view God as harsh and fear him (an attitude equivalent to the blasphemy against the Spirit, cf. 12:31), they will receive the very punishment he received. In this way, the readers are prepared for the theme of the concluding pericope (25:31–46) of this section (24:1—25:46) which will describe the blessing and the punishment of people who acted without knowing the mysteries of the kingdom.

25:31–46. The Last Judgment[26]

Since the preceding parables followed teachings regarding the coming of the Son of man (see 24:29–44), the readers can readily identify him as the "master" (24:45–51), as the "bridegroom" (25:1–13), and as the "man" of the preceding parable. Similarly, the servants and the maidens can readily be identified with "disciples." But the condemnation of the foolish servants (24:51) and the foolish maidens (25:12), which associates them with "hypocrites" and people that the Son of man does "not know," raises the question as to who does belong to the group of "disciples." Obviously, it is a mixed group involving faithful and wicked people (cf. 24:4–12); the border line that separates this group from outsiders is far from being clearly drawn. Once again, the decisive criterion for distinguishing those who belong from those who do not belong is the evaluation of what people do or do not do. Yet these parables did not specify the good actions that faithful disciples should perform. Rather, they emphasized the timing of these actions—they must be performed "at the proper time," before it is too late (cf. 24:45–51; 25:1–13)—and the importance of one's perception of the master/Son of man as the decisive factor leading one to perform good or wicked actions. In this context, the pericope about the last judgment is readily understandable as further unfolding the preceding points.

The oppositions through which Matthew makes new points in 25:31–46 are well marked. All the actions of the righteous vis-à-vis the Son of man

(25:35–36) are opposed to those of the cursed (25:42–43). A distinct opposition is found in the explanations provided by the Son of man which now emphasize what the righteous have done (25:40) and what the cursed have not done (25:45) "to one of the least of these." This means that the entire description of the judgment (25:31–34, 41, 46) is thematic; it is not directly involved in the oppositions. Notice how Matthew develops this theme.

25:31–34, 41, 46. The Son of man is described as coming "in his glory," with angels (25:31), very much as in 24:30–31. His "power" is now figuratively expressed by his sitting on a throne, suggestive of an eschatological judge with kingly authority; in fact, he is called "King" (25:34, 40). The next verse, 25:32, notes that he will judge "all the nations." For the readers, this mention of "all the nations" creates a tension; it suddenly broadens the group of those who are subject to judgment. So far this group involved only those who rejected the teaching of the Son of man, the "hypocrites" (cf. Matthew 23; 24:51), and the mixed group of disciples (24:4–12; 24:45; 25:1–13; 25:14–30). But now it involves "all the nations." Furthermore, the rest of the pericope indicates that all those who are judged, both the righteous and the cursed, know the Son of man or know about him. Thus "all the nations" seems to be much too comprehensive a phrase. Yet the readers can overcome this tension by remembering what was said about the end of time and the coming of the Son of man. Indeed, Matthew underscored that "the end will come" *after* the gospel of the kingdom has been "preached throughout the whole world, as a testimony to all nations" (24:14). Now it becomes clear that the servants and the maidens of the preceding parables are not to be understood as representing a relatively small and closed group of disciples but all those who heard the gospel— all the crowds and all the nations.

It appears that the reference to 13:12 in 25:29 was not accidental. Matthew wants his readers to conceive of those who are submitted to the judgment as crowds, all the crowds of all the nations to whom the gospel of the kingdom is preached in parables. They are those who might not know the mysteries of the kingdom, and thus exactly why what happens and will happen at the end of time occurs or will occur. Yet they have heard the gospel of the kingdom and were taught what was "hidden since the foundation of the world" (13:34–35). Consequently, they know that the Father has prepared a kingdom for them "from the foundation of the world" (25:34; cf. 13:31–33). Furthermore, since the preaching to the crowds also reveals to them the existence and role of the "enemy," the devil (cf. 13:24– 30), they should also know that the devil and his angels have prepared an eternal fire (25:41; cf. 13:30, 42). They should therefore be aware of the judgment—when the sheep will be separated from the goats (25:32b–33) according to the image of Ezek. 34:17—and what is at stake in it, blessing in the kingdom or punishment in the eternal fire.[27]

25:35–36, 42–43. Since the judgment is based upon what one has done or not done, one will want to do the right things in order to be blessed rather than punished. One will act for one's own benefit. But such actions are also for the benefit of the Son of man, just as the master in the parable of the talents benefits from the work of his servants (cf. 25:26). The first set of oppositions makes a similar point. The righteous gave food, drink, hospitality, and clothes to the Son of man and visited him (25:35–36), while the cursed did not do so (25:42–43). They have acted for the benefit of the Son of man, not merely for their own benefit (in order to be blessed).

This point has repeatedly been made in the Gospel, and first in 5:3–16. Striving to receive a blessing from God simultaneously brings blessing to God (or the Son of man). Since these actions are aimed at relieving hunger, thirst, isolation, nakedness, and the despair of sickness or imprisonment, it is clear that they are motivated by compassion or mercy, an attitude that the cursed lack. "Blessed are the merciful" (5:7)! Yet the new point is that by acting as they did neither the righteous nor the cursed were aware that they were or were not showing mercy to the Son of man (25:39, 44). Consequently, they were not even aware that they would be blessed (or cursed) for what they were doing (or not doing). They were not acting in order to be blessed or because they feared punishment: their only motivation was compassion, mercy.

25:40, 45. The second point expressed in the responses of the Son of man to the righteous (25:40) and to the cursed (25:45) emphasizes the identification of the Son of man with "the least of these"—with those who are hungry, thirsty, stranger, naked, sick, in prison, whoever these people might be.[28] The Son of man himself is merciful, so much so that when one does something to "one of the least of these" it is to him that one does it. In other words, in order to be faithful servants one needs to do something for the master who reaps where he did not sow and gathers where he did not winnow (25:26). It is the first duty of the servants and of the "disciples" (all those who hear the gospel) to serve (or "minister to") their Lord (25:44b). But because he is "the merciful," what benefits him is precisely showing mercy and compassion for those for whom he himself has compassion.

This pericope about the last judgment is therefore a warning that if one does not show mercy to those in need, then one will be cursed and punished at the eschatological judgment instead of being blessed (25:46). But it also emphasizes that fear of the judgment cannot be the motivation for acting properly (cf. 25:25); the only possible motivation is mercy, compassion. It is not a matter of doing something for people in need because one recognizes in them the Son of man. It is a matter of doing something for them because of one's mercy and compassion for these people.

This second opposition makes the point that the righteous respond with mercy and compassion to people in need, while the cursed do not. Seeing the Son of man in the least of these or failing to do so, is therefore inconsequential.

25:37, 44. Before we discuss this latter point, notice the astonishment of both the righteous and the cursed when they hear that they showed mercy or failed to do so *to the Son of man/king* ("Lord, when did we see thee . . .?" 25:37, 44). In fact, such an astonishment is shared by the readers. Up to this pericope, the discourse was focused on the coming (*parousia*) of the Son of man at the end of time—and on the delay of the parousia. In this way Matthew emphasized that one should not look for signs of his coming (24:5–35) and that watching involves doing the right thing before it is too late, before the coming of the Son of man (24:36—25:30). The parable of the talents had described the man as going away (25:14–15), and the Son of man was described as coming in his glory in 25:31. Nothing prepared the readers for another kind of parousia, for the *presence* (the primary meaning of "parousia") of the Son of man here and now before the end. The effect is to reject another of the presuppositions underlying the original question of the disciples (24:3), namely, that the parousia of the Son of man is exclusively associated with the end of time. It is true that the parousia in glory will take place at the end, but the Son of man is also present in the meantime.

25:40, 45. We now understand the point made through the opposition in 25:40 and 45. The presence of the Son of man before the end has a special character; he cannot be directly seen (repeated four times, 25:37, 38, 39, 44). The sign of his parousia (24:3), the sign of his presence, cannot be perceived as one perceives with one's eyes the physical presence of someone or of something. Actually one is in his presence only when one has mercy and compassion for "one of the least of these." Yet it is a mysterious presence, a presence that looks like an absence, a presence that goes unnoticed even for those who are in direct contact with it through their mercy and compassion. Alone the disciples to whom the mysteries of the kingdom have been revealed will eventually recognize it. But this is not the essential. The important thing is to be in his presence by showing him mercy in the persons of "the least of these," such as the poor, and this whether or not one recognizes him in them. Such are the righteous who will inherit the kingdom: "Truly, I say to you, as you did it to one of the least of these my brethren, you did it to me" (25:40).

NOTES ON 24:1—25:46

1. For a redaction-critical treatment of chapters 24 and 25 as a literary unity, see Lambrecht, "Parousia Discourse," 309–42; and Burnett, *Testament of Jesus-Sophia*, 183–360.

2. By contrast with Mark 13:1 and Luke 21:5 which indicate that Jesus' reply was in response to exclamations regarding the beauty and adornment of the Temple. There is an opposition of interpretations signaled by the phrase "You see all these, do you not?" Against Lambrecht, "Parousia Discourse," 317, n. 19.

3. The disciples have progressed in their understanding of Jesus since the request of the mother of the sons of Zebedee (20:20–21) which seemed to imply the expectation that Jesus, the Messiah, would take power as soon as he would reach Jerusalem.

4. This is one of the rare instances where Matthew makes the same point as Mark. Cf. Mark 13:5–6.

5. With BONNARD, 350; SCHWEIZER, 268; R. Pesch, *Naherwartungen*; Burnett, *Testament of Jesus-Sophia*, 136–47 (Burnett argues that there are apocalyptic enthusiasts within the community).

6. The term translated "sufferings" means literally "birth-pangs" (*ōdinōn*). This image designates the beginning of the end. Yet as the rest of the discourse shows, for Matthew this should not be understood as the sign that the end has begun and will necessarily arrive in the very near future, but rather as a first sign which is announcing that the end comes, but without specifying the time. This image is used in both senses in the Hebrew Bible (see Isa. 13:8; Hos. 13:3; Jer. 6:24; 2 Sam. 22:6; Pss. 17:5–6; 114:3).

7. With Lambrecht, "Parousia Discourse," 321; and Burnett, *Testament of Jesus-Sophia*, 247–56.

8. See Burnett, *Testament of Jesus-Sophia*, 277–300.

9. BONNARD, 351, notes these two possible interpretations and opts for the second. The warning to the readers is Matthew's way of underscoring that "the holy place" should not necessarily be taken literally. But the reference to Judea is then difficult to understand. So other commentators, such as SCHWEIZER, 452, and GUNDRY, 482, interpret "the holy place" as being the Temple. We propose to retain the ambiguity of Matthew's text in the interpretation, with Lambrecht, "Parousia Discourse," 321–23; and Burnett, *Testament of Jesus-Sophia*, 300–38.

10. With Hummel, *Auseinandersetzung*, 41; but against Lambrecht, "Parousia Discourse," 322.

11. Jeremias (*Parables*, 119–20) interprets the original parable of the fig tree as referring to the coming of the Messiah.

12. These remarks do not deny that the statement of 24:34 originally referred to the end of time (not merely to its preliminary signs). As we suggested, this is how Matthew expected his readers to understand it at first reading. Yet, by taking into account how the readers are led to resolve the tension between 24:34 and 24:36, the significance of Matthew's addition of the phrase "all these things" in 24:33 to the text of Mark 13:29 appears. For the modern reader, it remains that the expectation that the end will occur *soon* after "the beginning of the sufferings" ("immediately" in 24:29) was not fulfilled. For different interpretations, see BONNARD, 353–54; SCHWEIZER, 457–58; GUNDRY, 489–91.

13. Jeremias (*Parables*, 55–58, 166) classifies this parable of Jesus among those announcing "the imminence of catastrophe" addressed by Jesus to his opponents. For Matthew, it is quite clearly addressed to the disciples.

14. For a redaction-critical interpretation of this parable, see Donfried, "Allegory of the Ten Virgins," *JBL* 93 (1974): 415–28. See also Jeremias, *Parables*, 51–53, 171–75; and Via, *Parables*, 122–28.

15. Donfried, "Allegory of the Ten Virgins," 426–27, interprets this as an allegorical reference to dying before the parousia analogous to Paul's remarks in 1 Thess. 4:15–17. The general consensus of the scholarship is that the parable functions rhetorically to warn people to be ready in view of the possible eschatological consequences.

16. Donfried ("Allegory of the Ten Virgins," 423) suggests that the "oil" refers allegorically to good deeds on the basis of the thematic link between this parable and 5:14–16.

17. Against Donfried, "Allegory of the Ten Virgins," 427. He believes "it is impossible to transfer 'good deeds' or 'obedience' from one person to the other." We cannot accept such an interpretation even when taking into account the text in other manuscripts where the wise maiden's refusal is more abrupt. It would go against everything we have found to be true in Matthew's system of convictions through our structural analysis. The point of the parable is not that transfer of good deeds is impossible at all times. On the contrary, in Matthew, it is both possible and highly desirable. To be a "lamp" is precisely to transfer one's light (good deeds) to another. Rather, the parable asserts that there is a time *when it is too late*, when it is no longer possible. Matthew's eschatology motivates ethics precisely when one realizes that the possibility (i.e., time) for doing good is going to run out soon. The possibility of being too late lends an eschatological urgency to doing all the good one possibly can while one has the chance.

18. Even though the Greek verb for knowing is different in 7:23, the parallelism of 25:11–12 and 7:21–23 is noteworthy. So Donfried, "Allegory of the Ten Virgins," 422.

19. See Jeremias, *Parables*, 58–63; and Via, *Parables*, 113–22.

20. Since what the talents are is largely undefined, commentators have suggested a wide range of possibilities: natural gifts, spiritual gifts, faith, the gospel, and Jesus himself. But this kind of interpretation is beside the point Matthew makes, as BONNARD, 362, notes.

21. In the Greek text, this adverb is at the beginning of 25:16 and thus implicitly applies to the activities of the three servants since there is no indication to the contrary.

22. The Greek word (*argyrion*), which I translated literally "silver" (the metal), is also used in the sense of "money," the term used in most translations. But the literal meaning needs to be preserved so as to understand the points made by Matthew.

23. The Greek term (*oknēros*), usually translated by "slothful" or "lazy" in 25:26, is derived from a verb that means "to hesitate" (e.g., because of fear), a meaning that is quite appropriate in view of the explanation this servant gives of his action in 25:24–25.

24. It is not without irony that Matthew makes the master not only repeat the description that his servant made of him (see 25:26b) but also designates the talent "silver" as the servant did. In this way, he shows that by putting it to its right use, on the bankers' tables, even "silver" can be productive. This touch of irony conveys to the readers that the main problem for the wicked servant is not his confusion regarding the nature of the talent but his perception of his master.

25. See comments on Matthew 13.

26. See Jeremias, *Parables*, 206–10.

27. Recall that the mission of the disciples as described in 9:36—10:15 involved the proclamation both of the gospel and of judgment (see 10:14).

28. There is no reason to limit this identification of the Son of man to the "disciples" who are in such situations of need.

THE PASSION AND RESURRECTION
OF JESUS

THE MAIN THEME

The limits of this section are easy to identify. The first words of 26:1, "When Jesus had finished all these sayings," make it clear that the preceding section has come to a close and thus that a new section begins. Furthermore, the next verse (26:2) notes the proximity of the Passover, which is presented as the time of the crucifixion. It is soon confirmed that this section of the story embraces the crucifixion and even the end of the Gospel (28:20); the story of the resurrection is closely intertwined with the story of the Passion.[1]

The overall theme can be described as the Passion and Resurrection of Jesus. Throughout this section Matthew conveys to his readers his own view of the Passion and Resurrection even though his text closely parallels Mark 14:1—16:8.[2] In so doing he challenges aspects of his readers' earlier understanding of the cross and the resurrection and, for this purpose, makes use of the readers' presumed knowledge. Despite the unusually close parallelism with the text of Mark,[3] we need to remember that Matthew's entire text—including the parts that duplicate the text of Mark—expresses his point of view, since he chose to formulate his text in this way.[4]

Since it is a narrative section and since its beginning and end are clearly marked, we are in a somewhat privileged position for comparing the introductory (26:1–16) and concluding (28:1–20) parts in order to elucidate the main theme. Because this section concludes the entire Gospel According to Matthew, the identification of this theme will not necessarily account for all the prominent thematic features of the passage. Its themes as well as certain points should somehow echo those of the opening chapters of the Gospel, particularly Matthew 1 and 2. The conclusion of a work should express the fulfillment of what is announced and prefigured by its introduction. A meaningful discussion of the issues of relationship of end to beginning can take place only after we identify the theme of the concluding section and after we study the new points Matthew makes in each subunit. Furthermore, Matthew's points in this section are important; they address issues that previously made points of the Gospel have not yet resolved. In brief, the relations of the themes and points of the Passion story to those

of the rest of the Gospel can be fully presented only in a systematic presentation of Matthew's system of convictions (the subject for a subsequent
companion volume).

In order to identify the theme of the Passion and Resurrection story, one
should compare its introductory (26:1–16) and concluding (28:1–20) parts
so as to note what in the former has been transformed to make room for
the concluding state of affairs. We compare the features of these two parts
following the order in which they appear in 26:1–16.

The opening verses of the section (26:1–5) oppose Jesus (26:1–2) to the
chief priests and the elders of the people (26:3–5) in what seems to be a
clear-cut *confrontation* between Jesus and Jewish religious leaders. In the
concluding part, 28:1–20, we find a similar confrontation. The chief priests
and the Pharisees order the guards to spread the story that Jesus' body has
been stolen by the disciples (28:11–15), while Jesus (and the angel) orders
the women to announce his resurrection to the disciples (28:5–10). But this
confrontation is significantly transformed. In 26:1–5, Jesus describes himself
with passive verbs ("the Son of man will be delivered up to be crucified,"
26:2)—he will be submitted to the actions of others—while the chief priests
and the elders plan an action (26:4)—they are active agents. By contrast,
in 28:1–20, Jesus is the one who plans actions (in 28:10 he gives an order
to the women and then, in 28:18–20, he lays out a plan of action for his
disciples), while the chief priests and the Pharisees cannot act upon the
situation and thus try to save face by spreading a lie about it (28:11–15).
The respective situations of Jesus and the Jewish leaders are reversed: the
Jewish leaders, who were in control of the situation in 26:3–5, lose control
and are reduced to lying about it to save face in 28:11–15; Jesus, who had
no control over (or refused to control) the situation in 26:2, is in total control
at the end of the story—"All authority in heaven and on earth has been
given to" him (28:18).

It soon appears, however, that the overall theme of this section is more
complex. The *Jewish people* (over whom the "elders of the people" are
supposed to have authority) are presented in 26:5 as being on the side of
Jesus and thus against the Jewish leaders. But by the end of the story, they
are presented as accepting the story that Jesus' body has been stolen: "and
this story has been spread among the Jews to this day" (28:15). Paradoxically, the Jewish crowds pass from the side of Jesus to that of the Jewish
leaders precisely when their leaders lose control and a valid claim of authority, and when Jesus receives absolute authority.

Although it is difficult to understand what this means at a first glance,
it can be noted that in 26:6–13 an *unnamed woman* prepares the body of Jesus
for burial (26:12) and is rebuked by the disciples (26:8–9), while *named
women*, "Mary Magdalene and the other Mary" (28:1), meet the resurrected
Jesus and are charged to announce his resurrection to the disciples (28:5–
10), who apparently obey them (28:16). The relationship of authority between disciples and women seems to be reversed. The correlation of the

woman who had prepared the body of Jesus for burial (26:6–13) with Mary Magdalene and Mary is justified, for the readers would have expected these women to visit the tomb after the sabbath to prepare Jesus' body for burial (although after the fact); yet they do not do so: they only "went to see the sepulchre" (28:2). At the very least, this contrast means that women have a special role and status; they remain on the side of Jesus from the beginning to the end of the Passion and Resurrection story.

The main transformation involves passing *from* a time when Jesus is with his disciples in such a way that one can do something to his body (26:12) *to* a time when this will not be possible (a time when the disciples will have only the poor with them, 26:11a). During this latter time, the disciples will not have Jesus with them (26:11b) in a sense. But in another sense, he will be with them "always, to the close of the age" (28:20), as the one who has received "all authority in heaven and on earth" (28:18) and also as the one to whom one shows mercy when one takes care of the poor (see 25:31–46). So to speak, the "physical" Jesus is transformed into the "resurrected" Jesus.

The disciples themselves also seem to undergo transformation. In 26:6–13, they show themselves unreliable when they are indignant at the act of the woman (26:8); once again they have misunderstood Jesus' earlier teaching. Furthermore, it is one of the Twelve who accepts money to betray Jesus (26:14–16). But by the end of the story, and in spite of some doubt (28:17), they are deemed worthy of teaching others all that Jesus has commanded them (28:20a). One therefore wonders what kind of a transformation of the disciples took place.

Finally, the preaching of the gospel to the whole world is mentioned in 26:13, while in 28:19–20 the disciples are sent to "make disciples of all nations," to baptize them, and to teach them. In other words, all the aforementioned transformations have the effect of setting up a situation in which the proclamation of the gospel to the whole world will be possible.

In sum, the main theme of the Passion and Resurrection story in the Gospel According to Matthew is the transformation of the mode of the presence of Jesus, a transformation that involves a change of his relationship with everybody—his disciples, the Jewish leaders, the Jewish people—except women. The result of this transformation is to bring about the proclamation of the gospel to the whole world. Our study of each pericope will elucidate how Matthew unfolds this complex theme and what are the points (convictions) he conveys to his readers through this story.

MATTHEW'S CONVICTIONS IN 26:1—28:20

26:1–16. Pouring Ointment on Jesus' Head and Betraying Him for Thirty Pieces of Silver[5]

This passage is composed of four scenes which are juxtaposed with each other: (1) 26:1–2, Jesus and his disciples at the place where he gave the preceding discourse; (2) 26:3–5, the chief priests and the elders of the people "in the palace of the high priest, who was called Caiaphas" (26:3); (3) 26:6–13, Jesus, a woman, and the disciples, "at Bethany in the house of Simon the leper" (26:6); (4) 26:14–17, Judas Iscariot, and the chief priests, at a location where the latter are. These scenes introduce the main protagonists in the Passion narrative: Jesus, the Jewish leaders, the disciples, and Judas. They could have been introduced in any number of ways (the scene of Judas could have been directly linked with that of the Jewish leaders, the first scene could have been directly followed by the scene at Bethany, etc.). In short, this arrangement of the story into four juxtaposed scenes is not without significance for Matthew.[6]

This arrangement suggests that the Passion narrative will involve four story lines rather than simply being the confrontation of Jesus with Jewish leaders. By separating the scene in which the disciples are presented as actively intervening (26:6–11) from the scene in which Jesus alone is active (26:1–2), the text suggests that the disciples have a story line distinct from that of Jesus; they are not associated with Jesus as ideal disciples should be. Similarly, by attributing to Judas his own scene (26:14–17), the text isolates him from the story of the Jewish leaders; Judas will have his own story line. Thus we can expect that the Passion narrative will be a complex story in which at least four story lines will be interwoven: that of Jesus, Jewish leaders, disciples, and Judas.

Another effect of the literary arrangement is that the readers are invited to view the interrelations of the four story lines as more important than the unfolding of each individual story. Readers can thereby note that the scenes are thematically related. For instance, both Jesus and the Jewish leaders mention the Passover in relation to the time when Jesus will be killed, although they discuss the Passover in opposite ways (26:2, 5); a proper understanding both of the time of Jesus' crucifixion and of the Passover is therefore somehow important. Then it appears that the third scene is also linked with the preceding ones by the theme of *time*, since Jesus points out that the disciples confuse what should be done in another time (when he will not be with them) with what is appropriate for the present time (26:11). Furthermore, the *place* where the Jewish leaders meet, the "courtyard [of the palace] of the high priest called Caiaphas" (26:3, au.), is contrasted with the place where Jesus goes, the house of Simon the leper (26:6). While the Jewish leaders are associated with the outside of a location of religious authority and religious purity, Jesus is associated with the inside of a location without religious authority or religious purity (Simon the *leper*). These space representations remind the readers of the contrast between the Jewish leaders' concern for external purity (see 23:25–26) and Jesus' mercy for the sinners (see 9:10–13), which he expresses by associating with those who are impure (see 8:1–4, 17). Similarly, the third scene is linked with the fourth one by the theme of *money*. The disciples would have liked to sell the precious ointment for a large sum of money (26:9), and Judas, "one of the twelve," has a similar interest in money (26:15). Although money is to be used for different purposes in each case (helping the poor and delivering Jesus to the Jewish leaders), the disciples as a group, and not merely Judas, are nevertheless preoccupied with money!

These thematic features are suggestive of Matthew's points. The study of the oppositions will help us elucidate them. Due to the complexity effected by the juxtaposition of the four scenes we will pay special attention to the relations among the four oppositions found in 26:1–16 in order to discern these points.

26:2–5. Matthew links the two introductory scenes by opposing what Jesus says ("after two days the Passover is coming, and the Son of man will be delivered up to be crucified," 26:2) to what the Jewish leaders say ("Not during the feast, lest there be a tumult among the people," 26:5).[7] Since the Jewish leaders are described as "chief priests and the elders of the people" (26:3) who are planning to use deceit to arrest Jesus (26:4), they are shown to be deceitful religious authorities (cf. 21:23–27 and 23:1–30). By contrast, Jesus is shown to be the Son of man. The new point made by this opposition is to be found in the contradictory statements. For Jesus, it will be during the Passover that he will be crucified (26:2), while for the Jewish leaders it should not be during the feast (26:5). In contrast to Jesus, the Jewish leaders have an incorrect knowledge of the time when Jesus will be crucified, even though they are the ones who plan to arrest and kill him. Jesus calls this time the "Passover," while the Jewish leaders call it merely a "feast," and their only concern is the relation of this feast to the people; for them it is a feast celebrated by the people. We are left wondering what is the point made by these very suggestive contrasts, until we recognize the relationship of this first opposition to the next two.

26:7, 9. In these verses, the text opposes the woman's action, pouring precious ointment on Jesus' head (26:7), to the hypothetical action proposed by the disciples, selling the ointment for a large sum of money (26:9). Part of the point made by this opposition is that for the disciples a good action is primarily concerned with the need of the poor, while the woman's action is exclusively directed toward Jesus. Note also that for the disciples the ointment is viewed in terms of money—it is an "expensive" item—while the woman's attitude does not show any concern for its price. Although for her it is "very precious" (*barytimos*, 26:7), its value is not thought of in terms of money. The points of this opposition and of the preceding one appear when we consider their correlation; somehow the disciples are like the Jewish leaders, and the woman is like Jesus. Now the disciples' proposal is directly related to Jesus' preceding discourse, which emphasized that the primary concern of disciples should be to show mercy and compassion to the poor (25:31–46). Once again (cf. 24:3), the disciples are shown to be wrong precisely when they attempt to apply Jesus' teaching! It is not their concern for the poor that is deemed incorrect but rather their attitude. The disciples are like the Jewish leaders in that their attitude is pragmatic; they are so single-minded that everything around them becomes one-dimensional. Thus, for the Jewish leaders, Passover is not a religious festival that they should celebrate themselves; it is a hindrance to their projected action. Since the people will be gathered in Jerusalem to celebrate Passover, the arrest and killing of Jesus should not take place during this time, "lest there be a tumult among the people" (26:5b). In other words, because of their single-minded purpose they totally ignore this other aspect of their experience, their relationship with God; they do not envision that they should also "serve" (or "minister to," cf. 25:44b) God by celebrating the Passover. By contrast, for Jesus (26:2) Passover is precisely a time to serve God. His service is expressed by the way in which Jesus describes himself as totally passive (note the passive verbs in 26:2). During Passover, Jesus will be totally submitted to what will happen to him, a submission to the will of God (see 16:21). In this way, Jesus' first concern during Passover will be to serve God.

Similarly, even though their intention—serving the poor—is good, the disciples are single-minded in their proposed action. As a consequence they are like the Jewish leaders. They fail to perceive that the presence of Jesus, the Son of man, with them calls them to serve him, to minister to him, in the same way that the Passover is a call to minister to God. So they view "the alabaster flask of very precious ointment" (au.) as a means toward their single-minded goal of serving the poor. The woman, however, sees it as a means of ministering to Jesus, the Son of man, a means to "honor" him (a connotation of *barytimos*). The woman recognizes that in the present time, the time of Jesus' presence with them, the first duty is ministering to Jesus and honoring him.

26:8–13. The third opposition between what the disciples say (26:8–9) and Jesus' rebuke (26:10–13) underscores the point regarding time. This opposition concerns the contradictory evaluations of the woman's action by the disciples and Jesus. The disciples are "indignant" and say that it is a "waste" (26:8). Jesus calls it a "good deed"[8] (26:10), and then adds: "For you always have the poor with you, but you will not always have me" (26:11). So the disciples correctly think that serving the poor will be their primary responsibility. They fail, however, to recognize that this does not apply to the present time, the time when Jesus is with them. They fail to acknowledge that time and the circumstances it brings about are constraints to be taken into account in evaluating actions and in deciding what they should do. A good action is one that is fitting in the present time and circumstances (a point that Matthew repeatedly emphasized, and first in

3:15). By contrast, for the disciples, a good action is one that fits their plans and purpose, whatever might be the time and circumstances. Time and circumstances are to be submitted to their purpose.

The disciples once again look and act like the Jewish leaders who view themselves as being in control of time. They think they can decide in their council when Jesus will be killed and when he will not be killed (26:4–5). And yet they have an incorrect knowledge of the time of Jesus' death. Contrary to their decision, Jesus will be arrested and killed during the feast! Their illusion is that they control time because they view it in a one-dimensional way; they think it is merely human time, therefore something to be manipulated for their own purpose. When one recognizes the role of the divine in human experience, then it appears that time is really under the control of God, the Father. Indeed, not even the Son is in control of time, as in 24:36. So the Son of man submits to time (26:2), just as the disciples should also do.[9]

26:10, 13. Finally, the text opposes the disciples who cause "trouble" for the woman (26:10) and the preachers of the gospel who will tell what she has done in memory of her (26:13). The woman ministered to Jesus. As she honored him, so she will be honored. Furthermore, what she did fits fully what is demanded by the present circumstances. Jesus had just announced his death "after two days" (26:2). As Jesus lies down ("reclining" at table; *anakeimai*, RSV: "as he sat at table," 26:7b), she pours ointment on his head, a gesture that Jesus can then interpret by saying: "In pouring this ointment on my body she has done it to prepare me for burial" (26:12). In brief, her act is part of the gospel because she honors Jesus as the Son of man who will die during the Passover (and not as one who has supernatural power or is triumphant). Consequently, those who will preach the gospel in the whole world will also proclaim in their own words that Jesus needs to be honored as the one who died during Passover, as the crucified. These preachers will need to have an attitude that is opposite that of the disciples in the story. The latter failed to recognize that the Son of man who will be dying after two days is the one who needs to be ministered to and honored. They failed to recognize that he who is "one of the least of these" (since he will be delivered up to be crucified) is the one worthy of honor, the greatest among them (cf. 20:25–28).

26:14–16. The fourth scene, Judas' betrayal, is thematic (it neither involves nor is linked with any opposition). Here Matthew expresses preceding points in terms of his readers' knowledge or expectation. The readers already know that one of the Twelve, Judas Iscariot, will deliver up Jesus (see 10:4). That one of the Twelve would join Jesus' opponents is not surprising for the readers, although one might deplore it; the preceding verses have shown that the disciples' attitude was similar to that of the Jewish leaders. If they fail to heed Jesus' rebuke of their attitude toward the woman's good deed, if they fail to acknowledge that Jesus must be honored as he submits to the prospect of being crucified because they remain single-minded in a one-dimensional world, then they already have much in common with the Jewish leaders. Matthew suggests that Judas merely takes an additional step on the path on which the disciples already were—they who wanted money for the poor—by emphasizing Judas' desire for money. It is he who asks the chief priests: "What will you give me if I deliver him to you?" (26:15a).

Yet there seems to be a tension in the text; the chief priests pay Judas right away, before he does anything. This suggests that Matthew introduces a new theme, as is confirmed by the formulation of 26:15b: "And they paid him thirty pieces of silver." Matthew, counting on their knowledge of Scripture, expects his readers to recognize this quasi quotation from Zech. 11:12.[10] Judas' action fulfills a prophecy from Scripture! Judas' betrayal shows that it is God who is in control of the unfolding of the events of the Passion. Judas actually deprives the Jewish leaders of any control over the timing of the arrest and death of Jesus! They had decided this would not take place during the feast (26:5). But now it is Judas who will choose the time: "And from that moment he sought an opportunity to betray him" (26:16). Through Judas' betrayal, God manifests complete control over time, just as the prophecies also express.

26:17–29. Celebration of the Passover. The Last Supper

It is striking that the second part of the Passion and Resurrection story is almost entirely thematic; it contains a single opposition which contrasts what each of the disciples says (26:22) to what Judas says (26:25). As a result Matthew makes only one new point, one that is important for the understanding of the entire passage.

26:17–19. The verses that describe the preparation of the Passover on the first day of the feast ("on the first day of Unleavened Bread") form a first thematic scene which reexpresses in terms of the readers' knowledge points that have been made earlier and that can be recognized in the tension created by the text. First, and in contrast to Judas, the disciples show that they attempt to heed Jesus' teaching in their usual way after several of Jesus' discourses. Jesus had rebuked them because they failed to recognize the importance of honoring him, an attitude comparable to that of the Jewish leaders who failed to view the Passover as a feast to be celebrated. That the disciples take the initiative to prepare the celebration of Passover (26:17) and then do what he commands (26:19) shows that they have understood and accepted Jesus' earlier words, at least in part.

Jesus' command to the disciples (26:18) is concise. He asks them to say to "a certain one," "The Teacher says, My time is at hand; I will keep the passover at your house with my disciples." This should strike the readers as a demonstration of Jesus' authority over the disciples and also *over those to whom the disciples convey his command.* At first this affirmation of Jesus' broad-ranging authority is, for the readers, in tension with Jesus' passive submission (see 26:2). But the statement "My time is at hand" (26:18), closely associated with the description of Judas seeking an "appropriate time to betray him" (26:16b, au.),[11] makes it clear that Jesus does not claim authority over time; this statement once again expresses Jesus' submission to time, over which God alone has control. That his crucifixion is near and that he submits to it does not mean that Jesus is without authority. He does not have control over *when* these events will take place, but he has control over *where* he will celebrate the Passover, even over the person whose house will hold the celebration. It is as the one who is to be crucified in the near future that he claims authority over those to whom the disciples will transmit his command. This authority is that of a "teacher," of someone who transmits a teaching which needs to be obeyed.

26:20–25. Once again the disciples seem to be on the side of Jesus, taking the initiative for the celebration of the Passover and submitting to his authority. Yet despite all their goodwill, their stance on Jesus' side is most fragile, as the first part of the description of the Passover meal (26:20–25) shows. It is in this passage that Matthew finds the need to underscore a point by opposing what each of the disciples says (26:22) to what Judas says (26:25). Their words are almost identical. In response to Jesus' announcement that one of them will betray him, both Judas and the rest of the disciples formulate the same question: "It is not me, is it?" (RSV: "Is it I?"). But Judas addresses Jesus as "Rabbi" (RSV: "Master"), while the others call him "Lord."

The main difference between Judas and the rest of the disciples is that he already knows the answer to his question (the text designates him as the one "who betrayed him" and reports Jesus' response, "You have said so" 26:25), while the others do not know. The great sorrow of the (eleven) disciples (26:22a) and the formulation of their question show that the disciples do not exclude the possibility they might betray Jesus. The disciples strive to be faithful to Jesus and to follow his teaching as they have demonstrated by preparing the Passover meal for him (26:17–19) and eating it with him (26:20). Yet they cannot be sure whether or not they will betray Jesus. And in fact, the one who will betray Jesus is the one who is the most directly associated with him: "He who has dipped his hand in the dish with me" (26:23). Being associated with Jesus is no guarantee that one will not betray him.

So what is the basic difference between a betrayer and faithful disciples? It is expressed in Jesus' explanation of the situation: "The Son of man goes as it is written of him, but woe to that man by whom the Son of man is betrayed!" (26:24). This verse appears to be the application to a specific case of the teaching in 18:7:[12] "For it is necessary that scandals come, but woe to the person by whom the scandal comes" (au.). The scandal brought to the "little ones" (18:6) is here the betrayal of the Son of man (who identifies himself with the "least of these," 25:31–46); and it is specified that the coming of scandals is necessary because it needs to be according to Scripture. In 18:1–9 those who scandalize others are those who themselves have been scandalized *because they do not "turn and become like children"* (18:3); they do not perceive themselves to be lacking anything that they need to receive from someone else.

In this light, the point Matthew makes by the opposition contained in 26:20–25 appears. The (eleven) disciples who do not betray Jesus are those who really do not know whether or not they can be faithful and can avoid betraying Jesus. They are anxious and troubled "children" who pathetically need to be reassured by Jesus' answer: "It is not me, is it, Lord?" (26:22b, au.). By contrast, the betrayer does not need an answer to his question; he knows it: "You have said so" (26:25b). He is not a child anxiously needing an answer from someone else; he really does not expect to receive anything from Jesus. Woe to him! Indeed, his betrayal contributes to the departure of the Son of man, a necessity according to Scripture, because it and other scandals must happen (18:7). As the scandal of the persecutions of the disciples must happen in order that the gospel be proclaimed to the entire world (cf. 10:18; 24:14; and their contexts), so Jesus must be betrayed. But for the one who brings about the scandal, "It would have been better for that man if he had not been born" (26:24b; cf. 18:6).

26:26–29. In order to elucidate how Matthew understood the institution of the sacrament of the Lord's Supper (Eucharist), one needs to read it as an integral part of the Passover meal scene to which it belongs. Since it is a thematic passage (it does not include any opposition), it should be interpreted in terms of the preceding passage and the point it expresses.

The text simply says that Jesus gives bread and cup, his body and his blood, to "the disciples" (26:26). There is no mention whether Judas has gone away or not and his shadow lingers over this group, even if the readers conclude that he has left. As the eleven are not sure that they would not betray Jesus, so the readers are not sure whether the group to whom Jesus offers bread and cup includes the betrayer. In short, the disciples are perceived as people who, truthfully or not, have expressed their anxiety about their ability to remain faithful to Jesus. It then appears that the giving of bread and cup, of his body and his blood, is a way whereby the disciples' need is being met. The eleven needed reassurance that they would not be the betrayer. For Matthew, they are reassured when Jesus designates Judas as his betrayer (26:23–25). By their anxiety, however, they have expressed their lack of confidence in having the ability to remain faithful. In this light, the giving of bread and cup is to be perceived as providing them with what they need. Faithful disciples are those who see themselves to be in need of receiving from Jesus bread and cup, his body and his blood; they are those who obey his command to eat and drink. They are indeed anxious and troubled children who cannot envision being faithful disciples if they do not receive from Jesus what they need.

Beyond the preceding point, 26:26–29 specifies what the disciples need to receive from Jesus and therefore what is their basic need. In 26:26–27 Jesus twice repeats similar gestures;[13] Jesus "took" (bread, a cup), "blessed" or gave thanks, "gave it to the disciples," and then commanded them to either "eat" or "drink." In addition, both the bread and the cup are related to Jesus: "this is my body," "this is my blood." A discrepancy (tension) in the parallelism of 26:26 and 27 directs our attention toward it. In 26:26 we find the mention of "bread" which is taken, broken, and eaten—a sequence of acts which could be taken literally. Thus the parallel term for "bread" should be "wine" which could be taken, poured, and drunk. But the text refers to a "cup." Of course, the cup is to be interpreted as referring to the wine that it contains (the cup is a metonymy for wine). The discrepancy in the parallelism forces the readers to notice that this is a Passover meal characterized by the saying of blessings *over the cup* (several times during the meal). These verses need to be interpreted in terms of the celebration of the Passover.

This discrepancy also calls for a nonliteral (symbolic) interpretation of these verses. In other words, the need of the disciples is not for "bread" and "wine," food and drink for their physical bodies. Their basic need is expressed in 26:28: "for this is my blood of the covenant, which is poured out for many for the forgiveness of sins." The basic need of the disciples is for "forgiveness of sins," which is part of a "covenant" between God and many (disciples) established by Jesus' blood "poured out for many." In this way, the text invites the readers to see Jesus' death (the pouring of his blood) as a Passover sacrifice, related to the giving of a covenant between God and the people (many disciples), and for a deliverance from sins (instead of from Egypt). Forgiveness is indeed what the disciples need, they who have been described as lacking self-assurance that they will be able to be faithful disciples (26:20–25) and who constantly do the wrong thing despite their effort to apply Jesus' teaching (26:6–13).

But how will their need be met? How will they be able to participate in this covenant? How will they receive this forgiveness of their sins? "Take, eat; this is my body" (26:26b). "Drink of it, all of you; for this is my blood" (26:27b–28a). The readers are reminded of an earlier passage where Jesus spoke about drinking the cup that he is to drink (20:22–23), a passage that expresses in a general way that drinking means sharing Jesus' fate, possibly being persecuted as he is betrayed and crucified (20:18). In this light, it appears that the disciples are invited to associate themselves with Jesus' death, to make his (broken) body and his poured-out blood theirs. In brief, Jesus' death is offering to the disciples what will meet their basic need, provided they obey his command and associate themselves with his death. Bread and cup, Jesus' body and blood, are offered to them; in turn they have to take and eat that bread and drink that cup. With such an attitude, they will not be betrayers, but faithful disciples.

The concluding verse of this passage, 26:29, emphasizes that this meal is the last one Jesus will have with his disciples. This is the "last supper." This means that in the very process of providing his disciples with what they most urgently need—his death—in order to be disciples who do not betray their Lord, the disciples will be separated from Jesus. Paradoxically it is only when they will be separated from Jesus that the disciples can hope to be faithful to their Lord, because it is only through his death and their association with it that they will receive what they need to be faithful disciples. Yet Jesus adds: "until that day when I drink it new with you in my Father's kingdom" (26:29b). This separation is not permanent; they will be together in the kingdom of the Father. It is this very separation, Jesus' death, which will make it possible for the disciples to participate in the kingdom with Jesus—rather than being cursed, and thus rejected from the kingdom, as the betrayer is (26:24). Jesus' death and sharing of it is also a promise that the disciples will share in the feast of the kingdom with Jesus, because Jesus' death offers to the disciples what will enable them to be faithful (and not betrayers).

A central question remains without answer: In which sense are the disciples to associate themselves with Jesus' death? In the thematic passage, 26:26–29, the meaning of "eat; this is my body" and of "drink of [the cup] . . . ; for this is my blood" remains somewhat undetermined. The answer to this question is to be found in the Passion story, especially in passages such as 26:30–35 and 26:36–46 where Jesus criticizes the disciples for their attitude. These passages will show that accepting association with Jesus' death means: (*a*) being scandalized by him, accepting a stripping away of all that gives one the self-confidence that one can be a faithful disciple; (*b*) being scattered, and thus accepting separation from him; (*c*) watching and praying with him, in order to avoid the temptation of denying him. Through this sharing of Jesus' Passion, one is then paradoxically equipped to be a faithful disciple, one who is totally dependent on God's constant help for carrying one's mission.

26:30–35. Jesus Announces the Scattering of the Disciples

These verses in which Jesus prophesies that the disciples will "be scandalized by" him (RSV: "fall away because of" him, 26:31, 33) are closely linked with the Passover meal, whose last part, the singing of hymns (psalms), is mentioned in 26:30. The points Matthew makes in this passage prolong the themes we have just discussed.

We need to be aware that the text describes *two quite different* relationships between the disciples and Jesus during the Passion. On the one hand, the disciples "will be scandalized by" Jesus and "will be scattered" (26:31, au.). In this case the disciples are passive; this kind of separation from Jesus happens to the disciples. Nothing in the first part of the text (26:30–33) suggests that Jesus is reproving his disciples when he tells them that they will be scandalized and be scattered. Instead, he is reassuring them in two ways. First, he emphasizes that he is the cause of their being scandalized and scattered (26:31, 33) and that this is to be expected since it is prophesied in Scripture (26:31). Second, he promises them that they will be reunited after his resurrection (26:32). On the other hand, in 26:34–35 we read about denial, a separation of which the disciples are the active subject: "you will deny me" (26:34), "I will not deny you" (26:35). In this case, Jesus clearly reproves Peter for such a denial.

26:31–33. The scattering of the disciples is presented as happening according to Scripture (cf. the quotation of Zech. 13:7 in 26:31),[14] just like Jesus' departure (26:24) and Judas' betrayal (see 26:15). Yet these three fulfillments of Scripture are qualitatively different. Jesus' departure has been shown to be necessary for the sake of the disciples who, without it, could not be faithful (26:26–29). Judas is cursed because of his betrayal (26:24); he who brings about the departure of Jesus will be permanently separated from him. But when the disciples are scandalized by Jesus and are scattered (26:31) their separation from Jesus will not be permanent; they will be reunited in Galilee after his resurrection (26:32) before being reunited with him in the kingdom of the Father (26:29). Here Jesus does not reprove his disciples. It is Peter who objects and finds the suggestion that they will be scandalized by Jesus to be unworthy of them. The polemical exchange between Jesus and Peter in 26:31, 33 sets up an opposition through which Matthew shows that Jesus and Peter evaluate what will happen to the disciples during the Passion (namely, being, or not being, scandalized by Jesus) from two different perspectives.

In 26:33, Peter is incorrect. First, for him being scandalized or not is a matter of individual decision: "Though they all are scandalized by you, I myself will never be scandalized" (26:33, au.). Peter is *self-confident* that he will have the strength or courage to remain associated with Jesus despite everything. The point expressed by Jesus' words in 26:31–33 can then be perceived. On the one hand, "all" the disciples are in the same situation; no one can claim a different status, a different ability to remain with Jesus— "You all will be scandalized by me" (26:31a, au.). On the other hand, Peter's self-confidence contradicts the prophecy of Zechariah, according to which only one can be said to be in control of the situation—namely, God, who says, "I will strike the shepherd" (26:31b). Ideal disciples—disciples who would not contradict the prophecy of Zechariah—are those who, in contrast to Peter, would view themselves as being totally at the mercy of what will happen and thus as unable to avoid being scattered when Jesus will be struck.

A second point made in 26:31–33 can be seen when one notes that Peter considers being scandalized by Jesus in permanent and absolute terms ("never," 26:33). Jesus' words make the point that being scandalized by Jesus is limited in time ("this night," 26:31). It should not be construed as a once-and-for-all separation from Jesus; indeed, they will be reunited at a later time, after the resurrection (26:32).

In sum, because the disciples are associated with Jesus during "this night"—they are the flock of which he is the shepherd when he is struck (26:31)—they will be stripped of all their self-confidence. As Peter does, they believe that they have what it takes to remain with Jesus whatever the circumstances: strength, courage, tenacity which they have demonstrated by following Jesus since he first called them in Galilee (see 4:18–22).[15] In other words, while the Passion of Jesus is the loss of his life, the "Passion of the disciples"—being associated with Jesus' death, eating his body, drinking his cup and his blood—is the loss of anything that gives them the self-confidence that they can follow Jesus and be with him. They are stripped of what they might view as allowing them to be disciples; continuing to be disciples is not in their power. Stripped of anything that would give them self-confidence, they who are disciples associated with Jesus during his Passion are made to become like children totally at the mercy of others and of God. And since "children" are "the greatest in the kingdom" (18:4), their participation in the Passion (being scandalized by Jesus) during "this night" will make of them ideal and true disciples, the greatest in the kingdom, those who will sit on the thrones with the Son of man at the time of the judgment (19:28); they will drink with Jesus in the kingdom of the Father (26:29). And all this is God's doing, as Matthew emphasizes by his formulation based on Zech. 13:7, according to which God says: "I will strike the shepherd."

26:34–35. The point made in the last two verses of the passage is related to the preceding point, as suggested by the repetition of the phrase "this night" in 26:34. In his second statement approved by the rest of the disciples (26:35), Peter concedes that he is not in control of the situation; the first part of his answer can be rendered: "Even if it must happen to me that I should die with you" (26:35a). He acknowledges that he might not be able to do anything about the situation and that he might be destroyed by it. But he remains self-confident that he will want to remain by Jesus' side, even at the cost of his life. In other words, even if he is deprived of everything else, he is confident that he will still retain one thing, an unshakable will to be with Jesus: "Even if I must die with you, I will not deny you."

In this light, the point of Jesus' saying in 26:34 appears: "you will deny me three times" (26:34). A single denial could be construed as an involuntary lapse. But three denials in a relatively short time—"this very night, before the cock crows"—means that Peter will deny his wish to be associated with Jesus; he will lose even his will to be with Jesus. He will reject his identity as a disciple (see 26:69–75).

The significance of Matthew's points in 26:30–35 appears when one recalls how in 26:20–25 he has emphasized that faithful disciples, ones who do not betray Jesus as Judas does, are those who show a lack of self-confidence and therefore perceive themselves as needing something from Jesus. Throughout the Passion the disciples will be stripped of anything that leads to self-confidence that they themselves could be faithful disciples. They will need to acknowledge that their ability to be disciples depends totally upon help from God (or Jesus)—the condition for being faithful disciples. But simultaneously this passage is a warning. Through their participation in the Passion they might even lose their will to be disciples, their will to be associated with Jesus. In sum, instead of making them faithful disciples, the Passion could have the opposite result, making them lose their discipleship, denying Jesus, if they refuse to give up the self-confidence that they have what it takes to be faithful disciples (as Peter does in 26:33). This is what the next passage, 26:36–46, further expresses by showing what one needs to do in order to retain their identity as disciples (and as Son of God) through the Passion.

26:36–46. Jesus and the Disciples at Gethsemane

The theme of the scene at Gethsemane is twofold, as the tension between 26:36 and 26:37 suggests. The former verse indicates that even though Jesus went to Gethsemane with his disciples, nevertheless he is the only one who will go and pray; he asks his disciples to "sit here," as if he were the only one needing to pray. But in 26:37 he takes three disciples with him, Peter and the sons of Zebedee, asking them to "watch" with him (26:38) and to "pray" (see 26:41a). The meaning of this tension becomes clear by the end of the passage. In brief, being close to Jesus or being separated from Jesus does not make any difference in the disciples' response to the situation. Whether the disciples are with Jesus (Peter and the sons of Zebedee in 26:39; Jesus only goes "a little farther" to pray and in 26:38 he asks them to watch *with him*) or are separated from him as the other disciples are, the disciples do not pray. They just "sit here," sleeping, resting (26:45). As a consequence, and this is a first part of the theme, nothing changes for the disciples. In contrast, and this is a second part of the theme, something changes for Jesus; at first Jesus, who is very "sorrowful and troubled" (26:37), asks his Father that "this cup pass from" him (26:39), while he does not do so later on (26:42, 44). Since it is clear that these agonizing prayers of Jesus are a struggle to accept the will of his Father (four verses refer to "will," 26:39, 41, 42, 44), we suspect that by the end of the scene Jesus has made his own the will of his Father. But so should have the disciples! Yet they did not.

What is at stake in this twofold theme is expressed by Matthew's points made through three oppositions. Two of these oppose what the disciples should do, watching and praying (26:38, 41), to what they actually do, sleeping (26:40, 43, 45). The third opposition is expressed in Jesus' words: "not as I will, but as thou wilt" (26:39b).[16] One point concerns the disciples, and the other Jesus. Consider the latter first.

26:39b. The words "not as I will, but as thou wilt" (26:39b) oppose what would hypothetically happen according to the will that Jesus has in the first part of the scene (this cup, the crucifixion, will pass from him) to what will happen according to God's will. Matthew's point therefore concerns the discrepancy between Jesus' will and God's will, even though this discrepancy is erased as soon as it is mentioned, and by the very words that evoke it. Note how Jesus is described in the preceding verses. First, he is described as "sorrowful and troubled" (26:37), a point that is underscored when he says, "My soul is very sorrowful, even to death" (26:38). It is clear that he is sorrowful at the prospect of his death which he announced by quoting Zechariah in such a way as to express that it is God who will strike him (26:31). Yet Jesus is also described as praying to God and addressing him as "My Father" (26:39).

It is now essential to recall 26:30–35. Matthew underscored that in the Passion the disciples would be stripped of self-confidence and that they might lose their identity as disciples by denying Jesus—by losing the will to be associated with him. Thus it appears that the Passion has a similar effect on Jesus. It challenges his relationship with his Father to the point that he runs the risk of no longer identifying his will with that of God. In such a case he would no longer be in a Son-Father relationship with God. The tragedy of Gethsemane, Jesus' sorrow and distress, is that the Father, whose absolute trustworthiness and goodness Jesus proclaimed when preaching the kingdom, is now the one who strikes him. For Matthew, whatever will happen is according to God's will; in Jesus' prayers what is "possible" (26:39) or not (26:42) is totally identified with God's will.[17] Thus "this cup," the cross, is according to his Father's will. As the disciples will be scandalized by Jesus, so Jesus is scandalized by his Father: "My soul is very sorrowful, even to death" (26:38). As the disciples will be scattered, separated from Jesus, so Jesus is separated from his Father, abandoned by him (see 27:46). But unlike the disciples whose will to remain associated with Jesus will be shaken, Jesus' will to remain associated with this God who strikes him remains unshakable. He continues to address him as "My Father" (26:39, 42) and submits his will to his Father's will: "not as I will, but as thou wilt" (26:39b); "thy will be done" (26:42b). In sum, by watching and praying Jesus overcomes the temptation to deny his Father (see 26:41).

26:38–45. This last comment already alludes to the two other oppositions that contrast what the disciples should have done, watch (26:38, 41), and what they did, sleep (26:40, 43) and rest (26:45). In the light of the preceding, the point made by these two oppositions can readily be grasped. Unlike Jesus, the disciples—especially Peter here with the sons of Zebedee—in their self-confidence refuse the possibility that they might be scandalized. They do not share the tragedy of Gethsemane even though Jesus in his great sorrow asked them to do so: "watch with me" (26:38). And how could they be sorrowful at the prospect of being scandalized by Jesus and of being separated from him, they who are so confident of having the strength to avoid such a tragedy (26:3, 35). They rest (26:45)! "The spirit indeed is willing, but the flesh is weak" (26:41b). Ironically, they do not even have the strength to watch for one hour (26:40b). Watching and praying would have been the only thing that would have prevented them from entering "into temptation" (26:41a)—from denying Jesus, from losing their will to be associated with Jesus. Furthermore, even though Jesus takes them with him (26:37) and makes repeated efforts to be with them (26:40a, 43), by not watching with him and by sleeping the three disciples abandon Jesus; they separate themselves from him. In turn, Jesus leaves them (26:44) to their sleep.

26:45–46. Thus, the disciples are found sleeping, taking their rest, instead of watching when "the hour is at hand" (26:45) and when "the betrayer is at hand" (26:46). The verb "is at hand" was previously used to speak of the coming of the kingdom (3:2; 4:17; 10:7) and of the harvest (21:34). The mention of "the [unexpected] hour" being at hand recalls references to the coming of the Son of man (24:44, 50; 25:13). For the readers, these phrases therefore evoke many possible connotations.[18] But the point is clear: despite Jesus' warning, the disciples are caught sleeping at "the hour" when they should have been watching. This is the hour when Jesus will be betrayed (26:45–46) but also the hour when the disciples will be scattered and when Peter will deny him.

26:47–56. The Arrest of Jesus

26:47–50. The first part of the story of the arrest of Jesus (26:47–50) is thematic. Matthew simply tells it without attempting to make a new point. There is only one thing that might stop the readers, namely, Jesus' response to Judas in 26:50a. At any rate, it stops the commentators and the translators who are at a loss to render it! The RSV proposes two translations which represent well the range of possible meanings:[19] "Friend, why are you here?" or "Friend, do that for which you have come." Most likely this answer shows that Jesus resists neither Judas nor his arrest.[20] Of course, the readers are struck by the manner in which Judas betrays Jesus, the kiss (mentioned twice, 26:48, 49). Jesus is betrayed by one who is intimate with him, one of the Twelve (26:47).

26:51–54. The act of "one of those who were with Jesus" drawing his sword (and striking the servant of the high priest, 26:51) is opposed to Jesus' command, "Put your sword back into its place" (26:52). This first opposition underscores that the use of a sword (violence) is inappropriate for "those who [are] with Jesus" (26:51a). Matthew makes it clear that this point has a general application rather than an application limited to the time of the arrest of Jesus.[21] This is shown by the way in which Jesus justifies his command by a *general* statement about the outcome of the use of violence: "for all who take the sword will perish by the sword" (26:52b). Thus, whatever might be the time and the circumstances, the group of "those who [are] with Jesus" should not make use of swords and violence to protect itself. In short, Jesus' passive submission to his opponents during the Passion is a model for the attitude that his followers should have in similar situations.

A second point is made by the opposition of what Jesus says (26:52, 54) with what the follower of Jesus might think (26:53). This point is directly related to those made in the scene at Gethsemane (26:36–46). Once again, what is "possible" or not ("Do you think that I cannot . . . ?" 26:53b) is subordinated to what is according to God's will. If it were God's will that Jesus be protected from his opponents, he could appeal to his Father, who would at once send him all the help he would need, "twelve legions of angels" (26:53). But Jesus does not do so because he has made God's will his own will. Beyond the points made in 26:36–46, the will of God is here identified with "scriptures." In other words, all the fulfillments of the prophecies of Scripture (whatever they might be) are according to God's will; "it must be so" (26:54b).

26:55–56. The words to the crowds further develop the preceding point, as indicated by "at that hour" (26:55a)—Matthew uses such temporal phrases to signal a thematic continuity—and by the concluding statement about Scripture (26:56a).

The opposition between capturing Jesus (26:55a) and not seizing him (26:55b) underscores the transformation of the crowds' attitude toward Jesus and in this way develops further the point made by the former of the two oppositions in 26:51–54. That the crowds come to capture him with swords and clubs shows that they view Jesus as a dangerous man, a highway bandit. Like the person who struck the high priest's servant, they think that Jesus (and his followers) would use violence to defend himself. But this is a wrong view of Jesus. Defenseless, he "sat" among them many times ("day after day") teaching in the Temple. Far from being a violent man, he was teaching them the things of God "in the temple." For some reason, the crowds have abandoned this correct perception of Jesus and now mistakenly view him as one who would use or condone violence. He, however, is the one who rebukes the use of violence (26:52).

"But all this has taken place, that the scriptures of the prophets might be fulfilled" (26:56a) develops the latter of the two points made in 26:51–54. Here Matthew emphasizes that both ("all this has taken place") seizing Jesus with swords and clubs as if he were a robber and not seizing him while he was teaching in the Temple are fulfillment of Scripture. For the readers, this means that neither of these actions can be viewed as negative; both are according to God's will. Difficult as it might be for the readers, they should not view Jesus' arrest as a tragedy.

"Then all the disciples forsook him and fled" (26:56b) indicates that Jesus' prediction—that "all" the disciples would be scandalized by him and would be scattered (26:31)—has come to pass. They were ready to fight for him (26:51) and to stay by his side "even if [they] must die with [him]" (26:35). But when Jesus forbids them to use violence and emphasizes that he is not a highway bandit, they abandon him and flee; they are scandalized by such a nonviolent Jesus.

26:57–75. Jesus Before Caiaphas and Peter's Denial

This long pericope is composed of two intertwined stories: the story of Jesus before Caiaphas (26:57, 59–68) and the story of Peter's denial (26:58, 69–75). Each of these stories makes its own points and could be interpreted by itself. That they are intertwined requires us to interpret them together and in terms of each other. Their respective points complement and reinforce each other.

26:57–58. The entire passage is linked with preceding ones through these two verses which thematically introduce the two stories. Jesus is brought to the group that had gathered at Caiaphas' palace to plot his arrest and killing (26:3–5). The Jewish authorities are no longer designated as leaders of "the people." They are now constituted as a court, the Sanhedrin (26:59a), whose authority is no longer considered in terms of those upon whom it is exerted but in terms of its religious function of judging in the name of "the living God" (26:63) and according to the law of God—thus the addition of "scribes" to the list of participants in this group (26:57). By contrast, Peter, who follows Jesus as the disciples did throughout Jesus' ministry, represents the group of Jesus' followers. But it is "at a distance" that he follows Jesus. This warns the readers that there is something unusual in this verse which needs to be interpreted in terms of what they have read in 26:30–35. As he claimed he would do (26:33), Peter continues to follow Jesus at a time when the other disciples have been scattered and have fled

(26:31; 26:56); he does not allow himself to be scandalized by Jesus, despite the prophecy of Zechariah quoted by Jesus in 26:31. Peter, in his single-minded effort to carry out what he said he would do and what he considers to be true faithfulness to Jesus, is not unlike the Jewish leaders who pursue the implementation of their single-minded plan (see the comments on 26:3–13). One can then wonder whether these leaders do not defy by their actions the very law of God that they strive to implement, as Peter defies both the prophecy of Scripture and the teaching of Jesus (26:31) in his single-minded effort to be faithful to him.

26:59–60. Matthew makes a first point by opposing seeking "false testimony" (26:59) to not finding any (26:60a). This opposition underscores that, despite many false witnesses, "the chief priests and the whole council" (Sanhedrin) are unable to find false testimony that could serve as sufficient legal evidence for condemning Jesus to death. In order to uphold the law, the Sanhedrin cannot condemn Jesus without evidence acceptable according to the law. That such legally valid evidence would be "false testimony" shows that the chief priests and the Sanhedrin strive to fulfill faithfully their vocation in the same twisted manner that Peter strives to be faithful to Jesus. But they are prevented from carrying out this travesty of justice; they cannot find among the false testimonies any evidence that would meet the requirements for acceptable evidence for condemning Jesus to death (according to the law). Consequently, for the second time (see 26:14–16), events do not follow the plan of the Jewish leaders. In spite of them, Jesus will not be condemned on the basis of false evidence.

This point is confirmed by the words in 26:60b. First, note that this statement is separated from the preceding by a temporal notation, "at last." This signals that the two new witnesses should not be associated with the preceding ones, who are designated as "false witnesses." Second, these two persons are not called "false" witnesses. Third, this testimony is brought by "two" witnesses; Matthew has underscored in 18:16 (cf. Deut. 17:6–7; 19:15) the importance of the testimony of two (or three) witnesses for establishing the truth of a testimony. In sum, we conclude[22] that, for Matthew, the testimony presented in 26:61 is true! Jesus' condemnation will be based on true evidence.

Consequently the condemnation of Jesus to death is not the result of a corrupted application of the Jewish interpretation of the law. The circumstances, which are governed by God (as repeatedly emphasized in this chapter), force the Sanhedrin to exercise its authority in full legality. So by condemning the Son of man to death, the Sanhedrin condemns itself. In brief, it is the Jewish interpretation and application of the law, and not a corrupted form of them, which are rejected.

26:61–63a. According to Matthew, the statement of Jesus that is reported by the two witnesses is therefore true. However, according to this report, Jesus does not say that he *will* destroy the Temple of God and rebuild it in three days, but rather that *he can do it*: "I am able to . . ." (26:61). It is a statement regarding his power, not what he will do or will not do. While the Gospel does not report such a saying in any of Jesus' earlier discourses, for the readers such a statement is not unthinkable; after all, Jesus' divine power has been repeatedly demonstrated. Ironically, the issue that will bring about the condemnation of Jesus—he has been arrested while refusing to use his power and violence and is therefore powerless—has to do exclusively with his power and authority.

It is in this light that the opposition expressed by the high priest's question (26:62) and Jesus' silence (26:63a) needs to be interpreted. For the chief priest, Jesus should defend himself against such an accusation; he should either deny that he made such a statement ("Have you no answer to make?") or at least explain it ("What is it that these men testify against you?" 26:62). For the high priest, Jesus does not have such a power, and therefore the statement of the witnesses is false either because Jesus did not say it or because Jesus falsely claimed to have such a power. By his silence, Jesus refuses to deny that he has such a power.

26:63b–64a. The following exchange opposes the high priest, who asks Jesus to tell them if he is the Christ, the Son of God (26:63b), to Jesus, who answers that the high priest himself has said so (26:64a). For Matthew's readers, that the high priest raises the issue of knowing whether or not Jesus is "the Christ, the Son of God" is not surprising, even though it is historically unlikely that a high priest would use such a phrase.[23] In the Gospel the titles "Christ" and "Son of God" (or close equivalents) are used by people who are not disciples and by demons (8:29) in order to express their recognition that Jesus has divine power. Since Jesus did not deny that he has the power to destroy the Temple and rebuild it in three days, a power that can only be divine, Matthew's high priest can only wonder: Is he not implicitly claiming to be the Christ, the Son of God?

The point of this opposition concerns the high priest's attempts to put Jesus under the obligation to declare himself to be the Christ, the Son of God. He does so by putting Jesus under an oath: "I adjure you by the living God" (26:63). But as his answer shows, Jesus is not under any obligation to do so; the high priest has already said he is the Christ, the Son of God. This also means that such an oath is not binding for Jesus; it is actually wrong. Jesus has taught that oaths of any kind are against God's will (5:33–37). Jesus' answer involves therefore a rejection of the high priest's oath as a religious practice and a denial that the high priest has any authority over him.

26:64b–65. Another opposition is set by Jesus' second statement—

"moreover I tell you" (26:64b, au.)—and the high priest's response (26:65).
While Jesus does not need to say anything regarding his present status as
the Christ, the Son of God, he speaks about the authority of the future
("you will see") Son of man, in words combining those of Ps. 110:1 and
Dan. 7:13: "the Son of man seated at the right hand of Power, and coming
on the clouds of heaven" (26:64). By this statement Jesus claims even more
power and authority than the power to destroy and rebuild the Temple in
three days (26:61). Although he speaks in the third person about the Son
of man, it is clear for the readers and also for the high priest that he speaks
about himself. It is this claim of future power and authority which the high
priest and the Sanhedrin view as a blasphemy. The text removes any possible
ambiguity by presenting Jesus as speaking of sitting at the right hand "of
Power" rather than "of God." If the latter phrase had been used, one could
say that Jesus was accused of blasphemy because he used the name of God
improperly. His blasphemy is to claim that he will share in God's power.

Conversely, the text condemns the Jewish leaders for having declared
blasphemous what, from the perspective of the readers, is actually true.
Jesus has been shown to be trustworthy, and thus this new prophecy (cf.,
e.g., 16:27) concerning his future coming in power is true.

26:66–68. These thematic verses draw the conclusion of what precedes
in terms of the readers' expectations. Of course, once he is declared to be
a blasphemer, Jesus is condemned to death (26:66), as was expected (see
26:59). Furthermore, by their actions—spitting in his face, striking him,
asking him to prophesy—the members of the Sanhedrin deny that he has
any authority which should be respected, that he has any power which
would allow him to protect himself from their blows, and that he has any
messianic gift of prophecy which would allow him to tell who struck him,
let alone to say what will happen in the future (see 26:64).

26:69–75. The story of Peter's denial fulfills Jesus' prophecy (26:34); this
is underscored in the concluding verse (26:75). It provides, therefore, an
ironic response to the mocking words of Jesus' opponents who teased him,
saying: "Prophesy to us, you Christ!" (26:68). What Jesus prophesies comes
about! As a result, his prophecy that he will sit at the right hand of Power
and will come on the clouds of heaven (26:64) is trustworthy. Simultaneously, through the points made in it, the story of Peter's denial shows how
the points made regarding Jesus before the Sanhedrin apply to the disciples.

Each of the three denials sets up an opposition. In the first one (26:69–
70) the maid's statement is obviously true; Peter was with Jesus. Her words
are comparable to those of the two (true) witnesses (26:61). Both are true,
although each of them involves something odd which suggests antagonism;
the words of the witnesses have not been recorded in Jesus' earlier discourses; the maid calls Jesus a "Galilean." Peter's attitude should therefore

be comparable with that of Jesus when he was confronted with a true testimony which is potentially damaging for him; he should remain silent (26:63a). "Before them all" and confronted with the threat they represent, he should not anxiously seek for words that would protect him from this potential danger but rather wait for the words that the Spirit of his Father will speak through him (see 10:19–20). Yet Peter spoke: "I do not know what you say" (26:70, au.). As the high priest did when he asked, "What is it that these men testify against you?" (26:62b), Peter pretends that he does not understand the true statement of the maid. In brief, instead of being like Jesus, Peter is like the high priest.

The opposition set up by the second denial further underscores that Peter is like the high priest. As the high priest uses an oath ("I adjure you by the living God," 26:63), so does Peter: "he denied it with an oath" (26:72). Furthermore, the other maid's words are comparable to those of Jesus in 26:64. The maid does not speak to Peter but to the bystanders. Consequently, she speaks of Peter in the third person—"This [one] was with Jesus of Nazareth" (26:71b)—as Jesus spoke of himself in the third person—"you will see the Son of man" (26:64). As Jesus' words described the glory and authority of the Son of man, so, for a disciple, the words of the maid should be taken as a description of his glory and authority. What could be more glorious for a disciple than having people testifying about him: "This [one] was with Jesus of Nazareth"! But Peter denies it. By saying, "I do not know the man" (26:72), Peter denies both Jesus and the glory and authority of being a disciple.

In the third denial (26:73–74a) Matthew makes an additional point. It is because of Peter's way of speaking (or "accent," 26:73b) that the bystanders recognize him to be an associate of Jesus. Despite all his efforts to use words that would dissociate himself from Jesus, these very words identify him as one of the disciples! As all the members of the Sanhedrin condemned Jesus because of what they "heard" him say (26:65b), so people identify Peter as belonging to the group of followers of the condemned Jesus because of what they hear him say. But this also means that, despite his repeated denials—including the third one in which he once again uses an oath (26:74a)—Peter remains associated with Jesus; he remains a disciple. Unlike Judas, who is cursed because of his betrayal and is permanently separated from Jesus, Peter is prevented from irreparably separating himself from Jesus.

Peter is interrupted in his third denial. He was just beginning "to invoke a curse on himself and to swear, 'I do not know the man'" (26:74a) when the cock crowed ("immediately," 26:74b). Remembering Jesus' words, he stops denying Jesus: "he went out and wept bitterly" (26:75b). Despite his denials, Peter is still a disciple, but now a disciple who has been stripped of all his self-confidence—just as the condemned Jesus is powerless, mocked, and called a false prophet by his opponents.

27:1–26. Jesus Before Pilate and the Death of Judas

As in the case of 26:57–75, two stories are intertwined in this subsection and need to be interpreted together. That the story of Judas' death (27:3–10) is introduced into the story of Jesus before Pilate (27:1–2, 11–26) casts the latter story in a peculiar light, adding dimensions to it, just as the story of Jesus before the Sanhedrin gave meaning to the story of Peter's denial.

First, note that neither of the two stories is focused on Jesus. There is not even any direct reference to Jesus in the story of Judas (except in 27:9, a quotation). Similarly, in the scene before Pilate, it is in the introductory verses alone (27:11–14) that Jesus plays an active role, a role limited to two words! In sum, we have reason to suspect that the themes and points of this subsection concern the respective roles of Judas, the Jewish leaders, the crowd, and Pilate in the events leading to Jesus' death, and the various degrees of responsibility and guilt each of them has.

27:1–2. The introductory verses of this subsection are thematic. They express themes in terms of the readers' knowledge and, at this stage of the Gospel, primarily in terms of what they have read earlier in it. Even though historically speaking the first verse (27:1) might refer to the daytime formal condemnation of Jesus by the Sanhedrin (which could not make such decisions at night), Matthew's concern is elsewhere. The Jewish leaders are no longer presented as forming a court of law with scribes as in 26:57. Rather, we are reminded of 26:3, which emphasized the relationship of this group to "the people": these are leaders "of the people." Furthermore, it is "all the people" who, following the instruction of the Jewish leaders (27:20), play the central role in the concluding part of this subsection (see 27:21–25). It is as leaders of the people that the chief priests and the elders deliver Jesus to Pilate (27:2).

The use of the verb "to deliver" (*paradidōmi*, also translated "to betray") to describe the action of the Jewish leaders is significant. So far in the Gospel, Judas alone has been described as delivering or betraying Jesus (10:4; 26:15, 25), an action for which he was cursed when Jesus declared: "Woe to that man by whom the Son of man is betrayed!" (or delivered, 26:24). Here those to whom Jesus has been delivered by Judas in turn deliver him to Pilate. Does this mean that the Jewish leaders become betrayers of Jesus and are themselves under the curse that Jesus pronounced against whoever delivers the Son of man?

The validity of this question, although it is based on a possibly incidental use of a word, is confirmed by the following passage (27:3–10) and at the end of the subsection (27:25). "All the people" who submitted to the authority of the Jewish leaders—those who delivered Jesus to Pilate—put themselves under this curse by declaring: "His blood be on us and on our children!" (27:25). In sum, all those who carry on what Judas has begun are inextricably associated with Judas' action; they become betrayers of Jesus, and all of them are under the same curse.

27:3–10. This is the issue at stake in the confrontation between Judas and the chief priests and elders. A first opposition is set by what the repentant Judas says to the Jewish leaders (27:3–4a) and their response (27:4b). The point is that Judas recognizes that he has "sinned in betraying [or delivering] innocent blood," while the Jewish leaders do not recognize that they themselves have sinned. They do not deny that Judas has sinned, but they believe that they can dissociate themselves from his sin: "What is that to us? See to it yourself" (27:4b). It is not without irony that Matthew presents their claim that they do not share in Judas' responsibility for "betraying innocent blood" just after having condemned Jesus to death (27:1) and delivering him to Pilate (27:2).

A second opposition between Judas throwing down the pieces of silver in the Temple (27:5a) and the Jewish leaders removing them from there (27:6) underscores a complementary point. For Judas the pieces of silver are inextricably linked with the betrayal of innocent blood. By throwing them down in the Temple he symbolically expresses that the Temple and the chief priests (and elders) are inextricably associated with the guilt of betraying innocent blood. This is the point that the Jewish leaders attempt to deny by stating, "It is not lawful to put them into the treasury" of the Temple (27:6). But the explanation that they provide for the first part of their statement, "since they are blood money," actually confirms what they have attempted to deny. They acknowledge that the guilt of betraying innocent blood cannot be contained and isolated in the person of Judas. It contaminates what is around it. The money is contaminated. What the money serves to buy is also contaminated; what was the "potter's field" now becomes "the Field of Blood" (27:7–8). The Temple and consequently the Jewish leaders themselves would be contaminated by this guilt if the money would remain in the Temple.

But are not the Jewish leaders already contaminated by this guilt? Such is the additional question that the text raises through its thematic features. By throwing away the money, Judas attempts to free himself from this guilt and the curse attached to it. But he is unable to escape it; departing, he hangs himself (27:5b). In this way, the text shows that by his actions Judas does not merely fulfill the prophecy of Scripture (see 26:15 and 24a) but also that he fulfills the curse according to which "It would have been better for that man if he had not been born" (26:24b). How could the Jewish leaders hope to escape this guilt and its consequences, since, as Judas did, through their own acts they unwillingly fulfill a prophecy (27:9–10)?[24] This thematic question receives an answer at the end of the subsection. It is this guilt of the betrayal of the innocent blood that "all the people" finally take upon themselves in 27:24–25.

27:11–14. Jesus plays an active role only in these verses of this entire subsection (27:1–16). But this role is limited to the minimum. In response to Pilate's question, "Are you the King of the Jews?" (27:11a) Jesus merely answers: "You have said so" (27:11b). This response reminds the readers that Jesus answered Judas (26:25b) and the high priest (26:64a) by using exactly the same words. For the readers, the effect of this repetition is twofold. First, it means that as Jesus does not need to reveal to Judas that he will betray him, so he does not need to reveal to the high priest that he is the Christ and to Pilate that he is is the King of the Jews, because they already know it (or should know it). Second, it appears that by comparison with the exchange with the high priest (26:63–64), the exchange between Pilate and Jesus in 27:11 is not antagonistic. Jesus actually provides Pilate with the information he was seeking. There is no opposition in this verse.

By contrast, Matthew makes a point in 27:12–14 by opposing Jesus, who refuses to respond to the accusations of the Jewish leaders (27:12, 14), and Pilate, who urges him to do so (27:13). But what is the point Matthew makes by this opposition? Why does Jesus refuse to respond to the accusations of the Jewish leaders, while he answered Pilate's question? The text does not say anything regarding the specific content of the accusations that the Jewish leaders made *before Pilate*. It is only mentioned that there were *many* such accusations (27:13), a mention that precludes the possibility that the Jewish leaders were merely repeating the few accusations found in 26:59–67. Consequently, the point can only be that Jesus refuses to defend himself against these accusations because they are proffered by the Jewish leaders. We would be at a loss in attempting to grasp what this means if we had not read in the preceding verses that the Jewish leaders, against their will, have been inextricably associated with Judas; they share his guilt, and, as his actions do, their actions against Jesus fulfill the prophecies of Scripture. In fact, Jesus' attitude toward the Jewish leaders is the same as his attitude toward Judas. Since what they do must happen to Jesus "as it is written of him" (26:24a), Jesus does not resist them, as he did not attempt to prevent Judas' betrayal. As a consequence, the Jewish leaders put themselves under a curse similar to the one under which Judas put himself.

Since Pilate, the Roman governor, is contrasted with the Jewish leaders, he appears in a much better light. Jesus has answered him. Furthermore, when Jesus does not answer the charges of the Jewish leaders, he "wondered greatly" (27:14b), a phrase which suggests a positive attitude toward Jesus.

27:15–23. At first, the story that leads to the release of Barabbas unfolds thematically. Pilate hopes to take advantage of a custom in order to release Jesus. For this he needs the cooperation of the crowd, since the custom was that, during the feast (Passover), he would release the prisoner that the crowd wanted (27:15b). Yet he is confident that the crowd will ask for the release of Jesus rather than that of the notorious Barabbas, "for he knew that it was out of envy that they had delivered him up" (27:18). In other words, since it was the Jewish leaders who had delivered Jesus (27:2) and since they did so because of "envy"—presumably envy about the authority that Jesus had over the people—Pilate is confident that the crowd will be on the side of Jesus. Thus Pilate entrusts the crowd with the responsibility of releasing Jesus by choosing between him and Barabbas.

The point of this story appears in 27:19–20, verses that oppose the attempt by Pilate's wife to convince her husband not to do anything against Jesus (27:19) and the attempt by the Jewish leaders to convince the crowd to have Jesus put to death (27:20). The point is that Pilate's wife knows not only that Jesus is a "righteous man" but also that it is dangerous (dysphoric) to harm him in any way—she "suffered much over him" (27:19b). By contrast, the Jewish leaders are unaware that it is dangerous for them to seal Jesus' death by persuading the crowd to request it from Pilate.

In effect, this is the same point that was made in 27:4. There Judas acknowledged that he "sinned in betraying innocent blood" and the Jewish leaders affirmed that they were not a guilty partner. But this point in 27:4 was made by a rather dubious character, Judas, and therefore not to be fully trusted. So now, the same point is made by a woman—and throughout the Gospel women have been shown to be trustworthy (as at Bethany, 26:6–13)—to whom this was revealed "in a dream," a source of revelation that can be trusted (see chapters 1 and 2). Even though they are not aware of it, by betraying (delivering) Jesus and by convincing the crowd to have Jesus put to death, the Jewish leaders condemn themselves. They are guilty of betraying innocent blood and will "suffer" a curse similar to the one suffered by Judas and the one envisioned by Pilate's wife. That's the point.

A small bright spot in this dark picture emerges. That the woman is Pilate's wife, presumably a Roman woman, makes another point. While the Jewish leaders are unable to make a distinction between what is good and bad, dangerous or not, sinful or not, this distinction is revealed to a Gentile. But this small bright spot makes the rest of the picture even darker. It is to someone who is in no way associated with the Jewish leaders that such a revelation is made. One should therefore expect all those who are associated with the Jewish leaders to be contaminated by them, to be as blind as they are, and to condemn themselves with the Jewish leaders. By asking for the liberation of Barabbas and the crucifixion of Jesus (27:21–22), according to the Jewish leaders' instructions, the crowd condemns itself.

This point is underscored in 27:23. Pilate, who attempts to defend Jesus the Christ, is opposed to the crowd which demands that Jesus be crucified. It is the crowd which condemns Jesus to death.

27:24–26. The concluding verses of the subsection once again oppose Pilate and the crowd in a polemical dialogue. Pilate refuses any responsibility for Jesus' death, while "the people" assume this responsibility. Pilate acknowledges that Jesus is righteous (27:19) and without evil (27:23). He knows that to kill Jesus is evil, a guilt, a contamination with disastrous consequences; it is shedding "innocent blood" and thereby being under a curse as Judas was (27:4–5). By contrast, the people are not so aware, as already expressed by the preceding points. But here Matthew goes beyond these by contrasting Pilate and the people. He underscores Pilate's powerlessness—"Seeing that he is not accomplishing anything good" (27:24a, au.)—and the people's agitation and potential violence (27:24a). Pilate is described as abdicating his power and authority as governor to avoid violence. Not unlike Jesus, who could have called legions of angels to prevent his arrest (26:53), Pilate could have called the Roman legions but does not do it. He allows the people to take control of the situation. As Jesus acted so that Scripture might be fulfilled (26:54), so Pilate acts according to Scripture. By washing his hands and saying, "I am innocent of this man's blood" (27:24b), he performs the ritual prescribed in Scripture (Deut. 21:6–7). In this way, for Matthew, Pilate frees himself of the responsibility for Jesus' death. In contrast to the chief priests and the elders who deliver Jesus to Pilate after having decided in their deliberation that he should be put to death (27:1–2), it is against his best judgment and because "all the people" have taken this responsibility that Pilate delivers Jesus to be crucified (27:26).

By adding "see to it yourselves" (27:24b), Pilate lays the responsibility for Jesus' death on the crowd, who accepts it. The crowd could have refused it, as the Jewish leaders did by using the same phrase in their dialogue with Judas (27:4b). Contrary to the Jewish leaders, who thought they could remain uncontaminated by the sin of betraying innocent blood, "all the people" accept being contaminated by this sin: "His blood be on us and on our children!" (27:25).

Voluntarily, blindly, they put themselves under a curse similar to the one that Jesus proffered against the scribes and the Pharisees: "upon you may come all the righteous blood shed on earth" (23:35). This remark is important for understanding this terrible subsection. Matthew lays the responsibility and the guilt of Jesus' death upon the Jewish people as a whole ("all the people"), to the point that the Romans appear to be guiltless. And the Jewish people are cursed for it. But interpreting this passage as a justification for anti-Semitism is to contradict Matthew's story. First, recall that this theme was already expressed in chapter 23 where the cursing of the scribes and the Pharisees was addressed to those who follow Jesus, the crowds and the disciples. In brief, the discourse of chapter 23 was a warning that anyone can become the one against whom these curses are proffered. This is also true of the points made in 27:1–26. In fact, these points do not concern merely the delivering of Jesus to death but also and primarily the inability to make any proper distinction between what is good and what is bad, what is euphoric (blessing) and what is dysphoric (curse), and between who is contaminated by sin and who is immune to such a contamination.

For Matthew this is a characteristic of the Jewish people, a people led by "blind" leaders (23:16). But the persons who view themselves as being immune to such a sin deceive themselves and are in fact contaminated by this sin, as the Jewish leaders were (27:4). So the question is: Who is not under this guilt and this curse? Those like Pilate, to whom, through his wife, was revealed what is truly good and truly bad; those like Pilate who accept being powerless and abandon any control over situations where they are confronted with sinners and who submit to Scripture.

27:27–54. The Death of Jesus on the Cross

A first reading of this passage shows that what we take to be its central event, the crucifixion, is described in a short subordinate clause: "when they had crucified him" (27:35). What gives unity to the several scenes of this long subsection is the theme of the *mockeries of Jesus*, beginning with "the whole battalion" mocking Jesus (27:27–31), a theme that finally gives way to a positive assessment of Jesus by "the centurion and those who were with him" saying: "Truly this was the Son [or, a son] of God" (27:54). The text is primarily concerned with the way in which the soldiers (27:27–38), those who passed by (27:39–40), the Jewish leaders (27:41–43), the robbers (27:44), Jesus himself (27:45–50), and finally the centurion and those with him (27:54) interpreted both in words and in actions the significance of Jesus' crucifixion. An examination of the introductory scene (27:27–31) will allow us to see that the main theme of the crucifixion story concerns incorrect and correct views of Jesus' authority and its relation to power.

27:27–31. The scene of mockeries of Jesus by the soldiers is thematic; it does not include any opposition of actions.[25] This means that it needs to be interpreted in terms of the readers' knowledge, and especially in terms of the preceding passage with which Matthew links this scene through the use of the temporal notation "then" (27:27a)—a common Matthean technique. That we are dealing with a scene of *mockeries* also needs to be accounted for.

What does Matthew convey to his readers by this scene? What effect does a scene of mockeries produce for readers? Mockeries, like caricatures, involve portraying a person by selecting a few *actual* characteristics of that person and excluding his or her other characteristics. Through the exclusion of features that normally link them in a meaningful way, the selected characteristics are brought together in an artificial and odd way which makes them look grotesque and contradictory. While the overall portrayal of a person by caricature is false, it is necessarily based upon actual characteristics of that person. Otherwise one could not mock, laugh at, *that person.*

For the readers who are inclined to view Jesus in a positive way, the mockeries have a twofold effect. On the one hand, they emphatically display actual characteristics of Jesus. On the other hand, these mockeries show

how the mockers themselves are ridiculed because of their lack of understanding of the overall person of Jesus. In order to understand what Matthew
means to say by these mockeries we first need to identify the actual characteristics of Jesus that the soldiers use to mock him and that Matthew
expects his readers to recognize (from what they have read in previous
passages). Second, we need to identify in which way Matthew shows, for
the sake of his readers, that the mockers themselves are ridiculed.

Readers have no difficulty identifying the actual characteristics of Jesus
that are the basis for the mockeries. On the one hand, Jesus has been presented as "the King of the Jews," a title that he accepted by responding to
Pilate, "You have said so" (27:11). On the other hand, he is powerless, in
the hands of soldiers (27:27), and "delivered" to be crucified by the very
people to whom he is supposed to be king (27:22–23, 25–26).

For "soldiers of the governor" (27:27a), for people who are subordinated
to a political authority and thus who conceive of authority only in political
terms and in terms of power, such a situation can only be contradictory
and ridiculous. This is expressed through their actions and words. They
put a "robe" on Jesus (27:28), a symbol of royalty ("scarlet" in color) which
is simultaneously a symbol of subordination and lack of kingly power. The
Greek term for "robe" (*chlamyda*) designates a *soldier's* cloak in contrast to
the cloak of someone in a position of authority. They put a crown on his
head, but it is a crown of thorns (27:29a). They put a scepter in his right
hand, but it is a reed (27:29). They kneel before him, honoring him as a
king, saying "Hail, King of the Jews!" but do so in a mocking tone (27:29b).
And then they deny his authority as king, humiliating him by spitting on
him, using his reed/scepter to hit him on the "head" (a symbol of authority?), and stripping him of the robe (27:30–31a).

Matthew expects his readers to perceive not only that the soldiers are
insensitive and cruel in their treatment of Jesus but also that the soldiers are
ridiculous and thus wrong in their assessment of Jesus. Their designation
as "soldiers of the governor" (27:27a) is full of irony in the light of the
preceding passage. It indicates that the soldiers have authority over Jesus
because this authority has been delegated to them by the governor to whom
they are subordinated. The irony is that, in the case of Jesus, Pilate the
governor has just forsaken his authority, submitting to the will of "all the
people." The soldiers, apparently under the political authority of the Roman
governor, are actually under the authority of the Jewish people whose orders
they will carry out by crucifying Jesus. By mocking Jesus as the "King of
the Jews," in the person of its king the soldiers mock the Jewish people,
whose order they carry out; they mock the people who have authority over
them!

What is wrong with the soldiers' assessment of Jesus? They lack an understanding of the nature of true authority which prevents them from perceiving who really has authority. They fail to recognize that those who are

seemingly without authority—the crowd and Jesus—have authority, while the one who seems to have authority, the governor, has forsaken his authority. They also misconstrue the relationship between authority and power. For them, one has authority only insofar as one has the power to enforce it over other people; thus, for them, Pilate has authority because he has soldiers (and the crowd has authority because by rioting it can make Pilate do what it wants). While they recognize Pilate's authority, and while, by obeying him, they unknowingly submit to the crowd's authority, they cannot recognize any authority in Jesus because he is powerless, which is further demonstrated by his humiliation at their hands.

But what is the proper understanding of Jesus' authority? Does Matthew want to say that Jesus is the "King of the Jews" precisely when he is powerless, and therefore that his kingship does not involve having any power at his disposal? As the rest of the subsection (27:32–54) will show, this is not exactly what Matthew wants to convey; for him, as for the soldiers, authority and power are necessarily related. One who has true authority exerts it by using power. But for Matthew, this is not a power which belongs to the person in authority—who, in and of himself or herself, is thus powerless. One alone has power, God, so much so that he can simply be called "Power" (as Jesus did in 26:64). In fact, Jesus has true authority precisely when he refuses to use any other power than God's power. Consequently, Jesus' authority can be "truly" recognized only when he has been totally stripped of all his own power and is dead (see 27:51–54).

27:32–38. The description of the crucifixion is succinct, limited as it is to a subordinate clause in 27:35a. The readers' attention is therefore drawn to the thematic features that Matthew chose to describe in this thematic passage. He calls his readers to interpret these features as further developments of earlier themes.

The theme of the soldiers' power and authority is further expressed when they compelled Simon of Cyrene to carry the cross. The explanation of the name Golgotha as "the place of a skull" might further develop the theme of humiliation and lack of authority, since a "skull" is a "dead head"; Matthew seems to take "head" as a symbol for authority in 27:29–30. The inscription put "over his head" (27:37) further develops this theme; being "King of the Jews," the title that refers to Jesus' authority, is associated with the "head" of the one who undergoes ultimate humiliation and powerlessness by being crucified. Similarly, the description of the crucifixion of the robbers "one on the right and one on the left" (27:38) conveys that Jesus is associated with highway bandits (as in 26:55). As they were, so he is supposed to be characterized by the use of power (violence). As they also are, so he is now stripped of this power, hanging powerlessly on a cross. But the readers' attention is drawn to 27:34 where Matthew makes a point through an opposition and to 27:35, which, surprisingly for the readers, emphasizes the dividing of Jesus' garments instead of his crucifixion.

27:34. The text opposes the soldiers who would make Jesus drink wine "mingled with gall" (27:34a) to Jesus who refuses to do so after tasting the mixture (27:34b). For Matthew, the action of the soldiers is an additional mockery; while pretending to give him a good drink (wine), they give him a disgusting mixture. But this mockery goes beyond the preceding ones. Earlier the soldiers inflicted humiliation and suffering on a passive Jesus. Now they would like Jesus to inflict upon himself the humiliation and the suffering involved in drinking this disgusting and bitter mixture (see 27:48). Matthew's point is that, by refusing to do so, Jesus manifests that his submission to humiliation and suffering is not a masochistic attitude—a Matthean point. He does not willingly inflict suffering on himself. Furthermore, after he tastes the mixture, we read that he "did not want to drink" (literal translation of 27:34b); Jesus has not forsaken his will for he still acts according to what he perceives to be good or bad. This further shows that he submitted voluntarily to the preceding humiliation and suffering and now submits to the crucifixion, and this because he views it as the good thing to do. In effect, this point again expresses the point Matthew made in the arrest scene (cf. 26:52–56 to which the theme of 27:38 is also related), namely, that Jesus willingly submits to his arrest so that the Scriptures might be fulfilled. Here also Jesus willingly submits to suffering and the crucifixion because in so doing he does what is the ultimate good, namely, the will of God as expressed in Scripture.

This point is thematically expressed by two allusions to Scripture.[26] The description of the soldiers as giving him gall to drink uses the vocabulary of the Greek translation of Ps. 69(68):21(22); this event fulfills Scripture! This also helps us understand why Matthew emphasizes the dividing of Jesus' garments rather than his crucifixion. We read in Ps. 22:18(19): "they divide my garments among them, and for my raiment they cast lots." The essential feature for Matthew is not so much the crucifixion but that it happens according to Scripture; what the soldiers do with Jesus' garments fulfills Scripture. In sum, all of this demonstrates that Jesus voluntarily submits to humiliation, suffering, and crucifixion because it is the will of God that he do so.

27:39–44. The description of the mockeries by those passing by, the chief priests and the scribes, and the robbers involves other allusions to Scripture which further develop the preceding point. The description of the passers-by as "wagging their heads" (27:39) uses a phrase from Ps. 22.7(8); and the words of the chief priests include a phrase from Ps. 22:8(9): "He trusts in God; let God deliver him now, if he desires him" (Matt. 27:43a).[27] The mockeries to which Jesus is submitted are according to Scripture; it is according to God's will that Jesus submits to them.

The text also sets up two oppositions through which Matthew underscores two points. First, the text opposes what the passers-by (27:40) and the chief priests (27:42) mockingly suggest that Jesus should do (save himself) to what Jesus did (he saved others, 27:42a). The mockery (literally, blaspheming) of the passers-by (27:40), which suggests that Jesus should save himself *if* he is the Son of God, is similar to the temptations found in 4:1–11. Whether or not Matthew expected his readers to make this connection, the temptation form of this mockery shows that it concerns the way in which Jesus' will is established. Keeping in mind our discussion of mockeries (see 27:27–31), we conclude that, for the mockers, by not saving himself Jesus demonstrates that he is not the Son of God, because if he were, he would have the power to save himself—he implicitly claimed that he has extraordinary power by not denying that he could destroy the Temple and build it in three days (see 26:61). They do not envision that he might *not want* to use the power that is at his disposal to save himself.

The mockery of the chief priests and the scribes makes a slightly different point. Jesus had the (use of) power to save others, but he does not have the power to save himself (27:42a). Here again the mockers ridicule Jesus for not having the power to save himself, although they concede that in the past he might have had the power to save others. Conversely, the point that Matthew makes for the readers in these mockeries is that, as Son of God, Jesus has the (use of) power to save himself; he did save others, and thus it is voluntarily that he does not use it.

Matthew refines the preceding point by opposing believing in Jesus, as the chief priests say they will do if he climbs down from the cross (27:42b), to trusting in God, as Jesus does (27:43a). The new point made by this opposition appears when we remember that these verses are a mockery of Jesus. For the mockers, Jesus cannot be the King of the Jews because, as above, he does not have the power to come down from the cross. But now the chief priests also presuppose and express that the power which would be used by Jesus for coming down from the cross would be God's power. Unlike the soldiers who thought that a true King of the Jews has political power of his own and unlike the passers-by who thought that the Son of God is someone who has divine power on his own, the chief priests correctly recognize that the King of the Jews/Son of God could only make use of a power that he would have received from God—a power which is not his own. They acknowledge that one alone has power, God, who can simply be called "Power" (as Jesus did in 26:64). Consequently, for the chief priests, that Jesus does not come down from the cross shows that God does not intervene in his favor, and consequently that God does not want Jesus as the King of the Jews or as his Son: "let God deliver him now, if he desires [or, wants] him," (27:43). This is the point that Matthew makes for his readers: the mockers completely misunderstand the relationship between God's will and Jesus. God wants him as King of the Jews and as his Son when Jesus trusts in him and does his will ("thy will be done," 26:42) even though God's will for him entails being humiliated, suffering a crucifixion, and indeed being abandoned by God. Asking God to intervene and to deliver him "now," that is, at a time of Jesus' choice, as the chief priests suggest, would amount to testing God, as the tempter had suggested he should do (4:5–7). But Jesus does not want to test God and therefore does not want to make use of the power that is at his disposal.

27:45–49. In these verses, two oppositions extend the preceding point. First, the text opposes what Jesus says (27:46) *and* what bystanders understand (27:47); then one of the bystanders who gives a drink to Jesus (27:48) is opposed to the other bystanders who would prevent him from doing so (27:49).

The point of this second opposition is clear. Most bystanders only see in Jesus' cry a new occasion to mock him; they do not have compassion. By contrast, the gesture of the other bystander can only be interpreted as one of compassion, as expressed by his haste in doing something for Jesus: "And one of them at once ran" (27:48a). Here, "vinegar" (rather than a good drink such as wine) is given as drink; yet it should not be understood as a mockery. Rather, it shows that this gesture fulfills Scripture, since it alludes to Ps. 69(68):21(22), a text that had already been used with the opposite connotation in Matt. 27:34. In sum, for this bystander and despite a misunderstanding of Jesus' words, Jesus' cry is an expression of despair which moves him to perform a gesture of compassion.

The point expressed by the opposition between what Jesus said (27:46) and what the bystanders understood (27:47) is more complex. According to the bystanders' incorrect interpretation, Jesus calls Elijah, asking him to intervene and save him (27:49). This is a desperate cry for help; it moves one of them to make a gesture of compassion. Consequently, according to the text, Jesus' actual cry, which is opposed to what the bystanders understood, is not a desperate cry for help. But it remains a cry, indeed a "loud" cry (27:46a)! By it Jesus does not attempt to test God; he does not ask for God's intervention to save him from the cross. Moreover, this cry does not express a breakdown of the relationship between Jesus and God; he addresses him as "my God" (27:46b). Jesus still "trusts in God" (27:43a). Furthermore, as the address "My God, my God" shows, it is not a cry of rebellion against God or a refusal to continue to do God's will. Jesus fulfills God's will by using the words of Ps. 22:1(2); by his cry he fulfills Scripture![28] However, it remains a cry, an expression of a most profound despair.

That God has abandoned him is not in and of itself the cause of Jesus' despair. Rather, this despair is rooted in a lack of knowledge of the reason, the purpose of his suffering and death: Why? For Matthew, this despair indicates that Jesus is now stripped of everything—all the gifts and blessings of God—that could have been the basis for trusting God and for wanting to do his will. He is stripped of any mark of his authority; he is humiliated as the last mockery of the bystanders further shows (27:49). He cannot use the power that God put at his disposal during his ministry; to ask for God's intervention would be to test God. And because God does not intervene on his behalf, he powerlessly dies on the cross. Yet his trust in God and his will to do God's will could still have been solidly grounded in another gift from God, his knowledge of the purpose that will be achieved according to God's will by his crucifixion. According to Matthew, Jesus had such a knowledge; he attempted to communicate it to his disciples when he announced his coming crucifixion: "this is my blood of the covenant, which is poured out for many for the forgiveness of sins" (26:28). But now, in this hour of "darkness" (27:45), which symbolizes Jesus' agony, the knowledge of the purpose of God's will that he is carrying out is taken away from him. Why? At the moment of his death, Jesus is left without anything that could be a basis for trusting God and being willing to do God's will. Thus, in addition to physical suffering, Jesus suffers in his spirit; he despairs. And yet he still says: "My God, my God." In the midst of this despair, all that is left in Jesus is an unconditional trust in God and an unconditional will to do God's will. It is in the midst of this despair that he dies: "And Jesus cried again with a loud voice and yielded up his spirit" (27:50).

27:51–54. Following the absence of God's interventions throughout the crucifixion story, the readers should be struck by the sudden and amazing manifestations of God's power at the moment of Jesus' death. The curtain of the Temple was torn in two from top to bottom (27:51a). There was an earthquake so powerful that the rocks were split (27:51b). Tombs were opened and "many bodies of the saints who were asleep were raised" (27:52, au.).[29] This description of manifestations of divine power (27:51–53) is thematic (there are no oppositions). In these verses Matthew expresses his points in terms of his readers' knowledge, including that of apocalyptic symbolism and the preceding passage. Readers must therefore consider the story of the crucifixion in the new perspective opened by these manifestations of divine power. This is what the centurion and the soldiers do.

"When the centurion and those who were with him, keeping watch over Jesus, saw the earthquake and what took place, they were filled with awe, and said, 'Truly this was the Son [or, a Son] of God!'" (27:54). This confession forms a narrative opposition with each of the mockeries (27:29, 40, 41, 49). But Matthew clearly emphasizes its relationship with the first mockeries; he describes those who make this confession as the centurion *and the soldiers* who keep watch over Jesus—the "whole detachment" (27:27b, au.)[30] which led Jesus to be crucified (27:31b) and kept watch over him (27:36). It is striking that those who mocked and humiliated Jesus, denying that this

powerless person could be the King of the Jews, now confess that Jesus is
Son of God because they see *manifestations of divine power*: they "saw the
earthquake and what took place" (27:54). Following such events it is not
surprising that the soldiers are "filled with awe" or greatly afraid (27:54).
But one wonders why they concluded that Jesus is Son of God. Perhaps
they thought that these are manifestations of the wrath of God because his
Son had been killed.[31] But the text does not provide any explanation; Matthew is not concerned about describing the soldiers' state of mind. His point
is that the juxtaposition of Jesus' death with manifestations of divine power
leads the soldiers "truly" to recognize that Jesus is Son of God.

In order to understand this point, we need to remember that Matthew
has closely associated the titles "King of the Jews" and "Son of God," which
are interchangeably used by the chief priests in 27:42–43. For the readers,
the effect is that Jesus is worthy of being designated by these two titles.
The title "King of the Jews" connotes authority exerted by means of power
(as is clear in 27:27–31), and the title "Son of God" connotes someone who
has at his disposal supernatural power and who is desired by God (as is
expressed in 27:40–43). Consequently, the interchangeability of these titles
means that whenever Jesus is designated by one or the other such a designation expresses both that he has authority and that he is somehow associated with divine power. The question is: How is his authority related
to power and more specifically to divine power? Furthermore, by showing
that these two titles are equivalent Matthew closely links all the mockeries
with the soldiers' confession.

Now the soldiers (27:27–31), the passers-by (27:40), and the Jewish leaders (27:41–43), each in their own way deny that Jesus is worthy of being
recognized as having the authority of King of the Jews or Son of God because
he is powerless, and this, as the chief priests specify (27:43), because God
does not intervene with power in order to save him from the cross. This
view involves an incorrect understanding of the relationship between Jesus'
authority, his power, and divine power, as the soldiers' confession in 27:54
shows. He is properly recognized as Son of God, and thus as having the
authority of the Son of God, when, after his death, the power of God is
manifested without ambiguity in striking events. As we have seen, Jesus'
death demonstrates that he is stripped of all power—dignity, his physical
strength, the use of God's power, and even the knowledge of the purpose
of God's will—which would have been the means through which he could
have exerted such an authority *on his own*. Until his last cry, however, he
remains in relationship with his God ("my God"); he also retains the will
to do God's will. But then the manifestations of divine power associated
with Jesus' death demonstrate that *all his authority* and *the power* to exert it
that he displayed during his ministry and will display after his resurrection
(cf. 27:53; 28:18) *are not his own*. It is absolutely clear now that they belong
exclusively to God. Not only were they (and will they be) given to him

by God but they also remained (and will remain) exclusively God's authority and power. In other words, they should not be construed as gifts from God which become the possession of the receiver who can then use them for his or her own purpose and at his or her own discretion, as, according to Matthew, the Jewish leaders construe such gifts from God (27:41–43; see also the comments on 21:23–27 and 23:2–7). In such a case, God's authority and power are misused and are no longer truly God's, as possibly symbolized for Matthew by the splitting of the curtain of the Temple (27:51a). Since this curtain separates the holy from the profane, its splitting amounts to a demonstration that the Temple is profaned. But Jesus neither misconstrues nor misuses God's authority and power; he does not confuse his will and God's will (27:34, 39–43; cf. 26:39, 42).

The main point that Matthew conveys by his rendering of the crucifixion story now appears. Jesus' death on the cross, followed as it is by striking manifestations of divine power, is the ultimate demonstration that the authority and the power that Jesus displayed in his ministry are unambiguously God's authority and power. All of Jesus' preaching and teaching are unambiguously God's word, the expression of God's will and of its purpose— as is clear from the fact that when abandoned by God, Jesus no longer knows the purpose of the will of God that he is carrying out. The manifestations of power that characterized Jesus' ministry—his healings—are also unambiguous manifestations of God's power; without God, Jesus is totally powerless. Therefore, Jesus' entire ministry in the entire Gospel is to be taken as the unambiguous manifestation of God, of *his* authority and power. In one phrase, Jesus is truly "Emmanuel," "God with us" (1:23).

Jesus' death followed by manifestations of God's power also means that he is "Son of God." He is the one that God desires (or "wants," 27:43), and also the one with whom God is "well pleased" (3:17; 17:5). He is the one who trusts in God and continues to make God's will his own will even when he is deprived of all God's gifts and blessings. He serves rather than being served (20:28a). We also are in a position to perceive how Matthew understood the rest of that verse according to which Jesus came "to give his life as a ransom for many" (20:28b). If he had not given his life by dying on the cross, then it would be impossible for people to recognize and receive all that he taught in words and acts as an unambiguous and trustworthy revelation from God. It is only through this teaching and revelation that people can hope to be saved, namely, by doing this teaching. Because of his death he is therefore worthy to be Son of God and to receive from God all authority and power (as he will, 28:18).

Finally, note that the thematic description of the manifestations of God's power invites the readers to interpret them in terms of passages other than the crucifixion story. Indeed, these manifestations have an eschatological, even apocalyptic, character—darkness over all the earth (27:45), earthquake, tombs opened, resurrection of saints—which can only remind the readers of chapters 24—25 (earthquakes, 24:7, in association with darkness, 24:29; cf. 27:45). In addition, the splitting of the Temple curtain can be taken as a symbolic destruction of the Temple (see 24:2). All of this means that Matthew expects his readers to interpret Jesus' death as an eschatological event.[32] But as Jesus said in 24:8 concerning events such as wars, the destruction of the Temple, and earthquakes, "all this is but the beginning of the birth-pangs." Jesus' death is the beginning of the end-time, the time that will culminate in the coming of the Son of Man and of the judgment, and a time during which one needs to watch, as chapters 24—25 indicate. It is the time when Jesus' authority as Son of God can already be recognized without ambiguity. But it is not yet the time when he is manifested as the eschatological judge—the Son of Man coming in glory.

This description of eschatological events also asks the readers to look forward toward Jesus' resurrection (the saints were raised and were "coming out of the tombs *after* his resurrection [and] they went into the holy city and appeared to many," 27:53). This strange statement relates the resurrection of Jesus to all these manifestations of God's power. The manifestation of God's power through which Jesus is raised from the dead is also a demonstration that he is Son of God and that he is given by God an authority that is unambiguously God's authority. In addition, the descriptions of the resurrection of many saints indicate that the manifestations of the power of God that follow Jesus' death on the cross benefit "many."

27:55—28:20. The Burial of Jesus and His Resurrection

Like an earlier portion of the Passion story, the concluding subsection is composed of two stories that are intertwined: the story of the women, Joseph of Arimathea, Pilate, the angel, Jesus, and the disciples (27:55–61; 28:1–10; 28:16–20); and the story of the Jewish leaders, Pilate, and the guard of soldiers (27:62–66; 28:11–15). As shown by the comment "and this story has been spread among the Jews to this day" (28:15), through the story of the guard at the tomb Matthew expects his readers to be aware of Jewish objections to the church's proclamation of the resurrection of Jesus—his body would have been stolen by the disciples. Thematically and according to his readers' expectations, by intertwining the story of the guard at the tomb, Matthew underscores the validity of the church's proclamation of the resurrection of Jesus by showing that it would have been impossible for the disciples to have stolen the body. But this thematic proof of the factuality of the resurrection, which reflects his readers' expectations, is far from being the main point that Matthew conveys to them. His primary concern is to show the significance of the resurrection. Rather than describing the event of the resurrection itself, Matthew presents people—the Jewish leaders, the angel, Jesus—talking about it. By intertwining the story of the guard at the tomb, Matthew makes a series of points that underscore how the resurrection is to be properly interpreted. He also adds an ironical tone to this passage. The readers will easily recognize the irony involved in the description of the Jewish leaders' efforts to make the sepulchre secure and in their subsequent behavior (28:11–15) which ends up being a "fraud" while their purpose was to prevent the disciples from committing a "fraud" (27:63–64). But it soon appears that the text also directs its irony against the readers' expectations.

27:55–61. The burial scene is thematic (there is no narrative opposition). It therefore needs to be interpreted in the light of what precedes. Yet Matthew's new points can be recognized in what is surprising for the readers.

Following Jesus' death, a burial scene is to be expected. Nothing is really surprising in its description, according to which Joseph of Arimathea takes the initiative for claiming the body of Jesus from Pilate and he lays it "in his own new tomb" after having wrapped it in "a clean linen shroud" (27:58–60). He does not encounter any objection from Pilate, who had sympathy for Jesus. In view of the circumstances, this is the best burial one could have expected for Jesus. The only possible tension is that Joseph of Arimathea, about whom the readers have never heard a thing, is described as "a disciple" *and* "a rich man," terms that the readers had learned to consider as almost contradictory (see 19:16–26). But the mention that he is rich is necessary to explain why he owns a new tomb. Similarly, that "he rolled a great stone to the door of the tomb" (27:60b) prepares the next scenes.

By contrast, the presence of women[33] at the beginning (27:55–56) and the end (27:61) of this scene is puzzling for the readers. Furthermore, that there are "many women" at Golgotha is unexpected. First, even though the women were "looking on from afar" (27:55), it appears that Jesus was not completely abandoned by his followers after all! Second, the readers cannot remember any mention of a group of "many women" (27:55a) in the story of the journey from Galilee to Jerusalem. By recognizing, however, the name of "the mother of the sons of Zebedee" (27:56b; cf.20:20), the readers can easily overcome this tension by concluding that the crowds that followed Jesus from Galilee must have included many women. Except for the mother of the sons of Zebedee (who briefly appeared on front stage because of her inappropriate request), women stayed in the background, hidden in the anonymity of the crowds—that's the point. It remains that in 27:55 the women are described not only as following Jesus but also as serving him (or "ministering to him"), a description that tells the readers they should be viewed as disciples. Of course they do not have the same status as the Twelve disciples, who were prominently featured throughout the Gospel. Rather, the women remained anonymous and are merely characterized as those who serve instead of being served, even as Jesus "came not to be served but to serve, and to give his life as a ransom for many" (20:28). In other words, the women heeded what Jesus taught following the request of the mother of the sons of Zebedee; they serve rather than being served (20:20–28). Furthermore, for the readers, they remained invisible as they served, even as the Son of man who identifies himself with the poor and the needy remains invisible both to those who have compassion on the poor and needy and to those who do not (cf. 25:31–46). In this perspective they appear as ideal disciples, by contrast with the actual disciples, including Judas who betrayed Jesus and Peter who denied him. During the Passion, the actual disciples (excluding Judas) had become more like the women. Peter "followed [Jesus] at a distance" (26:58), even as the women are looking on from afar (27:55). The disciples have now become anonymous and invisible because they undergo a passion of their own by being scattered as Jesus had predicted (26:31, 56), even as the women have been anonymous and invisible all along. The difference is that because they were women ("the least of these" in a patriarchal society), they were serving in this anonymous and humiliated position from the beginning. Therefore, for Matthew, the women are those who are legitimately associated with Jesus at the moment of his death; they share in his death as the disciples were invited to do at the last supper and as the disciples do now by being scattered. The women also continue to play their discreet and humble role. They do not join the centurion and the soldiers in confessing that Jesus is Son of God. They merely look on from afar, passively and silently. They are merely there, as Mary Magdalene and the other Mary "were there, sitting opposite the sepulchre" (27:61) when Joseph of Arimathea put Jesus' body in the tomb. In both cases, they are onlookers at a distance. And once again in 28:1, the two women will be described as going "to see the sepulchre." Matthew does not provide us with a clue regarding their emotions, their thoughts, or their purpose. As they were discreetly serving Jesus while following him from Galilee without being mentioned in the story of the journey, so here they remain in the background.

27:62–66 (28:1–2). The scene in which the Jewish leaders ask Pilate for "a guard of soldiers," obtain it,[34] and make "the sepulchre secure by sealing the stone and setting a guard" (27:66) is closely intertwined with the preceding one through Pilate and with the following one through its last verse which sets a narrative opposition with 28:2. Its ironical tone is apparent to the readers in the words of the Jewish leaders who call Jesus an "impostor" and say that the proclamation of his resurrection is a "fraud" (27:64–65). This statement is all the more ironical in that they pay the soldiers to spread a lie (28:11–15). There is also irony in the words of Pilate: "go, make it [the sepulchre] as secure as you can" (27:65b, the RSV captures the irony).

This irony, which reflects Matthew's points expressed through a series of three narrative oppositions, needs to be taken into account for interpreting these oppositions. The main opposition is between what the Jewish leaders say to Pilate (27:63a) and what Jesus (27:63b) and the disciples (27:64b) said or will say. First, we need to consider another opposition expressed in the saying of the Jewish leaders between being raised (27:63b, 64b) and stealing the body (27:64), which is closely related to the third opposition between making "the sepulchre secure by sealing the stone" (27:66) and rolling back the stone (28:2).

Through the latter oppositions Matthew makes a twofold point concerning the contrasting characters of God's intervention and of human actions. The point made by the opposition between being raised (27:63b, 64b) and stealing the body (27:64)—two actions that would result in an empty tomb—simply contrasts what God and human beings can do. God alone can fulfill what has been announced by Jesus: "After three days I will rise again."[35] Acting on their own, human beings perform only fraudulent actions, as reflected by the use of the verb "to steal." Similarly, the opposition between sealing the stone (27:66) and rolling back the stone (28:2) contrasts divine action with human action. The earthquake manifests, as in 27:51, the awesome character of God's power, while the description of the "angel of the Lord" descending "from heaven" (28:2) makes clear what is the origin of this power. All that human beings can do is attempt to safeguard a situation as it stands, to preserve the status quo, a futile attempt because God's intervention is of an earth-shaking proportion, an intervention that shatters the status quo.

In sum, these two oppositions underscore that human beings by themselves can only do two things: they can either transform a situation in a fraudulent manner or strive to maintain the status quo. In contrast, God through his intervention radically transforms a situation and shatters the status quo. In short, the resurrection can be understood and accepted only insofar as one abandons a human perspective, which can lead one either to contradict the will of God (as stealing does) or to refuse God's intervention by striving to maintain the status quo that it would shatter.

We can now understand the point made by the opposition between what the chief priests and the Pharisees say (27:63a) and what Jesus said (27:63b) and the disciples will say (27:64b). The readers cannot miss the irony involved here: such a saying of the Jewish leaders is reported just after the crucifixion which has unambiguously demonstrated that Jesus is the Son of God. Jesus is not a deceiver (or "impostor," 27:63), and neither the prophecy of his resurrection nor the proclamation of the resurrection by the disciples is a deceit (or "fraud," 27:64). And yet Jewish leaders affirm it. On the basis of the preceding points, we conclude that they do so in order to preserve the status quo and their authority over "the people" (27:64).

The question remains: How is someone's authority over the people established and maintained? Conversely, what would threaten such an authority? It is striking that the Jewish leaders are primarily concerned with what Jesus *said* and what the disciples might *say*. In brief, what they view as the primary threat to their authority is words, not events. They are afraid that the disciples might proclaim to the people that Jesus is risen from the dead. With such a proclamation they would mislead the people, that is also, lead the people and have authority over them in the name of Jesus. The Jewish leaders thus understand the proclamation that Jesus is raised from the dead as a claim that he has authority, an authority to which the hearers of the proclamation should submit. Yet in order to be convincing and to have power over the people, such a proclamation needs to be plausible. But this only means that facts should not contradict the proclamation. Thus, if Jesus' body is still in the tomb, the disciples would be unable to proclaim that he has been raised from the dead, because their proclamation could be contradicted. On the other hand, if the tomb is empty, regardless of what brought about this state of affairs, the proclamation could not be contradicted and thus would be convincing for the people. The people would then acknowledge Jesus' (and the disciples') authority and follow him, instead of being submitted to the authority of the Jewish leaders. All this presupposes that, according to the Jewish leaders, a proclamation that establishes someone's authority is more than a simple retelling of the facts. It involves a claim of authority that one makes for oneself (as in the case of Jesus according to 27:63) or for someone else (as in the case of the disciples, 27:64).

Because of its ironical character, this passage is both true and false. But it is difficult to assess what is incorrect in the view of the Jewish leaders. It seems that the only thing wrong with them is that they want to prevent the proclamation of Jesus' resurrection by making sure it would be contradicted by the facts. Consequently, they want to make the sepulchre secure, "sealing" it as a sign that Jesus' body is still there (27:66). If this is so, their view that the proclamation of the resurrection is a proclamation of Jesus' authority is valid. It would also mean that the proclamation of Jesus' authority—the proclamation that he is raised—is more than a retelling of the facts. The retelling of the facts is necessary only to show that the claim that Jesus has authority is not contradicted by the facts. But the facts do not prove the resurrection and Jesus' authority. The proclamation does. That these are the points Matthew makes here is confirmed by the following passages.

28:1–6. The scene is set by the description of the women going "to see the sepulchre" "after the sabbath, toward the dawn of the first day of the week" (28:1)—a date specified to underscore that it is now the third day after Jesus' death—and by the description of the earthquake and of the angel who rolls back the stone and sits on it (28:2; see my comments above). Then Matthew sets a narrative opposition between the guards who tremble for fear and become "like dead men" (28:4) and the women who, according to the angel's words, should not fear him (28:5a). Both the guards and the women are confronted with the same situation, which involves the earthquake, the rolled-back stone, and the presence of the angel of the Lord who is "from heaven," whose appearance clearly shows his supernatural origin: "His appearance was like lightning, and his raiment white as snow" (28:3). It is clear that Matthew here contrasts two responses to the divine manifestation in the action and person of the angel. The point is that when one is confronted by such a divine manifestation, this event is devastating. As expressed in 28:4, it has the same effect on a person that an earthquake has on the ground; because of fear one shakes (RSV: "trembled" [seiō]; in Greek the same root as the noun earthquake [seismos]). Furthermore, one becomes as dead, one is paralyzed by fear. But if they listen to the word of the angel, the women should not fear him, and thus should not fear the divine manifestation that he is (28:5a). According to the text, the only difference between the women and the guards is that the angel speaks to the women but not to the guards. The angel gives a series of commands to the women: "Do not be afraid" (28:5a); "Come, see" (28:6b); "Go quickly and tell" (28:7a). It is an authoritative discourse through which the angel both asserts authority and interprets the event—the angel in the empty tomb means that Jesus is risen (28:6a)—as an authoritative event which demands certain actions from the women. The point Matthew makes now appears. By itself the divine manifestation represented by the angel and the action of the angel at the sepulchre can result only in a paralyzing fear. The events are not paralyzing, even though they might still engender some fear (see 28:8), if they are interpreted in an authoritative discourse by someone who is trustworthy—as the angel demonstrated he is by saying he knows why the women are at the sepulchre (28:5b). The facts and events of the empty tomb by themselves do not achieve or prove anything. Rather, they have a negative, incapacitating effect upon people, although they need to be observed: "Come, see the place where he lay" (28:6b). Alone, a proclamation of the meaning of the events prompts a positive response. But note that while such a proclamation is not contradictory of the facts—it is indeed based on the facts—it expresses more than can be observed since the resurrection is not described. Instead of incapacitating people, such a proclamation enables people to act; it proclaims the authoritative character of the event and thus has a claim upon people.

28:7–15. Matthew sets another narrative opposition by contrasting what the women are supposed to do according to the angel's (28:7) and Jesus' (28:10) command—announce Jesus' resurrection to the disciples (as they start to do, 28:8)—*and* what the soldiers are supposed to do according to the Jewish leaders' command (28:13)—tell that the disciples have stolen Jesus' body (as they do, according to 28:15). The contrast that Matthew sets between the respective actions of the women and of the guards in response to what happened at the tomb further develops the preceding point.

Both the soldiers and the women are charged to tell more than what happened, by contrast with the initial report of the soldiers to the chief

priests in which they do tell "all that had taken place" (28:11b)—nothing
more. Thus the soldiers are charged not only to tell that they were inca-
pacitated but also to explain it by saying that they were asleep; they are
charged not only to tell that Jesus' body has disappeared but also to explain
it by saying that the disciples have stolen it, something they could not have
seen because they were asleep (28:13). Similarly, the women are charged
to announce that Jesus is risen, although at first they have only seen the
angel and the empty tomb (28:7).

Both the soldiers and the women (will) act because they are commanded
to do so. The main difference between them is in the character of those
who send them. The soldiers are sent by people who are not trustworthy,
the Jewish leaders, who demonstrate their lack of trustworthiness by taking
"counsel" with the elders (28:12, a phrase the readers have learned they
should understand to mean "plotting") and by giving the soldiers a bribe
to convince them to do what they order them. Furthermore, the Jewish
leaders anticipate that the soldiers might feel uneasy telling such a story
since it involves admitting that they were negligent in their duties, something for which they could be punished by the governor. So the Jewish
leaders add: "we will satisfy him [the governor] and keep you out of trouble" (28:14b). Some sort of bribe or lie will possibly need to follow the
bribery of the soldiers, confirming the fraudulent character of both the
Jewish leaders and the rumor they ask the soldiers to spread. In contrast,
the angel is trustworthy due to his origin, heaven, and also because the
angel knows why the women are at the sepulchre. The women do not need
to be bribed! At once they begin doing what they were ordered to do. The
women run "to tell his disciples" (28:8). Although they are somewhat
afraid, it is clear they trust the angel's words; they welcome his announcement that Jesus is risen with "great joy" (28:8). Furthermore, as the women
begin doing what they were ordered to do, the angel's announcement of
Jesus's resurrection is confirmed to them. Jesus meets them (28:9) and repeats in part the order they have heard from the angel (28:10).

Finally, by accepting the order to deliver their respective messages, the
soldiers and the women change status, but in opposite ways. By telling that
the disciples stole Jesus' body while they were asleep, the soldiers do have
influence over the Jewish people—they convince the Jews their story is
valid so that in turn the people continue to spread that rumor "to this day"
(28:15). But in the process the soldiers are diminished in the eyes of the
people. They will be viewed as bad soldiers who neglect their duty and
sleep instead of keeping watch. By delivering a fraudulent message upon
the order of people who are not trustworthy, one is diminished and loses
worthiness even though one influences others. By contrast, by delivering
the message they were asked to transmit by the angel, the women find
themselves in a position of authority over the disciples. They who were
last, humbly serving Jesus and remaining during his ministry in the ano-

nymity of the crowds who followed him, are now first (and are named). They are those who, in the name of the angel and in the name of Jesus (28:10), will give an order to the disciples: "Go to Galilee, and there you will meet Jesus" (au.). And the disciples will meet Jesus only if they trust their message and obey them! They are invested with authority over the very people whom Jesus calls "my brethren." Thus, by delivering a truthful message and obeying people—the angel and Jesus—who are trustworthy, one in turn shares in the authority of Jesus, and one can be trusted.

In sum, beyond the specific point regarding the women and the soldiers, in 28:7–14 Matthew makes more general points which provide criteria to evaluate whether or not an instruction is trustworthy and authoritative. An instruction is trustworthy and authoritative (1) if the person who expresses it has authority and is trustworthy (the angel and Jesus, 28:5, 10), (2) if in the process of carrying it out one gains in status rather than being diminished (the authority of the women over the disciples), and (3) if its trustworthiness is confirmed as one carries out what it demands (the resurrected Jesus appears to the women, 28:9–10).

28:16–17. The concluding instructions of Jesus to his disciples[36] do not involve any narrative opposition.[37] It is most usually the case the conclusion of a book does not make new points but rather brings together in a thematic way major points that have been made earlier in the work. In Matthew's case, we can expect that the criteria for the validity of an instruction found in the preceding passage will apply to Jesus' instructions. We can also expect to find other points reexpressed here, and this especially in the tensions that the text creates for the readers.

Almost every phrase in the description of the disciples meeting Jesus in Galilee (28:16–17) evokes by means of tensions earlier features of the Gospel. The phrase "the eleven disciples" (28:16), instead of the customary "the Twelve," surprises the readers enough to recall Judas' betrayal and, by association, Peter's denials and that all were scattered, scandalized by Jesus (26:30–35). It is to these less-than-perfect disciples that Jesus gives the responsibility and authority to "make disciples of all nations" (28:19a)!

That they "went to Galilee" tells the readers that the women have carried out their mission and that the disciples trusted them and their message enough to obey them. This means that the disciples acknowledged the women's authority over them. They who were "first" and viewed themselves as such—Jesus promised them that they will "sit on twelve thrones, judging the twelve tribes of Israel" (19:28)—are now subordinated to the "last," women who remained during Jesus' ministry in the anonymity of the crowds. It is to disciples such as these that responsibility and authority will be given.

That the disciples and Jesus leave Jerusalem for Galilee reminds the readers of chapters 2 and 3—4, where it was emphasized that what is first manifested

in Judea needs later to be fully manifested in Galilee. Here the authority of
Jesus which has been manifested in Jerusalem on the cross that revealed the
true character of his authority as King of the Jews and Son of God is directly
manifested in the resurrected Jesus who reveals the full extent of his authority in Galilee. But what about the disciples? What is the significance of
their move from Jerusalem and Judea to Galilee?

What the disciples do goes beyond what is expressed in the women's
message. They "went to Galilee, to the mountain to which Jesus had directed
them" (28:16b) or "to the mountain where Jesus appointed them." The
ambiguity of the phrase is reinforced because the readers cannot remember
that Jesus directed them to a specific mountain or that he appointed them
on a mountain. Thus the readers are led to associate this mountain with all
the mountains mentioned in Jesus' ministry in Galilee: the mountain upon
which Jesus delivered the Sermon on the Mount (5:1), since here also he
will instruct them; the mountain of the feeding of the four thousand (15:29)
where Jesus had compassion on the crowd "because they have been with
me now three days, and have nothing to eat" (15:32), perhaps related to
the three days of the Passion after which Jesus has compassion for his disciples; the mountain of the transfiguration (17:1) where the authority of
Jesus was revealed to three disciples who were not to speak about it until
the resurrection (17:9), to be contrasted with the mountain (in Judea?) of
the temptation (4:8) where Jesus refuses false authority. Here also the authority of Jesus will be revealed to the disciples.

For the readers all these possible associations are more confusing than
enlightening until they are confronted with an even more puzzling verse:
"And when they saw him they worshiped him; but some [or, they]
doubted" (28:17); the last phrase could be translated "they who had hesitated."[38] Even if one chooses the translation that suggests that only some
of the disciples doubted, it remains that Jesus gives the responsibility and
authority to make disciples of all the nations to all the disciples, including
those who doubted. But the text clearly expresses that Jesus gives this
authority to doubting disciples, and as we shall see, meant that all the disciples doubted. At any rate, once again their attitude contrasts them with
the women. When seeing Jesus they worship him, even as the women did
(28:9), but unlike the women they doubt. The women were afraid, since
Jesus tells them "Do not be afraid" (28:10a), but to doubt is more than
being afraid. It involves not acknowledging the manifestation of God's
power through which Jesus was raised, something that the women never
questioned.

Here we need to remember that the women believed *because the angel
spoke to them* when they were confronted by the manifestation of divine
power. Despite the message that the women transmitted to them—although
Matthew does not mention the women speaking to the disciples—the disciples are similar to the guards at the tomb who were "like dead men." Of

course, since the disciples worship Jesus, the appearance of the resurrected Jesus, a divine manifestation, does not have as negative an effect on them as it had on the guards, possibly because of the women's message. But the text presupposes that Jesus' words remove their doubt and that they will indeed go and make disciples of all the nations. To repeat, before the resurrected Jesus speaks to them, the disciples doubt. It is only *after* he speaks to them that they will eventually believe.

The disciples' attitude, doubt, is not unlike Jesus' last cry, "My God, my God, why did you abandon me?" (27:46, au.). As Jesus still acknowledged that God is his God, so the disciples worship the resurrected Jesus, acknowledging his authority. As Jesus expressed doubt about the purpose of God's will, so the disciples doubt. As we noted, Jesus' cry demonstrated that his knowledge of God's will was given to him by God; it was not self-acquired knowledge. So the mention of the disciples' doubt expresses that even their belief in Jesus is given to them by Jesus; it is not a belief that they could have by themselves (as was already expressed in 16:17). It also appears that the disciples have shared in Jesus' Passion. They are the "eleven" who have been scattered and scandalized by Jesus ("they doubted") and who have even denied him (so Peter). In this way they have demonstrated that "the spirit indeed is willing, but the flesh is weak" (26:41). As the cross has shown that Jesus was willing to do God's will, even in the weakness and the powerlessness of a situation in which he was stripped of everything that could have helped him to carry out this will, so the disciples are willing to acknowledge the authority of Jesus (they worship him) and to do his will even though by themselves (the flesh) they are unable to do so. They shared in Jesus' Passion. As the Passion has shown that all of Jesus' power, ability, and knowledge was given to him by God, his Father, so the Passion demonstrates that the disciples cannot any longer claim to have anything that would allow them to carry out their mission as disciples. All this, including their belief in Jesus, is given to them by God through Jesus. As the crowd that was with Jesus for three days had nothing to eat and was hungry (15:32), so the disciples have been with Jesus for three days, sharing his Passion. They are stripped of their self-confidence that would allow them to carry out their mission. But now, by instructing them, Jesus gives them everything they need to undertake it. In brief, it is precisely because they doubted that the disciples are worthy to receive the responsibility and authority to make disciples of all the nations, as the women were given the responsibility and the authority to transmit the news of Jesus' resurrection because during his ministry they made no claim for themselves, humbly serving Jesus in the anonymity of the crowds.

28:18. "All authority in heaven and on earth has been given to me." It is not surprising for the readers that Jesus has received divine authority. The events following his death (27:51–54) already indicate that his authority is nothing else than God's authority. But these words are necessary for the disciples. Events by themselves are not sufficient to convey the significance of divine interventions. The disciples need to be told what Jesus' resurrection means: God has given to him "all authority in heaven and on earth." The new thing for the readers is the all-encompassing scope of this authority. It is not limited to the earth, as was the authority of Jesus during his ministry. What is the nature of this authority? It is not specified here, and thus the readers are invited to interpret it in terms of what has been said about Jesus' authority in the Gospel. First, his authority on earth might be similar to the authority he had during his ministry on earth, the "authority" (or "power," *exousia*) to teach or instruct, to preach the kingdom, and to heal every disease and infirmity (see 4:23). In brief, it is the authority to demonstrate the mercy of God (healing), to proclaim (preach) the goodness of God the Father, the goodness of his kingdom, and to teach what one needs to do in order to participate in the kingdom, God's will. But Jesus repeatedly spoke of another authority that he will have, namely, that of the Son of man who will come as the eschatological judge coming "in his glory, and all the angels with him" (see 25:31–46), and at the right hand of God (see 26:64). It is this kind of authority that he has now received, the authority "in heaven." But note that both kinds of authority are closely linked. Preaching and teaching, calling people to participate in the kingdom, become, when rejected, a judgment (see 9:36—10:15). And judging involves assessing whether or not people have observed all that is expressed in the teaching.

Obviously the rest of Jesus' words to the disciples emphasize the "teaching" rather than the judgment. As far as the disciples are concerned, Jesus has received "all authority." This means that the authority he displayed during his ministry is God's authority and therefore that his teaching was authoritative, God's word. His resurrection demonstrates his trustworthiness. The first criterion for the trustworthiness of an instruction (see 28:7–15) is therefore met.

28:19a. Consequently the instruction can continue: "Go therefore and make disciples of all nations." "Therefore." Since the resurrection demonstrates that Jesus' teaching is trustworthy and a direct expression of God's will, it follows that the disciples must transmit this teaching and "make disciples" as Jesus did. Furthermore, since Jesus has received "all authority," he has authority over the disciples. He can command them, and they must submit to his authority. Yet once again the trustworthiness of Jesus' authority is demonstrated. By submitting to Jesus' authority the disciples are not diminished, as when one submits to an authority that is not trustworthy (see 28:7–15); rather, they receive authority themselves. They share in Jesus' authority, a universal authority which applies to "all nations." The ministry that Jesus carried out in Galilee and Judea is the one they need to carry out among all nations. The second criterion for the trustworthiness of an instruction is therefore met.

28:19b. Thus the instruction that follows comes as a surprise for the readers: "baptizing them in the name of the Father and of the Son and of the Holy Spirit." Throughout the Gospel there is not a single mention of baptism except with reference to John's baptism (in 21:25 and in chapter 3); Jesus was baptized by John (3:13–17) but did not baptize anyone. Are the disciples commanded to baptize as John did? This seems unlikely, since John's baptism was not a baptism "in the name of the Father and of the Son and of the Holy Spirit." The only clue we have for elucidating how Matthew understood this instruction comes from the (eleven) disciples who will perform these baptisms; they are in the process of making "disciples of all nations." In other words, their ministry aims at making it possible for new people to have the same status that they themselves have. Now the status of the (eleven) disciples to whom these instructions are addressed is one of sharing in Jesus' authority and Jesus' ministry. Making disciples involves allowing people to share in Jesus' authority and ministry. In this light it appears that baptizing people "in the name of the Father and of the Son and of the Holy Spirit" means *baptizing them as Jesus was baptized*, so that in turn they might share in Jesus' authority and ministry. This means that the disciples' mission needs to be interpreted in terms of 3:13–17. This text is one of only two passages (see 10:17–20) in the entire Gospel that refer to the Father, the Son, and the Holy Spirit—all three. At Jesus' baptism the Spirit of God descends upon him; the "voice from heaven" is the voice of the Father; and Jesus is called by the voice the "beloved Son" with whom he is well pleased. By being baptized in the name of the Father and of the Son and of the Holy Spirit, people share in Jesus' baptism and share in Jesus' authority. God is their Father, as he is Jesus' Father. They are "beloved sons," as he is the "beloved Son"—and thus appropriately Jesus calls the disciples "my brethren" (28:10). And as the Holy Spirit descended upon Jesus, so the Holy Spirit descends upon the new disciples. This means that through baptism people are given to share in Jesus' ministry, as Jesus gave this authority to the Twelve in chapter 10 (where Father, Son, and the Spirit are all mentioned). As expressed in 10:17–20, disciples carry on their ministry in the name of Jesus and are persecuted because of it. But they should not be anxious, because the "Spirit of their Father" will be speaking through them. For Matthew,[39] being baptized of the same baptism with which Jesus was baptized does not primarily mean sharing his Passion by being persecuted. The emphasis is rather on sharing Jesus' authority and his ministry, a ministry that does include being persecuted.

28:20a. The last instruction, "teaching them to observe all that I have commanded you," emphasizes in a final way the importance of Jesus' teaching and of doing what it demands. Now that the cross and the resurrection have demonstrated the trustworthiness of this teaching, a direct expression of God's will, the instruction that this teaching be transmitted to new disciples so that they might practice it comes as no surprise.

The concluding words, "and lo, I am with you always, to the close of the age" (28:20b), confirm the trustworthiness of Jesus' instruction. As expressed in 28:7–15, a last criterion for the trustworthiness of an instruction is that it is confirmed as people implement it. This is what the presence of Jesus with the disciples will do. The crucifixion and the divine manifestations following it have shown unambiguously that during his ministry Jesus was God's manifestation, "God with us," "Emmanuel" (1:23). Now Jesus' presence with his disciples until the end of the ages is the continued presence of God with them. For the readers, this promise calls to mind two passages that refer to Jesus' presence with his disciples. It reminds them of the promise "For where two or three are gathered in my name, there am I in the midst of them" (18:20). This text underscores that the promise in 28:20b reads: "I am with you," a plural "you." Jesus' presence is promised for disciples who are with other disciples involved in the ministry of which they have been charged. Making disciples is therefore a means to ensure that one will be with other disciples and therefore in the presence of Jesus, as forgiving a brother or a sister is also a means of being in the presence of Jesus (see 18:15–22). Similarly, this promise reminds the readers of the judgment scene in 25:31–46 where the Son of man/king reveals to those who are judged that having compassion for people in need is having compassion for him. In other words, the presence of Jesus with the disciples until the end of the ages is also his presence in the poor. By observing all that he has commanded them, they will indeed show mercy and compassion for the poor and consequently be in the presence of Jesus; it is to Jesus that they show compassion. Jesus will not be with them in his body (as he was during his ministry), but he will always be with them since "you always have the poor with you" (26:11). Thus this presence of Jesus with his disciples is twofold: he is with disciples gathered in his name and he is with disciples who observe all that he commanded them and who thus manifest the mercy of God to those who need mercy, as Jesus did during his ministry.

NOTES ON 26:1—28:20

1. Our structural exegesis of the Passion and Resurrection narrative is to be compared with other semiotic analyses of this text: Marin, *The Semiotics of the Passion Narrative* (French 1971, Eng. trans. 1980); Pham Hüu Lai, "Production du sens par la foi," *RSR* 61 (1973): 65–96; Delorme, "Sémiotique du récit," *RSR* 73 (1985): 85–110; Calloud, "Entre les écritures et la violence," *RSR* 73 (1985): 111–28. My analysis is significantly different from each of them, yet I learned much from each and owe many of my insights to them. As their dates indicate, the first two studies were pioneering in the field. With them we made our first steps into semiotics.

Without them one could not have envisioned using semiotics for biblical studies. But since then semiotic theory and methods of structural analysis have progressed to the point of providing sharper methodological tools. The differences with the last two studies are due to my focus on the analysis of Matthew's convictions (narrative semantics and its discursivization), deliberately using for this our knowledge of the entire "generative trajectory"; furthermore, I come to this text at the conclusion of an analysis of the entire Gospel of Matthew. Delorme's and Calloud's studies have more narrowly focused goals.

2. Cf. Dahl, "Die Passionsgeschichte bei Matthäus," NTS 2 (1955):17–32; BONNARD, 368–69.

3. For a detailed study of the relations (parallelisms, omissions, additions) of Matthew's Passion story with Mark's Passion story, see Descamps, "Rédaction et christologie dans le récit Matthéen de la passion," 359–415.

4. He made his own text that he borrowed from Mark, even when he did not introduce any change in the text. It is important to be aware that Matthew's Passion and Resurrection story follows and further develops the points made in Matthew 24—25.

5. Our interpretation of this passage is indebted to the semiotic analysis of 26:1–16 by Delorme, "Sémiotique du récit," 85–110.

6. In Mark 14:1–11 the sequence of events is the same, but the first scene is missing and the other scenes are different.

7. Technically this opposition is set by the reflexivity of the verbs "you know" (the disciples are to attribute this message to themselves) and "they said" (as they were taking counsel together, and thus to themselves).

8. Rather than "beautiful" action (RSV). As we have noted, throughout his Gospel Matthew systematically emphasizes the goodness of actions. Since the Greek term (*kalos*) used here can have both the meanings "good" and "beautiful," the former translation is the only appropriate one.

9. The attitude of the Jewish leaders and the disciples is also similar to the attitudes of those who look for signs of the end (see chapters 24—25). Looking for such signs is an attempt to gain control over time.

10. On Matthew's use of Zech. 11:12–13 to interpret the story of Judas, see STENDAHL, 120–26.

11. The Greek term (*eukairian*) we translated "appropriate time" has for its root the term used for "time" in 26:18 (*kairos*).

12. As BONNARD, 376, suggests. Whether or not Matthew expected his readers to recognize the relationship between 18:7 and 26:24 is not significant here. All the elements of the point Matthew makes in 26:20–25 are in these verses. Our reference to 18:7 merely helps us to perceive it more clearly.

13. Repetitions, like tensions, manifest where in the text a point is underscored for the readers in a thematic passage.

14. As STENDAHL, 80–83, has shown, both in Matt. 26:31 and Mark 14:27, this quotation is modified so as to emphasize the activity of God by reading "I will strike the shepherd" rather than "Strike the shepherd."

15. The text presents the disciples as viewing their strength and courage as a special and permanent gift given to them by God rather than as their own achievement, since Matthew constantly presupposes that what people have is given to them by God; these verses do not suggest the contrary.

16. A fourth opposition, letting this cup pass from Jesus (26:39) and not letting it pass from him (26:42), could also be noted, even though it is not as clearly marked as the others. At any rate, it is subsumed by the preceding.

17. For Matthew, God's power and its manifestations (what happens) cannot be separated from God's will (in contrast to Mark 14:36 which is open to another interpretation). Thus whatever happens in life is according to God's will. This is why disciples should not be anxious insofar as they know that God is their Father in heaven (6:25–33).

18. With Edwards, *Matthew's Story*, 87. These remarks support Meier's proposal: "Matthew sees the death-resurrection as an eschatological event in which the king-

dom breaks into this area in a new, fuller way." MEIER, 38 and 30–40. In this way Meier follows and "tones down" the proposal of Bartsch ("Die Passions und Ostergeschichten bei Matthäus," 80–92). The results of our structural exegesis suggests that Meier still overstates the role of salvation history in Matthew. As we have noted, it is expressed in *thematic* passages where Matthew expresses his convictions in terms of their presumed knowledge. In other words, Matthew presupposed an audience with a strong salvation history perspective, a view that he does not reject but that is not his own main preoccupation.

19. For the history of the interpretation of these words, see BONNARD, 386.

20. Even when these words are taken to be an ironical statement it is difficult to see here a narrative opposition.

21. The commentators are divided on this point. Typical are the interpretation of BONNARD (386–87), which is against our interpretation but not directly justified in terms of Matthew's text, and that of SCHWEIZER (495–96), with whom we agree and who shows that such an interpretation is consistent with 5:39.

22. In agreement with SCHWEIZER, 498–99, and GUNDRY, 541–42; but against BONNARD, 389–90.

23. Cf. Klausner, *Jesus of Nazareth*, 342.

24. Concerning this prophecy and its relationship to the entire story of Judas, see STENDAHL, 120–26, 196–98; and GUNDRY, 554–58. It is a quotation of Zech. 11:13 with allusions to Jer. 18:1–2; 32:6–9; or Jeremiah 19 rather than a quotation from Jeremiah, as the text affirms. In telling the story of Judas, Matthew had in mind the prophecy that he believed it fulfilled. As Stendahl shows, because the Hebrew text had two versions, one referring to the "potter" and the other to the "treasury," the prophecy could be applied both to the buying of the potter's field and to putting the money in the treasury, and thus to the throwing of the money in the Temple. In other words, buying the potter's field does not prevent the money from remaining associated with the Temple. Finally, note that the Greek text of the quotation is not without problems. How should its last phrase—"as the Lord directed me"—be understood at the conclusion of a text in the plural? Gundry resolves the problem by reading it in the singular—"I took . . . I gave . . ."—on the basis of a weak variant. We leave this question open.

25. The actions of the soldiers stripping Jesus and putting a scarlet robe on him (27:28) and stripping him of the robe and putting his own clothes on him (27:31) are clearly the opposite of each other, but they are not *semantically opposed* actions. The same actors (the soldiers) are performing both actions, and they do not perform the second action because they changed their mind. The second action is demanded (according to the text) so that the crucifixion might be properly performed. Technically there is a "difference" (or "opposition") between the two actions, but they are in a relation of "implication" and not in a relation either of "contradiction" or of "contrariety."

26. Cf. Gundry, *Use of OT*, 62, 144–45. On the use of Psalm 22 in this passage, see also Aletti, "Mort de Jésus et théorie du récit," *RSR* 73 (1985):147–60.

27. Cf. STENDAHL, 140–41.

28. For the quotation in 27:46 and a discussion of the textual variants, see STENDAHL, 83–87.

29. For comments on the "full panoply of apocalyptic imagery," see MEIER, 31–33, and bibliography in the notes.

30. The Greek term (*speira*) means "battalion" (so RSV). In a technical military sense it would refer to a unit of six hundred soldiers. Yet it is certainly used here in an imprecise sense to designate the "detachment" on duty at the time which will carry out the execution and is led by a centurion.

31. So BONNARD, 407; and MEIER, 32–33.

32. With MEIER, 31–40.

33. See Anderson, "Matthew: Gender and Reading," 3–27.

34. We translate Pilate's response in 27:65, "Take a guard of soldiers," as a positive response rather than a negative one when it is translated, "You have a guard of soldiers." Both translations are grammatically possible. But the former, reading

the verb as an imperative, is suggested by 28:12–14, which indicates that the "sol-diers" who composed the guard might have to respond to Pilate concerning their acts. It is therefore a guard of Roman soldiers provided by Pilate. This means that the dialogue between the chief priests and Pilate does not set a narrative opposition.

35. As suggested by the passive form of the Greek verbs in 27:63b and 64b. This saying differs slightly from the announcements themselves (cf. 16:21; 17:23; 20:19). We find here "after three days" instead of "on the third day," a discrepancy that reflects different traditions primarily concerning the interpretation of the resurrec-tion in terms of various texts from Scripture. Cf. Lindars, *New Testament Apologetic*, 60–66; and R. L. Richardson, Jr., "The Function of the Scriptures in the Rise of the Easter Faith." In the announcements Jesus spoke of his resurrection in the third person ("The Son of man . . . will be raised"), a formulation that makes it clear that this is God's doing, rather than in the second person as reported in 27:63. Yet even in the present formulation the Greek verb (*egeiromai*) is in a passive form sug-gesting an action of God (as further expressed in 27:64b).

36. For a survey of the interpretations of the "apostolic commissioning" in terms of traditions and literary genres, see Hubbard, *The Matthean Redaction of a Primitive Apostolic Commissioning*, 1–23.

37. The only possible narrative opposition is between "worshipping" and "doubting" (28:17). Yet the text does not provide any description which would allow us to distinguish "worshipping disciples" from "doubting disciples." There is no semantic opposition associated with the possible narrative opposition. Thus we conclude that Matthew emphasizes the ambivalence of the disciples' attitude. The juxtaposition of "worshipping" and "doubting" is, therefore, a thematic ten-sion rather than a narrative opposition.

38. With Léon-Dufour, we need to emphasize that this "doubting" should not be homologated with the disciples' doubt in other Gospels. His suggestion to trans-late the verb by "hesitated" renders well what we have found elsewhere in the Gospel regarding "faith" and "doubt" according to Matthew as recognition or non-rec-ognition of Jesus' power. He also argues that the verb refers to an *earlier* doubting: "They who had doubted." Although this reference to the disciples' doubt evokes, for the readers, earlier situations when the disciples doubted, Matthew's primary concern is to express the disciples' doubt at the time when they worship Jesus (the three verbs in this verse are aorists). See Léon-Dufour, "Présence du Seigneur res-suscité (Mt 28, 16–20)."

39. By contrast with Mark. Compare Mark 10:35–45 and Matt. 20:20–23.

NARRATIVE OPPOSITIONS IN MATTHEW

The table of "narrative oppositions" is provided for the convenience of the users of this commentary who might want to identify more precisely the oppositions discussed in the commentary. It has been prepared in Greek because several of the oppositions are not transparent in translation. These oppositions have been identified by applying the principles discussed in the Introduction to this book and in D. and A. Patte, *Structural Exegesis*, 26–27, 52–59. There is no need to present these principles again.

Since a given narrative opposition contrasts a pair of "transformations" (the "object—receiver" relations), I have strived to include not merely the verbs manifesting the transformations but also the clauses expressing the "object" which is communicated and the "receiver" to whom it is communicated. Yet, for brevity's sake, I did not include the "objects" in the case of certain cognitive oppositions. I want to refer to the oppositions created by polemical dialogues. The opposed "objects" are the entire sayings of the protagonists. In most instances, they are much too long to be included in the present table. Yet, in order to help the users of this table to identify in the text the specific narrative oppositions, I have often included the "subjects" of the transformations even though they do not directly contribute to setting up the *narrative* oppositions.

1:20a	παραλαβεῖν Μαρίαν τὴν γυναῖκά σου	1:19	ἀπολῦσαι αὐτήν
1:20b	τὸ γὰρ ἐν αὐτῇ γεννηθὲν ἐκ πνεύματός ἐστιν	1:25	(οὐκ) ἐγίνωσκεν αὐτὴν
2:10	ἐχάρησαν χαρὰν μεγάλην	2:3	Ἡρῴδης ἐταράχθη
2:12	μὴ ἀνακάμψαι πρὸς Ἡρῴδην	2:8	ἀπαγγείλατέ μοι
2:19	Τελευτήσαντος τοῦ Ἡρῴδου (2:20 τεθνήκασιν)	2:16	ἀνεῖλεν πάντας τοὺς παῖδας τοὺς ἐν Βηθλέεμ
3:5	ἐξεπορεύετο πρὸς αὐτὸν Ἱεροσόλυμα	3:7a	πολλοὺς τῶν Φαρισαίων καὶ Σαδδουκαίων ἐρχομένους
3:8	ποιήσατε καρπὸν ἄξιον τῆς μετανοίας	3:7b	φυγεῖν ἀπὸ τῆς μελλούσης ὀργῆς
3:9b	λέγω ὑμῖν ὅτι δύναται ὁ θεὸς . . .	3:9a	λέγειν ἐν ἑαυτοῖς· πατέρα ἔχομεν τὸν Ἀβραάμ
3:15a	ὁ Ἰησοῦς εἶπεν αὐτῷ; ἄφες ἄρτι	3:14b	λέγων· ἐγὼ χρείαν . . .
3:15b	τότε ἀφίησιν αὐτόν	3:14a	ὁ δὲ διεκώλυεν αὐτὸν (3:14c ὑπὸ σοῦ βαπτισθῆναι)
4:1	ὁ Ἰησοῦς ἀνήχθη εἰς τὴν ἔρημον ὑπὸ τοῦ πνεύματος	4:5	παραλαμβάνει αὐτὸν ὁ διάβολος εἰς τὴν ἁγίαν πόλιν (4:8 εἰς ὄρος ὑψηλὸν)
4:4a	ὁ δὲ ἀποκριθεὶς εἶπεν	4:3	ὁ πειράζων εἶπεν αὐτῷ
4:4c	ἀλλ' ἐπὶ παντὶ ῥήματι (ζήσεται)	4:4b	ἐπ' ἄρτῳ μόνῳ ζήσεται ὁ ἄνθρωπος
4:7	ἔφη αὐτῷ ὁ Ἰησοῦς	4:6	λέγει αὐτῷ
4:10a	λέγει αὐτῷ ὁ Ἰησοῦς	4:9a	εἶπεν αὐτῷ
4:10b	κύριον τὸν θεόν σου προσκυνήσεις	4:9b	πεσὼν προσκυνήσῃς μοι
5:12a	χαίρετε καὶ ἀγαλλιᾶσθε	5:11	ὀνειδίσωσιν ὑμᾶς
5:15b	ἀλλ' (τιθέασιν) ἐπὶ τὴν λυχνίαν	5:15a	τιθέασιν αὐτὸν ὑπὸ τὸν μόδιον
5:17b	ἀλλὰ πληρῶσαι	5:17a	καταλῦσαι τὸν νόμον ἤ τοὺς προφήτας
5:19b	ὃς δ' ἂν ποιήσῃ	5:19a	ὃς ἐὰν λύσῃ μίαν τῶν ἐντολῶν τούτων τῶν ἐλαχίστων
5:22a	ἐγὼ δὲ λέγω ὑμῖν	5:21	Ἠκούσατε ὅτι ἐρρέθη τοῖς ἀρχαίοις
5:24	διαλλάγηθι τῷ ἀδελφῷ σου	5:22b	εἴπῃ τῷ ἀδελφῷ αὐτοῦ ῥακά (5:22c εἴπῃ μωρέ)
5:28	ἐγὼ δὲ λέγω ὑμῖν	5:27	Ἠκούσατε ὅτι ἐρρέθη
5:29a	ἀπόληται ἕν τῶν μελῶν σου	5:29b	ὅλον τὸ σῶμά σου βληθῇ εἰς γέενναν
5:32	ἐγὼ δὲ λέγω ὑμῖν	5:31	Ἐρρέθη
5:34a	ἐγὼ δὲ λέγω ὑμῖν	5:33a	ἠκούσατε ὅτι ἐρρέθη τοῖς ἀρχαίοις
5:34b	μὴ ὀμόσαι ὅλως	5:33b	οὐκ ἐπιορκήσεις
5:39	ἐγὼ δὲ λέγω ὑμῖν	5:38	Ἠκούσατε ὅτι ἐρρέθη
5:44	ἐγὼ δὲ λέγω ὑμῖν	5:43a	Ἠκούσατε ὅτι ἐρρέθη
5:44b	ἀγαπᾶτε τοὺς ἐχθροὺς ὑμῶν	5:43b	μισήσεις τὸν ἐχθρόν σου
5:47a	περισσὸν ποιεῖτε	5:47b	οἱ ἐθνικοὶ τὸ αὐτὸ ποιοῦσιν

6:4a	ὁ πατήρ σου ὁ βλέπων ἐν τῷ κρυπτῷ	6:1	πρὸς τὸ θεαθῆναι αὐτοῖς (6:2a δοξασθῶσιν ὑπὸ τῶν ἀνθρώπων)
6:4b	ἀποδώσει σοι	6:2b	ἀπέχουσιν τὸν μισθὸν αὐτῶν
6:6a	ὁ πατήρ σου ὁ βλέπων ἐν τῷ κρυπτῷ	6:5a	φανῶσιν τοῖς ἀνθρώποις
6:6b	ἀποδώσει σοι	6:5b	ἀπέχουσιν τὸν μισθὸν αὐτῶν
6:8	οἶδεν ὁ πατὴρ ὑμων ὧν χρείαν ἔχετε	6:7	ἐν τῇ πολυλογίᾳ αὐτῶν εἰσακουσθήσονται
6:13b	ἀλλὰ ῥῦσαι ἡμᾶς ἀπὸ τοῦ πονηροῦ	6:13a	(μὴ) εἰσενέγκῃς ἡμᾶς εἰς πειρασμόν
6:17	ἄλειψαι σου τὴν κεφαλὴν …	6:16a	(μὴ) γίνεσθε ὡς οἱ ὑποκριταὶ σκυθρωποί
6:18	μὴ φανῇς τοῖς ἀνθρώποις νηστεύων ἀλλὰ τῷ πατρί σου τῷ ἐν τῷ κρυφαίῳ	6:16b	φανῶσιν τοῖς ἀνθρώποις νηστεύοντες
6:25	μὴ μεριμνᾶτε (6:31,34 μὴ οὖν μεριμνήσητε)	6:27	μεριμνῶν (6:28 μεριμνᾶτε)
6:33	ζητεῖτε δὲ πρῶτον τὴν βασιλείαν καὶ τὴν δικαιοσύνην αὐτοῦ	6:32	πάντα ταῦτα τὰ ἔθνη ἐπιζητοῦσιν
7:5	ἔκβαλε πρῶτον ἐκ τοῦ ὀφθαλμοῦ σου τὴν δοκόν	7:4	ἐκβάλω τὸ κάρφος ἐκ τοῦ ὀφθαλμοῦ σου
7:11	δόματα ἀγαθὰ διδόναι τοῖς τέκνοις ὑμῶν	7:10	λίθον ἐπιδώσει αὐτῷ … ὄφιν ἐπιδώσει αὐτῷ
7:13a	Εἰσέλθατε διὰ τῆς στενῆς πύλης	7:13c	οἱ εἰσερχόμενοι δι᾽ αὐτῆς [πλατείας πύλης]
7:14	ἡ ὁδὸς ἡ ἀπάγουσα εἰς τὴν ζωήν	7:13b	ἡ ὁδὸς ἡ ἀπάγουσα εἰς τὴν ἀπώλειαν
7:17a	καρποὺς καλοὺς ποιεῖ	7:17b	καρποὺς πονηροὺς ποιεῖ
7:21b	ἀλλ᾽ ὁ ποιῶν τὸ θέλημα τοῦ πατρός μου	7:21a	ὁ λέγων μοι κύριε κύριε
7:23	ὁμολογήσω αὐτοῖς	7:22	πολλοὶ ἐροῦσίν μοι
7:24a	ἀκούει μου τοὺς λόγους τούτους καὶ ποιεῖ αὐτούς	7:26a	ὁ ἀκούων μου τοὺς λόγους τούτους καὶ μὴ ποιῶν αὐτοὺς
7:24b	ᾠκοδόμησεν αὐτοῦ τὴν οἰκίαν ἐπὶ τὴν πέτραν	7:26b	ᾠκοδόμησεν αὐτοῦ τὴν οἰκίαν ἐπὶ τὴν ἄμμον
7:29a	διδάσκων αὐτοὺς ὡς ἐξουσίαν ἔχων	7:29b	οὐχ [διδάσκων] ὡς οἱ γραμματεῖς αὐτῶν
8:4b	ἀλλὰ ὕπαγε σεαυτὸν δεῖξον τῷ ἱερεῖ καὶ προσένεγκον τὸ δῶρον	8:4a	(μηδενὶ) εἴπῃς
8:8	ἀποκριθεὶς δὲ ὁ ἑκατόνταρχος ἔφη	8:7	λέγει αὐτῷ
8:13a	ὡς ἐπίστευσας γενηθήτω σοι	8:10	παρ᾽ οὐδενὶ τοσαύτην πίστιν ἐν τῷ Ἰσραὴλ εὗρον
8:15	ἀφῆκεν αὐτὴν ὁ πυρετός· καὶ ἠγέρθη	8:14	τὴν πενθερὰν αὐτοῦ [Πέτρου] βεβλημένην καὶ πυρέσσουσαν
8:20	λέγει αὐτῷ ὁ Ἰησοῦς	8:19	εἰς γραμματεὺς εἶπεν αὐτῷ
8:22	ὁ δὲ Ἰησοῦς λέγει αὐτῷ	8:21	ἕτερος δὲ τῶν μαθητῶν εἶπεν
8:26	λέγει αὐτοῖς	8:25	λέγοντες· κύριε, σῶσον

8:29	ἦλθες ὧδε	8:28	μὴ ἰσχύειν τινὰ παρελθεῖν διὰ τῆς ὁδοῦ ἐκείνης
9:6	ἔγειρε ἆρόν σου τὴν κλίνην (also 9:5,7)	9:2	παραλυτικὸν ἐπὶ κλίνης βεβλημένον
9:4	ὁ Ἰησοῦς ... εἶπεν	9:3	τινες τῶν γραμματέων εἶπαν ἐν ἑαυτοῖς
9:12	ὁ δὲ ἀκούσας εἶπεν	9:11	οἱ Φαρισαῖοι ἔλεγον τοῖς μαθηταῖς αὐτοῦ
9:13a	ἔλεος θέλω	9:13b	(οὐ) [θέλω] θυσίαν
9:13d	ἀλλὰ [καλέσαι] ἁμαρτωλούς	9:13c	(οὐ) ἦλθον καλέσαι δικαίους
9:15	εἶπεν αὐτοῖς ὁ Ἰησοῦς	9:14a	οἱ μαθηταὶ Ἰωάννου λέγοντες
9:14c	οἱ δὲ μαθηταί σου οὐ νηστεύουσιν	9:14b	ἡμεῖς καὶ οἱ Φαρισαῖοι νηστεύομεν
9:17b	ἀλλὰ βάλλουσιν οἶνον νέον εἰς ἀσκοὺς καινούς	9:17a	βάλλουσιν οἶνον νέον εἰς ἀσκοὺς παλαιούς
9:18b	ἀλλὰ ... ζήσεται	9:18a	ἡ θυγάτηρ μου ἄρτι ἐτελεύτησεν
9:24a	ὁ Ἰησοῦς ... ἔλεγεν	9:24d	κατεγέλων αὐτοῦ
9:24c	ἀλλὰ καθεύδει	9:24b	(οὐ) ἀπέθανεν τὸ κοράσιον
9:30	ἐνεβριμήθη αὐτοῖς ὁ Ἰησοῦς λέγων· ὁρᾶτε μηδεὶς γινωσκέτω	9:31	οἱ δὲ ἐξελθόντες διεφήμισαν αὐτὸν ἐν ὅλῃ τῃ γῇ ἐκείνῃ
9:33	οἱ ὄχλοι λέγοντες	9:34	οἱ δὲ Φαρισαῖοι ἔλεγον
10:6	πορεύεσθε δὲ μᾶλλον πρὸς τὰ πρόβατα τὰ ἀπολωλότα οἴκου Ἰσραήλ	10:5	Εἰς ὁδὸν ἐθνῶν μὴ ἀπέλθητε, καὶ εἰς πόλιν Σαμαριτῶν μὴ εἰσέλθητε
10:8	δωρεὰν δότε (10:10 ἄξιος γὰρ ὁ ἐργάτης τῆς τροφῆς αὐτοῦ)	10:9	(Μὴ) κτήσησθε χρυσὸν
10:13a	ἐλθάτω ἡ εἰρήνη ὑμῶν ἐπ' αὐτήν	10:13b	ἡ εἰρήνη ὑμῶν πρὸς ὑμᾶς ἐπιστραφήτω
10:19b	δοθήσεται ὑμῖν ἐν ἐκείνῃ τῇ ὥρᾳ τί λαλήσητε	10:19a	(μὴ) μεριμνήσητε πῶς ἢ τί λαλήσητε
10:20b	τὸ πνεῦμα τοῦ πατρὸς ὑμῶν τὸ λαλοῦν ἐν ὑμῖν	10:20a	(οὐ) ὑμεῖς ἐστε οἱ λαλοῦντες
10:22	οὗτος σωθήσεται	10:21	παραδώσει δὲ ἀδελφὸς ἀδελφὸν εἰς θάνατον ... ἐπαναστήσονται ... θανατώσουσιν αὐτούς
10:28b	φοβεῖσθε δὲ μᾶλλον τὸν δυνάμενον καὶ ψυχὴν καὶ σῶμα ἀπολέσαι	10:26	(μὴ) φοβηθῆτε αὐτούς (10:28a [μὴ] φοβεῖσθε ἀπὸ τῶν ἀποκτεννόντων τὸ σῶμα, 10:31 [μὴ] οὖν φοβεῖσθε)
10:32	ὁμολογήσει ἐν ἐμοὶ ἔμπροσθεν τῶν ἀνθρώπων	10:33	ἀρνήσηταί με ἔμπροσθεν τῶν ἀνθρώπων
10:34b	οὐκ ἦλθον βαλεῖν εἰρήνην ἀλλὰ μάχαιραν	10:34a	ἦλθον βαλεῖν εἰρήνην ἐπὶ τὴν γῆν
10:38	ἀκολουθεῖ ὀπίσω μου	10:37	Ὁ φιλῶν πατέρα ἢ μητέρα ὑπὲρ ἐμὲ ... φιλῶν υἱὸν ἢ θυγατέρα
10:39c	ὁ ἀπολέσας τὴν ψυχὴν αὐτοῦ ἕνεκεν ἐμοῦ	10:39a	ὁ εὑρὼν τὴν ψυχὴν αὐτοῦ
10:39d	εὑρήσει αὐτήν	10:39b	ἀπολέσει αὐτήν

11:4	ὁ ᾿Ιησοῦς εἶπεν αὐτοῖς	11:2	῾Ο ᾿Ιωάννης . . . εἶπεν αὐτῷ
11:9a	προφήτην ἰδεῖν	11:7	θεάσασθαι; κάλαμον . . . (11:8 ἰδεῖν; ἄνθρωπον ἐν μαλακοῖς ἠμφιεσμένον;)
11:9b	λέγω ὑμῖν (also 11:11)	11:18	λέγουσιν (also 11:19)
11:21	μετενόησαν	11:20	οὐ μετενόησαν
11:23b	ἕως ᾅδου καταβήσῃ	11:23a	μὴ ἕως οὐρανοῦ ὑψωθήσῃ
11:28b	κἀγὼ ἀναπαύσω ὑμᾶς	11:28a	οἱ κοπιῶντες καὶ πεφορτισμένοι
12:3	ὁ δὲ εἶπεν αὐτοῖς	12:2	οἱ δὲ Φαρισαῖοι ἰδόντες εἶπαν αὐτῷ
12:7a	ἔλεος θέλω	12:7b	οὐ (θέλω) θυσίαν
12:11	ὁ δὲ εἶπεν αὐτοῖς	12:10	ἐπηρώτησαν αὐτὸν λέγοντες
12:15	ὁ δὲ ᾿Ιησοῦς . . . ἐθεράπευσεν αὐτοὺς πάντας (12:12 τοῖς σάββασιν καλῶς ποιεῖν)	12:14	οἱ Φαρισαῖοι συμβούλιον ἔλαβον κατ᾽ αὐτοῦ, ὅπως αὐτὸν ἀπολέσωσιν
12:23	παντες οἱ ὄχλοι . . . ἔλεγον	12:24	οἱ δὲ Φαρισαῖοι ἀκούσαντες εἶπον
12:25,28	εἶπεν αὐτοῖς . . . εἰ δὲ ἐν πνεύματι θεοῦ ἐγὼ ἐκβάλλω τὰ δαιμόνια	12:25,27	εἶπεν αὐτοις . . . εἰ ἐγὼ ἐν Βεελζεβοὺλ ἐκβάλλω τὰ δαιμόνια
12:30a	συνάγων μετ᾽ ἐμοῦ	12:30b	σκορπίζει
12:33a	ποιήσατε τὸ δένδρον καλὸν	12:33b	ποιήσατε τὸ δένδρον σαπρὸν
12:35a	ὁ ἀγαθὸς ἄνθρωπος ἐκ τοῦ ἀγαθοῦ θησαυροῦ ἐκβάλλει ἀγαθά	12:35b	ὁ πονηρὸς ἄνθρωπος ἐκ τοῦ πονηροῦ θησαυροῦ ἐκβάλλει πονηρά
12:39	ὁ δὲ ἀποκριθεὶς εἶπεν αὐτοῖς	12:38	ἀπεκρίθησαν αὐτῷ τινες τῶν γραμματέων καὶ Φαρισαίων λέγοντες
12:49	εἶπεν· ἰδοὺ ἡ μήτηρ μου	12:48	τῷ λέγοντι αὐτῷ· τίς ἐστιν ἡ μήτηρ μου . . . ;
13:8	ἄλλα δὲ ἔπεσεν ἐπὶ τὴν γῆν τὴν καλὴν	13:4,5,7	ἔπεσεν παρὰ τὴν ὁδόν . . . ἐπὶ τὰ πετρώδη . . . ἐπὶ τὰς ἀκάνθας
13:11	ὁ δὲ ἀποκριθεὶς εἶπεν	13:10	οἱ μαθηταὶ εἶπαν αὐτῷ
13:16	ὑμῶν δὲ μακάριοι οἱ ὀφθαλμοὶ ὅτι βλέπουσιν, καὶ τὰ ὦτα ὅτι ἀκούουσιν	13:13	οὐ βλέπουσιν . . . οὐκ ἀκούουσιν οὐδὲ συνίουσιν (13:14,15 μὴ συνῆτε . . . μὴ ἴδητε . . . μήποτε ἴδωσιν τοῖς ὀφθαλμοῖς καὶ τοῖς ὠσὶν ἀκούσωσιν
13:17a,c	ἃ βλέπετε . . . ἃ ἀκούετε	13:17b	οὐκ εἶδαν . . . οὐκ ἤκουσαν
13:23a	ὁ τὸν λόγον ἀκούων καὶ συνιείς	13:19	Παντὸς ἀκούοντος τὸν λόγον . . . καὶ μὴ συνιέντος (13:21 διὰ τὸν λόγον εὐθὺς σκανδαλίζεται)
13:23b	ὃς δὴ καρποφορεῖ	13:22	ἄκαρπος γίνεται
13:24	σπείραντι καλὸν σπέρμα (also 13:27b καλὸν σπέρμα ἔσπειρας)	13:25	ἐπέσπειρεν ζιζάνια (also 13:28b ἐχθρὸς . . . τοῦτο ἐποίσεν)
13:28a	ὁ δέ ἔφη αὐτοῖς	13:27a	οἱ δοῦλοι . . . εἶπον αὐτῷ
13:29	ὁ δέ φησιν	13:28c	οἱ δὲ δοῦλοι αὐτῷ λέγουσιν

13:30	ἄφετε συναυξάνεσθαι ἀμφότερα	13:28d	ἀπελθόντες συλλέξωμεν αὐτά
13:34a	Ταῦτα πάντα ἐλάλησεν ὁ Ἰησοῦς ἐν παραβολαῖς τοῖς ὄχλοις	13:34b	χωρὶς παραβολῆς (οὐδὲν) ἐλάλει αὐτοῖς
13:37	ὁ σπείρων τὸ καλὸν σπέρμα	13:39	ὁ δὲ ἐχθρὸς ὁ σπείρας αὐτά (ζιζάνιά)
13:57	ὁ δὲ Ἰησοῦς εἶπεν αὐτοῖς	13:54	ἐκπλήσσεσθαι αὐτοὺς καὶ λέγειν
14:16	ὁ δὲ Ἰησοῦς εἶπεν αὐτοῖς	14:15	οἱ μαθηταὶ λέγοντες
14:18	ὁ δὲ εἶπεν	14:17	οἱ δὲ λέγουσιν αὐτῷ
14:27	ἐλάλησεν αὐτοῖς λέγων· θαρσεῖτε ... μὴ φοβεῖσθε	14:26	οἱ δὲ μαθηταὶ ... ἐταράχθησαν λέγοντες
14:29	Πέτρος περιεπάτησεν ἐπὶ τὰ ὕδατα	14:30	ἀρξάμενος καταποντίζεσθαι
15:3a	ὁ δὲ ἀποκριθεὶς εἶπεν αὐτοῖς	15:1	Φαρισαῖοι καὶ γραμματεῖς λέγοντες
15:2	οἱ μαθηταί σου παραβαίνουσιν τὴν παράδοσιν	15:3b	ὑμεῖς παραβαίνετε τὴν ἐντολὴν τοῦ θεοῦ (also 15:6b ἠκυρώσατε τὸν λόγον τοῦ θεοῦ)
15:4a	ὁ θεὸς εἶπεν	15:5	ὑμεῖς δὲ λέγετε
15:4b	τίμα τὸν πατέρα καὶ τὴν μητέρα	15:6a	οὐ μὴ τιμήσει τὸν πατέρα αὐτοῦ
15:10	ἀκούετε καὶ συνίετε	15:12b	οἱ Φαρισαῖοι ἀκούσαντες τὸν λόγον ἐσκανδαλίσθησαν
15:11a	οὐ τὸ εἰσερχόμενον εἰς τὸ στόμα κοινοῖ τὸν ἄνθρωπον	15:11b	ἀλλὰ τὸ ἐκπορευόμενον ἐκ τοῦ στόματος, τοῦτο κοινοῖ τὸν ἄνθρωπον
15:13	ὁ δὲ ἀποκριθεὶς εἶπεν	15:12	οἱ μαθηταὶ λέγουσιν αὐτῷ
15:20b	οὐ κοινοῖ τὸν ἄνθρωπον	15:18	κἀκεῖνα κοινοῖ τὸν ἄνθρωπον (15:20a τὰ κοινοῦντα)
15:24	ὁ δὲ ἀποκριθεὶς εἶπεν	15:23	οἱ μαθηταὶ αὐτοῦ ἠρώτων αὐτὸν λέγοντες
15:25	ἡ δὲ ἐλθοῦσα προσεκύνει αὐτῷ λέγουσα (15:27 ἡ δὲ εἶπεν ... 15:28 ὁ Ἰησοῦς εἶπεν)	15:26	ὁ δὲ ἀποκριθεὶς εἶπεν
15:32	Ὁ δὲ Ἰησοῦς ... εἶπεν (15:34 λέγει αὐτοῖς ὁ Ἰησοῦς)	15:33	λέγουσιν αὐτῷ οἱ μαθηταί
16:2	ὁ δὲ ἀποκριθεὶς εἶπεν αὐτοῖς	16:1	οἱ Φαρισαῖοι καὶ Σαδδουκαῖοι πειράζοντες ἐπηρώτησαν αὐτὸν σημεῖον
16:3a	τὸ μὲν πρόσωπον τοῦ οὐρανοῦ γινώσκετε διακρίνειν	16:3b	τὰ δὲ σημεῖα τῶν καιρῶν οὐ δύνασθε
16:6	ὁ δὲ Ἰησοῦς εἶπεν αὐτοῖς (also 16:8a)	16:7	οἱ δὲ διελογίζοντο ἐν ἑαυτοῖς λέγοντες
16:12a	τότε συνῆκαν	16:9	οὔπω νοεῖτε (16:11 πῶς οὐ νοεῖτε)
16:12c	ἀλλὰ [εἶπεν] ἀπὸ τῆς διδαχῆς τῶν Φαρισαίων καὶ Σαδδουκαίων	16:12b	οὐκ εἶπεν προσέχειν ἀπὸ τῆς ζύμης

16:16	ἀποκριθεὶς δὲ Σίμων Πέτρος εἶπεν	16:13	λέγουσιν οἱ ἄνθρωποι εἶναι τὸν υἱὸν τοῦ ἀνθρώπου
16:17b	ἀλλ᾽ ὁ πατήρ μου [ἀπεκάλυψεν σοι]	16:17a	σὰρξ καὶ αἷμα οὐκ ἀπεκάλυψέν σοι
16:21a	ἤρξατο ᾿Ιησοῦς δεικνύειν τοῖς μαθηταῖς αὐτοῦ . . .	16:22	ὁ Πέτρος ἤρξατο ἐπιτιμᾶν αὐτῷ λέγων
16:21c	τῇ τρίτῃ ἡμέρᾳ ἐγερθῆναι	16:21b	πολλὰ παθεῖν . . . καὶ ἀποκτανθῆναι
16:23a	φρονεῖς τὰ τοῦ θεοῦ	16:23b	ἀλλὰ [φρονεῖς] τὰ τῶν ἀνθρώπων
16:25c	ὃς δ᾽ ἂν ἀπολέσῃ τὴν ψυχὴν αὐτοῦ ἕνεκεν ἐμοῦ	16:25a	ὃς ἐὰν θέλῃ τὴν ψυχὴν αὐτοῦ σῶσαι
16:25d	εὑρήσει αὐτήν	16:25b	ἀπολέσει αὐτήν
17:5	φωνὴ ἐκ τῆς νεφέλης λέγουσα	17:4	ἀποκριθεὶς δὲ ὁ Πέτρος εἶπεν τῷ ᾿Ιησοῦ
17:7a	ἐγέρθητε	17:6a	οἱ μαθηταὶ ἔπεσαν ἐπὶ πρόσωπον αὐτῶν
17:7b	μὴ φοβεῖσθε	17:6b	ἐφοβήθησαν σφόδρα
17:9	ἐνετείλατο αὐτοῖς ὁ ᾿Ιησοῦς λέγων	17:10	ἐπηρώτησαν αὐτὸν οἱ μαθηταὶ λέγοντες
17:13	συνῆκαν οἱ μαθηταὶ	17:12	οὐκ ἐπέγνωσαν αὐτόν
17:18	ἐθεραπεύθη ὁ παῖς	17:16	οὐκ ἠδυνήθησαν αὐτόν θεραπεῦσαι
17:20	οὐδὲν ἀδυνατήσει ὑμῖν	17:19	ἡμεῖς οὐκ ἠδυνήθημεν ἐκβαλεῖν αὐτό
17:23b	τῇ τρίτῃ ἡμέρᾳ ἐγερθήσεται	17:23a	ἀποκτενοῦσιν αὐτόν
18:4	ὅστις ταπεινώσει ἑαυτὸν ὡς τὸ παιδίον τοῦτο	18:3	ἐὰν μὴ στραφῆτε καὶ γένησθε ὡς τὰ παιδία
18:5a	ὃς ἐὰν δέξηται ἓν παιδίον τοιοῦτο ἐπὶ τῷ ὀνόματί μου	18:6a	ὃς δ᾽ ἂν σκανδαλίσῃ ἕνα τῶν μικρῶν τούτων τῶν πιστευόντων εἰς ἐμὲ
18:5b	ἐμὲ δέχεται	18:6b	καταποντισθῇ ἐν τῷ πελάγει τῆς θαλάσσης
18:8a	εἰσελθεῖν εἰς τὴν ζωὴν (also 18:9a)	18:8b	βληθῆναι εἰς τὸ πῦρ τὸ αἰώνιον (18:9b βληθῆναι εἰς τὴν γέενναν τοῦ πυρός)
18:13	ἐὰν γένηται εὑρεῖν αὐτό	18:12	πλανηθῇ ἓν ἐξ αὐτῶν
18:15	ἐὰν σου ἀκούσῃ	18:16	ἐὰν δὲ μὴ ἀκούσῃ (18:17a,b παρακούσῃ)
18:22b	ἀλλὰ [λέγω σοι] ἕως ἑβδομηκοντάκις ἑπτά	18:22a	(οὐ) λέγω σοι ἕως ἑπτάκις
18:26, 27a	μακροθύμησον ἐπ᾽ ἐμοί . . . σπλαγχνισθεὶς δὲ ὁ κύριος τοῦ δούλου ἐκείνου (18:33 κἀγὼ σὲ ἠλέησα)	18:30a	ὁ δὲ οὐκ ἤθελεν (18:33 οὐκ ἔδει καὶ σὲ ἐλεῆσαι τὸν σύνδουλόν σου)
18:27b	ἀπέλυσεν αὐτόν	18:30b	ἀπελθὼν ἔβαλεν αὐτὸν εἰς φυλακὴν
19:4	ὁ δὲ ἀποκριθεὶς εἶπεν	19:3	Φαρισαῖοι πειράζοντες αὐτόν καὶ λέγοντες
19:6a	ὃ οὖν ὁ θεὸς συνέζευξεν	19:6b	ἄνθρωπος (μὴ) χωριζέτω

19:8	λέγει αὐτοῖς	19:7	λέγουσιν αὐτῷ
19:11a	ὁ δὲ εἶπεν αὐτοῖς	19:10	λέγουσιν αὐτῷ οἱ μαθηταί
19:11c	ἀλλ᾽ οἷς δέδοται	19:11b	οὐ πάντες χωροῦσιν τὸν λόγον τοῦτον
19:12c	οἵτινες εὐνούχισαν ἑαυτοὺς διὰ τὴν βασιλείαν	19:12a,b	οἵτινες ἐκ κοιλίας μητρὸς ἐγεννήθησαν οὕτως . . . εὐνουχίσθησαν ὑπὸ τῶν ἀνθρώπων
19:14	μὴ κωλύετε αὐτὰ ἐλθεῖν πρός με	19:13	οἱ δὲ μαθηταὶ ἐπετίμησαν αὐτοῖς
19:17	ὁ δὲ εἶπεν αὐτῷ	19:16	εἷς προσελθὼν αὐτῷ εἶπεν
19:21	ἀκολούθει μοι (also 19:27 ἠκολουθήσαμέν σοι)	19:22	ἀκούσας δὲ ὁ νεανίσκος τὸν λόγον ἀπῆλθεν λυπούμενος
19:26	ὁ Ἰησοῦς εἶπεν αὐτοῖς	19:25	οἱ μαθηταὶ ἐξεπλήσσοντο σφόδρα λέγοντες
20:1	μισθώσασθαι ἐργάτας εἰς τὸν ἀμπελῶνα αὐτοῦ	20:7	οὐδεὶς ἡμᾶς ἐμισθώσατο
20:2	συμφωνήσας δὲ μετὰ τῶν ἐργατῶν ἐκ δηναρίου (20:13b οὐχὶ δηναρίου συνεφώνησάς μοι)	20:10a	οἱ πρῶτοι ἐνόμισαν ὅτι πλεῖον . . .
20:9,10c	οἱ περὶ τὴν ἑνδεκάτην ὥραν ἔλαβον ἀνὰ δηνάριον . . . καὶ ἔλαβον τὸ ἀνὰ δηνάριον καὶ αὐτοί	20:10b	πλεῖον λήμψονται
20:13	ὁ δὲ ἀποκριθεὶς ἑνὶ αὐτῶν εἶπεν	20:11	ἐγόγγυζον κατὰ τοῦ οἰκοδεσπότου λέγοντες
20:19b	καὶ τῇ τρίτῃ ἡμέρᾳ ἐγερθήσεται	20:18, 19a	κατακρινοῦσιν αὐτὸν εἰς θάνατον . . . καὶ σταυρῶσαι
20:22	ἀποκριθεὶς δὲ ὁ Ἰησοῦς εἶπεν	20:21a	λέγει αὐτῷ
20:23	οὐκ ἔστιν ἐμὸν τοῦτο δοῦναι, ἀλλ᾽ οἷς ἡτοίμασται ὑπὸ τοῦ πατρός μου	20:21b	εἰπὲ ἵνα καθίσωσιν οὗτοι . . . εἷς ἐκ δεξιῶν καὶ εἷς ἐξ εὐωνύμων σου
20:28b	ἀλλὰ διακονῆσαι	20:25	κατακυριεύουσιν αὐτῶν . . . κατεξουσιάζουσιν αὐτῶν (20:28a οὐκ ἦλθεν διακονηθῆναι)
20:30	ἔκραξαν λέγοντες (also 20:31c)	20:31b	ἵνα σιωπήσωσιν
20:32	ὁ Ἰησοῦς ἐφώνησεν αὐτοὺς (20:34 σπλαγχνισθείς)	20:31a	ὁ δὲ ὄχλος ἐπετίμησεν αὐτοῖς
21:13a	ὁ οἶκός μου οἶκος προσευχῆς κληθήσεται	21:13b	ὑμεῖς δὲ αὐτὸν ποιεῖτε σπήλαιον λῃστῶν
21:16b	ὁ δὲ Ἰησοῦς λέγει αὐτοῖς	21:16a	εἶπαν αὐτῷ
21:21	ἀποκριθεὶς δὲ ὁ Ἰησοῦς εἶπεν αὐτοῖς	21:20	οἱ μαθηταὶ ἐθαύμασαν λέγοντες
21:24	ἀποκριθεὶς δὲ ὁ Ἰησοῦς εἶπεν αὐτοῖς	21:23	οἱ ἀρχιερεῖς καὶ οἱ πρεσβύτεροι τοῦ λαοῦ λέγοντες
21:25	ἐὰν εἴπωμεν· ἐξ οὐρανοῦ	21:26	ἐὰν δὲ εἴπωμεν· ἐξ ἀνθρώπων
21:27b	ἔφη αὐτοῖς καὶ αὐτός	21:27a	ἀποκριθέντες τῷ Ἰησοῦ εἶπαν
21:29b	ἀπῆλθεν	21:30	οὐκ ἀπῆλθεν

21:29a	ὕστερον δὲ μεταμεληθεὶς	21:32c	οὐδὲ μετεμελήθητε ὕστερον τοῦ πιστεῦσαι αὐτῷ
21:32b	οἱ δὲ τελῶναι καὶ αἱ πόρναι ἐπίστευσαν αὐτῷ	21:32a	οὐκ ἐπιστεύσατε αὐτῷ
21:34	λαβεῖν τοὺς καρποὺς αὐτοῦ (21:41b ἀποδώσουσιν αὐτῷ τοὺς καρπούς)	21:35	ὃν μὲν ἔδειραν, ὃν δὲ ἀπέκτειναν, ὃν δὲ ἐλιθοβόλησαν
21:37	ὕστερον ἀπέστειλεν . . . τὸν υἱὸν αὐτοῦ λέγων	21:38	οἱ δὲ γεωργοὶ ἰδόντες τὸν υἱὸν εἶπον ἐν ἑαυτοῖς
21:41	κακοὺς κακῶς ἀπολέσει αὐτούς	21:39	λαβόντες αὐτὸν ἐξέβαλον ἔξω τοῦ ἀμπελῶνος καὶ ἀπέκτειναν
21:42b	οὗτος ἐγενήθη εἰς κεφαλὴν γωνίας	21:42a	λίθον ὃν ἀπεδοκίμασαν οἱ οἰκοδομοῦντες
22:3a	καλέσαι τοὺς κεκλημένους εἰς τοὺς γάμους	22:3b	οὐκ ἤθελον ἐλθεῖν
22:4	δεῦτε εἰς τοὺς γάμους	22:5	οἱ δὲ ἀμελήσαντες ἀπῆλθον
22:7	ἀπώλεσεν τοὺς φονεῖς ἐκείνους	22:6	κρατήσαντες τοὺς δούλους αὐτοῦ ὕβρισαν καὶ ἀπέκτειναν
22:12a	λέγει αὐτῷ	22:12b	ὁ δὲ ἐφιμώθη
22:18	ὁ Ἰησοῦς . . . εἶπεν	22:16	τοὺς μαθητὰς αὐτῶν μετὰ τῶν Ἡρῳδιανῶν λέγοντας
22:29	ἀποκριθεὶς δὲ ὁ Ἰησοῦς εἶπεν αὐτοῖς	22:23b	Σαδδουκαῖοι . . . ἐπηρώτησαν αὐτὸν λέγοντες
22:31	τὸ ῥηθὲν ὑμῖν ὑπὸ τοῦ θεοῦ λέγοντος	22:23a	Σαδδουκαῖοι, λέγοντες μὴ εἶναι ἀνάστασιν
22:37	ὁ δὲ ἔφη αὐτῷ	22:36	ἐπηρώτησεν εἷς ἐξ αὐτῶν νομικὸς πειράζων αὐτόν
22:43b	Δαυὶδ ἐν πνεύματι καλεῖ αὐτὸν κύριον λέγων	22:42	λέγουσιν αὐτῷ
22:43a	λέγει αὐτοῖς	22:46	οὐδεὶς ἐδύνατο ἀποκριθῆναι αὐτῷ λόγον
23:3a	πάντα ὅσα ἐὰν εἴπωσιν ὑμῖν ποιήσατε	23:3b	κατὰ δὲ τὰ ἔργα αὐτῶν μὴ ποιεῖτε
23:8	ὑμεῖς δὲ μὴ κληθῆτε ῥαββί (see also 23:9–10)	23:7	καλεῖσθαι ὑπὸ τῶν ἀνθρώπων ῥαββί
23:12b	ὅστις ταπεινώσει ἑαυτὸν	23:12a	ὅστις δὲ ὑψώσει ἑαυτὸν
23:13b	(οὐδὲ) τοὺς εἰσερχομένους ἀφίετε εἰσελθεῖν	23:13a	κλείετε τὴν βασιλείαν . . . ἔμπροσθεν τῶν ἀνθρώπων
23:15a	ποιῆσαι ἕνα προσήλυτον	23:15b	ποιεῖτε αὐτὸν υἱὸν γεέννης διπλότερον ὑμῶν
23:20	ὁ οὖν ὀμόσας ἐν τῷ θυσιαστηρίῳ ὀμνύει ἐν αὐτῷ καὶ ἐν πᾶσι τοῖς ἐπάνω αὐτοῦ . . . ἐν τῷ ναῷ ὀμνύει ἐν αὐτῷ καὶ ἐν τῷ κατοικοῦντι αὐτόν	23:16	οἱ λέγοντες· ὃς ἂν ὀμόσῃ ἐν τῷ ναῷ . . . ἐν τῷ χρυσῷ τοῦ ναοῦ . . . ἐν τῷ θυσιαστηρίῳ . . . ἐν τῷ δώρῳ
23:23b	ταῦτα δὲ ἔδει ποιῆσαι	23:23a	ἀφήκατε τὰ βαρύτερα τοῦ νόμου
23:26	καθάρισον πρῶτον τὸ ἐντὸς τοῦ ποτηρίου	23:25	καθαρίζετε τὸ ἔξωθεν τοῦ ποτηρίου

23:31	μαρτυρεῖτε ἑαυτοῖς ὅτι υἱοί ἐστε τῶν φονευσάντων τοὺς προφήτας	23:30	λέγετε· εἰ ἤμεθα . . .
23:34a	ἐγὼ ἀποστέλλω πρὸς ὑμᾶς προφήτας	23:34b	ἐξ αὐτων . . . διώξετε ἀπὸ πόλεως εἰς πολίν
23:37b	ποσάκις ἠθέλησα ἐπισυναγαγεῖν τὰ τέκνα σου	23:37c	οὐκ ἠθελήσατε
23:39	εἴπητε· εὐλογημένος ὁ ἐρχόμενος ἐν ὀνόματι κυρίου	23:37a	ἡ ἀποκτείνουσα τοὺς προφήτας καὶ λιθοβολοῦσα τοὺς ἀπεσταλμένους πρὸς αὐτήν
24:4a	ἀποκριθεὶς ὁ ᾿Ιησοῦς εἶπεν αὐτοῖς	24:3	οἱ μαθηταὶ κατ᾿ ἰδίαν λέγοντες· εἰπὲ ἡμῖν . . .
24:4b	βλέπετε μή τις ὑμᾶς πλανήσῃ	24:5	πολλοὺς πλανήσουσιν
24:13	ὁ δὲ ὑπομείνας εἰς τέλος	24:10	τότε σκανδαλισθήσονται πολλοὶ
24:16	οἱ ἐν τῇ ᾿Ιουδαίᾳ φευγέτωσαν εἰς τὰ ὄρη	24:17	(μὴ) καταβάτω ἆραι τὰ ἐκ τῆς οἰκίας αὐτοῦ (also 24:18 ἐπιστρεψάτω ὀπίσω . . .)
24:22b	κολοβωθήσονται αἱ ἡμέραι ἐκεῖναι	24:22a	εἰ μὴ ἐκολοβώθησαν αἱ ἡμέραι ἐκεῖναι
24:24	ἰδοὺ προείρηκα ὑμῖν	24:23	ἐάν τις ὑμῖν εἴπῃ· ἰδοὺ ὧδε ὁ χριστός (also 24:25 ἐάν εἴπωσιν . . .)
24:31	ἐπισυνάξουσιν τοὺς ἐκλεκτοὺς αὐτοῦ ἐκ τῶν τεσσάρων ἀνέμων	24:28	ὅπου ἐὰν ᾖ τὸ πτῶμα, ἐκεῖ συναχθήσονται οἱ ἀετοί
24:45	τοῦ δοῦναι αὐτοῖς τὴν τροφὴν ἐν καιρῷ	24:49	ἄρξηται τύπτειν τοὺς συνδούλους αὐτοῦ, ἐσθίῃ δὲ καὶ πίνῃ μετὰ τῶν μεθυόντων
25:4	αἱ δὲ φρόνιμοι ἔλαβον ἔλαιον	25:3	αἱ μωραὶ . . . οὐκ ἔλαβον μεθ᾿ ἑαυτῶν ἔλαιον
25:6	ἐξέρχεσθε εἰς ἀπάντησιν	25:10	ἀπερχομένων δὲ αὐτῶν ἀγοράσαι
25:9	ἀπεκρίθησαν δὲ αἱ φρόνιμοι λέγουσαι	25:8	αἱ δὲ μωραὶ ταῖς φρονίμοις εἶπαν
25:12	ὁ δὲ ἀποκριθεὶς εἶπεν	25:11	αἱ λοιπαὶ παρθένοι λέγουσαι
25:16	ὁ τὰ πέντε τάλαντα λαβὼν ἠργάσατο ἐν αὐτοῖς καὶ ἐκέρδησεν ἄλλα πέντε (also 25:17)	25:18	ὁ δὲ τὸ ἓν λαβὼν ἀπελθὼν ὤρυξεν γῆν καὶ ἔκρυψεν τὸ ἀργύριον
25:20	ὁ τὰ πέντε τάλαντα . . . λέγων (also 25:22 ὁ τὰ δύο τάλαντα εἶπεν)	25:24	ὁ τὸ ἓν τάλαντον εἰληφὼς εἶπεν
25:27	ἔδει σε οὖν βαλεῖν τὰ ἀργύριά μου τοῖς τραπεζίταις	25:25	ἔκρυψα τὸ τάλοντόν σου ἐν τῇ γῇ
25:35,36	ἐδώκατέ μοι φαγεῖν . . . ἐποτίσατέ με . . . συνηγάγετέ με . . . ἐπεσκέψασθέ με . . . ἤλθατε πρός με	25:42–43	οὐκ ἐδώκατέ μοι φαγεῖν . . . οὐκ ἐποτίσατέ με . . . οὐ συνηγάγετέ με . . . οὐ περιεβάλετέ με . . . οὐκ ἐπεσκέψασθέ με

25:40	ἐποιήσατε ἑνὶ τούτων τῶν ἀδελφῶν μου τῶν ἐλαχίστων, ἐμοὶ ἐποιήσατε	25:45	οὐκ ἐποιήσατε ἑνὶ τούτων τῶν ἐλαχίστων, οὐδὲ ἐμοὶ ἐποιήσατε
26:2	οἴδατε ὅτι μετὰ δύο ἡμέρας τὸ πάσχα γίνεται . . .	26:5	ἔλεγον δέ· μὴ ἐν τῇ ἑορτῇ
26:7	κατέχεεν ἐπὶ τῆς κεφαλῆς αὐτοῦ	26:9	τοῦτο πραθῆναι πολλοῦ
26:10a	γνοὺς δὲ ὁ Ἰησοῦς εἶπεν αὐτοῖς	26:8	οἱ μαθηταὶ ἠγανάκτησαν λέγοντες
26:13	λαληθήσεται καὶ ὅ ἐποίησεν αὕτη εἰς μνημόσυνον αὐτῆς	26:10b	τί κόπους παρέχετε τῇ γυναικί;
26:22	λυπούμενοι σφόδρα ἤρξαντο λέγειν αὐτῷ εἷς ἕκαστος	26:25	ἀποκριθεὶς δὲ Ἰούδας ὁ παραδιδοὺς αὐτὸν εἶπεν
26:31	Τότε λέγει αὐτοῖς ὁ Ἰησοῦς	26:33	ἀποκριθεὶς δὲ ὁ Πέτρος εἶπεν αὐτῷ
26:34	ἔφη αὐτῷ ὁ Ἰησοῦς	26:35	λέγει αὐτῷ ὁ Πέτρος
26:38	γρηγορεῖτε μετ' ἐμοῦ	26:40	αὐτοὺς καθεύδοντας
26:39b	ἀλλ' ὡς σὺ [θέλεις] (also 26:42)	26:39a	(οὐχ) ὡς ἐγὼ θέλω
26:41	γρηγορεῖτε καὶ προσεύχεσθε	26:43	αὐτοὺς καθεύδοντας (also 26:45 καθεύδετε)
26:52b	ἀπόστρεψον τὴν μάχαιράν σου εἰς τὸν τόπον αὐτῆς	26:51	ἀπέσπασεν τὴν μάχαιραν αὐτοῦ
26:52a	λέγει αὐτῷ ὁ Ἰησοῦς	26:53	δοκεῖς ὅτι οὐ δύναμαι . . .
26:55b	ἐν τῷ ἱερῷ ἐκαθεζόμην διδάσκων, καὶ οὐκ ἐκρατήσατέ με	26:55a	μετὰ μαχαιρῶν καὶ ξύλων συλλαβεῖν με
26:60	οὐχ εὗρον πολλῶν προσελθόντων ψευδομαρτύρων	26:59	ἐζήτουν ψευδομαρτυρίαν
26:63a	ὁ δὲ Ἰησοῦς ἐσιώπα	26:62	ὁ ἀρχιερεὺς εἶπεν αὐτῷ
26:64a	λέγει αὐτῷ ὁ Ἰησοῦς	26:63b	ὁ ἀρχιερεὺς εἶπεν αὐτῷ
26:64b	πλὴν λέγω ὑμῖν	26:65	ὁ ἀρχιερεὺς . . . λέγων
26:69a	μία παιδίσκη λέγουσα	26:69b	ὁ δὲ [Πέτρος] ἔμπροσθεν πάντων λέγων
26:71	εἶδεν αὐτὸν ἄλλη καὶ λέγει τοῖς ἐκεῖ	26:72	πάλιν ἠρνήσατο μετὰ ὅρκου
26:73	οἱ ἑστῶτες εἶπον τῷ Πέτρῳ	26:74	ἤρξατο καταθεματίζειν καὶ ὀμνύειν
27:3	Ἰούδας . . . ἔστρεψεν τὰ τριάκοντα ἀργύρια τοῖς ἀρχιερεῦσιν καὶ πρεσβυτέροις λέγων	27:4	οἱ δὲ εἶπαν
27:5	ῥίψας τὰ ἀργύρια εἰς τὸν ναὸν	27:6	οἱ δὲ ἀρχιερεῖς λαβόντες τὰ ἀργύρια
27:14	οὐκ ἀπεκρίθη αὐτῷ	27:13	λέγει αὐτῷ ὁ Πιλᾶτος
27:19	ἡ γυνὴ αὐτοῦ λέγουσα	27:20	οἱ δὲ ἀρχιερεῖς καὶ οἱ πρεσβύτεροι ἔπεισαν τοὺς ὄχλους
27:23a	ὁ δὲ [Πιλᾶτος] ἔφη	27:23b	οἱ δὲ περισσῶς ἔκραζον λέγοντες
27:24	ὁ Πιλᾶτος . . . λέγων	27:25	ἀποκριθεὶς πᾶς ὁ λαὸς εἶπεν

27:54	ὁ δὲ ἑκατόνταρχος καὶ οἱ μετ᾽ αὐτοῦ τηροῦντες τὸν Ἰησοῦν ... ἐφοβήθησαν σφόδρα, λέγοντες	27:29	[οἱ στρατιῶται] γονυπετήσαντες ἔμπροσθεν αὐτοῦ ἐνέπαιξαν αὐτῷ λέγοντες (also 27:40a λέγοντες, 27:41 ἔλεγον, 27:49a οἱ δὲ λοιποὶ εἶπαν)
27:34b	οὐκ ἠθέλησεν πιεῖν	27:34a	ἔδωκαν αὐτῷ πιεῖν οἶνον μετὰ χολῆς μεμιγμένον
27:42a	ἄλλους ἔσωσεν	27:40a	σῶσον σεαυτόν (also 27:42b ἑαυτὸν οὐ δύναται σῶσαι)
27:43	πέποιθεν ἐπὶ τὸν θεόν	27:42b	πιστεύσομεν ἐπ αὐτόν
27:46	ὁ Ἰησοῦς φωνῇ μεγάλῃ λέγων	27:47	τινὲς δὲ ... ἀκούσαντες ἔλεγον
27:48	εἷς ἐξ αὐτῶν ... λαβὼν σπόγγον ... ἐπότιζεν αὐτόν	27:49b	ἄφες ἴδωμεν εἰ ἔρχεται Ἠλίας σώσων αὐτόν
27:63b	ἐκεῖνος ὁ πλάνος εἶπεν (also 27:64b οἱ μαθηταὶ εἴπωσιν τῷ λαῷ)	27:63a	οἱ Φαρισαῖοι πρὸς Πιλᾶτον λέγοντες
27:63c	μετὰ τρεῖς ἡμέρας ἐγείρομαι (also 27:64c ἠγέρθη)	27:64a	οἱ μαθηταὶ κλέψωσιν αὐτὸν
28:2	ἄγγελος ... ἀπεκύλισεν τὸν λίθον	27:66	σφραγίσαντες τὸν λίθον
28:5	μὴ φοβεῖσθε ὑμεῖς	28:4	ἀπὸ δὲ τοῦ φόβου αὐτοῦ ἐσείσθησαν οἱ τηροῦντες
28:7	εἴπατε τοῖς μαθηταῖς αὐτοῦ ὅτι ἠγέρθη (also 28:8 ἀπαγγεῖλαι τοῖς μαθηταῖς, 28:10 ἀπαγγείλατε τοῖς ἀδελφοῖς μου)	28:13	εἴπατε ὅτι οἱ μαθηταὶ αὐτοῦ .. ἔκλεψαν αὐτὸν

BIBLIOGRAPHY

Aletti, Jean N. "Mort de Jésus et théorie du récit." *RSR* 73 (1985):147–60.
Allen, Willoughby C. *A Critical and Exegetical Commentary of the Gospel According to St. Matthew*. ICC. Edinburgh: T. & T. Clark, 1912.
Allison, Dale C. "Elijah Must Come First." *JBL* 103 (1984):256–58.
Anderson, J. Capel. "Matthew: Gender and Reading." *Semeia* 28 (1983):3–27.
Barth, Gerhard. "Matthew's Understanding of the Law." In Gunther Bornkamm, Gerhard Barth, and Heinz J. Held, *Tradition and Interpretation in Matthew*, 58–164. Philadelphia: Westminster Press, 1963.
Bartsch, Hans Werner. "Die Passions und Ostergeschichten bei Matthäus." In Hans Werner Bartsch, *Entmythologisierende Auslegung. Aufsätze aus den Jahren 1940 bis 1960*, 80–92. Hamburg-Bergstadt: H. Reich, 1962.
Beardslee, William. *Literary Criticism of the New Testament*. GBS. Philadelphia: Fortress Press, 1970.
Beare, Francis W. *The Gospel According to Matthew*. San Francisco: Harper & Row; Oxford: Basil Blackwell, 1981.
————. "The Mission of the Disciples and the Mission Charge: Matthew 10 and Parallels." *JBL* 89 (1970):1–13.
Beilner, Wolfgang. *Christus und die Pharisäer. Exegetische Untersuchung über Grund und Verlauf der Auseinandersetzungen*. Vienna: Verlag Herder & Co., 1959.
Berger, Klaus. *Die Gesetzesauslegung Jesu. Ihr historische Hintergrund im Judentum und im Alten Testament*. Neukirchen-Vluyn: Neukirchener Verlag, 1972.
Betz, Hans Dieter. *Essays on the Sermon on the Mount*. Philadelphia: Fortress Press, 1985.
————. "The Logion of the Easy Yoke and of Rest (Matt. 11:28–30)." *JBL* 86 (1967):10–24.
Bloch, Renée. "Juda engendra Phares et Zara de Thamar." In *Mélanges bibliques rédigés en l'honneur de André Robert*, 381–89. Paris: Bloud et Gay, 1957.
————. "Quelques aspects de la figure de Moïse dans la littérature rabbinique." *Cahiers Sioniens* 8 (1954):210–85.
Bonnard, Pierre. "Composition et signification historique de Matthieu XVIII. Règle ecclésiastique ou éthique du royaume?" In I. de la Potterie, *De Jésus aux Evangiles. Tradition et rédaction dans les Evangiles synoptiques*, 130–40. Gembloux/Paris, 1967.
————. *L'évangile selon saint Matthieu. Commentaire du Nouveau Testament* 1. Neuchâtel: Delachaux & Niestlé, 1963.
————. "Composition et signification historique de Matthieu 18." In *Anamnesis: Recherches sur le Nouveau Testament*. Geneva: Revue de Théologie et de Philosophie, 1980.
Bornkamm, Gunther. "End Expectation and Church in Matthew." In Gunther Bornkamm, Gerhard Barth, and Heinz J. Held, *Tradition and Interpretation in Matthew*, 15–57. Philadelphia: Westminster Press, 1963.
————. *Jesus of Nazareth*. New York: Harper & Brothers, 1960.
————. "The Stilling of the Storm in Matthew." In Gunther Bornkamm, Gerhard Barth, and Heinz J. Held, *Tradition and Interpretation in Matthew*, 52–57. Philadelphia: Westminster Press, 1963.
Brown, Raymond. *The Birth of the Messiah*. New York: Doubleday & Co., 1977.
Brown, Raymond; Donfried, Karl P.; and Reumann, John, eds. *Peter in the New*

Testament: A Collaborative Assessment by Protestant and Roman Catholic Scholars. Minneapolis: Augsburg Publishing House, 1973.

Brown, Schuyler. "The Matthean Community and the Gentile Mission." *NovT* 22 (1980):193–221.

————. "The Mission to Israel in Matthew's Central Sections (Matt. 9:35—11:1)." *ZNW* 69 (1978):73–90.

Burnett, Fredrick W. "Characterization in Matthew: Reader Construction of the Disciple Peter." Working paper for use of the group "Literary Aspects of Gospels and Acts," SBL meeting, November 1985.

————. *The Testament of Jesus-Sophia: A Redaction-Critical Study of the Eschatological Discourse in Matthew*. Washington: University Press of America, 1981.

Calloud, Jean. "Entre les Ecritures et la violence. La passion du témoin." *RSR* 73 (1985):111–28.

————. *Structural Analysis of Narrative*. Philadelphia: Fortress Press, 1976.

Carlston, Charles E. "Transfiguration and Resurrection." *JBL* 80 (1961):233–40.

Chilton, Bruce. "Jesus *ben David*." *JSNT* 14 (1982):88–112.

Cohn-Sherbok, D. N. "Jesus' Defense of the Resurrection of the Dead." *JSNT* 11 (1981):64–73.

Cope, O. Lamar. *Matthew, A Scribe Trained for the Kingdom of Heaven*. CBQMS 5. Washington: Catholic Biblical Association of America, 1976.

Cothenet, Edouard. "Les prophètes chrétiens dans l'Evangile selon Matthieu." In *L'Evangile selon Matthieu: Rédaction et théologie*, ed. M. Didier, 281–308. Gembloux: J. Duculot, 1972.

Crossan, John D. *In Parables: The Challenge of the Historical Jesus*. New York: Harper & Row, 1973.

————. "Kingdom and Children: A Study in the Aphoristic Tradition." *Semeia* 29 (1983):75–95.

Dahl, Nils A. "Die Passionsgeschichte bei Matthäus." *NTS* 2 (1955):17–32.

————. "The Parables of Growth." *Studia Theologica* 5 (1972):132–66.

Daube, David. *The New Testament and Rabbinic Judaism*. London: Athlone Press, 1956.

Davies, William D., ed. *The Gospel and the Land: Early Christianity and Jewish Territorial Doctrine*. Berkeley and Los Angeles: University of California Press, 1974.

————. "Knowledge in the Dead Sea Scrolls and Matt. 11:25–30." *HThR* 46 (1953):113–59.

————. "Matthew 5:17–18." In *Mélanges bibliques rédigés en l'honneur de André Robert*, 428–56. Paris: Bloud et Gay, 1957.

————. *The Setting of the Sermon on the Mount*. Cambridge: Cambridge University Press, 1964.

Delorme, Jean. "Sémiotique du récit et récit de la passion." *RSR* 73 (1985):85–110.

Descamps, Albert. "Rédaction et christologie dans le récit Matthéen de la passion." In *L'Evangile selon Matthieu: Rédaction et théologie*, ed. M. Didier, 359–416. Gembloux: J. Duculot, 1972.

Dillon, Richard J. "Towards a Tradition History of the Parables of the True Israel." *Biblica* 47 (1966):1–42.

Dodd, Charles H. *The Parables of the Kingdom*. New York: Charles Scribner's Sons, 1961.

Doeve, Jan W. *Jewish Hermeneutics in the Synoptic Gospels and Acts*. Assen: Van Gorcum & Co., 1953.

Donfried, Karl P. "The Allegory of the Ten Virgins (Matt. 25:1–13) as a Summary of Matthean Theology." *JBL* 93 (1974):415–28.

Duling, Dennis C. "The Therapeutic Son of David: An Element of Matthew's Christological Apologetic." *NTS* 24 (1978):392–409.

Dupont, Jacques. "L'ambassade de Jean Baptiste." *NRTh* 83 (1961):805–21, 943–59.

————. *Les béatitudes*, vol. 1: *Le problème littéraire*. Paris: J. Gabalda, 1969.

————. *Les béatitudes*, vol. 2: *La bonne nouvelle*. Paris: J. Gabalda, 1969.

————. *Les béatitudes*, vol. 3: *Les évangélistes*. Paris: J. Gabalda, 1973.

————. "Le point de vue de Matthieu dans le chapitre des paraboles." In *L'Evangile selon Matthieu: Rédaction et théologie,* ed. M. Didier, 221–60. Gembloux: Duculot, 1972.

————. "Repentir et conversion d'après les Actes des apôtres." In *Etudes sur les Actes des apôtres,* 421–57. Paris: Editions du Cerf, 1967.

————. "Vous n'aurez pas achevé les villes d'Israel avant que le fils de l'homme ne vienne (Matt. X:23)." *NovT* 2 (1958):228–44.

Edwards, Richard A. *Matthew's Story of Jesus.* Philadelphia: Fortress Press, 1985.

————. "Matthew's Use of Q in Chapter 11." In *L'Evangile selon Matthieu: Rédaction et théologie,* ed. M. Didier, 257–75. Gembloux: Duculot, 1972.

————. *The Sign of Jonah in the Theology of the Evangelists and Q.* London: SCM Press, 1971.

————. "Uncertain Faith: Matthew's Portrait of the Disciples." In *Discipleship in the New Testament,* ed. F. F. Segovia, 47–61. Philadelphia: Fortress Press, 1985.

Faierstein, Morris M. "Why Do the Scribes Say that Elijah Must Come First?" *JBL* 100 (1981):75–86.

Feuillet, André. "Les perspectives propres à chaque évangéliste dans les récits de la transfiguration." *Biblica* 39 (1958):281–309.

Fitzmyer, Joseph A. "More About Elijah Coming First." *JBL* 104 (1984):295–96

Frankemölle, Hubert. *Jahwebund und Kirche Christi. Studien zur Form und Traditionsgeschichte des Evangeliums nach Matthäus.* Münster: Aschendorff, 1974.

Gaechter, Paul. *Die literarische Kunst im Matthäus-Evangelium.* Stuttgart: Verlag Katholisches Bibelwerk, 1965.

Garland, David E. *The Intention of Matthew 23.* Leiden: E. J. Brill, 1979.

Gerhardsson, Birger. "'An ihren Fruchten sollt ihr sie erkennen': Die Legitimitätsfrage in der Matthäischen Christologie." *EvT* 42 (1982):113–26.

Gnilka, Joachim. "Das Verstockungsproblem nach Matthäus 13:13–15." In *Antijudaismus im Neuen Testament?* ed. W. Eckert, 119–28. Munich: Chr. Kaiser Verlag, 1967.

Goulder, Michael D. *Midrash and Lection in Matthew: The Speaker's Lectures in Biblical Studies, 1969–71.* London: SPCK, 1974.

Green, H. Benedict. "The Structure of St. Matthew's Gospel." *Studia Evangelica* 4/TU102 (1968):57–59.

Greimas, Algirdas J., and Courtés, Joseph. *Sémiotique. Dictionnaire raisonné du langage.* Paris: Larousse, 1979. Eng. trans.: Larry Crist, Daniel Patte, and others. *Semiotics and Language: An Analytical Dictionary.* Bloomington: Indiana University Press, 1982.

————, eds. *Sémiotique. Dictionnaire raisonné du langage,* vol. 2. Paris: Larousse, 1985.

Grundmann Walter. *Das Evangelium nach Matthäus.* Berlin: Evangelische Verlag, 1968.

Gundry, Robert H. *Matthew: A Commentary on His Literary and Theological Art.* Grand Rapids: Wm. B. Eerdmans, 1982.

————. *The Use of the Old Testament in St. Matthew's Gospel.* Leiden: E. J. Brill, 1967.

Held, Heinz J. "Matthew as Interpreter of the Miracle Stories." In Gunther Bornkamm, Gerhard Barth, and Heinz J. Held, *Tradition and Interpretation in Matthew,* 165–299. Philadelphia: Westminster Press, 1963.

Hiers, Richard H. "'Binding' and 'Loosing': The Matthean Authorizations." *JBL* 104 (1985):233–50.

Hill, David. "Son and Servant: An Essay on Matthean Christology." *JSNT* 6 (1980):2–16.

Holmberg, Bengt. *Paul and Power: The Structure of Authority in the Primitive Church as Reflected in the Pauline Epistles.* Philadelphia: Fortress Press, 1980.

Hood, Rodney T. "The Genealogies of Jesus." In *Early Christian Origins* (Studies in honor of H. R. Willoughby), 1–15. Chicago: Quadrangle, 1961.

Hubbard, Benjamin. *The Matthean Redaction of a Primitive Apostolic Commissioning: An Exegesis of Matthew 28:16–20.* Missoula, Mont.: Society of Biblical Literature, 1974.

Hummel, Reinhart. *Die Auseinandersetzung zwischen Kirche und Judentum im Mat-thäusevangelium*. Munich: Chr. Kaiser Verlag, 1963.

Jeremias, Joachim. *The Parables of Jesus*. New York: Charles Scribner's Sons, 1963.

Johnson, Marshal D. *The Purpose of Biblical Genealogies: With Special Reference to the Setting of the Genealogy of Jesus*. SNTSMS 8. Cambridge: Cambridge University Press, 1969.

――――. "Reflections on a Wisdom Approach to Matthew's Christology." *CBQ* 36 (1974):44–64.

Keck, Leander. "Ethics in the Gospel of Matthew." *Iliff Review* 40 (Winter 1984):39–56.

Kingsbury, Jack D. "The Figure of Peter in Matthew's Gospel as a Theological Problem." *JBL* 98 (1979):67–83.

――――. *Matthew as Story*. Philadelphia: Fortress Press, 1986.

――――. "The Form and Message of Matthew." In *Interpreting the Gospels*, ed. J. L. Mays, 66–77. Philadelphia: Fortress Press, 1981.

――――. *Matthew: Structure, Christology and Kingdom*. Philadelphia: Fortress Press, 1975.

――――. *The Parables of Jesus in Matthew 13*. Richmond: John Knox Press, 1969.

――――. "The Title 'Son of David' in Matthew's Gospel." *JBL* 95 (1976):591–602.

Klausner, Joseph. *Jesus of Nazareth: His Life, Times and Teaching*. New York: Mac-millan, 1925.

Kunzel, Georg. *Studien zum Gemeindeverständnis des Matthäus-Evangeliums*. Stuttgart: Calwer Verlag, 1978.

Lagrange, Marie-Joseph. *Evangile selon saint Matthieu*. Paris: Gabalda, 1927.

Lambrecht, Jan. "The Parousia Discourse: Composition and Content in Mt. XXIV—XXV." In *L'Evangile selon Matthieu: Rédaction et théologie*, ed. M. Didier, 309–42. Gambloux: Duculot, 1972.

Lategan, Bernard. "Structure and Reference in Mt 23." *Neotestamentica* 16 (1982):74–87.

Léon-Dufour, Xavier. *Etudes d'Evangile*. Paris: Editions du Seuil, 1965.

――――. "Présence du Seigneur ressuscité (Mt 28, 16–20)." In *A cause de L'Evangile: Etudes sur les Synoptiques et les Acts*, 195–209. Paris: Editions du Cerf, 1985.

Levine, Etan. "The Sabbath Controversy According to Matthew." *NTS* 22 (1975–76):480–83.

Lightfoot, Robert H. *Locality and Doctrine in the Gospels*. London: Hodder & Stough-ton, 1938.

Lindars, Barnabas. *New Testament Apologetic: The Doctrinal Significance of the Old Testament Quotations*. London: SCM Press, Philadelphia: Westminster Press, 1973.

Linton, Olof. "The Parables of the Children's Game." *NTS* 22 (1976):159–79.

Lohmeyer, Ernst. *Das Evangelium des Matthäus*. KEK. Göttingen: Vandenhoeck & Ruprecht, 1956.

――――. *Galiläa und Jerusalem*. Göttingen: Vandenhoeck & Ruprecht, 1936.

Lowe, Malcolm. "Who Were the IOYDAIOI?" *NovT* 18 (1976):101–30.

Luz, Ulrich. "The Disciples in the Gospel According to Matthew." In *The Inter-pretation of Matthew*, ed. Graham Stanton, 98–128. Philadelphia: Fortress Press, 1983.

Marin, Louis. "Essai d'analyse structurale d'un récit-parabole: Matthieu 13:1–23." *EThR* 46 (1971):35–74.

――――. *The Semiotics of the Passion Narrative: Topics and Figures*. Pittsburgh: Pickwick Press, 1980.

Meier, John P. "John the Baptist in Matthew's Gospel." *JBL* 99 (1980):383–405.

――――. *Law and History in Matthew's Gospel*. Rome: Biblical Institute Press, 1976.

――――. *Matthew*. Wilmington, Del.: M. Glazier, 1980.

――――. *The Vision of Matthew: Christ, Church, and Morality in the Fourth Gospel*. New York: Paulist Press, 1979.

Minear, Paul S. "The Disciples and the Crowds in the Gospel of Matthew." *ATR* Supplementary Series 3 (1974):28–44.

――――. *Matthew, The Teacher's Gospel*. New York: Pilgrim Press, 1982.

Nellessen, Ernst. *Das Kind und seine Mutter: Struktur und Verkündigung des 2. Kapitels im Matthäusevangelium*. Stuttgart: Verlag Katholisches Bibelwerk, 1969.

Nolan, Brian M. "The Heir Unapparent: Detecting the Royal Theology in the Parable of the Master's Son (Matthew 21:33–46)." *Proceedings of the IBA* 4 (1980):84–95.

———. *The Royal Son of God: The Christology of Matthew 1–2*. Göttingen: Vandenhoeck & Ruprecht; Fribourg Suisse: Editions Universitaires, 1979.

Panier, Louis. *Récit et commentaires de la tentation de Jésus au désert: Approche sémiotique du discours interprétatif*. Paris: Editions du Cerf, 1984.

Patte, Daniel. *Early Jewish Hermeneutic in Palestine*. Missoula, Mont.: Scholars Press, 1975.

———. "The Interface of Semiotics and Faith." *RS/SI* 2 (1982):105–29.

———, ed. *Kingdom and Children: Aphorism, Chreia, Structure. Semeia* 29 (1983).

———. "Method for a Structural Exegesis of Didactic Discourses: Analysis of 1 Thessalonians." *Semeia* 26 (1983):85–129.

———. "Parcours génératif." In *Sémiotique. Dictionnaire raisonné du langage* 2: 101–04. Paris: Larousse, 1985.

———. *Paul's Faith and the Power of the Gospel*. Philadelphia: Fortress Press, 1983.

———. "Reading Paul so as to Hear the Gospel Anew." *Chicago Studies* 24 (1985):339–56.

Patte, Daniel, and Aline Patte. *Structural Exegesis: From Theory to Practice*. Philadelphia: Fortress Press, 1978.

Paul, André. *L'Evangile de l'enfance selon S. Matthieu*. Paris: Editions du Cerf, 1968.

Pederson, Sigfred. "Die Proklamation Jesu als des eschatologischen Offenbarungsträgers (Mt. XVII, 1–13)." *NovT* 17 (1975):241–64.

Pelletier, André. "L'annonce à Joseph." *RSR* 54 (1966):67–68.

Perrin, Norman. *Rediscovering the Teaching of Jesus*. New York: Harper & Row, 1967.

Pesch, Rudolf. "Eine alttestamentliche Ausführungsformel im Matthäus-Evangelium." *BZ* NF 11 (1967):79–95.

———. *Naherwartungen. Tradition und Redaktion im Mark 13*. Düsseldorf: Patmos Verlag, 1968.

Pesch, Wilhelm. "Die Sogennante Gemeindeordnung Mt. 18." *BZ* 7 (1963):220–35.

Pham Hüu Lai. "Production du sens par la foi: autorités religieuses contestées/fondées. Analyse structurale de Matthieu XXVII, 57—XXVIII, 20." *RSR* 61 (1973):65–96.

Phillips, Gary A. "Enunciation of the Kingdom of Heaven: Text, Narrative, and Hermeneutic in the Parables of Matthew 13." Ph.D. dissertation, Vanderbilt University, 1981.

———. "History and Text: The Reader in Context in Matthew's Parables Discourse." *Semeia* 31 (1985):111–38.

Prabhu, George M. Soares. *The Formula Quotations in the Infancy Narrative of Matthew*. Rome: Biblical Institute Press, 1976.

Przybylski, Benno. *Righteousness in Matthew and His World of Thought*. Cambridge and New York: Cambridge University Press, 1980.

Richardson, R. L., Jr. "The Function of the Scriptures in the Rise of the Easter Faith." Ph.D. dissertation, Vanderbilt University, 1972.

Robbins, Vernon. "Pronouncement Stories and Jesus' Blessing of the Children: A Rhetorical Approach." *Semeia* 29 (1983):43–74.

Rothfuchs, Wilhelm. *Die Erfüllungszitate des Matthäus-Evangeliums. Eine biblische-theologische Untersuchung*. Stuttgart: Kohlhammer Verlag, 1969.

Sanders, J.A. "*Nazoraios* in Matt. 2:23." *JBL* 84 (1965):169–72.

Schrenk, Gottlob. "Entolē." In *TDNT* 2:545–56.

Schüssler Fiorenza, Elisabeth. *In Memory of Her: A Feminist Theological Reconstruction of Christian Origins*. New York: Crossroad Publishing Co., 1983.

Schutz, John H. *Paul and the Anatomy of Apostolic Authority*. SNTSMS 26. Cambridge and New York: Cambridge University Press, 1975.

Schweizer, Eduard. "'Er wird Nazoräer heissen' (zu Mc 1, 24; Mt 2, 23)." In *Judentum, Urchristentum, Kirche* (Festschrift for Joachim Jeremias), ed. W. Eltester, 90–93. Berlin: Töpelmann, 1960.

———. *The Good News According to Matthew.* Atlanta: John Knox Press, 1975.

———. "Matth. 5, 17–20. Anmerkungen zum Gesetzesverständnis des Matthäus." *TLZ* 77 (1952):479–84.

———. *Matthäus und seine Gemeinde.* Stuttgart: Verlag Katholisches Bibelwerk, 1974.

———. "Noch einmal Mat 5, 17–20." In *Das Wort und die Wörter*, ed. H. Balz and S. Schulz, 69–73. Stuttgart: Kohlhammer, 1973.

———. "Matthew's Church." In *The Interpretation of Matthew*, ed. Graham Stanton, 129–55. Philadelphia: Fortress Press, 1983.

Segbroeck, Frans van. "Les citations d'accomplissement dans l'Evangile selon Matthieu d'après trois ouvrages récents." In *L'Évangile selon Matthieu*, ed. M. Didier, 107–30. Gembloux: J. Duculot, 1970.

Smith, Charles W. F. "The Mixed State of the Church in Matthew's Gospel." *JBL* 82 (1963):149–68.

Stanton, Graham N. "The Origin and Purpose of Matthew's Gospel: Matthean Scholarship from 1945 to 1980." *ANRW* II. 25. 3., ed. H. Temporini and W. Haase, 1879–1951. Berlin: Walter de Gruyter, 1983.

Stemberger, Gunter. "Galilee—Land of Salvation?" In W. D. Davies, *The Gospel and the Land: Early Christianity and Jewish Territorial Doctrine*, 409–38. Berkeley and Los Angeles: University of California Press, 1974.

Stendahl, Krister. "*Quis et Unde*? An Analysis of Mt 1—2." In *Judentum, Urchristentum, Kirche* (Festschrift for Joachim Jeremias), ed. W. Eltester, 94–105. Berlin: Töpelmann, 1960. [It also appears in *The Interpretation of Matthew*, ed. Graham Stanton, 56–66. Philadelphia: Fortress Press, 1983.]

———. *The School of Matthew and Its Use of the Old Testament.* Philadelphia: Fortress Press, 1968.

Strecker, Georg. "Die Makarismen der Bergpredigt." *NTS* 17 (1970/71):255–75.

———. *Der Weg der Gerechtigkeit.* Göttingen: Vandenhoeck & Ruprecht, 1962.

Suggs, M. Jack. *Wisdom, Christology and Law in Matthew's Gospel.* Cambridge: Harvard University Press, 1970.

Tagawa, Kenzo. "People and Community in Matthew." *NTS* 16 (1969–70):149–62.

Thiering, B. E. "Are the 'Violent Men' False Teachers?" *NovT* 21 (1979):293–97.

Thompson, William G. *Matthew's Advice to a Divided Community: Matthew 17:22—18:35.* Rome: Pontifical Biblical Institute, 1970.

Tilborg, Sjef van. *The Jewish Leaders in Matthew.* Leiden: E. J. Brill, 1972.

Tolbert, Mary Ann. *Perspectives on the Parables: An Approach to Multiple Interpretations.* Philadelphia: Fortress Press, 1979.

Trilling, Wolfgang. "Die Taufertradition bei Matthäus." *BZ* 3 (1959):271–89.

———. *Das wahre Israel: Studien zur Theologie des Matthäus Evangeliums.* Munich: Kösel-Verlag, 1964.

Tucker, Jeffrey T. "On Following Jesus, Hardness of Heart, and the Goodness of God: A Structural Exegesis of Matthew 19:1—20:16." Unpublished paper, Vanderbilt University, 1985.

Via, Dan O. "Matthew on the Understanding of the Parables." *JBL* 84 (1965):430–32.

———. *The Parables: Their Literary and Existential Dimensions.* Philadelphia: Fortress Press, 1967.

Vigen, Larry. "To Think the Things of God: A Discursive Reading of Matthew 16:13—18:35." Ph.D. dissertation, Vanderbilt University, 1985.

Windisch, Hans. "Zyme, zymoō, azymos." *TDNT* 2:902–6.

Wink, Walter. *John the Baptist in the Gospel Tradition.* SNTSMS 7. Cambridge and New York: Cambridge University Press, 1968.

Zumstein, Jean. *La condition du croyant dans l'Evangile selon Matthieu.* Fribourg: Editions Universitaires; Göttingen: Vandenhoeck & Ruprecht, 1977.

(The index includes only those references to Matthew found outside of the sections dealing with a given passage.)